GUARDIAN OF THE LIGHT

PRAISE FOR GUARDIAN OF THE LIGHT

"Archbishop Hurley was one of our greatest South Africans. This biography reveals what gave him that stature—his integrity, fearlessness, gentleness of spirit and his magnanimity. It is a must read for all of us."

—The Most Reverend Desmond Tutu, Archbishop Emeritus of Cape Town, South Africa

"This book not only provides a glimpse into South African history during the apartheid years but a vivid, poignant story of a powerful yet humble man of God, committed to truth, justice and nonracialism. It should be read by every South African and many others too around the world, in order to understand our role as part of the human family."

—Ela Gandhi, Granddaughter of Mahatma Gandhi, Chancellor
of the Durban University of Technology

"Archbishop Denis Hurley's life, a life of immense courage, deep spirituality and prophetic leadership, deserves to be more widely known not only in South Africa, but throughout the world. His life was a superb example of the close unity between personal holiness and action for social justice."

—Albert Nolan, O.P., author of *God in South Africa*.

"Denis Hurley was an inspiration. This champion in the fight against apartheid in South Africa was a bishop ahead of many of his people. He was equally progressive in expressing his vision of the future of the Catholic Church. Himself an activist in the same cause, Paddy Kearney is well placed to tell the inside story. His book throws fresh light on the life and career of a great churchman."

—John Wilkins, editor, *The Tablet*, 1982–2003

"Chronicling a towering life that shaped earthshaking events in church (Vatican II and its aftermath) and state (apartheid in South Africa), this book informs and inspires. The keenness of Archbishop Hurley's mind was matched only by the greatness of his heart, the humor of his wit, the twinkling of his eye, the courage of his soul. For those who knew him, this text carefully fills in gaps in his story with documentation and personal interviews. For those who did not, a treat awaits as they meet this fascinating "lighthouse" person of faith."

—Elizabeth Johnson, Distinguished Professor of Theology, Fordham University

GUARDIAN OF THE
LIGHT

Denis Hurley: Renewing the Church,
Opposing Apartheid

PADDY KEARNEY

continuum

NEW YORK • LONDON

2009

The Continuum International Publishing Group Inc
80 Maiden Lane, New York, NY 10038

The Continuum International Publishing Group Ltd
The Tower Building, 11 York Road, London SE1 7NX

www.continuumbooks.com

Royalties from the sale of this book go to the
Denis Hurley Centre
Emmanuel Cathedral
Denis Hurley Street
Durban, South Africa
This multipurpose centre serves the social and educational needs of the cathedral parish, as well
as providing extensive pastoral outreach to refugees, homeless people and people living with
HIV/AIDS. For further details, see *www.archbishopdenishurley.org*

Library of Congress Cataloging-in-Publication Data
Kearney, Paddy.
  Guardian of the light: Denis Hurley: Renewing the church, opposing apartheid / Paddy Kearney.
    p. cm.
  Includes bibliographical references (pp. 356–58) and index.
  ISBN-13: 978-0-8264-1875-3 (hardcover : alk. paper)
  ISBN-10: 0-8264-1875-9 (hardcover : alk. paper) 1. Hurley, Denis E. 2. Catholic Church—
South Africa—Bishops—Biography. I. Title.

  BX4705.H87K43 2008
  282.092—dc22
  [B]

                                                                    2008044620

Printed in the United States of America
9780826418753

CONTENTS

ARCHBISHOP DENIS HURLEY'S FAMILY TREE   VIII

MAP OF SOUTHERN AFRICA   IX

ADVICE TO AN ARCHBISHOP   X

GUARDIAN OF THE LIGHT   X

ABBREVIATIONS   XI

PREFACE   XIII

ACKNOWLEDGMENTS   XV

———

PART ONE: "A BOY OF GREAT PROMISE"   1

CHAPTER 1 – *Skibbereen*   3

CHAPTER 2 – *Lighthouses*   9

CHAPTER 3 – *High School*   17

CHAPTER 4 – *Ireland and Rome*   25

———

PART TWO: PRIEST, BISHOP, ARCHBISHOP   39

CHAPTER 5 – *Cathedral and Scholasticate*   41

CHAPTER 6 – *Youngest Bishop*   52

CHAPTER 7 – *Out of the Shadows*   61

CHAPTER 8 – *Defying Verwoerd*   70

CHAPTER 9 – *How to Oppose Apartheid*   80

(Photo section following page 92)

———

PART THREE: "THE GREATEST EXPERIENCE OF MY WHOLE LIFE"   93

CHAPTER 10 – *Good News*   95

CHAPTER 11 – *Second Vatican Council*   106

CHAPTER 12 – *Archbishops Clash*   125

CHAPTER 13 – *Humanae Vitae*   134

CHAPTER 14 – *Implementing Vatican II*   144

CHAPTER 15– *Leader of ICEL*   161

CHAPTER 16 – *Close Encounters*   170

———————

PART FOUR: PROPHETIC LEADER   179

CHAPTER 17 – *Stirrings of Resistance*   181

CHAPTER 18 – *'No' to Apartheid War*   199

CHAPTER 19 – *Leading the Bishops*   208

CHAPTER 20 – *Namibia*   216

CHAPTER 21 – *In the Shoes of the Workers*   228

CHAPTER 22 – *Police Conduct in the Townships*   234

CHAPTER 23 – *New Policy Directions*   238

CHAPTER 24 – *Mobilising the Church*   245

CHAPTER 25 – *Reason to Believe*   252

CHAPTER 26 – *The Price of Prophecy*   256

(Photo section following page 220)

———————

PART FIVE: "IN OLD AGE THEY WILL STILL BEAR FRUIT"   261

CHAPTER 27 – *Last Years in Office*   263

CHAPTER 28 – *Civil War*   275

CHAPTER 29 – *A Painful Experience*   289

CHAPTER 30 – *The Perfect Chancellor*   297

CHAPTER 31 – *A Busy Retirement*   302

CHAPTER 32 – *Family*   311

CHAPTER 33 – *"The Departure Lounge"*   317

Notes   329

SELECT BIBLIOGRAPHY   356

INDEX   359

In memory
of my parents,
Jack Kearney (1911–2002) and
Margie Kearney, née Walsh (1909–2000)

Archbishop Hurley's Family Tree

Denis Hurley
married 18.2.1871 to
Helena Driscoll

- Eliza *b. 1872*
- Ellen *b. 1873*
- Mary *b. 1875*
- Patrick *b. 1876*
- Kate *b. 1879*
- **Denis** *b. 1880*
- Julia *b. 1882*
- Timothy *b. 1882*
- John *b. 1884*
- Daniel *b. 1886*
- Jane *b. 1889*
- Helena *b. 1895*

Denis Hurley
married 11.11.1913 to
Theresa May
O'Sullivan

- **Helena** Mary (Eileen) *b. 1914*
- **Denis** Eugene *b. 1915*
- **Jeremiah** (Jerry) *b. 1919*
- **Christopher** Edward (Chris) *b. 1922*

Jeremiah O'Sullivan
married 12.7.1866 to
Kate Collins

- Anne *b. 1867*
- Pat *b. 1869*
- Mary *b. 1871*
- Sarah *b. 1873*
- Kate *b. 1876*
- Johanna *b. 1878*
- Eugene *b. 1880*
- John *b. 1881*
- **Theresa** *b. 1884*
- Ellen *b. 1885*
- Harriet *b. 1888*
- Jerry *b. 1892*

Jerry Hurley
married 28.12.1946 to
Dorothy Leslie (Bobbie) Smith

- Mary *b. 1948*
- Anne *b. 1949*
- Jeremy *b. 1951*
- Julia *b. 1954*
- Leslie *b. 1956*
- Martin *b. 1959*
- Kate *b. 1962*
- Matthew *b. 1966*

Chris Hurley
married 1.8.1857 to
Maris Ursula Allpass

- Christopher *b. 1958*
- Ursula *b. 1959*
- Mikaela *b. 1960*
- Denis *b. 1962*
- Eeva *b. 1966*
- Helena *b. 1975*

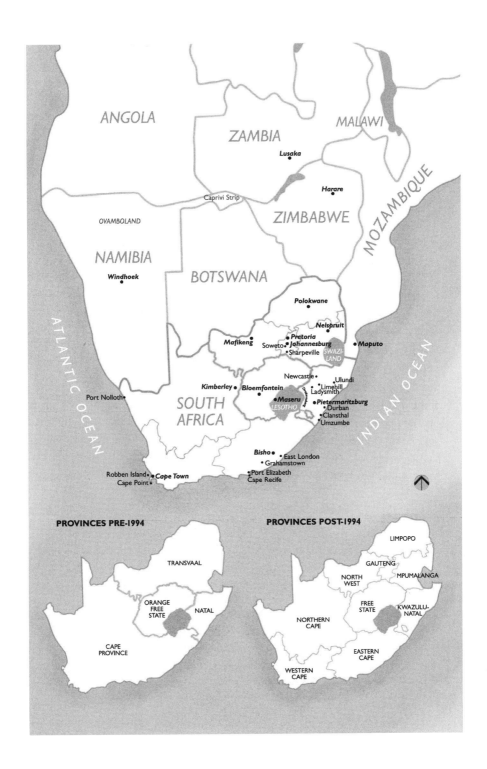

ANGOLA

ZAMBIA

MALAWI

● Lusaka

Caprivi Strip

OVAMBOLAND

● Harare

ZIMBABWE

MOZAMBIQUE

NAMIBIA

● Windhoek

BOTSWANA

ATLANTIC OCEAN

● Polokwane

● Nelspruit

● Pretoria

Mafikeng ●

Soweto ●

● Johannesburg

● Sharpeville

SWAZILAND

● Maputo

Newcastle ●

● Ulundi

Limehill

Ladysmith

Kimberley ●

Bloemfontein ●

● Maseru

LESOTHO

Pietermaritzburg ●

● Durban

● Clansthal

● Umzumbe

INDIAN OCEAN

Port Nolloth ●

SOUTH
AFRICA

Bisho ●

● East London

● Grahamstown

Robben Island ●

Cape Point ●

● Cape Town

● Port Elizabeth

Cape Recife

PROVINCES PRE-1994

TRANSVAAL

ORANGE
FREE
STATE

NATAL

CAPE
PROVINCE

PROVINCES POST-1994

LIMPOPO

GAUTENG

NORTH
WEST

MPUMALANGA

FREE
STATE

KWAZULU-
NATAL

NORTHERN
CAPE

EASTERN
CAPE

WESTERN
CAPE

IX

ADVICE TO AN ARCHBISHOP

Alcuin of York (735–804) was a celebrated adviser to Emperor Charlemagne on matters of religion and education. Here he offers advice to his friend Adelhard, who was about to be consecrated archbishop.

> Almighty God grant all go well with you.
> Be an honour to the Church, follow Christ's word
> Clear in your task and careful in your speech.
> Be yours an open hand, a merry heart.
> Christ be in your mouth, so that all may know life.
> Be a lover of righteousness and compassion;
> Let none come to you and go away sad.
> Go before God's people to God's realm,
> That those who follow you may come to the stars.
> Sow living seeds, words that are quick with life,
> That faith may be the harvest in all hearts.
> In word and example, let your light
> Shine in the dark like the morning star.
> Let not the wealth of all the world nor its dominion
> Flatter you into keeping silent about the truth.
> Neither king, nor judge, nor even your dearest friend
> Muzzle your lips from righteousness.

Appleton, G. (ed.) (1985), *The Oxford Book of Prayers*. New York: Oxford University Press.

GUARDIAN OF THE LIGHT

"Denis Hurley was not born in a lighthouse as some people imagine. His father was the keeper of the lighthouse at Cape Point, the guardian of the light that warns the sailors of dangers and guides them away from destruction.

Now the son did not follow in his father's footsteps. But he became a lighthouse keeper too; the guardian of the light that warns of dangers and saves us from destruction. The lighthouse has become a symbol of light and hope and our Archbishop has been doing this work of warning and guiding for the greater part of his [life]. And he has done it with great faithfulness for which today we give thanks."

Tribute on the occasion of Archbishop Hurley's 70th birthday celebration in the Durban City Hall, by Alan Paton, author of *Cry, the Beloved Country*.

ABBREVIATIONS

(Note: Abbreviations for the Notes are listed on page 329–330.)

AIDS – Acquired Immune Deficiency Syndrome

AMECEA – Association of Member Episcopal Conferences in Eastern Africa

ANC – African National Congress

AWR – Association of Women Religious

BCM – Black Consciousness Movement

BECLC – Black Ecumenical Church Leaders' Consultation

CAFOD – Catholic Fund for Overseas Development

CAU – Catholic African Union

CCFD – *Comité Catholique contra le Faim et pour le Développement*

CDF – Congregation for the Doctrine of the Faith

CDW – Congregation for Divine Worship

CIDSE – *Coopération Internationale pour le Développement et la Solidarité*

CIIR – Catholic Institute for International Relations

CJP – Christians for Justice and Peace

CODESA – Congress for a Democratic South Africa

CORDAID – Catholic Organisation for Relief and Development Aid

COSATU – Congress of South African Trade Unions

COSG – Conscientious Objector Support Group

CPC – Central Preparatory Commission

CSSR – *Congregatio Sanctissimi Redemptoris* (Redemptorists)

DRC – Dutch Reformed Church

DVC – Deputy Vice-Chancellor

ECAR – Education Council of Association of Religious

ECC – End Conscription Campaign

FMS – *Fratres Maristae a Scholis* (Marist Brothers)

GEAR – Growth, Employment and Redistribution

HIV – Human Immunodeficiency Virus

HMT – His Majesty's Troopship

ICEL – International Commission on English in the Liturgy

ICET – International Consultation on English Texts

ICJ – International Commission of Jurists

ICU – Industrial and Commercial Workers' Union

IFP – Inkatha Freedom Party

IHM – Sisters, Servants of the Immaculate Heart of Mary

IMBISA – Inter-Territorial Meeting of Bishops in Southern Africa

IRA – Irish Republican Army

JB – The Jerusalem Bible

JORAC – Joint Rent Action Committee

LP – Liberal Party

MAWU – Metal and Allied Workers' Union

MDM – Mass Democratic Movement

NCFS – National Catholic Federation of Students

NCLG – Natal Church Leaders' Group (from 1994: Kwa Zulu-Natal Church Leaders' Group)

NGO – Non-Governmental Organization

NIC – Natal Indian Congress

NIO – Natal Indian Organization

NP – National Party

NUSAS – National Union of South African Students

OFM – Order of Friars Minor (Franciscans)

OMI – Oblates of Mary Immaculate

OP – Order of Preachers (Dominicans)

OSA – Order of Saint Augustine (Augustinians)

OSB – Order of Saint Benedict (Benedictines)

OSM – Order of Friar Servants of Mary (Servites)

PAC – Pan-Africanist Congress

PACSA – Pietermaritzburg Agency for Christian Social Awareness

PBPSG – Permanent Black Priests' Solidarity Group

PP – Progressive Party

RDP – Reconstruction and Development Programme

RSM – Religious Order of the Sisters of Mercy

SA – South African

SAAF – South African Air Force

SABC – South African Broadcasting Corporation

SAC – *Societas Apostolatus Catholici* (Pallottines)

SACBC – Southern African Catholic Bishops' Conference

SACC – South African Council of Churches

SACP – South African Communist Party

SADF – South African Defence Force

SAIC – South African Indian Council

SAIRR – South African Institute of Race Relations

SAPA – South African Press Association

SASO – South African Students' Organization

SATV – South African Television

SAWCO – Sarmcol Workers' Co-operative

SC – Senior Counsel

SECAM – Symposium of Episcopal Conferences of Africa and Madagascar

SJ – Society of Jesus (Jesuits)

SMA – Society of Missionaries of Africa

SND – Sisters of Notre Dame de Namur

SPOBA – St Peter's Old Boys' Association

SPROCAS – Study Project on Christianity in Apartheid Society

SSC – State Security Council

StratCom – Strategic Communications

SVD – Society of the Divine Word

SWAPO – South West African People's Organisation

TRC – Truth and Reconciliation Commission

UCT – University of Cape Town

UDF – United Democratic Front

UKZN – University of KwaZulu-Natal

UP – United Party

UWUSA – United Workers' Union of South Africa

VMSG – Vaal Ministers' Support Group

WOSA – Women's Ordination South Africa

YCS – Young Christian Students

YCW – Young Christian Workers

PREFACE

I am not sure when I first thought of writing a biography of Archbishop Hurley. He had been a presence in my life from childhood, through his visits to St Mary's Church and St Charles' College, Pietermaritzburg, from the late 1940s. An exceptional personality, he impressed me as someone who was determined to make a difference in Church and society.

This impression was intensified from the time of the Second Vatican Council (1962–65) when he used every opportunity to explain the changes taking place in the Catholic Church. I could not help being swept along by his enthusiastic addresses to students at the University of Natal. Not long after that I became a member of the archdiocesan Justice and Peace Commission, which he had established, and was able to see the leadership he provided.

Because I was an active member of the Commission, he invited me to work for Diakonia, an ecumenical organization to promote social justice, which he had been planning from the early 1970s. I became directly involved in 1974 and 1975, when I worked with him in its establishment, and later I accepted the invitation to head the staff of Diakonia in 1976. This turned out to be a key decision for me because I continued in this post through extraordinary times in our country until 2004.

Throughout this period I witnessed Hurley's concern that work for justice should be an integral part of the Church's ministry. I saw his willingness to devote time and energy to make this happen, even if it was not a popular cause in some circles. I witnessed his efforts to implement the Council's vision in every aspect of diocesan life and in his contacts with the members of other churches and faiths.

By 1987, when he celebrated forty years as bishop, I realized that his efforts were not sufficiently known or understood, even within the Church. This motivated me to edit a special commemorative brochure, *Archbishop Hurley: Fortieth Anniversary as Bishop of Durban*. While doing research for this booklet, I discovered many interesting aspects of his life. Two years later, when he celebrated fifty years as a priest, I edited a book of tributes, entitled *Guardian of the Light*—a further journey of discovery.

In 1997, Professor Colin Gardner invited me to record interviews with the archbishop for the Oral History Project of Natal University's Alan Paton Centre. I welcomed this opportunity to learn more about the life of the archbishop and during the next seven years I completed over twenty interviews with him, each a fascinating experience. It must have been this experience which convinced me that it was time to begin working on a biography.

After Hurley's death in 2004, realizing that he had done much work on his memoirs, I discussed with his family and the Oblate congregation the editing and publication of this material. With their approval I prepared two books, *Vatican II: Keeping the Dream Alive* and *Memories: The Memoirs of Archbishop Denis E Hurley OMI*. This work provided an excellent foundation for a biography.

At the same time I began interviewing people in South Africa, Ireland and the United Kingdom, Europe, North America and Australia who had been associated with the archbishop. Eventually I had nearly 250 recorded and transcribed interviews. A great incentive to go ahead with the writing was the positive response of Frank Oveis, senior editor for Continuum in New York, the first publisher I approached.

My research has helped me to see how Denis Hurley opened himself to learning at every stage of his life, and so developed from a white South African youth with the racial prejudices typical of his time to an anti-apartheid activist; and from a young priest with conventional theological views to a vigorous campaigner for the implementation of Vatican II. He distinguished himself as a pastoral and prayerful bishop, a man of grace and compassion, not afraid to challenge the powerful whether in the Church or in society. By his own admission he had been a shy boy and perhaps never fully overcame that limitation, yet he disciplined himself to reach out to all sorts of people. My aim has been to let all this and more emerge from his own words, from the events of his life and from the stories and insights of people who experienced his ministry. In telling this story I have, as far as possible, used a chronological approach, except in a few instances where it seemed more appropriate to group material in themes.

Acknowledgments

Many people contributed to this biography: they assisted with funding the research; helped with accommodation and transport; made archives, libraries and private collections of letters, documents and photographs accessible; agreed to be interviewed about their memories of Archbishop Hurley; offered editorial assistance and advice about the text; and supported and encouraged me over years of research and writing. My thanks to all who helped in these ways; without their contribution this book would not have been possible. Although it is not feasible to list all who assisted, I would like them to know that I am grateful.

The story begins with the Diakonia Council of Churches, which gave me six months' sabbatical leave in 2003–4, as well as an initial research grant. At the end of that time they graciously accepted my resignation so that I could work nearly full-time on this book. Their farewell gift—a laptop computer—has been my constant companion over the past five years.

When Philippe Mayol of the French funding agency, *Comité Catholique contra le Faim et pour le Développement* (CCFD), heard about the biography project, he offered to approach some of his colleagues who had known and worked with Archbishop Hurley, so that their organisations could contribute collectively. I had much help from Costas Criticos in drawing up an attractive funding proposal and in reporting back at regular intervals. As a result, generous grants were given by the Catholic Fund for Overseas Development (CAFOD), Catholic Relief Services, CCFD, Catholic Organisation for Relief and Development Aid (CORDAID), Development and Peace, *Entraide et Fraternité*, *Katholischer Jugendwerk*, *Misereor*, Norwegian Church Aid, *Stichting Porticus*, the Swiss Catholic Lenten Fund and *Trocaire*. Their support reflected how much Denis Hurley was admired by international funders of justice, peace and development work.

Other grants and donations came from the University of KwaZulu-Natal (UKZN), Cluster Publications, Celia Dodd and Father Jean-Louis Richard OMI of Canada.

Because of the Archbishop's network of family, friends and associates, his studies overseas and extensive travels, it was necessary to visit Ireland and the United

Kingdom, Belgium, France, Germany, Switzerland, Italy, the United States, Canada and Australia. Also, of course, to travel within South Africa to Johannesburg, Pretoria, Grahamstown, Cape Town and Pietermaritzburg. I am indebted to people who accommodated me during these visits: Dennyo and Pauline O'Sullivan of Skibbereen, Marian Marist College, the Oblate Retreat House at Inchicore, the Cabra Dominican General House—all in Dublin; Petal O'Hea of Hereford, England; Mildred Neville (several lengthy and pleasant stays), Sue and Geoff Chapman, of London; the Sheehys of Oxford; Bishop Maurice Taylor of Galloway, Scotland; Jacques and Betty Briard of Namur, Belgium; Father Mike Deeb OP and the St Jacques Dominican Priory, Paris; Sr Geneviève-Marie OSA and the Augustinian Convent, Harcourt, France; the Eisners of Bad Homburg, Germany; Father Heinz Steegmann OMI of the Salvatorberg Oblate Guest House, Aachen, Germany; Marly Soltek of Cologne, Germany; the Scholasticate of the Scolopi Fathers and the Community of Sant'Egidio, Rome; the Oblates of St Francis de Sales, Washington, DC; Fr Chris Johnson OP and the St Joseph's Dominican Priory, Greenwich Village, New York; Peter and Ann Walshe, South Bend, Indiana; Archbishop Rembert Weakland OSB and St Francis Seminary, Milwaukee; Orlando and Joan Redekopp, Chicago; Rose Moss, Cambridge, Massachusetts; Alex and Marlene Campbell, Ottawa; Our Lady of Perpetual Help Redemptorist Community, Vancouver; Wolfram and Adelheid Kistner, The Grail and Douglas and Colleen Irvine, Johannesburg; Wendy Watson and Olive Douglas, Pretoria; Fr Peter-John Pearson and Di & Don Oliver, Cape Town; Bob and Maggy Clarke, Grahamstown. Their friendship and hospitality was much appreciated. Special thanks to those who, in addition, assisted with transport.

In an extraordinarily kind gesture, the Marist Brothers of Australia provided accommodation to Rev Tony Gamley and myself when we visited Perth, Adelaide, Melbourne, Sydney and Brisbane in September 2005 to launch two Hurley books and to interview the Hurley family and others who knew him. It was a fitting tribute to the Archbishop who had, in 1983, been made an affiliate of the Marist Congregation and thereafter always signed his correspondence with them as 'Brother Denis'. In each of these cities, we were able to stay with Marist communities. Another special opportunity was the Slater Fellowship awarded by University College, Durham University. This enabled me to spend the Spring 2006 term writing the early chapters in the inspiring surroundings of Durham Cathedral. Many thanks to Charles Yeats for nominating me for this award.

A number of people made archives, libraries and private collections of letters, documents and photos available: Petal O'Hea, who has a collection of Denis Hurley's letters spanning fifty years; Fr Richard Haslam OMI of the Oblate Archives at Inchicore, Dublin; Professor Matthijs Lamberigts of the Faculty of Theology, Leuven, Belgium; Jacques Briard, who assembled documents from the *Entraide et Fraternité* archives in Brussels; Sr Geneviève-Marie OSA who photocopied Hurley letters and documents in her possession; Valentin Moser of *Misereor*, Aachen, who prepared documentation about Hurley's long association with *Misereor*; Father Maciej Michalski OMI, archivist at the Oblate General House in Rome, who located much significant material, especially about Denis Hurley's academic achievements in Rome; and Wolfgang and Daisy Losken of Cary, North Carolina, who gave me copies of letters in their possession. Many thanks to members of the Hurley family, especially Chris and Jeremy, who patiently responded to numerous questions.

As for South African resources, I must first salute Professor Joy Brain, archivist of the Archdiocese of Durban, and Fr Eric Boulle OMI and Joicelyn Leslie-Smith of the Oblate Archives at Cedara. These archives have extensive collections of Hurley papers, and I am indebted for the access and assistance I was given—also by Johnson Khabelo, Librarian of the Southern African Catholic Bishops' Conference (SACBC), Khanya House, Pretoria, and Catherine Page of the Catholic History Bureau, Victory Park, Johannesburg, both of whom were most helpful.

Professor Julie Parle of the UKZN History Dept gave invaluable assistance in locating and interpreting documents in the KwaZulu-Natal Archives in Pietermaritzburg concerning Denis Hurley senior's mental illness. Bobbie Eldridge, formerly of the Campbell Collections, UKZN, gave much help with documents about South African political history. Other Durban libraries that were helpful were the Don Africana Library, where several staff assisted me; and the EG Malherbe Library at the UKZN, where Catherine Dubbeld made reference material available for an extended loan and Sipho Sibiya assisted me in locating information about the Bantu Education Act. Thanks are also due to Carol Davids and Senzo Mkhize at the UKZN archives in Pietermaritzburg for documents concerning the Archbishop's time as Chancellor of the university, and to Jewel Koopman of the Alan Paton Centre on the same campus, for assistance with materials relating to the Natal Convention. Carol Archibald, Assistant Curator of the Historical Papers Department at the William Cullen Library of the University of the Witwatersrand, made files on Christians for Justice and Peace available. Mark Coghlan, regimental historian of the Natal Carbineers, provided information about Jerry Hurley's involvement in that regiment. Sydney Duval shared with me a large suitcase of Hurleyana collected over many years. Thanks to the librarians of the Denis Hurley Library at St Joseph's Theological Institute for allowing me access to their unique theological and ecclesiastical collection.

I wish there was space to list all those interviewed in the course of research in Durban and the other places listed above. Some are mentioned in the text and some in the notes, but even those not named helped to fill out my picture of the life and times of Denis Hurley.

Special thanks to Monsignor Paul Nadal and Father Albert Danker OMI who were interviewed and consulted on a number of occasions and always gave their time most willingly. Many thanks to Maria Criticos for her expert assistance and patience in designing the Hurley family tree, drawing the map of southern Africa and doing the layout for the eight pages of photos. Patricia Cobbledick did fine work as a meticulous indexer of the whole book.

Two great admirers of Denis Hurley—his former secretaries, Julie Mathias (formerly Rainsford) and Pat Maycock—were remarkably helpful: Pat located documents and correspondence, especially of the last two years of the Archbishop's life; and Julie transcribed all the recorded interviews—a massive undertaking. Julie also helped by putting the text into the required format for the publishers and did a final proofreading of the manuscript.

I have had a distinguished panel to advise me: Colin Gardner, retired head of the English Department at the University of Natal, now the UKZN, Pietermaritzburg; Ian Linden, former head of the Catholic Institute for International Relations, London; Richard Steyn, former editor of the *Natal Witness;* Philippe Denis OP, Professor of History at UKZN, Pietermaritzburg; and Cos Desmond, anti-apartheid activist. I am most grateful for their wise advice, and in a special way to Margaret Lenta, retired Professor of English, who helped as a mentor for the whole process. Her availability, wit and patience were a great encouragement.

John Page, with assistance from Jim Schellman, made a huge contribution to my understanding of the International Commission on English in the Liturgy (ICEL), as did Fathers Giorgio Ferretti and Matteo Zuppi, together with Leone Gianturco, in relation to the Community of Sant'Egidio. Sue and Geoff Chapman kindly read the text and made important suggestions. Carmel Rickard, Bishop Michael Nuttall, Fr Larry Kaufmann CSSR, Dennyo and Pauline O'Sullivan helped with particular chapters, and Anthony Egan SJ made several suggestions of appropriate reference material—my thanks to each of them. Bishop Nuttall generously agreed to read the manuscript before the manuscript was finalised—and made wise and helpful suggestions.

Ultimately, of course, I must take responsibility for what appears in this book.

From my publishers in New York, I have had much support: particular thanks to Frank Oveis, who was enthusiastic about the project from our first meeting, and David Barker and Burke Gertenschlager, who took over when Frank retired towards the end of 2007. Gabriella Page-Fort, and Ryan Masteller who took over from her, were always helpful and cooperative about the design and layout. I am delighted that the book is co-published by the UKZN Press and thank Glenn Cowley, Andrea Nattrass and Sally Hines for all their help.

Let me conclude with thanks to my brothers Jack and Brian and Brian's wife, Rae. They were endlessly encouraging and gave every possible support through a long journey. This book has been enriched by their personal memories of Archbishop Hurley.

PART ONE

"A Boy of Great Promise"

—Father Richard Ryan OMI, Denis Hurley's Novice Master, January 1933

Skibbereen

Skibbereen is the main market town of West Cork on the south coast of Ireland.[1] The Atlantic Ocean has carved deep bays out of this coastline, and little towns like Skibbereen shelter under green hillsides. There are several theories about the name; the most popular is that it comes from the Irish word for 'little boat harbour'. It was here that Archbishop Denis Hurley's parents, Denis Hurley and Theresa May O'Sullivan, were born and where they met and married in 1913, before coming to settle in South Africa.

Skibbereen was one of the places hardest hit by the famine of 1847–51, when more than a million Irish people died of starvation and disease as a result of the failure of the potato crop, their staple food.[2] Ireland was still a colony of England, despite sending members to the Westminster Parliament. Although the government in London knew that the Irish potato crop was failing, they neglected the problem, and the situation had reached crisis proportions before any relief schemes were implemented. Even then, it had to take second place to ensuring that the economic policies of the day could continue unchecked. Ireland was still producing and exporting more than enough grain crops to feed her own population, yet thousands were dying. The grain crops were regarded as 'money crops', not 'food crops', and were not, therefore, used to prevent starvation and disease.

The Abbeystrewery Cemetery in Skibbereen bears grim testimony to this economic policy imposed by London: over 9,000 victims were buried there in mass graves. Famine victims are also remembered at the town's Heritage Centre, where a sobering exhibition helps to keep alive the lessons from that tragic period. Skibbereen became the place most associated with the famine in public imagination because the *London Illustrated News* based a journalist and artist there, who provided extensive and prolonged coverage of the famine for the publication's international audience, using sketches that graphically capture the suffering of that time.

Starving and sick people in their thousands made their way to places like Skibbereen, and the huge number of deaths and funerals during the famine brought home to the Irish the urgent need to rule their own country. It was not surprising, therefore, that in 1856 an Irish nationalist organisation known as the Phoenix National and Literary Society was established in Skibbereen.

The Phoenix Society was in turn absorbed into the Fenian movement, whose members were bound by a secret oath and dedicated to using force to achieve Irish independence. The Fenians believed that there was no way the British would be persuaded to give up control and that it was necessary to prepare for a military struggle. They were under no illusions about how strong Britain was but hoped to strike when the government was distracted by an international situation such as the Crimean War. The Catholic Church was totally opposed to Fenianism, especially Archbishop Paul Cullen of Dublin, who called it 'a compound of folly and wickedness'. Cullen persuaded Pope Pius IX to proscribe the Fenians in 1870. Nevertheless, in this part of Ireland, they built on the established structures of the Phoenix Society and went on to become a major force in Irish politics.

Denis Hurley, Archbishop Hurley's father, one of Skibbereen's residents who had left Ireland because of the poverty, decided to come home for an extended visit in 1913.[3] He had been working in the South African lighthouse service and had just been appointed assistant keeper at Danger Point in the Cape Province. His father, the Archbishop's grandfather—also named Denis—owned an 80-acre property known as Inchindreen, about five kilometres outside Skibbereen. Inchindreen had come into the Hurley family when the Archbishop's grandfather married Helena O'Driscoll, who had inherited it.[4] Before becoming the owners of the property, the Hurleys would probably have been a poor farming family, living not far from Ballynacarriga Castle. This castle had been owned by Randall Hurley. At the time of Oliver Cromwell he must have joined the Irish rebellion of 1641, because Cromwell's second in command, General Ireton, bombarded and wrecked the castle during Cromwell's brutal suppression of Irish dissent. In the area surrounding the ruined castle live a number of Hurley families, to whom the Inchindreen Hurleys are distantly related.

A newspaper report on the death of Archbishop Hurley's grandfather refers to him as 'closely identified with every phase of the Irish nationalist movement' and fully engaged in the Land League—established as a reaction to the worsening conditions for tenant farmers in the 1870s.[5] 'There was scarcely a nationalist public meeting for the past 45 years which he did not attend', continued the report. In fact, the archbishop's grandfather took such a leading part in organising the league's mass meetings that he was popularly known as 'General Hurley'. He lived to see much progress in the struggle to restore ownership of their own land to the Irish, yet as in the case of so many families his children were forced to emigrate to other parts of the world because of unemployment.

That was the fate of 18-year old Denis, who left his family home at Inchindreen and the strong strand of its radical tradition, and in 1898 set off across the fields to the neighbouring village of Castletownshend, where he took the first step to join the British navy. This entailed a visit to Vice Admiral Boyle Somerville, a leading member of what were known as the 'Anglo-Irish'. Somerville had written hundreds of recommendations for young men desperate for work, financial security and perhaps also the adventure offered by the British navy. His recommendation was essential.

Somerville would interview each candidate and, if satisfied, give him a certificate of good character together with train tickets to Queenstown (now Cobh), just to the east of Cork city, where there was a naval base. The successful recruit was also given some cash. This money, the 'Queen's shilling', had become infamous because it suggested acceptance of British control over Ireland. It is believed that Somerville received a payment of ten shillings per person for whom he provided such recommendations. He paid the ultimate price for recruiting young Irish men into the British navy when he was assassinated in 1936, probably by the Irish Republican Army (IRA).

Once at the Queenstown naval base, Denis would have introduced himself by means of the vice admiral's letter and been accepted for naval training. The significance of these simple steps was profound in the Ireland of 1898, particularly for a young man whose father had spent his adult life fighting so that the Irish people could once again enjoy ownership of their own land. One can imagine the old man's embarrassment that one of his own sons had 'taken the Queen's shilling'. Denis was told that he would not be welcome at Inchindreen in a British naval uniform. But he had not taken the drastic step of breaking with his family and joining the British navy in mere youthful rebellion; he could see no other way of ensuring his future. The second oldest of 12 children, he would not inherit the farm. His prospects looked bleak in the desperately poor Ireland of that time. However strongly Denis Hurley's family reacted against his decision, the British navy could offer him something that they could not: reasonably paid employment for the term of his service and a pension on retirement.

The 'Hurley Family Chronicle'—written by Archbishop Hurley's sister Eileen, after a visit to Ireland in the early 1950s—records that an uncle by marriage arranged for Denis to join the training ship *The Black Prince* at Queenstown. It seems, therefore, that not all members of the family were unsympathetic to his plight. The 'Hurley Family Chronicle' reports that from Queenstown Denis went to Devonport in England and joined a battle cruiser on a trip to the West Indies. The new cruiser broke down and the crew had to be picked up by an older ship. On returning to Devonport, Denis was sent to gunnery school for a year. After this training he was drafted to HMS *Pearl*, which was due to sail to Africa. When it reached Madeira, the news arrived that the Anglo-Boer War (1899–1902) had broken out in South Africa. For the next four years, HMS *Pearl* was based at Simonstown in the Cape Colony, from where it patrolled the African coast, going as far up the East Coast as Zanzibar and even visiting Mauritius.

In 1906 Denis Hurley decided to buy himself out of the navy by paying the standard fee of ten pounds, quite a substantial sum at the time. The 'Hurley Family Chronicle' records that he entered the South African Light Service on 2 April 1906 and arrived at the Cape St Francis lighthouse for his first duty on 7 April.

He was initially appointed a 'relieving keeper', who spent short periods filling in for keepers and assistant keepers on leave or ill. Between 1906 and 1913, he served in this capacity at fifteen lighthouses ranging from Cape Recife, near Port Elizabeth, and up the West Coast to Port Nolloth. On 15 June 1913, he was promoted to assistant keeper and assigned to Danger Point in the Western Cape, his last assignment before going home to Ireland for six months' leave. The family believes that his two married sisters, who were living in Cape Town at the time, urged him to find a bride while at home in Ireland since an engagement to someone in Cape Town had not worked out.

Meanwhile, Theresa May O'Sullivan, who had emigrated to the United States and was working as a seamstress in Salem, Massachusetts, had also made her way back to Skibbereen on long leave. Theresa, or 'Tess', as she was known, was the sixth of eight girls in a family of twelve children. Her father was a blacksmith with a forge in Skibbereen's High Street. The skill had been handed down for several generations. In addition, Jeremiah O'Sullivan received an annual payment from the government for veterinary services, despite not having any formal qualification: what he did have was extensive practical experience. In the Irish Census of 1901, he indicated his 'profession or occupation' as 'farmer, veterinary surgeon and master blacksmith'.

In his youth Jeremiah had been a member of the Fenians, and a family story describes how one day the British army searched the O'Sullivan house for arms. Jeremiah's two older sisters were working in the kitchen, one ironing and the other sewing. The soldiers went through the pile of ironing, pushing it out of place, and one of the sisters gave them a tongue-lashing for disturbing her work. The other scolded her quietly for being rude to men who were only carrying out their orders. The soldiers left and the two sisters had a good laugh: throughout the search, the quiet one had been perched sedately on her brother's pistols.

Jeremiah O'Sullivan had married the daughter of a nearby farmer, Kitty Collins, who was to become famous for her charity and assistance at births and deaths. Jeremiah's property included a smallholding nearly two kilometres from the house. There Kitty was in charge, keeping cows and pigs, fowls and geese, and growing potatoes and corn while her husband was working at the forge.

In 1885 Jeremiah became a member of the Irish National League, a successor to the Land League. The new body's object was to attain national self-government for the Irish, as well as to promote land law reform, local self-government, extension of the parliamentary and municipal franchises, and the development of Ireland's industries. The 'Hurley Family Chronicle' records that Jeremiah was a 'picturesque character, powerfully built, and his strength was a legend in Skibbereen. [He was] afraid of nobody but a good many people were afraid of him'. His failing, however, was 'the drink' and he is said to have given his wife 'many a sleepless night'.

Young Tess had left school after she passed the equivalent of Standard VII, or ninth grade. She would have liked to be a teacher or a nurse, but there were no opportunities. The only work she could find was an apprenticeship to a dressmaker for two years, after which she earned four shillings a week, working from 9 a.m. to 8 p.m. on Monday to Saturday, with an hour off for lunch.

There were several pretty girls in the O'Sullivan family, but Tess was thought to be *the* beauty. She enjoyed life and loved singing and dancing. Three of her sisters had left for the United States by the time she decided to set out for what was seen as the land of opportunity.

The O'Sullivan sisters who had already emigrated to Salem, Massachusetts, lived together in the home of their married sister, Sarah Draper. They looked after each other; with their help Tess soon found work with a Mrs Chapman, a high-class dress-maker who had a number of young women working for her. Mrs Chapman was so impressed with Tess's work that when she went to live in Canada, she invited Tess to go with her. Tess did not want to leave because she had family in Salem and knew that working conditions and pay were better in America, so she stayed. After three years she had saved enough to go home for a nine-month holiday. She returned to Salem after that holiday and just four years later had saved enough to go home to Skibbereen again. This was the 1913 holiday that found her there at the same time as Denis Hurley.

By the time of this visit, Denis had been accepted back by his family. He had long since left the British navy, and 15 years had passed since he had left home. His two Cape Town sisters, who must have seen a lot of him during his naval and lighthouse service, probably interceded for him even before he went home on holiday. According to the family story, during his holiday at Inchindreen his father sent him into town to have a horse shod at the O'Sullivans' forge. During this visit, a match was made between Tess and Denis, as was common at the time. They did not know each other, though Tess knew Denis's younger brother Dan quite well and his sisters by sight.

On 11 November 1913, within three weeks of the match-making, Denis and Tess were married at the Pro-Cathedral in Skibbereen. In an article entitled 'Wedding Bliss', a local newspaper described the event as a 'very pretty function' at which the bride had worn a dress of white silk and Irish lace with a hat of Irish lace and ostrich plumes. The report listed at length the details of who had given what gifts to the couple.

No wedding invitations were issued in those days, but the word would have gone out far and wide: relations, friends and neighbours of both families would know that they were expected and would be welcome. After nuptial Mass in the pro-cathedral, a great wedding party took place for several days at the O'Sullivan home, 45 High Street. Among those who would have attended were farmers bringing their dairy pro-duce to town, dropping in to join the celebration on the way to the creamery and then again on the way home. The next day or days they might repeat this procedure. To provide for the many guests, a pig would probably have been slaughtered, and there would have been much home baking. The central feature, though, would doubtless have been an abundance of the powerfully alcoholic Irish brew *poteen*.

It is recorded that the newlyweds commenced the long journey to South Africa by train from Skibbereen at 7:25 p.m. on their wedding day. Their luggage was sent on ahead of them to the station by pony cart; they walked the length of High Street, stopping at houses along the way to greet people and say farewell. They told every-one they would be back for a visit within a few years, but Skibbereen would never see them again. For their two families, it would have been an emotional time, and though the party continued for the next two days, it must often have seemed more like a wake, with the handsome couple gone. Farewells of this kind were all too common in Ireland at that time. The 1901 census put the country's population at about four-and-a-half million, a drop of over three-and-a-half million in just 60 years: a million had died in the famine of 1847 to 1851, and two-and-a-half million had emigrated.

The newly-wed Denis Hurley obviously knew the conditions he and Tess would find in South Africa, especially at the lighthouses where he had been a relieving keeper during the previous eight years, but those conditions would have been totally unknown to his wife. In addition, she must have been apprehensive about this complete break with her family. She had been brought up in the close Irish community of Skibbereen. Even when she went to Salem, Massachusetts, four of her siblings were there with her, living in the same house and able to help each other adapt to the new country. She was part of a lively young set who went to movies and enjoyed all the modern dances.

Denis and Tess were initially based at Cape Recife, near Port Elizabeth, where Denis returned to his position as assistant lighthouse keeper. Their first child, Eileen, was born there. Denis had the support of two married sisters in Cape Town but even they were quite far from Cape Recife. Tess had no relations in South Africa. Moreover, though today we view lighthouses as quaint and charming places, increasingly used for tourist and holiday accommodation, they must have seemed lonely and isolated nearly a hundred years ago.

2

Lighthouses[1]

When the Portuguese explorer Bartholomew Dias rounded Cape Point for the first time in his storm-battered ship in 1488, he called it *Cabo Tormentosa*, the Cape of Torments. Other explorers, with similar experience of raw winter rain and winds, called it the Cape of Storms. Howling north-westerly winds, torrential downpours and poor visibility made this one of the most dangerous and feared coastlines in the world. Few places could be more in need of a lighthouse to ensure that ships avoided these perils, especially in winter. Yet it was not until 1 May 1860 that a lighthouse was built at Cape Point. The first site was at the highest and most conspicuous point, 249 metres above sea level, from which there was a spectacular view over False Bay and the Atlantic Ocean. Yet this turned out to be the wrong choice of site, something brought home by a dramatic shipwreck early in the twentieth century.

The Portuguese steamer *Lusitania* (5,557 tons), was on its way from Lourenço Marques (now known as Maputo) to Cape Town on the night of 18 April 1911 with 678 passengers and 122 crew members. Captain Faria sighted the Cape Point lighthouse and charted a course that would give it a wide berth. Though conditions were calm, a gathering mist gradually made it impossible to see the lighthouse. Just over an hour later, visibility suddenly improved, but to his dismay Captain Faria found that he had drifted too close to the lighthouse. Turning quickly to port, he headed for the open sea, but fate brought the *Lusitania* to a grinding halt on Bellows Rock just before midnight. Most of the passengers and crew were saved, with the lighthouse keeper playing a key role in their rescue.

The wreck of the *Lusitania* had been caused by the siting of the lighthouse, which for an average of 900 hours a year was enveloped in fog. Lower down the cliffs, however, visibility was always good. A new lighthouse was eventually erected only 87 metres above the sea, 160 metres lower than the original structure. Work started in 1913 but, because of the difficult terrain, was only completed in 1919. The new lighthouse has one of the most powerful lights in the world and has saved many ships from destruction.

Denis Hurley senior was transferred from Cape Recife to become one of two assistant lighthouse keepers at Cape Point towards the end of 1914, shortly after Eileen's birth in September 1914.[2] The wreck of the *Lusitania* must still have been fresh in the minds of lighthouse staff at Cape Point when he and Theresa arrived there. Construction work for the new lighthouse had just begun and would continue for another six years, long after the Hurleys and their two children had left for their next posting. One can imagine that during Denis Hurley's time at Cape Point, the staff members were often on a state of high alert, especially whenever the lighthouse misted over.

Early in October 1915, Theresa Hurley travelled to Cape Town, a journey of about 60 kilometres, to prepare for her second confinement. She later told her daughter Eileen that she had never felt better than during that pregnancy. Denis Hurley's sister Lizzie had invited Theresa to stay with them for the last month. A Cape cart pulled by mules took her from Cape Point to Simonstown; from there she caught the train to Cape Town. The dirt track to Simonstown was notoriously bumpy and may have led to what Theresa regarded as a remarkably smooth delivery, the easiest of her four confinements. 'He came so easy, he just popped out. He cried at the right moment; breathed at the right moment; sucked at the right moment—he was just a perfect baby'.

The birth took place at 3:30 p.m. on 9 November 1915, and the baby weighed 8½ pounds. He was named Denis after his father and grandfather, and Eugene after the oldest surviving O'Sullivan uncle. Father John Colgan baptised Denis on 21 November 1915 at St Mary's Cathedral, near Parliament in Cape Town.

Once Theresa and baby Denis were back at Cape Point, a cow named Sarah was purchased to provide fresh milk so that the baby would not need to be weaned on condensed milk; everyone at the Cape Point lighthouse benefited from the supply of fresh milk. In fact, Sarah became a talking point at the settlement and on one occasion fell into disgrace because she ate all the bread belonging to soldiers in the nearby camp. They were encamped there to protect Cape Point, part of a major international shipping route round South Africa, under threat from the Germans during the hostilities of World War I. Denis and Eileen spent their first years there unaware that they were living in spectacularly beautiful but troubled surroundings.

Denis's father's next appointment was to another of South Africa's famous lighthouses, on Robben Island, to which he was transferred in 1918.[3] The family sailed there from Table Bay harbour on a small steamer named *Pieter Faure*, a converted tug that made the 9-kilometre trip several times a week. The island, roughly 2- by 3½-kilometres, is now internationally famous because for decades it was the location of a maximum security prison for political prisoners. Many members of the African National Congress (ANC) and Pan Africanist Congress (PAC) as well as the South West African People's Organisation (SWAPO), were held there from the early 1960s to the early 1990s; the most notable of them, Nelson Mandela.

Over the years the island has been used for various other purposes, but at the time the Hurleys lived there, from 1918 to 1923, it was the site of three major institutions: a mental hospital, a leper asylum and a big prison for black convicts serving long sentences. A fence across the island prevented anyone from crossing into the half occupied by the leper asylum. A small community of white people was in charge of these institutions. By the 1920s, there were estimated to be between one and two thousand people on the island, including patients, prisoners and staff. There were Anglican and Catholic churches, a school, a library, sports fields, tennis courts and recreation halls, a police force and a fire brigade; especially the last-mentioned made a big impact on the children.

The lighthouse had been completed in 1865, but there had been a much earlier way of warning ships off the Cape coast: in 1657, Jan van Riebeeck, the founder of the white settlement at the Cape in 1652, gave instructions for a platform to be built on the island's highest point, Mount Minto, the site of the present lighthouse. A fire was kept burning there at night to guide shipping.

During the period that the Hurleys spent on the island, two members were added to the family: Jerry (Jeremiah) born in 1919 and Chris (Christopher) in 1922. Theresa Hurley did not need to go to a maternity home because there was a doctor and a midwife on the island. The midwife moved in and took over the household before the birth and stayed on for ten days afterwards.

Denis's memory is that 'Father and mother were wonderful parents, and we became a deeply united family with a strong Irish-Catholic faith. Mother was the predominant influence in the matter of faith . . . She lived her faith and communicated it easily to her children. Father was devout but it was mother who created the deep spiritual atmosphere of our home'.

There was no church close to Cape Point, so Theresa used to lead prayers at home on Sundays. Perhaps Denis's first experience of faith led by a woman made it easier for him, much later in life, to support the idea of women's ordination.

His father had a tremendous sense of justice and fair play; he used to tell his children: 'No matter where people are, what level they are at, what colour their skin, you know that you are not to treat anybody badly in this house'. Denis remembered that his father was as good as his word and 'never allowed anyone to be treated badly'. This became an important factor in his own response to the injustices of South Africa. Combined with these qualities were his father's strong sense of duty and capacity for hard work, qualities that he also inherited. He must have often been at his father's side and seen what a difficult, strenuous and tiring job it was to be a lighthouse keeper, without the technology available today. He had one of his earliest spankings when, as a practical joke, he called out during the family rosary one evening that the lighthouse light had gone out.

Denis attended the little government school on the island. Sub A and Sub B were taught by Miss Hands, who was much loved by everyone; but about a year or so after Denis began his schooling, she left to get married in Cape Town. The whole school went down to the jetty to wave a tearful goodbye. Another teacher had Standards I, II and III and the headmaster, a Mr Newton, Standards IV, V and VI. Denis had a great admiration for Mr Newton. 'He was a very dignified person. He spoke very kindly . . . with a certain warmth in his voice. Children take to people in whom they sense a certain warmth and humanity and welcoming attitude, so I took to him for that reason'.

One day a teacher wrote down details of each child in Denis's class. When Denis was asked, 'What is your religion?' he replied, 'Irish'. He told his mother about this at home, but she said he should not say that too loudly. It was the time of the Irish rebellion of 1921 and 1922 against British control of Ireland. Theresa was aware that the Irish rebels were unpopular with loyal British subjects on Robben Island and in Cape Town.

Star of the Sea Catholic Church was an important place for the Hurley family. A priest came from Cape Town once a month to say Mass and attend to the spiritual needs of the Catholic population. Theresa, who must have felt sadly deprived of regular Mass at Cape Point, was delighted to have at least this monthly opportunity, and her enthusiasm rubbed off on her children. They also remembered occasionally taking part in the Sunday school activities of other churches, marching behind their banners and singing Protestant hymns such as 'All things bright and beautiful', which suggests a tolerance on the part of their parents unusual for that time.

Denis became interested in sport at an early age and would accompany his father to watch football and cricket. He was excited about this and would walk home a little faster than his father to get there first and let his mother know the results. At this time, young Denis also became keen to pursue a rather unusual career. Early each morning, a group of convicts would come round to each house to collect the night soil. Dressed in bright-red striped uniforms, they drove on a dashing mule cart, clanging and rattling buckets and shouting to each other. Denis found this activity most attractive and would have liked to join them as a convict on Robben Island— an ambition that did not last long.

His parents took turns to wash up at night. The one who was not 'on duty' would read aloud interesting articles from the newspaper. Often the items selected concerned conflicts in Ireland, and one name was particularly prominent. It sounded most ominous: 'devil era'. Later, Denis learnt that this was Éamonn de Valera, the elected representative of the Irish rebels. He was to hear no more about the name until the early 1930s, when he arrived in Ireland for his novitiate and discovered that de Valera was leading the *Fianna Fáil* party in the election and had emerged as the new Prime Minister of Ireland.

An event on Robben Island that caused great excitement, especially for children, was the arrival of planes. These were former de Havilland DH.9 fighter aircraft from World War I, which had been disarmed for civilian use but still had their two cockpits: pilot in the rear and navigator in the front. A commercial venture took people on short trips for ten shillings a flight. From Robben Island they flew to Table Mountain, giving their passengers an outstanding view of Cape Town, and then returning to land on the beach of Robben Island. Denis was also fascinated to watch ocean liners sweeping into Table Bay east of the island. The Union Castle liners were particularly impressive and he enjoyed sketching them.[4]

Soon the Hurley family would be on the move again, this time to East London to take up Denis senior's 1923 appointment as first assistant lighthouse keeper at the Hood Point lighthouse, 1,075 kilometres from Cape Town and about 5 kilometres south of downtown East London.[5]

Harold Williams, in *Southern Lights*, a study of South African lighthouses, says that Hood Point was one of the most popular stations in the service, perhaps because it was close to East London and not as isolated as many others. Denis was excited at the prospect of this transfer. At the Robben Island lighthouse richly illustrated magazines arrived regularly from England—*The Mirror*, *The Graphic* and *The Sketch*—from which he had learnt much about life in England, the royal family, cricket matches and so on. Now he would be seeing the real thing, he thought, not knowing that East London (in South Africa) was entirely different from London.

As some slight compensation, while the Hurleys were at Hood Point, three British battle cruisers, *Hood*, *Repulse* and *Renown*, visited East London. They were so big that they could not enter the Buffalo River harbour but had to anchor outside. Nevertheless, the family examined the ships closely through binoculars. In later life, Denis could give a detailed account of the battles these cruisers were involved in some 19 or 20 years later: his lifelong fascination with naval battles would have made his ex-navy father proud of him.

The school that Eileen and Denis attended was the East London West Bank Government School. Eileen found herself in Standard IV and Denis in Standard III, whereas they had expected to be in Standards III and II. Somehow, in the combination of classes on the island, two years had been telescoped into one for each of them. This would later have an effect: in high school Denis was one year younger than all the other boys in his class. He was already younger because of having his birthday at the end of the year. This was probably one of the reasons for his shyness and difficulty integrating into the high schools he attended: St Thomas's and St Charles's.

Once again, as on Robben Island, Denis went with his father to watch soccer matches, this time at the West Bank Football Club. By now he had become more partisan, giving his undivided loyalty to the side that he regarded as his own. Standing on the sideline with his father, he would try to coax the ball into the opponents' goal by forcing his head in that direction. He was so intent on pushing the ball up the field with his head that he would quite often go home with a stiff neck.

Perhaps the family member who was happiest at Hood Point was Theresa Hurley. For the first time the family had a resident parish priest, a delightful Irishman, Father Flanagan, and the family could attend all the services in the nearby wood-and-iron church. The children took part in the regular catechism classes on Saturday afternoons, and Denis was prepared for his first confession and communion. It was even possible to have home visits from Father Flanagan, events that caused a 'sense of joy and real exultation . . . A priest in the house was built up in our childish emotions and imagination as almost a visit from God himself'. Father Flanagan rode a motorbike, which added to the children's interest in him, and led his fellow priests to compose a jingle: 'On again, off again, gone again, Flanagan'.

Within a year at most, the stay at Hood Point was over and the family was transferred again, this time to Clansthal, near Umkomaas on the Natal South Coast, about 60 kilometres southwest of Durban.[6] This would prove to be the most isolated of all four lighthouses at which the young Denis lived with his family. Early in 1924, his father took up this appointment, a promotion to lighthouse keeper, with one assistant keeper, a Mr Gray.

In his memoirs, Jerry Hurley described what it was like to arrive at the isolated Clansthal. When their train stopped at the Clansthal siding, the whole family had to troop with all their luggage up a steep hill and through dense bush to the lighthouse, which stood on the crest. To make matters worse, they arrived at night. The way up was not a road, just a sandy track, too soft for any form of wheeled vehicle. Goods had to be brought up from the railway halt on a sledge made out of a large fork of a tree, pulled by oxen.

The Clansthal 'settlement' comprised the lighthouse, painted red and white, and houses for the keeper and his assistant. The lighthouse had a paraffin pressure lamp that shone through a series of lenses to create two powerful beams of light, sweeping a long distance over the Indian Ocean, across a reef known as Aliwal Shoal. The pressure lamp was placed on a platform that revolved because heavy weights pulled on a chain driving a series of cogwheels. When the weights reached the ground floor of the lighthouse, a long distance below, the platform would stop rotating unless a keeper was present to wind them manually to the top again. One of the two keepers had to be on duty from 6:00 p.m. to 6:00 a.m. every night to make sure the rotation never stopped.

Aliwal Shoal is a submerged mass of rock, approximately four kilometres long and one kilometre wide, about five kilometres from the coast and has caused the wreck of many ships. At the lowest tide, a white line of surf can be seen where the sea breaks over the exposed shoal. The Hurley family found it exciting to watch ships making their way to and from Durban on the coastal side of the shoal, especially the large Union Castle liners with their distinctive grey hulls and black-and-red funnels, which Denis had enjoyed sketching at Robben Island.

Denis imagined that the remoteness of the new home at Clansthal must have been a cause of great concern to his mother. Because of the racial prejudices of the time, the family did not regard the Indians and Africans who lived close to the lighthouse as their neighbours, and no whites were living nearby. The Hurleys' new home was situated on a two-acre clearing, ' . . . surrounded by trees and bush inhabited by monkeys and snakes, among which the green mamba appeared to be the most dangerous. There were black mambas too but not as numerous as the green ones, also antelope in the wild leafy area, the main species being bushbuck, duikers and the tiny ones we called "pities," after the Zulu word *ipithi*'.

There were monkeys in the bush around the house, who liked to visit a wild fig tree nearby. On at least one occasion some of them got into the kitchen and stole food. The children found them frightening, especially one that their father shot. They also occasionally heard shots in the night when he eliminated a snake or buck. Once when he had wounded a bushbuck, it charged him, and he had to fire a second shot in a hurry. On another occasion he shot a dog that was disturbing his sleep during his week off night duty. This led to a court appearance in Umkomaas, the outcome of which was not known to the children: they were discouraged from asking about the incident.

Schooling was the major concern for the parents. The closest government school was eight kilometres away and would have involved a daily walk up and down hills. The only solution was boarding school, but Theresa insisted that it must be Catholic. She began to look all along the coast for a suitable school. While she was engaged in this search, their father tried to keep Eileen and Denis's minds active by teaching them Morse code and how to signal with a lamp, as well as the points of the compass. But these two bright children were not wildly excited about naval skills and longed to get back to school. Eventually Theresa saw an advertisement in *The Southern Cross*, the national Catholic weekly newspaper, for a primary school at St Elmo's Convent, Umzumbe, run by the Newcastle Dominican nuns.

Theresa travelled the 50 kilometres to Umzumbe to meet the nuns and persuade them to take Eileen and Denis as their first boarders. There were only twenty pupils in this primary school, taught by three nuns. Eileen and Denis were accepted as boarders in June 1924, Eileen for Standard V and Denis for Standard IV. Jerry and Chris were accepted later, also as boarders. Chris described the convent and school as 'pretty primitive places, especially so in having pit toilets down a path into the bush. We learned to throw a stone in that direction in the hope that it would scare away any snakes that might be around'.

At the end of Standard V, Eileen was kept back to repeat that class. She thought it was because her arithmetic was poor, but Denis thought her poor health was the problem. Whatever the reason, the result was that they went into Standard VI together and completed the Standard VI School Leaving Certificate at the same time.

Neither Clansthal nor Umzumbe was socially stimulating for young people; they had to make the most of whatever rare excitement came their way. A real treat was a visit by Monsignor Frederick Kolbe, a prominent priest from Cape Town, 'Uncle Joe' of 'Children's Corner' in *The Southern Cross*. Monsignor Kolbe travelled the country to visit all his 'Cornerites', as he called them. He was so impressed by the four young Hurleys that he wrote a poem about them, which *The Southern Cross* published with a photo of them dressed in sailor suits.

Another great excitement was the visit of an 'Agricultural Exhibition Train'. In the coaches were lots of exhibits in bottles especially intended for schoolchildren, and the St Elmo's pupils examined it 'from top to bottom'. Denis remembered a pig's heart preserved in methylated spirits; Eileen recalled snakes in bottles.

Once again, as on Robben Island, aeroplanes aroused much interest. This time it was a newly-established airmail service between Cape Town and Durban. Like those they had seen at Robben Island, the aircraft were probably of World War I vintage. If the St Elmo's pupils were not in class, they would run out as far as they could into the fields and wave to the pilots, who would wave back.

Another example of how even a simple event could cause great excitement was the stir caused by a picnic at Hibberdene, a coastal resort just four kilometres from Umzumbe. The whole school went there by train, spent a few hours on the beach and then returned. This was such a sensational break from normal routine that the children chatted about it excitedly for weeks before and after.

Reflecting on what effect the isolation had on him at crucial stages of his development, Denis said many years later: 'I think it put me back a bit in growing up with sociable instincts. I think I found it rather hard to mix in with communities of boys later on and to make friends with [them] . . . Clansthal on the South Coast of Natal . . . was very lonely indeed because there were only two lighthouse keepers' families there [and only] one other little boy younger than myself. When I first went to boarding school, I found it hard to drift into the community life . . . I think I was very, very shy'.

By the time Denis and Eileen passed the Standard VI School Leaving Certificate, it was clear that Denis was already thinking about the priesthood. Schooling came to an end after Standard VI for many young people. They were expected to go out and look for work to boost their family income. That was not to be the case with Eileen and Denis because their parents were determined that their children should have better opportunities than they had had. In Denis's case a secondary education was essential because he was thinking about the priesthood.

When he wrote his memoirs, he found it difficult to remember how he had begun to think of becoming a priest even in his primary school days. It might have been an inspiration of his mother, perhaps promoted by the nuns, who had plenty of opportunity. Starting at the ages of 10 and 9 respectively, Eileen and Denis had lived in the convent at Umzumbe for 3½ years: 'We were the only two boarders, and we slept upstairs in the convent'. Eileen actually had a cubicle in the nuns' dormitory. It must have been a strange but influential experience for the two young Hurleys, a remarkable exposure to a life of prayer and religious discipline.

3

High School

When Eileen and Denis Hurley successfully completed their Standard VI School Leaving Certificate, it was not easy for their parents to organise high school education for them because St Elmo's, Umzumbe, did not go beyond Standard VI.[1] Life at a remote lighthouse and their parents' insistence on Catholic schooling meant that secondary schooling would have to be at boarding schools even further from home. The Dominican sisters ran two suitable schools in Newcastle, Northern Natal: the Newcastle Academy for girls went up to matriculation, and St Thomas's Boys' School went up to Standard VIII. So it was that Eileen and Denis began their high schooling there in 1928, while Jerry and Chris continued as boarders at St Elmo's. The parents found it hard that their children had to go so far away to continue their education. Two train journeys were involved: from Clansthal to Durban (60 kilometres) and from Durban to Newcastle (239).

There was no comparison between St Elmo's and the Newcastle Academy in terms of academic excellence and opportunities; St Thomas's also had more pupils and facilities. Denis was initially at something of a disadvantage in Latin because the other boys had already had two years of this subject, whereas it was new to him. He was able to catch up with extra lessons given by a Sister Enda who could not have had any idea of what an important foundation she was laying. A more complex disadvantage was his secluded childhood. One of his contemporaries at St Thomas's, Gerry O'Donovan, remembers him and his great friend, Pat Holland, as somewhat aloof. In O'Donovan's view, they seemed to regard themselves as superior; he thought it was because they were both considering the priesthood. He may, however, have been merely misinterpreting their underlying shyness.

St Thomas's was in some ways an ideal school for teenage boys since it was several miles outside Newcastle and surrounded by farmlands.[2] Attached to it was a large estate, the whole of the area now known as Lennoxton, with the Incandu River flowing through it. Though there was no swimming pool, the boys made the most of the river and swam as often as they could. On the far bank lay many picnic places in the foothills of the Drakensberg Mountains, to which the school made regular visits.

Films were shown every Saturday evening by a young man named Dawjee. The girls at the Academy would see the same film earlier in the week. Eileen recalled that Dawjee had been trained by the nuns to put his hands over the projector if there were any scenes the girls ought not to see: this led to much yelling by way of protest. Those were the days of silent movies, with the dialogue printed on the film. In bioscopes, as they were then called, a pianist would provide musical accompaniment appropriate to the excitement on-screen, but it is unlikely that any such arrangement was possible at these two boarding schools. Denis recalled *The Mark of Zorro* and *Rin Tin Tin* as his favourite films, while Eileen's were *Tom Mix* and *Tom Coleman*.

The classes at St Thomas's were taught by nuns; one of them, Sister Josephine Ryan, was also in charge of the boarders. She was a disciplinarian, with a knotted cane, and anyone who misbehaved felt its effect. Newcastle is cold in winter and, to protect themselves from the chill of undressing, some of the boys occasionally tried to get into bed without changing into their pyjamas. If this was discovered by Sister Josephine, they could expect a good spanking. Harold Dainty, a contemporary of Denis Hurley's, recalled another aspect of boarding school life: all the boys were given a dose of castor oil from time to time, a fairly common practice in the 1920s and 1930s and still happening even in the 1950s.

As so often in boarding schools, food was the great preoccupation. 'We often had sago pudding—it was dreadful stuff', complained Dainty. The boys were allowed individual vegetable patches where they grew carrots, radishes and turnips, 'anything we could eat without having to cook it'. They were also allowed to fish in the river, and the nuns would cook that day's catch for the successful anglers—though all they ever caught was barbell, not the tastiest of fish.

The St Thomas's chaplain was a young Frenchman, Father Charles Hugo OMI, who had come to South Africa in a last attempt to regain his health; he had a severe case of tuberculosis of the bone in his left arm, a condition that could have affected the rest of his body. Because Father Hugo was still learning English, but probably also as a way of exerting a spiritual influence over three boys who were considering the priesthood, he would bring Denis Hurley, Pat Holland and Joseph Surgeson together every Saturday evening to correct any mistakes in his sermon in English for the next day. This arrangement had the added advantage of helping the three to think about the readings and texts of the day. Denis Hurley described it as 'a nursery of priests'.

Bertie Simpkins, a close friend of Denis's, with whom he shared a double desk for his two years at St Thomas's, recalled a group photo of Hurley, Holland and Surgeson. He had no doubt that even at this stage Denis was serious about becoming a priest and, in his view, this photo of the three potential candidates for the priesthood indicated that they were seen as such by the school. Denis was certain that, 'the idea of the priesthood had already come to me. I don't know how these things come to you; they grow into you, and you grow into them'. He received a lot of encouragement from Father Hugo, who also passed on word to Bishop Henri Delalle OMI, the Vicar Apostolic of Natal, about these boys' interest in the priesthood. Some of Denis's school friends believe his commitment grew even more intense after a dramatic event in his first year at St Thomas's.

May 24 was a public holiday, Empire Day, and in 1928 St Thomas's celebrated the occasion with a picnic.[3] The boys went to Loxton's Drift, across the river and in the foothills of the Drakensberg Mountains, where they could play and explore. They were expected back at the Drift at 2:00 p.m. for a picnic lunch, after which they could spend the afternoon in further exploration. Denis was with two other boys, Colin Marshman and George Rossiter. In their pre-lunch wandering they came to the small entrance of a cave and decided to explore it. Denis assumed the other boys knew the cave after several years at St Thomas's and numerous picnics.

Denis described himself as the least enthusiastic about this expedition. As the three were going into the cave, somewhere between 10:30 and 11:30 a.m., he took off the broad-brimmed hat borrowed from a boy called Leslie Delease and left it outside, fearing that it would get in the way. It was dark in the cave and the only light they had was that of a torch. After exploring for a while and not finding anything exciting, they decided to come out. Denis was leading the group but suddenly took a wrong turn, stepped back and said, 'Oh, this is the wrong way'. As he did so, he trod on the hand of the boy holding the torch. The torch clattered down into the blackness of the cave, and that was the last they saw of it.

Without the torch, the cave 'was absolutely pitch black; you couldn't see the slightest indication of any light'. They did not know what to do or where to go but groped around, looking for the entrance. There were so many passages, all similar, that they could not work out which they had used to enter the cave, and they feared to take a wrong turn. Soon they began to feel the cold and to shiver; they huddled together to keep warm as they sat on the damp rocks. They had just their short-sleeved shirts and short pants, no jacket or jersey, and nothing to eat or drink.

By 4:30 p.m., when there was still no sign of the three, Leslie Delease, the boy who had lent his hat to Denis, told Sister Josephine that he had seen them going into a cave but that they had not come out while he was there. The other nuns calmed Sister Josephine, who was becoming anxious, telling her that the boys would surely be back soon. She wondered whether they had crossed the Drakensberg range but said to herself, 'Denis Hurley is such an excellent boy, and he being one of the three helped me to hope that they were not up to mischief'. Delease reassured her that the boys had been in that cave often before, so there was no danger; the boys knew every cave on those hills.

That evening, a search party set off, consisting of Father Hugo, the prioress, Sister Josephine and three boys, including Delease. They struggled to cross the Incandu River in the dark and found it difficult to climb up to the caves. Mother Prioress fell many times but was determined to continue. Delease, the only one who knew the location of the cave, was unable to find it in the darkness despite a two-hour search. Later, the other two boys and Father Hugo tried again. This time they located the hat and the cave, but because it was so dark, they could do nothing further until morning.

During that long night in the cave, the three lost boys heard a clattering over their heads and thought there must be people walking there. They decided to shout as loudly as they could, on repeated counts of three. But no one heard.

When the police arrived the next morning, they refused to believe that the boys could be in the cave, arguing that they must have gone off somewhere else. Sister Josephine was equally adamant that they must be there, because the hat was there. The police refused to go down into the cave, claiming that the opening was too small for them. Sister Josephine regarded this as sheer cowardice and rebuked them sternly, 'There is not a man amongst you'. Fortunately, one of the boys, Charlie Farr, offered to go down and was lowered with a cable fastened around his waist.

Denis described the night in the cave as the most terrible of his life; he hoped he would never experience anything like it again. Writing for the St Thomas's school magazine, he said, 'That night could be called a night of prayer. We, in the cave, prayed as we never did before, whilst those awaiting our return to the light of day prayed alternately for our safety, and for the repose of our souls, according as hope or despair was uppermost in their minds'. Marshman and Rossiter were Protestants, and they were praying out aloud while Denis was praying silently to a nineteenth-century French saint, Thérèse of Lisieux, who 'did a great job that night'. Many years later he visited her shrine at Lisieux to thank her for saving their lives. 'I had been owing her a visit for close on 75 years'.[4] Marshman and Rossiter 'prayed very hard; in fact, they were a good example to me about praying'. Denis would often refer to how much he had learnt about spontaneous public prayers from this ecumenical experience. Later on, he also became skilled at such prayers.

After Charlie Farr had been in the cave for about five minutes, he called out, 'Sister, Marshman's name is printed on a rock'. A few minutes later he called out again: 'Sister, Rossiter is here'. When she asked 'Is he alive?' he replied, sounding as if he were a mile away: 'I don't know; he is shouting, but I can't see him'. A little later, Sister Josephine called out again to Charlie to ask where the other two boys were, and he replied that they were all there, safe and well.

The boys were drawn up out of the cave, one after the other, eager hands helping them to the top. Within minutes they were all perched on the rocks, after 22 hours of darkness. Denis had great difficulty keeping his eyes open because it was such a shock to look at the sunlight. Sister Josephine described the three boys as, 'sights to behold, with clay in their eyes, in their mouths, clay everywhere, but they were really happy and grateful'. She asked whether they had been frightened, and they told her they had prayed all through the night, but they knew that Delease had seen them go into the cave and felt sure he would tell her and she would come and get them out. The police, embarrassed that they had done so little to save the boys, made a last-minute attempt to redeem themselves by giving them the sandwiches they had brought for their own lunch.

The next day, Denis's mother happened to see in the *Natal Mercury* a story about three boys lost in a cave, and reading further, learnt that one of them was Denis Hurley. She almost fainted, and her husband had to run to her rescue and revive her. Sister Josephine was ill for a few days after the incident, and the boys could hear her at night, calling out in her nightmares. At the St Thomas's athletics day there was a happy sequel: a gold medal for the heroic rescue was presented to Charlie Farr by the mayoress of Newcastle, Mrs W. M. Goodwin.

Many years later, the Marshman and Rossiter families insisted that their fathers, Colin and George, had told them explicitly about a promise that Denis Hurley had made: if they got out of the cave alive, he would definitely become a priest. According to Bertie Simpkins, Denis already had the intention of becoming a priest, but as a result of the cave incident, it became a firm commitment. Certainly the cave experience was immensely maturing, helping the young Hurley to become more courageous and later on to face up to the much more challenging experiences of a bishop struggling against the darkness of apartheid.

The night in the cave signalled that childhood was ending for Denis and that serious decisions would soon have to be made. But something even more disturbing was to happen just over a year later, with painful consequences for him and for his whole family. It thrust him into the world of adult cares and responsibilities. He recalled how he and Eileen were on their way home for the July holidays, on the South Coast train that went through Clansthal.

> Something very strange occurred. Father joined the train at Umkomaas, a small town before Clansthal . . . Father was very excited and spoke incessantly. This was not like him at all. A good deal of his talk was in religious vein, inspiring but perplexing. We left the train at the Clansthal halt . . . and began walking up the sandy path through the bush to the lighthouse. Father kept up his talk. Suddenly we were met by mother, carrying a lantern. One look at her face and my heart sank into my shoes. Eileen must have had the same experience. On mother's face was a look of sheer agony. Something had gone terribly wrong. That something was my father's mental breakdown. The evening was awful, with my father behaving most oddly. He even went off to collect some neighbours from quite a distance to join us in a 'family party' marking the return of his daughter and son.

After this deeply disturbing start to their July holidays, a 'relieving keeper' was appointed to take charge of the Clansthal lighthouse, and Denis senior was put on sick leave. Initially, the idea was that the whole family would go on holiday to Umzumbe as guests of the Dominican sisters. This would give their father a chance to rest and help him regain his mental health. During the journey, however, he became offended at some perceived slight and refused to leave the train when they reached Umzumbe. It was clear that the problem was serious.

Theresa Hurley was then involved in intricate legal steps to have her husband committed to the Pietermaritzburg Mental Hospital.[5] This finally happened on 6 July 1929, on the basis of a recommendation from two doctors who declared him to be suffering from General Paralysis of the Insane (GPI). With the endorsement of the local magistrate, they authorised the committal. Whatever physiological basis there may have been for this condition, the extreme loneliness and isolation of Clansthal, coupled with the responsible and demanding task of a lighthouse keeper, must have taken their toll. About two months later, Mr Hurley was transferred to the Pretoria Mental Hospital, which had just opened a special unit for treatment of GPI. There he was successfully treated over the next 16 months and released on 30 December 1930.

In 1929, the Wall Street Stock Exchange in the United States collapsed, leading to a great worldwide economic crisis. There could not have been a worse time for a bread-winner to lose permanent employment and be put off work at the relatively young age of 49, at which he would only be entitled to a much-reduced pension. The severely traumatised family spent a miserable July holiday; then Denis and Eileen returned to Newcastle to complete their Junior Certificate. Jerry and Chris continued their schooling as boarders at Umzumbe, and their mother went to live there as well. When the school year ended, the two older children joined them, so the whole family was dependent on the hospitality of the sisters, being temporarily accommodated in classrooms.

Despite everything, Denis and Eileen did well in their Junior Certificate exams, and Mrs Hurley was determined that they should matriculate. In all these decisions, and in other family responsibilities, she could not look to her husband for any help. She had no idea when or whether he would ever improve. He was so utterly absent that it was almost as if he had died. Once again, the Church came to the rescue. Because Denis was apparently certain that he wanted to become a member of the religious congregation known as Oblates of Mary Immaculate, Bishop Delalle offered to pay for his schooling as a boarder at St Charles's College in Pietermaritzburg. Some arrangement must also have been made with the Dominican sisters about Eileen's fees at the Newcastle Academy, and for Jerry and Chris to continue as boarders at Umzumbe.

Mrs Hurley faced an uncertain future with four children at boarding school, an inadequate pension and no family home. She worked for a short time at a Catholic orphanage in Durban but found it impossible to continue. Then she decided to look for a house in Pietermaritzburg, where Jerry and Chris could stay with her while attending school at St Charles's as day scholars; Denis could remain a boarder at the school.

She later told him about a day when she had spent many hours looking for a suitable house to rent, without success. Eventually she sat down on a bench and wept. 'A kindly gentleman passing by spoke to her and gave her some cheer and encouragement. He turned out to be a prominent member of the Catholic Parish of St Mary's in Pietermaritzburg'. Perhaps he did more than merely give 'cheer and encouragement'; he may have even helped the family find suitable accommodation. Denis goes on to say: 'In due course a humble, semi-detached house within the limits of the family budget' was found.

Eventually the mother and children came together for the July holidays of 1930—a family still without a father, who was only released to rejoin them six months later. Meanwhile Mrs Hurley had gone back to dressmaking to supplement the family income. Chris remembers that 'she could look at a blazer and then draw the pattern and make the blazer. She made our shirts, she made our shorts, she made our longs, she pretty well made everything'.

When Denis senior returned from Pretoria, Eileen and Denis were somewhat reserved with him. They remembered the circumstances that had led to his being taken away and were probably anxious about how he might behave. Chris, the youngest, however, had had no such experience. He just knew his father had been away and that he had missed him very much. He rushed into his father's arms, which really pleased Mr Hurley.[6] From this time on, Denis senior seems to have been less of a disciplinarian in the family and became softer and more affectionate.

The young Denis Hurley was being exposed to other challenging new experiences. On one of the many train trips he took to school in Newcastle, before moving to St Charles's, when the train stopped at Pietermaritzburg, he was surprised to see a young white woman in animated conversation with an Indian woman. That may not sound unusual, but Denis was a young white boy, a product of his times and of his secluded upbringing. This was the first time he realised that people of different races could relate to each other normally. He had not previously understood that black people have the same need for relationships as white people, that they laughed and conversed freely.[7]

Saint Charles's College in Pietermaritzburg, where Denis started his Junior Matriculation year in January 1930, was by far the biggest school he had attended, with boys from Standard I to matriculation (Standard X).[8] It had been started by the Oblate fathers in 1877, in town. In 1914, the Marist Brothers, a French teaching congregation, took over. They had been founded after the Napoleonic wars in what Hurley called an 'extraordinary re-flowering' of the Catholic Church. From the start, the Marist Brothers' hope was to find a more suitable site for the school, with adequate grounds for sports. In 1924 that dream became a reality when the college moved to a 56-acre property in the suburb of Scottsville.

The impressive buildings and extensive grounds and gardens were still relatively new when Hurley was there in 1930 and 1931. The atmosphere of the school 'really excited' him; he realised he had been under the supervision of nuns for too long. He was happy to be taught and supervised by men and to be with boys of all ages. The school played cricket and rugby against the most prominent schools in the province, and this gave him a sense of importance. St Thomas's and St Elmo's were cut off from such competition. In the case of St Thomas's, pupils had played the Irish game of hurling, like hockey, with sticks and a ball, and 'cage ball' with a large inflated ball that could be hit, thrown, or kicked. These games may have provided fun but would largely have been unknown in other South African boys' schools, so there was no chance of any external competition.

Hurley was not, however, impressed by the academic standard of St Charles's— except for Brother Florian, one of the French brothers who had come to South Africa in 1903 after being expelled by an anti-clerical French government. 'He wasn't a very emotional person; he wasn't a very friendly person; he didn't mix easily with the boys, but when he taught, teaching as a profession was at its highest peak'. Hurley had the good fortune to be taught by Florian for three of his seven matriculation subjects: English, Latin and chemistry. Though French, Florian had achieved a wonderful mastery of English. His logical, coherent and highly organised lessons greatly influenced Hurley, who regarded him as one of the most methodical persons he had ever known. At the beginning of each year, he would hand out meticulously prepared diagrams indicating exactly what he intended to cover. As the year unfolded, Florian covered everything he had planned.

What made the biggest impact on Hurley was Florian's insistence that the weekly English essay should flow logically from a good introduction to a substantial middle and then work up to a strong conclusion. Once that was reached, not a word was to be added. One weekend Hurley had been so busy with sport that his first opportunity to write the essay came only during the study period after Sunday night supper, by which time he was tired. When he had finished the essay, he suddenly realised that he had omitted a key point and simply added it *after* his conclusion. The dressing-down he received the next day taught him a lesson for life.

By contrast, Brother Henry, a disciplinarian and a good headmaster, was quite ineffective as a mathematics teacher. He would lose himself in the problems he was working on at the blackboard and forget all about his pupils. He also disappointed Hurley by deciding that since the matriculation class was not sufficiently strong at history, they would do bookkeeping instead. Hurley loved history and found book-keeping a poor substitute, though it gave him a useful skill. Apart from being deprived of history, a major disappointment was the catechetical instruction during those two years. Hurley felt that he did not learn anything about his religion which he had not already learnt from the nuns during his primary schooling.

A regular visitor to the school was Bishop Delalle. He made a point of meeting with Hurley and the other boys who wanted to become Oblates. As Hurley came to the end of his matriculation year, an arrangement was finalised between him and the bishop that he would leave for Ireland early in 1932 to begin his training for the priesthood. During this phase, the novitiate, he would learn the basics of religious life. Eileen Hurley claimed that Denis had talked about being a priest since his childhood, but that at St Charles's he became serious about it. She also said, however, that their mother was determined not to be like other Irish mothers who pressurised their sons into the priesthood. Those without a genuine vocation did not survive long. It had to be Denis's own decision, not hers. So when he was at St Charles's, his mother asked him whether he still wanted to be a priest. His reply was, 'Oh, more than ever now'.[9]

As the end of 1931 drew near, however, he was becoming aware that he had chosen a difficult path, and he had some hesitation about his choice. Girls had not previously been a feature of his life, but now he was finding them attractive. 'I lay awake some nights brooding over it and at least on one occasion there were tears on the pillow. The prospect of the priesthood was looking less inviting. I was beginning to experience what all young men experience in their fifteenth and sixteenth years of age, and life not bound by priestly restrictions began to look a little more tempting. I managed with the help of God to rise above the temptations'.

Having made up his mind, 'there was no stopping the process'. Arrangements were made by Bishop Delalle for him to sail from Durban on the Carnarvon Castle. The departure date was 21 January 1932, when the other young men in his matriculation class were enjoying freedom from school life. He, by contrast, was about to enter a way of life that would be more restrictive than school had ever been—and far from family, home and country. It was a significant feature of Denis Hurley's character that, though he might take some time to reach a decision, once he had done so, there would be no turning back.

4

Ireland and Rome

A passport photo taken in 1931 shows Denis Hurley as a gentle sixteen-year-old, but there is also great determination in his face: he looks like a young man who has begun to have a sense of destiny. The first step would be a long journey from Pietermaritzburg in South Africa to Cahermoyle in Ireland, where he would make his novitiate with the Oblates of Mary Immaculate.

As arranged, he sailed from Durban on 21 January 1932, just weeks after completing matriculation, accompanied by Ralph Hughes, who was also going to join the Oblates.[1] Bishop Delalle invited Hurley to stay overnight at the cathedral presbytery in Durban before his departure. The next day the Hurley family came down to Durban to see Denis off at the docks. Though his departure was an adventure for the young man, he heard afterwards that the family's return to Pietermaritzburg was sad. The youngest, Chris, remembers his mother holding his hand the whole way back on the train,[2] and Jerry wrote in his memoirs that they reached home 'exhausted, leg-weary and bereft'.

The *Carnarvon Castle* made three stops on its voyage to Cape Town: at East London, Port Elizabeth and Mossel Bay. Hurley soon discovered that he was still as prone to seasickness as he had been as a young child on Robben Island, and going ashore for each of these stops was a great relief. While staying for a few days with his father's relations in Cape Town, he wrote to his family about the journey thus far and displayed the racial prejudice so common among whites at that time: 'The only fly in the ointment is that we have Indians and coloureds on board, no Indian rajabs or Nabobs but common old sammy's [*sic*], and as dirty as they are common. They travel 3rd class like us and have the same cabins, lounge and everything!'

This was a time of deep economic recession after the Wall Street collapse of 1929, and hardly anyone could afford to travel. On this huge ship, which could accommodate a thousand passengers, there were only ninety, spread out over the first, second and third classes. Hurley and Hughes were in the third class, right above the engine and the propellers at the back of the ship. Seasickness was particularly severe for Hurley in the first three days after leaving Cape Town. After that, he enjoyed the 13½-day voyage to Southampton.

On arrival, Hurley and Hughes travelled by train and then by a small ship to *Dun Laoghaire*, the port of Dublin. They had resigned themselves to sleeping on deck in the chill of a northern night until a crew member told them that their tickets entitled them to a cabin. There they slept so soundly that they did not wake up even when their ship came into harbour the next morning. Loud knocking on the door eventually woke them: it was Angus Mackinnon, one of the thirteen South African Oblate seminarians, known as scholastics.

The two young arrivals were taken to the scholasticate at Belmont House and introduced to the superior, staff and students, especially the South Africans. Little did they or their newly-acquired friends in the scholasticate know that an arrangement had been made by Delalle that Hurley and Hughes should go directly to the novitiate at Cahermoyle in County Limerick.[3] Instead, the scholastics convinced them that they need only reach Cahermoyle a few weeks later to begin their novitiate. Until then they should visit friends and relations, of whom Denis had an abundance around Youghal in East Cork and Skibbereen in West Cork.

The scholastics' advice was happily followed, and the two young men set off on visits to Hurley's friends and family. They felt thoroughly welcome, though unfamiliar accents made communication difficult. Hurley was mercilessly teased about having been lost in a cave and forced to re-tell the story to everyone they met. As time moved on, the young South Africans decided it might be wise to send a telegram to Cahermoyle, to check whether the date they had in mind for their arrival would be suitable. Back came a cold and formal telegram: 'Arrive immediately unless otherwise arranged with your bishop'.

That was the end of the happy jaunt: they scrambled to get to Cahermoyle as fast as possible. Hurley was immediately plunged into a six-day retreat and then received as a novice on 16 March 1932 and made his first vows of poverty, chastity and obedience a year later on St Patrick's Day, 17 March 1933. These were temporary vows, for one year at a time over three years, after which he would make 'final vows' for life—part of initiation into the religious life rather than steps to the priesthood: the various stages of ordination would come later.

The Cahermoyle novitiate was situated on a property once owned by a wealthy O'Brien family, the main building being an impressive country mansion. Various additions had been made and more were on the way. Hurley approached his year there with trepidation because the very word 'novitiate' made him expect tough conditions. Cahermoyle had strict discipline and a rigorous programme, unchanging from day to day. The community rose early, began the day with a half-hour's meditation, followed by Mass and breakfast, manual work for two or three hours, and at midday the divine office of psalms, readings and prayers. This was followed by lunch, recreation and further manual work; in the late afternoon came a period of spiritual reflection as all listened to someone reading from a book or a lecture from the novice master, Father Richard Ryan. Then came a further half-hour's meditation, supper and a short walk in the grounds by way of recreation, followed by bed. Silence was observed throughout except during the two recreation periods.

The most extraordinary item on the programme was known as 'taking the discipline', which happened every Friday evening for one minute before going to bed. Whipping oneself with a leather thong was, Hurley wrote, 'quite a hair-raising legacy from more ascetic times'. According to Father Eric Boulle, who trained as an Oblate some years later, the discipline probably had a medieval origin. In Boulle's experience the bell would ring at the beginning and end of the minute. Each novice would do the 'whipping' privately in his own cell. Cries of pain were heard, but it seemed that some people whacked their pillows to make a loud, impressive sound, and so the cries might have been less than genuine.[4]

Hurley was initially caught up in what was known as 'first fervour' and felt that he was firmly on the road to sanctity and should invite his family and friends to join him. He said that, in the first three weeks, he had done more kneeling than in a whole year back in South Africa. But he 'wouldn't give it up for the world'. Hurley remembered Ryan as kind and loving and a good superior but was disappointed that he did not provide individual counselling, restricting himself to communal instruction through the daily reading or lecture.

Hurley could not remember the content of those lectures, but only the spiritual books Ryan favoured: *Christ, the Life of the Soul* and *Christ, the Ideal of the Monk* by the Benedictine Dom Columba Marmion. Part of the great rediscovery of St Paul's teaching on the Church as the body of Christ, these writings were beginning to have an effect on the liturgy and the lay apostolate.

At this stage, Hurley was ignorant about the politics of Ireland. Many people, hearing that his parents were born there, conclude that this explains his later interest in social justice and the zeal with which he would oppose apartheid. In fact, it was not like that. The intensity of the Irish dislike for the English came as a surprise to him. He had been brought up to view the English favourably. He did not understand what had been happening in Ireland: the warfare involving Irish rebels against the English forces, and the civil war that started in 1922. His fellow novices in the novitiate at Cahermoyle and scholastics at Belmont House had grown up with a strong antagonism against the English. They fully endorsed Ireland's resistance to English rule and the struggle through which the Irish had liberated themselves.

Hurley had not grown up with that political consciousness.[5] His parents and many other Irish people accepted, probably with some degree of resignation, that they were part of the British Isles, subjects of the British royal family and governed by England. 'Of course there had always been a simmering of revolution in certain minds and hearts', said Hurley. This came to the surface in Easter Week 1916, when a poorly organised rebellion tried to shake off English rule but, except in Dublin, was quickly quelled. The ringleaders were executed by firing squad—a ruthless response creating a new consciousness that Hurley's parents missed out on because they were already in South Africa. Those shot instantly became martyrs in the eyes of most Irish people. From then on, the new consciousness made it impossible for England to keep control over Ireland.

Hurley described himself, however, as being 'a divided personality' during his training in Ireland. Though he had Irish parents and many relations there, these did not alter the 'semi-British loyalty' he had. He avoided discussions with 'hot-headed Irish political students' and did not share their viewpoint because he had not yet studied Irish history and was not involved in Irish nationalism. Later he would read widely about the history of Ireland and come to sympathise with the Irish point of view far more than he did as a novice or a first-year scholastic. Nevertheless, it is likely that his family background—one grandfather a leading 'land leaguer' and the other an active 'Fenian'—had sensitized him, perhaps unconsciously, to social and political issues. Resistance to oppression must have been in the genes.

Though Hurley was disappointed by the novitiate, he did not consider leaving. He had never been a person to change direction easily or to desist from a course of action he had chosen. Ryan had a favourable view of Hurley, describing him in a report of January 1933 as of a 'serious disposition' with 'plenty of will power'. There had been no reason for any reprimand: in fact, Hurley was 'pious, humble, detached, mortified, charitable, sociable and attached to his vocation'. Ryan summed up the young religious as 'a most desirable subject [with] great gifts of intelligence and heart. He is a boy of great promise'.[6]

One of the 'gifts of heart' that Hurley was still to develop was a sympathy for other races in South Africa. Despite the ban on newspapers of every kind, political news about his home country filtered through. Hurley commented: 'I hear poor old South Africa is going to the dogs all together, with Hertzog and Smuts making a right mess of everything and Havenga going one better still. They'll soon have a war on out there, and then the nigs will step in and grab the reins of government and we'll all go back to the old days of cannibalism and 'eat or be eaten', and forget all about gold standards, war debts, tariff and income tax'.

Shortly after making his first vows on St Patrick's Day, 17 March 1933, his novitiate completed, Hurley went to Belmont House in Dublin to await the new scholastic year in September. He used the time to attend philosophy lectures at the scholasticate, which were 'very difficult for the average ex-schoolboy from a matric-ulation standard to grasp'. He could not understand why preparation for the active life of a priest, celebrating the sacraments, preaching and attending to the spiritual needs of people should begin with this dry, formalistic study of ancient philosophy. To make things worse, the subject was not well taught: the professor simply lectured from a manual of which he and the students had copies. Hurley wondered whether even the lecturer understood what he was speaking about. Some of the scholastics were studying at the National University of Ireland, where they had well-known and outstanding professors. Hurley had no idea whether he would have the good fortune to study there, but this would have been a much more stimulating prospect.

The summer holidays began in July, and the scholastics were off to Glencree in the Wicklow hills for two months. The holiday was mostly spent cycling. Hurley par-ticularly remembered the first trip, to Tara, the centre of the old high kings of Ireland. He exerted himself so much that day that he lay awake the whole night with cramps in his legs. The holiday also provided time to enjoy five or six novels by Dickens.

As with the novitiate, Hurley's overall feeling about the scholasticate was one of disappointment. It was not only the dryness of the philosophy and the difficulty of seeing a connection between that and the life and work of a priest, but the scholastics were not interested in their studies, perhaps because of the poor teaching, though more likely because of an anti-intellectual atmosphere. 'The students didn't discuss the ideas that came up in their studies . . . In fact it was frowned upon by the students themselves. It was . . . a sad atmosphere to have in a study house'.

Fortunately, relief was at hand. Towards the end of September, the Irish Oblate Provincial came to the scholasticate to announce that two Irish scholastics would be sent to Rome to complete their studies, together with Hurley, whose Provincial had requested this. No envy was shown towards the three who had been selected to go to the Continent—quite the contrary. Because of what the scholastics had heard from other Oblates who had studied at the Belgian Oblate Scholasticate, going to the Continent, whether to Rome or anywhere else, was like being sent to Siberia, a fate deserving only sympathy.

Just before the announcement that Hurley would be going to Rome, his fellow scholastics had elected him secretary of the De Mazenod Circle, an organization established in honour of the Oblates' founder, Bishop Eugene de Mazenod of Marseilles. The Circle was responsible for promoting interest in the worldwide Oblate congregation among the scholasticate community—and Hurley's election was a sign that his leadership was already being recognized. He was not, however, able to take up the task: within a week, he was on his way to Rome.

As he wrote to his family, he felt anything but sorry for himself. 'I am highly excited, any human being may well be, at the prospect of living in the very heart of Christianity, the ancient city of the Roman Caesars'. Indeed, he described himself as being quite beside himself with excitement. A lively and imaginative personality emerges from what he told his parents: 'Absolutely wondering if I should affect the pose of Antony giving his famous oration, or Horatius keeping the bridge, or Nero playing the fiddle, or Titus Blazus rolling home after a hectic night at the "Globe"'.[7]

He was not unaware of the challenges that lay ahead, such as having to learn Italian and French within the next month or two. Nevertheless, it must have been an immense relief to escape from the rather limited Irish scholasticate.

The journey from Ireland to Rome was more complicated in 1933 than now. It involved Hurley and his two colleagues from the Irish scholasticate, Michael McGough and Peter Paul Cronin, in two separate journeys by ship and three by train. He was astonished to arrive at the Oblate Scholasticate in Rome and immediately be confronted by the massive Colosseum on one side, and the Roman Forum at right angles to it, metres from where he would be living for the next seven years. No wonder he was able to say about his arrival: 'Oh what a relief it was—a happy release to be in the atmosphere of Rome, which was very different from that of Ireland'.

The three new scholastics were just in time for the retreat that opened the academic year in the Oblate International Scholasticate in Via Vittorino de Feltre.[8] They did not understand any French but had to try to follow sermons in that language. A much bigger challenge lay ahead: all their university lectures would be in

Latin. Though they had studied some Latin at school, it was hardly adequate for understanding complicated lectures about philosophy. In addition, wherever they went in Rome, they would need to speak and understand Italian. Newspapers were pinned up on the news-stands in the streets: to keep up with international news, one had to learn Italian.

How these new students must have struggled in their first six months, and how confusing it must have been to juggle three foreign languages. Fortunately, it was an international scholasticate with between twenty and thirty English-speaking students and priests, out of a total of seventy-six from the United States, Canada, Spain, France, Ireland, Scotland, Italy, Belgium, Germany, Poland, Czechoslovakia, South Africa and Ceylon (now Sri Lanka). These were obviously the brightest Oblate students from around the world, which made for a studious atmosphere. But Hurley found himself rebelling inwardly against the lectures because they seemed decades or even centuries away from the kind of training he felt was necessary. He asked his fellow students: 'What are we doing here? Why are we studying all this nonsense when it doesn't relate to our priesthood at all?'

Hurley continued to rebel against scholastic philosophy until he was in his third year, when he began to appreciate the great concepts on which human understanding is based, concepts such as 'being', 'truth' and 'the good'.[9] The breakthrough came quite suddenly in March 1935, when he was wondering why the students were being asked to reflect on what is meant by 'truth' and what constitutes 'the true'. For the first time he realized that he could think. From then on, he became enthusiastic about scholastic philosophy and even wrote a brief dissertation on it for his Licentiate, passing the whole course *magna cum laude*. Reflecting afterwards, he felt that philosophy had been important for training his mind to go to the essence of problems.

The scholasticate programme was not just a matter of learning foreign languages and an even more foreign philosophy, though it must have seemed like that initially. As described by Father Jacques Gervais OMI,[10] a French Canadian contemporary of Denis Hurley, the scholastics' day began at 5:30 a.m. with 15 minutes for dressing, followed by a half-hour's meditation, Mass, breakfast and immediately after that leaving for the university, a walk of approximately ten minutes, during which they were expected to practise their Latin and be on time for the first lecture at 8:00 a.m. Four hours later they returned to the scholasticate, had 15 minutes in the chapel before lunch, with various scholastics reading to them in different languages. An hour's recreation followed plus another half-hour after supper. They were able to play games such as tennis, basketball and volleyball in their soutanes, but no soccer because the grounds were too small.

On Thursday afternoons they went on long walks in pairs but had to be back by 5:00 p.m. for study, supper and evening prayers. Long walks were also part of the Sunday programme. Hurley often roamed through the Forum and the Palatine Hill next to it—the site of ancient palaces—becoming familiar with nearly every part of the ruins of imperial Rome. Though the scholasticate was within easy walking distance of St Peter's and the other major churches of Rome and he appreciated their architecture, he seemed more attracted to that of imperial Rome.

In letters[11] to his family he also described the beauty of parks and open spaces: 'The Piscine Hill is the greatest favourite. Usually some kind-hearted band comes along and renders a few classical tunes while we lazily recline on benches under the trees and listen to the splash of fountains. Talk of Elysian fields! All we lack is a few lire to provide the nectar!'

A lack of lire was not an obstacle to the young students' gaining admission to grand palaces and villas, as Hurley explained: 'Caretakers expect tips when they show people round, but we have not the wherewithal to supply them tips. What then, stay outside? Not on your life. We study with one eye and keep the other open for possible tourists. A few fine specimens come on the scene, the caretaker springs to attention, we get interested, the bulldog opens the door, the tourists enter and we follow. After that all is plain sailing. While the caretaker shows the tourists round, . . . we inspect as much as possible, and then clear out before the others, so as not to have to face that snarling guide with our empty pockets'.

There were also opportunities to attend great religious ceremonies. It was not long before he had his first sight of Pope Pius XI[12] in St Peter's, on 8 December 1933, the Feast of Mary's Immaculate Conception: '[The Pope was] carried in on the *sedia gestatoria* [a portable throne, later abolished]—the two large ornate fans, known as *flabella*, just above the level of his head, and the silver trumpets pealing out their music to a tempo expressive of the movement of the *sedia*. The congregation welcomed the Holy Father with their repetitions of "*Eviva il Papa*"'.

Some time later, when the Pope gave an audience for the Angelicum, a university run by the Dominicans, where Hurley was studying philosophy, Pope Pius XI passed through the crowd, greeting staff and students. As Hurley was about to kiss his ring, the Pope asked him in French whether he and his group were Oblates: '*Vous, Oblats?*' Hurley was so tongue-tied that he did not know whether to say 'Yes' or '*Oui*' or '*Si*'.

He gave his family a description of the Pope's appearance on another occasion: 'He is of small stature and has rather a small face . . . From the distance of about 20 or 30 yards he looks about 50 years of age, has a slightly stern expression and a firm chin that would be the envy of any movie actor. When one has a closer look at him, however, the deep lines of worry and age appear, and sometimes he seems so tired that I'd love to take him and put him to bed. There you have a short description of the one man whom Mussolini could not shift'.

Having completed a Licentiate of Philosophy at the Angelicum, Hurley began his four-year study of theology at the same institution. After the first year, the decision was made that the next three would be at the Gregorian University, run by the Jesuits. The Angelicum was not recognized as a university by the German government, so it was thought that exemption from military service would be more secure if the Oblate students attended the Gregorian, which did enjoy such recognition.

During his years at the Gregorian, Hurley focused on the Church's social teaching, a body of social principles and moral teaching concerning how to build a just society, set out in papal and other Church documents. The foundations of modern Catholic social teaching were laid by Pope Leo XIII's 1891 encyclical letter *Rerum Novarum* ('Of new matters'), on questions of labour and capital. In his fourth year of theology, Hurley chose an optional course on Pius XI's encyclical *Quadragesimo Anno* ('In the fortieth year'), written to mark 40 years since the publication of Leo's groundbreaking *Rerum Novarum*.

For his dissertation entitled 'Economic Domination by Credit Control,' Hurley chose a passage dealing with credit control. This involved research in the Gregorian University's library, including how the big mining houses and banks of South Africa were imposing a tyrannical domination over the country. He described this study as a 'great sharpening of conscience': he learnt what capitalism was doing in the Western world and how it disregarded the rights of the poor and workers. It was a revelation that economic oppression was going on at the highest levels and seemed to be a dominant feature of business in the West.

Hurley was impressed by the angry phrases that Pope Pius used against credit control: 'He was a real fighter, Pius XI' . . . Quite how much impact was made by the Pope on the scholastics is captured by Hurley's comment: 'We ate and slept and pondered over *Quadragesimo Anno*, the encyclical of 1931. And then the encyclicals of Pius XI against communism, against fascism and against Nazism. These things were our bread and butter, so I couldn't imagine a seminarian in those days not being influenced in that way'. Another student at the Gregorian at that time was Oscar Romero, later to be the martyred Archbishop of El Salvador, but Hurley and he did not meet. 'Perhaps we passed each other in the corridors', he said.[13]

Not included in the curriculum, but much discussed in Rome during Hurley's years of studying theology, was the 'see, judge, act' method of Canon (later Cardinal) Joseph Cardijn.[14] The scholastics heard about this method and about the Young Christian Workers who used it, from their French and Belgian colleagues. Public lectures on these topics were given in the various academic centres in Rome. For the rest of his life, Hurley would have the highest regard for the Young Christian Workers and their 'see, judge, act' method. Cardijn had trained young men and women to be apostles to other young people by reflecting in small groups, on their own lives, especially their lives at work, in the light of the Gospels.

The combination of these discussions and studying Pius XI's great social encyclicals made Hurley highly conscious of the major social issues the Church was facing. While the encyclicals tended to focus on addressing the consciences of those in power, the Young Christian Workers were helping working-class youth emancipate themselves, using Cardijn's method: learning by seeing, discussing and taking action to bring about change. By the end of his studies in Rome, Hurley was acutely aware that the conflict between labour and capital was a major issue for the Church.

Dramatic political developments were taking place in Italy, and the young and impressionable Hurley eagerly recorded what he saw: 'The whole Italian nation is mad with Fascism. Every second man in the street, quite literally and with no exaggeration, wears some kind of a uniform, principally the black-shirt variety. Soldiers carry rifles, revolvers, bayonets. Policemen sport sabres, rapiers, daggers and revolvers. A regular armoury is attached to each fellow's belt. Even little boys are togged out in black-shirts and wellington boots. The whole nation. Seems a bit childish, doesn't it?'

Other signs of Mussolini's rule, Hurley welcomed: impressive new roads and slum demolition projects, so that grand buildings could make a greater visual impact. In his enthusiasm for beautiful architecture, Hurley seems not to have been aware of the consequences that such demolitions brought for the poor.

Towards the end of April 1936, about the time of the Italian conquest of Abyssinia (now known as Ethiopia), Hurley saw Mussolini for the first time. He and another Oblate student, Joseph Fitzgerald, also later an archbishop in South Africa, remembered seeing posters announcing that Mussolini was to address a fascist rally in the Piazza Venezia next to his office. Hurley and Fitzgerald went along to listen:

> We found the Piazza full of people, shouting 'Duce, Duce, Duce' (pronounced DOO-chay), inviting Mussolini to come out and address them. After quite a long period, the French doors opened from the office to the balcony and out came Mussolini, alone. He stood there, looked at the crowd, threw up his hand in the Fascist salute. Left and right there were more cries of 'Duce', so that he held up his hand for silence . . . and began to speak. He had rather a husky voice at this time. He'd been a great shouter and very eloquent public speaker, a rabble-rouser in his young days.

Hurley told his friends Geoff and Sue Chapman that while studying in Rome he had seen how fascists behaved towards other people. It dawned on him that this was the contempt with which whites treated blacks in South Africa. He decided that he would have to behave differently when he returned home.[15]

On 3 May 1938 Adolf Hitler came to Rome on a six-day state visit to cement the alliance between Italy and Germany.[16] Hitler wanted to be received in the Vatican, but Pius XI showed his total disapproval of Nazism by leaving the city for his summer residence at Castel Gandolfo, saying, 'I cannot stay in Rome with a man who has raised the crooked cross against the cross of Christ'. He gave instructions that the Vatican museums should be closed and no member of Hitler's party allowed into the Vatican.

A big military parade took place along the Via dell'Impero, a broad, modern road between the Colosseum and the monument to Victor Emmanuel II. Hitler was given a place of honour in the reviewing stand. That morning, Hurley was in the study hall of the International Scholasticate, close to where these events were taking place. One of the scholastics came running into the hall and said to him: 'Come on quickly. You can see Hitler from the roof'. Following the Pope's example, Hurley said: 'No, I'm not going. I don't want to see that man'. In 1999 he said: 'By that time . . . we knew that Hitler was already something of an embodiment of evil. We didn't know about his attitude to the Jews, but we knew he had taken up the cudgels . . . against the Catholic Church and that Pius XI had published an angry encyclical against Nazism, called *Mit Brennender Sorge* [with burning concern] . . . I was very, very convinced of [Hitler's] evil influence in Europe at the time and saw him as a person to be utterly avoided'.

The scholastics had differing attitudes towards Mussolini, Hitler, and Franco. The Germans were so sensitive to any criticism of Hitler or of Nazism that open discussion of these topics had become impossible. The Italians were at least willing to discuss Mussolini's merits and demerits, so other scholastics would raise their concerns, but they learnt to expect a spirited defence. The one dictator that all regarded positively was Franco. Because he opposed communists and anarchists and supported the Catholic Church, they considered him beyond reproach. Only later did Hurley come to understand that Franco 'was not the knight in shining Christian armour that we had pictured'.

Pius XI, who had stoutly opposed Nazism, fascism and communism, was coming to the end of his life as Hurley was completing his studies in Rome in the late 1930s. He died in February 1939. Brother Pat Holland's diary listed seventeen occasions on which he had seen the Pope between 1935 and 1939 and three on which he saw the Pope lying in state. Because Hurley and Holland were such close friends, we can assume that they would have been together on most, if not all, these occasions. Hurley would also have seen the Pope several times between 1933 and 1935 before Holland arrived in Rome. Hurley developed an extremely high opinion of Pius XI; much later in his life he said that he regarded him as the second greatest Pope of the twentieth century, after John XXIII.

Hurley was in Rome for the election of Pius XI's successor, Cardinal Eugenio Pacelli, as Pius XII. On the afternoon of the first day of the election, 2 March 1939, watching in St Peter's Square, he saw the white smoke from the chimney of the Sistine Chapel, indicating that a Pope had been elected. He heard the announcement of the new Pope's name and recalled that no sooner had the name 'Eugenium' been announced than the crowd roared 'Pacelli, Pacelli'. Pacelli was well known in Rome as Secretary of State and had been considered likely to be elected.

For the coronation of Pius XII, Hurley and Holland managed to find a space at the back of St Peter's but went outside for a while because there was such a huge crowd that they could see little. Luckily an elderly French cardinal arrived, so they joined his entourage and were swept in at the side entrance to St Peter's—skills learnt, as earlier indicated, in dealing with caretakers at Roman villas and palaces. They had an excellent standing view of the Mass and coronation. Hurley's impression of Pius XII was that he was 'very austere and remote—not a person that would draw you by his humanity or warmth or sympathy'—an impression confirmed later in private audiences with the Pope in 1950 and 1956.

The great highlight of Hurley's seven years in Rome was 9 July 1939, when he was ordained to the priesthood as part of a group of about thirty, in the chapel of the Leonine College, by Archbishop Luigi Traglia, Auxiliary Bishop of Rome, and later Dean of the College of Cardinals. In a letter to his family, he described his feelings: 'It is a happy day, gloriously happy! In fact I am not quite sure if I have both feet on the ground yet'. Archbishop Traglia he described as 'a perfect gift, so solemn and so clear and conversational in the long Latin addresses and prayers. I felt well and truly ordained when he was through with me!'

The celebrations continued on the next day, when he said his first Mass in the chapel of Villa Rosa, the guesthouse of the Newcastle Dominican Sisters, a 'home [away] from home' because of their kindness to the Hurleys at the time of his father's mental illness, and his schooling with them at Umzumbe and Newcastle. The spiritual fervour that followed these ceremonies lasted for several months, much longer than his first fervour after being received as a novice at Cahermoyle.

Despite Hurley's happiness during those few months, war clouds were darkening over Europe. On 1 September 1939 Germany invaded Poland. France and England issued an ultimatum to Germany to withdraw all its troops from Poland by 11:00 a.m. on 3 September. Germany refused and World War II was launched. Because Italy did not immediately enter the war, it was possible for the scholastics to continue their studies as planned, returning to Rome from their country holiday house in Roviano, where once again they had enjoyed the mountains, fresh air, swimming and long walks. They were back in time for their annual retreat and the start of the academic year on 3 November.

In April 1940 the German army invaded Denmark and Norway; then on 10 May the Battle of France began, with disastrous consequences for the French. Mussolini showed signs of wanting to enter the war so the British Ambassador advised all citizens of the British Commonwealth to leave Rome as soon as possible. The Gregorian University allowed its students to advance the date of their oral examinations, and on about 17 May the Commonwealth students and priests left Rome by train for Bordeaux, hoping to sail from there to other countries. There were no ships at Bordeaux, so they travelled to Paris, where they stayed for a week while their travel agents tried to find a way for them to leave France. Finally places were found for them on a flight to London—Hurley's first air flight. After a month at the Oblate house in Tower Hill, London, he secured a passage on the *Warwick Castle* and sailed via Cape Town to Durban.

Looking back in 1999 on his years in Rome from 1933 to 1940, Denis Hurley felt that he had gained far more than he would have if he had stayed in Ireland for that time. Among his closest friends had been two brilliant Sri Lankan Oblates who caused him to alter drastically his attitude towards people of other races.

He had delighted in his exposure to imperial Rome. Contact with the Vatican and the great celebrations at St Peter's and other basilicas gave a 'greater depth to his Catholicism' than he could ever have experienced in Ireland or other countries. Rome was a great international centre, a world capital, whereas Ireland at that time, after decades of neglect by the British government, was a backwater.

He greatly admired some of his lecturers, especially a professor of moral theology, the Jesuit Franz Hurth, whose 'presentations were so clear, so vivid, so commanding that I scarcely ever took a note'. He also remembered a professor of History of Philosophy, Father Vincentius Kuiper OP, who exerted a profound influence on him as he traced the development of human thought. Hurley enjoyed Kuiper's classes immensely, but on one occasion the priest asked him why he was not taking notes: 'Father, I don't need to' was his reply; 'your presentation is so logical that I can remember all of it without a note'.

He was particularly pleased that towards the end of his stay in Rome he became aware of the revival of St Paul's teaching on the Church as the body of Christ. 'A dramatic moment in this development occurred when my superior in Rome asked me one day how I was getting on. I replied positively enough but mentioned there were times of discouragement which, I think, emanated from some hesitation about the religious vow of chastity and priestly celibacy. In his response he emphasized the need to realize the presence of Christ in one's life. At that psychological moment the words he spoke had an explosive significance for me'.

In the already quoted letter to his family written on his ordination day, he thanked them for their constant prayers, which had sustained him 'over the rough going of six stiff years in Rome'. When asked in 1999 why he had chosen those words, he said, 'We lived a very disciplined life; day after day was the same regime—it was also rather monotonous and very often the studies were not all that exciting'. They were too academic and too narrowly related to a few study manuals rather than encouraging wide reading on the topics covered. Worst of all, there was virtually no pastoral preparation, no experience of parish work. His French Canadian colleague, Jacques Gervais, deplored the fact that the scholastics were given no training in how to relate to the laity and actually had little or no contact with them. Monsignor Paul Nadal, a close friend of Hurley, comments that any young man studying for the priesthood at that time, was formed in a spirituality developed in isolation from the world, in an almost monastic existence. Hurley himself, said Nadal, admitted that in the most formative years of his life, from the age of 16 to 24, separated from his family, he lived without any contact with members of the opposite sex.

Also excluded from the curriculum was any training in preaching and public speaking—another extraordinary omission. To fill this vacuum, Hurley and a few scholastics from English-speaking countries had started what they called the 'Thomas More Academy', which met every Sunday during the three-month summer holidays and took turns in addressing and assessing each other. On one of these occasions, Hurley's sermon was kindly but firmly criticized by Hervé Marcoux, a Canadian Oblate from Ottawa University with considerable debating experience. Hurley was rather shaken by this critique, but afterwards asked Marcoux to help in overcoming the weaknesses he had identified. 'So we used to go down into the woods and shout away'.

Gervais enjoyed Hurley's sense of humour and the amusement he caused by imitating their professors. He described Hurley as 'a very easy confrere to live with . . . I was really glad to be with him'. A media profile compiled many years later described Hurley during his studies in Rome as 'known for his ability to compose and sing jocular songs, draw devilish cartoons of Hitler, Mussolini and his own professors, and devise comic skits which he induced other students to perform'.[17] At the same time Hurley was 'very quiet' and as a religious 'very faithful in everything'. Another of Hurley's former classmates, Antoine Humaine, also a Canadian Oblate, recalls: 'We always expected him to be made a bishop very soon'.

Hurley's superiors in the scholasticate spoke about his 'good reputation' and his being 'a good friend' (1935), and in 1939 reported that 'he takes religious life very seriously' and 'does what he should do, not what he wants to do'. In that same year, before his priestly ordination, he was described as 'an excellent influence' by Father Louis Peruisset, superior of the International Scholasticate.

Not long before he left Rome to return to South Africa in 1940, his authority over his fellow scholastics was recognized in a report by Father Hilaire Balmes, Oblate Assistant General.[18] Leadership was much needed in the Catholic Church in the South Africa, to which Hurley was now returning: it would not be long before he was chosen to provide it. Though he would have liked an opportunity to be a military chaplain to the allied forces in Europe, he was under obedience to return to South Africa.

Years later, reflecting on his studies overseas, he said that he had left South Africa in 1932 'very much as a white boy'. When he returned in 1940, he discovered that all the social teaching he had learnt in Rome challenged 'in a most striking way . . . the racial situation in South Africa'.[19]

PART TWO

Priest, Bishop, Archbishop

'I found myself in a lift that was going up'.
—Hurley to the author (undated)

5

Cathedral and Scholasticate

July 1940 was an extraordinary time for the Hurley family. On 16 July they welcomed Denis back with much joy after his 8½ years in Ireland and Rome—and had their first sight of him as a priest.[1] When he arrived in Durban on the *Warwick Castle*, his mother and Eileen waited for him at the cathedral, because in wartime it was difficult to have access to the passenger terminal. The next day the family said an anxious farewell to their second son and brother, Jerry, about to leave on *HMT Devonshire* for military service in North Africa.

On that day, Eileen, Denis and their mother went to Maydon Wharf, where the *Devonshire* was berthed, hoping that they would be able to see Jerry, who had already embarked with his battalion. Fortunately, through the intervention of a Catholic military chaplain, Father Williams, Jerry was allowed ashore for thirty minutes. He commented in his memoirs, 'It was a brief but fortunate meeting'. When interviewed in 2003, Hurley recalled that Jerry was 'dressed in a slightly nondescript uniform. I don't think they had enough . . . to go around that battalion of the Natal Carbineers, so they dressed them up as best they could and put them on the ship to . . . Kenya, and from their base [there] they moved into Somalia and . . . Ethiopia'.[2]

These were the first South African troops to serve in World War II. Before they left their camp in what was then known as the Transvaal, they had been addressed by the Prime Minister, General Jan Smuts. He encouraged them by telling them that his days in the army during World War I had been the best of his life. They then left by a train that brought them directly to Durban harbour. As the *Devonshire* set sail from Durban, its decks packed with troops, it sailed past each of the other ships in the harbour—and there were many, including warships. Each in turn sounded its siren and kept on sounding it. By the time it had passed all the ships, all were blasting a moving farewell. The Hurleys would not see Jerry again until 1945, when the war was over and he was back from North Africa and Italy.

After all the conflicting emotions of 16 and 17 July, Hurley spent two weeks with his family in Pietermaritzburg before reporting to Emmanuel Cathedral on 1 August as the junior curate.[3] Normally, a new priest arriving in the Natal Vicariate would be sent to a mission station to be immersed in a Zulu-speaking community, learning the language and culture. Hurley was expecting that he too would have this sort of exposure. One of the priests at the cathedral had, however, requested permission to become a military chaplain with the Union Defence Force; the administrator of the cathedral, Father Leo Sormany OMI, had agreed to release him provided the bishop found a replacement.

Hurley was the replacement, and so he missed a crucial opportunity to become fluent in Zulu and be exposed to missionary work. The 'biggest regret' of his life, he called it, and 'a great failure on their part (the vicarial and Oblate authorities) and on my own part'. It was symptomatic of all that was wrong with seminary training at that time that he should return from Rome fluent in Latin, French and Italian but was not given and did not insist on a substantial opportunity to learn the language that would be crucial for the rest of his life in a vicariate with a large majority of Zulus.

On the way to Durban after his family leave in Pietermaritzburg, Hurley called at the Inchanga mission, where he met the two Oblate novices, Dominic Khumalo and Jerome Mavundla.[4] Khumalo (later Auxiliary Bishop) remembered that Hurley told them, 'I would love to stay here and be a novice, . . . learning the Zulu language, but they don't give me permission'. More than once, after Hurley had become bishop, Khumalo urged him to take a few months off to become more fluent in Zulu, but there never seemed to be time for that.

When Hurley came to Emmanuel Cathedral in July 1940, Durban was becoming known internationally because of the number of servicemen and -women who passed through its harbour.[5] An estimated twenty thousand vessels called there during World War II, ferrying six million men and women to and from the war zones. In addition to having the busiest and most important harbour in South Africa, Durban was the premier holiday resort because of its long stretches of beach and its mild winters, which made year-round swimming possible. It was also becoming one of the main industrial areas in South Africa, with nearly 800 registered factories employing over 30,000 people in 1938.

As the headquarters of South Africa's sugar industry, it was, in addition, home to the biggest textile, soap, rubber and fertilizer factories, as well as the chief production centre for paint and food-processing industries. With the outbreak of war, Durban's engineering and ship-repair facilities had become strategically important because of the many battle-damaged ships that docked for repairs.

The 'Mayor's Minute' for the Council year ending 30 September 1940 reported that the city's population consisted of 69,913 Africans, 8,073 coloureds (people of mixed ethnic descent), 87,719 Indians, and 92,406 whites. Given the extent to which Afrikaners are generally held to be responsible for apartheid, it may come as a surprise that Durban, with a largely English-speaking white population, was responsible for originating the first apartheid-style 'Group Areas' legislation in South Africa decades before the National Party government came to power in 1948. Legal separation had already begun in Durban in the late nineteenth century, in response to the so-called 'Asian menace'.[6]

By the 1940s that early legal separation was regarded as inadequate by whites, who were increasingly concerned about prosperous Indian traders buying property in predominantly white areas. As a result of the Durban City Council's appeal to national government, the Trading and Occupation of Land (Transvaal and Natal) Act of 1943, commonly known as the 'Pegging Act', was passed. It prohibited any transfer of property from whites to Indians in the city of Durban for three years, giving the government time to investigate Indian 'penetration' of white areas. This legislation was followed by the Asiatic Land Tenure and Indian Representation Act of 1946 (the 'Ghetto Act'), which placed restrictions on the acquisition of land and property. Predominantly Indian areas were defined and reserved for Indian residence. This process culminated in the Group Areas Act of 1950, which divided the whole population of South Africa into race groups for the purpose of segregating them into distinct areas.

Though Hurley was disappointed about missing the opportunity to go to Inchanga and be a 'novice of the Zulu language', he soon immersed himself in the life of Emmanuel Cathedral. In the 1940s it was a vast and busy parish, subsequently divided into several parishes to serve the growing needs of Durban.[7] At that time it had masses on Sundays, at 6, 7, 8, 9, 10 and 11; Benediction of the Blessed Sacrament three times a week; the rosary daily and long queues for confession.

Father Sormany was not only administrator of the cathedral but also vicar delegate or second-in-command to Bishop Delalle. He had easy access to the bishop, whose office and residence were at that time in the cathedral presbytery, and Sormany was thought to have much influence over him. The most prominent member of the Natal Vicariate apart from the bishop, Sormany was in some ways even more of a public figure than Delalle because of his role as chair of the University Council. A French speaker, he was not a Breton like the majority of priests in the vicariate, but from the island of Jersey and was accustomed to working in an English-speaking environment.

In the absence of a bishop's house, the cathedral presbytery was the hub of the vicariate and, at a time when much thought was being given to who would be a suitable successor to Delalle, Hurley's talents were more visible there than they would have been on a rural mission. He was frequently called upon to be master of ceremonies for major liturgical events and thus was seen at the bishop's right hand.

The cathedral parish had few Zulu-speaking members, and Indians had their own church nearby: Emmanuel Cathedral was dominated by whites, though there was a sizeable group of coloured parishioners who lived in the inner city, within walking distance of the cathedral or in easy reach by public transport. The women worked in clothing factories, and the men were artisans and tradesmen, many working as welders in the shipyards. A few had their own businesses.

Coloureds and whites were ministered to separately; Father Joseph L'Henoret was specifically charged with responsibility for the coloureds. At Mass, they were expected to sit in the side aisles and were not allowed to be altar servers, ushers or choir members. They also had their own separate organization for young women. According to Father Albert Danker OMI, who was a member of the scouts and of the youth group that L'Henoret had started, the coloured members of the parish justifiably felt that they had second-class status. L'Henoret disagreed with Sormany because he (L'Henoret) wanted the coloured parishioners to have the use of all cathedral facilities, which Sormany was reluctant to allow, probably fearing complaints from the white parishioners. As we shall see, Hurley would challenge this sort of discrimination after he had been in the parish for a few years.

His first sermon in the cathedral was about the Feast of the Assumption, when Catholics celebrate their belief that, after her death, Mary was taken up into heaven, body and soul.[8] It was a complex and carefully reasoned address in which Hurley set out the close relation between the life and mission of Jesus and that of Mary. After Mass, he was accosted by a young woman named Petal Landers (now O'Hea), who came into the sacristy to complain. Though only 20, she had already completed a university degree and was lecturing at the Technical College. 'I thought I knew everything', she said, and had no hesitation in telling Hurley that his sermon had been difficult to understand: 'You'll have to come down from there', she said, partly perhaps comparing his lofty height with her own, 'and talk to us so that we understand what you're saying'.

Despite this difficult first encounter, they were to become good friends, visiting each other and corresponding right up to the time of Hurley's death. In the mid-1990s, he sent her a copy of the sermon, challenging her even at that late stage to pinpoint her difficulties. Since she was an intelligent woman, it is likely that she had no difficulty in understanding the sermon but was concerned that others might not follow such a highbrow approach, or perhaps she wanted an opportunity to talk to the handsome new priest.

Negative feedback for a different reason came from the all-white Catholic Men's Society, which invited Hurley to address one of their meetings. He used the opportunity to expose the many problems experienced by black people. In thanking him for his address, the members indicated that they would like to hear him speak again but not on such a topic. They had understood all too well what he said about the injustices of South African life. Nevertheless, he continued to raise such issues, using information provided by publications of the SA Institute of Race Relations (SAIRR).

His sermon notes for the fourteenth Sunday after Pentecost 1942 show that he preached about 'The Social Problem of South Africa': the great wealth and poverty that co-existed, and the miserable conditions under which many people had to live. He criticized the Catholic Church's failure to move from principle to application in its critique of these conditions and ended with a call to the congregation to get involved in small groups across racial barriers and in the action that he hoped would flow from such discussions.

In February 1943 he addressed the 'Tertiaries'—a group of lay people associated with the Franciscan Order—on 'Gospel Simplicity and the Colour Bar'.[9] To practise Gospel simplicity like St Francis, he said, it was necessary for 'the Catholic Church to act more vigorously, to support with greater force any attempts made to better the conditions of natives, coloureds and Indians in South Africa'. While the Catholic Church had a reputation for giving some recognition to people of all races—for example, they were free to go to the same confessional and approach the same altar rail for Communion—this did not go far enough. 'There is a colour bar. People of other races do not belong to the SV de P [Society of St Vincent de Paul, which cares for the poor], the Children of Mary, the Tertiaries'.

Hurley did not call for swift change to this situation and even conceded that sometimes it was necessary to keep such distinctions in order to avoid a greater evil, a sign that he was approaching the topic with some hesitation. Was this perhaps because of opposition previously experienced? Nevertheless, he challenged the Tertiaries: 'It should be the aim of Catholics to fight and work for the day when those distinctions will disappear completely'. This was the 'gradualist position' typical of liberal circles even later, in the early years of apartheid.

Two altar servers, Norman McNally and David Martin, remembered how Hurley had coached them in the Latin Mass responses.[10] He insisted that the Latin be recited with perfect accuracy and clarity—a meticulousness that would characterize his life as priest and bishop. But he also made being an altar server fun by introducing competitions and picnics at the north coast holiday resort of Genazzano.

McNally and Martin remembered that he could be stern, as when he noticed during Mass that eight-year-old McNally was secretly rolling a penny along the altar step to his friend, Martin. As soon as Hurley observed what was happening, he gave a "clip" to McNally. There was a similar response when McNally told an off-colour joke a few years later. Though Hurley told others that he regretted these punishments, McNally regarded him as a hero. He was 'very strong, charismatic, a wonderful person to have in company. Everybody loved Father Hurley . . . If he said something was OK, then it really was OK. If he said "no", then you knew it wasn't right'.

Another recollection of Hurley as the cathedral curate came from Hugh Eccles, a young British soldier who, in June 1943, came to the cathedral to find out whether he and his fiancée could get married while their troopship was in Durban. This was on a Monday, and the ship would sail that Thursday, so they knew they would have to move quickly. Hurley was the priest on duty, and they immediately took to him. He sympathized with them and smoothed the way for all the arrangements.

Hurley pursued his other parish duties with similar youthful energy and enthusiasm, using a motorbike for transport. He could be seen flying off with cassock flapping in the breeze, to act as chaplain to St Henry's Marist College, a primary and secondary school for white boys, and the Guild of Our Lady of Mercy, which made clothes for the poor.[12] Especially challenging was the chaplaincy to two prisons because most of the prisoners were Zulu-speaking, virtually his only contact with Zulus at that time.

At the Durban Point Prison, he had a moving experience with a dying convict. One day the prison warder told him that a sick convict wanted to see him. He found the man seriously ill with dysentery, being nursed by another convict who happened to be a Catholic. The Catholic convict told him that he had been talking to the sick man, who now wanted to be a Catholic. Hurley questioned the man briefly and decided to baptize him there and then. He told him about the Eucharist as simply as he could and promised to bring him Communion the next morning.[13]

Early the next morning, Hurley returned to the infirmary and found the man close to death. His convict friend said that the dying man had been suffering the whole night but had told him at midnight that he had seen a wonderful person surrounded with light who had said, 'I am coming for you tomorrow'. Deeply touched, Hurley gave him Communion and never saw him again, but said that he counted on him as 'one of my great heavenly supporters'.

Despite all his duties related to the cathedral, Hurley wanted to keep in touch with developments in the wider society. Because of his special study of the Church's social teaching, his antennae were out for matters relating to social justice. He saw an advertisement for a meeting concerning black workers, which was to take place at the Natal University College, as it was then known. Hurley felt it his duty as a priest to be informed about such matters so that he could guide the people for whom he was responsible.

He attended the meeting and was stimulated by the discussion. The academics present decided to meet again to pursue their initial discussion, and Hurley was keen to attend. A strike at the Dunlop rubber plant in January 1943 had led to a study of the conditions under which Africans were working, in the absence of union representation. Though there had been a union for African workers called the ICU (the Industrial and Commercial Workers' Union of Africa), founded in 1919, it had closed in the 1930s. The meeting that Hurley attended may have been part of an effort to revive unions for black workers.[14]

The ICU had begun with 24 members, but by the end of 1927 it was estimated to have more than 100,000 in over 100 branches. It was not favourably viewed by the white-led churches because it was widely suspected of being anti-white and anti-missionary. The white-led churches warned their people against joining and even fired employees who did. Many rural Africans, influenced by the ICU, left these churches and stopped carrying passes. This was part of a revolt that had taken place in the rural areas of South Africa during the 1920s. Poverty, low wages and increasingly tough laws drove rural communities into the arms of the ICU, which had made extravagant promises to its members, such as 'liberation before Christmas 1927'. It also threatened extensive land repossessions from white farmers.

The famous Mariannhill missionary Father Bernard Huss was alleged to have referred to the ICU as a 'deadly threat to the peace of the country'. Though he later claimed he had been misreported, his alleged remark was not out of keeping with the Catholic bishops' view of the ICU. In 1927 they had forbidden Catholics, on pain of excommunication, from having anything to do with the union; they gave their enthusiastic backing to the Catholic African Union (CAU), specifically established by Huss and another Mariannhill missionary as the only acceptable alternative.

Back at the cathedral, when Hurley spoke with enthusiasm about the meeting at the Natal University College, some of the senior priests made it clear that this was not the sort of gathering a young priest should attend. The elderly Father Le Voguer was the leading critic. The mere mention of trade unions for black workers would have brought back uncomfortable memories of how threatened the Church had been by the ICU during the 1920s. Hurley felt that he could not go against the advice of these priests, so much his seniors; as a result, he did not take any further part in the trade union discussions, much as he would have liked to do so.

Fortunately, in Father L'Henoret he found a kindred spirit with whom he could at least discuss the 'see, judge, act' method of the Young Christian Workers (YCW) and assess its appropriateness for the poorest part of the cathedral parish. The conditions under which the coloured parishioners lived were not unlike those in industrial areas of Belgium at the beginning of the century, when Father Joseph Cardijn began his ministry with young workers. If Hurley had stayed at the cathedral in 1944, he thought he would have started a YCW group there. Indeed, he would have liked to become a full-time YCW chaplain.

Hurley was deeply disappointed to find no interest at all when he spoke about the Church's social teaching with the other priests. It meant so much to him but so little to them. He was keen to discuss how all of this affected South Africa, but no one else at the cathedral was interested.

Yet he was grateful to Sormany for allowing the young priests to play badminton with lay people in the cathedral hall—and for something else: on Hurley's first Christmas Day at the cathedral, Sormany invited all the resident clergy to his office, went to a cupboard, took out a bottle of whisky and poured a tot for each. Hurley was 'converted' on the first sip, perhaps not 'as great a conversion as that of Saul on the road to Damascus . . . but certainly important'.

He eventually broke free of the influence of the priests who told him what sort of meetings a young priest should attend; in an interview of 2003, he said that this freedom was to come in his next appointment, when he became superior of the Oblate Scholasticate. While meeting people in Pietermaritzburg and talking to missionaries in that area, he acquired a far broader view of the role of a priest in South Africa than he had gained at the cathedral. Once he was at the scholasticate, his restricted days as junior curate were over.

When World War II made travel to and from Europe dangerous, the Natal and Transvaal Oblate provinces realized that they would have to train their candidates for the priesthood locally. Hurley had been able to return from Italy without too much difficulty in July 1940, but two years later his friend Pat Holland had an extraordinary 100-day voyage back to South Africa, taking in four continents.

Holland's experience underlined the urgent need to open a scholasticate in South Africa. The 14-acre St Joseph's Hermitage in Pietermaritzburg was chosen as the most suitable site. It was described by one of the early students as 'primitive' in some ways, poor in its resources and facilities, and only able to provide the simplest food for staff and students.[15] The students, however, made the best of the situation, conscious that they were the first Oblates to train for the priesthood in South Africa, and would not have to go so far from their families for their training.

When the scholasticate started classes on 8 March 1943, a respected elderly priest, Father Gabriel Viallard OMI, was appointed superior, with Holland as lecturer, but the latter was still on the high seas. Hurley was asked to come from Emmanuel Cathedral to take Holland's classes until he arrived, a situation that continued for just over a month, after which he was able to return to Durban. But he was not to stay at the cathedral for long because Viallard was finding it difficult to run a house for students much younger than himself. His health failed and in December 1943 he resigned. The 29-year old Hurley was appointed to take his place.

No longer a junior curate but a superior in his own right, Hurley decided to join the Pietermaritzburg Parliamentary Debating Society and take part in their debates.[16] His aim was not only to practise public speaking but also to meet people of different points of view. By taking part in the weekly debates, he was exposed to a wide range of lay people of various faiths and none. He found that debating helped him to present his views 'clearly, logically, systematically'.[17]

The debates were attended by between forty and fifty people, including a former mayor, several city councillors, one or two leading members of the African National Congress (ANC), Natal Indian Congress (NIC) and National Party (NP), as well as some army officers just back from the war. 'It [gave me] a vision of the world outside the Catholic Church', said Hurley, who became the 'Member for Howick' and, for short periods, 'Prime Minister' and 'Leader of the Opposition'. So prominent was he that his sister Eileen overheard a fellow member of the debating society saying: 'You see that young man: he'll be a Cardinal one day'.

There was often sharp conflict with one particular group, the 'Friends of the Soviet Union', an organization established to coordinate international solidarity with the Soviet Union. Because the Soviet Union had entered the war on the side of the Allies, members of this group felt able to assert themselves in the debates. The result was a clash between communist and anti-communist views, which Hurley thought a pity, though it never prevented the development of good friendships. Doughty opposition to the communist 'bloc' was provided by Eileen Hurley, who was qualifying as a librarian. Her profession gave her much scope to look up what was happening in Russia, information that she passed on to her brother or used for her own pointed questions. This put the Friends of the Soviet Union in an embarrassing situation since she often knew more about the Soviet Union than they did.

Among the impressive people Hurley came to know through the debating society were Professor Geoffrey Durrant, head of the English Department at the Pietermaritzburg branch of the Natal University College, and Ronald Albino, later to be Professor of Psychology. Hurley described Durrant, a Derbyshire man who had just come out of the army, as an 'outstanding personality' who listened sympathetically to what he had to say. Durrant described Hurley as 'a very outward-looking person . . . very much interested in the English language and in becoming a good speaker and writer of English . . . and encouraging the use of vigorous, clear language in the Church and elsewhere . . . a young man of great vigour, intelligence, boldness of mind as well as magnanimity. I was greatly impressed by him'.

One evening when Hurley was visiting Durrant's home in Scottsville, they discussed their philosophies of life late into the night. Durrant did not think Hurley was trying to convert him but rather 'sharpening his . . . thinking and no doubt strengthening his faith through his encounters with my own different views'. There was petrol rationing because of the war, and so no buses were available; Hurley had to walk back from Scottsville to Prestbury, about 8 kilometres. He seemed happy to do this because of the evening's stimulating conversation.

Albino describes Hurley as an 'extremely tolerant and decent person. I mean he put up with me, and in those days I was quite fierce and very anti-Church, but he tolerated it extremely well. [He was] a very admirable and clever person'. Hurley and Albino's greatest clash was a passionate debate in 1944 about whether Portugal under Salazar could be regarded as having a model economic system. Hurley was defending the motion as 'Prime Minister', praising Salazar, who had been influenced by two great social encyclicals that Hurley knew so well, Leo XIII's *Rerum Novarum* and Pius XI's *Quadragesimo Anno*. Albino was opposing the motion as 'Leader of the Opposition'; many years later he described the debate as 'a frightful, fierce debate' in which he (Albino) was 'taking a very atheistic, left-wing line'. However vigorous their exchanges, the members of the City Parliament got on well, and Hurley bore no grudge against Albino.

To promote debating at school level, the Parliamentary Debating Society organized an inter-school competition, the first round of which, in 1945, was between the only Afrikaans-medium school in Pietermaritzburg, Voortrekker Hoërskool, and Girls' Collegiate, a private English-medium non-denominational school.[18] Hurley was chairing this debate when an unexpected situation arose. The opening speaker from Voortrekker, Willem Schoombie, began to speak entirely in Afrikaans. At that time in Pietermaritzburg, there was great prejudice against Afrikaans, and Afrikaners did not feel free to speak their language in public. Mr Joliffe, one of the adjudicators of that evening's debate, made no secret about his irritation at being addressed in Afrikaans. Pushing back his chair, he turned to Hurley and said indignantly: 'I don't understand that language: get him to speak English'.

A few seconds of stunned silence followed, and then the chair spoke calmly: 'We will allow the young man to continue in his own language; he has every right to speak it wherever and whenever he chooses. So, will everyone please relax and will the young gentleman please start again'. Schoombie, paralysed by Joliffe's words, took a little while to regain his composure, but Hurley's quiet insistence and friendly manner helped him to start again, and then all proceeded smoothly: Voortrekker won that evening's debate and went on to win the competition. Hurley's intervention greatly impressed the captain of the Voortrekker team, Denise Ferreira (now Kocks). In her experience, no English speaker had ever publicly taken the side of Afrikaans, and she was amazed that it should be a Catholic priest, from whom she would have least expected such support. She concluded that this man would stand up for justice wherever he went.

In view of Hurley's criticisms of the lack of a pastoral dimension in his long years of priestly formation in Rome, the innovations that he introduced during his three years as superior of St Joseph's Scholasticate are significant. He insisted that speech training be included in the curriculum and sought the help of Petal Landers, his friend from Emmanuel Cathedral, in designing such a programme.[19] He also proposed to the scholasticate community that fortnightly parliamentary debates be held there, based on the city's Debating Society.[20] The proposal was eagerly accepted.

Hurley took on the role of speaker, and a government and opposition were elected, with two supporters each.

To ensure that these future priests would be aware of and concerned about the social situation in which they would be pastors, Hurley also introduced regular talks and discussions about South African issues.[21] His staff of young South African priests, Pat Holland, Wilfred Vogt and Brian Devitt, unlike the priests at Emmanuel Cathedral, were keen to discuss these issues with each other and with the students. Their conclusions later provided material for a three-day conference for missionary priests of the Natal Vicariate in 1948, Hurley's second year as bishop. The conclusions of that gathering were later used by the Southern African Catholic Bishops' Conference (SACBC) as the basis of their first statement on race relations, in 1952.

Keen as these young priests were to talk about South Africa's problems, they were reluctant to involve themselves as activists. They knew that major political change would have to come to South Africa—blacks could not forever be excluded from the political system—but they were not able to define too clearly how the change would come about or precisely what it should be. What seemed clear was that it could not be too rapid because in their view the educational level of black people was so low that they would not immediately be able to participate in a fully democratic society. Change would have to be gradual and come about by a process of education.

At that time these young priests would have had little contact with educated black people, and that limited their thinking. Nevertheless, a consequence of their discussions was the more formal inclusion of social issues in the curriculum. Thus the second term of 1945 saw Hurley inaugurating the grandly named 'Chair of Sociology, Catholic Action and Actualities' with one class per week, to be given by Holland. Another Hurley innovation was the establishment of a sixteen-page newsletter known as *Caritas*—for the benefit of friends and associates of the scholasticate. Compiled by the students, it gave them experience in writing, editing and publishing.

Life also became more interesting for the St Joseph's community because of the Italian prisoner of war (POW) camp established at Hay Paddock on the outskirts of Pietermaritzburg.[22] Hurley discovered that POWs were being released from the camp to work on local farms. It seemed that some of the POWs would be interested in coming to St Joseph's, which was not a farm but did have a large garden. During the week before classes commenced on 1 March 1944, Hurley cycled to the POW camp to see the commander about this possibility. His request was granted, and three POWs were assigned to live and work at St Joseph's: Piero Villani, a carpenter; Carlo Montanelli, a chef; and Franco Perego, a mechanic who helped as a handyman and worked in the grounds with Piero.

Many years later, Perego recounted how he and his colleagues had enjoyed being part of the St Joseph's family. They regularly played soccer and tennis with staff and students on Sunday afternoons and were involved in social gatherings on Sunday evenings and feast days, when wine was served. The POWs entertained the priests and brothers with the most primitive 'musical instruments': knives and forks, pots and pans.

'It was another life', said Perego. 'We were not prisoners of war . . . we were a family there'. For Hurley and Holland, the Italian POW presence must have brought back happy memories of their years in Rome and helped them remain fluent in Italian. It appears that the three POWs even played some part in the assessment of Hurley's suitability to be bishop.[23] Perego described how, while they were at St Joseph's, they were visited by 'a bishop'—it must have been Delalle—who asked them whether they were happy there and what they thought about Hurley. 'He's a very good man, a very good man', they said. Not long after that, they were interviewed by 'an archbishop'—probably the Apostolic Delegate, Archbishop Martin Lucas SVD. He asked the same question and was given the same response: they had a high opinion of Father Hurley.

Former students from that time described Hurley as serious about his role as superior and yet at the same time friendly, not someone who laid down the law but more like an older brother or companion, joining in the fun, in fact sometimes leading it. Father Jack O'Brien OMI summed up the atmosphere created by Hurley at St Joseph's: 'It was firm but friendly . . . a real Oblate spirit, the spirit of a family and the spirit of charity to one another'. But Father Charles Struve OMI offered a criticism: Hurley had imported what Struve thought must have been the practice of the Irish novitiate: the lecturers were given a breakfast of bacon and eggs, while the students, sitting at a table right next to them, had only porridge, bread and jam. Understandably, the students were not impressed with this aspect of scholasticate life.

Once a year, staff and students would go for a sport's day at Hurley's old school, St Charles's College. In a cricket match against the schoolboys, Hurley was bowled out before he was able to score a single run. As he made his way off the field, he passed the bowler, Gerard Viger, and issued a mock threat: 'I'll see you in confession'. Later when Viger went to him for confession, he was moved by Hurley's humility: 'That was an excellent ball, Gerard. For your penance, I would like you to pray for me'.

Hurley gave an important sign that he would not simply accept the prevailing social customs. He readily welcomed into the community—something unheard of at that time in South Africa, even in religious houses—its first black member, Jerome Mavundla, who had been studying for the priesthood in Lesotho but needed to leave there for health reasons. The experiment of having him join the all-white scholasticate worked so well that everyone was sad when he left to be ordained a priest.

6

Youngest Bishop

Sunday, 22 December 1946. Hurley was on his own at the Oblate Scholasticate in Prestbury; staff and students were away for the holidays. He had been invited to preach at St Mary's in Pietermaritzburg, have lunch with the parish priest, Father Angus Mackinnon, and visit St Charles's College for an afternoon's tennis.

As he set out for St Mary's, Hurley had no idea that there would be no tennis and that this day would change the rest of his life. While at St Mary's, a phone call came for him from Bishop Delalle. The elderly bishop had a rather abrupt manner on the phone: 'Father Hurley! Come to Durban'. Hurley asked whether he should come right away, and the Bishop said, 'Yes, immediately!'[1]

When Hurley shared this conversation with Mackinnon, the latter made clear why he thought the bishop wanted to see Hurley: 'Remember me when you come into your kingdom', he said. There had been much speculation about who would succeed Delalle now that his more than 40 years in office were coming to an end.[2] His resignation had been officially accepted in April 1946, and he had administered the vicariate since then, pending the appointment of his successor. Hurley had been teased that he was in the running but had not taken this seriously because he was convinced that the provincial superior of the Oblate Congregation, Father Joseph Kerautret, would be chosen.

Other high-powered, French-speaking Oblates who were the focus of speculation were Father Sormany, a man highly thought of by civic leaders, and Father Henri Cabon OMI, a great favourite of French priests, especially those working in the Ladysmith area. At this time the French priests in Natal were mostly Bretons who had been successful as missionaries, perhaps because they themselves were from humble rural families. They lived happily among the rural Zulu people, quickly became fluent in their language, were practical in their approach and had no claims to academic distinction. They had long been accustomed to the vicariate being under French control; this was how they would have liked things to continue.[3]

Hurley's name seemed, however, to come up with ever greater frequency: he had made a good impression as junior curate at Emmanuel Cathedral and was a great success as superior of St Joseph's Scholasticate. Most notable of those thought to favour him was Delalle himself, who had announced at the time of his retirement that he had found a successor. It was an open secret that this was Hurley. He seemed to have all the qualities needed, especially a striking physical presence, intellectual ability, dignity, eloquence and a deep spirituality. But even his supporters considered him at least ten years too young and lacking in pastoral or missionary experience. Hurley himself said, towards the end of his life, that he had been fifteen years too young.

He was, however, poorly rated by the Breton priests not only because of his youthfulness, but also his lack of missionary experience and the fact that he could not speak Zulu. Bishop Barry Wood OMI said that the Bretons 'didn't feel he had the qualities they wanted'.[4] Bishop Khumalo recalled that 'some of the French fathers openly criticized him. For them, he could not be anything other than racially prejudiced . . . just like [other] white South Africans'. One of them added: 'He is too clever. He cannot listen to us'. Khumalo's response to these criticisms was the wry comment that Hurley 'showed the love that I didn't see among those who were complaining against him'.

With some anxiety about why Delalle wanted to see him so urgently, and regret no doubt for the lost afternoon of tennis, Hurley travelled by train to Durban. Delalle was finishing his supper with some fruit when Hurley arrived. He offered a few grapes to the young priest, but Hurley was eager to know why he had been summoned and declined the fruit. Delalle simply said: 'Well, the Holy See wants to appoint you my successor. Are you going to accept?' Hurley's response was immediate and positive: he accepted, surprisingly without requesting time to reflect or consult.

The next day, Hurley went to inform Father Kerautret, his superior as Provincial of the Oblates, and could see tears in his eyes. They were tears of disappointment since he had been expecting to be appointed. Hurley felt sympathy for him: he thought the older man had deserved the appointment because of his competence and experience.

It was soon agreed between Delalle and Hurley that the episcopal ordination should take place on 19 March 1947, the Feast of St Joseph, and that Hurley should take over the vicariate officially from 1 February.

During this time of preparation for his ordination as bishop, an incident at the cathedral showed the sensitivity Hurley had developed in dealing with vocations to the religious life during his years at St Joseph's.[5] A girl of 15 was battling to decide whether she should become a nun. As she knelt in the cathedral one day, wondering how to resolve her dilemma, she decided to approach the first priest who came to hear confessions. If he told her that she should become a nun, that is what she would do. The first priest who came into the church was a tall, rather thin young man she had never seen before: Hurley, the bishop-designate. When she asked him, in the confessional, whether she should become a nun, he gently said she should come to the presbytery after Mass, and they would talk about it: it would take a long time to make such an important decision.

After Mass, when she went to the presbytery, he asked her some questions and spoke to her quietly and calmly, explaining that he would teach her to pray and to meditate, and in that process 'we'll come to what we think God is calling you to'. He arranged to meet her three times a week for about a half hour. Later, as their discussion became more intense, he increased this to four times a week, and this over the three or four months when he was extremely busy taking over from Bishop Delalle and preparing for his episcopal ordination.

Hurley treated her request with the utmost seriousness, whereas he could easily have referred her to others. He led her patiently to discern God's will, by discussing various Scripture passages and helping her to understand her own faith, with lots of prayer and meditation. Visits to various convents formed part of her discernment. Only at the end of that process did he encourage her to make her decision. By May that year she had made up her mind and was ready to join the Oakford Dominican sisters. Eventually she became Sister Marie de Lourdes OP, who worked with Hurley on several projects; she was always struck that, before he made any major decision, he would pray and reflect carefully, as he had taught her.

During this time Hurley was also working on his episcopal coat-of-arms with the assistance of Holland. Hurley chose the motto *Ubi Spiritus, ibi libertas*: 'Where the Spirit of the Lord is, there is freedom' (2 Cor. 3:17), having in mind the South African situation, especially the lack of freedom for black people.

The cathedral choir had been informed by Sormany, before his departure on an overseas trip, that for the ceremony on 19 March they would be expected to sing one of the four-part Masses in which they specialized. However, some young priests suggested to Hurley that it would be more appropriate to use Gregorian chant, led by a choir of priests. The proposal was accepted, and Hurley told the shocked and disappointed choir. They requested that at least they be allowed to sing a polyphonic *Te Deum*, a hymn of thanksgiving reserved for solemn occasions, which they assured him would fit in well with the Gregorian chant. They must have felt vindicated because the piece came right at the end of the 3½-hour-long ceremony, and the congregation was kept standing throughout its 22-minute duration. The choir's polyphonic efforts would not easily be forgotten.

The extensive use of Gregorian chant was a significant innovation, but much more so that Father Jerome Mavundla OMI, ordained the previous year, was an assistant to the bishop for the occasion. As we have seen in the previous chapter, he had been the first black scholastic at Prestbury and had fitted into the community so well that Hurley gave him this prominent liturgical role in a way not previously seen in the Natal Vicariate.

Delalle had been expected to preside over Hurley's episcopal ordination, but when he took ill, Hurley invited the Apostolic Delegate, Archbishop Martin Lucas SVD. Lucas took the opportunity of all the bishops being together in Durban for the episcopal ordination to hold the first bishops' conference in ten years. They assembled from 17 to 21 March at Mariannhill Monastery, just outside Durban, with 19 March set aside for Hurley's episcopal ordination.[6] Though the ceremony went well, one of Hurley's former students from Prestbury described the young bishop as 'tired and pale' at the end of the service, but nevertheless 'all smiles'.[7] Hurley himself remembered the day as tense, 'the culmination of a number of tense weeks'.

He gave no explanation of this tension, but it may have had something to do with resistance to his appointment by Breton clergy who had expected a Frenchman to succeed Delalle. Several years later they would petition Rome that part of the Natal Vicariate should become a new vicariate, with Father Henry Cabon OMI as bishop. Cabon is said to have built the large Ladysmith church on a prominent site over-looking the town, as his future cathedral.[8] Father Kerautret, as Provincial, visited these priests to explain that if they did not accept Hurley as bishop, they would have to return to France. Cabon was sent off to lecture at Roma University in Basutoland, now Lesotho, to prevent his becoming a focus for rebellion. Even then he apparently continued to propose the division of the diocese.

Another possible reason for Hurley's tension was that Sormany, who had been Delalle's deputy for many years and had in effect run the vicariate, must have found it difficult to accept this inexperienced new bishop many years his junior.[9] During the weeks leading up to the episcopal ordination, the bishop-designate informed Sormany that a young American, Father Frank Hill OMI, would replace him in the new administration both as vicar delegate and as administrator of the cathedral. This was a bold move for the new bishop, but it could not have been easy for Sormany to give up his power and influence.

During the week of his episcopal ordination, Hurley had several challenging experiences. He found himself catapulted into a conference of bishops on average twenty to thirty years his senior. Yet, talking about this in later years, he remembered feeling no sense of inferiority or shyness. Towards the end of the meeting, Lucas proposed that a permanent conference of bishops be established that would meet more regularly. Despite being the youngest of the bishops by far, Hurley was elected one of the four who would meet regularly with the apostolic delegate as the new confer-ence's Administrative Board.

Whatever the splendour of the rituals seen in the cathedral on 19 March 1947, Durban was at that time mostly taken up with pageantry of another kind: a royal visit. King George VI and Queen Elizabeth were in town with their daughters, the Princesses Elizabeth and Margaret, guests of Prime Minister Jan Smuts. Huge crowds turned out to greet them. The new bishop had to represent the Catholic Church at royal garden parties, receptions and military parades. At a reception in the Durban City Hall, King George VI seemed unable to cope in a series of one-to-one discus-sions with community leaders including Hurley. The exhausted King, who was sup-posed to converse briefly with this succession of leading public figures, simply sat with his head in his hands as Hurley waited to speak to him. Hurley felt he had no option but to discreetly withdraw.

After his ordination as bishop, the bishops' conference and the royal visit, Hurley was swept up in a round of events related to parishes, convents, schools and associa-tions: Masses, Benedictions, religious jubilees, parish bazaars and similar functions.[10] Everyone was keen to have a visit from the new bishop, not least the mission parishes, schools and outstations, where the pace was more leisurely but the needs vastly greater. Though the Church was expanding rapidly among Africans, finances for buildings, transport and teachers' salaries were in desperately short supply. Priests and people put pressure on their energetic new leader to provide churches, class-rooms, presbyteries and clinics. It must have been as a result of these experiences that Hurley began to plan a major overseas fund-raising drive.

During his visits to Indian parishes, people expressed their surprise that Catholic members of the Durban City Council were supporting the so-called 'Pegging Act', referred to earlier.[11] One of those who supported the Act was Leo Boyd, later to be the first Catholic mayor of Durban and a friend of Hurley. Hurley challenged Boyd and his fellow councillor on what he had heard. They listened carefully and respect-fully and then defended their position. However, Hurley thought that Boyd in partic-ular had taken the message to heart and had begun to change his attitude. Later he was to be one of a small group of opposition United Party (UP) leaders who left the party to pioneer the more liberal Progressive Party (PP).

Early in 1948, the young bishop addressed the Pietermaritzburg City Parliament, where he had often debated from 1944 to 1946.[12] This time it was not an exercise in public speaking: he had a message to convey about the political situ-ation. Unless whites were 'prepared to gracefully accept the end of white supremacy and the equality of all races in South Africa, the country was doomed to a future of strife and bloodshed'.

Like many others, Hurley was greatly shocked when the National Party (NP) came to power, having narrowly defeated the UP in the elections of May 1948. The new government made it clear that it would impose a rigorous form of racial segre-gation on every aspect of South African life. Though stunned and devastated by the NP's triumph in the all-white poll, Hurley was among those who thought the victory a flash in the pan that would be put right in the next election. He and others like him should have noticed, he later realized, that when it came to a parliamentary vote about whether to go to war against Hitler and the Nazis as early as 1939, Smuts had won by a mere thirteen votes. This showed how strong the NP had become; many Afrikaners were convinced that it was the only party representing them. There was also much support among Afrikaners for Hitler and his policy of racial purity, and uneasiness about Smuts's increasing stature on the international scene, as a member of Britain's War Cabinet. In addition, hosting the British royal family had done noth-ing for Smuts's prospects in the election.

Hurley knew that segregation was not a new feature of life in South Africa nor a purely Afrikaner policy. Before 1948, attitudes of English speakers had been less enlightened than they were after the elections. He believed that the rigid legaliza-tion of segregation that came with NP rule compelled many English speakers to examine their own racial attitudes and question their previous acceptance of social segregation.

The Catholic Church itself did not have a good track record as far as racial dis-crimination was concerned. The worst example in Durban was at St Joseph's Church, Stamford Hill Road, where there was a separate church for blacks (St Paul's) on the same site as St Joseph's for whites. Throughout South Africa, Catholic schools, hospitals and seminaries were segregated, as indeed were almost all of the Church's congregations.

The new young bishop wanted a more open and integrated society to develop, not through political activism but by a slow, evolutionary process. Catholics like Hurley, who realized the need for social change, still thought that the way to achieve it was by pastoral letters, statements and publications directed largely at the white establishment.

But even statements and pastoral letters dealing with racial matters were frowned upon by the Apostolic Delegate, Archbishop Lucas. Painfully aware of how the Catholic Church was seen as a troublesome minority, *die Roomse gevaar* (the Roman danger), and likely to be discriminated against, he wanted the bishops to avoid taking any public position on segregationist policies. Instead, they should dialogue with the new government. This was light years away from the African National Congress's (ANC) thinking at this time. Its Youth League, led by people like Nelson Mandela and Walter Sisulu, had become extremely influential and was promoting far more rapid change.

The other mainline churches, such as the Methodists, Anglicans, Presbyterians and Congregationalists, were more outspoken than Catholics about racial injustice because they had synods and assemblies where black lay people raised these issues. Many resolutions were passed, but little was done to implement them. There was the example of the famous Anglican activists Fathers Trevor Huddleston and Michael Scott, though their activism was rejected as too radical even by Anglican leaders.

The Apostolic Delegate wanted to ensure that the Catholic Church, which had been largely silent on political matters for the first half of the twentieth century, would continue to be so.[13] In a confidential letter of 28 July 1949, written only 'after lengthy consideration', he strongly advised Hurley 'not to criticize the Government at the moment'. Nothing would be achieved by criticism or public protest, he wrote, because the Catholic Church represented only a small minority, and one that was more 'tolerated than wanted'. The new National Party government was about to deal with the question of education and schools and was divided on the subject, some favouring the Catholic Church's having its own schools, supported by the government. In such a climate nothing should be done that could make the government less sympathetic to the Church's needs.

Lucas went on to assure Hurley that, if formal and informal approaches to government were not successful, he himself would not be silent but 'firm and audacious if necessary'.

In January 1949, not long after the National Party came to power, a violent disturbance occurred involving Africans and Indians in Natal.[14] It began close to the Indian Market in Durban, where an African boy stole from a shop. The owner struck the boy, who fell against the shop window, cut himself badly and began to bleed profusely. African people rose in anger, and the conflict spread rapidly. They marched on the leading Indian commercial area in Grey Street. The angry mood of the marchers became uglier as the march proceeded, and many properties in Grey Street were broken into and looted. Some whites were reported as having encouraged the Africans and taken part in the looting. Indian shopkeepers were assaulted, and the unrest spread in the evening to outlying shack areas.

Hurley remembered travelling back from Oakford Priory, on the north coast, on 14 January, the day this conflict started. Grey Street was covered in broken glass and deserted as he made his way back to the cathedral. As the conflict spread, homes were burnt and people attacked and killed, the worst massacre taking place in Cato Manor, where a row of Indian homes was close to African dwellings. Overall, the clashes left 142 people dead, more than 1,000 injured and 2,250 buildings damaged or destroyed.

The cathedral, situated in the Grey Street area where Indian people lived and owned shops and businesses, became immediately involved. From the bell tower, the priests were able to watch as shops in nearby streets were looted. Families were terrified and needed shelter. Hurley arranged that St Augustine's School (now the Denis Hurley Centre), next to the cathedral, should be made available as a refuge, as he would do with other church buildings in many subsequent crisis situations.

Popular explanations for the conflict were that Indians appeared to be suffering the effects of apartheid legislation much less than Africans and were favoured by whites. Africans felt exploited by Indian shopkeepers, whom they experienced as the interface of the dominant economic system that impoverished blacks. The Natal Indian Congress, which was closely linked with the ANC, blamed the Urban Areas Act, which had generated much anger among Africans by forcing them to live in shocking conditions in and around Durban.

Hurley felt that there was a deeper cause related to political developments: Africans were beginning to bear the brunt of the implementation of apartheid by the National Party government. In July 1949 the *Southern Cross* published a moving address by Hurley at a Catholic Action week in Durban. He confessed his own earlier racial prejudice: 'I speak to you as one who was born into the privileged race of South Africa, who grew up accepting . . . the fact that there were two kinds of men, utterly, completely, inevitably distinct; one superior, the boss, the master; the other inferior, the servant, the underdog; one with a white face, the real man; the other, one with a dark face, half a man; and with that dark face I associated, and I apologize to all those whom the words offend, all that was unpleasant and uncouth and uncivilized'.

He left his audience in no doubt about how difficult it had been for him to change that attitude: 'I speak to you as one in whom that conviction died slowly, one from whom it had to be torn in a slow-yielding, reluctant and painful process as when men tear out of the ground the steel rails they have sunk into it'.

He went on to claim that the colour bar had divided the Church into watertight compartments and asked whether Christ was divided because there were 'other Christs' on both sides of the racial divide. Young people were denied jobs and opportunities and simply left to rot on street corners because they were not white.

His speech ended with a rousing call to change this situation: 'Here is a splendid field for Catholic Action. Here is a problem to test the mettle of any man or woman who has gazed on the crucified Christ and called him Lord and Master'.

Despite the dramatic events in South Africa during 1948 and 1949, Hurley continued to plan an extensive fund-raising tour of Europe and North America, which became a reality in 1950.[15] For most of that year he was away from the vicariate, presenting its crippling shortage of funds to numerous Catholic parishes and institutions overseas. Though he visited England, Ireland, France, Germany and Italy, including leading a pilgrimage of South Africans to Rome for the Holy Year of 1950, he reserved most time for the United States.

There he stayed for six months, with some of his mother's relations in Salem, Massachusetts, in the house where she herself had lived for seven years before her marriage in 1913. He used this as his base for visits all over the United States, celebrating Mass in a different parish every Sunday, then meeting people in the parish hall. Visits to schools and colleges took up much time during the weeks. Hurley gave graphic accounts of the problems, especially the huge needs in rural missions and outstations.

For these occasions Hurley would have a stock of jokes to help everyone relax. He would be sure to inform himself beforehand about the prowess of local sporting heroes and quickly win their attention by some casual reference to their latest achievements. In this regard, his American relations felt he was rather like some of the more successful US politicians.

Being in the United States for this extended period meant that he got to know the people. They responded generously to his personality and the cause he represented. The visit laid the foundation for a direct mailing campaign that would begin after a second fund-raising tour in 1956 and continue through all his years as bishop; this campaign still provides a major source of revenue for the archdiocese.

Hurley had felt so welcome in the United States that when the time came to go home, it was difficult. Time spent with his relations and the innumerable gatherings he had addressed about South Africa had done wonders in overcoming his shyness and helping him become more relaxed and friendly.[16]

Early in 1951, while still in the United States, he received a telegram informing him that he had been appointed archbishop and that the Natal Vicariate would become the Archdiocese of Durban. This was part of the 'establishment of the hierarchy' in which the bishops would no longer be known as vicars apostolic and be under direct guidance from Rome. Their titles would change to 'archbishop' in the larger centres and 'bishop' in the smaller ones. All of them would have a higher status and more independence than vicars apostolic.

Denis Hurley was once more a record-breaker, this time as the youngest archbishop in the world at the age of 35. His vicar general, Father Frank Hill OMI, was determined to give him a worthy reception when he returned to Durban in March 1951. Family members, about thirty priests, and hundreds of lay people were at the Stamford Hill aerodrome when the first Archbishop of Durban touched down in a South African Airways Lockheed Lodestar.[17]

Hill had arranged that Hurley should dress in full archiepiscopal regalia. Unfortunately, there was another passenger also in an exotic outfit: a Scottish kilt. The excited crowd had been geared up to give three cheers as soon as their first archbishop appeared in the plane's doorway. However, the Presbyterian kilt wearer emerged first from the plane, astonished to receive a hero's welcome. Nevertheless, this served as a useful trial run, and the cheers were all the more convincing when the real archbishop finally made his appearance. A convoy of cars accompanied him to the cathedral, where he gave a brief account of his travels and a warm vote of thanks for the enthusiastic welcome he had received.

7

Out of the Shadows

'In my five years as a Vicar Apostolic from 1947 to 1952', said Hurley many years later, 'we were going through a process of coming out of the shadows, out of the inferiority complex of the past—and I suppose I played a little part in it at the time, being youthful and very confident . . . I don't know what gave me that confidence because I was a very shy child as a youngster. I suppose it was my success in study in Rome . . . I suppose I took part quite vigorously, almost unconsciously, in driving the Church up out of that sense of inferiority'.[1]

Being appointed superior of the Oblate Scholasticate at the age of 29, bishop at 31 and archbishop at 35 must have boosted that confidence, as also events of 1952. In that year Hurley presided over the highly successful Marian Congress, a national event held in Durban in May. He was also elected chair of the Bishops' Conference at their meeting in June and at that same meeting helped the Conference issue its first statement on race relations, breaking the Catholic bishops' silence on politics for the first fifty years of the twentieth century. The remainder of 1952 saw him in demand to speak about the Catholic Church's outlook on the South African political situation. It was like finding himself 'in a lift that was going up'.

The Marian Congress was organized to celebrate the centenary of the arrival of the first Oblate priests in Natal in 1852, and also the establishment of the Natal Vicariate.[2] Bishop Marie Jean François Allard, with a small group of Oblates, had arrived in Durban on 15 March 1852 as the first Vicar Apostolic. He established his base in Pietermaritzburg, the capital of what was then a British colony. To recall these events, a special committee was appointed to organize the Marian Congress; 21 priests and 24 lay people attended the first meeting. Surprisingly, there was not one Zulu among them, though two were later invited to join. Twelve sub-committees were established under this general committee, each chaired by a priest, one of these being an 'African Committee', whose task was to organize African participation in the Congress.

Hurley appointed Father Sheldon Kelly OMI, a dynamic priest from New York State, as full-time organizer, with another American, Father John Ochs OMI, as his deputy. These Americans 'thought big', according to Hurley, who admired their skills and went along with their imaginative proposals. There had been nothing like the Marian Congress in the South African Catholic Church. One can only wonder how the French priests, the most numerous in the vicariate—who had in 1852 pioneered the Catholic Church in this part of the world—felt about their new bishop's choosing two Americans, in addition to an American Vicar Delegate, Father Francis Hill, for the major organizing roles.

In the midst of the preparations for the Marian Congress came Hurley's official public installation as Archbishop of Durban, when he received the pallium from Archbishop Martin Lucas in Emmanuel Cathedral on 5 August 1951.[3] The pallium is a narrow strip of white woollen cloth decorated with black crosses, worn around the shoulders by archbishops as a sign of their office. Nowadays it is presented by the Pope to all new archbishops who head a province of the Church, in Rome each year on 29 June, the Feast of Saints Peter and Paul.

Planning for the Marian Congress moved ahead rapidly. Durban's Greyville racecourse was chosen as the principal venue with a specially constructed altar and a platform 212 feet wide in a prominent place opposite the main grandstand. A landmark feature was a 100-foot column surmounted by a statue of Mary, made locally of plaster over a framework, part of the public display of Catholic beliefs characteristic of the whole congress. The main pre-congress event was a passion play, directed by Father Noel Coughlan OMI and adapted from the famous Passion Play of Oberammergau in Germany. The local adaptation was presented five times in the Durban City Hall and then at the racecourse on the first evening of the congress. Once again, no fears of *Roomse gevaar* attitudes were allowed to keep the Catholic Church shyly in the shadows.

The congress had a busy programme, including a special welcome for the papal legate (Archbishop Lucas) at the cathedral, official dinners, a public reception in the city hall and the celebration of several outdoor Masses at the racecourse for various groups and categories of people. The opening Mass drew an estimated 18,000 people.

The climax and most public of all the events, in fact the most open display of Catholicism that Durban had ever seen, was the final procession from the Durban City Hall up the main street to Albert Park. Fifteen floats, each pulled by thirty volunteers, depicted scenes from the life of Jesus and Mary. In Albert Park, the procession ended with Benediction, the consecration of South Africa to Mary under the title 'Queen Assumed into Heaven' and a recorded message from Pope Pius XII. An estimated 30,000 people took part in the procession, including 210 priests and 480 nuns of fifteen congregations, with more than 50,000 spectators. Father Louis Stubbs, editor of the *Southern Cross*, commented on the 'superlative organization' of the congress, the wonderful co-operation of Catholics and non-Catholics and the lively downtown office presided over by Father Sheldon Kelly OMI and staffed by lay helpers. Looking back in later years, Hurley was, however, embarrassed at how whites had dominated the whole event.

The success of the congress helped Hurley with a major challenge. Mention has already been made of the total absence of comment on political and social issues by the Catholic bishops of South Africa in the first half of the twentieth century. Though there was no formal organizational structure to bring the bishops together regularly until March 1947, the Apostolic Delegate in the 1920s and 1930s, Archbishop Bernard van Gijlswijk OP, had assembled the bishops in 1924, 1927, 1933 and 1937. In 1927, as we have seen, they made a statement forbidding Catholics to take part in the ICU, their first and only political comment in the first half of the twentieth century.

Statements by Bishop Francis Hennemann SAC of Cape Town were the only exception to this silence.[4] In March 1939, in a letter to his priests, which he asked to be read to the congregations, he condemned 'any attempt of segregation on grounds of colour or race'. In 1948 he expressed concern about plans to segregate Cape trains, describing apartheid as a 'noxious, unchristian and destructive policy'.

There had been no further statement of this kind since Hennemann's, despite major political developments after the National Party had come to power: the ANC Youth League's 'Programme of Action', urging confrontation rather than moral persuasion, had been adopted by the ANC's annual conference in 1949; violent conflict between Zulus and Indians had taken place in Durban, as we have seen, in 1949; Hendrik Verwoerd had been appointed Minister of Native Affairs in 1950 and was establishing a systematic and all-embracing policy of total segregation. As a result, a series of Acts had been passed to entrench apartheid in every sphere of South African life.

Three major pieces of apartheid legislation were enacted in 1950 alone: the Population Registration Act, which classified all South Africans by race; the Immorality Amendment Act, which banned interracial marriages and indeed any sexual contact across the colour line; the Group Areas Act, referred to earlier—a major cornerstone of apartheid—which divided the whole country, apart from African townships and reserves governed by other apartheid legislation, into separate areas for particular race groups. It allowed government to move populations en masse from one area to another.

In 1951 these Acts were followed by the Suppression of Communism Act, which empowered the Minister of Justice to outlaw any person or organization viewed as 'communist'. In 1952 the Natives Abolition of Passes and Co-ordination of Documents Act did not in fact abolish passes: identity documents that had to be carried by blacks at all times, to prove that they had permission to be in a white area, but made them larger and more comprehensive.

These major developments on the political front led to a corresponding increase in acts of civil disobedience and protest. There was also police violence in response (on 1 May 1950 in Johannesburg, for example, during a stay-away organized by the Communist Party, the police fired into crowds, killing 18 people).[5] Nothing, however, was heard from the Catholic bishops. In writing his memoirs some forty years later, Hurley gave much thought to this episcopal silence and developed a detailed explanation, which is paraphrased here.[6]

The Catholic Church was aware of its status as an alien and minority community in an overwhelmingly Anglican and Protestant environment. It was almost totally dependent on bishops, priests and religious from overseas, and was therefore loath to jeopardize the religious freedom it enjoyed.

Vicars Apostolic appeared not to have absorbed the message of the Church's social teaching, especially the encyclical *Rerum Novarum* of Pope Leo XIII.

Though the Vicars Apostolic met from time to time when summoned by the Apostolic Delegate (as indicated above, only four times in the first half of the twentieth century), they had no permanent structure for corporate consultation and action. Only if the Apostolic Delegate thought the time was right was any meeting called, and he presided over all such meetings.

Similarly, there were no forums in which the bishops regularly heard the voice of lay people, unlike other churches which had regular synods or assemblies.

Because of the unecumenical attitudes of the time, the bishops were unwilling to join what was then known as the Christian Council of South Africa (later the South African Council of Churches, SACC), where joint action by churches was planned. The Catholic Church in South Africa had nothing comparable to this council to provide information and motivation concerning racial issues.

The centralization of papal administration during the nineteenth century had produced heavily dependent local churches that did not hold synods or have strong links between dioceses.

The Apostolic Delegate, Archbishop Martin Lucas, was opposed to confrontation with government and made this clear on a number of occasions.

Despite the obstacles identified by Hurley, after the National Party's election victory in 1948, the pressure for a response to the government's programme of discriminatory legislation increased. At the Administrative Board meeting in February that year, Archbishop Lucas announced that he was about to ask the lecturers at St Joseph's Scholasticate to prepare statements on racial segregation and Catholic doctrine; and the duty, task and position of the laity in church activity and social justice, with special reference to domestic and commercial employees.

At a meeting of the bishops on 9 and 10 November 1948, there were discussions about publishing a statement on human rights that would include reference to racial segregation. But with their usual caution, the bishops agreed that they would first canvass the government's attitude to the issues they wanted to raise. They therefore decided that Archbishop Lucas and Bishops Hurley, Garner and Whelan would informally discuss the issues with the Minister of the Interior. There is no record of such a meeting, and no statement on human rights was published by the bishops at the time.

In November 1949, the bishops asked Hurley to discuss 'with his group' (presumably the staff of St. Joseph's Scholasticate mentioned earlier) Lucas's suggestion of a 'Catholic political programme' to keep Catholic political principles before the public eye and bring them to the notice of political and parliamentary leaders.

There was a long delay in Hurley's response to this request because he was overseas from March 1950 to March 1951. Perhaps the passage of time was helpful because, by the time he returned, as we have seen, the hierarchy had been established, and he and two other South Africans were archbishops (McCann and Garner), equal in rank to the Apostolic Delegate. This may have encouraged the Bishops' Conference not to feel forever bound by Lucas's opposition to making statements. They could make their own decision about speaking out, even if Lucas was opposed—but 18 months passed before they did so.

Another encouragement to speak out may have come from the graduate conference organized by the Kolbe Association in July 1951 and described by the *Southern Cross* as 'the most important Catholic study conference' ever held in South Africa. The Kolbe Association brought together some of the brightest lay Catholics in South Africa, mostly academics and university graduates. The theme of their conference was the role that the Church should play in South Africa. The main paper was Hurley's 'A Catholic Social Programme for South Africa', which sounded like a response to Lucas's request for the Church to have its own 'political programme'. There is likely to have been much encouragement and even pressure from the Kolbe members for the bishops to issue a joint statement on the South African situation.

Immediately after the Kolbe Winter School, the bishops' Administrative Board met on 8 August 1951 and resolved that Hurley, with the aid of a sub-committee, should prepare a draft statement on race relations from the Catholic point of view. A draft was distributed to all members of the Board at their November meeting. At the same meeting the minutes record that 'mixed racial marriages' were discussed, presumably in response to the Prohibition of Mixed Marriages Act of 1949. The Board decided that such marriages were valid provided there was mutual consent, but that the bishop should be consulted in each case and 'that for obvious reasons, this [decision] should not be made known'.

Timidity nearly triumphed at the next meeting: the question of whether a statement about race relations should be issued at all was discussed again at length. Lucas made a last desperate effort to discourage the bishops from speaking out. He asked them to consider all the issues involved, such as the likelihood of a hardening of the government's attitude toward new foreign missionaries coming into the country and its attitude toward the registration of schools and hospitals. He reminded them that the government was determined that the Catholic Church's membership should not rise above 5 per cent of the population. The bishops should thus consider what further problems they might create for the Church by issuing a statement.

They decided to go ahead, with a two-thirds majority in favour. The statement, to be drafted by Hurley, should be 'forthright and comprehensive' but not contain anything 'that might be interpreted as partisanship or harmful criticism'. These contradictory instructions showed the bishops' anxiety about antagonizing the government and perhaps also a lack of consensus about the correct approach. They added a further restriction, though there is no evidence that this was carried out: 'it would be courteous to allow the government to know [the statement's] contents before publication'.

This first-ever joint statement on race relations by the Catholic bishops of South Africa was issued in June 1952.[7] It was a milestone in the Church's struggle in South Africa. Based on discussions with the staff of St Joseph's Scholasticate and conclusions reached at the 1949 meeting of missionaries in the Natal Vicariate, it had been the subject of much 'composition and writing, changing and revising' by Hurley. A draft had been circulated and amendments received and worked into the text. Hurley did not think it would ever have been passed if he had not personally pushed for its adoption. The Apostolic Delegate was not in favour: he wanted an understanding with the government.

The statement was far from revolutionary. Garth Abraham wrote that 'the matter . . . was approached with typical hesitancy and caution'. Hurley himself looked back on it 45 years later with embarrassment: 'It was a very primitive statement, in many ways, and one that I blush to read now. It's so patronizing, so horribly patronizing . . . It was written within the context of colonial Africa . . . We couldn't imagine blacks aspiring to equality except after a good deal of education and progress and upward movement of society, that looked a slow process and the goal a far-distant one'. He told Father Sean O'Leary SMA, 'We were way out of line with what was happening in South Africa at that time'.

Commenting on the 1952 statement, Hurley said: 'We seemed to be writing for a timeless and serene society, untouched by political agitation'. The statement began by asserting that bishops have a duty to teach Catholic doctrine but admitted that there was no easy solution to the racial problem. It bemoans the fact that race relations had become a plaything of party politics, whereas the subject should be kept at the 'highest level of prudent and earnest consideration'—an ideal that Hurley later described as 'episcopal wishful thinking at its best'.

The statement set out basic Christian teaching on creation, redemption, the dignity of human persons and therefore the love and respect due to them. Then it plunged into discussing relations between Europeans (the term used then for whites) and non-Europeans (the term for Africans, coloureds and Indians). It described the political, economic and legal 'colour bar' and the resentment, animosity and distrust it caused among non-Europeans. It would not be enough to simply condemn the attitude of Europeans; the problem was much more complex: 'Its complexity arises out of the fact that the great majority of non-Europeans, and particularly the Africans, have not yet reached a stage of development that would justify their integration into a homogeneous society with the European. A sudden and violent attempt to force them into the mould of European manners and customs would be disastrous. There must be gradual development and prudent adaptation. Nor must they be required to conform in every respect to European ways, for their own distinctive qualities are capable of rich development. Though the majority of non-Europeans are still undeveloped, there are many of them well qualified to participate fully in the social, political and economic life of the country'.

The statement went on to identify the racial problem of South Africa as deep-rooted prejudice on the part of most whites and resentment and distrust on the part of most blacks. Blacks were at different stages of development, the majority 'totally unprepared' for full participation in 'social and political life according to Western standards'. Major divisions bedevilled relationships among the various black groups.

What was the solution? The bishops called for prudent planning, Christian charity and justice. They drew a distinction between fundamental rights and 'secondary, derivative or contingent' rights, which could be granted to certain groups depending on their level of development. The fundamental rights listed by the bishops included 'the right to life, dignity, sustenance, worship, to the integrity, use and normal development of faculties, to work and the fruit of work, to private ownership of property, to sojourn and movement, to marriage and the procreation and education of children, to association with one's fellowmen'. The examples they gave of contingent rights were 'the right to vote in the election of legislative bodies, State-aid in education, unemployment insurance, [and] old-age pensions'.

The distinction between fundamental and contingent rights was drawn from the social teaching of the Catholic Church, which recognized a hierarchy among rights.[8] Some were considered more fundamental, the right to life being seen as the first and most basic. The right to human dignity, equality of all persons and religious freedom were also seen as fundamental. Other rights flowed from or were practical applications of these. The right to vote was among rights regarded as contingent rather than fundamental. In difficult situations, a slower process might be adopted towards the full achievement of such rights, though full achievement would always be the goal. There was no such hierarchy of rights in the Universal Declaration of Human Rights drawn up by the United Nations in 1948: clearly, the bishops had been influenced by Catholic social doctrine rather than by that Declaration.

The bishops had four conclusions. Racial discrimination was an offence against human dignity. Though most fundamental rights of black people were in theory respected in South Africa, legislation, convention and inefficient administration had seriously impaired their exercise. Justice demanded that blacks be permitted to evolve gradually towards full participation in the political, economic and cultural life of the country. In this gradual evolution, they would have to commit themselves to earnestly prepare for the 'duties connected with the rights they hope to enjoy'.

Despite the obvious shortcomings of the 1952 statement, at last the corporate silence of the bishops on issues of justice had been broken. Nevertheless, there was a long way to go to catch up with the realities of the South African situation. Moreover, close examination of the 1952 statement shows that the extent to which the bishops had broken their silence was limited. They had restricted themselves to speaking about political principles but remained silent on specific political policies.

In fact, throughout the 1950s little discussion of political matters was reflected in the minutes of the bishops' meetings, other than references to the Bantu Education Act, as we shall see in the next chapter. The bishops thought that this caution would prevent *Roomse gevaar* fears from getting out of hand. In this way, they hoped to gain some acceptance among Afrikaners and stave off possible deportations of bishops, priests and nuns from overseas, while mildly criticizing racial injustice in a general and vague manner.

The bishops would quickly discover that this was wishful thinking. After the publication of the 1952 statement, *Die Kerkbode*, the official publication of the three Dutch Reformed Churches, called for the widest possible publicity to be given to a pamphlet entitled *Die Roomse Gevaar*.[9] In this document, four specific proposals were made for combating the 'Roman danger' in South Africa: all schools, hospitals, orphanages and so forth should come directly under the government and should be based on Protestant principles; no more Catholic nuns, teachers or immigrants should be allowed to enter the country; all Catholic priests, teachers or members of the Catholic Church who attacked Protestants or who tried to undermine the government or South Africa's 'Christian national education system' should be immediately deported. Finally, no Catholic propaganda should be allowed to enter the country nor should such material be printed or circulated here.

The *Roomse Gevaar* pamphlet must have confirmed Lucas's worst fears about the dangers of making any statement about the South African racial situation. Hurley responded to the pamphlet in a remarkably friendly and tolerant way:

> We admire the old religious customs of their people [the Afrikaners], the family prayers and Bible reading, and we look back with gratitude to their great leaders of the past, to President Pretorius, who gave a site for the Catholic Church in Pretoria, to President Brand, who treated our early priests and sisters in Bloemfontein with such kindness. In our ideal of the Christian spirit of the home, we have much in common with the members of the Dutch Reformed Church. If we cannot agree on matters of religious dogma, could we not at least agree to differ in a Christian spirit of tolerance?

The 1952 statement could not have been more different in ethos and spirit from the Defiance Campaign mounted by the ANC in the same month.[10] In April 1952, while the white community celebrated the tercentenary of the arrival in the Cape in 1652 of Dutch settlers under the leadership of Jan van Riebeeck, many in the black community, led by the ANC and South African Indian Council (SAIC), refused to celebrate three centuries of white domination. They had been especially incensed by the legislation enacted by the National Party since coming to power in 1948. Black people were in no mood to celebrate the oppression they were experiencing.

After a number of successful mass protest meetings, the ANC and SAIC decided on more dramatic tactics: a civil disobedience campaign using Gandhian non-violent methods. In particular, they protested against legislation that required black people to carry passes; the Bantu Authorities Act, which provided black people with unrepresentative political structures; the Group Areas Act, the effects of which have already been described; the Separate Representation of Voters Act, which removed coloureds from a common voters' roll with whites; and the Suppression of Communism Act, which gave the government wide powers to deal not only with communism but also with much other political resistance.

At several places in the Transvaal and Cape (as they were then called), and to a lesser extent in the other two provinces, then known as the Orange Free State and Natal, the Defiance Campaign took the form of groups of protesters entering black locations without permits, burning identity documents known as 'passes', breaking curfew laws and defying 'Europeans Only' notices at railway stations and in post offices—generally in a way designed to invite arrest. By the time the campaign ended later the same year, 8,326 people had been arrested. Despite efforts to keep the demonstrations non-violent, 26 Africans and six whites had lost their lives. The outcome of the campaign was even tougher legislation to discourage any further such civil disobedience: a Public Safety Act, which gave the government the power to declare a state of emergency, and a Criminal Law Amendment Act, which imposed heavy fines, imprisonment and corporal punishment for breaches of the peace or incitement.

As the most outspoken of the bishops at that time, Hurley was much in demand after the 1952 statement. He addressed the Kolbe Winter School on 'Introduction to an Enquiry into South Africa's Social Problems', encouraging the members to spend the next twelve months focusing on a Catholic programme to tackle the race issue— a further indication that he had not forgotten Lucas's request. Hurley's paper clarified the distinction between fundamental and contingent human rights. The vote was 'to be used by very mature people'; Hurley would rather 'have seen it come at the end of the struggle than at the beginning'. From contingent rights flowed the idea of a qualified franchise, granting the right to vote as and when citizens reached a certain level of formal education and property ownership.

In an address to the Durban branch of the SAIRR in August 1952, Hurley explained once again the distinction between fundamental and contingent rights and said of racial discrimination, 'Surely a nation-wide system of discrimination with its luxuriant growth of 'Europeans Only' signs strikes a blow at something in the non-European which is profoundly and intensely associated with his condition of being human, his human dignity'. In a speech to the regional council of the CAU on 6 September 1952, on 'Some Aspects of the Bishops' Statement on Race Relations', once again in the context of the distinction between fundamental and contingent rights, he encouraged his largely black audience to acquire skills and abilities to exercise contingent rights.

8

Defying Verwoerd[1]

When the National Party (NP) came to power in 1948, it was deeply concerned about the direction of black education. The mission schools seemed to be preparing black pupils for a future little different from that of young whites. If these schools paved the way to an integrated society, they would inevitably create dangerous expectations: black people would end up competing for jobs meant to be white preserves. This was not at all what the NP had in mind: it wanted black schooling to underpin strict racial segregation. The new government was especially anxious because 15 per cent of black schooling was controlled by that great bogey *die Roomse gevaar*. As one of its first priorities, the NP set up a commission to look into how black schooling could be centrally controlled by government so that it would fit into the grand apartheid plan.

This became known as the Eiselen Commission from the name of its chairperson, Dr Werner Eiselen, former professor of Social Anthropology at Pretoria University.[2] The commission's main task was to formulate 'the principles and aims of education for natives as an independent race in which their past and present, their inherent racial qualities, their distinct characteristics and attitudes, and their needs under ever-changing social conditions are taken into consideration'. It is difficult to believe now, a little less than 60 years later, that any educationist could propose a system of education that would deliberately close the doors of opportunity for one group so as to protect another—but that was Eiselen's vision.

Appointed in 1949, the commission reported in 1951. It found that black schools were providing education for a relatively small proportion of what it called a 'backward population'. The dropout rate in the early stages of schooling was high and standards of achievement low. In general, the orientation of the schooling was thought to be too academic, not well related to the limited opportunities that would be open to black school leavers. The commission's conclusion was that the schools were 'not being used nearly as effectively as they ought to be' because they were poorly coordinated with the general development of black people.

There were two inherent weaknesses: that the schools were administered by the four provinces and controlled by churches, and that provinces and churches were not in any other way involved in black development. The commission thought that education should be a 'vital social service concerned not only with the intellectual, moral and emotional development of the individual but also with the socio-economic development of the Bantu as a people'.

The commission recommended that a general development plan should be drawn up for 'the Bantu' as soon as possible. This should be entrusted to a department of the Union government, with 'Union-wide jurisdiction', and education should be controlled by a specialist section of that department to be known as the 'Department of Bantu Education'. As soon as such a plan had been worked out, a clear picture would emerge of the sort of individual that the schools would need to produce.

The 'general development plan' Eiselen had in mind was the apartheid plan, in which black people would be subservient to whites and would, as far as possible, be contained in African reserves far from the cities. The man given the task of establishing the new system of education was Dr Hendrik Verwoerd. Born in the Netherlands and brought to South Africa by his parents at the age of 2, he became the supreme ideologue of apartheid. In Verwoerd's view, harmonious race relations were threatened by expectations developed through the 'wrong type of education'. Such relations

> cannot improve if the result of native education is the creation of frustrated people who, as a result of the education they have received, have expectations in life which circumstances in South Africa do not allow to be fulfilled immediately, when it creates people who are trained for positions not open to them . . . If the native in South Africa today in any kind of school in existence is being taught to expect that he will lead his life under a policy of equal rights, he is making a big mistake.

Another prominent Nationalist politician made the intentions of Bantu Education even clearer when he bluntly told Parliament: 'We should not give the Natives an academic education, as some people are too prone to do. If we do this we shall later be burdened with a number of academically trained Europeans and Non-Europeans, and who is going to do the manual labour in the country?'

The principal effect of the Bantu Education Act was to bring black education under centralized state control at a national level. Control over teachers, syllabuses and 'any other matter relating to the establishment, maintenance, management and control over government Bantu schools' was given to the minister. Three types of schools were to be allowed: community, government and private but state-subsidized schools, including those run by churches. Schools in the last category had to be registered and could only operate with government permission after consultation with the black communities concerned. Moreover, state subsidies were to be phased out over three years. Clearly, the National Party government wanted all such schools handed over to government and thought the removal of subsidies would do the trick.

By the time of the Eiselen Commission and the Bantu Education Act, the South African Catholic Church had been active in mission schools for over a century. Initially, it had to bear the main financial burden for these schools, but eventually the state had provided subsidies, and a 'fairly happy and productive partnership' had developed between church and state before the National Party came to power. State subsidies enabled the Church to train and employ great numbers of lay teachers: by 1953 the Catholic Church had 688 state-subsidized schools; 130 unsubsidized schools in the process of applying for subsidies; and 111,361 students. Of the schools, 377 were in the three Natal dioceses of Durban, Eshowe and Mariannhill, which meant that the future of mission schools was a particularly pressing question for Hurley and the bishops of Eshowe and Mariannhill.

The Bantu Education Act stipulated that the churches were to hand over their schools to the government, which would run them as community-based schools, or they could continue to run them themselves without government funding. The Anglican and Protestant churches were concerned about apartheid ideological control of the schools and not simply state ownership. In fact, some churches were relieved that they would no longer have to carry the financial responsibility for their schools.

The Catholic Church's problem with the Act was different: it had a huge investment in mission schooling, and most of the bishops opposed the takeover of schools on religious rather than ideological or political grounds. For them, the schools were essential evangelizing instruments. Giving them to the government would be suicidal for the Church's mission. Reflecting on this some years later, Hurley said:

> When you think of what happened afterwards, you know, that some of the politicians [in post-apartheid South Africa] are so grateful to Mariannhill, Inkamana [and] to other . . . schools that carried on and taught them. Maybe we were proved right in the end by preserving the schools and keeping this contact with people . . . We could see no sense in the decisions of other churches just to abandon the schools. If people are in need, stay with them; if their need gets steeper, stay with them. That was our attitude.

The bishops had been much influenced by Pope Pius XI's teaching that education is 'first and super-eminently the function of the Church—the supreme and surest teacher of men'.[3] They feared that if the mission schools were handed over to government, there would be no possibility of raising pupils in what they called a 'Catholic atmosphere'. The Church would lose its influence, many Catholics would fall away from religious practice and vocations would dry up. Schools had been successful in promoting conversions: a large number of these potential converts would be lost. The Church would also lose the greater acceptability and even popularity it had achieved by opening its schools to pupils of other churches and faiths.

Hurley was one of the few Catholic bishops who were also concerned about Bantu Education as an apartheid cornerstone, though less so than Ambrose Reeves, Anglican Bishop of Johannesburg, who felt that the only appropriate response to the Bantu Education Act would be to close the schools in protest. Hurley felt that the government would not succeed in ideological control through schooling: black teachers, he said, would never teach black children that they were inherently inferior. It was no surprise to him that after more than 20 years of Bantu Education, a huge revolt against apartheid came from the schools—in Soweto in 1976. In fact, as we shall see, he warned Verwoerd as early as 1954 that the imposition of Bantu Education would lead to great trouble.

The publication of the Eiselen Report in 1951 was, understandably, a cause of much anxiety for the Catholic bishops. What was to happen to their mission schools, which Hurley described as their 'most precious institutional jewels'? Because there was so much confusion on this subject, he asked Father Howard St George OMI, whom he had in 1950 appointed Secretary for Native Schools in the archdiocese, to study the report and write a series of articles explaining its implications. As secretary, St George also took an active part in many conferences held to understand the legislation and strategize on how to respond.

The most notable of these was organized by the SAIRR from 1–3 July 1952. It brought together 274 delegates from 159 organizations, including representatives of the Catholic Bishops' Conference. This delegation was led by Hurley, who chaired one of the sessions, perhaps the first time in South Africa that a Catholic bishop had played such a role in a secular event. It was part of the process of coming out of the shadows.

Despite St George's careful study of the Eiselen Report and its implications, it was only after the Bantu Education Bill became law in August 1953 that Bishop Whelan, Director of Native Education in the Bishops' Conference, and Bishop Riegler, Director of the SACBC's Native Affairs Department, met with Verwoerd in his capacity as Minister of Native Affairs to discuss Bantu Education. Riegler reported that the Minister was still willing to hold discussions, so it would not be wise to attack the legislation and thereby antagonize the government. Riegler was simply fitting into the established pattern for the Catholic Church in South Africa. To reduce the threat of being seen as *die Roomse gevaar*, you assured the government of your loyalty and kept far away from the other churches, making clear that you in no way supported their criticisms of government policy. Hurley, however, described 1954 as a 'year of truth', when the bishops discovered that they would achieve nothing by such a conciliatory approach.

From various interactions with the Under-Secretary for Native Affairs, F. J. de Villiers, one of Verwoerd's principal lieutenants, it soon became clear that sweeping changes were under way. Hence, St George concluded that the Church was likely to find itself in a 'no-win' situation, whatever it did. If it handed over the schools to the government, they would rapidly lose their Catholic character. If it tried to maintain the schools with its own resources, 'we are quite likely to struggle on miserably for a few years just to leave ourselves open to easy extermination in the end', given the three-year phase-out of subsidies. A third option was to close the schools in protest, as Reeves did with the Anglican schools in Johannesburg. The Catholic bishops could not see any point in that strategy.

One thing was clear: they had to make some decision, and soon. To devise a way forward for his own archdiocese, Hurley organized a special meeting of priests and nuns involved in African schools, held in Pietermaritzburg on 30 March 1954; he invited representatives also from the Mariannhill and Eshowe dioceses. Surprisingly, no lay teachers were present, indicating how little they were included in decision-making.

After much discussion it was decided that the Catholic Church would try to gain as much as possible for its mission schools by way of subsidies, appeal to the government for the maintenance of the status quo in the state-aided schools, try to enter the community school system subject to certain conditions and safeguards, suggest that the CAU administer the schools on a community basis, collaborate with the other churches in a nationwide appeal for preserving the status quo 'provided that Catholic principles be safeguarded'. If negotiations were considered necessary, the bishops would seek collaboration with the other churches 'provided that clear agreement could be reached with them on the conditions and safeguards considered absolutely essential'.

Hurley followed up the diocesan meeting of 30 March with a special plenary session of the bishops on 29 and 30 April. However optimistic Whelan and some other bishops were about the possibility of a deal with the government, Hurley correctly saw the writing on the wall for the Catholic mission schools. The minutes record a tough opening speech in which he gave no hint of conciliation:

> Apartheid had been elevated into a formal doctrine. As such we could not compromise with it; it was opposed to justice, charity, the unity of the human race and the unity of the mystical body. Some idealists who upheld apartheid might think we could compromise with it. That was out of the question. The sooner we clash, the better. It would be better to fight while our moral position was intact and strong instead of weakening ourselves by compromise. Apartheid could not last, it was doomed; and one day a new policy would arise to take its place. If we wanted the right to contribute to the formulation of a new policy, we must oppose apartheid now.

This was a remarkable statement for the early 1950s, though admittedly made within a closed church meeting. It showed a complete change of tone and approach on Hurley's part. The gauntlet had been thrown down for those, like Whelan, who kept on hoping—despite the Bantu Education Act having already been passed—that somehow a special deal would be possible for the Catholic Church if they were as conciliatory as possible.

Whelan replied to Hurley by calling for a further attempt at negotiation rather than the confrontation Hurley saw as inevitable:

> We must not get involved in party politics. Apartheid was practised in South Africa long before the present government came into power. Openly opposing it would not help us much. The Holy Father had indicated how, without surrendering our principles, we must be very tolerant towards others and take into account the situation in which we find ourselves. We must think very seriously before appearing to oppose authority.

The lines were clearly drawn for a full-blown argument between Whelan and Hurley. Ten years later their differing views on apartheid would explode in a public clash in the media. The debate in the special plenary session of April 1954 showed just how divided the bishops were in their approach to the government. The overwhelming majority believed that something could still be achieved by negotiation.

On 7 June 1954 Verwoerd clarified the Bantu Education policy when he addressed the Senate. According to the 1955 Survey of the SAIRR, he was quoted as saying:

The previous system of education blindly produced pupils trained on the European model, thus creating the vain hope among the Bantu that they could occupy posts within the European community despite the country's policy of apartheid. In terms of this policy, there was no place for them in the European community above the level of certain forms of labour. Within their own areas, however, all doors were open. Education should thus stand with both feet in the Reserves and have its roots in the spirit and being of Bantu society.

Those who were hoping against hope that the mission schools might survive through negotiation should have taken note of Verwoerd's view: 'Under the new system, education will be coordinated with the broad national policy which was impossible while the majority of schools were controlled by missions of many different denominations'.

As Hurley commented in *Memories*, 'The outlook did not appear too rosy for any submission that the Catholic bishops were likely to make'. The memorandum suggested by the bishops and drawn up by Hurley was ready early in August, and a copy was sent to Dr Verwoerd with a request that he receive a deputation of bishops to discuss it. The memorandum argued that the promotion of the Christian religion was essential for the civilization of the Bantu people.

The memorandum emphasized the contribution the Catholic Church had made to education in South Africa, the close contact of the clergy with mission teachers and schools, and the moderating influence of the Catholic African Teachers' Federation. The kernel of the memorandum came right at the end, where the bishops set out practical proposals concerning the retention of schools by the Church.

The Minister's private secretary replied that the Minister would be willing to receive a deputation on 2 September 1954 in the Union Buildings, Pretoria, but added ominously:

> He wishes to emphasize, however, that it must be quite clear to you that the proposals with which your memorandum concludes, contain the direct negation of the Bantu Education Act and of the objective with which it was introduced and accepted by parliament. . . . It is, therefore, obvious that consideration of such proposals cannot even be entertained and [the Minister] must feel that it is only fair to state this unambiguously in advance so that you can decide whether a deputation has any value for you under such circumstances.

On 2 September, the bishops' deputation led by Hurley consisted of McCann, Whelan (now also an archbishop, since his transfer from Johannesburg to Bloemfontein on 18 July), and St George. Verwoerd received them with great courtesy. From a distance, said Hurley, his face gave the impression of a perpetual smile, but from close up there was no smile and one became conscious only of the 'steely gaze of his pale eyes'.

> At his invitation we presented our memorandum with short addresses from all three episcopal members of the deputation. Dr. Verwoerd replied, regretting that he had to disappoint us completely. He was an extraordinarily coherent speaker. His voice,

slightly high-pitched, was not impressive, but the flow of his language, reflecting a masterful command of his thoughts and their logical sequence, was remarkable.

Without a single note he went through his points: the mission school system, for which he expressed appreciation, had to be replaced by a better organized system coming out of the community, linking education with the whole Bantu culture and giving the people more responsibility for their own system and its financing. He took two swipes at the Catholic Church, reminding the bishops that the Catholic school system of Mozambique was more discriminatory than what the South African government was planning, and recalling the riots and strikes that had taken place in some Catholic schools in South Africa, especially those with boarding establishments.

Hurley readily admitted that there had been problems, but they were as nothing compared to what the government would experience in its own schools. Verwoerd brushed this aside and said that the government would be able to manage. They knew how to control; they had a policy and methods of imposing the policy, and it would succeed. Verwoerd dismissed the delegation as people from overseas coming to tell South Africa how to solve its problems. Hurley replied that there was only one person in the room from overseas—a pointed reminder that Verwoerd had been born in the Netherlands, whereas the whole Catholic delegation was South African.

The deputation had failed in its main purpose, which should not have been a surprise to them after the negative response to the memorandum. Hurley moved swiftly to help the bishops decide the way forward: a special plenary session was summoned for 29 and 30 September 1954.

Opening the discussion at this plenary meeting was St George, accurately predicting that it would be impossible to maintain the mission schools on the reduced subsidies the government was offering; moreover, after three years there would be no subsidy at all. He suggested that the Church retain full control only of those schools that would be easiest to operate without subsidies: the minority staffed mostly by members of religious congregations. For the rest, they should provisionally accept the community school system; if this did not work out, the leases could be cancelled and the Church take back control of the schools.

Hurley opposed St George's proposal, urging an all-out effort to retain the mission schools. This proposal won the day, but by the barest two-thirds majority (16 out of 24 votes). Other important resolutions called for a pastoral letter asking the faithful to give their full support to the Catholic schools and mandated Whelan to write to Prime Minister Malan, informing him about the bishops' decisions and their motivation and expressing the bishops' grave disquiet at the implementation of the Bantu Education Act. Malan sent a completely negative reply: the government had its policy. and there could be no change.

At the next meeting of the Administrative Board, on 9 and 10 November, agreement was reached that the bishops should undertake a special fund-raising drive for the mission schools and the national seminaries and a pastoral letter should be drafted, explaining the decision to keep the mission schools.[4] This letter, drafted by

Whelan, was read from all pulpits on 5 December 1954 and was perfectly in keeping with 'the accepted Catholic episcopal style of the time', according to Hurley. When the rights of the Church were threatened (as in the case of the Bantu Education Act), there was no hesitation about taking up the issue strongly; when the issue was one of human rights in general, there was much caution. The bishops had said little about all the other legislation passed by the new Nationalist government, laws that were having a devastating effect on the human rights of most South Africans.

Faced with the major organizational challenge of how to raise a substantial amount of money to keep the mission schools going, it was to North America that Hurley looked once again. He had been told about an appeal system used in Canada and about a highly skilled fund-raiser from there, Father Peter Riffel OMI. Hurley invited Canadian Bishop John Bokenfohr OMI of Kimberley to explain the system to the Administrative Board. The bishops were so impressed that they invited Riffel to head the campaign.

Riffel arrived in South Africa in July 1955. Before the end of that month, he had held a week-long training workshop for diocesan directors of the fundraising campaign. The campaign was announced by the *Southern Cross* of 21 September, and a pastoral letter by each local bishop was read in all churches. In the second week, diocesan and parish action committees were set up in every part of South Africa. This was followed by five weeks of extensive advertising, as well as recruiting and training volunteers to collect pledges from as many people as possible. This phase culminated on 30 October, the Feast of Christ the King, when a launch Mass was held in every parish. After these Masses, the 8,000 volunteers (all men, and said to be a quarter of the country's Catholic wage earners) were sent out with the ringing of church bells to collect pledges for monthly payments to be made over two years. The campaign's success was a result of superb organization, as well as its emphasis that the future of the Catholic Church in South Africa was at stake.

The *Southern Cross* could not have been more generous in its publicity, devoting its lead story to this issue over eight successive weeks. It also published messages of support from Pope Pius XII, the Cardinal Archbishops of Westminster, Toronto and Sydney; letters of endorsement from local bishops and leading lay persons; photographs and articles about well-attended campaign events. It was 'just one huge phenomenon of publicity', Hurley said later. Before the end of the year, the total raised was over £976,000 (with an estimated value of at least R137,000,000 on 1 January 2009).[5]

Praise for this extraordinary effort came from unlikely quarters. In its monthly newsletter, *Contact*, the Liberal Party (LP) praised the Catholic Bishops' Campaign for having raised the 'fantastic amount' of one million pounds and said that this was evidence of how effective inter-racial efforts could be at a time of increasing racial separation. Even non-Catholics had 'grasped this opportunity of giving tangible evidence of their support for the stand the Roman Catholic Church has taken'.

Even more unexpected was a backhanded compliment from Verwoerd, showing a sneaking admiration for the Bishops' Campaign. In a statement criticizing the closing of the Anglican school at Sophiatown, he said that the school could have been kept open: 'If other churches were also eager to maintain their own education, they should also be prepared to put hands in their pockets and make a small offering'. It was clear that he saw the Catholic Church as a force to be reckoned with, not least because of its refusal to give in to his plan of handing over their schools to government.

In a speech to the organizers of the Bishops' Campaign, Hurley became almost lyrical in his praise: 'As the Campaign developed, one became conscious of a gigantic stirring of the Church in South Africa, an extraordinary mustering of unity, strength and generosity. The inward life and vigour of the Church became almost tangibly present in the external manifestation of disciplined and enthusiastic charity'.

He was also proud of the fact that 'to a world that knows South Africa as the last stronghold of official racial discrimination', the campaign came as an 'astonishing, unprecedented example of the fraternal charity of one race for another'. Despite the dramatic success of the Bishops' Campaign, Hurley realized, however, that the funds raised would only help the Church maintain the schools for a few years. With the money raised, teachers' salaries could not be more than 75 per cent of what they had previously been. The inadequacy of salaries would make the bishops increasingly uncomfortable and would have serious effects on the quality and morale of teachers in Catholic schools.

Knowing that he would need to be overseas for his next *ad limina* visit to Rome in 1956, Hurley decided to contribute to the campaign by a special tour of the United States.[6] His spirits rose as he set out from Durban on board the Italian liner SS *Africa* for what was to be his last journey by sea: 'As the ship headed out into the Indian Ocean, a great sense of relief came over me, the relief of getting away for a while from the crushing burden of the mission school problem under which I had lived for three worrying years!'

In a letter of 30 May 1956, he described his private audience with Pope Pius XII, who was 'intensely interested' in the schools' problem: 'I was very touched by the way he thanked all who worked for the cause. I wish I could convey . . . the tone of voice and the smile that accompanied his words. What a tremendous help it is to hear from the Holy Father himself words of appreciation, affection and encouragement'.

In addition to the *ad limina* visit to Rome, the Archbishop made other visits in Europe, the United Kingdom and Ireland, mainly to his Oblate colleagues. After these travels, he spent four months in the United States preaching appeals for the mission schools. The Americans 'responded well', but we have no record of how much was raised. Out of this visit came a suggestion that a regular mail appeal should be established to continue the fund-raising of 1950 and 1956.

During this visit, Hurley appealed to some of the biggest audiences of his career. At Notre Dame University, Indiana, he told the 3,700 delegates assembled for the seventeenth national convention of the Catholic Students' Mission Crusade that the experience of a concrete expression of Christian charity was the greatest need for the African people. He also mentioned that he was beginning to think of new mission strategies not dependent on schools—which had previously been 75 per cent of the Church's missionary effort. Clearly, the impossibility of sustaining the mission schools was much on his mind. In Philadelphia he addressed 6,000 people at the Vistarama Missionary Exhibition, the largest such exhibition ever staged in the United States at that time. 'The battle for the world's future', he said, 'will be won or lost on the issue of racialism . . . There [can be] no Church where there is racialism; where racialism rears its ugly head, there can be no true love'.

South Africa's Catholic bishops had been faced with a cruel dilemma as a result of the Bantu Education Act. They chose to keep their schools and raise the money to fund them, at least for a few years. As we have seen, in the first year of a three-year process through which subsidies were withdrawn, the bishops reduced the teachers' salaries by 25 per cent. This was done without consultation, the bishops apparently expecting that Catholic teachers would be willing to make a sacrifice for the survival of Catholic education. There should not have been any surprise that over the next ten years there was a continuing decline in teachers' salaries, working conditions, morale and prestige.

During and immediately after the Bishops' Campaign, however, the credibility of the Church increased because it seemed to have defied the government's intention to assume full control of all black education. 'The Catholics have stood by us, and we want our children in their schools', said a parent of Mazenod School, Chesterville, in the Durban area, whose principal, Raphael Mkhize, noted that 400 children had to be turned away from that school when it opened in 1954, the year after the Bantu Education Act was passed. Parents also flocked to many other Catholic schools to register their children.

The bishops had deliberately steered clear of any overt political challenge in their fund-raising because they did not want the government to interfere with the campaign. Despite this caution, the general perception was that the Church had successfully blocked Verwoerd's plan. In the long run, however, the government won the schools' battle. In 1953 there were 5,000 state-aided mission schools; twelve years later there were only 509 (the overwhelming majority of them Catholic) out of a total of 7,222 black schools. Nevertheless, the decision to keep its schools was a turning point for the Catholic Church: it had been strengthened by opposing the government plan and had at last learnt that conciliation was not the way to deal with the NP government.

9

How to Oppose Apartheid

If conciliation was not the way to oppose apartheid, what was? Interviewed by the media after his lengthy overseas visit of 1956, Hurley said that two thoughts had struck him forcefully while he had been away: how difficult it was to believe that people could still be formulating policies of racial discrimination, and how stupid it was to do so in a world in which black nations were rapidly becoming dominant. He had not found anyone overseas who had been impressed by the euphemisms that the South African government used for apartheid: 'separate development' and 'development along one's own racial lines'. He had been away for long enough to be shocked when confronted again by what he described as a 'fantastic outpouring of restrictive legislation' that left black people 'debarred, restricted, prohibited, insulted, without a voice or vote'.[1]

Resistance had been stirring in the black community, but the Catholic Church kept its distance, because the resistance came from a quarter that most bishops dismissed as 'revolutionary', 'communist' and 'Marxist'. The Congress Alliance, established in 1954 to link the ANC, the South African Indian Congress (SAIC) and the predominantly white Congress of Democrats, had a minority of members who could be described by these three words, but the Church was nervous even of this minority.

The Alliance organized the Congress of the People, a sort of national convention, in Kliptown outside Johannesburg in July 1955.[2] It was attended by 3,000 delegates from all over South Africa, the most representative gathering ever held in the country at that time. The delegates signed and adopted a powerful vision statement known as the 'Freedom Charter', a summary of thousands of suggestions sent in from every part of the country:

- The People shall govern!
- All national groups shall have equal rights!
- The People shall share in the country's wealth!
- The land shall be shared among those who work it!

- All shall be equal before the law!
- All shall enjoy equal human rights!
- There shall be work and security!
- The doors of learning and culture shall be opened!
- There shall be houses, security and comfort!
- There shall be peace and friendship!

Given what life was like for the black majority in South Africa in the 1950s, this must have seemed a remote but inspiring dream, certainly not one that would be realized without a struggle. Hence came the stirring call to action: 'These freedoms we will fight for, side by side, throughout our lives, until we have won our victory'.

Police watched the proceedings at Kliptown with great interest and intervened to search and interrogate the delegates until late at night. It was a warning of what was to come. Shortly afterwards, the homes and offices of 400 people and organizations involved in the congress were raided, on the grounds that they were taking part in treasonable activities. A whole year passed before 156 of them, including Nelson Mandela, were arrested and brought to trial for treason in 1956.

The Catholic bishops kept away from all of this. According to Hurley, they were not excited by the congress or its charter, seeing them as 'quite a thrust towards socialism', of which they were deeply suspicious. Their views must have been influenced by the Catholic Church's profound opposition to communism. Pius XII had made this opposition clear in speech after speech, on the basis of the Church's experience of Stalinist purges in the Soviet Union. The bishops declined even to be on Bishop Ambrose Reeves's committee to give material assistance to those on trial for the charge of treason.

The Congress of the People led to further repressive legislation to deal with black political activity. The Riotous Assemblies Act gave government the power to prohibit any outdoor political gathering that it thought might seriously endanger the peace. This was followed by the Bantu Administration Act, which enabled the government to serve banishment orders on 'undesirable persons'.

The legislation that caught the attention of the churches, however, was the Native Laws Amendment Bill proposed early in 1957, because it directly affected them. This legislation laid down that those churches, schools, hospitals, clubs and other institutions or places of entertainment established after 1 January 1938 which admitted black people would have to obtain the express permission of the Minister of Native Affairs. Part of this legislation, which became known as the Church Clause, directly interfered with freedom of worship and brought about the most intense church-state conflict South Africa had so far experienced.

The Catholic bishops, even the more conservative of them, seemed to have no problem in speaking out against the Church Clause.[3] If it became law, they would simply instruct their clergy and flock not to obey. There had been no remotely comparable response to other gravely unjust legislation. This illustrates the degree to which the bishops distinguished between 'the religious' and 'the secular', the latter being something they had been trained to avoid. Hurley and McCann led the Catholic Church's response to the Church Clause, and even such cautious bishops as John Garner of Pretoria and Clemens van Hoeck of Pietersburg made strong statements on the subject, describing the legislation as an 'unwarranted interference with our religion'.

Hurley said that if the law was passed, he would instruct his clergy to continue exactly as before without regard to the consequences: 'It is quite impossible for the Roman Catholic Church to exclude Africans from any of its places of worship. It would be contrary to the basic tenet concerning the unity of the Church'. Geoffrey Clayton, the Anglican Archbishop of Cape Town, protested in writing to the Prime Minister and shortly afterward collapsed and died. Hurley was surprised at how seriously Clayton had taken the proposed legislation. In his own view, the Church Clause was ridiculous and would not be implemented because of the adverse overseas publicity that would have followed. Hurley wanted the churches to focus on other aspects of the bill that would decrease the already-limited contact between blacks and whites. These were more likely to be implemented, with a consequent worsening of race relations.

Verwoerd paid no attention to protests about the Church Clause, dismissing them as propaganda against government policy and as coming from a few church leaders who did not represent lay views. This criticism backfired because it led the churches to encourage greater lay participation in protests. Major protest meetings organized ecumenically and presided over by lay leaders were held in several of the larger centres, including Cape Town, Durban and Pietermaritzburg, where thousands rejected the Church Clause, leaving the government in no doubt about lay opposition.

When the Administrative Board of the Catholic bishops discussed the slightly amended Bill, their opposition remained strong and unanimous. Despite continued protests, the Bill was enacted and published in the *Government Gazette* of 5 July 1957. The bishops, this time as a body, refused to accept its provisions relating to the churches, whatever the consequences; they required that the following statement be read at all Masses throughout South Africa on Sunday, 21 July 1957: 'The Catholic bishops, having taken note of legislation enacted in the last session of parliament through the Native Laws Amendment Act and the Group Areas Amendment Act, solemnly declare that no other authority than the hierarchy has the competence to decide on admittance of persons to Catholic places of worship, [and further] that Catholic churches must and shall remain open to all without regard to their racial origin. In consequence the bishops inform their clergy and flock that there is no restriction on attendance at any Catholic church and that they, the bishops, take full responsibility for admission to Catholic churches'.[4]

The Church had made such an uproar about the Church Clause that its provisions were, as Hurley had predicted, never strictly applied. Other provisions of the Native Laws Amendment Act prohibited the holding of classes and the provision of entertainment in white Group Areas if attended by blacks. The suppression of the already severely limited social and cultural contacts between blacks and whites was for Hurley the greater tragedy.

Nevertheless, the Church Clause was another turning point for the churches, especially the Catholic Church, on account of the strength and unanimity of its rejection, the leading role that it encouraged lay people to play in the protests and its support for Catholic involvement in ecumenical protest. Moreover, the Church openly declared its decision not to obey the law whatever the consequences, the first time it had ever adopted civil disobedience as a strategy.

Hurley's overseas visit in 1956 and his exposure to the intense criticism of apartheid common outside South Africa at that time may have been the main reason for his urging the bishops in 1957 to make a statement specifically on apartheid, whereas the earlier statement in 1952 was a general one on race relations. The experience of resisting the Church Clause gave the bishops courage. There seemed to be no difficulty in 1957 for them to decide in principle to speak out on apartheid. There was considerable debate, however, about precisely what they would say. Garner wanted a statement of Catholic principles: Hurley wanted specific mention and condemnation of apartheid policy.

The draft, prepared by Hurley for the Administrative Board, was eventually read and discussed in a plenary session. Some felt it irresponsible to indict National Party policy without giving an alternative. The Apostolic Delegate, the American Archbishop Celestine Damiano, like his Dutch predecessor Martin Lucas, urged the bishops to consider the possible consequences of making any statement: inviting a probable hardening in the government's attitude to immigration of missionaries and the registration of Catholic schools and clinics.

Opposition to the Church Clause had, however, stiffened moral fibres so that when Hurley argued 'strongly and persuasively', his draft statement was passed by eighteen votes. The conciliatory approach of the past had at last been rejected. The 1957 statement began by observing that in the five years since their 'statement on race relations', the situation had not improved; apartheid was being more strongly enforced than ever.[5] The bishops set out the theological principles that lay behind their opposition:

> It is a sin to humiliate one's fellow man. There is in each human person, by God's creation, a dignity inseparably connected with his quality of rational and free being. This dignity has been immeasurably enhanced by the mystery of our redemption. In the words of St Peter, we are 'a chosen race, a royal priesthood, a consecrated nation' (1 Peter 2:9 [JB]). Christ Himself said: 'I have called you [my] friends' (John 15:15 JB). No man has the right to despise what God has honoured, to belittle one whom Christ has called friend, to brand a fellow man with the stigma of inborn inferiority. It is an insult to human dignity, a slur upon God's noble work of creation and redemption.

The statement went on to call apartheid 'intrinsically evil' twenty-five years before it would be labelled a heresy by the World Alliance of Reformed Churches. But it conceded the difficulty of developing a fully integrated society immediately and called for gradual change to ensure the maintenance of order. The change should, however, start straightaway. The bishops challenged 'our beloved people of white race' about segregation in the Church's own institutions and said, 'This cannot be tolerated for ever'. 'We are hypocrites if we condemn apartheid in South African society and condone it in our own institutions'. The bishops seemed to accept that the situation would be tolerated for some time. White South Africans were, however, warned about the 'harvest of disaster' that apartheid would produce, but no message was addressed to the victims of the policy.

The bishops' statements of 1952 and 1957 appear to have had little impact on the overwhelming majority of white Catholics. Other than being read from the pulpit, no use was made of these statements; indeed, there is no firm evidence that they were read from the pulpit of every predominantly white parish. Some priests, fearing a negative reaction from their parishioners, might have chosen not to read the message or to read it selectively. There was no prepared programme of discussion or education to help priests and congregations wrestle with the issues raised and no opportunities for ordinary people to question or comment on what the bishops had said. Copies of the letter were not made available for people to read and reflect on privately or in small groups. This was partly because the role of the laity was still so circumscribed and partly because adult education methods were not advanced in South Africa at that time. Hurley, reflecting on this years later, said that the bishops' approach was rather like the Vatican approach to papal encyclicals: they were expected to filter down to the faithful, but no plan was in place to ensure that.

In condemning apartheid, the bishops made no mention of whether partition could be regarded as an acceptable alternative approach to the problems of South Africa provided it was carried out justly. Hurley's view was that integration had already progressed so far, despite all the efforts of National Party legislators, that it would be impossible to separate the races. Partition simply was not an option.

Proclaiming the view that 'the only possible Christian attitude was the fostering of integration', Hurley urged the Pretoria Kolbe Association to make contact with people of other races through the loopholes in legislation. 'There can be no finer apostolate than the apostolate of charity, trying to express Christian unity and communion in the teeth of tremendous opposition. Who knows what results will follow when the bridges have been built?'

Hurley did not believe that there was any support in the Scriptures for separate development. Everywhere in the New Testament he found backing for union and not separation, for breaking down and not erecting barriers. If St Paul were writing to Christians in South Africa, Hurley thought he would say, 'There is no more African or European, no more Indian or coloured; no one is civilized or uncivilized, no one is a slave or a free man; there is nothing but Christ in any of us'. However, at least one of his colleagues, Whelan, seemed to regard partition as an option, a view that would return to haunt the bishops a few years later.

No one else in the Bishops' Conference had such strong views on social justice as Hurley. In the early 1950s, he looked for an organization that would give him opportunities to share his concern about the South African situation, a place where he would meet like-minded people, be kept up to date on what was happening, analyse developments and work out how to respond appropriately.

Progressive Party (PP) policies were attractive to him, and he had friends in that party. It had been founded in 1959 by frustrated members of the UP, the official white opposition. They wanted policies more vigorously opposed to those of the NP and were committed to bringing black people into the political life of the country. As mentioned earlier, Hurley approved of their qualified franchise policy based on educational and property qualifications. Despite the 'moderation' of this policy, all but one of the first parliamentary members of the PP lost their seats to the UP in the all-white 1961 election, the only elections held at that time. The PP's qualified franchise nevertheless made more sense to Hurley than the universal franchise of the LP in which he also had a number of friends and with whose policies he was broadly in sympathy. It was not, however, appropriate for a bishop or priest to be an active member of any political party or movement because this could jeopardize their ministry to people from other parties.

The SAIRR was the most significant non-governmental organization committed to opposing apartheid from a liberal perspective. Hurley enjoyed its meetings, its pleasant and dedicated atmosphere; he admired its attitude and spirit and felt at home in its Durban branch.[6] Ultimately he would realize, however, that the SAIRR had a weakness similar to that of the churches: it believed that simply by publishing research and statements addressed primarily to whites, it could bring about change.

Nevertheless, it was through the Durban branch of the SAIRR that he met someone who was to expose him to activism for the first time: Professor Hansi Pollak from the University of Natal. An outstanding sociologist, she was much involved in research on Cato Manor, the black residential area closest to central Durban. Here a large number of Africans had been living in great poverty near an Indian minority, who were generally somewhat better off. By the late 1950s the National Party government had already moved the Africans from Cato Manor to the new townships of KwaMashu, on the northern side of Durban, and Umlazi to the south, far from the city centre, and was planning to move the 40,000 Indians living in Cato Manor to make way for a white suburb. These developments were all in keeping with apartheid town planning. Black people were to live in strictly segregated townships as far as possible from the city.

Pollak had research skills much needed in the campaign to prevent the Indians' removal. She found an influential ally in Hurley, and they developed what he called 'a mutual admiration society'. Hurley admired Pollak's expertise in research and dedication to finding out the facts of any situation. She admired his public-speaking skills and ability to marshal his thoughts with strict logic. They became committed to an intense joint effort to save the Indian areas of Cato Manor, working closely with the residents and their organizations.

The archbishop and the professor visited people in their homes, heard why they wanted to stay, and addressed protest meetings with the Natal Indian Congress (NIC) and the Natal Indian Organisation (NIO). This firsthand encounter with people and their problems motivated them to put together a submission to the Durban City Council, a proposal that became known as the 'Archbishop's Plan'. This suggested which parts of Cato Manor could be set aside for continued Indian occupation. The

City Council had meanwhile been considering their own compromise plan: they would recommend to central government that about 1,300 acres of the existing Indian section of Cato Manor be zoned for Indian use. Hurley and Pollak rejected this because the area under consideration was already overcrowded. They called for rezoning a much larger part of the Indian area of Cato Manor, if not the whole.

Despite Hurley's and Pollak's efforts, with those of the NIC and NIO, and despite some sympathy for the 'Archbishop's Plan' from the Durban City Council, there was no doubt that real power lay in Pretoria and that the apartheid juggernaut was moving forward relentlessly. It must have been disillusioning for Hurley that, despite his and Pollak's dedicated activism, they were not able to prevent the implementation of government policy, though their support had been much appreciated by the Indian community. Years later, Hurley was critical of his own Cato Manor efforts as rather 'individualist': he had not tried to involve either his priests or people but had just forged ahead with Pollak. The failure of the Cato Manor campaign was also a powerful reminder that there would be no real political change until black people had a direct say in the political system. This meant that the extension of the franchise needed to be at the centre of political discussion.

This issue had become more critical since the Congress of the People had opted for universal franchise.[7] Only the Congress Alliance and the Liberal Party accepted this view. Of the white parties, the NP had eventually succeeded in its long-held ambition of taking coloureds off the 100-year-old common voters' role for whites and coloureds in the Cape Province. When the party came to power in 1948, some 48,000 coloured men still retained a qualified franchise in the Cape. In the process of depriving them of the vote, the Nationalist government resorted to considerable interference with the independence of the judiciary. The UP's view was that blacks should continue to elect a small number of whites to represent them in parliament.

Hurley believed that a qualified franchise was the most appropriate solution because it took account of the vast educational disparities. In May 1959, in an address to the Durban Parliament, a debating society run along similar lines to the Pietermaritzburg Parliamentary Debating Society, Hurley said that there must have been at that time as many as one or two million blacks 'with a standard of education entitling them to take full part in the political, economic and cultural life of the country'.[8] He counselled blacks against adopting an 'all-or-nothing' stand, which would make negotiations with whites impossible. He urged them not to make the Liberal and Progressive positions impossible for whites but rather to encourage and help them by being prepared to negotiate. By this time, however, Ghana was independent, and political change was taking place in many parts of Africa, so the gradualism he was advocating was not popular in the black community.[9]

The 1957 statement had strongly condemned apartheid. By 1960, the bishops felt that they needed not only to condemn the policy but also to present an alternative vision, so they published a joint pastoral letter for this purpose.[10] For the first time they proposed that an educational programme should promote its message.

Each diocese was asked to organize a series of sermons to be preached in every church, concerning the content of the letter:

- The principles of the Gospel need to be applied to all aspects of human life.
- God's will is that human beings should live in unity, since they are all one.
- Prayer is needed to find a solution to South Africa's problems.
- Even politics must be subject to God's law.
- God's providence has brought together a great variety of people in this country, each with dignity and human rights.
- The good of such national groups should be subordinate to that of the whole community.
- Christ's teaching is that we should seek first the kingdom of God and God's justice.
- There should be individual change of heart leading to a change of national policy to be more in alignment with God's will.
- A new vision of society is needed.
- Justice requires the payment of proper wages and provision of decent living conditions.
- All should be able to acquire skills and to use them without consideration of colour.
- People should not be prevented from having contact with each other.
- In the light of the above, political participation should be accessible to all, through a system of qualified franchise.

Perhaps it would have been more effective for the Bishops' Conference to provide sermon outlines on these themes for the whole country. Hurley himself drew up such outlines for his own diocese. Once again, there is no way of knowing how extensively they were used or what effect they had.

With hindsight, it is difficult to understand why Hurley and his colleagues clung to the idea of a qualified franchise and even seemed to make it a theological principle. How could they fail to see that there could never be equality in South Africa until all blacks had the vote and government was answerable to them as well as to whites? Why did they not see the universal franchise as a fundamental human right? Was it because the bishops inherited nineteenth-century modes of thought about democracy or the need to 'civilize the natives'? Or was it because, fearful of communism, they allowed themselves to be influenced by friends in the PP, which they saw as the only hope?

At this time, the *Southern Cross* began to report addresses given by the Natal leader of the PP, Leo Boyd, in which he explained the party's policy—an unusual step for a Church newspaper.[11] It was not long before there was a complaint about the cosiness that seemed to be developing between the Catholic bishops and the PP. *Contact*, the LP's fortnightly publication, praised aspects of the 1960 pastoral letter because for the first time it was 'getting down to brass tacks' and not just speaking in general terms about justice. But it also criticized the bishops for aligning themselves so closely with the PP by promoting the idea of a qualified franchise. It was acceptable, they said, for a political party working in the field of white power to 'compromise with apartheid' by calling for a qualified franchise, but they wondered whether the Catholic Church would not be in danger of 'estranging [itself] from the rising generations of non-white democrats? . . . The questions are asked in a spirit of real admiration for a church which has shown itself to an increasing extent the friend of African freedom'.

Given the national crisis that overtook South Africa about a month after the publication of the 1960 pastoral letter, its overall message and the recommended programme of sermons could not have been more timely. The pastoral letter began on a sombre note: 'We are gravely concerned about the future of our country and all its people' and ended with 'We view the situation with gravity'. What happened on 21 March 1960 would give weight to those words. On that day, police opened fire on a 5,000-strong unarmed crowd at Sharpeville, the black township outside Vereeniging, in the province then known as the Transvaal.[12] The crowd was engaged in a pass law protest organized by the Pan-Africanist Congress (PAC), an offshoot of the ANC, though more Africanist in its policies.

The pass laws required all adult Africans constantly to carry pass books to prove their authorization to be in so-called white areas. The crowd had marched to the police station, some of them deliberately to be arrested because they refused to carry pass books. Others were expecting to hear an important announcement about the pass laws: perhaps the government had yielded because of all the protests. The subsequent enquiry described the crowd as 'noisy but not hostile'.

The police, fearing that the crowd was getting out of hand and that the fence around the police station would collapse under the weight of numbers, panicked and began shooting before receiving any instruction. They killed 69 Africans and injured 180. It did not seem that this could be regarded as a calculated massacre, but the position of the gunshot wounds indicated that most of the dead and wounded had been shot while fleeing from the police. Hurley noted that, just weeks before, a number of police conducting anti-liquor raids in Durban's Cato Manor had been ambushed and killed by a hostile crowd. He felt that this might have contributed to the panic leading to violent retaliatory action by the police at Sharpeville.

The shootings caused an international outcry and attempts by the United Nations to impose economic sanctions against South Africa. Britain and the United States prevented this with much help from top South African business leaders, like Harry Oppenheimer, head of the Anglo-American empire. There was, nevertheless, a serious withdrawal of foreign capital from South Africa for several years. McCann called for a judicial enquiry into the shootings; Hurley made a statement that Sharpeville was a clear indication of the breakdown of understanding between white and black in South Africa, which could lead to things far worse if not remedied in time.

A wave of unrest swept over many parts of South Africa in protest at the shootings. At dawn on 30 March, and over the next few days, over 18,000 people were detained under emergency regulations. These regulations gave the government power to prohibit gatherings, impose curfews, detain suspects, seize publications, search premises and do whatever they felt was necessary to maintain public order. Many detainees were questioned and set free, but over 5,000 were convicted and sentenced for various offences, and some were held for several months. The police used violence to break up a growing stay-away. In response, major protest marches to city centres were staged in Durban and Cape Town. In the latter city, 30,000 protestors set off for parliament, which was in session, but were persuaded to march instead to the Caledon Square police station.

On 8 April 1960 the ANC and PAC were banned. Non-violent protest and civil disobedience had completely failed to change increasingly harsh Nationalist government policies. The ANC decided to adopt a restrained form of armed struggle by their military wing, known as *Umkhonto we Sizwe* (Spear of the Nation). This took the form of sabotage and attacks on strategic targets to bring the government and its supporters to their senses, before the country was plunged into civil war. Mandela regarded the formation of *Umkhonto* as necessary to channel the anger of young black radicals, and it served this function until the mid-1970s. Hurley commented that there was a 'great deal of moderation on the part of the ANC because the sabotage would be carefully executed to avoid any injury or killing of persons'. That was not how the authorities viewed it: the police retaliated with even greater repression, and most black leaders such as Oliver Tambo and Nelson Mandela either fled from South Africa or ended up in jail.

The NP government had long wanted to transform South Africa into a republic with an executive state president rather than a largely ceremonial Governor General appointed by the British monarch—a painful reminder of the colonial past. Given international pressure in the wake of the Sharpeville shootings, the banning of the ANC and PAC and the mass detentions that followed the state of emergency in 1960, the government decided to pursue with greater urgency the idea of becoming a republic. The first step was a referendum to test white opinion, held on 6 October 1960; 52 per cent were in favour of South Africa becoming a republic, a majority of 75,000 votes. Only Natal had a majority of votes against the proposal.

The bishops did not give any guidance about how people should vote because they felt that no moral issue was involved. Hurley nevertheless said—many years later—that he had personally been opposed to the idea of separating from the British Commonwealth.[13] This view may have been influenced by those, including his brother Jerry, who had fought in World War II as part of Commonwealth armies. These ex-soldiers were among those who mounted a vigorous campaign against South Africa becoming a republic. They helped to create a strong climate of opinion in Natal, where 93,399 people voted 'no', a majority of three to one, some no doubt hoping that the multiracial Commonwealth would be a restraining force on the government's racism. South Africa applied to remain part of the Commonwealth at the Prime Ministers' Conference of March 1961, but Verwoerd, by that time Prime Minister of South Africa, failed to have the conference's final communiqué changed so that it would not condemn apartheid. He then walked out of the Commonwealth leaders' conference in a huff, and as a result, South Africa ceased to be a member of the Commonwealth. No new application was made for membership as an independent republic.

Late in 1960, after a majority of the white population had voted that South Africa should become a republic, a public meeting was held in the Pietermaritzburg City Hall to reflect on the highly successful campaign that had led to defeat of the referendum proposal in Natal. People of different political viewpoints had worked closely together, and there was a strong feeling that this should be taken further. Hans Meidner, a member of the LP from the University of Natal, proposed that a 'Natal Convention' should be held to map the way forward towards a common society—the opposite of the apartheid plan that the NP was imposing. A planning committee with representatives from all races was elected, including Hurley.[14]

He involved himself fully in this 'Natal Convention', which was attended by over 200 delegates of all races and religions from 17–19 April 1961, the numbers deliberately limited so that the delegates could work in groups not exceeding 30. Nearly 70 organizations sent either representatives or observers. Held at Natal University in Pietermaritzburg, the theme was 'Sharing the Future: Natal Takes Stock', under the headings: political, social and economic. In a moving opening address, Edgar Brookes, professor of politics and history at Natal University, who chaired the planning committee, declared, 'We who are gathered together in conference here determine that never again shall we be separated. If we mean this, nothing in the whole earth can beat us. We will not be wheedled or dragooned into hating and fearing one another any more'.

Brookes was happy that African, Indian and coloured leaders of standing participated fully in the convention, also that Anglicans, Catholics, Congregationalists, Methodists and Presbyterians were all represented, as were many non-political organizations and non-aligned individuals. Weaknesses were the refusal of the official opposition, the UP, to send delegates, and the absence of Afrikaner representation. Nevertheless, said Brookes, the 'convention was able to come to clear decisions and formulate a fighting programme. Those who attended were greatly strengthened by the spirit of very real friendship in it'.

Hurley was asked to present the final report in an open public session, summarizing what had been done in committees. The delegates, he said, had unanimously agreed that the franchise should be extended to black people but had disagreed strongly about whether it should be qualified or universal. No firm recommendation could therefore be made on this topic because it had been decided only to present recommendations for which there was overwhelming support.

The convention recommended that racial discrimination be systematically removed; education be compulsory, equal and free; segregation abolished in entertainment, public transport, sport and places of worship; influx control in urban areas and pass laws done away with so that there could be freedom of movement; the industrial colour bar and job reservation abolished and trade unions encouraged. Wages should be above the poverty datum line and no discrimination allowed on grounds of race or colour. Finally, all races should be entitled to freehold ownership of land. These recommendations were not all unanimous, as Hurley explained, but all reflected 'the general mass of opinion of that large section of Natal life represented in the convention'.

At a report-back meeting held a week later in the Durban City Hall and attended by 2,000 people, Hurley said that the Natal Convention had helped many people of all races to reach agreement on a new vision for South Africa. Those who had not learnt anything new had nevertheless been inspired to find that there was support for their views. Many discovered that people of all races shared a common humanity. Though it was only a beginning, the convention had brought about 'an extraordinary sense of community. Racial barriers and colour prejudice seemed to melt away'.

In conclusion, Hurley suggested that the organizing committee find out which organizations would be willing to participate in inter-racial consultations. These organizations, he suggested, should be given practical help by way of programmes, discussion outlines, discussion leaders and contacts with other interested groups and persons. Central to this would be all religious groups working on a common programme of race relations.

Sadly, little or nothing came of these promising ideas. Brookes acknowledged a 'serious error of judgment'. The Natal Convention Committee had received an invitation from an influential group in Johannesburg to discuss the possibility of a National Convention. This group came down to Natal and appeared to be highly enthusiastic, especially a man whom Brookes refers to as 'Mr X'. Arrangements were made to meet a wider group in Johannesburg. The Natal Committee, which had been asked to stay in office, discovered, however, that Mr X had gone into voluntary exile in England just the previous day. Without him, the meeting 'was visibly racked by fear among some of the most influential Johannesburg delegates'. Brookes's 'error of judgment' was to give the Johannesburg group time to recover their morale. While this was happening, the Natal Committee lapsed. What he should have done, said Brookes, was co-opt a few of the Johannesburg group onto the Natal Committee and proceed on that basis. 'I feel that this was one of the lost opportunities of the struggle, and I regret my share in it'.

Not long after the Natal Convention, Hurley was off to Rome for the inaugural meeting of the Second Vatican Council's Central Preparatory Commission on 13 June 1961, which, together with the sessions of the Council from 1962 to 1965, would require him to spend much time away from South Africa over the next five years. No equivalent of the Natal Convention was held in any other province or nationally until CODESA (Congress for a Democratic South Africa) helped to bring about a new democratic dispensation in the early 1990s. The Vatican Council, however, would, in its own way, provide a huge impetus to the Catholic Church's involvement in work for justice, peace and development and help it to play a leading role in the churches' struggle to end apartheid and introduce democratic government.

PART THREE

'THE GREATEST EXPERIENCE OF MY WHOLE LIFE'

—Denis E. Hurley, *Vatican II: Keeping the Dream Alive*, p. 2

10

Good News

Before looking at Hurley's involvement in the Second Vatican Council, it is necessary to reflect on some developments of the 1950s that helped to prepare him for that event. The mission schools crisis caused him to think deeply about how the faith would be passed on to future generations. He realized that each year the proportion of Catholic children who could attend Catholic schools was diminishing. The Church, which had long regarded schools as its primary method of evangelization, desperately needed to find a more effective way to reach the majority of its children and young people.

Through his reading, Hurley discovered that the catechetical movement in Europe had long moved on from the days of the 'Penny Catechism'—a rather dry set of questions and answers about every aspect of the faith—which generations of Catholic children had learnt by rote. He began to see that a new approach was much needed in South Africa. This made him re-examine the bishops' decision to retain the mission schools: if he had had information about the new catechetics at that time, he might have urged a more sustainable approach, based on developing a dynamic parish life and a system of continuing education for Catholics at all stages of life.

He discovered that the new catechetics amounted to a journey of faith, during which it was hoped that children, adolescents and adults would receive the 'good news' about how to develop a loving relationship with God through Scripture, liturgy and being part of a Christian community.[1] This was intended to help the individual live out a commitment to Christ in everyday life. Sister Theodula Müller CPS of Mariannhill, who had been studying and practising the new catechetics in her native Germany after World War II, helped to expose him to this new way of learning the faith. After her arrival in South Africa in 1952, she had conducted workshops on catechetical renewal throughout the Mariannhill diocese and so became well known in Natal church circles.

In 1957, the Association of Men and Women Religious in the Archdiocese of Durban organized a workshop on whether the concept of mortal sin should be

95

taught to young children. According to William E. May mortal sin 'is the sort of sin whereby human persons truly rebel against the Lord and, by their own self-determining choice, oppose themselves to his love and his law'.[2] Müller was invited to lead one of the discussion groups. Thanks to her catechetical studies, she felt at ease with this question. She was shocked, however, by the conservatism of the group she had been asked to lead, all of whom insisted that young children should be taught about mortal sin.

When Müller's turn came to report back, she faithfully presented the conservative views of her group and then explained why from a theological and pedagogical point of view, she would not teach young children about mortal sin. When we talk about mortal or deadly sin, she said, we are also talking about hell and eternal punishment. This gives the wrong impression to a child. It does not show God as a loving but as a punitive parent. Her view was that young children should not be burdened with such an image of God. Many of the workshop participants reacted negatively to Müller's comments. When they heard that she was opposed to teaching the concept of mortal sin to young children, some of them stamped their feet in protest.

After all the groups had reported, Sister Brigid Flanagan, who was chairing the meeting, turned to Hurley and asked: 'Your Grace, but how will we teach mortal sin to young children?' Hurley looked around to see whether Müller was still there. He feared that she might have left because there had been such a negative reaction to what she had said. Müller had not left but had gone to sit at the back, firmly resolved not to say another word, given the hostility to her views. Hurley invited her to come out to the front: 'Sister, please share with this audience your catechetical background and experience', which she then did. She thought that it showed extraordinary courage on Hurley's part to ask her to give another presentation to the meeting, despite their earlier rejection. Clearly, he thought the participants might be more sympathetic if they knew she was an authority on the new catechetics and if she was given more time to explain her views.

An even bigger surprise followed. Hurley wrote to her provincial superior, asking whether Müller could give a course on catechetical renewal to the religious women and men of the archdiocese, that is, members of religious orders or congregations who live in community and take vows of poverty, chastity and obedience. Despite Müller's reluctance, he pressed ahead with the plan, and six weeks later she received a letter from him saying that about sixty religious—mainly sisters—wanted to attend her catechetical renewal course. The course took place every Sunday afternoon for the whole of 1958 and was followed by a similar year-long training programme for about twenty lay leaders during 1959.

Hurley wanted to promote the new catechetics not only in his own archdiocese but also in the whole territory served by the SACBC (South Africa, Botswana, Namibia and Swaziland). The vehicle for this was a National Catechetical and Liturgical Commission, which he persuaded the bishops to establish in 1959. He had been so delighted with the two year-long courses Müller had given that she was one of the first people he invited to join the new commission. He was also excited to discover that a leading light of the international catechetical movement—the German

Jesuit Father Johannes Hofinger—was planning to visit South Africa as part of an African tour.

Hofinger was a 'world authority on catechetics', according to Colin Collins's SACBC announcement of the visit. Hurley arranged for Hofinger to address audiences in Pretoria, Johannesburg, Durban, Port Elizabeth and Cape Town. 'Father Hofinger was a 'godsend' to South Africa', said Müller, 'a priest who saw eye to eye with Archbishop Hurley . . . Things began moving fast'. She attended Hofinger's Johannesburg public meeting and was astonished—and no doubt also delighted—to hear him say in his opening remarks: 'I'm told there are people who believe that we should teach mortal sin to young children . . . *Nonsense!*'

In January 1960, Archbishop McCann was elected to succeed Hurley as president of the Bishops' Conference, and Hurley was chosen to head the new Catechetical and Liturgical Commission. Over the next ten years it drew up a new syllabus for schools, from grade one (six-year-olds) to matriculants (seventeen- and eighteen-year-olds). Having had first-hand experience of Hurley's vigorous leadership of the catechetical movement in South Africa, Hofinger recruited him as a speaker for his next major project, the Study Conference on Mission Catechesis to be held at Eichstatt near Munich in Germany in July 1960. The gathering was intended 'to adapt modern catechetical experience to the needs of the missions and to . . . establish basic principles of catechesis . . . and outlines of religious textbooks'.

Eichstatt, as the conference came to be known, was attended by cardinals, archbishops, bishops and internationally known catechetical experts, many of them from Germany and France. Among the lay delegates was a noted publisher from the United Kingdom, Geoffrey Chapman, who was there to learn more about catechetical renewal and to look out for publishing opportunities and potential authors. He was to become a close collaborator with Hurley in catechetical and liturgical publishing—and a lifelong friend. His view on the conference was that 'unless you had been at Eichstatt, you hadn't been anointed'.

Hurley was definitely one of the 'anointed'. Not only had he participated; he had also given a significant paper on 'The Role of the Bishop in the Catechetical Renewal',[3] in which he said that three things were necessary to promote catechetical renewal effectively: 'a realization by the hierarchy that catechetical renewal was an urgent necessity, experts to do the job and a catechetical institute through which to do it'. This form of renewal, he believed, should involve biblical scholars, theologians, religious and lay teachers, people involved in Catholic Action, as well as priests and lay people from parishes with a strong liturgical tradition. Above all, seminarians should be trained 'to make the renewal a universal reality' once they had been ordained.

This caused Hurley to include a favourite topic in his address: the reform of seminary education. Priestly studies needed to be aimed at 'announcing the glad tidings of Christ's Redemption', which would require the future priest to receive 'proper training to become a zealous and effective herald of the gospel, . . . filled to the brim with a conviction and fairly vibrating with enthusiasm to communicate it'.

This address made an impact, especially on the sixty-three episcopal delegates from many countries. Hurley was inspired by Eichstatt and the opportunity it provided for discussions with experts like Hofinger. He returned to South Africa keener than ever to speed up the development of new catechetical syllabuses. So enthusiastic was he to secure the bishops' approval for these that he was frustrated when Bishop Ernest Green of Port Elizabeth asked for an extra month to discuss them with his newly-established Catholic Schools' Association. Hurley's somewhat impatient response was that the Association was unlikely to come up with anything that had not already been discovered by the National Catechetical Commission in their three-year preparation of the syllabuses. Moreover, he feared that allowing for an additional month as requested by Green could open a Pandora's box of similar requests from other dioceses. Hurley was even less happy with Bishop Clemens Van Hoeck of Pietersburg's request that each bishop be given the chance to comment on the new syllabuses. Hurley urged Green and Van Hoeck to trust the work that had already been thoroughly done by the commission.

However, later that year, in a letter to Müller, he gave an interesting account of a meeting with Van Hoeck:

> We had a very straight, heart-to-heart talk about all sorts of differences [of opin-ion], and I think we both came away from it resolved to change our attitudes here and there. I am perhaps a little too impetuous in pushing things through and dis-regarding the feelings of other bishops, so Bishop Van Hoeck has done me a lot of good in pointing that out. He, on the other hand, showed great humility and readi-ness to collaborate.[4]

Father Dominic Scholten OP, who worked for many years for the SACBC, including as its general secretary from 1976–82, said that Hurley often spoke about the need for dialogue, but in his eagerness to get things done and perhaps also in what Scholten called his 'failure to display a supple or flexible personality', some of his colleagues felt that he did not always practise such dialogue in relation to them. Yet according to Scholten, Hurley's work on catechetics was rather more appreciated by conservative bishops than his anti-apartheid views.[5]

Once the syllabuses had been approved by the bishops, a series of catechetical study weeks was held in each of the major South African centres in January 1962 to launch the new documents. Father Oswald Hirmer (later Bishop of Mthatha) recalled how Hurley was so keen to ensure the success of such workshops that he would often be the first to volunteer for any tasks. This, said Hirmer, showed his 'great pastoral heart'. If there were posters to be displayed, he was the first to jump up and help. When a volunteer was needed for a demonstration on how to prepare an adult for baptism, Hurley readily made himself available; and to his own amusement and that of the participants, he enjoyed kneeling down and receiving a blessing from his 'sponsors'.

But Hurley also made a significant intellectual contribution to the Study Weeks, explaining the origin of the new catechetical movement. In the first half of the twen-tieth century, he said, several renewals were taking place in the Catholic Church. In addition to the new catechetics, there was a fresh emphasis on the importance of Scripture and on participating in and understanding the liturgy. These three renewals began to influence each other and were joined by a fourth, the lay apostolate. They would pave the way for the Second Vatican Council.

It was probably the success of Hofinger's visit to South Africa in 1959 and of the Eichstatt Catechetical Study Week in 1960 that inspired in him (Hofinger) the idea of organizing an African equivalent of Eichstatt, including both French- and English-speaking countries. This took place at Katigondo, near Kampala in Uganda, in September 1964—by which time the Second Vatican Council was well on its way.[6] Katigondo's theme was how to adapt and present the Christian message in Africa. The subjects covered were how Scripture, liturgy, music, art and literature could be used in catechetics; how the cooperation of clergy could be won; how catechists should be trained and how to use modern teaching methods.

The most senior bishop present at Katigondo was Africa's first cardinal, Laurian Rugambwa of Tanzania, but Hofinger asked Hurley to chair the conference. Geoff Chapman described his contribution: 'He was head and shoulders above anyone else there, and as a man, not just by his rank or his height'. Müller commented that 'Archbishop Hurley, with his sense of humour, with his intelligence, with his patience and good guidance brought [the conference] to a very happy and good conclusion'. The reverberations of Katigondo travelled far and wide, according to Chapman's wife, Sue. Some years later when she told people on a catechetical course that Geoff had participated in Katigondo, they reacted 'as if he had received the tablets of stone directly from Moses'.

Hofinger came to regard Hurley's presence as an essential ingredient for the success of these study weeks.[7] Katigondo inspired the idea of an Asian conference to be held at Hofinger's headquarters, the East Asian Pastoral Institute in Manila, Philippines, in 1966. Hofinger invited Hurley to participate, but he declined because 'the great work of implementing the council's decisions has to be pushed at home'. When the study week was postponed to April 1967, Hofinger tried again. Hurley replied: 'You are the hardest man in the world to say no to, but I am afraid I have to'. He told Hofinger about the meeting of the bishops' Administrative Board that he had to attend and why it was so difficult to refuse his request: 'I still remember with gratitude how much Eichstatt helped me in the Second Vatican Council'.

Hofinger was not easily put off, even by two refusals. When he organized a Latin American study week in 1967 in Medellín, Colombia, he tried to tempt Hurley to attend by reminding him that his (Hurley's) great surprise at the Second Vatican Council was discovering the progressive attitude of Latin American bishops. Hofinger promised that the Medellín study week would give him a further opportunity to interact with the very bishops who had so impressed him. Once again Hurley replied that he was unable to accept, this time because of frequent absences from Durban. In his next letter, Hofinger tried another ploy, reminding Hurley: 'Since you gave the address to the bishops at Eichstatt, you are "the man" to address the Latin American bishops'. But Hurley stuck to his decision. This seems a pity because he never visited Latin America, a continent whose small Christian communities fascinated him and greatly influenced his later promotion of pastoral planning and the networking movement 'Christians for Justice and Peace'. Professor Francis Wilson of UCT felt that if Hurley had been able to spend time in Latin America, it would have been 'like learning a new language', and would have greatly enriched his prophetic ministry.[8]

Once he had ensured that new South African catechetical syllabuses had been drawn up for grade one to matriculation, Hurley set his sights on a new religious education programme: the People of God series, which appeared in 1969.[9] He had long been determined that South Africa should have such a programme of its own that would reflect the culture of the country and not be based on material imported from Europe or the United States. At the time, books for African children tended to be different in content and quality from those for English- and Afrikaans-speaking children. Hurley and Chapman decided that all the translated texts would be identical in quality to the English and Afrikaans editions—a revolutionary step for that time. The books were to have mixed-race illustrations, in colour, as good as anything published overseas. According to Monsignor Paul Nadal, Hurley told Chapman: 'Don't stint on anything; go ahead and get the best'. Anything that Nadal and Müller needed to develop and promote the texts was also provided.

Six volumes were prepared in four colours and eleven languages: English, Afrikaans, Zulu, Sotho (for South Africa and Lesotho), Xhosa, Pedi, Venda, Tsonga, Tswana and two other African languages used in South West Africa (now Namibia), Otshivambo and Rukuangali. For the first time, all Catholic children would use the same books for religious instruction throughout South Africa and even beyond its borders. They had been designed for use in homes, parish classes and Catholic schools. The English and Afrikaans editions sold at 30 cents a copy, and all others at 20 cents, a remarkably low price made possible through sponsorship from the Swiss Catholic Lenten Fund.

Hurley's role in this vast project was to provide the overall vision and to drive the whole effort, persuading the bishops to use the texts in every diocese, raising the necessary funding and liaising closely with the publishers. Preparing the texts was largely in the hands of Nadal and Müller, though the first book in the series was written by Fathers Fritz Lobinger and Oswald Hirmer, who were later to become bishops in the Eastern Cape. They impressed on Hurley the need for an illustrated booklet that parents could use at home to teach their children the basic aspects of faith. Hurley immediately accepted their idea as the basis for the first book, *You Are My Children*. 'Denis was the master spirit', said Chapman, 'but others produced the books'. The title of the series, People of God, and of the individual books, *You Are My Children, You Are My Family, You Are My People, You Are My Friends, You Are My Witnesses*, showed the influence of Scripture and Vatican II.

When asked what it was like to work with Hurley on such a complex project, Sue Chapman said:

> Painless. . . . Hurley worked with you as an equal and he worked as an honest man . . .
> [He would] never second-guess [or] go behind your back. If there [were] any prob-
> lems, . . . we would have sat down and talked about them, you know. The only other
> people like that that we ever worked with were Tutu and the CPSA [Church of the
> Province of Southern Africa]. Same thing, . . . absolutely straight forward. A really,

really difficult project, really difficult, but it went through as it was meant to go because everybody dealt honestly with each other.

The new syllabuses, textbooks and methodology represented a profound change in how the Catholic faith was presented to young people in southern Africa. As noted earlier, the new catechetics was an important preparation for the renewal that Vatican II would promote. Along with Hurley's theological reading in the 1950s, it helped to prepare him not only to understand the thrust of key debates in the Central Preparatory Commission but also for the council itself. Right from the start, he had understood what was at stake.

'Providentially', he wrote in his memoirs, 'the good Lord had provided me with an unforeseen yet quite remarkably apt preparation for [Vatican II] in the form of reading that came my way during the '50s'.[10] What he gained from this reading was a more scriptural and historical theology than the neo-scholastic tradition in which he had been trained during his studies in the 1930s. The American publication *Commonweal* and the Irish theological journal *The Furrow* brought to his attention many changes taking place in theology and whetted his appetite to learn more about the new theology. Most important for him was the discovery of the Church as the body of Christ. There had been some reference to this idea even during his studies in Rome: the Church was not just an association of people but was full of Jesus' presence. Mention has already been made of Emile Mersch's *The Whole Christ* and François Xavier Durwell's *The Resurrection*, both of which greatly influenced him.

Another part of his 'providential preparation for the council' was the short book *Humanisme Intégrale*, by the French layman Jacques Maritain. Maritain distinguished between a 'secular society', which does not promote any specific religion, and a 'sacral society', in which the individual needs to belong to a specific religion in order to be a citizen. Hurley found this distinction liberating because of its relevance to the many secular societies that grant their citizens religious freedom. *Humanisme Intégrale* was especially important for anyone who wanted to take an intelligent part in the council's debates about religious freedom.

Another brief book that influenced Hurley was *The Work of Our Redemption*, by Clifford Howell SJ, which he had borrowed from Father Albert Danker one Sunday in 1957 after a long morning of confirmations at the Machibisa mission in Pietermaritzburg. Hurley had intended to have a siesta, but Howell's book allowed him no rest. He had to finish it in one session, entirely captivated by its message: Jesus is at the heart of all liturgy; all liturgy is his action, in which we join him.

Hurley was also delighted by a book on the history of the Catholic Church in the nineteenth century, written by the Belgian historian Roger Aubert. From Aubert he learnt that many things he had been taught to regard as sacrosanct were historically debateable. There were other books too 'that somehow educated me out of the straightjacket of the old philosophical, scholastic theology to a much broader, easier view. I just felt it was part of an evolution, not a rebellion, from what I had accepted, to broader, deeper, more heart-warming, more exciting aspects of theology. And these were all things . . . we were to talk about in the council'.

Reading the new theology was 'good news' for Hurley, but the best news of all was discovering Teilhard de Chardin.[11] While studying in Rome, Hurley had come across the name in a footnote about Teilhard's 'daring views on evolution'.[12] This was the beginning of a lifelong fascination with a man whom he came to regard as 'a great hero'. He was disappointed not to have met Teilhard when the latter was briefly in Durban during 1951. It was only in the late 1950s and early 1960s, after Teilhard's death, that Hurley was able to read his famous works *Le Milieu Divin, Hymn of the Universe* and *The Phenomenon of Man* because, while Teilhard was alive, the Vatican had prevented their publication.

Hurley said that Teilhard won 'my heart completely'. He seemed to provide the all-embracing vision of creation and redemption for which Hurley had been searching, perhaps even from the time of his studies. As a scholastic in the 1930s, he may have been asking with others whether redemption can be presented in a way that focuses not only on the cross but also on resurrection. Is it possible to speak about theological dichotomies such as this world and the world to come, matter and spirit, body and soul, nature and grace, science and faith, Christ and the universe, in their essential unity rather than in dualistic opposition?

Hurley set a high value on freedom to engage in intellectual exploration of such questions. As he learnt about Teilhard's life and work, he felt increasingly indignant about the censorship of Teilhard's writings and the two periods when he was exiled from France by the Jesuit order and the Holy Office.[13] After Teilhard died in exile in New York in 1955, his admirers did not feel bound to honour the restrictions imposed on his writings during his lifetime. As a result, they were extensively published and translated into many languages. 'The vision of Teilhard burst upon a delighted world', said Hurley, 'with the publication of his books . . . just in time to make [their] contribution to the Second Vatican Council'.

So great was Teilhard's popularity and influence that, in June 1962, months before the start of Vatican II, the Holy Office felt it necessary to issue a formal warning that his writings 'present ambiguities and even grave errors in philosophical and theological matters which offend Catholic doctrine'. This warning urged all bishops and heads of religious institutes, rectors of seminaries and presidents of Catholic universities to 'defend souls, above all the young people, from the dangers inherent in the works of Father Teilhard de Chardin and of his followers'.

Hurley's response to this warning was complex. While he admired Teilhard's views, he admitted that 'the warning was, and is, necessary, for this is a time of much re-examination of traditional ideas, and the danger is that in our enthusiasm for the new we may abandon too much of the old'. It was necessary, he said, to 'bow to the wisdom of the Church in cautioning us against an over-enthusiastic and insufficiently critical acceptance of every Teilhardian statement'. Teilhard was a poet and a mystic, writing as a visionary, not as a theologian or philosopher.

As Hurley stated in a review of *Hymn of the Universe*: 'One must not look for theological exactness in these writings. Here Teilhard is not writing with scientific sobriety' but 'with the insight of a genius, the sensitivity of an artist and the spiritual depth of great holiness'. A powerful combination indeed, which could easily lead to misunderstanding and misinterpretation. Nevertheless Hurley felt that 'once the various facets of Teilhard are better understood', the danger of erroneous interpretation would be lessened.

At the same time, Hurley described himself as 'furious' about the Holy Office's warning and resolved that, should he ever have the chance, he would speak up for Teilhard. This, as we shall see, he did at the Second Vatican Council. Delighted by the publication of Teilhard's books, especially *Le Milieu Divin* and *The Phenomenon of Man*, he read them repeatedly so that he could grasp their meaning and share it with others. 'When these two books in their English translation fell into my hands, the world fell into place'.[14]

Despite the difficulty of interpreting Teilhard's writings, Hurley was greatly attracted to his new and more positive attitude towards creation as a process of evolution activated by God, through Christ. After centuries in which the created world was seen by the Church as a place of trial, sorrow and temptation, a 'vale of tears' before we pass into the next life, Hurley rejoiced in the vision of creation that Teilhard presented. He was delighted too that after 'long years of estrangement' the mystery of creation had, in Teilhard's writings, been reconciled with the mystery of redemption. This was part of Teilhard's compulsion to seek unity: 'The love of Christ and the love of rocks were not merely two great inspirations. They were one consuming passion. They would be fused in Teilhard's thirst for unity, for a single all-embracing vision of reality, reality seen and reality unseen'.[15]

How excited Hurley was by Teilhard is captured in a story by his friend, Sister Geneviève-Marie OSA.[16] She had told Hurley that she would be on holiday for a few days at the Augustinian holiday house at Widenham on the Natal South Coast and that if he wanted to come for a visit, he would be most welcome, never imagining that he would find the time. Then suddenly the phone rang one day: it was Hurley to say he was free that afternoon. Could he come for tea?

No sooner had he arrived than he and Sister Geneviève began speaking about Teilhard. In fact, they had become friends out of a shared enthusiasm for the French priest's writings. Sister Geneviève asked Hurley if he would like her to read 'The Mass on the World' in the original French. They went outside on this beautiful sunny day, and Hurley lay on a grassy bank while she sat and read to him. He had told her he would not be able to stay for longer than an hour. So she read for about half that time, pausing regularly. They had their tea and Hurley's little break was over; inspired and refreshed, he made his way back to Durban.

Admiration for Teilhard fuelled another of Hurley's friendships, with one of South Africa's most famous palaeontologists, Professor Phillip Tobias. They had first met on anti-apartheid platforms in the early 1950s, when Hurley was leading the Catholic Church's struggle against apartheid legislation, and Tobias was president of the National Union of South African Students (NUSAS). In 1951 and 1953 Tobias had the pleasure of meeting Teilhard repeatedly during the latter's visits to South Africa.

Hurley was envious to hear about Tobias's contacts with Teilhard, after the unsuccessful efforts he personally had made to meet the priest.[17] It symbolized the fact that much of Teilhard's life was taken up with scientists and comparatively little with church leaders. The Church was responsible: Teilhard's superiors had repeatedly told him to stay away from theology and devote himself to science. Nevertheless, Tobias remembers Hurley as being especially pleased by Teilhard's bridging of the chasm between science and faith.[18]

Tobias's and Hurley's admiration for Teilhard came to the attention of the Pierre Teilhard de Chardin Association of Great Britain and Ireland, which approached them to start a Teilhard study group in South Africa. Though in some ways the ideal people to undertake such a task, they were both far too busy. No formal Teilhard association or study group has been established in South Africa, but Hurley and Tobias had chance encounters from time to time, generally when travelling by plane between Durban and Johannesburg. On these occasions they would rekindle each other's admiration for Teilhard. When Tobias was on his way to East Africa in 1966 to visit fossil sites, he received a letter from Hurley: 'I suppose you will be going to Olduvai [Gorge] and that you will be seeing a lot of Leakey. What a glorious prospect this must be, to be in contact with the unfolding data of science. I never cease to thank God that science and theology are on sisterly terms in our days, and that people like Teilhard were given to us to bring about this happy situation'.

In 2001 Hurley and Tobias were filmed by SATV in conversation in St Joseph's Church, Morningside, Durban, with Teilhard inevitably a major topic. 'Even in his eighties', wrote Tobias, 'Hurley was as clear-minded as ever. The spirit of his faith, his enthusiasm and his Teilhardian love of synthesis was as puissant as it had shown itself when our friendly discussions had begun decades before'.

Throughout his adult life, Hurley believed intensely in the importance of intellectual freedom, whether related to science, theology or philosophy. This was an important part of what his motto, *Ubi Spiritus, ibi libertas*, meant to him: where the Spirit is present, there should be freedom to explore ideas. Is the Spirit not in fact the inspiration of such exploration? Hurley believed that the Church could only develop and grow through intellectual pioneers willing to take risks. This is why he so enjoyed intellectual debate and was always troubled by the activities of the Vatican's Congregation for the Doctrine of the Faith, which has regularly recommended the disciplining, restriction and even excommunication of certain innovative thinkers in the Church.

Few such thinkers can have suffered as much as Teilhard de Chardin: he was forbidden to speak or publish on theological or philosophical topics from 1924 until his death in 1955, and even then his writings were the subject of a formal warning.[19] Hurley, who would himself pay a price for his commitment to truth and intellectual freedom, boldly challenged the efforts to silence Teilhard. In a speech made on 22 October 1964 before all the bishops assembled in the Second Vatican Council, he publicly declared Teilhard an 'illustrious son of the Church' and praised his 'splendid vision, religious and scientific, evolutionary and eschatological'.

Hurley was delighted by the traces of Teilhard's thinking that can be found, especially in the Vatican II Constitution on the Church in the Modern World (*Gaudium et Spes*), pages of which he believed could have been written by Teilhard because of their positive, evolutionary view of the world. Hurley was angry when he thought about Teilhard's enforced periods of exile and the repeated rejections of his message, but had been especially moved by the humility with which Teilhard accepted these restrictions.

In seeking to understand why Teilhard's writings became so popular after his death that he quickly became a legend, Hurley was obviously speaking first and foremost about his own response when he wrote:

> It is undoubtedly because his vision brings together in one flaming embrace things very dear to us and which up to the present we have uneasily suspected were in some sort of irreconcilable opposition to one another: the world we live in and the world to come, matter and spirit, nature and grace, science and faith, Christ and the universe. Matter is alive with God and God reveals Himself in matter.[20]

It would not be an exaggeration to say that Hurley's careful study of Teilhard in the late 1950s and early 1960s was the most important part of his preparation for the Second Vatican Council. Nevertheless, it seemed to leave some of his missionary priests far behind. Bishop Fritz Lobinger was told by one of these priests that Hurley 'thought about Teilhard de Chardin all the time and for them cement was more important. So he had a bit of difficulty, I think, to talk to an ordinary missionary who says, "Look, I need 5-inch screws".'[21]

Theo Kneifel, a German theologian who had lectured at St Joseph's Scholasticate but had been deported in 1986 for his anti-apartheid activism, had a different reason for querying Hurley's enthusiasm about de Chardin. His concern was that de Chardin's creationist theology was so caught up with vast sweeps of evolution that it would be aloof 'from the concrete suffering of people where one year of suffering is enough'.[22] Clearly de Chardin's thought did not have that effect on Hurley. It seems to have made him even more engaged with human suffering as will be shown.

Second Vatican Council[1]

Ninety days after his election, Pope John XXIII on 25 January 1959 startled the Catholic world by announcing his intention to call a general council of the Church.[2] If the small group of cardinals present on this occasion were excited to hear his historic announcement, they did not show it. In fact, the pope was struck by what he wryly described as their 'impressive and devout silence'. Many others were, however, surprised: most councils had been called when there was a crisis in the Church, especially when a heresy needed to be countered. There seemed to be no such need in the Catholic Church in the late 1950s. Hurley himself was puzzled because from his knowledge of the Church in the English-speaking world, there was no crisis. Everything seemed to be fine: parishes and schools were flourishing, with vocations to the priesthood and religious life abundant.[3]

The first council was that of Jerusalem, as described in Acts 15. Faced with deciding whether Christians should be required to obey the Judaic law, the apostles and elders of the Church 'gathered together to consider this matter' (Acts 15:6). They decided to abandon the prescriptions of the old law and to proclaim the freedom of the gospel.

Thereafter, from time to time in the early Church, such councils were summoned, mainly in the Eastern Church in places such as Nicaea, Chalcedon and Ephesus. These first councils dealt with doctrinal issues that had arisen through the encounter between Christianity and Greek philosophy. Crises of belief and doctrine were thrashed out by the bishops who assembled, together with other prominent leaders of the Church and theologians.

A few councils were held in the Eastern Church when the Turks were threatening Constantinople. In more recent times, councils have, however, only been held in the Western Church. The four Lateran Councils, particularly the fourth (1215), were of considerable historical importance. By far the most important, however, was that of Trent (1545 to 1563), called by the Western Church to respond to the challenges of the Reformation. Thereafter, there was no council for three hundred years until the truncated First Vatican Council of 1869–70, which declared the dogma of papal infallibility and then hurriedly adjourned during the Franco-Prussian War, never to re-convene.

The surprise that greeted Pope John XXIII's announcement in 1959 can be readily understood. Not only had he been considered a 'caretaker pope' who, because of his age, was not expected to do anything as dramatic as convening a council, but also, on the surface, there did not appear to be any major issue to be resolved. Hurley later realized, however, that John XXIII had his ear to the ground years before he became pope, as papal envoy based in Bulgaria and Constantinople and as papal nuncio in France. Hurley thought it must have been his French experience, in particular, that convinced him a council was needed. France was going through a theological crisis while he was there: a tug of war between a strongly neo-scholastic element, who saw theology in terms of fixed dogmas, and theologians who were more open and said it was time for Catholicism to recognize that it had undergone historical changes, not always for the better, and needed to revisit its sources in the Bible and the early fathers of the Church.

John XXIII realized that the Church needed to face up to the modern world that had been the product of a political, scientific and philosophical revolution and was drifting further and further from Christianity. Theologians, such as the two famous French Dominicans, Yves Congar and Marie-Dominique Chenu, felt an urgent need to reformulate Catholic doctrine as an invitation to salvation in Christ within a community based on a living tradition rather than on ossified formulas. John XXIII had come to accept that change was needed but that it would not be easy to convince the tradition-bound Roman Curia, the various departments that make up the Vatican. Perhaps the only way was to call a council representing the whole Church.

THE COUNCIL AGENDA

One of the first steps was to find out from the bishops what they thought needed to be discussed. In June 1959, Cardinal Tardini, Secretary of State and number two to the Pope, sent a formal announcement of the council to every bishop, inviting each to submit agenda suggestions. Hurley was away when this circular arrived, attending the Eichstatt catechetical conference in Germany. On the way to Eichstatt, he and Gerard van Velsen, the Bishop of Kroonstad, had a memorable private audience with John XXIII. He greeted them with his arms extended in a warm welcome and these words: 'We all have problems, and I have far more than you, so let us talk about our joys'. They then had about 20 minutes of joyful conversation before the Pope looked at his watch and realized that he would have to leave them for another group. He ended with a blessing, to which he added the words, in Latin, 'I have much more need of this than you', and the audience was over. This jolly encounter could not have been more different from Hurley's private audiences with the solemn and austere Pius XII in 1950 and 1956.

Returning to Durban after his visits to Rome and Eichstatt, Hurley had so much catching up to do that he was not able to reply to Cardinal Tardini's invitation before the deadline of 1 September 1959. Then came another letter from Rome, reminding bishops that they had been asked to send in suggestions and urging them to do so before the end of April 1960. Hurley took this as a sign that there must have been a disappointing response to the first invitation. He decided to use the new opportunity and submit agenda suggestions.[4] His reading during the late 1940s and 1950s was a great advantage: it had made him aware of what theologians were saying about the Church, about the liturgy, Scripture and catechetics. He was also aware, from the limitations of his own studies in Rome, how the training of priests needed to change.

In his submission he first set out five 'theological points' that he thought needed to be discussed:

1. The Church as the mystical body of Christ, with its liturgical and apostolic activity.
2. The hierarchy as a college of bishops united to the Pope in the government and teaching office of the Church.
3. The joint responsibility of priests and bishops expressed in their teaching office and pastoral care.
4. The laity's participation in the priesthood and mission of Christ, with special attention to Catholic Action.
5. Human freedom in relation to requirements of the Church and the authority of the state.

Then followed five 'practical points':

1. The need to create a closer unity between the Pope and bishops in governing the Church.
2. In the liturgy, more extensive use should be made of the vernacular, so that the laity could participate with understanding.
3. Lay involvement in the Church and in society should be promoted vigorously.
4. The laity should be given a vision of the mystery of Christ, drawing on Scripture and liturgy to inspire mind and heart.
5. Seminary formation was too theoretical and should be adapted to pastoral requirements.

CENTRAL PREPARATORY COMMISSION

Hurley's submission was one of 9,300 received from all over the world. What makes it significant is that it was remarkably similar to what emerged as the council's agenda. He received a friendly letter of acknowledgment for his contribution and, a little later, a letter from Cardinal Tardini saying that he had been appointed by Pope John XXIII to the Central Preparatory Commission (CPC). The CPC consisted of 101 members: 58 cardinals, 5 patriarchs, 29 archbishops, 5 bishops and 4 superiors general of religious orders. Fourteen specialized commissions were set up to develop and submit position papers. Philippe Denis OP believes that Hurley was chosen for the CPC because of his impressive agenda submission.[5] Hurley's view was that the

Vatican had not yet caught up with the fact that he was no longer president of the SACBC but had been replaced by Archbishop McCann. Whatever the reason for his selection, Hurley was delighted.

The task of the CPC was to coordinate and finalize the position papers received from the fourteen commissions. It studied these, drew up comments and suggestions and then voted on them. The first meeting of the CPC took place in June 1961, one of six visits Hurley paid to Rome over the next twelve months for CPC meetings.

It was not long before he discovered a big division between the supporters of neo-scholasticism and those on the commission, like himself, who were open to the new theology.[6] Neo-scholasticism was a particularly dry and rigid interpretation of scholasticism, a school of thought based on an interpretation of the writings of St Thomas Aquinas, an interpretation which became more sterile towards the end of the nineteenth century. The CPC members who lived in Rome, mainly cardinals, some of whom headed Vatican departments, were strongly neo-scholastic in their theological attitudes and views on the training of priests. They were adamant that the Church should continue in the established nineteenth-century tradition, despite Hurley's efforts to disseminate new ideas on seminary training.

By contrast, the *transalpini* cardinals, from countries north of the Alps—like Alfrink of the Netherlands, Frings of Germany, Liénart of France and König of Austria—had been influenced by the great theological resurgence in Western Europe. Hurley found himself in sympathy with the *transalpini*. Though much younger and from a remote and little-known archdiocese, he immediately felt comfortable with these leaders of great dioceses of northern Europe. He found it easy to engage in theological discussion with them: 'It was like playing tennis. I hit the ball to them, they returned it to me, and I found I could hit it back'.

Because of his theological reading in the 1950s, Hurley could readily identify the sources of progressive views in some members of the CPC; from his studies in Rome, he also knew well the origins of the conservative or neo-scholastic view of the Church. Since the Council of Trent, the Church had fought a rearguard action after the great shock of the Reformation. Subsequently, it had been in a defensive mode: against Protestantism, the scientific revolution, the industrial revolution, the Enlightenment, political revolutions and the twin ideological revolutions of capitalism and socialism. All these developments of thought and culture had been kept at arm's length by the Church. The conservatives in the CPC were convinced that this 400-year-old approach was right and should continue.

As the Church had moved into the twentieth century, however, there were various exciting signs of renewal referred to earlier: scriptural, theological, liturgical, catechetical and apostolic, involving particularly the lay apostolate. The cardinals on the CPC who were open to new ideas, including Montini (later Pope Paul VI), were aware of this resurgence in the Church: it made them want to be more in touch with the world. This was, in fact, what John XXIII was calling for when he spoke of *aggiornamento*, updating. Hurley described John XXIII as 'not really a theologian, but . . . a well-read person. I think he had a saintly, spiritual, divine instinct telling him that the Church was out of touch'.

The sessions of the CPC were, however, anything but an attempt to be more in touch with the modern world. As members offered comments and suggestions about the draft documents prepared for the council, a hidden core group seemed to be making all the decisions, regarding the other CPC members simply as consultants whose opinions did not need to be taken seriously. This core group was apparently composed exclusively of conservative members of the Roman Curia. After the progressives had gone home, the conservatives sifted through the suggestions and amendments to formulate the final text in keeping with their own opinions. This experience helped Hurley understand why a council of the universal church was needed: John XXIII must have intuitively realized that only such a council could break the curial stranglehold.

Hurley found himself 'extremely perplexed' by the manipulations of this core group. The CPC continually received minor papers on disparate themes and topics, without any system or order, all of them representing the old defensive way of thinking. The CPC had no overall vision or clearly specified aim.

This issue came to a head at the time of the second meeting attended by the newly-appointed Archbishop Suenens of Malines-Brussels early in 1962. Suenens had simply listened and observed at his first CPC meeting, but at the next, in March 1962, he proposed a way of grouping the various themes and topics, beginning with the Church as a central theme and dividing other topics into those dealing with its internal life and those that related to the Church and the world. At the end of this session, Hurley went straight over to Suenens to congratulate him. Unfortunately, the Suenens proposal did not seem to make any difference. The CPC continued to drift from one unrelated theme or topic to another, completely under the control of the 'hidden group'.

By May 1962, though Hurley was still convinced about how necessary the council was, he was despondent about the kind of event that would emerge from such disorganized preparations. He even thought the council should be delayed so that better preparations could be made. He unsuccessfully requested a private audience with the Pope to express his concern. Then he visited the progressive cardinals on the Commission one by one and shared his despair. He discovered that they also were concerned but seemed powerless to do anything about it. 'Let's wait and see what the Holy Spirit will do once the council assembles', they said.

Hurley's memoirs indicate that, on his return to South Africa during June of that year, he wrote to Cardinal Suenens, setting out at length his anxiety about the council. He told the cardinal that he expected the gathering to begin with a vast number of documents unsuitable for discussion in such a large assembly and with a totally impractical procedure for discussion. He noted from his reading of Roger Aubert that this was exactly how Vatican I had started, and that it had led to a waste of three or four months. He enclosed a detailed memorandum, setting out how he thought discussions in the council could be more effectively organized.

The Roman style would allow endless unrelated monologues, the main points emerging from which would be looked at by commissions. In contrast, Hurley suggested what he called an 'Anglo-American model', with twenty different commissions,

Denis and Theresa Hurley on their wedding day in Skibbereen, Ireland, 11 November 1913.

Oblate Archives, Cedara

Denis and Theresa Hurley with Eileen and Denis at Cape Point.

Oblate Archives, Cedara

Outside the cave where three boys were lost for 22 hours. Clockwise from front left: Denis Hurley, Charlie Farr (wearing gold medal for bravery), George Rossiter, Colin Marshman. The hat that saved the day is next to Marshman's foot.

Oblate Archives, Cedara

Passport photo 1931.

Oblate Archives, Cedara

After Hurley's first Mass on 10 July 1939, in the Chapel of Villa Rosa – guesthouse of the Newcastle Dominicans in Rome. On right is Pat Holland OMI.

Oblate Archives, Cedara

Assisting Bishop Henri Delalle OMI as he blesses an ambulance for use in the Second World War, 1940.

Natal Mercury

Football team at St Joseph's, Prestbury, 1945.
Front: Karl Struve, Charles Murray, Jack O'Brien, Denis Hurley, Robert de Sylva, Carlo Montanelli (Italian POW), dog "Papandreou", Remigius Scheuber.
Back: Brian Devitt, Patrick Holland, Wilfred Vogt, Gerard Coleman, Hugh Dalton, Franco Perego (Italian POW), Kevin Cawte.

Oblate Archives, Cedara

First blessing as bishop, 19 March 1947.

Archives, Archdiocese of Durban

Playing pool – Marian Centre, Pietermaritzburg. At right, Mayor CB Downes.

Oblate Archives, Cedara

The first Archbishop of Durban, arriving by SA Airways Lodestar, at Stamford Hill Aerodrome, Durban, 17 March 1951.

Archives, Archdiocese of Durban

Greeted by Hurley family at Stamford Hill Aerodrome. From left, Jerry, Mother (Theresa), Eileen, Father (Denis).

Archives, Archdiocese of Durban

Receiving the *pallium*, sign of his rank as an archbishop, from Apostolic Delegate, Archbishop Martin Lucas SVD, August 6 1951.

Archives, Archdiocese of Durban

Helping erect tents for the community of Limehill who had been forced to move. At left is Cos Desmond.

Oblate Archives, Cedara

Confirmation in the Valley of a Thousand Hills.

Oblate Archives, Cedara

Hurley's anti-apartheid role seen through the eyes of cartoonist, Jock Leyden.

Independent Newspapers

in all the main languages, each having 150 members who would be able to have real exchanges of opinion. Their findings could be coordinated for plenary sessions. His memoirs do not indicate how Suenens responded, but Hurley's idea was not adopted.

Nevertheless, on a flight back to South Africa, he read with growing excitement the draft document on the liturgy. Here at last was a paper that was worth presenting to such an important gathering. In his view, it provided a model of what was needed, and he was delighted when it was chosen as the first item for the council's agenda.

But there was still no improvement in procedure at the final meeting of the CPC in June 1962. A great variety of topics was presented, mostly tangential aspects of issues already discussed. A major conflict erupted in the commission related to Church-state relations and freedom of religion. Hurley wrote a paper on this subject, supporting Cardinal Augustin Bea's 'progressive' intervention. Hurley's neighbour in the CPC was the intransigent Archbishop Marcel Lefebvre, who later led a schismatic movement in opposition to Vatican II decrees, ordaining its own priests and bishops without Roman authorization. After Hurley had delivered his paper, Lefebvre remarked caustically: 'What the Archbishop of Durban has said is not Catholic doctrine'.

OPENING OF THE COUNCIL

Several months passed before the opening of the council in October 1962.[8] St Peter's Basilica had been prepared as the venue, with the nave curtained off from the aisles. Tiers of seats had been arranged on either side for approximately 2,500 council members. An excellent public address system had been installed, with microphones conveniently placed wherever necessary. The nave of St Peter's had been transformed into a most impressive *aula*, the Latin term for hall.

On his arrival in Rome for the opening, Hurley met Father Yves Congar OP for the first time. Congar had been known to Hurley by his writings and, more recently, through correspondence. It was fortunate that they met so early, given the intense lobbying taking place to ensure that the council would fulfil the vision of John XXIII. Congar and his colleague, Marie-Dominique Chenu OP, developed a high regard for Hurley, listing him as one of sixteen bishops, and the only one from Africa, who could be regarded as key allies in the fight for an open council.

Another short list which included Hurley was Notre Dame, Indiana's 'The Men Who Make the Council'—a series of booklets about the 24 most prominent bishops out of the 2,500 attending Vatican II. Of these council leaders, 17 were cardinals, 5 archbishops and 2 bishops. Only 2 were from Africa—Hurley and Rugambwa.[9]

The council commenced on 11 October 1962 with a great procession of all the assembled bishops through the piazza and into St Peter's Basilica. The organizers had instructed some of the bishops, including Hurley, to assemble in a hall of the Vatican Museum before linking up with the main body of the procession. There they were forgotten by an assistant master of ceremonies. Hurley joked afterwards that, as someone who regarded himself as a progressive, it was a galling experience to be left behind in a museum. Subsequently, this group of bishops was linked up with the main procession as it entered the basilica, to be greeted by the impressive sight of nearly 2,000 bishops filling the rows of benches rising on both sides of St Peter's in what Hurley called 'a canyon of mitres'.

Pope John XXIII used his opening address to set out what he expected the council to do. It should emphasize Christ as the centre of history and, where necessary, bring the Church's methods up to date. He described as 'prophets of doom' those who looked upon everything modern as 'ruin and prevarication'. There were not a few such prophets in the CPC. It was clear, however, that the Pope did not support their gloomy forecasts but favoured those who were more optimistic and open-minded, who would later emerge as the majority. Nevertheless, the Curia was still in control—a major preoccupation of the first session.

Something dramatic happened on the first day of business, 13 October, which would start reducing curial control.[10] The first item on the agenda was the election of council commissions. The preparatory commissions that had been in session in the lead-up to the council had been wound up, and new commissions had to be elected to function throughout the council. These were important structures that would revise position papers on the basis of submissions made during plenary sessions. If a commission consisted of a majority of conservatives, the outcome would be substantially different from what it would be if there were a majority of progressives.

The Curia, largely responsible for selecting the members of commissions in the pre-conciliar phase, expected the bishops simply to endorse the choices they had made for the preparatory commissions. The progressives wanted time for the bishops to get to know each other and to discuss and lobby for suitable candidates. A total of 160 bishops needed to be elected, 16 for each of 10 commissions. A small group, including Hurley, was aware that Cardinal Achille Liénart of Lille, France, had been primed to stand up at the beginning of proceedings and propose a delay to give the bishops time to consult about which of their colleagues would be the most suitable.

When Liénart made this speech, there was great applause, showing that the council fathers had a mind of their own and would not allow themselves to be dictated to by the Curia. Three days were set aside for discussion before the elections would be held. On those days, the bishops met in groups, nationally and by continent, to get to know each other and to propose candidates. When the elections were subsequently held and the results published, Hurley was one of the 160 elected. With 930 votes, he was the eleventh of those chosen for the Commission on Seminaries, Academic Studies and Catholic Education. It seems that he was elected because he was known to the *transalpini* who had been on the CPC; his article in the *Furrow*, on how seminary education needed to change, had been translated into several languages and read by many bishops; he had also impressed bishops at the Eichstatt catechetical conference; not least, perhaps his anti-apartheid stands in the 1950s had not gone unnoticed.

COMMISSION ON SEMINARIES, ACADEMIC STUDIES AND CATHOLIC EDUCATION[11]

Hurley's article in the *Furrow* called for priests to be above all 'competent communicators of the faith'. He felt that the overall aim of seminary formation, the training of pastoral priests, should be made clear from the beginning. It should include an introductory year, during which seminarians would receive 'a thorough initiation into the mystery of Christ'. The philosophy and theology courses should be integrated into one, with a strong pastoral component. Seminaries should not see their task as promoting academic knowledge but 'communicable knowledge'.

Given the predominantly conservative composition of the Commission on Seminaries, it was not surprising that Hurley's proposals were seen as too radical: 'By and large I think they were considered slightly "crackpot"', he said. He had made the fundamental mistake of departing too radically from the document's previous order and arrangement. This was not how things were done in Rome. He persevered, however, and 'by hard arguing' managed to have some amendments accepted, but he hoped that the full council would completely reject the document from the CPC.

Having failed to achieve any substantial revision, Hurley must have been deeply frustrated, but at least he had succeeded in having the need for pastoral training accepted, as well as the idea of an introductory year focusing on the mystery of Christ. He had also persuaded the commission to define the purpose of pastoral training.

When the council reassembled for its third session in September 1964, the commission was asked to give more flesh to the document, after which it would be subjected to discussion by the full council. The commission secretary, Father Augustin Mayer OSB, a clever strategist, feared there would be a difficult debate and so requested a few leading members of the commission, Hurley among them, to prepare responses to issues that might be raised. At the end of the debate, Hurley spoke on what he regarded as the key aspect: the integration of pastoral, intellectual and spiritual aspects of priestly training. Once again he tried to have philosophy and theology merged into one course, saying that even Thomas Aquinas supported this approach.

Contrary to what Father Augustin Mayer had expected, the document was well received by the conciliar fathers, with only forty-seven opposing votes. It 'breathes the spirit of Vatican II' was the view of Bishop Alexander Carter, of Sault Sainte Marie, Ontario, Canada. Philippe Denis OP claims, '[This] was due, in no small measure, to Hurley's influence in the commission'. He had spent many hours editing and re-editing, drafting and re-drafting, making sure the document was in line with the thinking of the conciliar majority. What especially seemed to make it acceptable was its first paragraph, which delegated responsibility for seminary programmes to episcopal conferences, thereby lessening the power of the curial Congregation for Seminaries and Universities. Hurley was one of those responsible for this proposal: it fitted in well with his enthusiasm for collegiality and decentralized control.

THE FIRST SESSION

Hurley was by far the most prominent South African bishop at the council, addressing plenary sessions 10 times and submitting 4 written interventions. Of the 300 or so bishops from Africa, he was second only to Cardinal Laurian Rugambwa of Tanzania, who made 15 oral interventions. Two other bishops from Africa, Sebastiano Soares de Resende of Beira in Mozambique and Elias Zoghby of Nubia in Egypt, gave the same number of speeches as Hurley. Oral and written interventions were one of the chief ways in which he influenced proceedings, and his speeches invariably provoked discussion.

Hurley wasted no time in getting on to his feet and addressing the first plenary session, which debated the 'Message to the World', the council's first public statement. With his customary ecumenical sensitivity, he called for the reference to papal primacy to be omitted so as to take account of non-believers and members of other churches and faiths.[12]

The next item on the agenda was the document on the liturgy prepared by Father Annibale Bugnini. It was well received in the initial vote of acceptance and sent on its way through the various stages of amendment before it would reach its final form. Hurley was so frustrated by the endless series of monologues in plenary sessions that he did not deliver his prepared speech, but simply handed it in. His prepared text said that liturgical reform should not be separated from catechetical and moral renewal. For this reason, it was important to encourage lay participation in the liturgy by adapting its structure and language.

In the last few weeks of the first session, two crucial debates took place in the plenaries. Since the thirteenth century, Catholic theology had been influenced by the thought of the Greek philosopher Aristotle, which had been introduced into the Church by St Thomas Aquinas. Aristotelian or Scholastic theology held sway for the next 400 years, and for all of that time the Church was on the defensive. A clear decision needed to be taken by Vatican II to adopt a more open approach to the world and human society.

The two debates that brought this issue to a head were about revelation and the Church.[13] The conservative approach to revelation spoke of two sources: Scripture and tradition. The council majority opposed this. They believed there was really only one source of revelation, God's Word, given to the apostles and passed on by them through Scripture and tradition, supporting and complementing each other. The document on revelation prepared by the Theological Commission was based on the conservative view: it simply re-stated old doctrines.

Hurley took the opportunity provided by these debates to criticize the council's agenda and procedure.[14] The preparatory stage had lacked central direction, he said. Everyone agreed that the Pope wanted the council to be pastoral, but there was no person or group to interpret what the Pope had meant by that or to coordinate the work of commissions to ensure that his vision was achieved. The agenda should be revised either by a general discussion and voting in plenary or by a special commission. This should be given the widest possible mandate to revise documents so that they captured the pastoral thrust of the council. It should also abbreviate them when necessary and arrange them in a logical order.

When the vote was taken on whether the document for the Dogmatic Constitution on Divine Revelation, with its conservative emphasis, should be set aside, the required two-thirds majority was not achieved. Pope John intervened and ruled that it should be re-written. Hurley regarded this as an 'epoch-making' event: 'the Church would never be the same again'. The conservative view was being officially set aside by the highest decision-making body of the Church.

The second crucial debate was about the Church. Once again, there was a strong reaction against the document: the critics said it was too scholastic and defensive and had not captured the new pastoral and open approach that was becoming so strong in the council. Many of the criticisms had previously been aired in the CPC, but the conservatives, who controlled that body, had paid no attention. Hurley's intervention supported the criticisms of the majority taking part in the debate. Once again, the pope intervened and said the document should be revised.

Nevertheless, Hurley described the rest of the first session, up to December 1962, as 'disastrous'. A random series of unsuitable documents was put before the bishops, all of which had to be referred back for re-drafting. Hurley's view was that they should have been weeded out before ever reaching the council. Pressure was put on Pope John XXIII, who was very ill by this time, to put in place a proper organizing committee to prepare a programme for the council and revise all the remaining schemas, something that Hurley had long recommended. On the day these papal decisions were announced, he wrote a huge 'Thank God!' in his notes.

He had another reason to be thankful: Cardinal Suenens had repeated in plenary his proposal to the CPC, that the council's central theme should be the Church, with sub-topics on its internal and external life. This proposal was received with great applause in the plenary session, whereas it had been ignored by the curial group who controlled proceedings in the CPC. The real highlight of the first period, however, was the discovery that the majority of bishops favoured an attitude of openness. Only as the voting repeatedly favoured their view did those who shared this openness realize that they enjoyed the support of all but about 300 of the 2,200 bishops.[15] Moreover, in some really significant decisions, they had received the backing of Pope John. Perhaps the session had not been as 'disastrous' as Hurley feared.

All of this must have come as quite a shock to the CPC's 'insider group', who had controlled the preparatory stage and had intended to run the council along similar lines. They imagined there would be the briefest discussion on the documents they had drawn up, some slight revisions made, and then a vote would be taken on each. They had not foreseen any great difficulty and expected the council to be over in one session. The bishops would all go home, they would be left to run the Church as before, and life could get back to normal. Nothing had prepared them for the power and influence of the majority. The breakthroughs achieved by this majority helped Hurley to believe that the Holy Spirit was indeed active in guiding this huge assembly.

A GREAT EXPERIMENT IN ADULT EDUCATION

Something else strongly confirmed that belief. While the formal sessions took place each morning in St Peter's Basilica, the late afternoons and evenings were available for informal gatherings. This provided a wonderful opportunity for bishops to attend talks by experts on the topics under discussion. Hurley called this 'the biggest, most famous, historical adult education project ever held'.[16] It helped to update the bishops and thereby ensure that the majority regularly voted in favour of *aggiornamento*. One of the most remarkable aspects of these lectures and seminars was that many of those invited to address the bishops had previously been disciplined by the Church for their views. Now those views were eagerly sought, and the bishops sat at the feet of Scripture scholars, liturgists, historians, philosophers and theologians: 'It was a wonderful experience, self-organized by the bishops' conferences, a kind of university education on the cheap', said Hurley.

Robert Blair Kaiser, *Time* magazine's Rome correspondent during the council, gives an example of the use Hurley made of these occasions: 'He would hear that maybe Rahner would be going to talk to the Canadian bishops, and so Hurley would [get] himself over to the Canadian College. He was like a sponge, soaking all that in'. Kaiser himself was making a unique contribution to this 'massive experiment in adult education' by organizing gatherings in his apartment every Sunday evening. Bishops, theologians and journalists participated in what Hurley called 'The Bob Kaiser Academy'.[17] Kaiser's *soirées* provided something more than the informal lectures organized by bishops' conferences: an opportunity to engage with leading bishops or theologians in smaller groups and a more intimate setting. Kaiser described it as a real learning process. Teachers would be learners, and learners teachers. Kaiser described some of the activities that took place during these gatherings:

> It was a large apartment, so in one corner there would be people singing Irish songs [accompanied by Archbishop Hallinan of Atlanta on the piano] and at the other corner Hans Küng would be deep in conversation with Denis Hurley and maybe one of the Jesuit editors of *America* magazine, Thurston Davis. So it was a kind of challenge for me to make sure everybody was fed and had drinks, and [to] handle the logistics and also keep an ear cocked over in one corner and look in on the bedroom conversation where Gregory Baum was helping somebody write a speech [for] the coming week.

Patrick Akal who was studying in Rome during the council recalls being asked several times by Hurley to make trips on his scooter across town to fetch or deliver something from Küng. Akal thought these may have been drafts of speeches Hurley was preparing to make in the council. 'I realised that the Archbishop was right in the thick of all the behind-the-scenes formulating of stands and policies and positions on the Council.'[18]

A French Canadian Oblate priest, Pierre Hartubise, former Vice Chancellor of St Paul's University in Ottawa, who was also studying in Rome at the time, had been invited to write a weekly column for a Canadian newspaper. He discovered that

Hurley, who was also accommodated in the Oblate headquarters, was an excellent source of information and analysis for these columns, so he met with him practically every week. These discussions gave Hartubise not only a good understanding of the council, but also insights into how Hurley's language skills—in French, Italian, Latin and English—gave him access to a variety of groups and helped him to 'bring together all kinds of people around certain ideas which . . . he thought were important for the future of the Church'.

In this way Hurley was able to introduce people who would not otherwise have met and to interpret to each what others were saying. Most bishops were totally identified with their own national group. Not so Hurley: 'He was not in a closed group of any kind . . . but was going from one group to the other and building an international network of bishops'.

The two theologians who made the greatest impact on Hurley at the Council were Chenu and Congar. More than 20 years after the council, when these two French Dominicans were both old and not in good health, Hurley decided to pay a special visit to each while he was in Paris.[19] Chenu was blind and staying in the St Jacques Dominican community; he was in bed when Hurley arrived with his friend, Sister Geneviève. Hurley said in French: 'Father, I have come to thank you in the name of the Church for all that you have suffered for the Church' (a reference to the long years in which their theological ideas had been frowned upon by the Vatican); then he knelt next to the bed, and they said the 'Hail Mary' together and spoke about a talk that Chenu was preparing. Because of his blindness Chenu had to memorize the text. Then Hurley and Geneviève went to the hospital of St Louis des Invalides, where they found Father Congar in a wheelchair. Once again, Hurley said the same words about the purpose of his visit. They prayed together, and Congar gave him a copy of his book about the council, in which he wrote a dedication. According to Geneviève, all three men were very moved by these visits.

FOUNDING OF ICEL

Possibly the most important fruit of Hurley's ability to network with bishops and theologians from a variety of countries was the establishment during Vatican II of ICEL, the International Commission on English in the Liturgy.[20] As the council fathers assembled in Rome just before the opening on October 11, 1962, bishops began to discuss their hopes for a vernacular liturgy and the possibility of bishops' conferences where English was spoken, collaborating in preparing translations. Among these were Archbishops Denis Hurley, Paul Hallinan of Atlanta, USA, and Guildford Young of Hobart, Tasmania. There is uncertainty about who first proposed a structure to produce uniform translations for all English-speaking countries. Hurley thought it was Hallinan.

During the first session of the Council, these discussions continued. At some stage it was thought important to involve Archbishop Francis Grimshaw of Birmingham, because it would have been strange to discuss English in the liturgy without having the 'mother country' represented.

When the bishops were about to return to their own countries in early December 1962, Grimshaw agreed to draw up and circulate an agenda for those English-speaking conferences that were interested, to discuss a common translation project when the bishops returned to Rome for the second session in September 1963.

By February or March 1963, Grimshaw had not done anything about this commitment, so Hurley took it upon himself to develop such an agenda because he and others felt that a vernacular liturgy was definitely on the way. There could be no better time to set up a structure to coordinate English liturgical texts than during the conciliar sessions, when all the bishops were gathered in Rome and it was relatively convenient and inexpensive to meet regularly. So in April 1963 he had written to Grimshaw, Hallinan and Young to propose such a structure. This time he suggested that the more dynamic Hallinan should, together with Grimshaw, convene the group.

Grimshaw was not in the best of health and had proved ineffective, slow moving, and confused as to the purpose of the group—he thought it was an informal discussion group about translations that would be done by each conference of bishops working independently. Determined not to lose time, Hurley suggested that consultants be used and research undertaken before September 1963, so that more rapid progress could be made when the bishops were together again during the second session. These steps were not taken, probably because of Grimshaw's inadequacies.

A major obstacle to bishops from English-speaking countries working together on common English translations was the different linguistic traditions of those countries. Yet it was recognized that a much higher standard of translation could be achieved through pooling their resources, with the larger countries coming to the aid of smaller and poorer ones. Hurley was probably the most highly motivated of the four bishops who pioneered the establishment of ICEL: he was concerned that, unless common translations were drawn up, the less well resourced countries like South Africa would be overwhelmed by a variety of translations and missals of all kinds coming from the United States, England, Ireland, Scotland and Australia.

On October 2, 1963, Hurley called together Grimshaw, Hallinan and Young during a lull in one of the plenary assemblies, for what he called a 'liturgical caucus' just outside the *aula*, in St Peter's. This gathering finally succeeded in getting Grimshaw to set the date for a first formal meeting to be held at the English College in Rome: 17 October 1963.

The meeting on that date was effectively the first meeting of ICEL. The bishops present represented Australia, Canada, England and Wales, India, Ireland, New Zealand, Pakistan, South Africa and the United States. An eleventh member, the Philippines, joined ICEL in 1967. In later years, fifteen other conferences were added as 'associate members' with full involvement in the consultation phases and full access to the texts produced.

The significance of this initial step becomes clearer when it is realized that the creation of ICEL preceded by six weeks the council's promulgation of the liturgical constitution, *Sacrosanctum Concilium*, which made provision for the use of the vernacular, and came a full year before the Vatican's encouragement to conferences of bishops sharing the same language to form joint commissions to prepare uniform liturgical translations. The English-speaking bishops, with what Hurley called 'typical pragmatism', had acted as examples to their colleagues of other languages, especially the French- and German-speaking bishops, who later established similar structures.

In the light of the initiatives Hurley took in relation to the establishment of ICEL and his later successful leadership of the organization from 1975 to 1991, it is puzzling that he was not chosen as an office-bearer at the time of ICEL's establishment. Monsignor Frederick McManus described him as probably the most vigorous, creative and outspoken of the bishops involved in ICEL. Though he was not elected to any office at the meeting of 17 October 1963, he invariably seemed to give the right push at the right time, but at the first meeting, it was Grimshaw who was elected to the chair, with Hallinan and Young as vice-chairs.

This international episcopal committee had three more meetings during the second session, largely about which translation of the Bible would be most suitable. Further extensive discussions during the third session of the council focused on finalizing a formal mandate, the first draft of which had been prepared by Hurley. This described the aim of the bishops' conferences in setting up this new structure as 'achieving an English version of liturgical texts acceptable to English-speaking countries, bearing in mind the ecumenical aspects'. When this mandate was submitted to the hierarchies concerned for approval, they gave it without hesitation. Hurley saw this new initiative as a fine example of the collegiality that the council called for, with a 'tremendous emphasis on collaboration, cooperation and exchange of ideas'.

Given later controversies about the work of ICEL, it is important to note that the involvement of expert consultants was part of the mandate from the start and that the idea of originating new English texts, and not simply translating existing Latin ones, was seen as crucial for a fully renewed liturgy. The original ICEL mandate also had a clear ecumenical dimension that took account of other churches' centuries-long experience with the English vernacular.

THE SECOND SESSION

Hurley discovered that the two coffee bars set up inside St Peter's for the use of the bishops (popularly known as Bar Jonah and Bar Abbas) were often much better sources of information than the most attentive participation in plenary sessions. They were also good places for lobbying. Hurley would make his way there every day at about 10:30 a.m. There he found that 'the agitation for a change of procedure is fermenting satisfactorily—bishops wander about the coffee-bars fuming, muttering, turning purple and coming close to blasphemy and other things' in their frustration at the ponderous procedures of the council.[21]

By 19 September 1963 when the bishops assembled for the second session, Pope John XXIII had died (3 June 1963) and Pope Paul VI, elected on 21 June, had succeeded him. Not only did Paul VI indicate that the Council should continue; he also publicly aligned himself with John XXIII's *aggiornamento*.

Hurley described the first two weeks of this session as the most important of the whole council.[22] In the first week, the nature of the Church was discussed, with many speakers using the image 'People of God', a profound change from the previous philosophical and structural emphasis and from the image of the Church as a fortress, inherited from Reformation times. Now it was to be a more engaged Church, reaching out to the world.

The second week was devoted to the hierarchy, particularly the collegiality of bishops. Did the bishops form a corporate body with the Pope? Did they derive their power from the Pope or directly from Christ as a body united with and under the Pope? The minority were afraid of the doctrine of collegiality: to them it weakened papal primacy. By contrast, the majority held that the leadership of the Church was weakened by the lack of close cooperation between the bishops and the Pope in governing the Church.

In the final version of the document on the Church, this collegial relationship is described in these words:

> The order of bishops is the successor to the college of the apostles in their role as teachers and pastors, and in it the apostolic college is perpetuated. Together with its head, the Supreme Pontiff, and never apart from him, it is the subject of supreme and full authority over the universal Church, but this power cannot be exercised without the consent of the Roman Pontiff.

Hurley made two oral interventions during this session, when the document on the Church was under discussion: about priests and about laity. In a speech, which is said to have made a deep impression, he deplored how inadequately priests had been treated in the document. They are responsible for just about all the Church's work of teaching and sanctifying, he said, and have the most direct influence on the great majority of Church members. 'They are the bishop's hands and feet, his eyes and ears and voice'. To do his work, the bishop therefore needs to give his priests the best possible leadership and support.

Hurley made a similar point about the laity: they make the greatest impact on the world, and that is their special role in the Church. If so, they should feel trusted by bishops and priests and allowed to exercise initiative. As they became better educated, more critical and vocal about the relationship of Catholic doctrine to social, economic and domestic issues, bishops would need to train their priests and seminarians in more mature ways of relating to the laity.

When the document on religious freedom was discussed in plenary for the first time, Hurley made a third, written intervention. Drawing on his reading of Maritain's *Humanisme Integrále*, he argued that in the modern world the Church no longer had any power over the state, and this was a good thing. There was no need for Church and state to be linked.

One of the greatest surprises of the council took place during this second session, at a time when the council seemed to be running out of energy. As Cardinal Josef Frings of Cologne began to speak in the debate on the Church and collegiality, participants suddenly realized that he was criticizing what was then known as the

Holy Office and is now called the Congregation for the Doctrine of the Faith, the Vatican's watchdog on orthodoxy. The bishops were on the edge of their seats as Frings chided the Holy Office for reproving and condemning authors without giving them the basic right of being heard in their own defence. Many *aggiornamento* theologians, who had suffered at the hands of the Holy Office, could hardly believe what they were hearing.

The second session ended on a high note, with the promulgation of the Constitution on the Sacred Liturgy, *Sacrosanctum Concilium*, with 2,147 votes for and only four against.

THIRD SESSION

A key debate of the third session, which commenced on 14 September 1964, was on the lay apostolate.[23] After the Reformation, so much attention had been devoted to the hierarchical nature of the Church that the role of the laity had been badly neglected. In the decades before Vatican II, however, there had been a great revival of concern about the lay apostolate, and a number of lay organizations had come into existence. One of the most important was the Young Christian Workers. Though Pius XI had seen the lay apostolate as assisting priests and bishops in their work, by the time of the council it was increasingly recognized that the laity's more important role was in influencing human society.

Vatican II was the first council where the relationship between Church and world was faced. The document *The Church in the Modern World* was debated under five headings: human destiny, the Church at the service of God and humanity, the dignity of the human person, the unity of the human family, the preservation of peace. During the debate Hurley gave the ringing endorsement (referred to earlier) of his favourite theologian, Teilhard de Chardin—a remarkably brave speech when one recalls the Holy Office's formal warning about Teilhard's writings as recently as June 1962.

Later the South African bishops realized that they had, however, missed an excellent opportunity to speak about racial injustice. The subject was raised by four bishops, two American, one Indian and one African. Given the rules for participating in debates, it was then too late for the South African bishops to take up the theme. Perhaps Hurley had been so engaged with the new theological ferment in the Church that even he did not immediately see the opportunity provided by the council for a resounding condemnation of apartheid. He regretted this omission.

There were several other disappointing aspects of this third session. First, Pope Paul VI removed the question of birth control from the agenda, reserving it to his own special commission. Nevertheless some bishops, especially Cardinal Suenens, still wanted to have their say without actually mentioning birth control. Subsequently, Suenens denied having justified birth control, but the world media and many bishops thought he had done exactly that.

Then an appeal had been made to the Pope to prevent the teaching on collegiality from being included in Chapter 3 of 'The Church'. This did not succeed, but an 'explanatory note' was added to the text that weakened what the Council said on this topic.

The third disappointing aspect, which suggested once again that the Pope was buckling under conservative pressure, came with the announcement that voting on the 'Declaration on Religious Liberty' was to be postponed to the fourth and final session. The American bishops, who had taken up the issue of religious liberty with special vigour, were outraged and alarmed at the likely effect on public opinion. Bishops from Eastern Europe and communist countries were likewise keen that there should be no delay in stressing religious freedom. The American bishops rapidly collected signatures to petition the Pope to overrule this postponement. The Pope, however, refused to go against the decision of the council presidents, and so the vote was postponed for almost a year, becoming the last taken in the council.

FINAL SESSION

These three interventions by Pope Paul were not well received by the council majority for they seemed intended to pacify the minority. In an effort to ensure that the fourth and final session, which commenced on 14 September 1965, would start on a more positive note, right at the beginning an announcement was made that a permanent Synod of Bishops would be established.[24] This was a response to many calls from council fathers including some prominent cardinals even before the council. It was also the fulfilment of promises that the Pope himself had made.

The formal establishment of the Synod of Bishops took place the day after the initial announcement, with the Pope present in the *aula* to hear the founding document read, to prolonged applause. Cardinal Paolo Marella informed the council that, in establishing the synod, the Pope 'had asked the advice of many bishops and listened to the counsel of experts'.

What the council fathers had requested was a structure that would promote collegial government of the Church by the Pope and bishops. Was this what Pope Paul had given them? On the positive side, it could be noted that the synod was established as a permanent body, with assemblies called together from time to time. The bulk of the membership of these assemblies, all but 15 per cent nominated by the Pope, were to be elected by bishops' conferences and would represent the bishops of the entire world. On a less positive note, it was clear that the 'will of the Pope' would be 'sovereign' within the synod. According to the late Peter Hebblethwaite, the noted English-speaking Vaticanologist: 'The pope calls the synod when and as he chooses, confirms its membership, determines its agenda, appoints its president and secretary, decides how its results are to be communicated, settles where it will be held, and presides over it (if necessary through a delegate). It is, moreover, said to be "immediately subject to the Roman pontiff"'.

Hebblethwaite was disappointed that no reference was made to collegiality in the founding document, and that there was no explicit reference to the Council document on the Church, *Lumen Gentium*.

Major debates of the final session were the second rounds of discussion on Religious Freedom and *The Church in the Modern World*.[25] Many bishops felt that Religious Freedom was a make-or-break issue. Hurley submitted a written intervention at the beginning of the session, strongly in favour. He wrote about how Christian revelation taught that the spiritual order was distinct from the temporal. The state had no competence in religious matters. Though from the time of Constantine to the twentieth century, the Church had accepted the idea that temporal society had to recognize and uphold the spiritual, this should no longer apply. 'Now we are almost unanimous in rejecting state competence in religious matters and its obligation to the true Church'.

The minority, mainly from so-called Catholic countries, could not understand why the Catholic Church should not enjoy special recognition. After all, it was the one true Church. How could any other church or religion receive comparable recognition? Their favourite slogan was, 'Error has no rights'. The vote was, however, overwhelmingly favourable. There were still amendments to be dealt with and then the ceremonial vote of promulgation, which took place only on the last day of council business, 7 December 1965, indicating how strong a rearguard action there had been about this declaration.

Much else remained to be debated on *The Church in the Modern World*, including controversy about whether the prime purpose of marriage was procreation and the education of children (the minority clung to this traditional view) or whether marriage should be regarded as a 'community of life and love'. This latter view Hurley had first heard from one of his lecturers at the Gregorian, Father Franz Hurth SJ. Hurth quoted a German, referred to only as 'Father Doms' in Hurley's writings, probably Father Heribert Doms, a theologian from the early 1900s, whose view of marriage had been rejected by Rome at that time. When signing the final text of *The Church in the Modern World*, Hurley had felt like adding a 'PS' to say, 'Doms, you were darn well right'.

Another significant discussion in this second round of debate on *The Church in the Modern World* concerned war and peace. The document spoke strongly about the horror of war, declaring that atomic, biological, chemical and conventional war was grossly immoral, yet conceding that there were occasions when force might have to be used against an aggressor. The balance of terror between nations that possessed atomic weapons was deplored, yet given grudging recognition for keeping the peace. Though every effort should be made to disarm and to outlaw war, in the meantime, to deter others, nations might possess atomic weapons. These moral juggling acts were not satisfactory for the French hierarchy, several of whose leading lights spoke passionately in favour of an outright condemnation of war and the outlawing of nuclear weapons. Yet not even the French were able to satisfy the Christian pacifists, including Dorothy Day, who were fasting and praying in Rome that the bishops would speak out for unilateral disarmament. They did not.

Hurley was one of nine bishops who signed a document drawn up by Archbishop Philip Hannan of New Orleans, specifically opposing the idea of such disarmament because they wanted to emphasize the value of deterrence. The signatories were, however, perceived to be favouring atomic weapons and came in for much criticism.

One of the last interventions by Pope Paul VI was similar to his three in the third session. This time it was clerical celibacy that he had decided would also not be debated by the council. There seemed to be relief among many bishops, judging by their applause when this was announced. Perhaps they were weary after so many fractious debates. The papal move, however, caused what Hurley called an 'angry sensation' among media representatives, who saw it as another blow against freedom of speech, like taking birth control off the agenda. The council had begun with several positive interventions by Pope John XXIII in favour of the majority; now it seemed to be ending with his successor's efforts to pacify the minority, an ominous trend for the post-conciliar implementation stage. Many years later, Hurley expressed the view that it was a serious error not to have discussed birth control and celibacy at the council; it had weakened the Church's moral authority.

Nevertheless, the achievements of Vatican II were considerable. In particular, it had given the bishops a new vision of their collegial role together with the Pope, and a powerful experience of that role in the commissions and plenary sessions. In addition, informal lectures and seminars achieved a remarkable degree of theological updating for many. The impressive official documents approved by the council presented a fresh vision of the Church and its mission emphasizing the idea of the Church as a living community, a people on pilgrimage through history.

CLOSING

The Second Vatican Council came to a rousing conclusion at a great Mass in St Peter's Square on 8 December 1965, with a vast congregation participating heartily according to the new liturgy, but largely in Latin and through Gregorian chant, though much use of vernaculars would have been possible by this time, as Hurley noted. The celebration, wrote Hurley,

> ended with the final blessing of the Holy Father and his ringing valediction, 'Go in peace', evoking a more explosive *Deo gratias* than most of us had ever heard before. The bishops made their way along Bernini's colonnade and rode off in their buses for the last time—through a forest of waving hands and a chorus of farewells. They had begun their journey back to their dioceses and their endeavours to lead the great effort of bringing the council to life in the communities they had been ordained to serve.

The remaining chapters of this biography reflect the efforts Hurley made to 'bring the council to life' especially in the promotion of justice and peace in his own archdiocese, more generally in South Africa, and even in other parts of the world.

42

Archbishops Clash

Towards the end of the Second Vatican Council's second session in 1963, Hurley received a letter from his friend Father Pat Holland OMI.[1] Holland told him that Dr André de Villiers, a leading Presbyterian, had suggested that an 'ecumenical act of witness' should be held in the Durban City Hall just before Christmas to focus on 'united belief in Christ's incarnation'. De Villiers had set two conditions: first, that Hurley should support the event and be one of the main speakers; second, that the occasion should be 'multi-racial'. 'The whole plan is being held in abeyance until an answer is received from Your Grace', wrote Holland. We don't have any record of Hurley's reply but can assume that it was an enthusiastic 'yes'.

Three days before Christmas, the Durban City Hall and its galleries were packed for the service, believed to be an historic first for South Africa. On the stage were nearly a hundred clergy, including Hurley, Anglican Bishop A. H. Cullen and a number of Catholic priests. The prayers and carols were in English, Zulu and Afrikaans. In his address, Hurley said that though there were still differences of belief in doctrine and in liturgical and sacramental life that made impossible the full expression of Christian unity, there was a new spirit breathing over the earth. The tremendous response to this service by the Christian churches of Durban was evidence of that spirit.[2]

Early in 1964 Hurley took another ecumenical step that was bold for the time, allowing Holland to accept an invitation from de Villiers to preach in the Frere Road Presbyterian Church at one of their Holy Week services. This was reported in newspapers around the country. As far as de Villiers was concerned, the service was good news, and the public should know about it. For Hurley, the publicity created a slightly awkward situation: his brother bishops had not yet worked out a common policy on pulpit exchanges. He had given his permission in advance of such an agreement because the service had been billed as 'unofficial', which he thought meant that it would not receive publicity because of its experimental nature. He gave an assurance to his colleagues in the SACBC that no further experiments of this nature would take place in the Archdiocese of Durban until the bishops had drawn up a code of rules for such exchanges.

One of Hurley's fellow archbishops, John Garner of Pretoria, chair of the bishops' ecumenical committee, took him to task in the *Southern Cross*.[3] A lengthy article by Garner appeared, not mentioning Hurley or Holland or even Durban by name, but leaving no doubt about its targets. A report about ecumenical activities, said Garner, had appeared in the *Rand Daily Mail*, and there had been similar reports a few weeks previously, presumably referring to the unity service in the Durban City Hall. Garner was upset that Hurley had taken these initiatives without discussing the matter with the Bishops' Conference and its Committee on Ecumenism. Shadow-boxing it might have been, but the punches came thick and fast. Garner's overall assessment was that 'the [ecumenical] movement has been dogged by muddle-headedness, bursting with goodwill, but confused to an exasperating degree'.

Hurley must have been less than pleased to be called 'muddle-headed' and 'confused' and to be criticized for actions that 'may well lead to disaster, the ruin of the whole movement'. Garner's criticism, however, seems not to have diminished Hurley's ecumenical enthusiasm: a month later he said the opening prayer at a second 'interdenominational demonstration of unity' in the Durban City Hall, on 5 April 1964, this time to give witness to a common belief in the resurrection. Once again, there was an excellent attendance.

Garner's clash with Hurley in the pages of the *Southern Cross* was mild in comparison with another clash between archbishops, which had begun early in 1964. Since 1962, much of the bishops' time had been taken up with the Council. Nevertheless, they were aware of political developments back home, especially a subtle shift that had taken place in apartheid policy. Since Verwoerd had become Prime Minister and leader of the National Party in 1958, he had put a new 'spin' on policy: the reason why Africans could not take part in South Africa's political system was not that they were inferior but that they were not really South Africans. Government policy did not discriminate on the basis of race or colour, Verwoerd held, but on the grounds that the African population consisted of different nations: Zulu, Xhosa, Sotho, Tswana, Tsonga and Venda. He promised that all these ethnic groups would be given political rights ('self-determination') in their own ethnic areas.

Once this vision had been fully realized through the independence of the 'homelands', there would no longer be any black (African) South Africans. Whether or not they had ever lived in their particular 'homeland' or had even visited it, that was the only place where they would be able to exercise political rights. South Africa would still be able to draw on these independent homelands as labour reservoirs, though such migrant workers would not enjoy any political rights in the white urban areas. The Promotion of Bantu Self-Government Act No. 46 of 1959 was introduced to give homeland citizens the opportunity to govern themselves, supposedly without intervention or external control.

This may have made the policy of apartheid look rather like 'partition', which some considered a respectable way of dealing with diverse populations, provided certain conditions were met to ensure justice. Those who had sternly opposed apartheid presented as a policy of white domination over the whole of South Africa were given pause by this new approach. Aware of this confusion, Hurley addressed the issue directly when invited to give the eighteenth annual Hoernlé Memorial Lecture at the South African Institute of Race Relations conference in Cape Town in January 1964.[5]

Hurley had been elected president of the SAIRR at the conference. Press reports said that he was given a great ovation by the large audience when he arrived at the University of Cape Town's Hiddingh Hall for the lecture: 'Apartheid: A Crisis of the Christian Conscience', and loudly applauded again at its conclusion. The main purpose of the speech was to respond to apartheid apologists who argued that the policy, properly understood, was acceptable to the Christian conscience. Though such apologists readily admitted that separate development was not perfect, they claimed that it was the best solution in difficult circumstances. Whites feared that in an integrated society they would lose out totally. There was only one solution: provide separate areas for each race, where they could develop in their own way in just and peaceful separation from other races: surely this was ethical and Christian, they said.

Hurley proposed four conditions that separate development should meet before it could be considered morally acceptable: the policy must be feasible; it must be freely consented to by all parties involved; in its implementation, there must be a proportionate share of sacrifice for all affected groups; and while the policy was being established, the rights of all parties must be adequately protected.

He then applied these four criteria to separate development in South Africa, stating that the policy could not be a vague goal that might only be achieved in some distant future. Those who were asked to accept it had to be assured that there was a real possibility of separate futures for (as the population statistics were at that time) eleven million Africans, three million whites, a million-and-a-half coloured people and a half-million Asians, 'so that each group and all the individuals constituting it may be provided with political, social, cultural and economic conditions under which to pursue a decent livelihood'.

One of the problems about separate development, said Hurley, was that the feasibility of the policy depended on what was meant by the term, and no one had spelt it out with any clarity. The reality was that the South African government treated Africans, Asians and coloureds as subject races who could only be granted human rights compatible with safeguarding the racial identity and supremacy of whites. There was no evidence that any of the race groups, including even whites, had accepted the idea of partitioning South Africa. To assess whether there was a proportionate share of the sacrifices involved in such partition, it would be necessary to submit the whole matter to a neutral arbitrator.

As to the fourth criterion, that the human rights of all concerned should be protected during the transition, Hurley said, 'We all know what is happening under the Group Areas Act, the Job Reservation Act, and the comprehensive range of laws which have deprived the African population of practically all civil rights in 87 per cent of South Africa'.

Hurley concluded that not one of the four conditions needed for a just implementation of separate development had been fulfilled at that time or showed any likelihood of being fulfilled in the future. There was no evidence that the policy would succeed; there would be no consultation with the parties most concerned to obtain their consent. No independent arbitrator would be called in to ensure that there was a proportionate share of the sacrifices involved in implementation. Finally, there was no guarantee that rights would be protected during the transition. Separate development as contemplated in South Africa could 'not be pursued without injustice and is, therefore, not in accord with the Christian ethic'. The real problem in South Africa was, according to Hurley, that 'white Christian society has grown up in the firm conviction that the law of love does not apply to non-Europeans, except in special and unusual circumstances'.

Hurley's Hoernlé Lecture, one of the most intelligent and devastating analyses of apartheid by any Church leader up to that time, received extensive media coverage. Little did Hurley realize what an intensely negative reaction it would stir up, not only, as one would expect, among ardent members of the National Party but also from one of his closest colleagues in the SACBC, Archbishop William Patrick Whelan of Bloemfontein.[6] Whelan's mother was an Afrikaner, and he had considerable feeling for the Afrikaners. Though known to be more conservative than Hurley in his social and theological views, as noted earlier he had been greatly aroused by the government's efforts to take over the mission schools. When the Church's rights were under attack, said Hurley, Whelan could be a tiger: it was not quite the same when human rights were affected—he was not convinced that was an area for Church involvement. Nevertheless, Hurley said, Whelan had been the first to call apartheid 'heretical', as early as 1957.

McCann later informed Hurley that Whelan had told him that he had long been irritated by Hurley's actions and statements on apartheid and by the considerable media attention his colleague received.[7] 'Archbishop Hurley is talking too much off his own bat and you should warn him'. Hurley was surprised because he was 'really fond' of Whelan, and they had been 'very good friends'. But Whelan's irritation, and perhaps envy, must have been all the greater by 1964 because of Hurley's prominence in the Second Vatican Council. Hurley had, however, been entirely unaware how his colleague was reacting.

When Whelan read the Hoernlé Lecture, his irritation reached boiling point, and he swung into action. Claiming to have been approached by a number of people to present an alternative view of apartheid to Hurley's, he decided to publish his views in the form of an interview, but would not divulge how it was put together.[8]

Writing in his official capacity as Director of the Department of Press, Radio and Cinema of the Bishops' Conference, Whelan said that he foresaw a 'happy issue' out of South Africa's 'current social and political difficulties' that would 'not necessarily' involve abandoning apartheid.[9] Questioned as to whether apartheid was an injustice that must go, Whelan replied that the issue was whether or not injustice was 'inherently involved in the policy of separate development as it is being currently pursued'. Asked whether apartheid or separate development was not in itself vicious, his reply indicated that he had been influenced by the change of National Party policy to emphasize self-determination for all ethnic groups in South Africa: 'There is no teaching of the Church in opposition to the idea of a state composed of a number of national groups, maintained in their separate and distinct identity by the state of which they form a part'. He noted moreover that 'the Church regards as immoral any policy aimed at levelling such ethnic groups into an amorphous cosmopolitan mass'.

Whelan dodged the question whether apartheid had been officially condemned by the Church, referring only to a statement by the president of the Bishops' Conference in 1958 (Hurley) that Catholics were 'perfectly free to vote for any of the parties contesting the general election' that year. This response, Whelan said, could not have been given 'if any party had been judged to be advocating a policy that, considered as a whole, was immoral'.

His only reference to the bishops' statements of 1952, 1957, 1960 and 1962 made it seem that these were exclusively directed at legislation causing hardship and injustice. Most people would have interpreted those statements as condemning the policy of apartheid as a whole, especially the 1957 statement that apartheid was 'intrinsically evil'. Equally unsatisfactory were Whelan's responses to questions about the violation of human rights implicit in apartheid, which he confused with the inevitable restrictions 'necessarily and increasingly imposed on individuals' in all societies. Coming to the central point of Hurley's Hoernlé Lecture, that the Christian law of love should have a profound influence on public policy, Whelan disagreed. The influence of Christian love was only for individuals and their motivation, not for public policy.

The chief question that Whelan avoided was how there could be a just partition of the country when the population group most affected had not been consulted. Indeed, many of its members had been banned, imprisoned or exiled precisely for expressing critical views of such partition.

Whelan gave the text of his interview to the *Southern Cross*, which used it in full, and to a number of daily papers, where it also received extensive publicity.[10] The interview represented a totally new approach to apartheid by the Catholic Church. The full text was issued by the SA Press Association and carried at length by most papers, in many as the front-page lead. It received special prominence in newspapers supporting the government, and many devoted editorials to it. Nationalist papers accepted it as official policy and hailed it as a welcome change on the part of the Catholic Church.

Opposition papers gave greater prominence to statements by McCann and Hurley declaring that Whelan's interview simply reflected his personal opinion. The *Cape Times* said that Whelan 'was contemplating an ideal, hypothetical state': Hurley's lecture, by contrast, 'concerned the real world'. The London-based *Catholic Herald* said that Whelan's statement 'has brought joy to the enemies of God, confusion to the honest and a deeper sense of abandonment to the Africans'. This theme was also taken up by a leading Catholic layman in South Africa, Drake Koka, who stated in the *World* that Whelan's 'views on apartheid will shake the faith and confidence of thousands of African Catholics'.

As soon as he had become aware of Whelan's statement, Hurley was on the phone to McCann, then president of the Bishops' Conference, and told him that he would be flying to Cape Town on the first available plane to discuss with McCann what steps the bishops should take to deal with the embarrassing situation Whelan's statement had created.[11] On arrival, Hurley urged McCann to call a plenary session of the bishops as soon as possible, whereas McCann had planned merely to speak to Whelan on the phone. For Hurley, the matter was far too important to be dealt with in that way. Eventually Hurley prevailed and the bishops did meet, though the official line was that they were meeting to 'deal with liturgical matters'.

The first official Catholic reaction to Whelan's interview was the statement by McCann that Whelan had spoken as Archbishop of Bloemfontein, not on the authority of the Conference. Hurley spoke more strongly: any reports that Whelan's views represented the official attitude of the Church were 'completely erroneous'. He added: 'Just as when I make my speeches, I do not expect my views to be binding on the Church, so are Archbishop Whelan's views in no way the official attitude'.

The only Catholic editor of a secular paper in South Africa, Donald Woods of East London's *Daily Dispatch*, sent a telegram to Hurley: 'Thank God for you. If you had not repudiated Whelan's statement, I would have left the Church. Keep on advocating real Christianity. Many are praying for you and depending on you'.

The *Southern Cross* reported McCann's request that no editorial comment be published until after the bishops' meeting. It is thought that he may have been requested to impose this ban by the Apostolic Delegate, Archbishop Joseph McGeogh, who had been nervous that the Bishops' Conference would be split down the middle by the conflict. The Catholic population of South Africa was abuzz: never before had there been such a public disagreement among the bishops. According to Hurley, at the beginning of the plenary session, McGeogh intervened personally 'to make sure that it didn't turn into a prairie fire'.

After the session a brief statement was made that the official policy of the SACBC in regard to race relations was as set out in their 1952, 1957, 1960 and 1962 statements: statements by individual bishops were made on their own responsibility. Under the heading 'Discussion Closed', the *Southern Cross* of 4 March 1964 declared: 'In accordance with a directive received, as the South African Catholic Bishops' Conference has issued a statement on race relations, discussion is now closed in this paper on the relevant matters recently raised'. No further coverage was carried about the contrasting views of Whelan and Hurley, nor were any further letters published on this subject. The newly-established independent monthly *Challenge*, edited by Catholic laity, regretted the ban and called for it to be lifted, but censorship prevailed.[12]

Colin Collins, a former staff member of the SACBC, who was present for the discussion on Whelan's statement, said that though the bishops officially endorsed their previous statements, behind closed doors there had been surprising support for Whelan's position.[13] The Church should not rock the boat in relations with the government, a number of bishops said, because this might cause problems for Church institutions. 'Let's be more careful about what we say' seemed to be their attitude; a repudiation of Hurley's Hoernlé Lecture rather than Whelan's interview. Collins walked with Hurley immediately after the meeting and found him distressed by the lack of support, especially from the expatriate bishops.

Hurley's own recollection was that, though dismayed that the bishops were not taking seriously enough the issues that were troubling South Africa at the time, he was not going to change either his outlook or his practice of speaking out.

'I maintained friendships with all the bishops very closely and just let that episode slide off my back as something that was not going to affect the future very much. But I suppose there was a lot said that I didn't hear and of which I was unaware, . . . luckily, fortunately'.

Hurley promised McGeogh to give serious thought to 'whether or not the policy of separate development could, in principle, be accepted or whether it was intrinsically immoral'.[14] He forwarded to McGeogh a brief paper on the subject, titled 'The South African Policy of Separate Development', adding that he was more convinced than ever 'as a result of writing this that the policy in itself is wrong, and totally unacceptable to the Christian conscience'. In the same letter he mentioned that the Bishops' Conference would have to deal with the issue arising from Whelan's statement 'and the encouragement it has given to great numbers of white Catholics to believe that the acceptance of apartheid is reconcilable with Catholic principles'.

Unfortunately, it seems that McGeogh himself may have adopted Whelan's view because late the same year, while still in Rome for the third session of the Vatican Council, Hurley wrote to the Vatican's *Sostituto* (substitute) for Extraordinary Affairs, Archbishop Antonio Samorè, one of two deputies to the papal Secretary of State. He enclosed a copy of his paper on apartheid and separate development, the purpose of which was 'to provide an explanation of terms and give information to the Secretary of State of His Holiness'. Hurley's purpose becomes even clearer from the next paragraph: 'From the manner in which His Excellency the Apostolic Delegate to Southern Africa has expressed himself, it would appear possible that he represents separate development as justifiable in principle and leaves the matter there'. Hurley then makes clear that his own view was that the South African application was 'morally indefensible'. He made himself available to discuss the matter further with top Vatican officials during the remaining week that he would be in Rome. An identical letter was sent to Cardinal Agagianian, Prefect of the Sacred Congregation for the Propagation of the Faith. There is no record of whether these offers were taken up. Monsignor Paul Nadal was told by Hurley that McGeogh had sent negative reports to the Vatican about Hurley's views.[15]

In a letter to Colin Collins, written about the same time, Hurley noted that the South African Embassy in Rome was still circulating Whelan's statement: 'The matter must be cleared up soon. I think poor Archbishop McCann hates to face up to the show-down. I am not relishing it myself but, the way things are, something must be done'. In a letter to McCann, Hurley suggested that the paper he (Hurley) had written 'could very well serve as the first step towards elaborating more formal documents. If we decide to do this, I think we should get a very broad sweep of opinion, both clerical and lay, in order that the facts we assemble are correct and our conclusions justified by them'.[16]

In Chapter 11 we have noted the bishops' disappointing failure to use the opportunity that the Second Vatican Council provided to promote global awareness of racial discrimination in South Africa.[17] Was this perhaps because they were reluctant to risk exposing their internal divisions in this international forum? They were, however, quick to apply the council teachings to the South African situation, publishing a special joint pastoral letter on the topic at their first plenary session, in July 1966, just six months after the end of the council. The main purpose was to introduce *The Church in the Modern World (Gaudium et Spes)* to their people and to draw to their attention chapters of particular significance for South Africa and its problems. The whole pastoral letter was a tour de force of Hurley's enthusiasm for the council message, his knowledge of its documents, his orderly and logical flow of thought, and profound concern about the South African situation.

The letter presented The Church in the Modern World as a charter for the dignity of human persons, their rights and responsibilities. The bishops, however, limited themselves to commenting on a few paragraphs from the chapter on 'The Community of Mankind'. Speaking directly to the South African situation, they referred to the 'innate sense of unity and interdependence' among human persons, which should know of no 'impediment of colour, creed or class' because there is a natural right to free association 'which cannot be either diminished or taken away on racial grounds, on the pretext that such association will damage the common good'. This unity was underlined by our Christian belief in one Creator, one human race, one Redeemer. 'This is the groundwork of our Christian faith; without it, the redemption can have no meaning'.

These were not new principles for the Church; they had been taught in various places and forms, said the bishops, reminding the faithful in South Africa that they had been referred to in their previous joint pastorals. Now they took on a special significance because they came from what the bishops called the 'supreme assembly of the Catholic Church': the Pope and bishops in council. The bishops therefore felt it appropriate to specifically make the point once again to the people of South Africa:

> It is a grave violation of the dignity of the human person to prevent anyone, on grounds of race or nationality, from choosing his own mode of living, to restrict his choice of employment, his right of free movement, his place of residence, his free establishment of a family. If any laws make the exercise of these rights unnecessarily difficult or almost impossible, all legal means should be used to have them changed.[18]

The 1966 pastoral[19] also quoted Pope John XXIII's encyclical letter *Pacem in Terris*: 'If any government does not acknowledge the rights of man, or violates them, it not only fails in its duty, but its orders completely lack juridical force'; this was a new thought for an SACBC pastoral, with far-reaching implications for civil disobedience in South Africa. These were, however, not spelt out.

The bishops stressed that Vatican II condemned everything that offended against the dignity of the human person 'such as sub-human living conditions, arbitrary imprisonment, deportation, slavery, prostitution, the selling of women and children, as well as disgraceful working conditions', all of which it called 'infamies indeed'. The bishops noted that the council did not regard racial discrimination as more important than other forms of discrimination, but said that, in racially pluralistic countries, racial prejudice took on a 'crucial prominence'. They quoted the council's own words: 'Discrimination is to be eradicated as contrary to God's intent'.

This pastoral letter showed that the bishops were once again able to move ahead after the bruising Whelan-Hurley conflict, strengthened by their experience of the council and determined to implement its message. The conflict had taken a great toll on Whelan, whose health declined so sharply that he was unable to attend the final session of the Vatican Council from October to December 1965 and died suddenly on 10 February 1966. Hurley's determination to continue his friendships with all the bishops was nowhere more strongly shown than in his magnanimous tribute to Whelan, when he preached the panegyric at the funeral in Bloemfontein's Cathedral of the Sacred Heart, built during Whelan's 12 years as archbishop.

He spoke of Whelan:

burning himself up in the service of God, preaching, instructing, confessing, offering the daily sacrifice, serving on welfare committees, inspiring the lives of university students, fostering the apostolic spirit of the laity, preparing the way for the Grail and the Young Christian Workers in South Africa, turning as editor of the *Catholic Times* from the myriad occupations of the day to the reading and writing of the night hours. Yet always ready to sit and talk to a confrère, clerical or lay, to talk deeply, sympathetically, searchingly. Always ready to respond to a soul in trouble, to mental anguish and bodily distress. One wondered how he survived. He was driven by a great love—for God, for his Church, his priesthood, his religious family, for people.[20]

13

Humanae Vitae

As we have seen, Hurley was not afraid to challenge leading members of the South African government on the policy of apartheid and also members of his own Church who supported that policy. A crisis at the end of July 1968 showed that he was willing to speak his mind in an altogether more difficult context, when a decision taken by the Pope did not seem to be in keeping with the spirit of Vatican II. This crisis resulted from Pope Paul VI's encyclical letter *Humanae Vitae* (Of human life), which upheld the Church's traditional ban on artificial birth control.[1] This decision went against the majority view of the seventy-five-member birth control commission established by Pope John XXIII in 1963. As indicated in Chapter 11, Paul VI had announced in June 1964 that birth control would not be discussed in the Council, but reserved to this papal commission. Once he had received their report, he would issue a formal papal statement setting out his views. This was *Humanae Vitae*.

The encyclical was all the more controversial because the birth control commission's report had been leaked, so it was common knowledge that the commission had recommended a change in the Church's teaching. This had led to tremendous expectations that the Church would indeed change its teaching on birth control. Surveys and reports showed that millions of Catholic couples were already using artificial birth control. Prominent theologians had said that despite any stand that the Pope might take, it remained a matter for couples to decide on the basis of conscience. There had also been enormous pressure on the Catholic Church to permit birth control as a way of easing population growth in poorer parts of the world.

In *Humanae Vitae* the Pope referred to previous documents on birth control issued by his predecessors and stated that the continuity of papal teaching did not allow him to make a change. A key sentence of the encyclical declared that 'every matrimonial act must remain open to the transmission of life' and that to 'destroy even only partially [the] significance [of intercourse] and its end, is contradictory to the plan of God and to His will'. The Pope was, however, careful to say that the encyclical was not infallible and should be implemented with sensitivity.

Widely differing responses were elicited; for example, the Australian bishops issued a joint statement: 'To refuse to accept the decision . . . would be a grave act of disobedience', and accordingly 'every member of the Church must be considered bound to accept the decision given by the Pope'. Father Hans Küng, the Swiss-born theologian who had been a star of the Council and was teaching at the University of Tübingen in Germany, declared: 'Those who reach the conclusion, after mature deliberation with themselves, that to preserve their marital happiness they cannot be guided by the principles enunciated in this encyclical, must follow their own consciences'. A diversity of opinions was also heard in South Africa: McCann (since 1965 a cardinal) said that the Holy Father had spoken and he was the supreme teaching authority. Garner of Pretoria commented: 'The surprising thing is that so many are surprised that the Holy Father should have reaffirmed the constant teaching of the Church on the subject'.

Hurley put out a full statement, which appeared in the *Southern Cross* of 7 August 1968. This began by stating that Paul VI had mentioned that this was the hardest statement he had had to make as Pope. Hurley agreed that it must have been agonizing and went on to say that responding to the Pope's statement had also been difficult. 'I don't think I have ever felt so torn in half'. On the one hand were reasons clamouring for immediate acceptance of the Pope's decision. On the other were reasons that made the statement hard to accept. Hurley frankly explained that from 1962 to 1965 he had argued with many bishops, theologians and lay men and women in defence of the traditional view, only to find that after the Second Vatican Council, early in 1966, he became personally convinced that the Church's attitude had to change. That was still his conviction.

Another reason why the Pope's statement was hard to accept, said Hurley, was that, during the council, the bishops had seen what 'magnificent results' could be achieved by full and open debate. The birth control issue had not been handled in the same way at all. The papal commission had received written submissions and made its own recommendation. Then the Pope decided that it would be wiser not to heed that recommendation. Obviously Hurley accepted that the Pope had a right to take a decision, but 'I would not be honest if I said I agreed with the method of the consultation—and with the result'.

It was, Hurley's statement continued, a time for earnest prayer and great love and loyalty in the debate that would take place about the decision itself and the manner in which it was taken. He expected that in many countries clergy and laity would urge their bishops to take part in the debate as corporate episcopates: 'As brothers of Pope Paul in the episcopate, they cannot shirk the issue of how they think the authority of the senior brother should be exercised. To discuss it with him is not disloyalty but "speaking the truth in love"'.

Yet he fully realized the gravity of his situation as an archbishop whose disagreement with a papal encyclical had been widely publicized. As he told Danker, one of the senior priests of the archdiocese, 'I am ready to lose my mitre, but I will stick to what I have said and written' on *Humanae Vitae*.[2] Albert Nolan OP remembers

Hurley's 'honesty and openness to the truth no matter where it came from, no matter what it was, no matter how much it seemed to upset all previous ideas about faith or anything else like that.'[3] A French Oblate priest of the Archdiocese of Durban said, however: 'If he doesn't obey the Pope, I will not obey him.'[4]

As indicated in Chapter 11, birth control was not the only item removed from the council agenda by Pope Paul VI, much to the alarm of some council fathers like Hurley: the other was clerical celibacy.[5] That issue also came strongly to the fore in South Africa during 1968. At a meeting of priests involved in seminary education held at Mariannhill from 26–28 September, a resolution was passed unanimously by the seventy priest delegates, calling for priestly celibacy to be made optional. Three bishops— Hurley, Fitzgerald and Van Velsen—had also been present, but had not voted. After the conference, in a lengthy interview with the *Sunday Times*, Hurley declared his strong support for the resolution: it was his view that priests should be allowed to marry and continue serving as priests. The interview was described by the paper as 'probably the most frank public statement by a South African Catholic leader on this delicate subject'. Hurley explained that the views of the Mariannhill conference would be forwarded to the Bishops' Conference and if they were in support, also to Rome.

Hurley's opinion was that the change in the 1,000-year-old celibacy rule should be made in phases, the first of which could see local bishops being able to give permission for a priest to marry rather than the matter being referred to Rome, a system that caused agonizing delays. Ultimately Hurley thought that the decision to marry should be left to the priest concerned, with no permission required. Ever in favour of due process, he said that this proposal would take careful study and preparation: it should not simply be sprung on people. Hurley said he could see two reasons for making celibacy optional for priests. One was that the decision about celibacy had to be made early in a seminarian's life, before ordination. Later in life some priests discover that they are not suited to a celibate life, though they are keen to continue being priests and might be well suited to that vocation. His second reason was the great shortage of priests in Africa, Asia and Latin America.

When Hurley had an audience with Pope Paul VI, together with a group of bishops from Africa, on 11 October 1967, during a session of the Synod of Bishops, he indicated to the Pope that several issues were of concern to him. He was encouraged by Paul VI to write to him 'on any points I thought worth bringing to your attention'.

He had taken up the Pope's invitation by writing a letter on 16 October 1967, in which he dealt with the issue of birth control.[6] He shared that he had been particularly touched by the 'humility and sincerity' with which the Pope had extended his invitation, also by the reminder of the 'dialogue in search of truth in which I have had the honour to be associated with Your Holiness since the days of the Central Preparatory Commission'. He expressed sympathy about how, if the Pope were to reach a different decision on birth control to that of his predecessors, there would be some embarrassment about the Church changing its teaching.

Hurley pointed out, however, that on several occasions Vatican II had come to different conclusions from the Church's former teaching. And there were other instances where 'our premises in the nineteenth century were faulty and our conclusions wrong. We see that clearly now. There are other matters too, like the Temporal Power [the Pope's political control of certain territories in Italy, which had come to an end under Pope Pius IX in 1870] and the Syllabus of Errors [a list of writings officially banned by the Church], that we would like to forget'.

Hurley's letter of 16 October 1967—written about nine months before the publication of *Humanae Vitae*—was (as mentioned above) written during a Synod of Bishops. He went on to make the bold suggestion that Paul take the 200 bishops at that very synod into his confidence on the subject of birth control:

> I am absolutely convinced that the response will be magnificent. I am sure there will be a special presence and guidance of the Holy Spirit in such a gathering, and that the outcome will be for the good of the Church and of those whose consciences are deeply troubled and confused in the present situation. . . . Do not let the opportunity pass, Holy Father. If necessary, ask us to stay on for a few days after the date fixed for the closing of the synod. Invite us to discuss the question with you. Be present with us when we discuss it. Appeal to us to observe all the secrecy and discretion that you feel is desirable. Put the case to us yourself.

Hurley felt confident that the effect of such a collegial consultation with the Synod of Bishops would convince the Pope that in future this would be the best way to deal with all such major decisions. There is no record of the Pope's response to this letter, but it is clear that he did not accept Hurley's suggestion, because in July of the following year, he issued *Humanae Vitae*. This led Hurley to write a further letter to the Pope on 12 April 1969. In it, he set out his thoughts openly and honestly about the implications of what the council had said concerning collegiality. Now the situation was all the more difficult because of the strong reaction to *Humanae Vitae*. He began by referring to a communication he and the Pope had in October 1968 at a papal audience. Hurley got to the point of the letter directly in his third paragraph: 'A situation of great uneasiness has arisen in the Church over a number of issues, in regard to which there is a deep difference between what has been laid down authoritatively by Your Holiness and what appears to be the attitude of a significant and vocal section of the Church. Two obvious examples are the questions of contraception and compulsory celibacy'.

He went on to say that the whole Church suffered and grieved with the Pope on these two issues because he was clearly so affected by both. Hurley expressed his 'profound and sincere regret' if his own words had added to the Pope's personal suffering. He was probably referring to his own statement, 'I was torn in half', after the publication of *Humanae Vitae*, which would surely have been drawn to Paul VI's attention.

Hurley then began a section of his letter headed 'Reconsideration of the Primacy', stating that the post-Vatican II emphasis on collegiality and the responsible participation of all the faithful in the life of the Church required that the papal primacy be looked at anew. The fundamental theological question was whether provision should be made for the exercise of collegiality on a permanent and universal basis. In addition to collegiality, there was also the question of various forms of consultation: with theologians 'whose special calling is to investigate divine truth';

between bishops and their priests; with those who have special experience in some sphere of Christian living, such as married couples and people engaged in industry.

The question, said Hurley, was whether the Pope has a 'charism' for discovering truth without consultation or whether he should 'preside over the search for truth, ensuring that use is made of all the means that faith and prudence suggest'. With regard to both teaching and legislation, 'the basic question is whether or not the exercise of papal power is qualified by the right of others, and in a special way, [the right] of the episcopal college, to be heard . . . on what the truth of the Church is in regard to some specific problem: to be heard in regard to proposed legislation'.

Hurley claimed that Vatican II showed how much could be gained by theological investigation and what a wonderful resource the Church had in its theologians. What they had done for the council, they would be willing to do for the papal primacy. In a time of 'the great crisis of authority in the Church', they would surely be willing to help formulate a theology of authority for our time, and likewise for the primacy.

The final section of Hurley's letter was headed 'Immediate Practical Measures'. Obviously the theological exploration he was calling for would take time. Meanwhile urgent thought should be given to whether issues of major importance should be decided on the basis of the Pope's own authority 'without the effective collaboration of the episcopal college and reasonable consultation of theologians and other categories [of people] in the Church'.

He repeated his earlier statement that the council had called the whole Church to responsible participation in Christian life and apostolate and to the dialogue required for such participation. 'When people are summoned to dialogue and responsible participation, they find it hard to give of their best, if experience shows that authority over them is likely to refuse dialogue on the very matters that concern them most deeply', probably a painful reference to Paul VI's removing both birth control and obligatory celibacy from the agenda of the council. In a 2002 letter to Dr John Marshall of the Birth Control Commission, Hurley made his feelings known more bluntly: 'What a great pity the council was silenced on the issue. A good conciliar discussion could have produced a result that might have spared the Church much confusion and much embarrassment'.[7]

In the same letter Hurley recalled that in a speech of 19 March 1969, the Pope had asked whether the Church could actively put into practice the idea of ecclesial co-responsibility 'if it is troubled by internal protests'. Hurley suggested, with great respect, that the question was not whether internal unity was a pre-condition for collegial co-responsibility but rather whether collegial co-responsibility was a necessary pre-condition for achieving internal unity. He admitted that the Pope might see his [Hurley's] appeal for a reconsideration of the primacy as 'impertinent'. Nevertheless he took his advice a step further by reminding the Pope of a conversation they had in a private audience of 1966, when Paul VI had pointed to a picture of Christ and said: 'I have offered my life to him that I may find a solution' for the birth control controversy. On that occasion Hurley had replied that he thought Christ was asking for more than Paul's life, in fact asking from him 'the courage . . . to lead the Church into a new vision of the primacy and of the exercise of authority in the Church'. Such a change could bring the exercise of authority into greater conformity with the Gospel precept about the greatest behaving as the youngest, the leader as one who serves (Lk. 22:27).

Hurley recommended that a representative commission of theologians be appointed as soon as possible to study the theological implications of papal primacy, and that a document on collegial consultation be drafted for the extraordinary session of the synod to be held in October that year. He ended by expressing the hope that he had not written anything that might cause offence 'for my only purpose in writing is to make my humble contribution to the solution of pressing problems in the Church'. Given the culture of Rome, this was an extraordinary intervention, one that showed great confidence and courage.

A little over three months later, Hurley received a full, personal reply from the Pope, dated 25 July 1969 and written at the papal summer residence, Castel Gandolfo. This indicated that the Pope had probably given more careful and sustained attention to the letter than would generally be possible. The Pope accepted Hurley's 'sentiments of complete loyalty' to the papal office 'and of deep affection' for the Pope himself. He nevertheless chided Hurley for 'expressions which a less well-disposed reader might find somewhat wanting in respect for the Apostolic See', and gave as an example a passage where Hurley seemed 'to admit the possibility that [the Apostolic See] might intend to use its universal power in an unreasonable and unjust manner' or 'at least that it has done so in the past'. The Pope's letter was extremely polite and diplomatic, but at the same time cautious and defensive.

Paul VI welcomed the idea of a 'genuine and objective theological inquiry' into the relationship between the Pope and the episcopal college. But such an inquiry 'not only ought not [to] go against, but [also] cannot prescind from the definitions and teachings of the supreme *magisterium* of the Church, especially those found in the dogmatic documents of the last two Ecumenical Councils'. Moreover, he pointed out that there was another limitation on the role of theologians: 'on the points on which the Second Vatican Council, after long and deep discussion, did not consider it possible to reach unassailable conclusions that could be proposed for the assent of the faithful, the opinions and affirmations of theologians, however eminent and qualified, could not now suffice to resolve such questions'.

With regard to what Hurley had called a 'right' of the episcopal college and others 'to be heard', Paul VI replied: 'No one more than Ourself—like Our predecessors—has taken it to heart to inquire far and wide, and to give ear to the thoughts, proposals and suggestions of truly competent persons in the Church who are animated by a *sensus fidei* [understanding and grasp of the faith], in particular the Bishops, whenever We have had to exercise the mandate Christ gave Us to teach the truth in the service of, and with binding force upon, the whole Church'.

But Paul VI stressed that this still required that the Pope form 'his own personal meditated judgment'.

Referring to what Hurley had described as a 'situation of great uneasiness' caused by *Humanae Vitae* and his assessment that 'there is a deep difference between what has been laid down authoritatively' by the Pope 'and what appears to be the attitude of a significant and vocal section of the Church', Paul VI says that would also have been the case if he had announced an entirely different decision. Then he gave an account of how he reached his decision about the birth control issue:

> We invited Our brothers in the episcopate freely to make known to Us their views, as many of them did. We conscientiously meditated upon the opinions of theologians and experts, listened to the voice of the people of God, and personally reflected and invoked the light of the Holy Spirit in prayer. And then, humbly and with trepidation, yet conscious that We were acting in accordance with the mission given to us by Christ, We took upon Ourself the responsibility, which pertains to Our supreme ministry, of declaring on the point at issue, what is the law of God.

He strongly rejected as a distortion of history the implication that the Pope might 'lay down laws for the community' without 'a good knowledge of the needs and conditions of the community'. Likewise, in referring to his encyclical letter about celibacy, *Sacerdotalis Coelibatus*, published in 1967, in which he strongly reaffirmed the tradition that priesthood and celibacy should continue to be linked, he said, 'This cannot be called, without injustice, an act of solitary primacy'. To make such a claim would be to forget that the encyclical confirmed the explicit pronouncement of the Second Vatican Council in the decree *On the Ministry and Life of Priests*, which upholds the law of celibacy. However, the Pope did not refer to the fact that as a result of his own intervention celibacy was not discussed in the council in open session.

In reply to Hurley's urging the Pope to change the way of exercising papal authority so as to bring it more into conformity with the Gospel precept: 'The greatest among you must behave as if he were the youngest, the leader as if he were the one who serves' (Lk. 22:27), Paul replied that he was constantly seeking to live according to that precept, but then strongly endorsed the papal authority first given to Peter:

> We should seriously belie this mission of humble service were We to forget that Christ Himself has formed out of Our weakness the rock upon which the Church is founded. The same would be true were We to lose confidence in the efficacy of His continual prayer for Us to the Father, that Our faith fail not, that it enable Us to confirm that of Our brothers: or were We to withdraw from the mission of love entrusted to Us by the Lord . . . or were We to fail to exercise the power of the keys, though it be a burden We often feel, but cannot renounce without betraying Our office. We have to exercise this power with conscientious prudence, and having recourse to the helpful advice and collaboration of Our brothers, successors of the Apostles, but we can never renounce the responsibility which is and will remain Ours personally, by divine disposition.

In a reply to Pope Paul VI's letter, dated 18 September 1969, Hurley expressed his gratitude for 'such a kind and paternal letter' and said that he was touched and deeply moved that the Pope 'went to such trouble to give a thorough and painstaking reply'. Yet he did not abandon his concern about what he called 'the great problem, as many of us see it', how the papal office can be exercised 'less in isolation and more in the context of corporate leadership of the whole hierarchy under the primacy of Peter'. He also urged the Pope to participate as fully as possible in the forthcoming synod, which would have a bearing on the issues of primacy and collegiality.

I was not able to find any reply to Hurley's letter of 18 September 1969, but in a further letter of 6 November 1970 he referred to the joy and gratitude with which the news had been received that the Synod of Bishops in 1971 would focus on the ministerial priesthood. As Hurley noted, however, he thought it inevitable that the synod would 'give a good deal of attention' to priestly celibacy as well, which he realized would be painful for the Pope. He also expected that there would be much discussion on how 'the ranks of full-time priests can be supplemented by the ordination of married men involved in secular vocations'. He said that to help the Pope face these difficult discussions, the Church 'had reached a stage of very open and courageous dialogue', which 'owes much to the lead given by Your Holiness in your first encyclical, *Ecclesiam Suam*. We can only rejoice that loyal members of the Church experience this freedom to speak their minds and thus make themselves the vehicle of the Spirit of Truth'.

With that, this fascinating correspondence on key issues for the post-conciliar Church came to an end. There was, however, a sequel when Hurley was invited by Father Walter Burghardt SJ to write for the American Jesuit journal *Theological Studies*. His article was to appear in the March 1974 special issue on the UN World Population Year. Hurley wrote about 'Population Control and the Catholic Conscience: Responsibility of the Magisterium'. He forwarded his contribution to Burghardt and, probably as a courtesy, also to Pope Paul VI because it continued the exchange of ideas they had been having for some years in person and by correspondence. The article challenged the *magisterium* to approach the population issue in all its dimensions and with broad vision; otherwise it would have no right to teach.

Hurley began the article by saying that family planning and population control were rapidly becoming commonplaces of world society. This was happening without any systematic opposition other than from the Catholic Church, and even that was not to the principle but to most of the methods. His conclusion was that for the vast majority of the world's population, not even cultural and religious attitudes offered any resistance to technological methods thought necessary for what was fast becoming a worldwide population policy.

This meant that the Church would have to be 'vitally and vigorously' concerned about the world population programme, because it would affect every married couple as well as most communities and governments. The population problem and related issues, such as unequal distribution of the world's resources, had to be a major area of concern for the Church. It was already accepted in principle that the Church should be involved in solving such global problems, but the population problem had not yet received the attention it deserved because of Catholic teaching on family morality.

Thus 1974, the year of a special UN Conference on Population, seemed to provide the opportunity to grasp the nettle. The Church's *magisterium* had not been effective in communicating on such issues. According to Hurley, it seemed to expect that simply announcing principles would be enough to ensure that they would be taken up enthusiastically. The Church had been good at saying what needed to be done but not how it ought to be done. All over the world people would be promoting family planning and population control. Central to these would be contraception and abortion, which were directly in conflict with official Catholic morality.

It would not be enough for the Church to keep saying that these were illicit and thereafter wash its hands of the whole population issue. For example, take the case of South Africa, said Hurley, where because of white exploitation, urbanization and migrant labour, 60 per cent of African children were illegitimate. In these circumstances, did the Church have the right to simply proclaim its teachings on marriage ... if at the same time it did not move heaven and earth to have the whole social situation changed? No, the Church could be guilty of a grave injustice if it allowed a situation in which people would be under such social pressures with regard to family planning and population control that only the heroic would be able to cope.

The Church, and especially the bishops and the Pope, would have to prepare for a situation of this kind, said Hurley. The Church should mobilize all available resources—social scientists, theologians, educators and communicators—who could assemble information, draw practical conclusions and formulate a pastoral plan. This would require great courage on the part of the Pope because some traditional Catholic attitudes could be shattered in the process. One of the first would be the traditional Catholic concept of absolute moral values.

Moral theologians were, according to Hurley, increasingly accepting that there could be conflicts of moral values, leaving a justifiable choice to the person caught between two values. As a result of the concentrated mobilization of resources he had recommended, Hurley saw the possibility of the Church coming to terms with forms of contraception not involving abortion. He could not imagine the Church ever approving of abortion, but it could develop such a convincing case against abortion 'that we could win the world to our way of thinking'. Most important of all would be to encourage international sharing of resources between rich and poor countries in a Christian spirit: solving the population problem would depend on improving the economic plight of vast third-world populations.

Hurley ended the article with a stern warning for the Church not to sidestep the difficult moral questions if it wanted the *magisterium* to be respected:

> If the *magisterium* does not see to it that this total ecclesial effort is mobilized and deployed, it will not have the right to teach; for, invoking our old ally, natural law, no authority has the right to command the impossible, and it will be impossible for pastors and people to cope with the population issue without very full and effective leadership from the *magisterium*. We must avoid at all costs incurring the reproach of Jesus: 'You load on men burdens that are unendurable, burdens that you yourselves do not move a finger to lift' (Luke 11:46).

In March 1974 Burghardt received a telex from Father Vincent O'Keefe SJ, one of the assistants to the Jesuit Superior General in Rome. It indicated that the Papal

Secretary of State had expressed his desire that Hurley's article not be published and that all the other articles in the special 'population issue' of *Theological Studies* be carefully examined for their fidelity to Church teaching.[8] With what he called 'a sigh of relief', Burghardt was able to inform O'Keefe that *Theological Issues* had come out the previous day. He also stressed how much care had gone into the preparation of that issue, especially the choice of authors. Burghardt had selected people who were not only competent in theology but also likely to write pastoral and practical articles. From what he had heard about Hurley, and from articles of his that he had read, Burghardt thought he was 'a first-rate author to write on population and *magisterium*'.

Burghardt never heard any more from Rome about the Hurley article or the population issue of *Theological Studies*, and happily continued in his position as editor for the next 16 years. There is no way of knowing whether Hurley's article caused much of a stir: it might have if it had been generally known that the Papal Secretary of State had wanted it to be censored. We will return to the article in Chapter 14 because it had consequences for Hurley in relation to his attending the Synod of Bishops.

14

Implementing Vatican II

Describing the conclusion of the Second Vatican Council on 8 December 1965, we have noted that Hurley wrote about the great work that lay ahead for the bishops in 'bringing the council to life in the communities they had been ordained to serve'.[1] This was a task he had begun in the earliest days of the council, giving talks after each session, sending out a pastoral letter about what was achieved in each; and writing lively and witty reports for the *Southern Cross*. It seems likely that he was also the principal author of the joint pastoral letter published by the bishops after the council in July 1966: 'His fingerprints are all over the document', as Mervyn Abrahams, formerly of St Joseph's Theological Institute, Cedara, puts it.

Hurley regarded the informal talks that theologians gave the bishops as one of the most important aspects of the council. In his keenness to make such opportunities available in South Africa, he promoted the idea of holding theological winter schools as part of the Pastoral Institute, a new initiative chaired by Hurley that the bishops had taken to implement the council. Other projects of the Institute were *Fons Vitae*, an adult education institution for nuns, initially run by Franciscans and later by Jesuits under Father John Gillick, and *Khanyisa*, a national catechetical institute open to nuns and lay people involved in catechetical work and run by Father Paul Nadal. Hurley was key to all these initiatives

The winter schools, intended primarily for priests and begun in 1968 with Father Noel Coughlan OMI as national director, brought many prominent theologians to South Africa to run week-long lecture and workshop sessions in each of the main centres, with public forums in the evenings. Among the well-known speakers who visited South Africa as part of this programme were Barnabas Ahern, Christopher Butler, Charles Curran, Godfrey Diekmann, Piet Fransen, Bernard Häring, Adrian Hastings, Elizabeth Johnson, Enda McDonagh, Roland Murphy, Ladislas Örsy and Carroll Stuhlmueller. Others like Edward Schillebeeckx responded warmly to Hurley's personal invitation but could not fit the winter school into their busy schedules: 'How much I would have loved to come to South Africa next year, not only to give lectures, but also to continue our "Roman talks" during the period of the council', he wrote.

Elizabeth Johnson, a feminist theologian who was at the time involved in a battle to secure tenure at the Catholic University of America in Washington, DC, had particular reason to be grateful for her participation in the South African winter schools of 1987. During that visit, she had explained to Hurley that a number of questions had arisen as a result of some of her writings that had been submitted to Rome. Hurley wrote a glowing testimonial explaining how the whole Catholic Church in South Africa was in her debt because of her lectures to the winter schools. Cardinal Joseph Bernardin of Chicago, who presided over the meeting of six US cardinals to reach a decision about her tenure, waved Hurley's letter triumphantly and quoted from it when she came in to be questioned by this formidable panel. The result of Hurley's endorsement was that the cardinals voted to give her tenure despite Rome's hesitations. Hurley would later have another reason for gratitude to Johnson. Reading *She Who Is*, her book on feminist theology, he regarded as a turning point in his thinking, according to Father Hyacinth Ennis OFM.[2]

Hurley himself also took part in explaining the Council's theology, especially to women religious and to seminarians. Sister Marie-Henry Keane remembers how 'as a young Dominican sister I, among thousands of others, was blessed to sit at the feet of Denis Eugene Hurley as he proclaimed the good news of the council's teaching.[3] What I heard was enough to whet my appetite for more'. Sister Michael Mdluli OP of Montebello said that the decrees of Vatican II formed 'a thick book and it was difficult for us to read, but we knew he [Hurley] would make it a little bit easy for us when we met. It was very helpful'.[4] Bishop Barry Wood OMI, who was in the Oblate scholasticate during the council, said, 'He really set us all afire with the whole spirit of Vatican II'.[5]

In 1985, twenty years after the council, Pope John Paul II called a special session of the Synod of Bishops to assess the extent to which the Council's vision and teaching had been implemented by the Church globally and locally. One of the striking features of those years was that many of the tensions that dominated the council had resurfaced and how it should be interpreted had become a subject of debate. There was a pervasive sense in the Roman Curia that since the council the Church had deteriorated.

Hurley's view was quite different: in his report on his diocese and on the South African Church over those years, he highlighted major positive developments: a more active participation by lay people in the Church's liturgy, the publication of new catechetical books and the adoption of religious education methods in keeping with the theology of the council, the establishment of diocesan structures and the promotion of lay ministries that reflected the idea of the Church as a community and encouraged lay people to share responsibility with bishops and priests, a more direct and intense involvement in social justice.

The South African bishops had been concerned about lay participation in liturgy even before the council, several of them suggesting that the council should discuss having the liturgy in the vernacular. Within two months of the Constitution on the Sacred Liturgy being promulgated in 1963, the SACBC met in Pretoria to work out how to implement the document. Hurley had invited the noted English liturgist Father Clifford Howell SJ to help prepare the South African church for the changes. Two years after the council, the vernacular Mass was in widespread use in South Africa.

Hurley was keen that there should be as much participation as possible by way of vernacular singing. He realized, however, that there was little suitable Catholic Church music available in English. He set to work with the help of a university lecturer in music, Moira Birks, to write new hymns and to compose more scriptural and theologically sound lyrics to accompany popular Catholic hymn tunes. Hurley and Birks went through hymn books of other churches, selecting and adapting hymns suitable for Catholic liturgy; they put these, new and old, into the *People's Hymn Book* published by the Archdiocese of Durban in 1965. Birks composed music for major feasts such as Easter and Christmas. A number of the hymns, for which the lyrics were composed by Hurley, are now to be found in the *Celebration Hymnal*, extensively used in English-speaking countries. Among the best new lyrics for old tunes were 'As we remember, Lord, the word, / Which Peter your apostle heard' to replace the peculiar Victorian hymn 'Full in the panting heart of Rome'. Another popular hymn that Hurley amended was 'I'll sing a hymn to Mary' for which he composed a new refrain which puts the emphasis on Jesus rather than on Mary. Among the most popular hymns written by Hurley are 'God our Maker, mighty Father' to the tune of Schiller's 'Ode to Joy' from Beethoven's Ninth Symphony; and 'Come with wonder and delight' to the tune of the Zulu hymn *Wozanini nonke*. When asked how she thought Hurley had found the time to compose words for about forty hymns and adapt many others, Birks replied, 'Perhaps he regarded it as a hobby'.[6]

Hurley was known to be a stickler for liturgical correctness and thorough preparation. To ensure that congregations could take part wholeheartedly in liturgical celebrations, he frequently insisted that new musical items be rehearsed before ceremonies began. He wanted the liturgy to be carried out to the letter, which irritated some who favoured more creative and spontaneous worship.

Hurley, as we have seen in Chapter 10, had begun to be actively involved in catechetical renewal before Vatican II, in particular from 1960, when he was elected chair of the bishops' Department of Catechetics and Education. During and after the council he gave much impetus to training in the new catechetics, as well as to new syllabuses and textbooks informed by the council's theological and scriptural emphasis.

The third issue highlighted in Hurley's response to the questionnaire for the 1985 Synod of Bishops was the establishment of diocesan and parish structures and the promotion of lay ministries reflecting the conciliar spirit of co-responsibility. Traditionally, lay people had been largely seen as those who 'pray, pay and obey'. Even their involvement in Catholic Action was as helpers to the bishops and priests, not based on their own call received at baptism. The Vatican II Constitution on the Church refers to the laity as sharing in the priestly, prophetic and kingly functions of Christ. They have responsibility, together with bishops and priests, for the mission of the whole Christian people to Church and world.

Hurley was keen that this vision be encouraged by new diocesan structures to promote lay leadership and involvement in the Archdiocese of Durban. After considerable consultation with clergy and laity, the first structures set up were parish councils.[7] Hurley's intellectual and linguistic skills were a great asset: on long plane journeys he spent many hours in drafting constitutions—perhaps another of his hobbies. The constitution he drafted for parish councils set out basic rules for their establishment and smooth running and provided a flexible structure for experimental purposes. Parishes were encouraged to submit amendments, so that the draft could be revised in the light of experience. The purpose of the new councils was to formulate and make known lay opinion about all aspects of parish life, as well as to promote and coordinate, consult and collaborate on all matters in which clergy, religious and laity could assist each other. Parish councils were expected to work for improved race relations and to cooperate with other local churches in common ecumenical projects. Parishioners were encouraged to contribute to community and civic affairs.

A system of separate councils was provided for African and non-African parishioners living in the same parish, apparently because of language and educational differences; the Zulu speakers in such parishes were mainly domestic workers. Each council was to elect two of its members to liaise with the council of the other language group, and there was to be at least one joint meeting of the two councils each year. This seemed a less than satisfactory arrangement especially in the context of apartheid.

A diocesan pastoral council was established to share responsibility for, and help shape, the pastoral strategy of the diocese. It would have lay and clergy representatives who would meet quarterly with the archbishop.

The most dramatic innovation was the establishment of a diocesan synod to discuss diocesan policy; it would meet biennially, bringing together all clergy with lay representatives of every parish and representatives of religious sisters and brothers.[8] To publicize and implement synod resolutions, diocesan commissions were established for catechetics and education, ecumenism, justice and peace, the lay apostolate and liturgy.

Durban's first synod was held from 16–17 December 1968, long before any other diocese in South Africa took such an initiative. In fact, 40 years later, other South African Catholic dioceses are only now starting to hold synods. Other Christian denominations have long been accustomed to such events which enjoy considerable decision-making power.

At the 1968 synod of the Durban Archdiocese, 100 priests, 280 lay men and women and religious sisters and brothers took part. More than 80 of the delegates were African; the proceedings were conducted in both English and Zulu, with simultaneous translation. Observers from other churches were also present. Opening the synod, Hurley said that in the past the word 'Church' meant only those who had authority in the Church. Now it meant all members of the Church, the whole community—a change in large part due to the Second Vatican Council.

Professor Otty Nxumalo, who was regularly asked to translate for the early synods, said: 'The synod gave an opportunity for many people to express themselves responsibly and to come up with solutions'. Another perspective was that of Sister Michael Mdluli of Montebello, also a translator, who recalled that synod delegates said: 'Now we can feel we are Church . . . Somehow people came out with something concrete to work on'. A third view was that of Professor Eddie Higgins, a key speaker at the first synod: ' [The Archbishop] managed to pull together so many . . . in that archdiocese, you know, the rural missionaries, the urban clergy, the religious, the laity, Indians, whites, Zulus, the whole tutti. . . . I think it was a great morale booster for many of the laity'.

The synod elected members for the diocesan pastoral council and established the five commissions referred to earlier. According to canon law, a diocesan synod is consultative, not legislative like those of other denominations. Its resolutions can only be enforced if the bishop approves them. After each biennial synod, Hurley made a point of promulgating, without exception, the synodal resolutions.

Reflecting on Hurley's promotion of the Council's vision in his own diocese, Auxiliary Bishop Jabulani Nxumalo (now Archbishop of Bloemfontein) said that over the years some priests asked what Hurley knew about pastoral work, because he had never been a parish priest. The irony, said Nxumalo, was that Hurley was a great pastoral innovator despite this lack of experience. His promotion of new parish and diocesan structures gave lay people a taste of involvement: 'The pastoral fervour that exists in the Archdiocese of Durban was triggered during his time . . . [As a result] it is a diocese that expects progress all the time. He excelled in leading the diocese in the very thing he is accused of not having had'.

Hurley went further: parish and diocese should not be inward-looking Catholic enclaves, he believed, but focus on creating a more just society. Flowing from this belief was a particular commitment to the struggle against apartheid for which Vatican II gave him an inspiring theological foundation. It must also have heartened him to find that many council fathers shared his concern about injustice. The council challenged him to take action for justice in a more concrete and direct way, less cerebral and academic. He seems especially to have taken to heart the opening words of the constitution *The Church in the Modern World*: 'The joys and hopes, the griefs and anxieties of the people of this age, especially those who are poor or in any way afflicted, these too are the joys and hopes, the griefs and anxieties of the followers of Christ. Indeed, nothing genuinely human fails to raise an echo in their hearts'.

Hurley had his own griefs at this time. His father died in April 1967, and his mother just ten weeks later, in July. His sister Eileen was struck by meningitis in the week that their mother died. She came out of a lengthy coma paralysed from the waist down and was never again able to walk, though she lived until 2003. Her disability created an even greater bond between these two siblings, who had been close from their earliest childhood.

LIMEHILL – A CASE STUDY OF ACTIVISM

By the late 1960s, the National Party government of South Africa was proceeding with all deliberate speed to implement its grand vision of consolidating the homelands as supposedly independent nation states, in keeping with the policy of separate development. This meant forced removals of Africans to consolidate areas known as 'reserves' or 'homelands'—only 13 per cent of the land for 70.2 per cent of the population, according to the 1970 census. Coloureds and Indians were also moved to group areas set aside for them. By 1984 over three million people had been forcibly removed without any consultation, causing human suffering on a colossal scale. A further two million were due to be moved. The issue came to Hurley's attention in 1968, particularly through Father Cosmas Desmond OFM, who was at the time stationed at Maria Ratschitz Mission in northern KwaZulu-Natal. One of the outstations of the mission was Meran, from which people were to be moved to Limehill.[9]

As a case study of removals, the story of Limehill is instructive, not because it was the first or worst removal, but because it was one of the best documented. Desmond passed on information about the threatened removal to Hurley and other Church leaders. As a result, a Committee of Church Representatives on Bantu Resettlement was established, with Hurley as chair. It included the Anglican Bishop of Natal, Vernon Inman, and leaders of the Congregational, Evangelical Lutheran and Methodist Churches. The Black Sash, Christian Institute, Institute of Race Relations and Natal Council of Churches were also represented. Desmond liaised between this structure and the people, regularly visiting Limehill so that he was up to date on developments.

At the beginning of November 1967, Father Paschal Rowland OFM (later Bishop of Dundee), who was parish priest of Maria Ratschitz Mission, was notified that the people on his mission and two other 'black spots' known as Meran and Wasbank, approximately 12,800 people in all, were to be moved on 29 January 1968. 'Black spots' were African settlements, once secured by title deeds, tribal or mission tenure, which were to be moved from what was described as 'the white area of South Africa'. The Maria Ratschitz removal had been rumoured for some time but could take place only after formal notice had been given. As it turned out, it was the people from Meran who were moved on 29 January, not those from Maria Ratschitz: their turn came later.

The Committee of Church Representatives tried to prevent the removal or at least have it postponed until basic facilities had been provided. While they continued their negotiations, including a lengthy memorandum to the Minister of Bantu Affairs and Development setting out the problems they foresaw, they carefully avoided media publicity until it became clear that their efforts to persuade the minister were fruitless. Though they received a detailed reply, the minister refused to meet them.

On 17 January 1968, the committee made a last desperate attempt to have the removal postponed; Hurley sent a telegram to Minister M. C. Botha: 'Perturbed removals imminent while provision for shelter and welfare of people completely uncertain. Postponement of removal imperative pending your investigation. Impossible [to] suppress publicity much longer'. When only an acknowledgment of this telegram had been received by 27 January, the media were notified about the impending removal, and Hurley sent another, more strongly-worded telegram to the minister: 'Committee of Church representatives on Bantu Resettlement deeply concerned about people to be moved Monday. Appears heartless to lodge families with little children under tents. Summer storms likely, health endangered, furniture unprotected, supplies and basic amenities precarious. Before God, how can you bear the responsibility?'

Limehill was a distinctly unattractive area, the only development being a few dirt roads and the foundations for a school, which would clearly not be ready when the people arrived. Classes had to be conducted in tents, and the people had to provide their own accommodation while building their new houses.

Four days after the telegram to the Minister, Hurley was rebuked by Minister M. C. Botha. '[It] never occurred to him that he would have to warn you not to call in [sic] the name of God so easily, something which was exploited for publicity purposes'. The department had lots of experience with resettlements over many years and would see that this one would be performed 'in a fair and satisfactory manner'.

On the day the removals started, 29 January 1968, Desmond and nine other local priests were present at 7:30 a.m., but since nothing was happening, they returned later, after lorries had arrived with officials of the Bantu Affairs Department to transport the people. Members of the security police stood on the opposite side of the road and photographed the clergy. Desmond and his colleagues deliberately did not assist the people to strip their homes so as not to cooperate with their forced removal. Later—when Hurley and his party, including members of the Black Sash, arrived after a three-hour drive from Durban—they all went on to Limehill, about 32 kilometres away. There they found the first arrivals sitting in the veld, 'surrounded by their belongings, looking . . . bewildered and utterly lost'. Hurley was among those who helped them erect tents.

Experiencing the conditions in this way motivated the visitors to appeal to the churches for material help: a Resettlement Aid Fund was established under Church auspices; a soup kitchen was organized at Limehill; fortified biscuits and firewood were provided; and wheelbarrows, picks and shovels were loaned to help in building houses. While the South African Broadcasting Corporation (SABC) presented a rosy picture of the move to Limehill and the preparations made there, Hurley and the clergy had seen for themselves the total lack of infrastructure. For months the people had to live, and their children go to school, in tents. No provision had been made for buying food; there was no clinic and no sanitary arrangements.

Speaking in the House of Assembly in early February, M. C. Botha made crude remarks about the clergy's presence at Limehill, describing them as *booswigte*, villains, who 'in their long black and white dresses . . . had rummaged around among the maidservants'. Much media attention, however, continued to be devoted to the plight of the Limehill people, especially when cases of typhoid and gastro-enteritis were reported. A tremendous quarrel erupted with government officials over the number of deaths, especially of young children. Desmond and Hurley visited the five cemeteries in the Limehill complex, and Desmond took photos of the pathetic headstones. Hurley gave a full list of names and ages to the press. It was difficult to quarrel with such evidence, but it made him even more of an enemy in the eyes of the government.

The Minister of Health, Dr Carel de Wet, turned down a request for an inquiry into the health situation at Limehill, calling those who had shown concern about the Limehill situation 'enemies of South Africa . . . who wished to put the country in a bad light'. Hurley picked holes in de Wet's statement that there had only been 19 deaths between September and December and that such a number was normal for a community of 6,000, whereas Hurley and Desmond had evidence of 73 deaths in the first five months after the move to Limehill.

As Desmond wrote: 'There can be no doubt about the completely inadequate preparation at Limehill and the suffering this caused thousands of people. These people were subjected to all this because it had been decreed that the land on which they had lived for generations was for whites only'. Desmond reported that this was happening to many thousands of people, all over South Africa, in places mostly far removed from media attention and therefore probably under much worse conditions than at Limehill.

Hurley's involvement in Limehill was new and different from his involvements in the past. He worked closely with leaders of other churches and social agencies in an ecumenical effort to delay or ameliorate the removals. With accurate information supplied by Desmond, he adopted an activist role, allowing himself to be influenced by direct contact with the appalling conditions at Limehill. His indignation at the suffering caused by apartheid policy was not to be watered down by diplomatic niceties. Yet at that time he did not feel able to defy a pernicious law: 'We cannot oppose the removal itself, since it is provided for by law. What we are campaigning for is that the law be carried out with more consideration for the people it affects'.

Over the next few years after the Limehill removal, Desmond involved himself ever more deeply in the issue of forced removals, including as researcher for the ecumenical Christian Institute, carefully documenting removals in many parts of South Africa. This information was compiled in his book *The Discarded People*, widely read in South Africa and overseas. By June 1971 the South African government had had enough of Desmond's embarrassing research and activism. They imposed a five-year house arrest and banning order to silence him. He was not allowed to be away from his home between 6:00 p.m. and 6:00 a.m. on any weekday, or at any time over weekends and public holidays, nor to have any visitors except his parents (who lived in London). Hurley, however, broke the rule and visited him.

The banning order prevented Desmond from speaking in public or having any of his writings published or quoted. He could not attend any meeting or visit any educational institution. Most significantly, he was not allowed to preach or conduct services. He decided, however, to continue preaching and celebrating Mass in public and got away with it. Speaking at a protest meeting in Durban against these restrictions, Hurley said that Desmond was being persecuted because he tried to share with the world 'the truth about the resettlements and removals that are going on in this country. I say to Cos Desmond: Thank you for being a representative of the Church, thank you for being a representative of the Christian priesthood, and thank you for all that you have done for those who believe in conscience'.

A few university students in Pietermaritzburg were outraged that a so-called Christian government could ban a priest from preaching and conducting services without widespread protest from the Church. Jeremy Hurley, a nephew of Archbishop Hurley, decided to dramatize Cos Desmond's situation.

On Sunday, 15 August 1971, Jeremy and two other Catholic students 'chained' themselves to the altar rails in St Mary's and said they would remain there until the priest allowed them to speak about Desmond's banning, or until the priest himself spoke about the issue. Eventually the priest agreed to let the students address the congregation. Jeremy told them that he and his two colleagues were protesting about the poverty of the African people and against Desmond's banning. That brought the protest to an end, but it led to an uproar in the parish. Parishioners urged the priests to complain to Hurley and to insist that something be done about the protest. Hurley's solution was to have a public meeting in the church hall, where the protestors could explain their point of view, followed by the offended parishioners. Finally, Hurley himself would give some sort of judgment.

Hurley listened carefully to how the students explained what they had done, and then to the parishioners who had been upset by the 'invasion' of their church and Sunday Mass. Finally he said that, all things considered, especially in the light of the situation in the country, he felt that the protest was justified and in no way disrespectful to the Church. Some years later Jeremy's comment on his uncle's verdict was, 'We were just blown away that he supported us . . . We really didn't expect it'.

IMBISA

One of the emphases of Vatican II that Hurley was keenest to promote and implement was collegiality: the bishops working with the Pope in leading the Church. So far we have only considered collegiality in relation to the Second Vatican Council itself and, to a lesser extent, to the local conference of bishops known as the SACBC. Another important body came into existence some years after the council, to promote collegiality among the bishops' conferences of the southern African region. Known as IMBISA, the Inter-Territorial Meeting of Bishops in Southern Africa, it promotes liaison and pastoral cooperation between the bishops' conferences of Angola and São Tomé e Príncipe (Portuguese-speaking islands off the coast of Africa), Lesotho, Mozambique, Namibia, South Africa (linked with Botswana and Swaziland) and Zimbabwe.

The idea of IMBISA was first proposed during the 1974 Synod of Bishops, when Bishop Donal Lamont of Rhodesia (now Zimbabwe) twice invited all the synod delegates from southern Africa for informal discussions on the situation in their region. Hurley and Fitzgerald were the two SACBC representatives.[10] Fitzgerald, at that time SACBC president, was mandated to explore the possibility of a meeting of representatives from all eight countries. If the response was positive, he was asked to convene a meeting.

The response was positive, and the first meeting took place in April 1975. The three representatives of the SACBC were Fitzgerald, Archbishop Peter Butelezi and Hurley, who gave a presentation on the situation in South Africa. On several later occasions he was co-opted on to the IMBISA committee, and, when each country gave an update on its own situation, he was regularly asked to report on South Africa.

According to Father Ted Rogers, an English Jesuit who was Director of IMBISA, Hurley was valued for his chairing and reporting skills as well as his outstanding writing ability. Only once, in 1988, has IMBISA published a joint pastoral letter, and Hurley played a leading part in its compilation and publication. This was one of the great success stories of IMBISA, but it took a long time to reach an agreement on the text because of language, theological and political differences between the English-speaking and Portuguese-speaking bishops.[11]

It may have been the visit to Zimbabwe by Pope John Paul II in 1988 that galvanized IMBISA into finalizing the letter so that it could be presented at the final session of IMBISA's second general assembly, in the presence of the Pope. Hurley was a member of the 'redaction committee'. In a letter to Ian Linden of CIIR (Catholic Institute for International Relations), he spoke about lengthy consultations he had with the Mozambicans and Angolans to reach agreement on the pastoral letter.[12]

A media release said that IMBISA's second general assembly ended 'with a strong call for justice and peace'. This was the joint pastoral to which they had eventually agreed. It was to be read in every Catholic church in the region. 'Unanimously we have resolved to work more actively to bring about justice and peace in southern Africa', declared the assembly participants, including 3 cardinals, 13 archbishops and 57 bishops who affirmed that 'the way the Church transforms society is part of her message'.

Speaking about the conflicts that existed between the Portuguese- and English-speaking members of IMBISA, Linden said that the former tended to be more conservative than even the most conservative of English-speaking bishops from the region. Because of their difficult experiences with the post-independence Marxist government of Angola, they were suspicious of the bishops of South Africa, whom they thought naive in their enthusiasm for Mandela and the ANC-led government of South Africa.

Linden believed that the political contexts of Angola and South Africa were too different for any serious progress to be made by IMBISA. As he saw it, the situation was remarkably like the East European bishops trying to understand their Latin American colleagues. Nevertheless, he was impressed by Hurley's calm way of dealing with the conflicts. Hurley, he said, appeared to be the person to whom everyone looked to hold IMBISA together. He carefully avoided taking up a partisan, South African position and, according to Linden, deserved credit for any success that IMBISA had in its collegial efforts.

Cathy Corcoran, a former CAFOD desk officer for South Africa, said that Hurley had initially tried 'extremely hard' to convince the Mozambican and

Angolan bishops about the importance of justice issues and working on the side of the people, especially the poor. His conclusion was, 'It just doesn't work; we don't speak the same language'. On one occasion he used a poster quoting Archbishop Helder Camara of Brazil: 'If I give the poor food, people call me a saint. If I ask why the people are poor, they call me a communist'. It was only as he held up the poster, looked at the word 'communist' and then at the Angolans and Mozambicans, that Hurley realized this was the worst possible way to convince them. What they were quite sure about was that their governments were communist and that they had to be opposed.

The Angolans and Mozambicans would often say, according to Dr Gunter Thie of the German bishops' agency *Misereor*, that they knew what communism was: they were experiencing it but the South African bishops did not know communism, so they did not know to whom they were giving their allegiance. The Angolan and Mozambican bishops were convinced that the future government of South Africa would be Marxist, which was not what happened. In reply the South Africans would say, 'And you don't know what the situation is like in South Africa'.

Michael Hippler, head of *Misereor*'s Africa desk, was struck by how difficult it was for the two groups to work together. The Portuguese colonial way of organizing the Church was totally different from the South African way: it was closed and hier-archically oriented and, surprisingly, more colour conscious. The two groups were quite separate and even addressed each other in a formal official way.

Hurley suggested to the IMBISA executive that they should stop arguing in the plenary assemblies, when large numbers of bishops were present, because this did not help. Instead, they should visit each other's countries in small groups and share their lives, experiences and insights. He set the example by being one of the first to go in a group to Angola. On his return he said he could understand why the Angolan bish-ops were so against Marxism: what he saw in Angola 'really was disastrous'.

He also suggested that two English-speaking bishops should learn Portuguese and vice versa, so that there could be more direct communication. A third Hurley ini-tiative to break the impasse was to broker an arrangement between the two bishops' conferences for seminarians from Angola to study at a South African seminary. This took years to organize, but eventually the first Angolans came to the Cape Town diocesan seminary in the late 1990s.

As a result of Hurley's suggestions for promoting greater mutual understanding, the Angolan bishops, according to Hippler, began to feel more at ease about attend-ing IMBISA meetings: they did not 'think they were going to meet enemies any more'. They appreciated the efforts Hurley made to understand them and to help the other South African bishops do so.

In his keenness to promote collegiality, Hurley was not only concerned that there should be a better understanding between the Portuguese-speaking and English-speaking bishops of southern Africa, but also that the bishops of Africa would be understood and respected by the Church internationally. This is nicely illustrated by an incident at a 1996 meeting in Harare, the capital of Zimbabwe, organized by the Pontifical Commission for Justice and Peace and attended by a delegation of southern African bishops from IMBISA and East African bishops from AMECEA (Association of Member Episcopal Conferences in Eastern Africa).[13] Present from the Pontifical Commission were its president, Cardinal Roger Etchagaray, and general secretary, Bishop Diarmuid Martin. The meeting was a follow-up to the African Synod that had brought bishops from all over Africa to meet with Pope John Paul II in Rome in 1994. They had strongly recommended that Catholic social teaching be used to advance the cause of justice and peace in Africa. The time had come to work out practical ways of implementing that proposal.

During the Harare gathering, word started going round that there was a special committee, chosen by the Vatican Justice and Peace Commission, preparing a set of resolutions from the meeting, though the group reports had not yet been given. Some AMECEA delegates, led by Father Pete Henriot SJ, were meanwhile working on their own set of resolutions, based on what was coming out of the group discussions. The last day of the meeting arrived, and the resolutions were to be presented in a plenary session to be attended by Robert Mugabe, President of Zimbabwe. The delegates found that they had two sets of draft resolutions in their places: those of the official committee, selected by the Vatican officials rather than by the delegates, and those of AMECEA.

Bishop Martin was not happy with this: as far as he was concerned, only one set of resolutions could be considered, those that his official Vatican-selected committee had prepared. Hurley said that the delegates had another document before them that reflected what had come from the participants, and this should be looked at. Martin was determined that the plenary should look at the 'official' resolutions. Hurley was on his feet again, suggesting that the matter be put to a vote. This was done, and the majority were strongly in favour of the AMECEA document. Father Henriot said some years later, 'To be honest, ours had a little more bite'.

A lengthy discussion followed: what should be done about these two rival documents. Eventually Martin conceded that they would use the 'official' one but see how it could be 'enriched with some of the comments' from the AMECEA statement. Hurley, not wanting the African Church's perspectives to be short-changed, disagreed and said that the AMECEA recommendations should be used as the basis for discussion, and the delegates would 'see how some of your comments might be melded into it'. Hurley was determined to resist what he had learnt from experience was standard Vatican behaviour on occasions of this kind.

Henriot felt that Hurley was right to follow the 'principle of subsidiarity', derived from Catholic social teaching: what can be done at a lower level should not be superseded by a higher level. The local Church in Africa was perfectly competent to prepare its own statement about how Catholic social teaching should be used in the struggle for justice and peace. Nevertheless, Henriot recognized that Hurley was a formidable opponent and was grateful that he was supporting AMECEA because 'he was a very big man and he said things in a very commanding way and people paid attention'. On this occasion, 'he [Hurley] wanted people to know that Africa had a lot to contribute . . . Africa has some rather pertinent points that need to be heard, challenging the North, as well as challenging the Church'.

Years later, Martin, by this time Archbishop of Dublin, said he felt that Hurley and Henriot had misinterpreted what had happened at the justice and peace conference in Harare as a 'planned coup'. As a result, Martin considered that the final statement agreed to by the conference was weaker than it should have been. Not so, said Henriot: the strength of the AMECEA statement was that it reflected the views of the local Church, and surely that was what the Harare meeting was about.

SYNOD OF BISHOPS

Potentially the most significant international institution for the implementation of Vatican II is the Synod of Bishops, which (as we have seen) was established by Paul VI at the start of Vatican II's final session in September 1965.[14] In setting out how the synod would function, Paul had made clear that it would be controlled by the Pope. As mentioned earlier, since its institution it has been a *consultative* body (advisory to the Pope), though it could be *deliberative* (able to make decisions) if given this power by the Pope. Even then, its decrees or resolutions could only be promulgated by the Pope. McConville, writing in *The New Dictionary of Theology*, says there continues to be an ambiguity about how significant the synod is. This reflects the ambiguity of the Council itself about papal primacy and episcopal collegiality. Some scholars hold that the synod is simply an extension of papal primacy, others that it is 'a true exercise of the collegial dimension of the episcopal office'.

This ambiguity, according to McConville, is reflected in the documents produced after synods. Thus *Familiaris Consortio*, produced after the synod of 1980 (held during Pope John Paul II's pontificate) and focusing on the family, 'seems to reflect almost none of the concerns brought to the synod by bishops'. Synods held under Paul VI, for example the synod of 1969, strengthened the role of bishops' conferences. The synod of 1974 provided an opportunity for bishops of the younger, third-world churches to express their views on mission and evangelization. Many of their concerns were taken up by Pope Paul VI in the document he produced after the synod, *Evangelii Nuntiandi*.

McConville's conclusion is that 'it remains for the Church to reflect more deeply on [the synod's] significance and to provide for more effective structures and procedures', to which Hurley would have said a heartfelt 'Amen'. Having been elected by his colleagues in the SACBC to attend the synods of 1967, 1974, 1977, 1980 and 1985, he was aware of the defects in its structures and procedures, also that it had not lived up to the hopes for a collegial instrument to promote collaboration between the bishops and the Pope.

The 1967 synod was important mainly because it was the first. In some ways it completed the work of the Second Vatican Council, particularly in regard to liturgical reform, which was being strongly contested by the right wing, in which Archbishop Marcel Lefebvre was already active. Eventually Lefebvre would found the Society of St Pius X, a schismatic movement, which has recently commenced discussions with Rome about healing the rift.

But perhaps this first Synod of Bishops was most notable for two issues that were not on the agenda: celibacy and birth control. As we have seen in Chapter 13, Hurley believed that the synod could have provided a most helpful consultative forum on both topics which he had strongly urged Pope Paul VI to consider. Instead, these two topics were the subject of papal encyclicals, *Sacerdotalis Caelibatus* (1967) on celibacy and *Humanae Vitae* (1968) on birth control, both prepared without formal collegial consultation. This seemed to suggest, according to Hebblethwaite, that collegiality was in abeyance.

The synod of 1969 was intended to deal with the fallout from *Humanae Vitae*. Hurley was not elected by his colleagues to attend: given his views on that encyclical, he might have been a controversial presence. For the first time, the synod broke up into language-based groups. These gave more scope for communication than the long series of monologues (8-minute speeches) made by individual bishops, which characterize the first few weeks of each synod. Another important development in synod structures took place in 1970. On 23 March, a synod council was established, which would consist of 15 members, 12 elected by the synod (3 per continent) and 3 named by the Pope. It would meet twice a year and prepare for the next synod.

Hurley was also not elected to represent the SACBC bishops for the 1971 synod on the ministerial priesthood and justice in the world, although both topics were of considerable interest to him. The 1971 synod was the first to involve lay experts like Barbara Ward and to consult lay people in advance through the national Justice and Peace Commissions. It produced what was commonly regarded as one of the best synodal documents, *Justice in the World*. There was, however, much unhappiness at the end when Pope Paul seemed to sweep aside the idea of ordaining suitable married men, as if such an idea had not enjoyed any support in the synod, whereas it had received a substantial number of votes (87 for, 107 against).

Though Hurley was not present at this synod, he commented to Petal O'Hea:

It seems the synod has been going on for about three weeks on problems of the priesthood and has just ended up with a resounding vote in favour of so-to-speak unadulterated celibacy. Well, that may settle things for a while, but I wonder, I really wonder. If that is the final word, the Lord is being very categorical and asking his Church for an all-or-nothing attitude. Somehow I don't think it's going to work, but I could be horribly wrong. I hope I am.[15]

The next synod was in 1974. This was one that Hurley came close to not attending, despite the fact that he had been elected one of the two SACBC delegates, whose names were forwarded to Rome. Writing to Burghardt many years later about the *Theological Studies* article on population development, Hurley said that he remembered the occasion well. After the Vatican's attempt to censor his article, he had received notification that his membership of the synod was likely to be cancelled. Hurley did not allow himself to be bullied but replied that if this were the case, he would publish the reason for it.[16] 'Nothing more was heard' and Hurley attended the synod together with Archbishop Fitzgerald. It must have been something of a surprise that he was invited to a meal in the Vatican by the Secretary of State, Cardinal Villot, the very man who had instructed the Jesuits to remove Hurley's article from *Theological Studies*. 'It was quite an experience eating under 'the golden roof' and within 'the marble halls' . . . Other guests were the Cardinal Patriarch of Lisbon, Cardinal Marty of Paris, a bishop from New Caledonia in the Pacific, and the Administrator of Esztergom in Hungary'.[17]

The preparations for this synod had, for the first time, been entrusted to the new synod council elected in 1971. The theme was evangelization, and the proceedings were made extremely difficult by a dispute between those who regarded evangelization as purely spiritual and religious, and those who saw it as also concerned with human development. Because of this disagreement, the synod for the first time was not able to produce a document of its own or even to reach any conclusion. As Hebblethwaite put it,

> It simply dumped a series of confused propositions in the papal lap and invited the pope to sort them out. . . . This he did magnificently, in *Evangelii Nuntiandi*, published on 8 December 1975 . . . It can be considered the high point in the history of the synod so far. For here was a text that was at once synodal and papal, and therefore deeply collegial. The synod provided the raw experience and many of the insights, while Paul VI articulated them, using his 'charism of discernment'.

Hurley's conclusion about the procedural problems experienced at this synod was that

> they should hand over the procedure and meeting order to the Anglo-Saxons and recognize that no other group of human beings really has that charism. We are not theologians, philosophers, canon lawyers, saints or mystics, but we can run meetings, and from a fairly wide experience I would say categorically nobody else can. The gift does not appear to accompany papal infallibility.[18]

Hurley was given an opportunity to influence the shape of the following synod because of his election as one of three Africans on the synod council. He told his family how the newly-elected members 'hope to insist on better preparation of synods, better procedure and better follow-up'. He was realistic, however, about how much success they might enjoy, having learnt the hard way from a number of Vatican committees and events that 'Rome has ways of resisting Reformers. We must be satisfied with achieving about 25 per cent of what we set out to accomplish'.

During the 1974 synod, Hurley and Fitzgerald, his fellow delegate representing the SACBC, were summoned to the offices of the Congregation for the Doctrine of the Faith. The purpose was to discuss the official response of the SACBC to *Humanae Vitae* which allowed some latitude for the exercise of conscience in relation to the use of contraception. Hurley was grateful that Fitzgerald was 'in a particularly combative mood' that day and did not allow any browbeating by the CDF representatives who interviewed them.

The 1977 synod focused on catechesis: how the Catholic faith is passed on, especially to children and young people. Once again, Hurley was there as an SACBC representative and was elected to chair the 'English B' discussion group. This meant having to 'keep order among Cardinals Hume [England], Manning (Los Angeles), Freeman (Sydney), Knox (Rome) and an assortment of bishops from Thailand, Fiji,

Beira, New Zealand, Nigeria, Liberia, Tanzania, the Philippines and a few other places'. After Hurley's election as chair, Cardinal Freeman, a fellow cricket enthusiast, leaned over and whispered to him, 'Denis, bring on the fast bowlers immediately'. Hurley said, 'In the way it happened, the first speaker turned out to be a fast bowler par excellence, Cardinal Hume. From there things rolled on merrily'.[19] At the end of the synod, Hurley was re-elected to the synod council, which once again had the task of preparing for the next synod.

By the time of this synod, Paul VI was showing signs of aging; he had reached his eightieth birthday and was not well enough to respond to the mass of synodal material presented to him for the drafting of a synod document. His health deteriorated so much that he died the next year. The task of putting together the synodal document had to be undertaken by Pope John Paul II who, as Cardinal Wojtyla, had represented the Polish bishops at the 1977 synod, and had been elected Pope on 16 October 1978.

Hebblethwaite's view was that the Synod of Bishops grew to maturity during Paul VI's pontificate. Thanks to Paul's compromises, the synod had always been somewhat ambivalent: was it the organ of the bishops or of the Pope? 'Of course, a dialectic was involved . . . But in the pontificate of John Paul II, one-half of the dialectic seems to have been suppressed, and the synod became simply the organ of the pope'.

At the 1980 synod on the Christian Family, Hume was elected to chair the English B discussion group and Hurley to be its *rapporteur*. The highlight for Hurley was that the Pope invited the delegates in batches of ten to have a meal with him, 'an experience which I never thought would be mine'.[20] Hurley's batch consisted of ten bishops from Africa, the synodal representatives from South Africa, Nigeria, Liberia, Ghana and Sudan. 'We duly presented ourselves, were most cordially and joyously welcomed and entertained to a simple but very tastefully cooked and served meal. The Holy Father took the opportunity of filling himself in on a good deal of information about our various countries'.

It was not all serious, as Hurley reports: 'At one stage I mentioned that I had first met him in the Church of the Nativity at Nazareth in 1964. He replied, "I wasn't there in 1964; it must have been 1963". I replied, "I can't argue. The Pope is infallible". He takes such remarks with great good humour—but how humiliating for me to be caught out on a date. I still feel like checking it, despite the infallibility'.

The last synod for which Hurley was elected as an SACBC representative was that of 1985, which (as indicated at the beginning of this chapter) focused on the twentieth anniversary of the Second Vatican Council. In describing the first week of the synod, which had involved listening to 139 eight-minute speeches given back to back, he said, 'Synods develop the [cricket] test match temperament in their participants'.[21]

Hurley had a more negative opinion of the Synod of Bishops than Hebblethwaite: 'There was no room for evolution', and 'synods have conformed to the prescribed requirements from the beginning': he meant that they were not collegial nor likely to be in the future.

In regard to the Synod becoming a deliberative organ [able to make decisions rather than just being consultative], I do not think there is any hope of this in the lifetime of Pope Paul VI. It is quite clear that he sees the collegiality of bishops purely as an advisory role and insists that all decisions, even quite minor ones, involving the Synod, are referred to him.[22]

By contrast, Hebblethwaite was hopeful that the synod might develop into a more collegial body under some future pope: 'The synod, as founded by Paul VI, is a permanent body, and when some pope wants to try the adventure of collegiality, he will have recourse to it with gratitude'.

Hurley was more positive about the overall implementation of Vatican II, which he confidently believed would happen, but he realized that the message would take decades to permeate the whole Church. He was ready for delays and setbacks in the process. These did not prevent him from remaining faithful to the task of implementation until he ceased to be Archbishop of Durban in 1992 and even thereafter. In fact, 'Implementing Vatican II' could describe his life's work over the 38 years from the end of the council to the time of his death in 2004.

45

Leader of ICEL

As one of the founders of the International Commission on English in the Liturgy (ICEL) during the Second Vatican Council, Hurley played an important part in its work.[1] His great love of language and liturgy and the opportunity to serve the international Church in implementing the post-conciliar liturgy were satisfied by this involvement. His colleagues on ICEL's episcopal board recognized this by electing him as their chair in 1975 and repeatedly re-electing him to that position for the next 16 years.[2]

The board was responsible to the eleven member-conferences for oversight of ICEL's work. They approved membership of the advisory committee, the scope of the work done by various sub-committees and the annual budget. Most important, they accepted, modified or rejected every liturgical text submitted by the advisory committee.

This committee was chosen from various countries for its members' expert knowledge of English, liturgy, Scripture and theology. Its members debated matters of language, translation style and how liturgical texts could be laid out and designed to ensure maximum user-friendliness. They critically examined each translation, recommended the composition of prayers not available in Latin and passed on each liturgical book for approval by the episcopal board.

Day-to-day handling of ICEL's work was entrusted to ICEL's staff in Washington, DC. They organized all ICEL meetings, implemented advisory committee proposals for the editing and layout of liturgical books, administered copyright and publishers' contracts, and prepared reports, newsletters and routine correspondence. In addition, ICEL developed a lengthy list of consultants who received copies of draft texts for comment. Drafts were also submitted to all the bishops of the English-speaking world, about 700 in all.

Much of ICEL's work involved sending sample texts to hundreds of voluntary consultants. The secretariat distilled what came out of these consultations to present to the advisory committee, which then made recommendations to the episcopal board. This 'arduous and intense process', as ICEL itself described it, meant that each text was reviewed by scores or sometimes hundreds of people before presentation to the episcopal board. Even after the board had given their approval, documents would still have to go to the eleven bishops' conferences for each to give their own separate *approbatio* or approval. This was the complex process over which Hurley presided for 16 years.

All texts would finally be presented to the Congregation for Divine Worship (CDW) for the *recognitio*: an assessment of whether the text was in keeping with the Church's liturgical laws and was doctrinally sound. Checking the doctrinal soundness would sometimes mean the CDW's consulting the Congregation for the Doctrine of the Faith (CDF). Over the years, the process of securing the *recognitio* became increasingly vexed, especially when the CDW suspected that ICEL's approach to some aspects of translation—for example, the use of gender-inclusive language— revealed what they regarded as a dubious theological agenda. Then the CDW strayed into territory already covered in the approval given by the bishops' conferences by making its own judgment on the text—effectively vetoing what had already been approved by hundreds of bishops.

Dr John Page, Executive Secretary of ICEL throughout Hurley's 16 years as chair, said that Hurley oversaw the completion of the first stage of ICEL's work, most notably the full breviary (the official prayer of the Church recited daily by priests, monks and nuns). His first term began after the completion of ICEL's translation of the Roman Missal (all the liturgies for the entire year). The archbishop had some reservations about that work. He was especially happy when in 1982 he had a major hand in ICEL's immense task of revising the Roman Missal comprehensively. On the occasion of Hurley's fortieth anniversary as a bishop in 1987, the bishops of ICEL and their advisers dedicated the revision of the Roman Missal to him. After 1991, when he stepped down as chair of ICEL, he continued to be involved as a member of the episcopal board, representing the South African bishops.

Hurley's 16 years in ICEL's top leadership position and just under 40 as a member of ICEL's board gave many people, both bishops and their advisers, much opportunity to observe his personality. Father Gil Ostdiek of the advisory committee described him as 'a gentleman to the core'. Father John Fitzsimmons, a former chair of the advisory committee, said: 'He was vivacious, he was amusing, he had a ready response for anything that came his way'. John Page discovered what a moving experience it was to sit next to Hurley when the board said the morning prayer together: 'You could tell that this was a man of intense and deep prayer'. Mary Fowler, a member of the secretarial staff, described him as 'the personification of a priest, . . . still a humble person, he didn't let his role as an archbishop make him any different'. Jim Schellman, associate executive secretary to John Page, found working with Hurley an inspiring experience because of his link with the Second Vatican Council: 'One felt one was involved in a great enterprise . . . directly tied in to the conciliar roots'.

According to his ICEL colleagues, Hurley would arrive thoroughly prepared for meetings, having studied the many documents that had been sent out. He used the long flights from South Africa to catch up on documents he might not already have read. He would ensure that he arrived in time to sit down with staff and go over the whole agenda, issue by issue, to work out what type of discussion would be needed for each item and where any difficulties might arise. Because of his council experience, his having been a founder of ICEL and his having served on the liturgical Consilium established by Pope Paul VI to implement the council's liturgical constitution (1965–68), as well as having been a member of the CDW (1969–74), he brought a clear understanding of liturgical issues, as well as a sense of stability and continuity to the whole ICEL effort. It would be difficult to find a more accurate exponent of the original ICEL mandate, in whose drafting he had played a central role.

As a result of his experience and his careful preparation, ICEL meetings had a sense of purpose: Hurley had everything at his fingertips. Nevertheless, he was patient to a fault in allowing discussions to run their course and never short-circuiting a debate. Some, like his successor, Archbishop Daniel Pilarcyk of Cincinnati, felt that this was a weakness and that occasionally he allowed discussions to become too protracted. Hurley, however, seemed to relish the discussion. 'He learnt from it, he could contribute to it easily, and he wanted to see it have the time it needed', as Schellman put it.

Though Durban was far from Washington, DC, Page was impressed that Hurley developed a hands-on style as chair. Even before the age of faxes and email, he kept his involvement strong through many meetings, not just the annual board meeting. A special telex machine was purchased for his office in Durban so that he could have swift and easy communication with the ICEL office. He had regular telephone conversations with Page and maintained an extensive correspondence.

Although Hurley had been excited by the presence and participation of scholars at the council and greatly appreciated their role in ICEL, there was never any doubt that it was the board that made the final decisions on all ICEL matters. Hurley would sometimes question the experts closely, in order to be sure that he had fully understood what they were saying, but always with courtesy and in an atmosphere of dialogue. During a meeting, he would be willing to change his opinion on a matter if he had been thoroughly convinced, but even if he had not, he would remain 'polite, gracious and appreciative'. He was thoroughly professional in his approach to all aspects of ICEL's operation, including the finances, and wanted to know the purpose of any expenditure and how it had been accounted for.

In the mid-1970s, Hurley re-introduced the practice of having the board meet every other year in joint session with the advisory committee, before the separate meeting of the board. This was to ensure that there was a good understanding between these two committees. There had been several such meetings in the early years of ICEL, but over time, the practice had lapsed. His approach to the advisory committee and the secretariat staff helped to develop a sense of community and shared purpose, a 'spirit of openness, trust and friendship'. In joint meetings, Schellman observed that Hurley was able to exercise his episcopal leadership with an 'easy parliamentary procedure, . . . a collaborative style of taking part'. He did not stress the different standing of the participants: he wanted all to feel part of a common enterprise and important to its success.

Just as he had loved the debates at Vatican II, it was clear that he derived great intellectual pleasure from the discussions with ICEL's experts in various fields. Sister Theresa Koernke, a guest participant in several advisory committee meetings, had the impression that for Hurley 'coming to ICEL was like dessert, you know, or tea when you have a large chunk of bread, slathered with butter and jam. He just couldn't get enough of it; he loved to engage us in conversation'. As a scholar himself, Hurley was always at home with scholars.

In 1989, Hurley's fifteenth year as chair of the board, ICEL was given a special award by the University of Notre Dame's Centre for Pastoral Liturgy. In the citation, the organization was described as 'a model of collegiality, collaboration and consultation for the universal Church'. Sister Kathleen Hughes said it was Hurley who had created that collegial atmosphere. Hurley's view was that collegiality had been present from ICEL's foundation. The organization had been started by representatives of the English-speaking bishops' conferences who had imbibed the collegial spirit of Vatican II, and in that spirit the founders intended it to be accountable to the member bishops' conferences.

Monsignor Anthony Boylan, a member of the advisory committee, saw ICEL's collegiality in the fact that no one hierarchy dominated 'all the others in any way'. Fitzsimmons remarked that ICEL made 'sure that every bishop [of the member English-speaking conferences], was fully apprised of everything that ICEL was doing'. Ostdiek saw collegiality in the way the bishops of the episcopal board worked with priests, nuns, laymen and -women on the advisory committee. 'I experienced a great sense of collegiality in that we were empowered by the episcopal board, at whose pleasure we served . . . They trusted us to do the work'. It was this sense of collegiality that had also impressed Fitzsimmons: 'The father-figure [Hurley] had created a sense of family, a sense of cooperation and a sense of the search for excellence in everything that we did, which lasted the Commission for years and years and years . . . His contribution to ICEL was inestimable'.

Hurley's international experience of the Church, through the numerous Vatican and other committees he had served on, broadened ICEL so that it was easily able to operate as a 'trans-national, true international collegial enterprise of the English-speaking world', according to Schellman. The collegial atmosphere was enhanced by the relaxed evening gatherings of the bishops, committee members and staff. Here there was an opportunity to learn about the life of the Church in many parts of the world, and for much laughter and sharing of stories and reminiscences. Hurley's skills as a 'masterful and witty raconteur' were well to the fore.

With regard to the serious side of ICEL's work, it was the bishops' conferences that gave the *approbatio* (approval) for texts, while the CDW gave the *recognitio*, a general agreement that the text could be published and used. At least, that was how it was done until the mid-1990s—but we will return to that later. Here it is important to indicate what was achieved by ICEL in happier times. Possibly in the early years of ICEL, Page said, 'the language [used in ICEL translations] was too spare and too concise and some of it not too memorable'. Great efforts were made, however, to improve these translations under Hurley's leadership, moving back to 'more elaborate patterns in the

prayers, . . . more poetic reverence, more formal diction, a language that was more res-
onant with people in the last part of the twentieth century, but still proclaimable'.

In keeping with its original mandate, ICEL tried to work closely with the English-
speaking bishops' conferences, through the members of the board. Page notes, however,
that the link with the conferences was not always as strong as it should have been.[3]
Chapman recalls that there were occasions when the English, Scots, Irish, Australian,
New Zealand and Canadian hierarchies elected not to use ICEL material and made
their own translations, which were later used in South Africa. This was particularly true
of the Divine Office, but there were also other instances.

Obviously, in a small bishops' conference it would be easier to keep the members informed than in a large one like that of the United States. A particular problem for some of the US bishops, according to Page, was that they felt ICEL was not
sufficiently under their control and also that it was something of a bully. In an
effort to keep ICEL texts uniform for all English-speaking countries, individual
conferences had, in the final instance, either to accept or reject the ICEL text as a
whole, without amendment. If they objected to a text, they could supply their own,
but they could not alter the proposed ICEL text itself. This could be seen as limit-
ing the rights of individual bishops' conferences. Page felt that ICEL should have
been more flexible and allowed individual conferences to make changes in the final
texts presented to them.

Archbishop Rembert Weakland OSB, of Milwaukee, chaired the US Bishops'
Committee on Liturgy for a number of years, but had never been on ICEL, though
he supported their work. He agreed that the link with the bishops' conferences was
not strong enough and felt that it would have been stronger if chairs of bishops' conference liturgy committees served on ICEL. Weakland said that it would have been
easier for him to defend ICEL when it was criticized by the US bishops if, as a member of the board, he had known exactly what was happening there. He tried to convince Hurley that this change should be made to ICEL's structures but did not
succeed, perhaps because Hurley was aware that a number of conferences changed
their liturgical chairs frequently, so there would have been little continuity.

If there were weaknesses in the relationship between ICEL and the conferences,
the relationship with the CDW was much more problematic and would eventually,
towards the end of the twentieth century, lead to the Vatican's systematic dismantling
of the 'old ICEL' (founded by Hurley and others in 1963) and the creation of a 'new
ICEL', more directly influenced and controlled by the CDW. In the early ICEL years,
it seemed that tensions with the CDW could be resolved by Hurley's gracious way of
approaching the CDW officials, but his success depended on who was in charge. This
person, known as the 'Prefect', was generally a cardinal, not necessarily with any
expert knowledge of liturgy, but with considerable power in the Vatican.

The cause of the tension seemed to be ICEL's independence. It regarded itself as
answerable not to the CDW but, in keeping with its own constitution and mandate,
to its member bishops' conferences in a spirit of Vatican II collegiality. Probably the
CDW had been somewhat wary of ICEL from its foundation, as the first such structure established to help in the preparation of vernacular texts. While there may have

been some admiration for the English-speaking bishops' customary decisiveness and practicality in setting up such a structure on their own initiative, said Page, 'there would no doubt have been some apprehension on the part of the cautious, slow-moving world of the Vatican'.

As a courtesy, ICEL maintained a low-key, informal relationship with the CDW but focused its attention on its direct link with the bishops' conferences through the episcopal board. This was in marked contrast to the French and German translation commissions. Because they were geographically much closer to Rome, and because there was a German-speaking priest and a Frenchman on the CDW, it was easier for these translation structures to have more frequent dialogue with the CDW. As a result, they seemed to have an easier relationship. They visited the CDW offices once a month or once every two months, whereas ICEL tended to visit Rome not more than once a year and generally only when there was an issue to be resolved.

A growing perception in the CDW was that the bishops involved in ICEL had ceded their authority over the organization to the experts, members of the advisory committee and their consultants, and perhaps in particular to the staff. This was linked to a criticism in some quarters that Hurley lived too far away to be an effective leader of ICEL, so that the staff were left to make the decisions that Hurley and the other bishops merely rubber-stamped. Page strongly denies this assertion and emphasizes the frequent telephonic contact he had with Hurley to ensure that between meetings decisions would only be made with the chair's approval.

Fitzsimmons insists that during his 14 years as advisory committee chair, ICEL always operated as a commission of bishops' conferences, each of which took their own decisions on the basis of material provided by the experts. The advisory committee's recommendations had to have the approval of the episcopal board before texts could go on to the conferences and then in turn to Rome for further checking. 'All we did was provide [the bishops] with material, and if they liked it, fine. If they didn't, well, we went back to the drawing board and started again'.

Because English is the major language of international communication, and ICEL had considerably more human and financial resources at its disposal than the CDW—and because its translations were used by vastly more people than the German or French translations—it grew in power and influence over the years. This made it a threat to the CDW, especially when, at the request of its constituent bishops' conferences, it composed new texts and promoted agreed ecumenical texts for the Eucharist, in terms of its original mandate. Perhaps most threatening of all was that bishops' conferences from less well resourced countries began to use ICEL's translations from Latin into English as the basis for vernacular translations into their own local languages, rather than going back to the Latin originals. ICEL's power and influence may have led some members of the CDW to conclude that ICEL was in danger of regarding itself, and being regarded as, the equivalent of a CDW for all those countries which use English translations of the liturgy.

The CDW was supposed to restrict its role to giving the *recognitio* to texts that had already been approved by the bishops' conferences, provided they were in keeping with the Church's universal liturgical law and Church teaching. Gradually, however, it began to assert itself by becoming directly involved in issues related to language and translation, which were properly the role of the conferences. This seemed to be its way of dealing with the apparent threat that ICEL posed.

One of the texts produced by ICEL during Hurley's years as chairperson, the Order of Christian Funerals, provides a case study of the sort of problems that increasingly bedevilled the work of ICEL. This text included about forty specially composed prayers for a wide range of pastoral situations, including, for example, funerals of suicides, the burial of ashes, the burial of stillborn infants and young children as well as of people who had died after a long illness. Prayers for some of these situations were available in Latin but were thought to be too generic and bland. For other situations, no special prayers were available.

The additional prayers had been composed at the specific request of the bishops' conferences but were frowned upon by the CDW because it wanted ICEL to restrict itself to translating existing Latin texts. The Order of Christian Funerals had, as usual, been through a rigorous process of discussion in the advisory committee and the board before being submitted to the eleven bishops' conferences.

After the conferences had each given the official *approbatio*, this new liturgical text was sent to Rome, and two years elapsed while the CDW mulled over it. There was a great uproar when, after those two years, Rome's response was to send ten pages of suggested 'modifications', though the CDW conceded that none of the changes were reason for refusing the *recognitio*. It was widely felt that this was simply an attempt to put ICEL firmly in its place and was breaching the CDW's own regulations by moving into what was officially the domain of the conferences.

This time, according to an unsigned and undated draft letter in Hurley's ICEL files, an outraged Cardinal Basil Hume of Westminster wrote on behalf of the Bishops' Conference of England and Wales:

> The modifications suggest that a small group of consultants at the Congregation [CDW] are more competent than the bishops of England and Wales. What is more, the Congregation's action implies that the Congregation is a surer guardian of the prayer life of the Catholic people of England and Wales than the bishops of that conference whose judgment the Congregation has superseded with a list of corrections.[4]

In the same draft, Hume wrote that the modifications proposed by Rome were also a repudiation of the work of about sixty experts from various scholarly disciplines and numerous consultants representing all parts of the English-speaking world. Hume's closing sentence showed his determination in the face of Rome's clear breach of correct procedure: 'Your Eminence, [the cardinal prefect of CDW], the Bishops' Conference of England and Wales believes that it is now time to proceed with the publication of the Order of Christian Funerals in the form approved overwhelmingly by the Conference on 10 April 1986 [two years earlier]'.

Father Chris Walsh, a member of the Advisory Committee who later became chairperson, was less polite in his response:

Even if the CDW were stuffed with gifted people, wise pastors, experienced hospital chaplains, first-class liturgists, all of them native English speakers and renowned litterateurs, such modifications would still be totally unacceptable because, constitutionally, it is quite simply not their function to second-guess the conscientious and considered consensus of the local churches of the English-speaking world, arrived at after exhaustive examination, revision and approval through all the proper constitutional channels. When the Congregation numbers but one English speaker, who is none of these things, it is a breathtaking arrogance, a constitutional outrage, a most sinister abuse of position and influence and from every point of view intolerable.[5]

According to Page, the perpetual dispute over whether the CDW or the bishops' conferences should have authority for vernacular texts arose from the first instruction on implementing Vatican II's Constitution on the Sacred Liturgy. Entitled *Sacram Liturgiam* (1964), this instruction effectively took away the authority that the Second Vatican Council (in *Sacrosanctum Concilium*, art. 36.4) had given the conferences for approval of vernacular texts without needing to send them to Rome. *Sacram Liturgiam* appeared just weeks after the council had approved *Sacrosanctum Concilium* once the council fathers had gone home. 'It was the revenge of the old Congregation of Rites [CDW's predecessor]', says Page, 'still trying to upset the apple cart. Unfortunately, Paul VI approved it, and it stands as authoritative even though it more than appears to trump the council'.[6]

In his sixteen years as chair of ICEL, Hurley only once missed the annual meeting of the board: the 1984 meeting held in London. He could not be present for that meeting because all the Catholic bishops of southern Africa were at that time attending a special IMBISA assembly in Harare, Zimbabwe, and, as president of the SACBC, it was crucial that he be there. From a letter to Page explaining why he would not be able to attend the ICEL board meeting, it is clear that his involvement in that body was much more than a duty: 'It just breaks my heart to think I can't be with you at this meeting. How I would enjoy that discussion on the style of translation of the prayers. This is one of the biggest privations I have suffered in years—worse than all the politico-religious brickbats that come my way from time to time'.

He gives a fascinating reason why he would particularly like to have been present: his concern about the fidelity of translations to the Latin originals [though he was not in favour of a literal translation, which would later be the Vatican's choice of translation methodology]:

My own reaction these days . . . is to try to reproduce as much as possible of all the nuances of the Latin in our English translations. I get the impression not a few of our translations preserve not so much the substance as the skeleton of the Latin original. I should like to see translations that could be translated back into Latin and not be too far from the mark when they got there.

This quotation reveals how there was already internal self-criticism within ICEL long before the Vatican intervened in a high-handed manner as we shall see in Chapter 29.

Hurley's absence from the London meeting did not pass without notice. All present signed a brief statement, dated 28 August 1984:

Dear Archbishop Hurley

Your presence here has been very much missed.

With affectionate and prayerful greetings,

The members of the Episcopal Board and Advisory Committee

and Guest Participants. [29 people in all]

Chapman comments that 'the fact that the original ICEL survived together as a functioning group and survived [pressures from] Rome for so long was due in considerable measure to [Hurley's] skills. He was the outstanding bishop associated with it'.[7]

46

Close Encounters

How was Hurley perceived back home in his own archdiocese? Usually those who get to know bishops best are their vicars general and secretaries and other diocesan staff members. This chapter on 'close encounters' with Hurley is based on interviews with two of his surviving vicars general, Father Eric Boulle OMI and Monsignor Paul Nadal; one surviving secretary, Julie Mathias (formerly Rainsford); Deacon Lawrence Mthethwa, who works on pastoral development for the Zulu-speaking parishes; Tony Cooke, the financial administrator of the archdiocese; Andy Piper, who worked in the chancery for several years as part of the Renew team; Father Raphael Mahlangu and Philip Mabaso, a diocesan catechist, both of whom frequently interpreted for Hurley.

Father Boulle was vicar general and chancellor (head of the diocesan office) from 1962 to 1968, during the Second Vatican Council years and the early years of implementing its message.[1] During those years Boulle 'got to know the person behind [Hurley's] exterior aloofness; his wit, his understanding of human weakness, his ability to accept praise and humiliation, his courage and spiritual fortitude, his sense of justice and his warm friendliness'. What Boulle concluded was that in his training for the priesthood, Hurley had learnt not to show emotion, which may have created a first impression of aloofness; yet his true feelings became apparent when he reached out to people in any kind of suffering. Aloofness was certainly not what his close friends experienced, according to Geoff Chapman, who recalls Hurley saying that 'his capacity to relate to people had been "knocked out" of him' during his training.[2]

Boulle recalls the day when Father Ernest Canevet OMI died in his sleep at the township parish of St Clement's in Clermont, Durban. As soon as he received the news, Hurley went with Boulle to be with the parishioners who were gathering in great numbers outside the priest's house. Grief about their pastor's sudden death was compounded by the deaths of three young parishioners struck by lightning just a few days earlier.[3] Realizing how traumatized the people were, Hurley walked up and down among them, leading them in reciting the rosary aloud in Zulu. Soon emotions were calmed and everyone was united with their chief pastor in expressing their grief.

On another occasion Boulle, by this time administrator of the cathedral, had experienced a personal crisis one weekend when he was due to preach at all the Sunday Masses. The crisis made him reluctant to preach, and on the Saturday morning he told Hurley over the phone. Hurley said that he would come straight away to see him. He drove to the cathedral, where they chatted for about an hour. Boulle was able to explain his feelings fully, and Hurley calmed him, offering encouragement and support. At the end of the conversation, Boulle felt able to go ahead with his preaching commitments.

This was just one of many occasions when Boulle saw that though Hurley was extremely busy, he would always make time for people who wanted to see him.

> Whenever and wherever trouble, tragedy or sorrow struck whether political or otherwise, such as removals, violence or death, Denis Hurley was one of the first to go to the scene to comfort the afflicted, to be with them in their suffering, to show them that Christ and his Church supported them. He never excused himself from his duties as shepherd and pastor, no matter what the cost to his person.

Boulle was also impressed by Hurley's humility and quoted a letter he had discovered while doing his retirement work as Oblate archivist, sorting through the late archbishop's correspondence. It was a reply, dated 18 October 1978, to a scathing letter from one of the priests, whose harsh judgement had deeply hurt Hurley, yet he was able to accept that in the sharp criticism of this man was a message to which he should pay attention:

> Your letter of the 4th October has been with me nearly two weeks. I am sure you understand it is not an easy one to answer. In fact, it is probably one of the most devastating I have ever received. But the voice of the Lord comes through it, and so I must thank you for being the instrument of his message. For too long I have been deaf to it . . . It takes a real explosion to shake some of us out of the habits of life and action we have settled into, and to force us to re-think our priorities.
>
> It is not an easy matter of course to cut a swathe through a thousand and one involvements that have grown up over the years and which accord with one's personal attitudes and inclinations. Pray for me that what you have said and written may be the launching pad for a real conversion. Conversion it must be, for by nature, I fear, and this has become clear to me in later years, the personal touch and concern do not come easy to me.

Julie Mathias became Hurley's secretary in March 1976.[4] After trying the job for three months, she decided that she had had enough and was ready to leave:

> Initially I found it horrendous. I hated it. There was virtually no communication at all. [The Archbishop] would arrive in the morning, leave stuff on my desk and go. I would work flat out all morning, and then whatever I had finished by lunchtime I would leave in his office while he was at lunch, so . . . we had no communication. It was like working in a morgue: you just worked flat out and saw practically no one from morning to night. The equipment was antiquated, and there were no systems in

place. I think there were only two ancient filing cabinets, packed full of buff folders, and the rest of the stuff rose in piles on the floor, like stalagmites.

When Hurley had been told that Mathias wanted to leave and why, he could not have been more apologetic. Things began to improve, the atmosphere relaxed; he and Mathias discussed ways of streamlining the work, put some systems in place, bought new equipment and built up such a good working relationship that she was heartbroken to leave this work when she emigrated to the United Kingdom 11 years later.

Those 11 years gave her a rare glimpse into Hurley as a person. She said that only once did she see him really angry. A priest had been doing door-to-door selling of household detergents and had proved to be such an effective salesman that he had won an expensive car as a prize. This he drove around ostentatiously, causing scandal among his parishioners. Hurley asked him to stop selling these products and give back the car. The priest disobeyed. He was then asked to come in for a chat, and Mathias caught a glimpse of what was happening as, his face white with anger, Hurley gave the priest a severe dressing down.

On another occasion Hurley was on the same plane as the Natal rugby team, who became increasingly rowdy as the journey progressed and liquid refreshment flowed. Despite the fact that they were using crude language, Hurley quietly continued working at his papers. But then one of them said loudly: 'Jesus!' and Hurley simply raised himself in his seat, looked round at the team, and there was instant silence.

By contrast she also saw that he was often amazingly kind and thoughtful. He would always send letters or handwritten notes of congratulation when these were due. If people were in trouble and he could not help directly, he would put them in touch with the right person or agency, making the introductory phone calls himself and following up if necessary. Most moving of these incidents occurred when a little boy at a mission station near Bergville tugged at Hurley's robe in order to catch his attention. Hurley discovered that the boy was one of several in the area who were profoundly deaf and thus had great difficulty in communicating; as a result they were denied any opportunity of formal education and training. This led to Hurley's establishing a school for the deaf known as KwaThintwa, a name that captures the literal and figurative meaning of being touched by the little boy. Mathias recalls that establishing the school was 'a large and complex undertaking', but Hurley had a particular interest in it and 'steered it from concept to completion with his usual gusto and enthusiasm, ably assisted by Beryl Jones and the King William's Town Dominican nuns. I think it had a special place in his heart'.

Hurley could take on new projects like KwaThintwa because he was able to prioritize. Mathias saw that when many things were happening at the same time, he could immediately focus on the most important, deal with that and then move on to other issues, even if it meant changing his entire schedule. And so he would go from one situation to another, without any carry over from the last or anxiety about the next, giving each his undivided attention.

Like Boulle, Mathias knew from her own experience that personal tragedies would always claim Hurley's immediate attention: she had gone to the Drakensberg Mountains with a friend for a weekend break. On the way they had a head-on collision with another vehicle and ended up in hospital in Pietermaritzburg, 80 kilometres from Durban. The next morning Hurley was at the hospital, having picked up Mathias's friend's mother and brought her to visit her daughter. For the duration of Mathias and her friend's stay in the hospital, they had various priests and other contacts come to visit them—all arranged by Hurley.

Mathias discovered that you could tell by his eyes if he was amused but it was not appropriate to laugh out loud. On the day of Dominic Khumalo's ordination as Durban's first auxiliary bishop, there was a gathering in the dining room at Archbishop's House in Innes Road, Durban, before the clergy left for King's Park Stadium (now Absa Stadium), where the ordination was to take place. Hurley came through to Mathias's office and said that Cardinal McCann wanted a cigarette— could Mathias help? She offered a full pack of cigarettes to Hurley, and he asked her to take them to the cardinal. She did so but was nonplussed when the cardinal took the cigarettes, helped himself to one, lit it, put her pack and lighter in his pocket and turned away. Hurley had seen the whole incident, and she could tell from his eyes that he was highly amused but was discreet about it.

She saw that he lived an extremely frugal life, seldom spending money on himself except for books or small gifts for friends or family, or occasionally taking people out for a meal. One of Mathias's last tasks at the end of each year was to wrap Christmas presents he had bought for all his nephews and nieces, the children of Jerry and Bobbie, and Chris and Ursula. She was impressed by his ability to select gifts that would appeal to young people of different ages. If he received money as a gift, most of this would be passed on to people in need. His housekeeper, Marie-Therese Bonelle, would nag him to buy new clothes, especially when he was going to Rome, but he would often forget or not have time, and Bonelle would then ask Mathias to buy replacements as close as possible to the original.

Working so closely with Hurley for 11 years, Mathias came to realize that he would never make a public pronouncement without thinking thoroughly about it. Nothing ever just came off the top of his head. He would not go into a meeting, gathering or liturgical celebration for which he had not thoroughly prepared. Part of that preparation was prayer. Often when Mathias went to see him in his office, he would be deep in prayer, either at his desk or in the chapel. 'If at his desk, he would be sitting very still, with his elbows on his blotter and his forehead resting on his folded hands'. If he was praying, she would quietly leave files or trays of correspondence, or whatever she had brought, at the top of the steps and go back to her office.

Many people experienced Hurley as shy, but Mathias felt that he had made a concerted effort to manage this. Nevertheless he did not find it easy to communicate freely with people, especially not on an emotional level, unless he knew them well. She felt that he had never fully overcome his shyness and that on some occasions he was 'slightly too hearty, almost theatrical, as if he were playing a role that did not come naturally to him'.

Not only was he a big man physically, but he had an even bigger presence and could not be easily ignored. If you wanted to discuss something with him, you had to be sure of your facts. 'You had to get up quite early in the morning and do your homework if you wanted to take him on . . . If someone was flannelling around, he would make them, in the kindest possible way, wish they had been better prepared before voicing an opinion'.

There were some tasks, that if he did not do himself, he feared would not be done at all. Because he was a perfectionist, he found it difficult to delegate. But Mathias noticed that it was not humanly possible for him to handle all the correspondence that came his way, and so some of it would not be dealt with and would wait for months. Sometimes he did not answer letters that she would have thought a priority, for example, a complaint about a priest or a problematic situation in a parish. Mathias would have answered these straight away because it was clear that a problem was brewing which would be better to nip in the bud than allow to fester. 'It baffled me that he left those letters ticking away like time bombs. This may have been out of his fear of confrontation, or perhaps he hoped the problem would resolve itself before he had to do anything'.

It was easier for him, she said, to deal with priests who helped themselves to parish funds, had an alcohol problem, or drove their cars into the ground, than with those who were having sexual affairs. 'That was real tiger country for him', and she felt he seldom did anything about such cases until there was mounting pressure from the parishes concerned. Then he would be very gentle, caring and understanding. 'Embarrassed, yes, but very kind'.

The reader may wonder whether Hurley was as reluctant to deal with cases of paedophilia. Such cases have been disastrously mishandled in a number of other countries, as revelations in recent years have shown. According to Monsignor Paul Nadal and Father Albert Danker OMI there were 'no known cases' of paedophilia in the Archdiocese of Durban during Hurley's term of office, so it is not possible to say how he might have handled them. It is fair to assume that, out of his strong sense of justice, he would have responded firmly.

Being secretary to a workaholic did have its difficulties for Mathias. She used to dread Mondays when he had not had any confirmations or other major engagements over the weekend, because he would use the time to make inroads into piles of correspondence, and it would not be unusual to find five or six full dictaphone cassettes on top of a great mound of correspondence on her desk. She thought he found it difficult to relax at home in the midst of piles of unanswered mail on his desk. That was why he enjoyed invitations to visit local friends or have a meal with friends from overseas. If you invited Hurley for a meal, said Mathias, he really knew how to relax: 'He would be able to shake off the official persona, . . . switch off and be a real *Mensch*'.

He did not seem to have the need for as much sleep as the average person so he had more working hours and would fill them first of all by tackling his correspondence. Mathias recalls that sometimes it would take her a full hour to open the post—and that was just his own diocesan mail, apart from all the international correspondence especially related to ICEL, and national correspondence mainly related to the Bishops' Conference. Though his desk 'looked like a bomb site', he liked his mail to be sorted in a certain way and always presented in the same sequence: books and periodicals at the bottom, then minutes and reports and notices of meetings, then correspondence . . . first of all from the Bishops' Conference, then ICEL, then clergy and religious, with letters from lay people right at the top of the pile.

As Mathias grew in confidence, she suggested to Hurley that perhaps it would help if she presented him with a set of files each morning to cover the appointments for that day. It was a simple system, but he was happy to consider this and other suggestions. He loved organization and good presentation and was famous for his insistence on grammatical English: he wanted documents and correspondence to be concise and unambiguous.

He loved to hear about new and interesting things; if something intrigued him, he would find out all he could about it. When the term 'humiture' was first used in the press, he asked Mathias to phone Durban airport to find out as much as possible about what it meant and how it was measured.

Apart from being a stickler for accurate language, he insisted on people keeping their appointments, otherwise the schedule would be messed up and subsequent appointments affected. He would say something 'quite direct and pointed' to late-comers. He once said to Mathias that the only religious in the diocese who had a valid excuse for being late were the Little Sisters of Jesus because they did not have their own transport and had to hitch-hike everywhere—but oddly enough, he noted, they were the ones who always seemed to be on time.

Some people were critical about how Hurley allocated his time. They thought he neglected his diocese in favour of national and international commitments, and that even in relation to his own local work, there was a bias in favour of justice issues and invitations from organizations like Diakonia. Mathias's response to this criticism was that the diocese's loss was the universal Church's gain, and that time spent at national and international events and local gatherings about social justice issues immensely enriched the life of the diocese, keeping it in touch with the latest thinking and developments. She also felt that despite Hurley's frequent trips overseas or to other parts of South Africa, the archdiocese had a lot more going on than many other dioceses. Though Hurley may have had a natural inclination to involve himself in what really stirred him, he 'managed to keep all the plates spinning in Durban'.

A third person who was able to observe Hurley's life and work from close quarters was Monsignor Paul Nadal, one of Hurley's best friends.[5] As a young priest Nadal had lived at Archbishop's House for a few years in the 1960s when he had been working for the national Catechetical Commission. Later he was Hurley's vicar general in the years leading up to the archbishop's retirement in 1992. He was struck by the fact that Hurley did not have any conventional hobbies. His life, his work, his pleasure, his entertainment all seemed to revolve around the Church, his role as bishop and as priest.

According to Nadal, he readily admitted that for most of his ministry as a bishop, he was too much of a 'desk man' and not sufficiently a 'people's person'. His taste was for theology, discussion and reflection, and he felt that he had not given sufficient time to developing personal relationships with his clergy and people. It was not that he had no interests outside of his work. He had many as well as an interest in people, which grew as he became older. Perhaps the closest thing to a hobby was his keen interest in his favourite sports, cricket and rugby. He was so interested in local teams succeeding in international matches that he would occasionally give some advice to coaches.

Once, when the Natal rugby team, the Sharks, was doing disastrously in a Super 12 season in Australia, Hurley wanted to speak to the coach, Hugh Reece-Edwards, and phoned Patrick Akal, his chancellor from the 1960s, to find out how to contact him. The problem, as Hurley saw it, was that the Sharks had become highly predictable: 'Why don't they do a few up-and-unders? I have to speak to the coach to tell him he's doing things wrong'. Akal managed to find out Reece-Edwards's email address in Sydney, and a message was duly sent.[6]

Hurley was not interested in films or theatre, said Nadal, but in serious books. Among his favourite leisure reading, oddly enough, were books about military strategy and great battles. This was a contradiction in his personality since he was essentially a man of peace. On one rare occasion he invited Nadal to see the film *Waterloo* with him and expressed regret that he had not re-read the *Encyclopaedia Britannica* account of this battle before seeing the film because then he would have been sure that there was a fundamental error in it: one of the generals was depicted as having attacked from the left, but the historical record showed that he had done so from the right.

Nadal observed that Hurley loved researching such items of information. He had 'the eye of a hawk' when it came to proof-reading. If there was a mistake in a text you could be sure he would find it. This personality trait sometimes led to embarrassing situations, particularly in liturgical celebrations. He could stop a celebration to correct a small mistake in ritual, which might not otherwise have been noticed. Perhaps the most embarrassing incident concerned a concelebrated Mass with fellow bishops when he stopped a bishop from seeking a blessing from the presiding bishop before reading the Gospel. Bishops do not seek a blessing from fellow bishops. Hurley was humble enough to tell this story himself.

Perhaps it was Hurley's attention to minute details that also led to a great interest in science. He would often say that if he had not been a priest, he would have liked to be a scientist. Quantum physics had a special attraction, and this sometimes astonished his brother priests, as when he included in a sermon a reference to the sub-atomic particles known as 'quarks'. Hurley tried to speak about these as simply as possible but, Nadal says, Bishop Khumalo battled to translate such matters into Zulu. The priests exchanged puzzled glances as if asking each other, 'What on earth is Hurley talking about now?'

Nadal concurred with Mathias that Hurley did not like to reprimand or confront people for misdemeanours or poor work performance. Nadal said that this was one of his shortcomings as a bishop. If it was a small misdemeanour, he would prefer just to cast a blind eye and let it pass, a weakness that some priests and lay people abused.

If it was a major issue and Hurley had to do something, things would build up, but he would eventually take sudden, decisive action, nicknamed the 'karate chop', according to Nadal.

Nadal says that Hurley always made himself available to those who needed to see him. Long after the diocesan offices had closed for the day, he would still be seeing people, greeting them with a smile and a word of welcome. He instructed Nadal that if any priest wanted to speak to him on the phone, he should be put straight through.

Lawrence Mthethwa was chosen by Hurley to work on Christian stewardship in the Zulu-speaking parishes and ordained a permanent deacon for his home parish. Though Hurley was not a fluent Zulu speaker, Mthethwa discovered that he had a good theoretical knowledge of the language so that he could correct spelling and grammatical mistakes in the translations Mthethwa did for him. But he was shy about speaking Zulu spontaneously, and so he always wanted a text when he had to preach or give an address. Sr. Michael Mduli OP of Montebello felt that this had been a major obstacle for Hurley in really getting to know and understand Zulu people: 'Without the language of the people you cannot touch the people. So that was something that we always felt he just lost there . . .' It may have been a major problem for Hurley in resolving a conflict between the German superior of Montebello and her congregation of Zulu-speaking nuns.[7]

Nevertheless according to Mthethwa, Hurley was much loved by Zulus, including those who were not Catholics.[8] He had been given the Zulu name *Umehlwemamba*, which means 'mamba eyes'. This needs some explaining for English speakers who might think it has sinister connotations. Mthethwa's explanation was that Hurley looked at people with a sharp, penetrating gaze when he was listening to them, and he would then ask questions that made them realize that he was aware of things they had not said but which were on their minds.

And yet Mthethwa and others were concerned that some who came to the diocesan chancery for assistance took advantage of Hurley's kindness. 'He would not be able to close his ears if somebody was really in need'. Mthethwa thought that even if some of the stories that people told Hurley in order to get assistance were not entirely true, he responded to their background of poverty and need; he found it difficult to refuse help in the light of those circumstances.

One of Hurley's great strengths, said Andy Piper, was that he was able to embrace change and move with the times, and to let people know exactly where he stood and why.[9] He could stand firm even if he was the only priest in the archdiocese taking up a certain position. 'So, we could never say we didn't know how he felt, what he was doing and where he was going. He gave clarity and vision'.

Piper also referred to his difficulty in dealing with issues related to sexuality. She remembered an occasion when a priest who was having an affair was being discussed, and Hurley 'sat in total silence and he was bright red and you could just feel this total embarrassment all the way through'. She also recalled discussing one of André Brink's books with him, and the only negative aspect Hurley mentioned was an explicit sexual reference, which he felt was totally distasteful. That was 'an absolute no-go zone, . . . and I don't know that anyone could broach that with him at all', but he was able to have great empathy with his priests: even when they were really out of line, they were still able to feel his loving support.

Another great embarrassment for Hurley, according to Tony Cooke, was to have to ask for money—though he had been a highly successful fund-raiser for the archdiocese and for a number of Church and other organizations for many years.[10] He was particularly apologetic if he had to appeal to the parishes, and especially the poorer ones. He had a flourishing direct mailing appeal, the inspiration for which had been extensive fund-raising trips to the United States in 1950 and 1956. However, he had not kept the parishes informed about how much was received from these campaigns: 'he felt acutely embarrassed about it for reasons I could never understand', said Cooke. It was only in about 1990–91, when he was in his last years as archbishop, that he was forced to turn to the parishes for support. The archdiocese was suddenly in a poor financial situation because the direct mailing appeal was in difficulty. Hurley called a big meeting, where he made a direct plea to the parishes: 'We are in dire financial straits, and the parishes are going to have to chip in now and help'.

Philip Mabaso describes a rather different experience of Hurley: his visits to rural and semi-rural parishes.[11] The people would respond as if to their father:

> They would really like to meet him from afar, so that as he came he would leave his car; . . . maybe a priest or someone else would drive his car and then he would walk . . . into the parish with people dancing, ululating, clapping. . . . All that showed me that he had the heart of a pastor, you know, to be with his people. He really brought consolation to the people, you know, he was a caring man. . . . He would sit there with [the poor people], talking with them, eating with them, drinking with them.

It was not always like this.[12] Father Raphael Mahlangu, who also accompanied the archbishop as a translator, felt that Hurley sometimes had so many things to do, that after confirmations in the morning, he would excuse himself at about 3:00 p.m., when the people wanted him to stay right through a special concert they had prepared. Mahlangu, who was a great admirer of the archbishop, also felt that he would have benefited from spending more time in individual discussion with his priests, listening to their problems and perspectives. This might have led to a more enthusiastic response to his pastoral vision and initiatives. This was not, however, an aspect of a bishop's work that Hurley found easy. Moreover he was extremely busy and thrived on stimulating meetings, writing reports and so on. As a result there were not enough of such close encounters with his clergy other than at times of crisis when his generous response could not be faulted.

PART FOUR

Prophetic Leader

When I spoke out, it was because I couldn't help it: apartheid was so obviously wrong.
—Hurley to author, 1 December 2002

17

Stirrings of Resistance

The role of prophets in the Old Testament was not, as is commonly thought, to fore-tell the future, but rather to draw attention to what was already happening—and what sort of response God was calling for. The prophets' communication with God through prayer and contact with the sufferings of ordinary people in times of great crisis gave them authority to challenge political leaders to end oppression and estab-lish justice. We have looked in some detail at Hurley's enthusiastic involvement in the Second Vatican Council. Now we must retrace our steps to the situation in South Africa in the early 1960s to see how he responded as a prophetic leader.

Nationwide protests about the Sharpeville massacre in 1961 led to a massive onslaught on all forms of black resistance, which the security forces were successful in weakening for the remainder of the decade. Black leaders were either imprisoned on Robben Island or forced into exile, and the two main liberation movements, the ANC and PAC, were banned. The Nationalist government believed that apartheid was succeeding: black people seemed to 'know their place', and the government was firmly in control. It was not until the late 1960s that there were new stirrings of resist-ance, through the Black Consciousness Movement (BCM), industrial action and, later, massive protest from black schools.

BLACK CONSCIOUSNESS

Towards the end of the 1960s, Black Consciousness, deriving to an extent from the Black Power movement in the United States, began to fill the vacuum created by the banning of the ANC and PAC and the imprisonment of their most significant leaders.[1] Its aim was to bring about a psychological transformation in the minds of black people, helping them to realise that they had the power to free South Africa.

Black Consciousness began among university students. Several black students, the most influential of them Steve Biko, a medical student, decided that the National Union of South African Students (NUSAS), dominated by whites, could not advance the interests of black students. So in 1969 they formed the all-black South African

Students' Organization (SASO), with Biko as its first president. Biko believed that until black people had confidence in themselves, they would never gain their freedom. They would have to end their dependence on whites and become self-reliant. The ripple effects of this thinking spread rapidly. Black people felt a new sense of pride about being black as the movement helped to expose the inferiority complex experienced by many at that time. It was a most important turning point in the South African struggle for freedom.

As one of the groups influenced by Black Consciousness, young black priests were frustrated by the gap between the bishops' statements on apartheid and exceptionally slow change within the Church itself.[2] Five priests who served on the executive of St Peter's (Hammanskraal) Old Boys' Association (SPOBA)—Fathers Smangaliso Mkhatshwa, David Moetapele, John Louwfant, Clement Mokoka and Anthony Mabona—put together a manifesto entitled 'Our church has let us down', which was published in the *Rand Daily Mail* on 23 January 1970.

Their complaint was that, despite their status as priests, they were treated as 'glorified altar boys' by the Church. They called for the Africanization of the Church in South Africa and for avenues to be opened up for black promotion, suggesting that a black bishop be appointed for the vast black townships known as Soweto, south-west of Johannesburg. Despite the South African bishops' statements about apartheid, the SPOBA executive said the bishops had done little to move away from racial discrimination in their own structures.

Two weeks later, the Administrative Board of the Bishops' Conference, including Hurley, met with these priests accompanied by nine laymen to discuss the manifesto. The delegation complained that black priests were given subservient roles; they called on the bishops to adopt a firmer stand against apartheid and associate themselves more closely with their people, 80 per cent of whom were African. They asked the bishops to establish some form of permanent liaison with black priests and laity. Defensive in their response, the bishops concentrated on the leadership opportunities that had already been offered to black priests, a number of whom had apparently been invited to take positions in the hierarchy but had declined, though this was not generally known.

The SPOBA delegation was not satisfied with this response. A year later they had additional reason to protest: Cardinal McCann, while in Australia at the time of Pope Paul VI's visit there, was asked whether he supported a universal franchise for South Africa. His reply was that he was in favour of a qualified franchise based on each individual's readiness for democracy. If blacks were given immediate and total control, he said, there would be chaos. These comments infuriated SPOBA: they seemed to be a perfect illustration of the priests' complaint.

They requested an opportunity to present their case to the plenary session of the bishops' meeting in July 1971, but were turned down by Father Dominic Scholten OP of the Bishops' Conference staff, who claimed that the agenda was already full. The priests decided to dramatize their protest by interrupting the bishops' deliberations to read out a memorandum condemning the Catholic Church for condoning racist practices and discrimination in its own ranks. The memorandum called on Bishop

Hugh Boyle of Johannesburg to resign and make way for a black bishop. Boyle was accused of having shown indifference when black members of his clergy and laity had been victimized by the government. The memorandum also called for a black cardinal to be appointed, because all confidence had been lost in McCann.

The bishops' own words in the 1957 joint pastoral were quoted back to them: 'We are hypocrites if we condemn apartheid in South African society and condone it in our own institutions'. The protestors pointed out that at a time when there were a million black Catholics and only 170,000 white, there were twenty-five white bishops and only one black apostolic administrator, Peter Butelezi, of the remote rural diocese of Umzimkulu.

Garner, who had been chairing the plenary session at the request of the president, McCann, described the protest in a statement published in the *Southern Cross* of 28 July 1971. The bishops, he said, were discussing justice and peace matters when the conference door suddenly opened; the protesters entered with their placards and remained standing in silence while the work of the conference proceeded. After some time the group's leader said it was not their wish to interrupt the bishops' discussions. He then read out the memorandum, of which copies were given to the bishops. According to the *Southern Cross*, the placards carried the following slogans: 'Must we tolerate white bosses in the Church as well?' 'Whose Cardinal is McCann?' 'Christ is Black—Bishops act for White interests'. 'We have no Cardinal'.

Mkhatshwa gives a livelier account of the event, including reference to bus-loads of lay supporters waiting outside while the delegation came into the conference room. He describes the protestors as deciding 'to storm the plenary session of the Conference [that] fateful Saturday afternoon'. What they wanted from the bishops was to be taken more seriously; to let them know that there was a lot of unhappiness, not only among black priests but also among black lay people.

Garner reported that as the group prepared to leave, Hurley rose briefly to say that he would like to express gratitude to all missionaries from overseas who had left their homes to serve the people of southern Africa. This was his response to the criticism levelled at Boyle and to some other aspects of the protestors' memorandum. When Hurley had finished speaking, nothing more was said and the group left.

Once again, Mkhatshwa's recollection of what happened was different. The protestors, he said, explained why they had barged in on this meeting. One of the laymen began accusing the bishops of condoning apartheid practices in the Church. Hurley was the only bishop who responded, which made the group angrier, and they addressed a number of rhetorical questions to him. Hurley, however, remained calm and dignified and won Mkhatshwa's respect because of his leadership and fearlessness in this difficult situation in which, despite being under attack together with all his colleagues, he must also have felt sympathetic to the protestors.

On a lighter note, Mkhatshwa described how the delegation celebrated later at the Tembisa parish, where Father David Moetapele was parish priest: 'I think we literally danced through the night, so relieved were we after the great tension of the build-up to the protest and of the day itself'.

The slow process of appointing black bishops in South Africa came under attack in the *Sunday Tribune* of 5 August 1971. Hurley's reply, titled 'You can't just rush blacks into power', warned that though black bishops definitely would be appointed, doing this too rapidly in 'an agonizingly complex situation' could be 'an injustice to [those chosen] and those they lead'. Nevertheless, despite Hurley's defensive response, the pace definitely needed to be accelerated, as was stressed in an article by Father Mandlenkosi Zwane (later Bishop of Swaziland from 1976, and a powerful influence on the SACBC before his tragic death in a car accident in 1980). Published in the *Southern Cross* of 23 February 1972 under the title 'An act that would electrify black South Africa', Zwane called for a black coadjutor bishop with the right of succession to be appointed for the Johannesburg diocese. Yet in 1971 there were 1,552 priests in South Africa, of whom 1,380 were white, 144 African and 28 coloured or Indian; hence the pool of those from whom black bishops could be chosen was relatively small.

THE 1973 STRIKES

As the Black Consciousness Movement was inspiring a new mood of confidence and resistance against apartheid in society and in the Church, there were significant stirrings among workers in Durban.[3] During the 1960s, the average number of blacks involved in strikes was only about 2,000 per year. By the early 1970s, black trade unions were still not recognized or registered. Strikes by African workers continued to be illegal and were routinely broken up by the police, who kept a careful watch on all worker activities. In this context, the victimization of workers was rife, and Durban dock workers decided they should seek support from Hurley, whose anti-apartheid stance was well known. Rob Lambert, at that time National Secretary of the Young Christian Workers (YCW), was asked to organize a meeting with Hurley, at which the workers could bring their problems to his attention.[4] When asked by Lambert whether he would be willing to meet such a delegation, Hurley replied, 'I'm ready as soon as they're ready', and the meeting took place with minimal delay. A delegation of about twelve came to see Hurley, three of them union organizers, the others shop stewards at the docks, all dressed in the best clothes they could find.

The worker delegation began to explain to Hurley in detail the problems they were experiencing. They thought they would first have to persuade him to support their cause. He reassured them, however: 'I'm fully behind you; let's not waste time with you explaining to me what you are doing'. The remainder of the hour-long meeting was about various kinds of support the Church could offer and how Hurley himself could help. The workers requested public statements that could arouse sympathy for their plight, as well as material assistance for victimized union leaders such as those who had been dismissed after a strike by dockers in 1969. According to Lambert, Hurley made clear his 'absolutely unambiguous commitment' to support the workers publicly and to give material support, because 'what you are doing is very important for South Africa'.

As they came out of the meeting, the workers said to Lambert: 'What a man! He is with us'. Hurley's immediate pledge of support had taken them by surprise. Lambert said that there were many subsequent encounters between Hurley and worker leaders. These reinforced the sense that the workers were building something new, something constantly under threat by employers and security forces, as well as enduring harsh public opinion.

As a result of Pope Leo XIII's encyclical *Rerum Novarum* and Pope Pius XI's *Quadragesimo Anno*, both of which spoke strongly about worker rights, Hurley was comfortable at this point to intervene on behalf of workers, but as we have seen, he had a more equivocal position on the political process, especially in relation to universal franchise.

Hurley's commitment to the worker cause was as 'firm as the rock of Gibraltar', said Lambert. This was hugely important for finding a non-violent pathway to change. The worker leaders who met with him early in 1971 successfully organized a major dock-worker strike in October 1972 for higher wages, voluntary overtime, shorter working hours and more hygienic living conditions. From this strike an important lesson was learnt: that united mass action was possible, but that worker representatives should not be elected so that they could not be individually victimized.

The October 1972 dock-worker strike gave the workers new confidence, which spread like wildfire during the massive 1973 strikes. The number of workers involved in strikes rocketed to 100,000 by the end of the year. The 1973 strikes were difficult for companies and government to stop because they were short, sharp, mass walkouts. The police were surprisingly restrained in their response and did not carry out large-scale arrests as so often in earlier strikes. The result was that the 1973 strikes were successful in winning better wages, not only for the strikers but also for many other workers. This breathed life into the black trade union movement. Hurley's commitment to the dock workers' cause, and the encouragement he gave to successive delegations that came to see him, contributed to the confidence needed to take these bold steps.

Speaking at the University of the Witwatersrand about the 1973 strikes, Hurley said that 'if the strikes were an example of what blacks could achieve in a generally peaceful and orderly fashion, they should be welcomed enthusiastically'. Hurley was delighted that workers were coming alive, and he expressed his full support for the organizing that Lambert and others were doing. This was totally in keeping with the Church's social teaching. Black awareness was increasing, and the oppressed were speaking out again. 'When the oppressed speak, it is God [who] speaks', said Hurley.

THE CHURCH AND JUST WAGES

The 1973 strikes and Hurley's interactions with workers and union leaders had a profound effect on his response to the increasingly acute financial crisis of the Catholic Church's mission schools. These had been kept in existence by funds raised during the Bishops' Campaign of 1954. By 1973, those funds had long been exhausted, and there was little or no chance of a re-run because by this time a number of white Catholic schools were also closing due to a financial crisis. As the campaign funding ran out, the Church could only keep its mission schools by paying inadequate salaries. This greatly reduced the quality of the education and meant that the schools became a counter-witness to justice. There was such a strong emphasis on just wages, particularly as a result of the 1973 strikes, that Hurley felt obliged to take bold steps.

At this time he was close to Chief Mangosuthu Buthelezi, leader of what was then known as the KwaZulu Territorial Authority and was later to become the KwaZulu homeland. Though Buthelezi had accepted this position in a homeland structure, he steadfastly refused to accept full independence. As a result, he enjoyed political respectability because he had once been in the ANC Youth League and had been encouraged by the ANC leadership in exile to take part in homeland politics. After the massive crackdown on black political activity that followed the Sharpeville massacre, the homeland experiment seemed to offer some limited opening in a highly repressive situation. Such was his friendship with Hurley at this stage that Buthelezi even paid a special visit to the Archdiocesan Synod of 1972, where he was warmly received and addressed the delegates. For all these reasons, it seemed acceptable for Hurley to suggest handing over control of the mission schools to the KwaZulu authorities. It meant that the schools would no longer compromise the Church because of their unjust salaries. Yet it also involved compromise of another kind—association with the homeland system—and Hurley agonized long and hard about the decision.

A special clergy meeting, attended by seventy priests, several religious and lay people, reached a final decision. Addressing this gathering, Hurley said there had been much discussion since 1971 about the future of the schools. It was painful for the Church to hand over the schools because of the role they had played as centres of Catholic influence and a key means of instruction in the faith. Wages, however, were becoming a crucial issue, Hurley said, as shown by the Durban strikes earlier that year. If the Church could not afford to continue running the schools, other means of passing on the faith would have to be developed. The meeting voted strongly in favour of handing over the schools to the KwaZulu Territorial Authority.[5]

A week later, a similar decision was taken by the bishops in plenary session.[6] The mission schools in dioceses outside Natal would, wherever possible, be handed over to government or community. The bishops said that it was with regret that they had reached this conclusion after carefully studying the various options. In the case of schools run by religious congregations, efforts would be made to save at least some schools by arranging for several religious congregations to run them jointly. With regard to religious who would, as a result of the closure of schools, no longer be engaged in teaching, the bishops looked forward to their involvement in parish and home cate-chetics, adult education, literacy, development programmes and similar activities.

CONFRONTING THE SECURITY POLICE

One of the key methods the National Party government had used since Sharpeville to keep control of black political activity was incommunicado detention without trial. During the 1960s, there had been much public protest, in which Hurley had been active, about such detention being lengthened. The government paid no attention to mass protest meetings, however, and the periods of detention allowed by law were steadily extended until indefinite detention became the practice. The government was determined to keep this legislation on the books because it helped the security police extract information from detainees.

There was no more graphic index of the desperate decline in human rights in South Africa than the number of activists who died in detention. With the new stirrings of resistance as a result of Black Consciousness and industrial unrest, there were more detentions and a greater determination on the part of security police to break the spirit of activists by using torture. It was not difficult for security police to overstep the mark in interrogating detainees separated from family and friends and without access to legal or any other form of support or protection. When people died in detention, the security police claimed they had fallen down steps by accident, slipped on soap in the shower, jumped to their deaths or in other ways committed suicide. Between 1963 and 1985, sixty-one people died in detention under mysterious circumstances.[7] Ahmed Timol, a teacher and anti-apartheid activist, arrested in country-wide detentions, was one of the first. He died in police custody on 27 October 1971, allegedly having jumped to his death from the tenth floor of police headquarters in Johannesburg.

Fatima Meer, a lecturer in sociology and well-known Durban activist, was in touch with the families of Natal students detained at this time.[8] She understood their anxiety about their detained family members and bravely decided that pressure should be put on the security police, by informing them that community leaders were monitoring the situation. Her plan was to visit Colonel Frans Steenkamp, the head of the security police in Durban, together with other community leaders. The first person she invited to accompany her was Hurley: 'Of course I will come' was his response. She also persuaded a senior professor from the university and a leading attorney to be part of the delegation. The latter two withdrew at the last minute, but Hurley had made a commitment and kept to it.

Fatima Meer later described herself as 'a very short, small person' and Hurley by contrast as 'a great big person. We were from different religious groupings, and I had been fairly well known by the Special Branch as some sort of troublemaker, but he took nothing of that into consideration. To him, the mission was the important thing'. In a 45-minute interview with Hurley and Meer, Steenkamp assured them that he would see 'that nobody was tortured or ill-treated in a manner to disturb the community at large', a promise that would hardly have inspired confidence in Hurley and Meer.

PILGRIMS AGAINST MIGRANT LABOUR

Hurley's willingness to be associated with protests of various kinds was shown also in the encouragement he gave to a group of white clergy and laymen, who decided to walk from Grahamstown to Cape Town, a distance of 950 kilometres, to draw attention to the breakdown of family life caused by the migrant labour policy.[9] The group consisted of François Bill, Trevor de Bruyn, Norman Hudson, Athol Jennings,

Victor Kotze, David Russell, Augustine Schutte and Francis Wilson. Their aim was to urge the government to make it legal for every South African husband and wife to live together with their children in a family home. Beginning on 16 December 1972, the group walked between 25 and 40 kilometres per day. As they passed through various centres, they held religious services to help local communities understand the purpose of this 'Pilgrimage for Family Life'.

The walkers wanted to focus the attention of white people throughout South Africa on the hundreds of thousands of families who were forcibly separated by the country's race laws. Wives and children were not allowed to live with their husbands and fathers in the urban areas, and there was no work for the husbands in the home-lands, to which wives and children were confined by law. The walkers' aim was not to accuse anyone, but to confess that they themselves shared responsibility for the migrant labour system, which even the Cape Dutch Reformed Church Synod had, on 25 October 1965, described as a 'cancer' festering in the life of the nation. The pilgrims invited fellow white South Africans to confess their common guilt for allowing such a situation to continue and then to commit themselves to changing it. This protest was a form of 'White Consciousness' parallel to the Black Consciousness promoted by Steve Biko.

Robert Selby Taylor, as the Anglican Archbishop of Cape Town, Beyers Naudé of the Christian Institute and Hurley had agreed to lead the final service on Rondebosch Common on 14 January 1973, the day the walkers reached Cape Town. However, when the walkers were warned that their lives would be under threat from a right-wing group known as Scorpio the three leaders decided to walk in solidarity with the pilgrims from their overnight stop at Athlone to Rondebosch Common. Rev Athol Jennings, a Methodist minister who spent some time that day talking to Hurley as they walked the last few kilometres, said: 'He was a man that anybody with ideals, anybody with hopes, anybody with faith would want to be walking with . . . not only on that walk but [also] in other things he was engaged with'. Hurley and Jennings discussed 'commitment to the social implications of the gospel . . . and [to challenge] so many other evils in our system'.

Addressing the 6,000 people who attended the service on Rondebosch Common, Hurley pleaded with them not to allow what the walkers had done to end there. 'Let their pilgrimage spread throughout the land into the life of churches and the nation'. He recommended that a fund be established to help re-unite families divided by migrant labour and suggested that everyone sacrifice one meal per week and give the savings to the fund.

As soon as possible after the pilgrimage, Hurley arranged for migrant labour to be debated by the Durban Parliamentary Debating Society, and he supported the motion: 'That citizens should spare no effort in ridding the country of the migratory labour system which, next to slavery, is the worst form of exploitation and oppression'. He gave a graphic description of the social and moral decay that had 'permeated the life of the migrant labourer—prostitution, bigamy, illegitimacy, homosexuality, drunkenness, violence, family insecurity, the breakdown of parental discipline and juvenile delinquency'.[10]

DEFYING SCHOOL SEGREGATION

At their plenary session in January 1976, the Catholic bishops decided to open Catholic schools to all races—a long overdue decision.[11] The bishops had already indicated in their 1957 joint statement that some day such a policy would have to be implemented. Nothing had been done, however, about integrating the schools until 1973, when a survey was conducted by an American nun, Augusta Neal SND. Hurley, as head of the Bishops' Department of Catholic Schools, had invited her to South Africa to have a close look at Catholic education. The bishops wanted only the white schools to be surveyed, but when Neal discovered this on arrival in South Africa, she refused to go ahead unless the black schools were included. Hurley immediately agreed to this change, and the greatly expanded survey proceeded.

Neal found that religious sisters and brothers were heavily concentrated in schools for whites, with 70 per cent of the Church's education resources devoted to only 30 per cent of the school population, at a time when there was a growing realization that 80 per cent of Catholics in South Africa were black. Once the national picture had been made clear by Neal's survey, Sister Kathleen Boner OP said that younger members of her congregation, the Cabra Dominicans, who had come to South Africa from Ireland in the 1950s and 1960s to teach black children, admitted how surprised they had been to find themselves mainly assigned to white schools.

Vatican II created a new climate of freedom in the Church, in which silent acceptance of such a situation gave way to open criticism of the Church's focus on white education, which these young sisters regarded as 'a luxury freely available in government schools'. Because there were legislative barriers making it difficult for the Church to open black schools, the only way nuns could teach black pupils would be by admitting them to white schools. Moreover, these nuns felt that it was unacceptable for Catholic schools to be segregated. Similar discussions were taking place in other congregations, leading to a feeling that the situation was intolerable: a growing number of religious felt they could no longer in conscience teach whites only.

The Association of Women Religious (AWR) took up the issue and in 1975 resolved,

> That the time had come for those Catholic schools which had hitherto accepted only white pupils to give practical Christian witness to social justice by accepting non-white Christians into their schools. The policy should be one of quiet infiltration, with no sought-after publicity and that it should be adopted by all Catholic schools. The AWR requested the Bishops' Conference to give this resolution explicit support and approval.

The irony was that the South African government had itself encouraged the opening of the schools, by its 1973 request to certain convent schools to accept the children of black diplomats from other African countries and from so-called independent homelands. At that time the government was desperately cultivating more pliable African governments as part of its détente policy and wanted the ambassadors of its own so-called independent homelands to be taken seriously. When the children of such diplomats were accepted by a few Catholic schools, black South African parents began to pressurize those schools to accept their children as well. The dilemma for the nuns was all the more acute: on what grounds could they accept foreign black pupils and deny locals?

Mother Geneviève Hickey OP, Regional Vicar of the Cabra Dominicans in South Africa and an executive member of the AWR, was a 'woman of great integrity and determination', according to Boner; she wanted the 1975 AWR resolution to be put into action as soon as possible, at least in schools under her jurisdiction. The topic was still under discussion in the Bishops' Conference and ECAR (the Education Council of Associations of Religious), which brought together sisters' and brothers' congregations. The brothers were cautious, feeling they needed to stay within the law so as not to lose their schools. They were, nevertheless, keen to campaign for the law to be changed. No final decision about the opening of the schools had yet been taken by either the Bishops' Conference or by ECAR, and Hickey was afraid that the 'talking would go on for ever'.[12] She and a number of her sisters wanted to seize the moment. They decided that Springfield Convent in suburban Cape Town would admit eight coloured girls in January 1976.

Hickey was not willing to wait for another year, given the immense frustration among her sisters. On 20 November 1975 she had written to Cardinal McCann to say: 'We are concerned that the time is ripe and opportune for radical action'.[13] When Hurley heard about the step taken by Springfield Convent, he was concerned that the Cabra Dominicans had gone ahead before the bishops had officially agreed to the policy and phoned Hickey to find out why. It was characteristic of him to want things done in an orderly, systematic way, with clear communication and everyone on board. The Catholic schools should move forward as a body and with adequate preparation, he believed. There is, unfortunately, no record of what was said in his conversation with Hickey, each of them a leader with considerable determination, integrity and concern for justice, but differing in their view of the appropriate strategy and timing.

Clearly, there was impatience among the nuns: 'After so much high-minded discussion, so much verbal protest by the Church, it was a relief to be involved in real action, however small the scale'. Boner said that the nuns were excited by the action they had taken. Both the government and the bishops had to respond to a situation that was no longer hypothetical: children of other races had been admitted to several Catholic schools registered as exclusively white. The law had definitely been flouted, but there was not much the government could do about it. They feared there would be much bad publicity internationally if they demanded that the black children who had been admitted were made to leave these schools.

The AWR was also aware that, in future, adequate preparation should be undertaken. A number of schools began this preparation with a view to accepting pupils of all races from 1977. According to Sister Margaret Kelly OP:

> In 1976 we became involved in the exciting project of integrating the school. We began to prepare the staff by opening ourselves to the Scriptures, to the African aspects of

our South African history, and to the riches of different languages, cultures and traditions. But while the new knowledge helped, we became aware that the real problem lay in what [W. B.] Yeats called 'the foul rag-and-bone shop of the heart', where the junk of wrong attitudes and feelings of superiority cluttered our openness to others.[14]

Among the schools that undertook these preparations were Holy Rosary Convent and St Dominic's Priory in Port Elizabeth, which took an even bolder step in January 1977 by enrolling thirty-three African pupils in primary and secondary classes. After the admission of African pupils, the attitude of government became much more threatening: the Administrator of the Cape, Dr Munnik, warned that the government would consider closing these two schools 'forthwith' if they continued to admit black pupils. The black pupils already admitted were to be asked to leave immediately. But what could the government do if the Church refused?

After a week in which there was much debate in the media about open schools, Dr Piet Koornhof, the national Minister of Education, together with the Cape and Transvaal Administrators, declared that they were willing to discuss the problems of church institutions in order to find solutions. They warned, however, about the consequences if schools continued to disregard the law: they might lose their registration. And so began a period of continuous and intensive negotiations that lasted well into the 1980s.

Mother Marian O'Sullivan, successor to Mother Geneviève, gives a fascinating account of the delicate balancing act that a *verligte* (enlightened) politician like Koornhof performed, because of the opposition of his more conservative colleagues, most notably Dr Sybrand van Niekerk, Administrator of the Transvaal. In private meetings with Sister Marian, Koornhof, sitting on one of the sofas in his office with his legs crossed under him, revealed that he supported the nuns' decision to admit black pupils and promised to take up the issue with the cabinet. But, faced with a high-powered delegation led by Hurley and in the presence of more conservative government officials, he vigorously defended government policy and gave no hint of his support for what the nuns had done. He also made a press statement (*Cape Times*, 26 January 1977) that 'continued disregard for the law would have serious consequences'.

From time to time over the next year, O'Sullivan, who lived near parliament, would encounter Koornhof on his way to sittings. If he was on his own, she would remind him of his promise to take up the matter with the cabinet and ask what progress he was making. Most often he would tell her that he had not been able to have a cabinet discussion of the issue because the time was not yet ripe. If he was with colleagues, he would make sure he did not see her.

The result of the prolonged negotiations was that, over the next decade, the open schools' movement went through three phases. The first might be called the civil disobedience phase, when some schools simply took the initiative and admitted black pupils, though they knew such admissions were illegal. In the second, the government tried to control the process by requiring a detailed application for each child. In the third phase, confronted by increasing numbers, the government abandoned that system and tried to control the situation by imposing quotas linked to subsidies: if the proportion of black students exceeded the quota, the entire subsidy could be withdrawn.

Throughout these negotiations, Hurley led delegations to members of the national cabinet and administrators of provinces. Marist Brother Jude Pieterse, who as chair of ECAR organized such delegations, paid tribute to his 'ready availability at even the shortest notice'. Hurley's willingness to shoulder responsibility on behalf of the Bishops' Conference and to back the schools throughout the lengthy negotiations' period was 'a source of great encouragement and support'. Hurley's response would be immediate and unconditional: 'I'll be there', he would say without hesitation, whatever commitments he might need to re-arrange.

When the ECAR leaders were drafting a memorandum to present to Koornhof, they first met with Hurley in Durban to discuss at length what it should contain, before going to Hibberdene on the Natal south coast to work out the detailed wording. Then they returned to see Hurley in Durban to finalize the document with him. Sister Evangelist Quinlan RSM, who was chair of the AWR, remembers this experience: 'You knew that if you were bringing something to Archbishop Hurley you had better have . . . your homework done . . . It had to come in an acceptable form, one that would justify your putting such proposals . . . I always found Archbishop Hurley . . . a very good listener and sometimes an incisive questioner to what it was you were proposing'.

Quinlan was impressed by the quality of leadership Hurley gave to the open schools' movement, especially in leading delegations: 'He represented the Church so very well. When he saw that something was right, he was quite fearless and he was able to . . . pass on that whole spirit to others . . . It gave the whole movement a quality and a conviction and a worthwhileness that was very precious'.

Koornhof was clearly also impressed by Hurley. He thought him a friendly and able man—'a fine gentleman'. Hurley in turn thought that 'we were very lucky to have [Koornhof], because he didn't want to take up any sort of aggressive stand against us'. By contrast, Sybrand van Niekerk, Administrator of the Transvaal, 'was very aggressive. And he wanted to stop everything in his Transvaal Province', but Koornhof, according to Hurley, 'played it coolly, didn't get too excited. He wanted to discuss. He wanted to negotiate, he wanted to dialogue, and the more he dialogued, of course, the more the children began to filter into the schools . . . he left all the gaps we needed'.

The bishops discovered that Koornhof 'was surprisingly easy to talk to and very friendly'. In one of the many meetings, when there was a break in the negotiations, Archbishop Fitzgerald deliberately asked Hurley about his time on Robben Island. Koornhof was shocked to hear that Hurley had been on the island but amused when he discovered the context. Nevertheless, it took the bishops a long time to realize that, as Hurley commented many years later, 'had we been better politicians, we would have known that they were more afraid of us than we of them'. The reach of the Catholic Church was global. The government would have been aware, for example, that Pope Paul VI had personally declared his support for the open schools in South Africa.[15]

How significant was the open schools' movement? Pieterse thought it had given the Church 'tremendous credibility' in the eyes of ordinary people and had encouraged the Church to take stronger action against apartheid. In a way, it broke what might be called a 'civil disobedience barrier'. Previously the Church had been reluctant to break the law, but now it began to see such action as an important way of bringing about change in the face of government intransigence. The success of the open schools' movement gave the bishops courage to tackle other racial injustices within the Church. Thus, in 1977 they made a twenty-one-point 'Statement of Commitment' to remove racial discrimination within the Church. The statement began, 'We are encouraged by the support given to our policy of opening Catholic schools to all pupils regardless of race; . . . now, after prayerful reflection and in humble reliance on the wisdom and strength that comes from God's Spirit, we commit ourselves to the following programme'.

However, in the lengthy negotiations spread out over more than ten years, some of the prophetic edge of civil disobedience seems to have been blunted. Being obliged to apply officially for each admission, and later to comply with racial quotas, curtailed the number of black pupils admitted. These requirements inevitably involved compromise in the interest of holding on to the schools' registration and subsidies, and some black children lost out.

The Permanent Black Priests' Solidarity Group (PBPSG) was establidhed in 1975 to give support to Father Lebamang Sebidi, the first black rector of St. Peter's seminary, Hammanskraal, who came under pressure when he involved himself with Black Consciousness and Black Theology. Though the PBPSG remained a small group because many priests were afraid to join it, it was nevertheless influential on account of the support it received from Black Consciousness. Though the PBPSG accepted that the open schools were an important witness to the Gospel, it recommended extending the policy in four ways:

1. It was only white Catholic schools that had been opened. The PBPSG wanted to see the facilities at black Catholic schools improved so that white pupils could also be admitted to those schools.

2. They urged that the number of black children admitted be greatly increased and financial assistance provided for those who could not afford the fees.

3. Staff should also be integrated; all pupils should learn an African language and be educated to be critical of South Africa's social and political structure.

4. There should be preparatory programmes for all involved in open schools—parents, children and staff—so that they would be more aware of what was at stake.[16]

Attention was given to these suggestions, especially the last, by a special three-person resource team set up by the Department of (Catholic) Schools. This team, consisting of Marylyn Aitken of the Grail, Father Kevin Dowling CSSR (now Bishop of Rustenberg) and Sister Jane Frances OP, responded to appeals for assistance from schools that were preparing to admit children of all races.

SOWETO, 16 JUNE 1976

One of the most dramatic events in the long history of resistance to apartheid took place on 16 June 1976.[17] It was the most important event of the 1970s and a watershed in South African history. The protest that began in Soweto marked the height of Black Consciousness as the dominant form of internal resistance, but also the beginning of its decline. On 16 June some 20,000 Soweto school pupils marched against the government's imposition of Afrikaans—a third language for most blacks, in which many of their teachers were not qualified—as a medium of instruction at secondary level. When this protest was brutally suppressed, it developed into a total rejection of Bantu Education and of apartheid itself.

The marchers were described as 'good-humoured, high-spirited and excited'. They carried placards with slogans like 'Down with Afrikaans!' 'We are not Boers!' 'If we must do Afrikaans, Vorster [the prime minister] must do Zulu!' Eyewitnesses claimed that violence began when police tried to seize the posters and stop the march. Taunted by the students, they responded with tear gas. It is difficult to say what happened next, whether shots were fired or stones thrown first; but in either case, no verbal warning was given to students to disperse, and no warning shots were fired. 'All hell broke loose' when several pupils were shot dead.

Within the next 24 hours, shooting and violence spread through all the 28 townships that make up Soweto. A total of 143 vehicles and 139 buildings were partially or completely destroyed by fire. Vorster reported to parliament that orders had been given to 'maintain law and order at all costs'. Within a week, 146 people had died in the violence, and over the next few weeks unrest spread through many parts of South Africa. It was the biggest crisis since the Sharpeville massacre of 1960.

A few weeks after these events, the SACC held its annual conference at Hammanskraal. Hurley had been selected as the keynote speaker, and his address, 'Mobilization for Peace', was inevitably a response to the crisis. The events in Soweto had been no surprise to him; he had been expecting a showdown of this kind for some time. In fact, as we have seen, he had predicted to Verwoerd in the early 1950s that there would one day be a massive rejection of Bantu Education.

In his address to the SACC delegates representing a wide range of member churches from all over South Africa, Hurley urged them to work ecumenically to prevent an even more catastrophic explosion.[18] He began by comparing the South African situation to that of San Francisco expecting a cataclysmic earthquake along the St Andreas fault. That earthquake had been predicted and feared for many years, yet San Francisco appeared to be paralysed by its inevitability and had taken no steps to prepare. South Africa had long been expected to descend into overwhelming racial conflict. What happened on 16 June 1976 was a warning that such conflict was just a matter of time. The crisis demanded from the churches an 'all-out mobilization for peace', involving three aspects, said Hurley.

1. An honest and sober description of the present condition of South African society, emphasizing the explosive resentment of the black population [faced with] white privilege, white domination, white intransigence. There was no

shortage of material that could be drawn on for this description. Unless something was done about resentment of this kind, there would be violence, and
responsibility 'would fall squarely on the shoulders of the white population'.

2. Setting out the kind of change that would be needed in South Africa to avoid
violence. Majority rule was inevitable and whites should prepare themselves
psychologically for the change, while blacks had to prepare psychologically and
technically. Hurley was under no illusions about how difficult this would be:
'It involves coming to grips with moral, educational, economic and political
problems of the first magnitude'. Once again he stressed that special research
would not be needed. Much had already been done in particular by SPROCAS
(Study Project on Christianity in an Apartheid Society), of which he had been
part. What was needed was a brief presentation of the educational, economic
and political options that SPROCAS had identified.

3. Communicating the above to each sector of the white population of South
Africa, both the Church and the wider society. For the Church, there would need
to be different presentations for leadership, clergy, congregations and church
organizations. With regard to the secular world, the message should reach
government, the professions, the media, universities, industry, commerce, the
farming community, the trade unions, ratepayers and housewives as well as
cultural, social and welfare groups. The purpose would be to describe the
situation and its dangers, persuade the white community to face the facts and
indicate the requirements for peaceful change. This message would need to be
communicated by every possible means.

Hurley proposed that an ad hoc agency be set up under the SACC, involving
as many churches as possible, including those that were not members of the SACC.
Key to the whole operation would be an executive and advisory body of ten to
twelve full-time staff, with voluntary helpers and branches in many centres. By
Hurley's own admission, the proposal was highly ambitious, but because of the
crisis, he felt sure that the churches would be willing to 'support the undertaking
with personnel and finances'. The whole effort would need a 'mobilization of
prayer from end to end of our country'.

One wonders whether Hurley had sufficiently prepared key players in the SACC
for this ambitious proposal. In the absence of such careful lobbying it seemed to fall
flat. The SACC apparently misunderstood what he was calling for. Its response was
limited to commissioning a high-powered audio-visual presentation of the South
African situation. Though this was made and was shown to many groups around
South Africa, Hurley had been calling for much more.

Many years later, the SACC admitted that Hurley had spoken a prophetic word
at their 1976 conference which should have been 'picked up and acted on with great
zeal and urgency'.[19]

The government had seen the full power of the Black Consciousness Movement
(BCM) in the student protests of 16 June and the widespread unrest that followed its
harsh suppression. This led to the detention of Steve Biko, who had become a symbol

of the struggle, and to his death in detention on 12 September 1977. One month after Biko's death, the government banned seventeen groups associated with Black Consciousness, including several newspapers. Though new Black Consciousness organizations subsequently came into existence, the overall influence of the BCM steadily waned, as the ANC returned to its leading role in resistance to apartheid.

DIAKONIA

A few months before Hurley's address to the SACC's 1976 conference, he had launched a new initiative similar to the one he suggested to the SACC, but with its focus restricted to the Greater Durban Area. This was known as Diakonia (the Greek word for 'service'), an ecumenical social justice agency, which he had first proposed three years earlier in an address to the annual general meeting of what was then known as the Natal Council of Churches. The proposal fell on fertile ground there, as well as at the 1974 Synod of the Archdiocese of Durban.[20] On the latter occasion, Hurley explained that the idea of Diakonia arose from four 'converging considerations':

1. The need for full-time personnel if anything was to be achieved in promoting social justice.
2. That in responding to human needs, there was a considerable overlap in welfare, development and liberation. Therefore, they should be worked on in tandem.
3. That no church should ever do on its own what could be done with others. Christian service, or *diakonia*, 'offers the best opportunities to the churches to engage in ecumenical collaboration'.
4. That wherever there is a social problem, there is the side of the haves and the side of the have-nots. The haves need to become aware of the injustices and privations for which they are responsible, and the have-nots must have opportunities for development and liberation.

In the light of these four considerations, Hurley called for an agency that 'could give welfare, development, liberation and ecumenical collaboration their rightful place in Christian endeavour to meet human need'.

A new kind of 'deacon' would help the Church meet such needs. As the early Church had handed over the distribution of relief for the poor to seven specially chosen deacons, the Church in this age should look for people 'with ability, training and time at their disposal' to staff agencies like Diakonia. The effort would need to concentrate on a manageable geographical area because 'to give a single agency too wide a field of operations would be to frustrate and to dissipate'. Hurley suggested that the Greater Durban Area would provide a suitable area for the initial experiment, after which Diakonia could be replicated in other areas.

After receiving unanimous support from the Natal Council of Churches and the Synod of the Archdiocese of Durban, widely representative ecumenical consultations were held in 1974 and 1975. The purpose was to flesh out Hurley's basic proposal and to enable the seven denominations that had expressed an initial interest to take ownership of the proposal and strengthen its ecumenical dimension. This was not to be a marginal effort by a few activists: Hurley wanted welfare, development and liberation to be mainstreamed as an integral part of Church life. As Diakonia's draft constitution put it, the purpose would be 'to activate the concern of its member churches in the social field, and focus this on problem situations and on welfare, development and liberation projects'.

Diakonia was not intended to work on behalf of the churches, but to conscientize churches and church groups so that they would themselves become involved. Hurley sounded a warning note that 'a vigorous and effective Diakonia that would scarcely touch the lives of Christian congregations and their members would be a failure'. He wanted Diakonia to guard against spinning off from the churches, leaving them untouched by its concerns and activities. How to guard against this danger? By 'constant review, regular self-examination of its success or otherwise in activating the social conscience of its member churches'.

Once sufficient consensus had been reached by the consultations, a steering committee was established. Under Hurley's leadership, it set about finalizing the constitution and the plan for initial funding and staffing, and rented office accommodation in the St Andrew's Centre of the Durban Central United Church, which linked the Presbyterian and United Congregational Churches.

Diakonia came into formal existence in 1976, some months before the events in Soweto that year. The longstanding sufferings and frustrations that boiled over on 16 June had been the reason for Hurley's establishing the organization and had been much in his mind throughout the lengthy preparations.

The inaugural meeting was held on 25 March 1976 at St Andrew's Centre.[21] The seven founding members were the African Methodist Episcopal, Anglican, Catholic, Evangelical Lutheran, Methodist, Presbyterian and United Congregational Churches—all of whom were also members of the Natal Council of Churches. Diakonia worked closely with the Natal Council and eventually merged with it to form the Diakonia Council of Churches in 1994.

At the inaugural meeting, Hurley was elected chair, a position he held for the next 4 years. Addressing the meeting, he thanked the German Catholic mission aid organization, *Misereor*, for meeting Diakonia's financial needs for its first year of operation. Hurley's name and reputation had been key to securing this funding and continued to be a great asset. Diakonia hoped, he said, 'to contribute a humble share to the growth of awareness of social evil and to the intensification of efforts, particularly within Church communities, to replace that evil with good'. Its main concern would be 'information, communication, inspiration': motivating its members to action rather than acting on their behalf.

A week before Diakonia's inaugural meeting, the media reported that Joseph Mdluli, a political activist from one of Durban's oldest townships, Lamontville, had died in security police custody the day after being detained. There was much suspicion that Mdluli had been tortured to death during interrogation. At Diakonia's inaugural meeting, Hurley called for a full judicial inquiry into his death and announced that Diakonia would be holding a special 'Evening of Reflection on the Death of Joseph Mdluli' in Emmanuel Cathedral on April 5. It was Diakonia's first public event, and over a thousand people filled the cathedral. They voted unanimously in favour of Hurley's call for a judicial inquiry, and a letter to that effect was sent to the Prime Minister.

This focus on Mdluli's death put Diakonia on the map—bringing the new organization to the notice of the ever-vigilant security police, and developing expectations especially in the black community. During Hurley's four years as chair, Diakonia continued its prophetic focus on the injustice of incommunicado detention and the grave human rights violation of death in detention, as well as the housing crisis in the Greater Durban Area, where about 50 per cent of the population lived in shacks without water, electricity or proper sewerage. The plight of workers and their unions was also brought under the spotlight by Diakonia's publication of a 'Worker Rights Statement', endorsed by the churches.

18

'No' to Apartheid War

By 1974 St Peter's Catholic Seminary at Hammanskraal, north of Pretoria, was becoming well known as a conference venue. In Catholic circles it already had a reputation for the radical views of its students and past students, all of whom were black. Soon it began to attract equally radical conferences. It was to become especially famous as a result of the SACC national conference held there in early August 1974. Unlike previous SACC conferences, this was fully residential, which meant that the white delegates, though in the majority, were more exposed to black concerns than at any previous conference.[1]

Many black people in South Africa were excited by the victory of the liberation movement, FRELIMO, over the Portuguese colonial forces in Mozambique, anticipating that this would spell the end of apartheid. Much else was happening in southern Africa that raised the political temperature at the 1974 SACC conference. A border war was taking place in South-West Africa (now Namibia) and Angola.[2] On the one side was South Africa with its allies, UNITA (the National Union for the Total Independence of Angola), backed by the United States. On the other were the MPLA (Popular Movement for the Liberation of Angola), SWAPO (South-West African People's Organization), and their allies, the Soviet Union and Cuba. South Africa's aim was to prevent SWAPO from using Angola as a base for infiltration into South-West Africa. Guerrilla warfare was also escalating in what was then known as Rhodesia (now Zimbabwe). Internal developments, such as the extensive labour unrest of 1973 and the widespread influence of Black Consciousness, had encouraged black people in South Africa to be more outspoken.

All these factors had led to South Africa arming itself as never before, at least not since the end of World War II.[3] Military training and service for young white men were intensified, and the defence budget grew beyond recognition. Indeed, during the 1960s and 1970s South Africa had been steadily transforming itself from a police to a military state. By 1972, the initial national service period for white conscripts had been increased from 9 to 12 months, with an additional 19 days service annually for the next 5 years.

Before the 1974 SACC Conference, the churches had not come to grips with this trend. In the heightened atmosphere of the conference, Douglas Bax, a white Presbyterian theologian who had been reflecting on conscientious objection to military service for a number of years, decided to propose a resolution that would cause the member churches of the SACC to face up to an escalation of events 'that might soon engage southern Africa in a holocaust'. The proposal opened up major issues for the churches. The core of the lengthy resolution was that South Africa was 'a fundamentally unjust and discriminatory society' and therefore a threat to peace throughout southern Africa.

Military might was being mobilized to defend this unjust and discriminatory society. Inevitably the question arose: Was it right for Christians to participate in that military effort? They could not regard military service as an unquestioned duty simply because it was demanded by the state. The traditional view of both the Catholic and Reformed churches was that taking up arms was only justifiable, if at all, in order to fight a just war. The resolution proposed by Bax and seconded by Beyers Naudé of the Christian Institute ended with these words:

The Conference therefore:

1. deplores violence as a means to solve problems;
2. calls on its member churches to challenge all their members to consider in view of the above whether Christ's call to take up the Cross and follow Him in identifying with the oppressed does not, in our situation, involve becoming conscientious objectors;
3. calls on those of its member churches who have chaplains in the military forces to reconsider the basis on which they are appointed and to investigate the state of pastoral care available to the communicants at present in exile or under arms beyond our borders and to seek ways and means of ensuring that such pastoral care may be properly exercised.[4]

The resolution also stated: 'The Conference prays for the Government and people of our land and urgently calls on them to make rapid strides towards radical and peaceful change in our society so that the violence and war to which our social, economic and political policies are leading, may be avoided'.

The resolution, though highly controversial at the time, was passed unanimously by the 100 delegates after a 5-hour debate. When it was reported in the media, there was an uproar, especially from the government. The general secretary of the SACC, John Rees, observed that 'the negative reaction has come so far from white media, white newspapers, white politicians and certain white churchmen'. He said they had accepted apartheid propaganda that the South African Defence Force (SADF) was shielding South Africa's citizens from a military threat posed by enemy forces massing on the frontiers of South-West Africa and Angola. For the black majority, said Rees, the resolution accurately reflected the situation.

P. W. Botha, as Minister of Defence, moved swiftly to have defence legislation amended to provide for a fine of up to R10,000 or ten years' imprisonment or both for anyone trying to persuade anyone else to avoid military service. Not only was conscientious objection unacceptable to the state, but any positive discussion of it would be illegal.

Hurley's initial response to the SACC's conscientious objection resolution was that the clash between the Prime Minister B. J. Vorster and the SACC about the resolution indicated that the time of crisis for South Africa was close. Aware that the SACBC would undoubtedly discuss the resolution at their next plenary meeting, he held back from expressing his own views and simply said that, in whatever discussion might take place among the bishops, they would have to be guided by what the Second Vatican Council had to say about war, especially such passages as this: 'It seems right that laws make humane provision for the case of those who, for reasons of conscience, refuse to bear arms, provided, however, that they accept some other form of service to the human community'.

The Administrative Board of the SACBC spoke out strongly against the Defence Further Amendment Bill.[5] They agreed that, should it become law, they would 'be bound in conscience to disobey it and would expect clergy and people of their own and other Churches to do likewise'. This was the first time since the Church Clause of 1958 that the bishops had threatened civil disobedience.

Caroline Clark, writing in the *Sunday Times*, described Hurley's next statement as the most radical on this topic by any church leader.[6] He had reached the conclusion, said Hurley, that the people of South Africa should at all costs avoid getting involved in a border war; in fact, there 'should be conscientious objection to getting involved in such a war', and 'conscientious objection should be adopted as a principle by the churches' even 'at the risk of confrontation with the Government. Confrontation has to occur sometime'.

It is interesting to compare this approach with that of the SACC. While Hurley fully supported the Hammanskraal resolution, his emphasis was different. The SACC put the responsibility on the individual facing the call-up; Hurley felt it was the responsibility of the churches to help the individual by declaring the war to be just or unjust. If it was unjust, the Church should conscientiously object to it. He believed that:

1. If South Africa gets involved in a border war, this war will have been provoked by the policy of apartheid.
2. To defend white South African society by force of arms is to defend the policy of apartheid.
3. To defend apartheid is to defend an unjust cause.
4. It is not permissible for Christians to fight an unjust war.

But the essence of Hurley's statement was that 'we should start negotiating in South Africa before the armed conflict really starts', because 'unless we can claim that a strenuous effort has been made to reach understanding between blacks and whites, including liberation movements, conscientious objection seems the only possible stand. . . . I appeal to all individuals to go into this matter in conscience'. He did, however, state that he 'would be obliged to respect the conscience of anyone who thought deeply about it and decided he was morally obliged to fight'.[7]

On the Sunday when this statement appeared in leading papers, Hurley preached over the radio from Durban's Emmanuel Cathedral.[8] He spoke about the prophet Jeremiah, in words that could describe his own opposition to involvement in the border war. Hurley's view was rejected by many, including priests and laity of his own archdiocese and even his fellow bishops. Jeremiah, said Hurley over the radio, was 'gentle and retiring by disposition [but] thrown into the maelstrom of politics and war . . . In his frustration at a God who made him do the impossible, the prophet cried out':

You have seduced me, Lord,

And I have let myself be seduced . . .

Each time I speak the word,

I have to howl and proclaim, 'Violence and ruin!'

The word of the Lord has meant for me

insult, derision, all day long.

I used to say: 'I will not think about him,

I will not speak in his name any more'.

Then there seemed to be a fire burning in my heart,

imprisoned in my bones'.

(Jer. 20:7–9 JB)

Hurley continued, 'Anybody who reflects and prays on the gospel sympathizes with Jeremiah. We know exactly how he felt . . . In our own small way we recognize the situation: God's word is like a fire burning in my heart, imprisoned in my bones, calling me to do the impossible'.

Hours later, the storm began to crash around Hurley, and he experienced something of the 'insult and derision' known by Jeremiah. Defence Minister P. W. Botha called him a 'lackey of communism' and a 'liar' for his statement about conscientious objection. Senator Denis Worrall described Hurley's statement as 'irresponsible in the extreme and devoid of any serious religious, ethical or philosophical justification. . . . For one man to declare a whole society unjust to the point where it should not defend itself is an enormous judgment'.[9]

Priests, especially those working with white Catholics, most of whom were solidly behind the SADF efforts in the border war, said Hurley's statement was unacceptable and untimely. Many white lay people were shocked and angry about it, in particular those who had sons on the border.[10] It was an agonizing time for Hurley, because although he had called for conscientious objection, he felt acutely the plight of young white men doing military service, and he understood the anxiety of their parents.[11]

Even Hurley's good friend Nadal was critical: Hurley, he said, had reached an intellectual conclusion without seeing the emotional uproar that would be caused by his statement. Public support for Hurley from his brother bishops was limited to a statement from Peter Butelezi, Auxiliary Bishop in Johannesburg, the only black bishop at that time. While Butelezi did not 'automatically agree with' Hurley's call, he said that it had 'served a good purpose' in that it highlighted such a breakdown in communication between whites and blacks that each did not know what the other was thinking. Fitzgerald of Johannesburg, while saying that he held Hurley in the highest regard intellectually and as a loyal churchman, stated that 'Catholics, no matter which country they are in, have always risen to the call to defend the country. I am quite sure that in the future they would play their part in the defence of this country'. McCann of Cape Town, though declining to state whether he supported Hurley's refuse-to-fight call, urged P. W. Botha to withdraw his allegation that Hurley was a liar.

Leo Boyd of the Progressive Party said that basically what Hurley was trying to convey was the urgent need for negotiation among the races to start without delay. Boyd fully supported that part of Hurley's statement but did not agree with what he had said about not serving on the border. That should be decided in conscience by each conscript.

Despite much opposition, Hurley refused to withdraw his statement and said that, like Beyers Naudé, he would be willing to face conviction and imprisonment for his stand. It was not, however, church leaders like Naudé or Hurley who were charged and imprisoned for their stand, but young men who individually objected to military service. Some of the more notable were Anton Eberhard (1977); Peter Moll (1979); Richard Steele (1980); Charles Yeats (1981); Michael Viveiros, Neil Mitchell and Billy Paddock (1982); Etienne Essery, Adrian Paterson and Peter Hathorn (1983). The legislation was changed in 1984: those who could prove they had genuinely religious reasons for objecting were allowed to do alternative service of a non-military nature. Others, whose grounds for objecting were seen to be mainly or exclusively political, continued to be sentenced, as in the case of Ivan Toms, David Bruce and Charles Bester (1988); and Saul Batzofin (1989).[12]

Raymond Slater, the Headmaster of Hilton College, one of the leading private schools in Natal, was approached by Charles Yeats, a former head boy of the school and captain of the Natal Schools' rugby team.[13] Yeats was faced with call-up papers a month after completing his final undergraduate examinations in 1977; he had a dilemma in conscience about military service and wanted advice. Slater, a Presbyterian, remembered Hurley's brave statement about conscientious objection in 1974. He suggested that Yeats, an Anglican, should request his advice and arranged for the young man to meet Hurley.

Yeats remembered little of this first meeting except that

> I was drawn into a great love for the tall man, who beamed at me kindly from behind his thick-framed spectacles and who calmed my sense of fear. In the coming years, that calming was to be very important, for while I never lost the fear of confronting the issue of military service under apartheid, I was emboldened by the sense that this great Christian figure was with me.

Loek Goemans, who was active in the Durban Conscientious Objector Support Group (COSG), said that many other objectors—not only Catholics, Christians, or even believers, but from across the spectrum—had similar meetings with Hurley. They too were fearful of the course on which they were embarking and wanted his support.[14] Hurley said little more to Yeats than that Christians have a duty to follow their conscience and that there is a more important duty than obedience to the state. 'I found that very reassuring', said Yeats, 'because it was the truth I had worked out for myself but which few leaders of the time were actually saying publicly'.

Yeats hesitated about declaring his objection to military service and decided, in 1979, to go overseas for further study. With an MBA from the University of the Witwatersrand, he was able to take up a trainee position in an accounting firm in London. Nevertheless, he informed the South African Defence Force of his where-abouts. They told him that his call-up could be deferred. The British media, however, kept the nightmare of apartheid repression powerfully in his mind, including the trials and imprisonment of the cousins Peter Moll and Richard Steele, pioneering conscientious objectors. Yeats felt an acute sense of guilt that he was in England while others were bravely giving witness to their beliefs and taking the consequences. Unable to resist the pull of conscience, despite the attractiveness of a promising financial career in London, he decided to return to South Africa and follow the exam-ple of Moll and Steele.

Once home again in 1980, Yeats immediately wrote to inform the SADF exemp-tion board of his return and his willingness to perform an alternative, non-military form of national service but not to serve in the army. While waiting to see how the Defence Force would respond, he decided to model the sort of alternative service he had in mind by working for Diakonia in Durban.

The Defence Force sent their military police to arrest Yeats at Diakonia on his twenty-fifth birthday in 1981. The startled military police were invited to join in prayers for Yeats before they arrested him. Later, Yeats said his arrest had been the result of a 'muddle' because the letter he had sent from England indicating his atti-tude to military service had not been passed on by defence headquarters in Pretoria to the regiment to which he had been assigned in Natal, nor had his letter informing the Defence Force about his return to South Africa. Natal Command had therefore been looking for him for two years, despite the fact that he had made no effort to hide his whereabouts: in fact, just the opposite. Once Natal Command became aware that he was actually asking to be tried as a conscientious objector if they would not allow him to do alternative national service, he was released pending his trial.

Yeats then chose an even more appropriate form of alternative national service by becoming secretary to the Anglican Diocese of Namibia, a position that required him to travel in the war zone as an unarmed civilian. In visiting the Anglican missions, he would frequently have to drive through areas 'strewn with landmines'. He was able to witness 'at first hand the cruelty and wastefulness' of the war.

By May 1981 he had been re-arrested and faced court martial for refusing to do military service. Here again Hurley came into the story. He was invited to give expert evidence about the Church's teaching on conscientious objection, along with the recently appointed Anglican Archbishop of Cape Town, Philip Russell.

According to Chris Swart, Yeats told the tribunal how his views on military service had developed since his decision to 'accept Christ as my Saviour and Lord' while still at school. Hearing about the army's role in the shooting in Soweto in 1976 'together with subsequent prayer and study' had led him to become a Christian pacifist. His objection to the South African war was that it was avoidable by negotiation. He argued that there was a civil war in South Africa and that South Africa's presence in Namibia was illegal. Yeats quoted from an Anglican synodical statement that South Africa was morally indefensible.

When Hurley was called to give evidence, Chris Swart said that he did so in 'powerful, concise and moving answers'. Hurley said that the Church should not involve itself in politics in the narrow sense of party politics. Because it promoted moral values, however, it was inevitably involved in politics in the broadest sense. In questions of conscience involving moral law, the Christian had an obligation to choose the Church before the State. He stressed that though Christ's teaching was thoroughly in favour of non-violence, the human instinct was for self-preservation and self-defence. The Church had compromised itself in accepting this position and had found a way of accommodating violent self-defence to the teachings of Christ. As a result, he believed the Church had failed to live the law of love and non-violence. Pacifists, however, played a prophetic role towards the Church, reminding it of Jesus' message, which was strongly non-violent.

Though Hurley conceded that the government had a right to decide whether to defend a country with force of arms, he added that an individual could differ from this view and follow the higher ideal of the teachings of Christ. That, he said, was why he admired 'the stand taken by the accused in this court. Some of the greatest progress in human history has come from individuals who felt they could not bring themselves to accept laws that conflicted with their consciences'. The president of the court martial, Colonel P. J. de Klerk, asked Hurley whether he agreed with Yeats that apartheid was morally indefensible. Hurley responded, 'In the light of how apartheid has worked out in the last 30 years, I would consider his judgement that apartheid is indefensible to be the judgement of an informed conscience'.

Having given his evidence on the second day of Yeats's trial, Hurley chose to stay on for a third day for the verdict and sentence to be given. It was clear that the verdict would be 'guilty' and the sentence severe, so he wanted to support Yeats at this difficult moment. Yeats reported:

> Again the force of his being there was to bring calm, to keep back the fear. In an earlier recess, he said to me that he had asked the sisters at the convent where he was staying, to pray, and that when the sisters get praying, no earthly power need be feared. [His] humour and their prayers were enough to help me meet the first moments of captivity when it came, after which the rest could be endured . . . As before and as he had done for so many others, he was able to still the storm of apartheid then raging about me and to impart the courage to go on.

Hurley's support for conscientious objection, shown in his dramatic call of 1974 and his support for individual objectors, 'earned him a sack full of hate mail', as Yeats put it. 'It struck at the heart of the minority white population's fear for their security in a post-apartheid South Africa' . . . and resulted in Hurley's being 'vilified by conservative groupings in Church and state'. Hurley, however, remained resolute in his defence of conscientious objectors and in his belief that their witness was one of the most significant ways of making peace in southern Africa. He readily lent his name to a statement by nine top church leaders who expressed their concern that Yeats had been sentenced to twelve months in detention barracks. These leaders, who included the national heads of the Anglican, Catholic, Congregational, Methodist and Presbyterian churches, urged the government to provide alternative forms of non-military national service for the many young men facing the same dilemma as Yeats.

Just over a year later, Hurley praised a young high school teacher, Neil Mitchell, the first Catholic objector to be sentenced to one year in detention barracks.[15] In a media statement, he spoke of Mitchell having joined 'the select band of conscientious objectors who are prepared to pay a heavy price for their adherence to the noblest ideals of non-violence. All honour to him'. Mitchell treasures a personal letter received from Hurley while serving his sentence in detention barracks at Voortrekkerhoogte. He thanked Mitchell for his 'splendid witness' and promised that he would be mentioned in prayers and discussions at the Bishops' Conference: 'May the Lord be good to you and sustain you as you undergo your period of trial for his sake and the sake of his people'.

As the number of young men opposed to taking part in an apartheid war grew steadily in the early 1980s and many went overseas to escape the call-up, a new organization came into being. Unlike COSG, this did not campaign only for a more just deal for objectors, but also for a bolder and more radical objective, as was clear from its name: the End Conscription Campaign (ECC). Speaking at an ECC Festival held at Wits University in June 1985, Hurley outlined how the South African military effort was linked to injustice:

A huge military effort has to be mounted in Namibia to contain guerrilla activity. A vast system of security has to be arranged to guard against sabotage. Even at a time when South Africa is in great danger of incurring economic sanctions, it is felt necessary to mount cross-border raids into neighbouring countries. Soldiers have to be drafted to assist the police in quelling township unrest. All because of the injustice perpetrated in the name of apartheid. The resentment of those suffering under the system has reached the point where violence seems unquenchable.[16]

In this context, said Hurley, thousands of young men found it 'utterly distasteful to be mobilized into the military machine designed to maintain this policy over the angry reactions of the victims'.

He indicated the full support of the Catholic Bishops' Conference for the ECC:

We are concerned at the growing numbers of young men faced with a crisis of conscience caused by their conscription. The choices for them are

1. Serving in an army with whose mode of operation they cannot agree.

2. Doing 6 years alternative service if they are recognized as religious pacifists.

3. Serving a 6-year sentence if they object to the war on the grounds that they believe it to be unjust.

4. Leaving the country and living in exile.

Therefore we join our voices with those who have already asked for an end to conscription.

By 1988, though it was becoming clear that apartheid might be on its last legs, the plight of objectors had not been substantially improved. A nationwide group of 143 young men simultaneously announced, in several centres, that they would not serve in the South African Defence Force because it upheld an unjust system. Nineteen of these, mostly university students and graduates, told a press conference in Durban, on 3 August, that they were patriotic South Africans keen to make a constructive contribution to changing the country. They chose to announce their stand at Hurley's office and invited him to chair their media conference and make some introductory remarks.[17] He took the opportunity to warmly congratulate the group: 'I would like to express from the fullness of my heart my congratulations, my full moral support for them, and the intention to do all I can to further their cause'.

Given Hurley's strong support for conscientious objectors and his firm rejection of South Africa's military effort in the absence of any substantial efforts to promote genuine negotiations with the black majority, his attitude to military chaplains may come as a surprise.[18] Should the Church provide military chaplains? Should such chaplains be allowed to wear military uniforms and accept payment from the defence force? These issues were frequently debated by the bishops. On one occasion, when the argument had become intense, the full-time chaplains were summoned to a bishops' meeting. Father (later Bishop) Reginald Cawcutt said, 'I think we'd made them mad because we actually attended the meeting in uniform. . . . All the bishops were there and they asked questions and embarrassed us and put the big sweat on us'.

It was a great surprise to Cawcutt and his fellow chaplains, who had tended to see Hurley as a strong opponent of their position, that at the end of a lot of wrangling, it was he who said: 'Look, these men are only there because we put them there. We must give them our support; they have got to stay there'. The majority voted in favour of that position. Cawcutt said, 'That was when I began to see what a just man he was, how he would always defend the underdog'. Presumably Hurley also gave this support because he was aware of how much anxiety there was among white parents about their sons in the army: this would have been exacerbated if the bishops had withdrawn the chaplains.

19

Leading the Bishops

The 1980s saw the height of apartheid repression in South Africa—and of resistance.[1] After the widespread strikes of 1973 and the Soweto uprising of 1976, the government was under great pressure to move away from apartheid. To co-opt more conservative members of the black community and win credibility in the eyes of an increasingly hostile international community, the government had to make concessions. But the changes it made led to the most extensive revolt in South Africa's history and a worsening of the international climate.

The first of the reforms, in 1979, legalized black trade unions, giving them the right to negotiate pay and working conditions. Some apartheid laws, such as the Mixed Marriages, Immorality and Separate Amenities Acts, were scrapped, as well as the Pass Laws. These changes, however, were regarded as superficial; the pillars of apartheid like the Group Areas Act and the homeland policy were kept in place. The government handed over control of black townships to black local councils, arguing that this met the demand for a more democratic South Africa. These councils were, however, regarded as government agencies, especially since they were expected to do apartheid's dirty work, for example, collecting rents.

The year 1983 saw disastrous constitutional changes: coloureds and Indians were given their own separate chamber in what was known as the 'tricameral parliament', which was dominated by the all-white chamber. In a move that the political analyst Allister Sparks described as 'sharpening the edge of racial discrimination in an especially provocative way', the African majority was totally excluded from these new constitutional provisions, limited as they were. Apart from having the vote for local government in urban areas, their only political right was a vote in the homelands, whether or not they lived there or had ever done so. The majority of whites thought the constitutional changes a 'step in the right direction'; to black people, they were totally unacceptable and deeply offensive. They did, however, sense the weakness and desperation that lay behind these steps; this made them all the more certain that the end was in sight for apartheid.

In August 1983, more than 500 organizations—community, religious, professional, sports, worker, student, women and youth—formed an alliance called the

United Democratic Front (UDF). Its purpose was to campaign against the tricameral constitution and the Koornhof Bills, which legislated for black control of urban councils; by this time Koornhof was Minister of Constitutional Development. Black politics was ignited by the new legislation: soon 700 more organizations had joined the UDF, including a number with Indian, coloured and white membership. In total, the UDF represented more than two million people.

For a year the UDF campaigned against Botha's reforms with relative freedom, addressing mass rallies in every corner of South Africa. It was the most sustained and widespread political campaign the country had ever seen and could hardly have been more successful. All the elections, whether for the tricameral parliament or the local black councils, were heavily boycotted. Black, coloured and Indian people—and even some whites—gained a powerful sense of what they could achieve as a united, non-racial movement. The overwhelming majority wanted to work together rather than allowing themselves to be divided by the new constitution or fobbed off with petty concessions.

There was much anger in the African townships against those who involved themselves in the local council system. This was the start of what Sparks called 'the great black revolt', provoked by rent increases imposed by the councils. Few blacks had been willing to make themselves available as candidates. Those who did were often corrupt and despised as collaborators with the government. In September 1984, protests against the rent increases were met by the police's indiscriminate use of firearms, beatings and unprovoked assaults. The protestors then turned on black councillors, killing some of them on their own doorsteps and burning their expensive houses and cars.

From the Vaal Triangle, the resistance spread all over South Africa, to rural and urban areas. Heavily armed riot police were constantly on the move in the townships; the young stone-throwing 'comrades' scattering when they appeared and rapidly re-grouping once they departed. The violence worsened in 1985. At Uitenhage in the Eastern Cape, a massacre took place on the twenty-fifth anniversary of the Sharpeville shootings. Riot police opened fire on a crowd at a funeral, killing twenty and wounding twenty-seven, most of them shot in the back. The UDF continued its protests, and the unrest increased. In Natal—known today as KwaZulu-Natal—rivalry between the UDF and Chief Mangosuthu Buthelezi's Inkatha movement, which collaborated with the government on many matters but refused to accept homeland independence, led to the worst violence of all, as we shall see in Chapter 28, reaching a climax just before South Africa's first democratic elections in April 1994 and continuing for some years after that.

In July 1985, the government declared a state of emergency in parts of South Africa. This was extended to the whole country a year later, days before the tenth anniversary of the Soweto uprising. Media restrictions made it difficult to know the full scale of what was happening. About 34,000 people were detained—a number of them priests, nuns and lay church workers—in a desperate effort by the government to quell resistance. In some areas the police appeared to give up trying to maintain law and order; the vacuum was filled by 'people's courts', which dealt out a rough and ready form of justice. The 'necklace' became a method of punishment, used especially by youth against people suspected of passing information to the police: a rubber tyre filled with petrol was put around the condemned person's neck and then set alight, leaving the victim to die in a most horrible way.

The township unrest of 1984 and 1985, shown on TV screens all over the world, destroyed business confidence in South Africa and gave new vigour to the campaign for economic sanctions. Faced with this threat from abroad and industrial unrest at home, as well as government's failure to make any positive impact on the situation, business and other leaders began to visit Lusaka to see what common ground could be found with the ANC-in-exile. Power was slipping away from the white minority.

This series of events in the early and mid-1980s formed the backdrop to Hurley's second spell as leader of the SACBC, from January 1981 to January 1987, and challenged him to provide exceptional leadership, examples of which are set out in this and subsequent chapters. There was a national crisis, and Hurley's example helped the Catholic Church to face up to it as never before.

SACBC PRESIDENT

Archbishop George Daniel of Pretoria thought it was providential that the bishops chose Hurley, a man conspicuous for prophetic leadership, to lead them through a time of national turmoil. When he took over as president in 1981, nearly 30 years had passed since Hurley first led the bishops, from June 1952 to January 1960.

By the 1980s a huge change had taken place among the bishops: they had become convinced that apartheid was evil and that a strong and clear response was needed.[2] They did not always know how to proceed, nor were they always brave enough, but as a group they had become 'crusaders' against apartheid, whereas in 1952 they were just beginning to suspect that the system was wrong. The changed outlook had come about largely because of the dramatic political developments in South Africa over nearly three decades. The political events of the 1960s and 1970s made the bishops more practical and realistic in rejecting apartheid and promoting justice. The Church had also been profoundly changed by the experience of the Second Vatican Council.

But Hurley recognized that despite efforts to implement the vision of Vatican II, there had been a failure to get the message through to the parish level, because the Church continued to rely on statements. Some organizations adopted a more activist role, in particular the Young Christian Workers (YCW), the Young Christian Students (YCS), the Justice and Peace Commissions and the National Catholic Federation of Students (NCFS). The Church generally, however, had not been much changed. Even some years after his second presidency, Hurley was not convinced that 'we have yet discovered how to promote such changes on a large scale'.

What sort of man had the bishops elected to lead them, and how was he viewed by his brother bishops?[3] His colleagues were aware of his intellectual ability and how he grasped the essence of issues rapidly and could summarize even the most complex debate. That ability helped him also to raise the debate to a larger vision of the Church and its mission in solidarity with the poor and oppressed. His exceptional leadership was based not only on intellectual but also on physical strength. This gave him a calm and tranquil manner that inspired confidence, as well as stamina for hard work and extra responsibilities, the endurance needed to cope with long meetings and difficult situations and to follow up the many tasks assigned to him. He was always willing to volunteer for committees and commissions and would give his full attention to each.

Archbishop Jabulani Nxumalo of Bloemfontein, who had been involved in SACBC work for many years before he became a bishop, said that the bishops acknowledged Hurley as the one who prepared most thoroughly for meetings, going through the documentation carefully, meticulously drafting any presentations he needed to give, working out his position on issues coming up for discussion. Cardinal Wilfrid Napier OFM respected the fact that, in general, Hurley could not easily be persuaded to change his view unless by a strictly logical argument. Not everyone in the conference was, however, able to meet that requirement.

The combination of intellectual ability and thorough preparation made him a tough opponent, and there were times when it seemed that his brother bishops felt somewhat overwhelmed: 'Because he was so strong, so exceptional', said Archbishop Buti Tlhagale of Johannesburg, 'he probably didn't realize his impact on others, and therefore didn't try to cushion it . . . Hurley [was] a gentleman but others became intimidated precisely because of his sharp mind'. 'When Hurley presented something that he really believed in, his presence and passion made most of the bishops afraid to challenge him', said Father Sean O'Leary SMA of the Justice and Peace Commission. There was, however, general recognition that Hurley did not use the force of his personality or his intellectual strength for that purpose.

A skilled chairperson, he would try to draw out opinions so that all could be involved in formulating policy. His belief in collegiality made him particularly keen to achieve consensus, but on occasion that consensus may have been a little artificial. Though some bishops disagreed with motions Hurley proposed, they could not think of a strong-enough argument to counter his. Hurley had an impressive command of English, which discouraged those for whom it was a second language. They conceded, however, that he was a good loser; when his view did not prevail, he graciously moved on to the next issue.

Though Hurley sometimes disagreed with the Church's official position, Bishop William Slattery OFM of Kokstad said that his loyalty to the Church was strong and obvious. He had bonded with it from childhood. He knew nuns, priests, bishops and cardinals from many countries and was attached to them. The Church was a second family to him, and he did not want to cause friction or to embarrass it in any way.

At the same time, according to Slattery, his view of the bishop's role had been influenced by his knowledge of the early Church, in which bishops had freedom to adopt independent positions on issues. Through many years of reciting the Divine Office he had been steeped in readings from the church 'Fathers'. 'He modelled himself on the great bishops of antiquity, . . . Cyprian and all those who . . . bowed their head to Rome but . . . had to work out their own theological positions, and did so proudly and with personal responsibility'. This fitted in well with Hurley's concern for truth—rather than ingratiation with authority in the interest of promotion.

A man who thrived on great plans, schemes and campaigns, Hurley flourished at the time of the Marian Congress, the bishops' campaign for the mission schools, the People of God catechetical series, the establishment and development of ICEL, and as we shall see, the Pastoral Plan and Christians for Justice and Peace (CJP). Nxumalo said that Hurley wanted to see things on the large scale, fully-fledged from the beginning, and 'had difficulty in accepting that they might need to start small and gradually emerge'.

He was also rather more successful in reaching out to intellectuals than ordinary people. Since he had never been a parish priest before his retirement and had never worked in rural areas before he became a bishop, he did not always think through how what he was proposing could be implemented in a rural setting, according to Napier. Slattery said, 'He was totally committed to the ordinary people, but he wasn't all that at ease [with them]'.

NO CAUSE FOR CELEBRATION

One of the first challenges to Hurley, as the newly-elected president of the SACBC, was the twentieth anniversary of South Africa becoming a republic (1981). Many government-sponsored celebrations took place around the country. A number of organizations, however, decided not to participate. The Catholic bishops issued an official statement 'that the vast majority of the people see no cause for celebration, since they are deprived and oppressed in the land of their birth and have no meaningful say in the government of the country and in the decisions that affect them so closely and intimately in their human dignity. We believe that, as their spiritual leaders, we must associate ourselves with them'.[4]

Hurley sent out a pastoral letter to all the parishes in his archdiocese, setting out fully his reasons for boycotting the republic celebrations.[5] When the majority of South Africans reflected on the policy and laws of the country, he said, the image that came to their minds was of 'people uprooted from their homes', the 'appalling misery of life in rural areas', the 'constant humiliation of being discriminated against' and 'arrest, detention and banning'. Nevertheless, the decision to boycott was not an easy one because it seemed to show hostility towards South Africa. However, 'if indeed the whole national community were rejoicing in this festival, the church would be happy to participate by publicly demonstrating its love for all the people of South Africa and by offering prayers of thanksgiving, blessing and petition'. But the majority were deeply opposed.

Hurley ended by commending a suggestion made by the Durban ecumenical agency, Diakonia, that people be invited to gather in local churches on 1 June, when a parade of South Africa's military might would be held in Durban. The prayers, which Diakonia suggested should wherever possible be ecumenical, were 'to ask God to guide us all to a peaceful solution of our problems and to give witness to the fact that we hope to be supported not by guns and tanks, 'not by power, nor by might', but by God's Spirit'.

So much controversy and debate was generated by Hurley's call for a boycott of the Republic Festival that the world-famous author, Alan Paton, was moved to write an article for the *Daily News* in which he asked ironically, 'Has the shepherd lost his way?'[6] Paton had seen from letters to editors that some lay Catholics believed Hurley had indeed lost his way, and that these readers thought he did not understand the Church's function.

One of the fiercest critics was Clive Derby-Lewis, a Catholic who was a key member of the Republic festival committee in Edenvale, Johannesburg. Derby-Lewis, who is serving a life sentence for his involvement in planning the 1993 assassination of the SA Communist Party's general secretary, Chris Hani, questioned Hurley's right to discourage participation in the festivities: 'He is more concerned with politics than with the Christian calling'.

Paton noticed that those who were complaining about Hurley's stance were white, whereas black people would applaud Hurley's call for a boycott. The archbishop's words reminded him of the prophet Isaiah: 'Learn to do good, search for justice, help the oppressed, be just to the orphan, plead for the widow' (Isa. 1:17 JB). His answer to the question about whether Hurley had lost his way was to advise him that millions of South Africans did not think so at all. On the contrary, they believed that he was trying to find a way, for the republic and all its people, 'out of the morass into which Apartheid has led us'. His advice to Hurley? 'Carry on, Your Grace'.

'ICH WILL EIN MENSCH SEIN'

A number of European and North American Catholic funders of justice, peace and development in South Africa hold their main annual collections for these causes during the 40 days of Lent leading up to the celebration of Easter. Lent is a time of prayer, fasting and giving to the poor. For years, funders have used this season to help Catholics, and the public generally, become more aware of third-world socio-political problems, and how first-world countries contribute to these. To help raise this awareness, these funders invite 'witnesses' from Africa, Asia and Latin America to travel to Europe and North America during Lent to share their third-world experience. Posters, discussion outlines, videos and slide presentations are produced to help familiarize congregations and small groups with the focus country or countries.

Hurley took part in a number of such campaigns, for example in Canada as a guest of Development and Peace in 1987, and in Belgium as a guest of *Entraide et Fraternité* in 1988. I have chosen to focus here on an earlier visit made to Germany in 1983 as a guest of *Misereor*, which was then celebrating its twenty-fifth year. In 1983 *Misereor* focused its Lenten campaign on South Africa, with the theme *Ich will ein Mensch sein*, 'I want to be a human being', a theme that captured the demand of black people to have their human dignity recognized.

Long before the campaign started, *Misereor* alerted the South African bishops that there would be opposition in Germany—from big business, politicians and South African diplomats, and from conservative members of the Church. Many Germans had contact only with white people in South Africa, and this shaped their views. The Lenten Campaign would be based more on the black majority's experience of South Africa, which would be new to these groups. It would be essential for the SACBC to provide accurate information about South Africa to counter the arguments that would inevitably come from conservative quarters.

Hurley was well known to *Misereor* since he had been involved with the organization from its foundation in 1958, when it had helped to save the mission schools.[7] Over the intervening years, like a number of other funding agencies, its staff had regularly consulted him about their South Africa policy. Because of his extensive contacts, he was able to recommend suitable recipients for their funding, both inside and outside the Catholic Church. They respected his knowledge of the situation, his analytical gifts and his willingness to challenge injustice. They also appreciated that he did not have a hierarchical approach but was friendly to everyone, willing to meet with ordinary members of staff, not just the top officials, and to treat all as equals.

Together with him, *Misereor* developed a conviction that apartheid was a 'structural sin': an evil arising from economic, social and political structures, and for that reason could not be reformed but had to be ended. He backed the choice of South Africa as their 1983 focus: in fact, he was delighted. If there was any hesitation about whether *Misereor* had made the right decision in such a controversial choice, he would encourage them to go ahead with their plan.

He was their guest at the campaign launch in the German city of Fulda, preached at the opening Mass in its cathedral and took part in a large public meeting on the theme *Ich will ein Mensch sein*. Doctor Ulrich Koch, former head of *Misereor*'s Africa section, said that Hurley 'gave detailed, understandable analysis of the South African situation, showing why it should be seen as a case of "structural sin"'.

After the opening of the campaign in Fulda, Hurley toured parts of Germany, giving media interviews and addressing church gatherings with six other 'witnesses', who had come from various parts of South Africa to speak about their own experiences of apartheid. Among them was Thora Perez, a teacher from Cape Town who was active in the SA Catholic Laity Council.[8] She remembers how much attention Hurley gave the team:

> He was so concerned and so protective of us, . . . and he would make sure that we were comfortable, make sure we were involved, [and] that we were present at all the meetings that were arranged for us . . . He was really our backbone there . . . He was able to include all of us, [whenever] we were at one of these big meetings where all these bigwigs were, where there were bishops and . . . politicians.

Hurley urged the South Africans: 'Speak from your heart, don't worry about anything. Tell them exactly what is happening; tell them exactly what you feel . . . Others read about it. Others hear about it. But you experience it, so do speak out'. And when the South Africans spoke out and the accuracy of their stories was questioned, Hurley would back them up with his own experiences.

There were some moving moments: for example, when they met young South African exiles living in Germany, some of whom had formed a music and drama group known as Sounds of Soweto, which performed at various campaign events.

One young man cried when he told them, 'I left without even saying goodbye to my mother. I left the house and I never went back and I can't go back now'. The archbishop wept with them and said, 'I'll make sure that all the mothers in South Africa who have children abroad that are in exile know that you . . . are thinking about them'.

Prominent Germans were opposed to the campaign, as *Misereor* had predicted. The strongest opposition came from Franz Josef Strauss, leader of the Christian Social Union, the most powerful party in Bavaria, a staunchly Catholic part of Germany. Strauss was highly critical of what Hurley had to say about the situation in South Africa. There were also threats from major industrial concerns, such as the chemical manufacturer Hoechst, who had previously given donations to Catholic parishes and institutions in Germany. 'If you go ahead with this political campaign against our partners [in South Africa], we will stop giving to the Church'. But Cardinal Joseph Höffner of Cologne, head of the German Bishops' Conference, publicly defended Hurley and his colleagues: 'We are, as a German Church, on the side of the Catholic Bishops' Conference of South Africa'.

Heribert Zingel, a key organizer of the Lenten campaign who had also travelled around Germany conducting awareness programmes about South Africa for parishes, clergy meetings and other groups, recalled that he and other members of the *Misereor* team were repeatedly told by conservative German Catholics that they should 'Go East' to what was then known as the German Democratic Republic— because of their perceived 'communist bias'. But despite these challenges and criticisms, many people were also learning that being active on political issues and belief in God were not separate, but two sides of the same coin.[9]

The campaign marked the beginning of a new era for *Misereor*, in which it would be more outspoken and political in its approach. This was not a change in its official policy. Even at its launch in 1958, Cardinal Josef Frings of Cologne had said that Lent was not only a time for fasting and showing compassion by financial contributions to the struggle against poverty, but also for the Church to exercise its prophetic role through criticism of unjust structures that caused poverty. The main focus of the first 20 years of *Misereor*'s Lenten campaigns was, however, on collecting money. In 1975 the German Synod stressed that the Church should do more by way of political lobbying. The Lenten Campaign of 1983 was the first big test of the new approach.

Hurley helped *Misereor* take the risk. For the first time, the prophetic message was given the same weight as fasting and giving money. Zingel had experienced the German bishops as tending to focus exclusively on their own dioceses. They were not as strong or clear in their political analysis as Hurley, who was able to convince *Misereor* and the German bishops to engage in lobbying, according to Koch. 'Do it, it's not as difficult as you think', he would say. Previously *Misereor* and the bishops thought it would be too dangerous to adopt this approach, but 'he motivated people to see the joy in undertaking this prophetic action', Koch said.

As a result, the campaign had a big influence on *Misereor*'s future work. Having introduced a more thorough political analysis into the 1983 Lenten campaign, it maintained this in later years as it focused on other countries and themes.

20

Namibia

Namibia, previously known as South-West Africa, is South Africa's northern neighbour on the West Coast, lying between Angola (to the north) and what was then known as the Cape Province (to the south). About one-and-a-half times the size of France, Namibia is largely desert. It has a small population, only about 1.4 million people in the early 1980s. Diamonds are mined on the coast, and it has the world's largest open-cast uranium mines, important for nuclear power and the manufacture of atomic weapons, hence its strategic importance.[1]

It was first settled by Europeans in the 1880s, when it became a colony known as German South West Africa. In 1915, a few months after the start of World War I, South African troops invaded the colony, and the German troops surrendered. In 1920, after the end of World War I, the League of Nations gave Britain the mandate to govern Namibia, exercised by South Africa on her behalf.

After World War II, the United Nations became officially responsible for Namibia. It maintained that Namibia was a Trust Territory, which should be prepared for independence. South Africa contended that it had acquired full responsibility for the territory when the League of Nations came to an end, and thus the UN had no claim to it. After the 1948 elections, which brought the National Party to power in South Africa, the government simply treated Namibia as a fifth province. It arranged for the white residents, only 5 per cent of the population, to be divided into constituencies that elected representatives to the all-white South African parliament. In 1966, the UN instructed South Africa to withdraw from the territory and give Namibia its independence. South Africa refused, saying once again that Namibia had nothing to do with the UN.

The introduction of apartheid laws in Namibia and South Africa's refusal to consider independence for that territory led to the growth of SWAPO (South West African People's Organisation), which began a war against South African occupation in 1966. In 1971, the International Court of Justice in the Hague ruled that South Africa was occupying Namibia illegally. The strength of SWAPO's guerrilla war against South Africa increased greatly in 1974, when Namibia's northern neighbour,

Angola, was granted its independence, and a left-wing government took power with support from Cuban troops as well as Soviet and East German advisers. When SWAPO developed bases in Angola, the South African Defence Force (SADF) illegally invaded that country, supposedly to destroy the SWAPO camps. The war against SWAPO and the raids into Angola proved expensive for South Africa, with many soldiers killed and millions spent on military procurement.

As SWAPO grew in strength and influence, the South African security forces became more brutal in their repression of the local population, especially in Ovamboland, the northern part of Namibia. Atrocities were also committed by SWAPO.

As Hurley began his second presidency of the SACBC, he had no idea that Namibia would be one of its dominant themes. It was one of the four countries served by the SACBC, together with South Africa, Swaziland and Botswana; hence that body took considerable interest in the territory.[2]

Father Heinz Steegmann OMI, parish priest of the best-known Windhoek township, Katatura, who was a member of the SACBC's Justice and Peace Commission based in Pretoria, was responsible for initiating Hurley and the SACBC into the struggle for Namibia's independence. The information he gave to the Commission led its full-time secretary, Marylyn Aitken of the Grail, to contact an influential overseas ally, Ian Linden of the London-based Catholic Institute for International Relations (CIIR). She suggested that they visit the territory to learn more. Linden agreed, and towards the end of 1981 he and Aitken arrived in Windhoek as guests of Steegmann, who took them to Ovamboland. Some white farmers had been killed there and a big manhunt for guerrilla fighters was under way.

Wherever the visitors went, there were roadblocks and searches. Alongside the road, every 2 kilometres or so, they saw cars that had been blown up by landmines. Missionaries were used to these sights, but they came as quite a shock to the visitors. Aitken and Linden heard many accounts of detention, torture and other atrocities committed by the security police and the police paramilitary unit known as *Koevoet*—an Afrikaans word meaning crowbar—who were frequently accused of torture and assassinations. Whole villages were being wiped out by the SADF 'just because it was suspected there were some SWAPO guerrillas there'.

Once back in South Africa after this harrowing visit, Aitken gave the bishops' Administrative Board a detailed account of what she and Linden had seen. The bishops, particularly Stephen Naidoo of Cape Town and Hurley, were appalled. According to Aitken, Naidoo pleaded passionately that the bishops should take up the issue; Hurley and Daniel of Pretoria supported him.

The Board agreed to hold a special meeting at which a Church delegation from Namibia would be invited to brief them from 23 to 26 June. The Board was so disturbed by what the Namibian delegation told them that it decided to organize a special plenary session where all the bishops could hear what they had heard. This took place on 26–27 August. Once again a delegation from Namibia spoke frankly about the situation. But this time some of South Africa's bishops did not believe that the SADF would do the sort of things the delegation was reporting. This was insulting and demoralizing for Steegmann and the senior church leaders from Namibia.

However, it gave an opening to Hurley to propose: 'Well, then, we need to go ourselves to see whether these stories are true or not'.

According to Steegmann, this was the best thing that could have happened. Hurley was determined that there should be a strong consensus among the bishops about what was happening in Namibia. So it was agreed that a delegation of six bishops would go: Hurley as president, Archbishops Peter Butelezi of Bloemfontein and George Daniel of Pretoria, Bishops Mansuet Biyase of Eshowe, Manfred Gottschalk of Oudtshoorn and Monsignor Marius Banks of Volksrust, chair of the bishops' Justice and Peace Commission.

The visit took place from 21 to 29 September 1981, and Steegmann accompanied the bishops wherever they went. The delegation first visited the Namibian capital, Windhoek, and then spent four days travelling in the northern war zone. They conducted seventeen detailed interviews with groups of people, numbering 180 in all. Everywhere they found fear of the security forces, who had been empowered by the emergency laws to detain and interrogate people, frequently in solitary confinement, with beatings and torture. 'They break into homes, beat up residents, shoot people, steal and kill cattle and often pillage stores and tea rooms', the bishops heard. It was particularly dangerous for the local communities when SWAPO tracks were discovered by the security forces.

This led to even harsher measures, including blindfolding people, taking them from their homes and leaving them beaten up or dead by the roadside. 'Women are often raped', the bishops were told. 'It is not unknown for a detachment to break into a home and, while black soldiers keep watch over the family, white soldiers select the best-looking girls and take them into the veld to rape them'. The bishops were told that the security forces drove around with the bodies of SWAPO guerrillas dangling from their vehicles, as a warning to locals not to join the movement. Despite all this intimidation, the delegation found massive civilian support for SWAPO guerrillas—while the South African troops and police were commonly known in the Ovambo language as *omakakhunya*, 'blood-suckers' or 'bone-pickers'.

Steegmann was impressed by Hurley's ability to listen attentively for hours to the groups they were visiting, only occasionally taking a note. At the end of the day, when the delegation would debrief themselves about all they had heard, Steegmann said that he had forgotten many of the details they had been told. But not Hurley: he had it all in his head.

Steegmann said that Hurley was highly effective in the way he ran the seventeen group interviews, giving everyone the opportunity to speak, expressing his own feelings and affection for the people in their suffering and helping them to feel secure. Moreover Hurley asked the right questions and he promised the people that their names would not be given to anyone. 'During this week in Namibia, he knew exactly what to do and how to do it'. Steegmann felt it was also a great advantage that two of the bishops, Butelezi and Biyase, were black. This helped the witnesses to trust the group and openly share information.

The overwhelming picture that emerged from the interviews contrasted strongly with the one generally presented in South Africa that its troops were protecting civilians from SWAPO guerrillas, who were portrayed in the South African media as ruthless terrorists, trying to wipe out their democratic opponents and take over the territory on behalf of their Soviet backers.

Despite the careful record that Hurley and Gottschalk compiled during the daily debriefings, once they were back in South Africa, it took some time for the full report to be published.[3] There was a long delay because some bishops insisted that there should be a meeting with the Prime Minister, P. W. Botha, before the document was published. Despite a number of attempts, the best that could be done was to meet with the administrator general in Windhoek and to publish, as part of the report, two lengthy letters from P. W. Botha setting out the South African government's attitude towards the Namibian question and its response to the bishops' report. The Defence Force commented that the bishops' allegations were 'a mere repetition of the one-sided propaganda regularly churned out by the SWAPO terrorist organization and its Communist allies'.

When the bishops' report was finally published on 14 May 1982, Hurley told a press conference that the findings would come as a shock to many. Though the bishops had not found any direct evidence of atrocities, the accounts they had heard 'had the ring of truth about them', with a 'convincing amount of circumstantial evidence'. Their report detailed six cases of brutality, two of which are recounted here. The first was about a man who, after being blindfolded, beaten up and subjected to electric shock treatment was taken with others, including girls, to a dam. The girls were indecently assaulted by the security forces, and then all were thrown into the water still blindfolded. The narrator swam to safety and helped the others out of the water.

The second story was about a woman who told how, during detention, she was constantly beaten and given electric shocks, while chained to a chair. During that time she was gagged: a cloth soaked in salt water was placed across her open mouth and tied tightly at the back of her neck. The shock treatment caused haemorrhages and affected her kidneys. After being taken to a hospital for an operation, she was jailed in a hot and dirty iron shack. The wound from the operation festered.

People in the operational area regarded such events as characteristic, not exceptional. As a result, the bishops said, 'it is easy to understand them when they say they fear the South African security forces rather than the SWAPO guerrillas'. With regard to South African claims that SWAPO was a communist organization, the bishops said that, while it did receive arms from communist countries and made use of some ideological rhetoric, most people saw it as a national liberation movement.

The media tended to focus on what the bishops had to say about atrocities: it made for sensational news. The charges later brought against Hurley for his remarks about *Koevoet* confirmed this emphasis. But more important were the overall conclusions to the report, especially about the political future of Namibia:

> There is a universal consensus, with South Africa virtually the only dissenting voice, that South Africa has no right to be in Namibia. To dismiss as biased or irrelevant the decision of the United Nations and the opinion of the International Court of Justice is to discard everything, however imperfect, which has been slowly built up in

mankind's agonizing search for institutions designed to promote and safeguard peace. It also seems clear to us that the great majority of Namibians have one overriding desire and that is the implementation of UN Security Council Resolution 435, resulting in a cease-fire, the withdrawal of South African Security Forces and the holding of elections under United Nations auspices.

Hurley and Gottschalk, who were already scheduled to be overseas in November 1981, were asked to discuss the bishops' findings on Namibia, with what was known as the Western Contact Group: Britain, Germany, France, the United States and Canada, all of whom were trying to negotiate a settlement.[4] Individual meetings were held with leading representatives of each. In addition, a presentation was made to the Vatican. Hurley and Gottschalk said they had been well received in government circles and that all the church representatives supported their meetings with the Western Contact Group. Several of the Catholic groups involved in development, justice and peace said, however, that this was not enough: economic pressure should be applied to South Africa. On their return, Hurley and Gottschalk urged the Bishops' Conference to make every effort to develop a sanctions policy.

So great was the interest generated by the bishops' report that the Justice and Peace Group at Christ the King Cathedral in Johannesburg organized a public meeting on 30 January 1983.[5] They invited Hurley and the newly-appointed Bishop of Windhoek, Bonifatius Haushiku, to be the speakers. The purpose was to explain the bishops' position on Namibia, which they did in a lively meeting attended by a thousand people, the first of its kind organized by any of the mainline churches.

Hurley stressed that the six bishops who visited Namibia in September 1981 had discovered that SWAPO members were regarded as liberators and would win any election hands down. All the observations the bishops had made in their report were corroborated by independent sources. Haushiku, who described himself as a member of the Okavango tribe in Northern Namibia, gave a graphic description of how the war was affecting the lives of ordinary Namibians and told the large gathering about their fears, losses and sufferings. He had visited all forty-six missions and outstations in the Diocese of Windhoek and everywhere heard about the atrocities people had experienced.

At times the atmosphere of the meeting was tense and emotions ran high. In contrast to the mood of the meeting, Hurley remained calm. Most questions were hostile to the bishops, but three-quarters of the audience appeared to be in favour. At the end, Hurley and Haushiku were given a standing ovation for the SACBC's stance on Namibia.

At about the same time, it was announced that the Bishops' report on Namibia had been banned by the SA government.[6] At first it was thought to be the entire forty-page document, but later it became clear that it was the four-page summary, which had been prepared for mass distribution to parishes and did not contain the two letters from P. W. Botha. The Minister of Internal Affairs, Mr F. W. de Klerk (later to be state president), described the 'whole tone of the document [as] negative in the extreme and [bordering] on high treason'.

Each year after the bishops' plenary session, a media conference is held to inform the public about the main topics discussed. On 3 February 1983, Namibia was high on that list.[7] In reply to a question, Hurley mentioned that, since the bishops' visit there, he had received reports of further atrocities by *Koevoet*. These allegations came in the wake of a major public relations campaign by the South African government to rehabilitate *Koevoet*'s reputation and must have greatly angered the authorities. In the light of what subsequently resulted from Hurley's remarks at this press conference, it is important to note his words on this occasion:

> Nothing can be proved in . . . these cases because we have no eyewitnesses. But everybody drew the conclusion that they [the victims] had died at the hands of a certain unit, a unit that is looked upon as most ruthless, up there—*Koevoet* . . . We are quite prepared to accept that in any guerrilla war this [sort of] thing does happen. Men get edgy, men get panicky, men react this way and there are atrocities. Our point of view is this: the organization or country responsible for keeping the war going is responsible for letting young men do this horrifying kind of thing.

The next day, Hurley's comments about *Koevoet* were in the news. Lieutenant-Colonel Leon Mellett of the Ministry of Law and Order announced that police would investigate possible charges against Hurley and 'any newspapers or media that published or disseminated the Archbishop's allegations' under Section 27B of the Police Act. This section dealt with the 'prohibition of publication of certain untrue facts' in relation to any action by the police, without reasonable grounds for believing that the statement was true.

The onus of proof rested on the person making the statement; and the penalties on conviction were a fine not exceeding R10,000, or imprisonment for a period not exceeding five years, or a fine and imprisonment. Police warned the South African Press Association (SAPA) that they were investigating charges against it for issuing reports in which atrocities by police in South West Africa were alleged. Hurley commented that he would welcome 'a good court case' but doubted that he would be prosecuted because of the amount of evidence that would come out.

In July, a police officer called on Hurley, saying that the Attorney-General of the Transvaal, the province where the SACBC media conference had been held, was opening a docket on Hurley's statement because it might have contravened the Police Act as mentioned above. Hurley put the matter in the hands of his legal advisers and heard no more about it until 9 October 1984. On that day, after returning from an ecumenical visit to Namibia, another police officer called on him with a summons to appear in court on a charge arising out of the alleged offence.[8] If Hurley was perturbed, he did not reveal it but engaged the police officer in a discussion about how the Springbok rugby team was faring.

The court appearance was scheduled for 31 October, when Hurley was due to be overseas, so arrangements were made to move it forward to 19 October.[9] At this first appearance, Hurley pleaded not guilty, and the case was remanded until 18 February 1985. The magistrate announced that the case might continue for four weeks before the accused was convicted or acquitted. The state was expected to call fifteen witnesses to give evidence against Hurley. This first court appearance was not without its lighter moments. When the magistrate asked the defence advocate how he should address the accused, the advocate replied, 'Your Grace, Your Worship'.

Hurley's legal team for his High Court trial was to be Denis Kuny SC with Hans Fabricius, instructed by Brian Currin of the firm Savage, Jooste & Adams. Currin said that it took some time for him to convince the archbishop of the seriousness of the charges, that there actually was a case to answer. He was 'slightly dismissive of the whole thing, as if he was saying: "Do we really now have to sit and spend time seriously and prepare for this because . . . what have I got to answer?"'[10]

A different perspective is provided by Geoff Chapman, who relates how he had once asked Hurley how he felt about the case. Was he worried? 'He looked grave for a moment and said that he was indeed concerned because it had very unpleasant possibilities'. Once he saw that the trial provided an extraordinary opportunity to present evidence about what was happening in Namibia and to say things in court that could not be said under normal circumstances, he became more enthusiastic.

Currin spoke highly of the experience of representing Hurley:

> I know that I speak on behalf of the entire legal team when I say it was a privilege and a career highlight to represent His Grace. His questions during preparation were always insightful and relevant. His answers were always short and to the point. He understood law and he understood politics. His quiet but unflinching resolve to succeed with his case gave us all grit and determination.[11]

In preparing Hurley's defence, his legal team set out to gather as much information as they could concerning *Koevoet* to use extensively in the trial. With this in mind, the whole team went to Windhoek to interview possible witnesses. They were greatly helped by a local Namibian attorney, Hartmut Ruppel, who had appeared in cases concerning *Koevoet* and was experienced in police and political matters. With Ruppel's help, the legal team was able to assemble a large volume of documentation concerning brutalities inflicted by *Koevoet*. In his report to Hurley, however, Currin referred to Ruppel pointing out 'the practical difficulty [of] proving the matters in a Court of Law, in that he is afraid that the witnesses may be terrified into not testifying'.

According to Currin, it seems that, by the time of the trial, they had not found anyone willing to testify in South Africa.[12] It might have been necessary to ask the court to go to Namibia and take evidence on commission there. That would have made it easier for people to give evidence, but there would still have been much fear about the possible consequences of testifying against *Koevoet*, especially when the witnesses would be returning to communities where that unit was still all-powerful. A more basic problem, according to Currin, was that the court would most probably not readily agree to this request.

Yet as the trial date approached, Currin became aware that the prosecution was growing increasingly anxious.[13] They had all heard about Hurley but had not met this man who seemed to epitomize the much-feared *Roomse gevaar*. Currin had noticed this anxiety in discussions with the prosecutors who were 'shuffling papers and glancing at one another'. This anxiety grew as the prosecution became aware of international interest in the trial. The embassies, the international media, the International Commission of Jurists (ICJ) and Amnesty International were all monitoring the case, not to mention bishops, priests and nuns from many parts of the world. The prosecution would have been aware that the defence team's strategy was to put the state on trial.

Meanwhile, Currin seemed full of confidence. 'Having this opportunity to present the evidence was a gift from heaven. To be precise, it was a gift from St Denis. The biggest mistake the prosecuting authorities made was to serve the summons on the day they did: 9 October is the Feast of St Denis [we were defending Denis Hurley], and the Senior Counsel was Denis Kuny SC. How could we lose with a triumvirate like that?' In any case, as far as the defence team was concerned, said Currin, 'it was not Archbishop Hurley who was on trial. The security forces were on trial. In fact, the Minister of Law and Order was on trial, as well as the President, P. W. Botha. In my own mind, His Grace had become the prosecutor, and I was totally focused on getting a conviction'.

Hurley seemed in no way intimidated by the charges. He had gone on another visit to Namibia in October 1984, as part of the ecumenical delegation referred to earlier. He reported his impressions of that visit at the SACBC plenary session on 30 January 1985. Conditions in the territory had worsened since the Conference's previous visit in 1982: there was increased poverty and unemployment, accompanied by growing militarization. He might have been expected to be reserved in his criticism of *Koevoet*, given the trial he faced just over two weeks later, but he spoke even more strongly. 'In contrast with 1982, the name of *Koevoet* . . . is on everyone's tongue'.

As the trial date grew closer, Father Smangaliso Mkhatshwa and Sister Brigid Flanagan, the two top staff members of the SACBC, put out a circular to bishops, priests and religious superiors all over South Africa, urging them to give as much support as possible to Hurley and suggesting a variety of activities. A campaign began to take shape, led by the SACBC Justice and Peace Commission, with WE SUPPORT HURLEY stickers, prayer vigils and meetings of all kinds. Major solidarity services were organized for Pietermaritzburg, Durban and Johannesburg. Thousands of prayer cards were distributed with a photo of Hurley and the following prayer:

Look with favour upon Denis Eugene Hurley, our bishop.

You have given him to us as our father and teacher.

Protect and defend him.

Inspire him with courage, bless him with health and strength.

Let him, who is called to leadership in your Church,

Always champion the cause of the poor.

In the midst of Hurley's preparations for the trial a message came from a famous prisoner—Nelson Mandela. Writing from Pollsmoor Prison to Stephen Naidoo CSSR, recently appointed Catholic Archbishop of Cape Town, Mandela said: 'Archbishop Hurley is often in my thoughts, especially now. I would like him to know that'.[14]

Pressure was growing for the charges to be withdrawn. Hurley's extensive files of letters, telegrams, telexes and cards from well-wishers all over the world reveal that many were calling on the South African government to back down. Father Robert Drinan SJ, a former member of the US Congress, used the opportunity of a function at the SA embassy in Washington to take the SA Ambassador aside.[15] He warned him that Hurley was held in high regard by many church people in the United States. 'You should know', he said, ' that if you people put Archbishop Hurley on trial, there'll be moral revulsion all around the world and you will suffer'. Bishop James Malone, of Youngstown, Ohio, president of the US National Conference of Catholic Bishops, gave a similar warning to P. W. Botha, who by this time had become state president, as well as to the US Secretary of State. There were also pressures from within South Africa: for example, from Peter Gastrow, Progressive Federal Party MP. Gastrow had been approached by concerned Catholics in Durban and had contacted the Minister of Justice, Mr Kobie Coetsee.[16]

These and other initiatives finally made a decisive impact on the South African government. On Friday, 15 February 1985, Hurley was phoned by Gastrow and told that Minister Coetsee had informed him that the charges would be withdrawn by the Attorney-General of the Transvaal. Since Hurley had already been formally charged, the state would be obliged to give reasons for not proceeding with the trial when Hurley appeared in court on Monday, 18 February. Before that appearance in the Pretoria Magistrate's Court, solidarity masses for Hurley were scheduled for Pietermaritzburg, Durban and Johannesburg. Hurley agreed that these should go ahead, but that they should obviously take on a note of thanksgiving as well as a continuing emphasis on the need for justice in Namibia.

More than 2,000 people gathered at Emmanuel Cathedral on Sunday, 17 February, many of them hearing for the first time that the charges were to be withdrawn. Hurley used his address to respond to those who wondered why the bishops were 'interfering in politics' by getting involved in issues like Namibia: 'Firstly', he said, 'because of suffering. The Church must be wherever there is suffering, and the bishops must take the lead in this. The gospel tells us that suffering is one of the most vivid revelations of God. We are told we can find Jesus where there is hunger, thirst, nakedness, sickness, imprisonment. Those of us who went to Namibia found Christ in the suffering of the Namibian people. The Church must be with that suffering'.

The second reason was that 'the Gospel is political', a statement that Hurley knew would startle many, but he explained: 'The law of love applies to all human behaviour, political as well as personal and domestic. It may be surprising to hear that politics is also subject to the law of love, but it is true. It is also true that in its vision of itself and the social behaviour of its members, a society must try to live the justice practised by Christ. Christian love, Christian justice, these are essential in the life of human society, and that is why the gospel is political'.

Crowds thronged the archbishop after the Mass, congratulating him and rejoicing that he had been vindicated by the withdrawal of the charges.

When Hurley entered the Pretoria Magistrate's Court the next day, 18 February 1985, it was packed with supporters, who overflowed into the corridors, many of them wearing WE SUPPORT HURLEY stickers. Bishops, priests, nuns and lay people had come from many countries, as well as representatives of other churches, legal and human rights experts, diplomatic representatives and a large media contingent.[17] As Hurley entered the court, they gave him a standing ovation, and the magistrate, W. J. van den Bergh, had to call for order. Senior Catholic bishops from as far afield as Ireland and Australia sat in the public gallery with Bishop Desmond Tutu and the president of the Lutheran World Federation.

Hurley stood in the dock as the lead prosecutor, Mr Frans Roets, made a short statement indicating why the charges were being withdrawn. He said that the state had not been able to find a recording of the February 1983 press conference about atrocities reportedly committed by *Koevoet*. They had therefore based their case on a report written by a journalist from SAPA. Roets said that the reporter, Ray Faure, had sworn in an affidavit that he had quoted Hurley correctly in saying 'security forces in SWA/Namibia were still perpetrating atrocities against local blacks'. The state, however, said they had only recently acquired a tape of Hurley's statement, and this differed from Faure's report. 'It is clear that what Bishop Hurley was quoted as in fact having said differs from what he actually said, to such an extent that the State was satisfied that he had not contravened Section 27B of the Police Act'.

The crowded court listened quietly during Roets's statement until he accused Hurley of 'wallowing in the glamour attributed to him' as a result of the case. Then 'there was a roar from the whole court; . . . people were so surprised by his remark and so indignant that they all shouted him down'. They booed and hissed in what Hurley described as a 'spontaneous outburst of disbelief and protest'. There was, however, applause when the regional magistrate acquitted Hurley.

Present in the court was Bishop Donal Lamont, formerly of the diocese of Mutare in Zimbabwe. He attended on behalf of *Co-opération Internationale pour le Développement et la Solidarité (CIDSE)*, an organization that links European Catholic funding agencies active in South Africa. Lamont was one of the most famous bishops in modern times to have been charged, tried and found guilty—allegedly for assisting guerrillas. He had been deported from Rhodesia by the Smith regime and returned to his native Ireland. In thanking Lamont for coming all the way from Ireland, Hurley joked about his embarrassment that his own court appearance had been so much less dramatic and so much shorter than Lamont's. The latter's speech from the dock had been published in a full-length book, *Speech from the Dock*, whereas Hurley's aborted trial was all over in less than 30 minutes.[18]

Hurley did not speak in the court at all, except before proceedings began, when he chatted to various friends and associates who had come to support him and light-heartedly invited Bishop Tutu and his wife, Leah, to join him in the dock. Speaking on Hurley's behalf, Denis Kuny SC said that the prosecution against his client should never have been instituted: 'This prosecution was unfortunate, ill-advised and causes grave disquiet'.

The hearing over, the crowd of supporters walked with Hurley to the nearby Khanya House, the SACBC headquarters, where a media conference was held. Hurley described it as 'bright and cheery. Everybody was in a great and wonderful mood. It was like a crowd after winning a rugby test match'. Hurley began the conference by speaking about his relief that the case was now over, but also his disappointment that the behaviour of the security forces would not be made public. His legal team had assembled a 'devastating' collection of findings at trials and inquests involving the security forces in murder, rape, assault and robbery, as well as 'damning' newspaper reports.

Hurley went on to quote extensively from a memorandum of the South-West African Bar Council, which said, among other things, that the nearest *Koevoet* and the special police came to being policemen was 'in name'. They measured their success by 'body count': 'We see the profession of policeman as a noble one without which justice cannot prevail, but then their task must remain the protection of society, the bringing of alleged offenders to trial and not that of programmed and licensed killers'.

After thanking his legal team, Hurley expressed

> the hope and the prayer that the aborted trial may be used by God in hastening the day when the horror of Namibia may come to an end, when the good name of the security forces so grievously tarnished, when the designation of 'policeman' so sadly disgraced, will be reinstated and rehabilitated and when freedom and peace will come to a country subjected to the distress and cruelty of a war for which unfortunately South Africa is mainly responsible. May God grant the grace of repentance to the offending party and the grace of forgiveness to the offended, that reconciliation may result and peace and friendship come into their own.

When the media were given an opportunity to ask questions, Hurley referred jokingly to the legal advisers on either side of him 'to tug my coat in case'. Asked what he thought was the basis of the state's case against him, since it had 'such flimsy grounds' on which to prosecute him, he replied, 'To enhance my glamour', quoting the prosecutor's words, to much applause and laughter.

While most people were relieved that Hurley did not have to go through the ordeal of a trial, there was also concern that *Koevoet* atrocities would continue unless they were exposed in court. After the charges had been withdrawn, the only option was for Hurley to sue the police for malicious prosecution. This would mean that the atrocities he had revealed and the evidence against *Koevoet* would have to be reviewed in court. A civil claim would thus provide an opportunity to speak out with the court's protection. This was the motive for Hurley's instituting, on 1 July 1985, a claim for damages of R124,047 from the Ministers of Law and Order and of Justice, and from the Attorney-General of the Northern Transvaal.[20] Hurley's interest, as Currin put it, was definitely not financial but 'that if the truth could be published via a high-profile court case, perhaps public opinion would change and perhaps future atrocities would be curbed'.

The civil claim was due to come to court on 2 March 1987. The day before, however, the state asked for the matter to be settled out of court, and R25,000 was agreed to by both parties, without the state admitting any liability. Currin had been surprised that the government 'threw in the towel so quickly when we decided to proceed with a civil trial'. The legal team thought it best to accept, as the case could have been a long, drawn-out one, and there might have been some difficulty in finding witnesses so long after the event. Once again it was clear that the state did not want the evidence against *Koevoet* to be aired in court.

With all legal recourse exhausted, the only other avenue was for the collected evidence to be published, for example, by the Bishops' Conference. It would not have enjoyed the protection of evidence produced in the course of a court case. Another avenue would have been to publish overseas, through a body like the Catholic Institute for International Relations (CIIR), which had shown enormous interest in and support for the whole process. Strangely, there is no evidence that the option of publication, either locally or overseas, was ever considered, and so the extensive evidence collected by Currin, Kuny, Fabricius and Ruppel remained unpublished.

24

In the Shoes of the Workers

Hurley realized that he and his brother bishops, despite extensive experience of conditions in South Africa, could always learn more about what was happening. That led to what became known as 'study days', when the bishops' normal agenda was set aside and they delved into an issue, with the assistance of experts and those who were deeply involved.

The first of these study days during Hurley's second SACBC presidency focused on the plight of workers and trade unions. Organized by the Church and Industry Department of the SACBC, it was held on 30 January 1982, during the bishops' plenary session.[1] The day began with talks by researchers and trade unionists, followed by group discussion in which all the bishops participated, together with lay members of the various SACBC commissions and the union representatives. What came out of the talks and the discussions was a greater awareness of the plight of workers and their feeling of helplessness in the face of oppression. At the same time, the bishops were impressed by the unionists' lack of bitterness, their determination to carry on the struggle for worker rights and their confident appeal to the Church for understanding and help.

Addressing the media conference that followed the plenary session, Hurley said, 'We want to throw the moral weight of the Church behind their struggle'. The bishops had decided to give practical assistance to workers who suffered and were victimised. He expressed the hope that this decision would not lead to confrontation with government but added, as he did on many occasions, 'If it has to come, it has to come'.[2]

The new president was sure there would be controversy within the Church about the bishops' decision. Most black members would support their stand, but whites were nervous of trade unions, and those in management were often 'humane and Christian people' but caught up in heartless structures. Nevertheless, Hurley described trade unionism among black workers as critically important for the country and had high praise for those who had addressed the bishops. 'I am convinced that the great majority of trade unionists are not political revolutionaries. Just listening to them, I feel wholeheartedly on their side'.

In October that year, Diakonia, founded by Hurley, published a 'Worker Rights Statement' endorsed by several of its member churches and a number of other church structures, both local and national. 'It is our belief', said the document, 'that, in South Africa, both legislation and industrial practice are so heavily loaded against workers that the Church has no option but to come to their defence, as a first priority in industrial mission'.

Hurley, one of the strongest supporters of the statement, was happy to champion it at the media launch, together with Rob Lambert, researcher for the Church and Work Department of the Bishops' Conference, and June-Rose Nala of the Metal and Allied Workers' Union (MAWU). 'Without a strong labour organization', said Hurley, 'management in South Africa tends to exploit workers, with little regard for considerations of health, family or social life'.[3]

True to its promise to support victimized workers, the SACBC established the St Joseph the Worker Fund, which played a key role in sustaining the labour movement through the 1980s.[4] Hurley was able to find overseas donors, and large sums were made available to unions and workers in difficult situations. As far as possible, the fund operated in a non-bureaucratic way. Unions needing assistance contacted Rob Lambert, who would pass on the request to Hurley. If the application was approved, within a few hours, or days at most, the money would be on its way to those who needed it.

Sometimes a more detailed explanation was needed, and the trade union would make direct contact with Hurley. Alec Erwin, a key union organizer in Durban and a post-apartheid Minister of Public Enterprises, would visit Archbishop's House in Durban and walk with Hurley in the garden to avoid security police eavesdropping. The support Erwin was requesting was 'shelter in the terrible years of violence' or 'support for strikers or the families of those who were arrested or detained'. Erwin observed Hurley closely on these occasions. 'What I saw was a man of feeling who had been able to discipline himself because a greater cause seemed to need him. This is a rare and even austere trait. Madiba conveys it. Like Mandela, there is always a smile and a welcoming embrace: behind these you know there is steel that has withstood the hottest furnaces'.

In the early 1980s trade unions in Durban did not have adequate buildings or properties and were often prevented from using what few community halls there were in the townships. Yet they needed places for large numbers to meet since this was essential to keep workers united in the struggle for just working conditions. The Church, by contrast, had numerous properties and buildings; the unions often turned to them to make these available for worker gatherings. After the study day of January 1982, the SACBC issued a statement that all Catholic buildings would be available for worker meetings. It was, however, not always easy to carry out, as two stories from 1985 will show.

In August that year, a racial conflict—one that many suspected was promoted by the security police—broke out between Africans in the vast Inanda area north of Durban and the tiny minority of Indians living there, many of them traders and business people. Within a few days, all the Indians had been driven out, their homes and shops burnt down. The Gandhi Settlement, where Mahatma Gandhi had lived for 11 years at the beginning of the twentieth century, was also laid waste, apart from its clinic. There was an urgent need to call trade union leadership together because their disciplined structures could play an important role in stopping the chaos. At the height of the conflict, on a Sunday, Erwin contacted Lambert to find out whether Emmanuel Cathedral would be available for an emergency meeting that afternoon. Several times Lambert tried to contact Hurley to ask his permission, eventually discovering that he was at a rural mission for the day. By this time, the workers were already on their way to the cathedral in large numbers, so the meeting would have to go ahead.

Not only had no arrangements been made for such a gathering in the cathedral, but at 3:00 p.m. on Sundays the cathedral had a Mass in Zulu, which drew a large congregation from far and wide. Father St George, who ministered to that congregation, arrived to prepare for Mass shortly before 3:00 p.m. and was furious to discover that a trade union meeting was already underway in the church and that the Mass would have to be delayed until the meeting was over. St George tried to turn off the lights, fans and loudspeakers: 'There's no permission for this. It can't happen'. Lambert stood in front of the switchboard to prevent St George from getting at the switches, and the worker meeting proceeded, but St George and the other priests at the cathedral were outraged.

Lambert was eventually able to speak to Hurley only at 8:00 p.m.. He apologized about the upset that had been caused. It had been impossible to do anything other than continue with the meeting, given the urgent need for worker leaders to develop a strategy to end the violence. Hurley understood this and told Lambert not to worry. He assured Lambert that, given the circumstances, he had done the right thing and that he (Hurley) would take responsibility for dealing with the aftermath. Priests demanded that the archbishop call a clergy meeting where they could express their concerns. Hurley agreed to their request and invited Erwin to address the clergy meeting and explain the critical circumstances that had led to the union meeting.

According to Father Eric Boulle OMI, St George requested with some emotion that such an incident not be allowed again. Most if not all the priests supported his complaint. Hurley then tried to explain what had happened and said that, if such an occasion arose again, he would give permission for the workers to use the building, in accordance with the resolution of the Bishops' Conference. According to Boulle, 'Everyone present was stunned and felt for Father St George, who just sat down and shook his head'. Boulle disagreed with Hurley, not about allowing the cathedral to be used for worker meetings, but because of how he had responded to St George, one of the most senior and respected priests in the diocese. Hurley was, however, trying to help his priests understand what was happening in Durban at the time, how lives were threatened by the violence and the unions were trying to calm down an extremely volatile situation. He asked his priests to look beyond the narrow confines of the Church's needs and accept that in a time of crisis, 'business as usual' might not be possible.

The use of church buildings by workers was also an issue in a different part of the diocese at that time. On 1 May 1985, workers at the BTR-Sarmcol rubber factory in Howick, outside Pietermaritzburg, had embarked on a wildcat strike.[5] The issue was a recognition agreement for the Metal and Allied Workers' Union (MAWU). After 19 months of negotiations, industrial action and disagreement over the signing and content of the agreement, management had refused to recognize the union. The workers went on strike, and the following day management fired all 970 strikers. This led to one of the longest and most violent struggles in South African labour history. The community of Mpophomeni (the black township of Howick) was torn apart by the conflict between strikers and the scab labour hired by management to replace them.

The dismissed workers tried to meet in the Mpophomeni Community Hall, but an interdict was brought against them. Then they requested the use of the Catholic church in the township, the biggest building in that community. Permission was given by Father Larry Kaufmann CSSR, who worked both in Mpophomeni and Howick. He had consulted Hurley and gained his full support. The workers began to meet in the church every Wednesday evening. Once a month, it was also used to distribute food parcels to the striking workers.

After each meeting, time was reserved for dealing with individual problems— and these were many, according to Philip Dladla, a part-time pastor and shop steward. Workers' furniture was being repossessed because they could no longer pay instalments. Children could not go to school because their parents had no money. Families could be evicted for not paying their rent. There was no money for funerals. The poorest could not even afford to buy firewood to cook the meagre rations in their food parcels. Families were breaking up because the men could no longer play their role as fathers of families. On one occasion, owing to harassment by the police, the church in Howick had to be used rather than the one at Mpophomeni. The Mpophomeni church had to be vacated a few times on a Wednesday evening because it was under attack by armed members of Inkatha from neighbouring rural communities.

In December 1985 the MAWU chief shop steward, Phineas Sibiya, a key witness for the strikers in the ongoing industrial court inquiry into the mass firing, called members of the strike committee together at his house to discuss strategy. But armed Inkatha members burst in on the meeting and abducted the four committee members, took them to the Mpophomeni community hall, where they were tortured, and then drove them to a deserted stretch of road on the way to Lion's River. When they stopped the car, one of the MAWU members, Micca Sibiya, the brother of Phineas, escaped. He was shot in the hand but rolled down a bank, under a barbed-wire fence and fell a few feet into a river, where he hid for the whole night. Nearby, the other three MAWU members, two men and a woman, were individually executed and their bodies burnt in a car owned by another MAWU representative. The next morning Micca risked leaving the river and reporting the assassinations to the police. He then made his way to Durban, where Hurley arranged safe accommodation for him, and later he was employed at a church institution.

When the time came for the funerals of the assassinated trade union leaders, the workers asked that the services be held at the Catholic church in Mpophomeni because two of those killed were Catholics. Kaufmann agreed and informed Hurley, who spontaneously offered to come and help in what were likely to be extremely tense events. The police imposed tight restrictions: instead of one mass funeral, which would have been the workers' choice, there had to be three separate funerals. The police only allowed the bodies to be released one at a time from the funeral parlour in Pietermaritzburg after they had received a message that the previous funeral was over. In Dladla's words, 'we were not allowed to sing or have slogans; . . . one could see that if we were just going to be out an inch, they were ready to shoot or to kill'.

There was a roadblock at the entrance to Mpophomeni, and when Hurley arrived, his car was thoroughly searched by police and army, as if looking for weapons. Once at the church, as Hurley prepared in the sacristy, he took out his mitre, a tall headdress worn by bishops, looked at it and said to Kaufmann, 'I think we should give the people the dignity of the mitre, don't you?' Kaufmann readily agreed. 'Bishop Hurley conducted that funeral and he approached the soldiers', said Dladla, 'trying to be a mediator; . . . should anything they see not be within the rules that were laid down for us to bury these people, they must communicate with him. It was very, very difficult, very difficult'. Kaufmann described Hurley as going to the cemetery, 'surrounded by 'hippos' [armoured personnel carriers] and guns trained down on us; he just ignored them and carried on with the burial rites'.

Between the first and the second funeral there was a 1½-hour delay before the next body arrived from the funeral parlour. Hurley 'waited with such graciousness, chatting to the people'. Kaufmann and he sat in the sacristy, had a cup of tea, spoke about many topics other than the funeral: 'His very presence was . . . enough to give me hope and confidence'. However, Hurley had to leave after the second funeral for another engagement.

But it was not long before he was back in the area because there had been much polarization between the black-worker congregation in Mpophomeni and the white congregation in Howick, a number of whom were involved in management at BTR Sarmcol. The Howick parish council wanted to protest against the Church's 'involvement in politics' and requested Hurley to come and meet with them so that they could inform him how angry they were with Kaufmann.

On the day of this visit, Hurley first met with senior management of BTR Sarmcol, who put pressure on him to 'get this meddlesome priest out of politics and stop using your church for worker meetings', a similar message to the one Hurley received from the parish council. Hurley defended Kaufmann, saying that he was merely implementing the policy of the Bishops' Conference on the use of church buildings, especially in situations of struggle and suffering. He called for continued dialogue, searching for ways forward and keeping reconciliation as a primary goal. The meeting over, Hurley enjoyed a 'lovely Italian supper' with the priests, chatting in a relaxed way about life and Vatican II, anything and everything except the tense meeting with the parish council.

Whenever MAWU ran out of funds for food parcels, they would turn to Hurley for assistance, and the St Joseph the Worker Fund always came to their relief. They also secured permission from the Oblates of St Francis de Sales to plough their small-holding in Merrivale, near Howick, and plant vegetables to supplement the food parcels and to give the striking workers employment. Hurley obtained funds from *Misereor* to purchase the farm on behalf of what was known as the Sarmcol Workers' Co-operative (SAWCO).[6] SAWCO also arranged for the workers to make T-shirts and to buy in bulk. They put together a play known as 'The Long March', which told the story of their lengthy legal battle. This was performed overseas to raise funds.

Their case was taken to the Industrial Court, the Natal Supreme Court (now known as the High Court), the Labour Appeals Court and the Supreme Court of Appeals. Finally, 13 years after the strike began in 1985, the Supreme Court of Appeals in 1998 found in favour of the dismissed workers, ruling that BTR Sarmcol had unfairly dismissed them. It found that BTR Sarmcol management's desire to break the union, was the main cause of the strike, which they had used as an opportunity to replace all the unionized workers with non-unionized ones. Judge Pierre Olivier described the workers' 13-year battle as a simple attempt by the union to gain legal recognition. He said that no responsible employer, knowing the consequences to an entire community, would dismiss a workforce of nearly 1,000 people, each with an average service of 25 years, after giving them only 1 hour to return to work.

Dladla described Hurley as

> like a father to the whole strike. Whenever . . . someone who passed away . . . had [left the family with] no income . . . he would gladly and positively respond. [He would say,] 'This is what you do'. He was always behind our cause . . . He was very generous and he was very sympathetic and he was also very clear on the oppression that the workers were facing . . . He put himself squarely into the shoes of the workers and walked along with all of us.

22

Police Conduct in the Townships

On 3 September 1984, rage and frustration exploded in the five black townships of Boipatong, Bophelong, Evaton, Sebokeng and Sharpeville, which together form an area known as the Vaal Triangle, 60 kilometres south of Johannesburg.[1] The immediate cause was the rent increases proposed by black-run town councils, whose members (as we have seen) were regarded as sell-outs. On 3 September three black township officials were killed in mob violence. One of them was Kuzwayo Jacob Dlamini, deputy mayor of the Vaal Triangle, who was attacked and killed by an angry crowd. The mob approached him at his home, taunting him to join them in a march to the local administration to air their grievances. Dlamini had begun firing at the crowd, injuring at least one. The crowd was incensed and burnt his house and car, and then stoned and burnt him.

This incident led to a case against five men and one woman, who became known as the 'Sharpeville Six'. They were arrested, tried, convicted and sentenced to hang for having 'common purpose' with Councillor Dlamini's killers, who remained unknown. Such mob violence was the climax to years of public contempt for government-sponsored councillors, who were thought to be lining their pockets at the expense of the community. One of those who championed the release of the Sharpeville Six was the Catholic parish priest of Sebokeng, Father Paddy Noonan OFM, who had been in the Vaal Triangle for seven months. He and his colleagues from other Catholic parishes in this area, as well as pastors of other denominations involved in the Vaal Ministers' Solidarity Group (VMSG), witnessed and recorded the escalation of events that continued over the next few years. These are well documented in Noonan's book *They're Burning the Churches*.

Noonan and the other clergy were horrified by the South African government's decision to send 7,000 troops and police into Sebokeng in the course of 'Operation Palmiet', a 'peace offensive' launched on 24 October 1984. Though this was officially described as an effort 'to restore law and order and to get rid of criminal and revolutionary elements', it was actually what Noonan called a desperate attempt to restore apartheid's 'disintegrating regime'. For Noonan, the Vaal Triangle was the place where 'the liberation revolution began in earnest—the first shots in the final phase of the country's struggle for freedom were fired there—by the police'.

So disturbed were Noonan and his colleagues by the police conduct that they began to share their reports with the SACBC and SACC and were regularly invited to brief officials of both. Noonan said, 'There's a madness in the air and the whole structure of the townships is falling asunder . . . We found ourselves as clergy trying prayerfully to interpret the signs of the times'.

In the police's desperation to re-assert control over these townships, they resorted to every possible tactic, many of them illegal. As these facts came to the attention of the SACBC, the general secretary, Father Smangaliso Mkhatshwa, informed Hurley as president. They decided that the Conference should collect information about what was happening, publish a full report on police conduct, and disseminate it as widely as possible, especially overseas.[2] Between October and December 1984, the clergy of the Vaal Triangle collected affidavits of police brutality from those who had been arrested, detained and tortured. As Noonan said: 'We had the ears of the people, the trust of the people. They came to us, they reported to us, and we sent many people out to bring back . . . names, times, addresses, information on what was happening, . . . and we collected a massive amount of information [including] affidavits which we had to do secretly because the security branch [officers] were extremely active in those days'.

They also decided to share the information with foreign journalists because there were so many restrictions on the local media. 'So we would take the opportunity to give interviews. To bring people from the townships and whisk them up to upper rooms in big hotels and put them before cameras to tell the world what was really happening . . . while the police were chasing us and trying to find out what we were up to'. Economic sanctions had long been discussed overseas: for this campaign to be effective, it was necessary for people to be accurately informed.

Hurley presented the thirty-eight-page document 'Report on Police Conduct during Township Protests: August–November 1984' to the media in Pretoria on 6 December 1984.[3] The most scathing critique of police conduct published at that time, it quoted sworn affidavits relating to cases of gratuitous violence, rape, theft, indiscriminate shooting, beating and tear gas use, and called for an immediate inquiry into the abuses, followed by appropriate disciplinary action. Both black and white police were said to have been involved, but mainly young white police. The report accused the police of indiscriminately using firearms, birdshot, rubber bullets and tear gas, assaults and beatings, damage to property, and callous or insensitive conduct. It also referred to 'particularly provocative' conduct at funerals of people killed by the police, who seemed to be 'at war' with the residents.

To be fair to the police, the bishops noted that there had also been cases of mob violence and instances where the police had been provoked or had to act in self-defence, but added: 'That cannot justify unwarranted or illegal conduct on the part of the police'. They estimated that, in the 3 months since 3 September, there had been more than 150 deaths due to the violence, while the injured 'may run into thousands'.

The most disturbing finding was that 'the police are now regarded by many people in the black townships as disturbers of the peace and perpetrators of violent crime' . . . They seemed to say, "The people are our enemy, and we are out to impose our will upon them by any means that we find effective"'. The report warned that 'the legacy of bitterness and resentment that this wanton violence engenders, serves only to postpone a just and lasting settlement of the issues dividing our country'. The Police Act prohibited the publication of unproven accusations against the police. To avoid prosecution in terms of this legislation, the evidence came from sworn affidavits made by individuals before a commissioner of oaths.

During the week before the media conference, the bishops made a number of efforts to present the report to Mr Louis le Grange, Minister of Law and Order, but he was 'too busy'. The police's official response, once they had studied the report, was that it contained 'untruths as regards detail, chronology and events'. They found it regrettable that the bishops had not condemned or even mentioned 'the victimization and brutal murder of innocent people by callous and lawless rioters'. Despite this strong response to the bishops' claims, the report provoked 'an intense public debate in the national English and Afrikaans press on the methods, outlook, perceptions, activities and equipment used by the police in the black ghettoes', as Noonan noted.

The bishops wanted to do more than just issue a report on the police violence; they decided to go as a group to Sebokeng to demonstrate their solidarity with the community. Noonan and other local clergy, who were asked to organize the liturgy, arranged that the bishops would walk in procession through the grim and dusty streets of Sebokeng to Emmanuel Church, Unit 14, where a great Mass of solidarity would be celebrated. On the day, the twenty-eight robed and mitred bishops, led by Hurley, were accompanied by many visiting priests and nuns, who had come to show solidarity. Such a procession was illegal, but the whole event was kept low-key, and it was over before the police realized what was happening. The bishops made their way to the church 'with great serenity, as they smilingly walked up the street amidst the crowds'. A large contingent of local and foreign journalists had been invited to make sure the story went around the world.

A special offertory procession provided another powerful focus for the media, as symbols of the township situation were brought to the altar and held up by the bishops for the whole congregation to see. These included a list of people in detention, a rent invoice, school books, a tear-gas canister, a list of those killed in the violence, a change of clothes for a detainee and the bishops' report on police conduct—as well as rubber bullets. The media even dubbed the service 'The Mass of the Rubber Bullet'. It was a friendly and peaceful 'invasion', unlike the one by police and army on 4 October 1984. The people gave the bishops a rousing cheer as they emerged from the church at the end of the Mass, and crowds rushed forward to shake their hands.

After the lengthy emotion-charged Mass, the bishops spent the day in small groups, visiting sites where conflict had taken place and the homes of victims of police violence. Hurley was greatly impressed by the work the local churches were doing: 'It is not enough just to preach to people during a crisis. The Catholic

Church's response to [the] unrest in the Vaal townships is an example of crisis ministry. During the unrest, priests worked closely with the people, often acting as their representatives'.[4]

The local authorities, angry at being taken unawares by the bishops' visit to Sebokeng, summoned a policeman known to them, to find out what had been going on 'at the Roman church' the previous day. 'What was that Hurley talking about?' they wanted to know. With a broad smile the policeman told them that the archbishop had been 'talking about love'. Quite true, of course, though their informant could perhaps have added that Hurley had been explaining the implications of love in the present situation. 'There must be change', Hurley had said, 'for without it there can be no peace, and without change my greeting to you is a complete and utter mockery'.

At the time of his court appearance in the Namibian case in Pretoria on 18 February 1985, Hurley also arranged to go with a delegation of the SACBC and the VMSG to discuss the police conduct report with Colonel Steyn, the Divisional Commander of the South African Police.[5] The police insisted that the SACBC provide them with statements and affidavits relating to police brutality. The bishops' concern was that if they made the statements and affidavits available to the police, they would have to ensure that those who had made them would have adequate protection. The SACBC insisted that any questioning take place on church property and that a priest or lawyer be present throughout. Ultimately the police would not accept this procedure. Nevertheless, Noonan recalled how civil, friendly and controlled Hurley was in his contacts with the police, how much the delegation trusted his leadership, and how his figure and standing also had to be respected by the police.

Looking back on Hurley's central role in the compilation of the report, its media launch, the solidarity Mass in Sebokeng and the interaction with the police that followed, Sarah Crowe, media officer for the SACBC, said:

> You could see that [Hurley] was a man who was driven. He had a passion, he had a sense of purpose. [He was] so single-minded about where he was going with the Bishops' Conference that . . . nobody . . . who had any doubt in their mind could really say anything else . . . Hurley put together some completely convincing arguments as to why these acts should be done, . . . convincing them that the church could not remain silent, and doing it in such an eloquent way . . . He was a natural-born media player. It just came to him as mother's milk. He fitted into an interview situation, he knew how to pace himself, what words to use . . . I think in another life he would have been a . . . brilliant politician. He had very . . . clear qualities of leadership and great oratorical skills.

23

New Policy Directions

Three major policy directions undertaken by the SACBC during Hurley's second presidency made a huge difference in how the Catholic Church related to the political situation in South Africa. We have already seen the first of these, which was that the Church gave its full backing to the worker struggle.

The second related to altering the fundamental orientation of the bishops' efforts to bring about change, which up to that time had been largely by trying to influence the National Party government and the white population of South Africa. By the 1980s it was clear that this was not working, and the bishops had to accept that the liberation movements were the major force for change.

The third new policy direction was that after decades of relying on pastoral letters and statements, the bishops decided that the situation was so critical that sanctions were the only effective non-violent strategy. Hurley strongly promoted these policy changes and led the way in implementing each despite not being enthusiastic about sanctions.

MEETING THE ANC

In 1983 for the first time, the head of the Catholic Church in South Africa and the leader of the ANC-in-exile met for secret and informal talks.[1] This was before the time when large delegations, including trade unions, leaders of the Afrikaans community and business leaders began publicly meeting the ANC in Lusaka and elsewhere for informal talks about the growing crisis in South Africa and a vision for post-apartheid South Africa.

Hurley as president of the Bishops' Conference and Oliver Tambo as president of the ANC had each expressed interest in meeting. Ian Linden of CIIR and Albert Nolan OP arranged the first meeting in London. Thabo Mbeki (former president of South Africa) was present as secretary to Tambo. The venue was the Railway Hotel at Paddington Station, which had several doors leading onto the busy station, where the encounter would hardly be noticed. 'The meeting was very jolly', said Linden, 'like

With Pope John XXIII and Bishop Gerard van Velsen OP of Kroonstad, 1960.

Archives, Archdiocese of Durban

Happy days for ICEL – presenting liturgical translations to Pope Paul VI.

Oblate Archives, Cedara

Celebrating the ordination of a new priest – Fr Raphael Mahlangu, 1976.

Fr Raphael Mahlangu

Praying with an old woman outside her makeshift shelter in 1989 after 30 families were evicted from their Weenen homes and forced into the open veld.

The Witness

A birthday celebration with learners at KwaThintwa School for the Deaf – which he founded.

UmAfrika

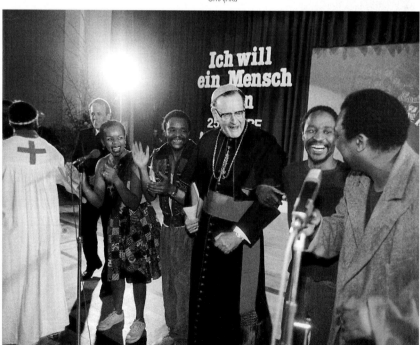

With "The Sounds of Soweto" at the opening of the German Lenten Campaign, organised by *Misereor*, 1983. The banner reads "I want to be a Human Being".

KNA – Bild, Bonn

Freedom March, 22 September 1989. From left: The Revd. Joe Fourie, Saydoon Sayeed (second row), Bishop Stanley Mogoba, Archbishop Hurley, Bishop Michael Nuttall, The Revd. John Borman, Muslim leaders.

Independent Newspapers

In the dock at the "Koevoet Trial", 18 February 1985. At left, Sr Brigid Flanagan HF.

Carmel Rickard

With Mikaela (niece) and Denis York, and their children, Helena and Theodore.

York family

Enjoying the Chancellor's joke — Professor Brenda Gourley, Vice-Chancellor of the University of Natal. On this occasion President Mandela was given an honorary doctorate.

Oblate Archives, Cedara

Last meeting with Pope John Paul II. In centre is Bishop Vincenzo Paglia, of the Community of Sant'Egidio.

Community of Sant'Egidio

Archbishop Hurley was an honorary member of the Black Sash. Here they stand in his honour during the lying-in-state in Emmanuel Cathedral, 27 February 2004.

Sherilee Clarke, Independent Newspapers

brothers seeing each other after a long absence'. From their warm and effusive greetings, Linden concluded that they might have met in South Africa before Tambo went into exile in 1960, but I have found no evidence of such an earlier meeting.

For the Paddington meeting there had been a lot of 'subterfuge' and 'pantomime clandestine arrangements' to ensure secrecy. 'It was all sort of cloak and dagger but [in fact] a lot of cloak and no dagger', according to Linden. Much of this, on the ANC side, was caused by the fact that the London representative of the ANC at this time was seen as 'dodgy'—he later turned out to be an informer—so he had to be kept out of the arrangements, which were brokered by Ishmael Coovadia of the South African Communist Party.

Linden was full of admiration for how Hurley handled the 3-hour meeting under these awkward circumstances: 'He was magnificent in that [meeting], you know. When he met Oliver Tambo, he was just fantastic . . . I think it meant a lot to Tambo that he [Hurley] came, and it meant a lot to Hurley that he had that meeting with Tambo, and my sense was that he was able to handle it absolutely brilliantly, and that was terribly important for the future, . . . affirming what he [Hurley] was doing, but in a strange way they both affirmed each other'.

By 1986, when South Africa was in the grip of a protracted state of emergency, it had become clear to the bishops that they needed to have formal talks with the ANC-in-exile. The government had expressed anger at the legitimacy such meetings were giving the ANC but was unable to do anything effective to stop them, despite the fact that the ANC was still banned.

Speaking at the end of the bishops' plenary session in January 1986, Hurley indicated that the bishops were about to change their approach in response to what was happening in South Africa: 'We have to relate to the liberation movements'.[2] The change appeared to have been influenced by the *Kairos Document* (1985), a discussion paper reflecting on the crisis in South Africa, produced by a large group of theologians led by pastors and priests working in Johannesburg and the townships of Soweto. They had been appalled by the state of emergency and felt that it was time to re-assess the type of activities the Church engaged in and to develop new forms of action that would make a real difference to the future of South Africa.

Although the Church seemed, until then, to have aimed its exhortations largely at the whites and the government, now the bishops deemed it necessary to talk to the black liberation movements.[3] Because the ANC was set to play an important role in any new government, the bishops realised they would need to negotiate with it. Hurley could see that the ANC was the 'most powerful factor in regard to the pursuit of black liberation in South Africa, and had great support'.

On 14 April 1986 a four-person SACBC delegation flew to Lusaka, the capital of Zambia, for formal talks with the ANC-in-exile. The delegation consisted of Hurley as president, Napier as vice-president, Bishop Mansuet Biyase of Eshowe and Father Mkhatshwa as secretary general. As they stepped off the plane at Lusaka, they were met by Tambo and later introduced to the rest of the ANC delegation: Thabo Mbeki—in charge of publicity, Ruth Momphati, 'Mac' Maharaj, Steve Tshwete, John

Nkadimeng and Peter Ramokwa. The visitors were immediately plunged into a media conference.

The conversations with the ANC began that afternoon at 2:00 p.m., with the SACBC representatives giving their evaluation of the situation in South Africa. This was followed by the ANC delegation taking turns in presenting the overall strategy of the ANC, with a particular focus on the armed struggle, negotiations and sanctions, what the ANC's post-liberation policy would be, the ANC and communism, and the ANC's view of the churches' role. From these discussions, it appeared to the bishops that the ANC had a multifaceted strategy that was succeeding; meanwhile President P. W. Botha was floundering and obviously had no clear plan.

Hurley formed a positive impression of the ANC leadership: 'I found them very friendly, very open and easy to talk to, easy to debate with. . . . There was a sociability about them, a friendliness that was very impressive'.[4] He brought up the question of communism: 'Mr Tambo, you are deeply involved with the Communist Party and communists are strong in the ANC. Don't you fear that when you have . . . taken over, that in the end the communists will win out and impose a system in South Africa similar to the system in Russia and in Eastern Europe? A system of tyranny?' Tambo replied, 'I haven't noticed that at all . . . I don't think it worries us because we don't think it works out that way'.

This was not the only provocative question that Hurley asked. Napier remembered that he questioned the ANC delegation about economic policy, which at the time was socialist. How would they be able to impose that on an economy that was capitalistic without causing confusion? He also asked how the ANC would be able to change the bureaucracy controlling South Africa, again without causing confusion. According to Napier, Hurley's questions exercised the minds of the ANC team for the next two hours.[5] When the SACBC delegation raised their fears about sanctions causing an increase in suffering, poverty and unemployment, the ANC replied that the suffering caused by apartheid was far greater. The ANC's feeling was that the victims of apartheid were clamouring for sanctions.

With regard to the role of the Church, the ANC called for a more positive involvement in the South African political scene. There was a clear choice between apartheid and liberation. If the Church was opposed to apartheid, it should be working for liberation. It should take sides with the people in campaigns concerning rents, bus fares and boycotts. The Church should clear up misconceptions about the ANC and its policies.

In summing up their impressions, the SACBC report, probably drafted by Hurley, said:

> We found the ANC delegation extremely well informed and practised in the art of responding to questions and difficulties.
>
> We came away satisfied that the ANC is not communist although it admits communists to its ranks and works with communists. Essentially it could be designated the spearhead of a popular liberation movement.
>
> We found some responses rather unconvincing: in the matter of communists taking power; in regard to how managerial and technical services would be found for

a post-liberation civil service and nationalized industry; the matter too of atrocities such as the 'necklace of fire'.

Otherwise ANC delegates made out a case which is not easily dismissed especially in regard to the claim that the choice lies between apartheid and liberation and that anybody not doing anything to oppose apartheid is in fact supporting it.

The talks continued throughout the afternoon and evening of 15 April, as well as the next day until lunch time, an estimated 8 hours in all. Then the SACBC delegation returned to South Africa. In a 'Joint Communiqué' issued by the SACBC and the ANC on 16 April 1986, they indicated that they had reached a most significant agreement:

> The Pretoria regime cannot be an agent for change. Rather, it is the principal obstacle to the emergence of a democratic government representative of all the people of South Africa . . . Moved by a common concern to see all the people of South Africa, both black and white, living together in peace and as equals, the SACBC and the ANC agreed that they would continue to maintain contact with each other.

In an interview with Vatican Radio, Hurley called on the SA government to negotiate with the ANC. The bishops had come a long way from the distance and suspicion that had characterized their attitude towards the ANC from the 1950s until the early 1980s.[6]

SANCTIONS

Given the harsh repression in the Vaal Triangle in late 1984, Hurley was faced with one of the most difficult questions of his whole career as a bishop: whether to support economic sanctions as a way of ending apartheid. He feared that sanctions would cause more unemployment and poverty, leading to greater suffering and hardship.

Since the 1960s there had been calls to impose sanctions against South Africa.[7] Sports boycotts began with the country's exclusion from the Olympic Games. The Gleneagles Agreement, signed by Commonwealth prime ministers in 1977, discouraged all sporting links with South Africa. A cultural boycott was also started by artists in the early 1960s. This was commended by the United Nations, which tried to dissuade artists from performing in South Africa. Though such boycotts showed that the world was opposed to apartheid, they caused only inconvenience. Economic sanctions, increasingly called for in the 1980s, were meant to damage South African trade and industry and force the government to abolish apartheid.

What put economic sanctions against apartheid on the agenda for many countries was P. W. Botha's famous 'Rubicon' speech in Durban on 15 August 1985. Advance publicity had indicated that he would announce a major change in policy. This created huge expectations. When the speech contained no such policy shift, despite widespread calls for change in South Africa and an international clamour for apartheid to be scrapped, the sanctions debate took on new urgency. Many countries wanted to know what the view was inside South Africa. This was not easy to determine, given that the ANC and PAC were banned and some of their most important leaders imprisoned on Robben Island. Many turned to the churches to find out their view.

Hurley's role was crucial in formulating the SACBC stance.[8] At the time of taking office as president of the Conference in 1981, he had said that the bishops had in mind an 'altered strategy' that would include 'external economic pressure', but it was only after the Vaal Triangle crisis of 1984 and the first state of emergency in 1985 that formal policy statements on sanctions were published. At the end of the 1986 plenary, Hurley reported that the bishops had concluded that violence was 'becoming so characteristic of our country that unless an alternative way of bringing about change is found, the country will be devoured by violence'. The alternative could not be moral persuasion since that had been tried unsuccessfully for a long time. Something with greater impact was needed. This could include such 'non-violent measures as boycotts, passive resistance and economic pressure—the pressure of divestment, disinvestments, sanctions'.

'The sort of violence we have been seeing since September 1984' made the choice clear for the bishops, but they realized that the non-violent strategy of sanctions could not be pursued without increased unemployment and economic distress or hardship resulting from state repression of protest. The bishops were frank about their fear: 'We dread what this may mean for many people'. Nevertheless, they urged their people to consider that economic sanctions might be the only alternative to uncontrolled violence and reminded them that when confronted with the choice between two evils, 'love dictates the choice of the lesser'. They came to the conclusion, therefore, that, 'while still open to dialogue, we see no choice but to envisage forms of non-violent action such as passive resistance, boycotts and economic pressure to move our country away from its present state of racial conflict and set it firmly on the road to justice and full participation of all its inhabitants in the structures of government'.

The bishops resolved to hold an extraordinary plenary session in May 1986, at which sanctions would be discussed further and decisions taken. In the run-up to that session, knowing how controversial the issue was, they invited written submissions. Many were received, but almost exclusively from whites strongly opposed to economic pressure. African opinion has not tended to be expressed in terms of written submissions.

Hurley must also have been disturbed that over forty of his own priests met in Durban, on their own initiative, just before the bishops' meeting, to air their views on sanctions.[4] The overwhelming majority questioned the motives behind the Church's public and official support for economic pressure and dialogue with the ANC, which they saw as snubbing the more moderate Chief Mangosuthu Buthelezi, who was implacably opposed to sanctions. The chairperson of the priests' meeting, Father Angus Mackinnon OMI, said that the gathering offered the priests an opportunity to discuss, debate and comment on the bishops' attitude. In a secret ballot, thirty-five voted against disinvestment and six in favour. Four abstained and two ballot papers were spoilt. Those who had voted against disinvestment said that it would lead to a climate of revolution. Priests, they said, could not preach such a doctrine as a Christian solution, knowing that it would lead to more unemployment, hardship and violence.

Three full days were set aside for the bishops' special plenary on sanctions a few days after the Durban priests' meeting.[10] On the first day, arguments were put forward by five speakers addressing different aspects. Most spoke strongly in favour of disinvestment, though Hurley had made sure that there was at least one opponent: Noel Pistorius, an attorney. In order to stimulate debate, he gave Pistorius all the information he needed to argue the case against sanctions. In the plenary discussions that followed the expert presentations, there were strong arguments for and against. Hurley remembered bishops saying: 'I just think of my diocese and the increase in unemployment that is going to result from this. I can't support sanctions. We will have hundreds of people coming to the door, asking for charity'.

On the third day and late into that night, the bishops met in closed session with their theological advisers. Brian Gaybba, who facilitated the discussion, said that the bishops' decision in favour of sanctions was ultimately collegial. He focused the discussion on what the bishops wanted to say and its theological implications. Father Kevin Rai, another theological adviser, said that the bishops' final decision showed considerable restraint. The kind of pressure they agreed to would have to satisfy three conditions: it should not destroy the economy; it should keep further job losses to a minimum; it should enjoy the support of the people most affected.

Even this conditional support was not presented as something 'of universal obligation' but of 'discernment', meaning that individual members of the Church could disagree with the bishops. But those who disagreed should only do so after careful and serious consideration of what the bishops said. Their pastoral letter on sanctions 'pressurizes no one into conformity. But it does force everyone to think and to take the necessary action', said Rai.

In order to help members of the Church understand exactly what the bishops were saying, special public meetings were held in various parts of the country, where the bishops invited questions and comments.[11] Each of these meetings, from 19 to 27 May in Pietermaritzburg, Durban, East London, Port Elizabeth, Cape Town, Bloemfontein and Johannesburg, was addressed by a local bishop together with Gaybba.

The pastoral letter on sanctions stated:

> It is the unprecedented seriousness of our present crisis, the enormity of the present suffering of the oppressed people of South Africa, the horrifying spectre of escalating violence that has led us to take this stand. Anyone who does not appreciate the untold daily sufferings of the people, the pain, the insecurity of starvation, the horrors of widespread unemployment that are associated with the present system, will also not appreciate the need for drastic and extraordinary measures to put an end to all this misery as quickly as possible . . . It seems that the most effective of non-violent forms of pressure left is economic pressure.

Ian Linden of CIIR, who travelled with Hurley to various meetings in the United Kingdom where sanctions were discussed, described him as a 'wobbly' advocate of the policy. When the microphone was switched off at the end of the meeting, he would make remarks about how he was really not sure about sanctions. Though his mind said 'yes' to economic pressure, he did not like advocating sanctions because they would cause a lot of suffering among poor black people. Napier felt that there was another reason for Hurley's hesitation: his concern about the negative response of his clergy. Just as he was keen to achieve collegial consensus with his colleagues in the Bishops' Conference, he was anxious to have collegiality with his priests, and the Durban priests' meeting described earlier indicated that this was far from the case with regard to sanctions.[12]

Enthusiastic campaigners for sanctions were Desmond Tutu, the Anglican Archbishop of Cape Town, and Dr Beyers Naudé, former Director of the banned Christian Institute.[13] Hurley was concerned about maintaining collegiality with his brother bishops and priests and bringing the lay constituency along with him as far as possible in his prophetic stance, but Tutu appears not to have had this concern. He had become committed to sanctions long before he became head of the Anglican Church in South Africa though his call for comprehensive sanctions was made just 12 days before his election as Archbishop of Cape Town.[14] Naudé had been expelled from the Dutch Reformed Church, so he did not have to worry about a church constituency but simply to lead his band of committed followers.

The leader of the Liberal Party in South Africa and famous author, Alan Paton, opposed sanctions because, like Hurley, he feared they would cause more unemployment and hardship for those already over-burdened. Unlike Hurley, who came to accept that there was no peaceful alternative, Paton remained totally opposed. There were also some, like Cos Desmond, who argued that foreign investment destroyed more jobs than it created. For example, the mechanization of agriculture, with the aid of imported technology, led to the 'resettlement' of 1.1 million black people who had been rendered 'superfluous' on white farms. Fears that sanctions would cause unemployment were therefore overblown, Desmond thought.[15]

24

Mobilizing the Church

During his second presidency of the SACBC from 1981 to 1987, Hurley devoted renewed effort to mobilizing the Church for a deeper involvement in social justice through a pastoral plan launched in 1989 and by involving the churches in Christians for Justice and Peace (CJP).

PASTORAL PLANNING

After the Second Vatican Council, many dioceses and bishops' conferences embarked on 'pastoral planning', working out how the Church should respond to the social situation. It was the 'see, judge, act' method of Joseph Cardijn, writ large for a whole diocese or country. The most famous pastoral plans emerged from Latin America, where bishops' conferences of the whole continent developed a common pastoral approach in the general assemblies of Medellín in Colombia (1969) and Puebla in Mexico (1979).

This approach was deeply influenced by Vatican II documents like *The Church in the Modern World*. However, because Latin America's social situation was one of overwhelming economic inequality and injustice, their bishops developed an important additional dimension: the 'option for the poor'. In a situation of such economic oppression, the Church could not be a neutral referee: it would have to take the side of the poor. This, they were convinced, was how Christ would have responded to their reality. Medellín and Puebla popularized the idea of pastoral planning, especially in third-world countries faced with similar situations of profound injustice and inequality. South Africa was more than ready for pastoral planning, but it took years to formulate a plan because the bishops were determined to prepare the document in a participatory way so as to ensure a high level of ownership.

In 1977, hard on the heels of the Soweto uprising, the SACBC held a special study day on social justice.[1] For the first time, the bishops deliberately focused on how racial discrimination within the Church mirrored the injustices of the society as a whole. This led them to commit themselves to making specific changes in the

Church's life and institutions. Their *Declaration of Commitment on Social Justice and Race Relations within the Church* was impressive, but many felt that it did not really succeed, since follow-up and implementation were weak.

Nevertheless, one of the most important discoveries of the 1977 study day was that much could be gained if bishops, priests, religious and laity jointly assessed where the Church was going. The idea was accepted by the SACBC, and dates were set for 1980, giving time to survey all parishes, groups and dioceses to find out their needs and priorities. These were fed into an Inter-diocesan Pastoral Consultation held at Hammanskraal. Though two priorities emerged clearly, social justice and building community, these headed a lengthy list, and the SACBC was overwhelmed by the findings. The joint discussions and conclusions involving bishops, priests, religious and laity were, however, an important step on the way to a pastoral plan.

Nevertheless, something more rigorous and systematic was needed. Little progress was made until the SACBC focus on the Namibian situation intensified in 1981. Although the bishops were impressed by the stand their Conference was taking about that country, some asked why they were not paying equal attention to South African issues demanding attention. In the plenary session of 1983, they decided that similar attention should be given to South Africa's problems.

As they were preparing a study day with that focus, further questions were asked by some bishops. It was all very well, they said, to focus on South Africa's social problems, but what about the internal life of the Church in this country? Was that healthy? They acknowledged that it had many weaknesses, such as increasing ignorance of the faith, especially among young people, and much falling away in Christian living. The bishops decided that they would need two study days: on the social issues facing the country and on the internal life of the Church; both would be crucial for the eventual shape of their pastoral plan.

During the study day on the internal life of the Church, the bishops concluded that the methods of teaching the Catholic faith that had served the Church well in earlier years—preaching, encouraging various sodalities and organizations, and running Catholic schools—were not working any more. What seemed more effective in the modern world were small neighbourhood groups that reflected on life and faith in the light of the gospel. Such groups, where pastoral planning was done at micro-level, were crucial to Medellín and Puebla. It became clear to the SACBC that one or two study days would not be enough to develop a pastoral plan for South Africa: a huge task lay ahead. The bishops decided to set up a committee, chaired by Hurley, to formulate a pastoral plan that would respond to both the internal and the external scene. It would, however, take a further six years before that plan would be launched and several more before its implementation.

In 1984 a Pastoral Planning Working Paper was issued by the SACBC; thousands of copies were sent to parishes and groups, asking them to make suggestions for a pastoral plan. Only a hundred replies were received. These were collated and the results presented to the SACBC plenary session in January 1987. Hurley was keen to ensure that pastoral planning was solidly established as the way forward for the Catholic Church in South Africa. But he realized that, for himself, time was running out. At that January plenary, his second presidency of the SACBC would come to an end. He arranged that 2½ days would be spent on pastoral planning.

Reports were received on what had been done, especially the collated responses to the working paper. The comments focused on two key aspects: building community and being involved in action to bring about change: not separate activities but brilliantly combined in the theme 'Community Serving Humanity', which was officially adopted. Agreement was reached that the remainder of 1987 would be used to seek the views of all parishes and groups (May to October) and then those of all dioceses (in November).

When asked about Hurley's role in developing the pastoral plan, Bishop Oswald Hirmer of Mthatha said, 'He was the driving force at all stages'. But he added that Hurley had the humility to accept that the plan would be different from what he had originally envisaged. Hurley's view had been that a few bishops would each draft a section; these would then be put together into a plan. 'But all that was thrown overboard . . . and the whole approach changed', said Hirmer.

Bishop Fritz Lobinger of Aliwal North also believed Hurley's role to have been crucial. One of Hurley's key talents, he said, was to provide a bird's-eye view of the whole project and to keep all the phases in mind. Another was that he had learnt over the years to ask searching questions rather than propose solutions, so he would ask: 'Now that we've more-or-less got an idea of a pastoral plan, how do we go ahead?' or 'Who is talking to whom in this plan?' Lobinger sensed in the older Hurley a man who 'was already a bit used to having an idea rejected. I heard from others that in earlier times he would fight for one issue'. In the older Hurley he saw 'a shrewd man, holding back at times . . . He would let others speak and wait until the air clears slowly, . . . not push an idea immediately so that the opposition doesn't grow, . . . although he knows the opposition is there. He would surely play down his own opinion, . . . rather letting someone else express a conclusion that he might have already come to'.

Hirmer felt that 'by accompanying the Pastoral Plan, by his listening attitude, . . . he [Hurley] made an essential contribution'. This showed 'the greatness of the man'. Though his idea of the methodology had been rejected, he did not say: 'Well, you haven't accepted my idea, so I'll just leave you to do it'. He remained keenly engaged in the process.

CHRISTIANS FOR JUSTICE AND PEACE[2]

'If only you had known the things that make for your peace' (Luke 19:42) was the theme chosen by the SACC for its national conference in 1983.[3] One of the speakers invited to address the theme was Hurley, who ended with a call for a major new Christian justice and peace programme at the national level. At this time hundreds of non-governmental organisations were coming together in the United Democratic Front (UDF). Perhaps he was influenced by this example.

Hurley asked whether South Africa knew the things that make for peace any better than Jerusalem in the time of Christ. His answer was that it did not, 'because we have not thought, prayed, searched and consulted enough together to find out what we should know and do'. As a result, no systematic programme of peacemaking had been worked out by the Church. Once again, as with pastoral planning, Latin America was Hurley's source of inspiration. The Church there had for a long time been supportive of the rich and powerful, but now had confidently set out on a new course. The change had come about through Medellín and Puebla's 'preferential option for the poor'. This, said Hurley, gave a powerful impetus to the small Christian communities of the poor, which emphasized building community, as well as dealing with spiritual and material concerns. They had given a whole new dynamism to the struggle for justice and peace.

Though the Church in South Africa could not simply adopt this model from Latin America, Hurley felt several features were worth considering: the importance of combining spiritual inspiration and social concern; systematic effort in theology, leadership, development of programmes and training; recognition of the need for people to participate and to express their needs and insights, and for the theologians, organizers and trainers to discern what action the Holy Spirit wanted. This would require two or three years of prayer and extensive consultation so that great numbers of Christians throughout South Africa could be involved.

For a start, Hurley suggested, the aim of the South African justice and peace programme should be to hold a large conference in 1986. Church leadership should assume overall responsibility for this event, using the SACC for executive and secretarial services. Consultation within participating churches should begin as soon as possible.

Hurley's proposal was discussed at the next meeting of national church leaders in February 1984.[4] He spoke about the conference he had proposed for 1986 as a 'massive effort to . . . get people to open their hearts to what the Holy Spirit is trying to say to them', but observed that the word 'conference' was perhaps not the most appropriate because what he had in mind was more of an ongoing process, with lots of preparation before the event and extensive follow-up. A committee was appointed to propose the way forward: Rev Dr K. Mgojo (Methodist), Mr I. C. Aitken (Presbyterian), Rev M. Wessels (Congregational), Bishop D. Tutu (at this time general secretary of the SACC, as convenor) and Hurley.

When this group met on 13 March 1984, they agreed that the aim of the project should be 'Transformation of South African society through Christian education and action'. Policy and general oversight would be the responsibility of a church leaders' committee, which would in turn appoint a research and action committee to draw up the plan for countrywide prayer and consultation. A suggested name for the process was 'Christians for Justice and Peace'.

A 'group of interested persons' from the Durban area met Hurley on 8 May 1984 to develop ideas that could be forwarded to the next church leaders' meeting.[5] This group urged that the conference be postponed to 1987, to allow more time for consultation. The target for participation in this process should be 'those small groups already grappling with issues. They could be greatly strengthened and encouraged by discovering their numbers right across the country, and should begin to be involved in the preparations as soon as possible so that they could "own" the

Conference and be committed to follow-up. Both black and white people would need to be involved'.

From early on it was realized that full-time staff would be needed to bring the vision to fruition. Initially, Peter Kerchhoff, organizing secretary of PACSA in Pietermaritzburg, acted as coordinator, and later Sue Brittion, a staff member of Diakonia in Durban. Eighteen months after the proposal by Hurley in June 1983, the church leaders decided to proceed with 'Christians for Justice and Peace', on the basis of extensive consultations.

Gradually, over the next year, regional CJP groupings emerged in Cape Town, Johannesburg, Durban and Pietermaritzburg and fleshed out the basic concept of CJP.[6] From the leaflet prepared during 1985 on the basis of these regional discussions, it seemed that a high level of consensus had been reached about CJP's purpose and how it would operate. The organization would call together people committed to transformation to share resources and experience, develop strategies and build a network with other individuals and groups working for justice and peace'. The proposed conference was described as a 'national gathering' whose form and content 'will be determined by those individual Christians, Christian groups and Christian agencies participating' in CJP.

The purpose of gathering these groups regionally and nationally was to share experiences, reflect theologically, develop a vision of transformation, exchange information and resources, build common strategies, plan for crises, give each other mutual support and encouragement, stimulate networks, and then encourage further growth and multiplication.

According to Brittion, 'There were already at that time a whole lot of Christians who were organized in various ways but . . . were all working disparately . . . because the security apparatus was so good [at dividing organizations]'. Some justice and peace groups did network but only at the diocesan or local level, not nationally.

Soon it was possible for a national consultation about CJP to be scheduled for 22 to 24 November 1985. This was preceded by regional consultations in the four areas where CJP groups had been meeting. These regional consultations focused on questions about the future of CJP, including whom they thought should be involved, what structure and staffing should animate the organization at national level, what sort of national gathering would be appropriate and when it should be held.

The general response was positive; it seemed that the delegates could see the value of the networking that CJP would offer. A warning note had, however, been sounded by Rev Frank Chikane of the Institute for Contextual Theology (since 1994 director-general in the Office of the Presidency), who said, 'CJP needs to be extraordinary if it is going to take root in [the] black community'. Much earlier in the process, Rev Peter Storey, president of the Methodist Conference, had expressed his concern at the Church leaders' meeting of February 1984. He had heard an opinion 'that the churches would split before the end of the decade [presumably along racial lines]'. It would be difficult for a programme like CJP to take off in such a climate.[7]

Days before CJP's first national consultation, a Black Ecumenical Church Leaders' Consultation (BECLC) was held in KwaZulu-Natal, attended by eighty church leaders, ministers and lay people. Brittion made a presentation about CJP. The meeting raised many concerns about the proposed programme, and participants decided not to be involved in any way.[8] The delegates felt that the original CJP idea had been 'hijacked' and 'skilfully sidestepped'. They were also 'gravely distressed' that requests made by a black caucus had been 'flagrantly ignored'. These had called for a black programme with its own aims, methodology and perspective of education 'that should run parallel with a white programme [yet] under one umbrella'—a methodology common in the days of Black Consciousness. In addition, CJP had been urged by the black caucus to 'listen to our black people' and 'obtain from the blacks the mandate to determine such an agenda'.

The BECLC felt that the CJP programme was being imposed from the top rather than developing from grass roots. This was 'intolerable oppression' at a time when 'the entire black community was experiencing untold suffering'. The words 'Christians', 'Justice', 'Peace' and 'Transformation' as used in the CJP programme 'are those of people suffocating from affluence [and] totally unaffected by township life'. The BECLC's conclusion was that 'the CJP is not dealing with our agenda at all and as such we feel morally bound to dissociate ourselves from this programme forthwith; and call on all black Christians, here and elsewhere, to support us in this stand'. The BECLC was aware that CJP was already raising funds and said that any resources procured on behalf of black people should be given to black people to use for their own programme.

When delegates assembled for the CJP national consultation, on the evening of 22 November 1985, the first item on the programme was the BECLC resolution. After this had been presented and discussed, the meeting adjourned to enable a caucus of black CJP delegates to discuss their own response. This they presented the next morning: 'In the light of the Black Ecumenical Church Leaders' Consultation's statement', they said, 'black delegates to the present CJP consultation, in solidarity with its sentiments, find it impossible to participate further in the conference'.

One delegate then made a statement expressing sadness at the decision of the black caucus but also understanding their position. Black delegates withdrew from the consultation, which was then considered closed. No further meeting under the banner of CJP was ever held. Brittion sent a letter to the members of the church leaders' group explaining what had happened. She ended with the comment, 'My heart is heavy. I had really believed that here at last was a programme with which the Church could become relevant to the realities of the South African situation'. Brittion has no recollection of receiving any replies, which added to her feeling of isolation.

There is no record of how Hurley felt about this rejection of a plan in which he had invested much time and commitment and which appeared so promising. Reflecting on this rejection, it seems clear that more care should have gone into consulting about the aims and methods of CJP, and more attention to ensuring the diversity of those involved in key roles. It was unfortunate that in an organization proposed by a white church leader, its main decision-making structure—the Research and Action committee—was chaired by another white (Beyers Naudé), and the only full-time member of staff—the coordinator of the programme—was also white. In Brittion's view, the original committee that had set up CJP should have looked at itself and realized that it consisted primarily of whites and therefore needed to check out more rigorously whether there was real support from black people.[9] Ironically, it was a case worthy of the lament: 'If only you had known the things that make for your peace'.

25

Reason to Believe

One of the best-known human rights lawyers in Durban, Victoria Mxenge, was gunned down outside her home in Umlazi, on 1 August 1985, while returning from work. During a memorial service held for her in the Umlazi Cinema on 8 August, according to the Truth and Reconciliation Commission's report, hundreds of armed Inkatha vigilantes stormed into the cinema and began randomly stabbing and shooting the mourners, killing fourteen and injuring many others. In response to the death of Mxenge and this attack on the mourners, widespread unrest broke out in the Durban townships. The security police, in an effort to pin the blame on the UDF, arrested a number of UDF leaders and others associated with them.[1]

The detainees were held under Section 29 of the Internal Security Act, which provided for indefinite incommunicado detention: no lawyers, no visits, no contact or messages were allowed. No one would know where they were held or what was happening to them. There was nothing that anyone, supposedly also including the courts, could do about it. South Africa remained a strangely legalistic society, with the law and the courts still functioning and Section 29 providing the legal cover for indefinite detention.

I was among those detained at this time, arrested at the Diakonia offices on Monday, 26 August, as staff members were gathering for the weekly staff worship. Hurley was informed that the security police had placed me under arrest and were searching my office. He immediately came to find out what was happening. The security police unceremoniously pushed him out of my office and refused to allow him to speak to me.

The next person who came to find out what was happening was Advocate Chris Nicholson, who was Director of the Legal Resources Centre, one of the other tenants of the Ecumenical Centre, and now Deputy Judge President of KwaZulu-Natal. He asked the police under what provision they were acting and was angered when they told him. He knew that Section 29 was supposed to be used against people suspected of being terrorists or having information about terrorists that they had refused to divulge to the authorities. Nicholson said that he would challenge this detention in court. '[The security police] told me to get out of the office', he said, 'and as to my threat about court action, that I should do whatever I liked. Clearly, they paid no attention at all to what I said, as they believed they were immune from any court order'.[2]

As soon as he returned to his office at the Legal Resources Centre, Nicholson began preparing the legal action he had threatened. His first step was to contact Hurley to find out whether he would be willing to back a Supreme Court (now High Court) application for release. Hurley said that he was keen to do whatever would help, and the process of drafting papers got under way. This would be the test case that Nicholson had been mulling over for some time. He was convinced that there had to be a way of challenging Section 29.

Two crucial clauses of that Section would have to be tackled. Section 29 (6), the so-called 'ouster' clause, prevented courts from enquiring into detentions. This clause read: 'No court of law shall have jurisdiction to pronounce upon the validity of any action taken in terms of this section, or to order the release of any person detained in terms of the provisions of this section'. Section 29 (1) was equally important: 'Any commissioned officer . . . of or above the rank of lieutenant-colonel may, if he has reason to believe that any person [has committed terrorism or is withholding information about terrorism], without warrant, arrest such person and detain such person for interrogation'.

Nicholson detected a loophole in the phrase 'reason to believe' in Section 29 (1). He thought this meant there had to be objective facts or reasons on which the police officer had based the belief that it was necessary to arrest the suspect. It would not be enough to simply 'believe' that there were grounds. He correctly foresaw that the police would not accept this argument. They would refuse to disclose their 'reasons' for the decision to detain and justify their silence as necessary to protect their informers. He would then need to make an 'unanswerably persuasive case', as legal journalist Carmel Rickard described it, 'with a strong set of facts which would then stand unchallenged, because (as he expected) the police would put up nothing to rebut them'.

To persuade the court that it was not bound by the 'ouster' clause, Nicholson's argument would be that it was true that a court could not enquire into action 'taken in terms of this section'. If, however, the police had no 'reason' for their belief, then their action in detaining someone could not be said to have been ' in terms of this section'.

This is where Hurley's role would be crucial. He would have to make an affidavit with facts so strong that they would persuade a court, faced with either silence or innuendo on the part of the police. As Nicholson recalled, 'He rose to the occasion brilliantly. He was absolutely willing to say, with the utmost confidence, that he knew this detainee extremely well, had known him from birth and was utterly certain that there could be no good reason, as defined in the law, for the detention'. Hurley 'was a figure of great stature, and he made these statements in a commanding way. We felt that coming from him, it would have an impact against the things that the police were saying in their feeble reply'.

The legal battle took place over two days in the Durban Supreme Court before the Acting Deputy Judge President of the Natal Bench, Judge Ray Leon, who heard the application that the detention be declared invalid. The argument centred on the meaning of 'reason to believe' and on whether the court was entitled to hear the application at all, given the 'ouster' clause. Rickard said of Hurley, 'He seemed enthralled by the feint and parry, the intellectual skill involved'.

In a letter to his family, Hurley said that his legal team had

> put their heads together to build up a big case around 'if he has reason to believe'. These words became so important that we are considering [asking] a pop composer to put them to music . . . The whole thrust of the legal argument prepared by the team was to convince the judge that the phrase in question means that the police officer must have an objective reason, not just something that he cooks up subjectively, and once a person is required to have an objective reason, this must fall under the scrutiny of the court.

At the end of the second day's argument, Judge Leon reserved his judgment. Six days later, on 12 September, he was ready. When the court convened, he spoke gravely about the importance of the case. 'It raises matters of great constitutional importance affecting the liberty of the subject, the security of the State and the jurisdiction of the courts'. He took two hours to read the judgment, but Hurley felt it was 'pretty clear almost from the first sentence in which direction he was heading'.

Leon had decided that he did have the power to test whether or not the arresting officer really had 'a sound reason to believe'. An affidavit had been handed in to the court from the police officer in question, Lieutenant Colonel Ignatius Coetzee, head of the security police in Durban, certifying that his information (about the detainee) was confidential and that he would not reveal it. The judge therefore pronounced the detention unlawful and ordered the release of the detainee. 'We wanted to jump up in our seats and roar our hurrahs', said Hurley, 'but that is not done in court, and we observed due decorum'.

The state's lawyers made one last desperate effort to keep the detainee in detention, and that was to argue that my release should be put on hold, pending the state's appeal. Nicholson had expected this and had his argument ready to convince Leon that it would not be in the interests of justice for the execution of the order to be any further delayed. Then, as Rickard described, 'Archbishop Hurley led a triumphant procession to the security police headquarters to demand the release of the first Section 29 detainee ever freed on the say-so of a court'. Natal University Law professor and human rights lawyer Tony Matthews commented that this was 'the most important civil rights ruling for several decades'. A number of people were assisted by the legal loophole and were released from detention on the precedent set by what became known as the Hurley case.

Hurley attended the state's appeal against Leon's judgment heard in Bloemfontein on 13 March 1986.[3] Just over two months later, the Appeal Court announced its decision to uphold Leon's judgment and dismissed with costs the appeal by the Minister of Law and Order, the Commissioner of Police and the

Divisional Commissioner for Port Natal. The impact of the judgment was modified when the government changed the wording of security legislation to counter the effect of the court's decision. Later, the government declared a state of emergency (June 1986), with detentions made much easier under different regulations and legislation.

Nevertheless, Rickard said: 'Judge Leon's decision is still seen as a high point of judicial courage, and the reasoning in part of the appeal judgment—particularly on "ouster" clauses—is an important standard in administrative law even today'. 'The case has gone down in the legal record books as *Hurley and Another versus the Minister of Law and Order*, and is still taught in law classes and cited in judgments, even though Section 29 and the rest of the security legislation dreamed up to maintain apartheid have long since been scrapped'.

The Leon judgment would certainly not have been possible if Nicholson had not brilliantly identified the loophole in the law and Hurley had not lent his considerable stature and integrity to the application. Rickard comments that it was 'just one example among many of how Hurley helped people affected by unjust apartheid laws. During those terrible years, it was always reassuring and encouraging to have him on—and at—one's side: as Nicholson often quipped, "When you're in the hurly-burly, it's good to have the burly Hurley"'.

26

The Price of Prophecy

Hurley's second presidency of the SACBC, from January 1981 to January 1987, was the most prophetic period of his life in the biblical sense of that word, which (as we have seen earlier) means speaking out clearly and making courageous interventions in current events. Inevitably there was a price to pay, most notably through being charged and brought to court for statements about the activities of *Koevoet* in Namibia, but Hurley also had other experiences of the price of prophecy.

As a result of Hurley's sharp critique of security force involvement in Namibia and in the townships of the Vaal Triangle, Brian Edwards, a member of the Natal Provincial Council representing the conservative New Republic Party, in 1984 publicly described him as an 'ecclesiastical Che Guevara'.[1] He accused Hurley of encouraging church groups to show a video of security force atrocities. A particularly gruesome scene in the video portrays a group of soldiers in brown uniforms walking into a village and later leaving, their bayonets dripping with blood. Edwards claimed that this could not have been footage of the SADF, but was possibly of Cubans, because the film had clearly been dubbed from Spanish into English, and South Africa had stopped issuing bayonets to its soldiers over ten years earlier.

Hurley said that he had no knowledge of this video and, therefore, could not have promoted its use. Edwards, he said, appeared to have based his story on the right-wing *Aida Parker Newsletter* of 27 April 1984. According to Parker, Hurley had been present when the video was shown in Benoni. Hurley's response to this allegation was, 'It is a complete and utter fabrication that I was present'. Though there were widespread calls for Edwards to retract his remarks and apologize to Hurley, he refused.

Edwards's criticism, as he told me in an interview in 2004, was that Hurley was 'hearing the worst from everyone and that's what he put across all the time'. He complained that Hurley did not look at things in a balanced way but 'went overboard in the types of statement he made'. No charge was brought against Edwards, but he did receive a letter from Hurley's lawyer.

Something more sinister may have been behind Aida Parker's negative propaganda. As a result of the Truth and Reconciliation Commission's investigations into the former South African government's State Security Council (SSC), the TRC discovered that some church leaders who were thought to be making things difficult for the government had been targeted in various ways.[2] In a list of names presented to the SSC on 8 September 1986, Hurley's name appeared with those of Desmond Tutu, Allan Boesak and Wolfram Kistner. The recommendation was that Boesak have his passport taken away, Kistner be banned, Tutu be 'cut off' from overseas funding and have 'StratCom action' taken against him, as should also happen to Hurley. StratCom (Strategic Communications) specialized in intelligence gathering and 'dirty tricks'. According to one of its former operatives, speaking at a TRC hearing, it used propaganda, front companies, surrogate organizations, assassinations, theft, blackmail, subversion and a 'host of other activities'. Among these tactics were concerted campaigns to undermine prominent democratic leaders. Was Aida Parker employed by StratCom for campaigns against Hurley?

Another anti-Hurley smear appeared in an overseas publication, the Southern Californian *Family Protection Scoreboard*, a magazine distributed free to a wide range of clergy.[3] As part of a general attack on liberation theology, it published a photo of Hurley presiding at a Mass at which a black priest was seen holding up petrol bombs. The caption read, 'Two petrol bombs are held aloft by a Black priest at a "Mass for peace" . . . intended to strengthen the people's fight for liberation'. In the accompanying article, the *Family Protection Scoreboard* alleged that Hurley and three other 'celebrity' church leaders (Tutu, Naudé, Boesak) had at one time or another 'advocated or hinted at the violent overthrow of the SA government'. The article claimed that all three had 'a nominal in-country religious constituency, most of which disapprove of their political activities and their spending of church funds'.

Hurley criticized the *Family Protection Scoreboard* for 'misinforming' its readers by distorting the truth for its own purposes. He explained that the picture of the priest with petrol bombs had been taken in January 1986, at a special Mass in Mamelodi East, near Pretoria, at which prayers were said for peace with justice. 'During the service, objects symbolizing the prevailing violence were offered up and then put aside to represent the need for reconciliation in South Africa'. These objects, which included petrol bombs, rubber bullets, stones, a tear-gas canister, a *sjambok* (whip), and a *knobkierie* (a stick with a large knob at the end), were first held aloft, a prayer of repentance was said, and then they were dumped in a drum as a sign of rejection of such weapons'. The magazine had deliberately falsified the photo and the service, said Hurley. The significance of a slur of this kind in a publication widely circulated especially in the United States was the damage it could do to the Archdiocese of Durban's direct mailing campaign to raise funds for the missions. The problems experienced by that campaign in Hurley's final years in office may have been related to the negative publicity spread by the *Family Protection Scoreboard*.

The entire decade of the 1980s was a difficult period in South Africa, but 1986 was especially so because of the national state of emergency declared by P. W. Botha's government in a desperate attempt to control growing resistance. As indicated earlier, tens of thousands of people were detained, including priests, religious and lay Catholics working for the Church. On 9 and 10 July, the bishops held a special plenary session to assess the crisis and how they should respond.[4] Early that year, they had turned down the idea of contact with the government: such meetings had not produced results in the past. Faced with the severity of the crisis, however, the bishops had second thoughts and decided to seek a meeting with the state president as soon as possible. To demonstrate to the government and the whole Church that the bishops were united, it was suggested that all take part in the meeting. If the state president agreed only to meet a delegation, the Administrative Board would represent the Conference.

Much thought was given to what should be included in a memorandum to be discussed in this meeting. Crucial would be an emphasis on the 'non-negotiable' changes needed to bring the crisis to an end. These included lifting the state of emergency, releasing all political prisoners, completely dismantling all apartheid legislation and initiating dialogue with authentic leaders in order to introduce a democratic non-racial government.

The growing determination of the bishops was clear from their decision to make public the full text of the memorandum, whatever the outcome of the meeting with the president, even if he refused to meet with them. They were particularly keen that the public should know that the SACBC, as a united body, had requested the meeting and were united about the issues to be discussed. In an interview in 2005, Cardinal Napier explained this emphasis on unity: the bishops had become aware that the National Party government was trying to drive a wedge between Hurley and the rest of the bishops. Apparently the government was saying, 'We know the Catholic bishops are sensible men; they wouldn't hold a position like that. It's this Denis Hurley who is doing these things'.[5]

The bishops' memorandum was drawn up in August 1986 and published in September under the title 'An Urgent Message to the State President from the Southern African Catholic Bishops' Conference'. The meeting with the government took place on 17 November at the Union Buildings in Pretoria. In addition to Hurley as SACBC president, the bishops were represented by Cardinal Owen McCann, Archbishops Stephen Naidoo of Cape Town, George Daniel of Pretoria, and Peter Butelezi OMI of Bloemfontein, as well as Bishop Wilfrid Napier OFM (vice-president of the SACBC). They met with the State President, P. W. Botha; the Minister of Constitutional Development, Chris Heunis; the Defence Minister, Magnus Malan; the Minister of Law and Order, Adriaan Vlok; and others.

According to the bishops, in the 2-hour meeting, they emphasized to the president that, unless the fundamentals of apartheid were dismantled, violence would increase.[6] P. W. Botha did not, however, respond to this issue but stressed that the reforms his government was implementing were welcomed by most black South Africans in the face of the communist threat. As Hurley said in an interview in 1998, 'He wasn't going to yield or bend in any way . . . What he was doing was the right course and that was that'.

According to Napier, Botha tried to bully each member of the delegation. No matter what Botha said, Hurley came back at him with a reply that he could not answer. As a result, Hurley was subjected to one of Botha's famous finger-wagging sessions: 'I'm very disappointed with you, as a South African'. 'He was very annoyed with me', commented Hurley. 'I think my very presence there annoyed him. It must have been the build-up from the past'.

Rev Dr Peter Storey of the Methodist Church recalls an ecumenical delegation which met with P.W. Botha. Storey says that Botha dealt with Hurley in 'a brutal and outrageous manner'. 'I won't talk to you at all,' he said, claiming that Hurley was an apologist for the communists. Storey observed that Botha was surrounded by top security police who passed him files about various members of the church delegation. 'I know what you've been saying', was his snide comment to Hurley.

Hurley's last plenary session as president of the Conference took place in January 1987. As usual on such occasions, the Apostolic Delegate, at that time Archbishop Jan Mees, was invited to give a message on behalf of the Pope. Mees, a Belgian who had previously been a Vatican diplomat in Paraguay, had been close to General Alfredo Stroessner, Paraguay's right-wing military dictator, who had decorated him. On this occasion Mees's message, that the bishops should keep out of politics and leave it to lay people, was rather like what his predecessor, Archbishop Martin Lucas, had said in the 1950s.[7]

Although Mees did not directly refer to the South African bishops, the implication was clear. He quoted Pope John Paul II: 'It is not for the pastors of the Church to intervene directly in the political construction and organization of social life. This task forms part of the vocation of the laity acting on their own initiative with their fellow citizens'. What Mees said seemed like a rejection of all that Hurley had stood for since the joint statement of 1952, but more particularly the many important initiatives he had either inspired or backed, especially as SACBC president since 1981.

These same words of the Pope had been quoted to the bishops by P. W. Botha during their meeting the previous November. Hurley responded to Mees immediately. In giving a vote of thanks, he told SACBC delegates, official representatives of other churches and other faiths, members of the diplomatic corps and a large media contingent: 'We cannot dispense ourselves from the obligation of preaching justice and love, not only in individual encounters . . . but [also] in the great encounters between the great communities of mankind, where so far the success the Church has in preaching justice and love [has been] about 0.1 per cent'. He warned that the Pope's view strengthened the hands of 'our friends on the right'—which was taken as a reference to Botha's use of the same quotation.

Hurley called for the Pope to clarify what he meant by 'politics', saying that in a private meeting with John Paul II he had urged the Pope to put out a statement 'explaining the difference between promoting social justice . . . in socio-political life . . . and taking an active part in the pursuit of and exercise of power'.

There was some consolation for Hurley in the fact that Mees was transferred not long afterwards. The man left in charge at the Apostolic Delegation until a new delegate had been appointed, Monsignor Mario Cassari, took the first possible opportunity to reaffirm the SACBC position. He was given a standing ovation for telling the bishops: 'You, more than others, know your people, you live among them, you share their anxieties and their sorrows as a result of their everyday conditions. For all this you must shout even from the roof tops—in the name of God—that the time has come that South Africa really becomes a New South Africa'.

PART FIVE

'IN OLD AGE, THEY WILL STILL BEAR FRUIT'

—Psalm 92:14, sung at Hurley's ordination as bishop, 19 March 1947

27

Last Years in Office

After Hurley ceased to be president of the SACBC in January 1987, he had a few years left in office as Archbishop of Durban before he officially retired in October 1992. They were significant years because of political developments in South Africa and because the Catholic Church's Pastoral Plan was launched after many years of consultation and preparation. Hurley continued his active involvement in the life of the Church and in its ministry to society.

PROTEST MARCHES

In the late 1980s, the South African crisis seemed insoluble.[1] The white population was divided into those who were clinging to apartheid at all costs and an increasing number who were becoming aware of the need for change. The black majority was determined that nothing would stop them from achieving their freedom. In its desperation to smash this growing black resistance, the National Party government had resorted to successive states of emergency and large-scale detentions. In 1988, using emergency regulations, it banned the United Democratic Front. The banning failed. Instead of being crushed, the UDF appeared in a new guise—the Mass Democratic Movement (MDM)—a loose coalition of anti-apartheid activists with no constitution, no official membership rolls, no national or regional governing body and no office-bearers, making it virtually impossible to ban.

The official response by Church leaders to the crisis of the late 1980s was to call a 'Convocation of Churches in South Africa' in 1988. In addition to the usual SACC member churches, this brought together international church representatives, several non-member churches of the SACC, and people of other faiths. It was the brainchild of Rev Frank Chikane who at that time was General Secretary of the SACC. He acknowledged that his thinking had been influenced by several aspects of Hurley's Christians for Justice and Peace (CJP). Chikane recognized that useful discussions had taken place under the CJP banner, so that not much new ground needed to be covered before the convocation could conclude that a 'Standing for the Truth Campaign' should be started.[2]

Standing for the Truth was a national civil disobedience programme that worked closely with the MDM's 'Defiance Campaign', making the latter significantly different from the earlier Defiance Campaign in 1952 (see Chapter 7), when there had been a total lack of high-level support from any of the faiths. Though Standing for the Truth was not able to mobilize the local parish and church involvement originally hoped for, it did bring together many Christians and people of other faiths in what was described by the SACC as 'acts of public witness to the truth of righteousness as against the lie of apartheid. It involved church leaders in a way not previously seen in South Africa'. Along with the MDM's Defiance Campaign, it became 'one of the last straws to break the back of intransigent authorities' and 'played a prominent part in eventually bringing the government to the negotiating table in 1990'.

Government intransigence was also broken in a different and unexpected way when the stubborn P. W. Botha, whose policies were failing, suffered a stroke on 18 January 1989. Instead of resigning from office, as many expected, Botha tried to hold on to power as head of state, but gave up leadership of the National Party. F. W. de Klerk was elected to replace him in the latter role, and a bitter struggle developed between them. Eventually the irascible Botha was forced by de Klerk and other members of the cabinet to resign on 10 August 1989, and de Klerk was elected state president in addition to heading the National Party.

Although the state of emergency continued, there was a new recognition that major change was inevitable. This was signalled by de Klerk's personal intervention to allow a mass march through the streets of Cape Town, jointly organized by the MDM and Standing for the Truth. This march, from St George's Anglican Cathedral to the Cape Town City Hall, was the first government-sanctioned anti-apartheid march.

Similar marches had been planned for other centres.[3] They were meant to take place in defiance of the law but, in the light of de Klerk's allowing the Cape Town march, were unlikely to be broken up by police. One of these was the Freedom March in Durban on 22 September 1989. Hurley was asked to lead this, together with representatives of other faiths. It began with an interfaith service in Emmanuel Cathedral and ended with a mass rally outside the Durban City Hall.

In addition to religious leaders, the estimated crowd of 20,000 included city councillors, teachers, business and professional people, members of political organisations, and students—a good-humoured assembly, waving banners and posters. The aims of the march were to call for an end to the state of emergency and the sweeping powers given to the security forces, which had led to many detentions and deaths. There was a large, low-profile police presence, including a helicopter that kept a watchful eye on proceedings.

For Hurley and his Anglican colleague Bishop Michael Nuttall, the only jarring note was that activists carrying flags of the South African Communist Party took up a prominent place immediately behind the religious leaders. Hurley and Nuttall threatened to withdraw from the march, and Hurley would only speak at the City Hall after the flags had been moved.

Hurley and Nuttall's threats caused quite a stir among local leaders of the MDM, who later requested a meeting to express their disappointment that such significant church leaders were opposed to being associated with the South African Communist Party (SACP) flag, despite the important role played by the SACP in the struggle to end apartheid. There were also critical letters in local newspapers, and Hurley wrote to defend his views: 'The track record of communism in power is almost 100 per cent a tale of totalitarian suppression of social, political, economic and religious freedom . . . In regard to those who have made great sacrifices under the banner of communism, I have no less admiration than your correspondents for their courage. I just regret that in their anger and frustration they adopted an ideology so destructive of freedom and human rights'.[4]

He was not in favour of suppressing the SACP, saying that history had proved that where democracy was strong, communism did not come to power. 'All I ask is that we be logical and not ask people to march for freedom under a flag so symbolic of oppression. It is particularly embarrassing for clergymen who participate in . . . their campaign of Standing for the Truth'. Nuttall recalls Hurley's concern that Pope John Paul II would be deeply offended if he were to see photos of Hurley marching in front of the hammer-and-sickle flag.

'*COMMUNITY SERVING HUMANITY*'

Hurley was not just concerned about the political situation in South Africa. He also knew that he had only a few more years to ensure that he could hand over a healthy diocese to his successor. In those years, as we have seen, he was determined to see the Pastoral Plan become a reality. Though no longer president of the Bishops' Conference, he still chaired their Pastoral Plan Advisory Committee. That put him in an influential position to finalize and launch the plan before he retired.

Thanks to Hurley, the Pastoral Plan was high on the agenda of the SACBC and began to gain momentum in 1987, with its simple but powerful theme: 'Community Serving Humanity'. This captured the two dimensions: the internal, about increasing community spirit in the Church; and the external, about building a better society, which meant improving the quality of life, working for human dignity and social justice and promoting human development. It was important, however, for each community or parish to discover the needs in its own area and to build a better society in its own way.

Thus 1987 was devoted to extensive consultations about these two aspects of the Pastoral Plan.[5] The question on building community was, 'What kind of division between people will your parish have to overcome?', that on serving humanity, 'If your community wants to help build a better world, what can it do?' Between 1987 and 1993, the Pastoral Plan Advisory Committee met about twenty times, with Hurley guiding the process.[6] The committee developed a booklet, posters and training kits for parishes throughout South Africa.

Meanwhile, Hurley had also been giving much thought to how he would implement the Pastoral Plan in his own archdiocese. Once again, his admiration for American organizing skills led him to a process known as 'Renew'.[7] He had discussions with several overseas bishops who had used Renew in their dioceses and learnt that it had helped them to develop community, strengthen faith and inspire more active witness to Jesus and his message. The Renew process extends over three years, with an initial six-month preparation followed by five six-week sessions, offered twice a year. Parishioners share in the experience through the Sunday liturgy, the use of materials for individual or group reflection at home, and most important, small faith-sharing groups meeting in homes. In one comprehensive process, Renew offers basic formation in prayer, Scripture, community building, action for justice, liturgy, evangelization, family life, and support for adults wanting to become Catholics.

After taking a close look at the Renew materials, Hurley decided that this would be a suitable methodology to implement the Pastoral Plan in his archdiocese. He sent a diverse team of nine people (priests, laity of different races, with Monsignor Paul Nadal as leader) to be trained at the Renew headquarters in Plainfield, New Jersey, in July 1987. This was a four-week course, going through the Renew process thoroughly, with lots of prayer, liturgy and experience of small faith-sharing groups. To pay the airfares and training costs, Hurley used funds given to him by Georgetown University in Washington, DC, when they conferred on him an honorary doctorate in "Humane Letters" earlier that year.

After the Durban team returned from their Renew training, a faith-sharing group was established in the diocesan chancery, and Hurley took part in it, together with Nadal. According to Sister Donna Ciangio OP, one of the American Renew staff, Hurley was touched by people sharing what Scripture was saying to them in their own lives. He described these years when Renew was being implemented in the archdiocese as the 'honeymoon' of his episcopacy. Andy Piper, a key member of the Durban Renew team, said that Hurley, who had previously been rather reluctant to kiss or embrace lay people, 'is now like a hugger'. 'It took fifty years of my priesthood to get to this stage', he said.

When he visited the parishes for Mass or confirmation, he was keen to hear what aspect of Renew they were working on and how they liked the process. If a parish seemed to be struggling, he would visit the priest or invite him to come and discuss how the diocese could help. Monsignor Tom Kleissler, one of the Renew founders, and Sister Donna, who had both worked with hundreds of bishops involved with Renew, said, 'This [their experience with Hurley] gets as close to perfect as it can, you know. . . . Anyone who from our place [Renew headquarters] had any dealings with him [is] just in awe of his goodness and . . . everything about him.' 'He was bigger than South Africa in some sense, in terms of his style of leadership, and certainly bigger than any one diocese. I think that's why he functioned well on the national and international levels'.

The third season of Renew had a particular focus on justice and peace. When Hurley saw the special discussion outlines that the Durban team had drawn up on these topics 'very close to his heart', he phoned Piper to thank her and the team for all the work they had put into this. She could hear how moved he was: the outlines gave him hope about the effect Renew could have in the diocese. Piper was also impressed by the support he gave Renew in other ways, speaking about it at clergy study days, diocesan pastoral council meetings, and in his sermons for confirmation and other special parish occasions, urging everyone to become involved. He did not, however, want to compel any parish to participate.

Deacon Lawrence Mthethwa, another member of the Renew team, realized that one of the reasons why Hurley had chosen Renew was that it gave clear guidelines and training for every parish leader. These showed exactly what they had to do and gave all the materials needed. All it required was for any priest to say that he wanted Renew for his parish and to let people go for the training offered by the diocese. The Renew team would then swing into action.

One area of the diocese reluctant to be involved in Renew was the Umvoti deanery, a group of rural parishes mainly served by elderly French (Breton) priests, who (as noted in Chapter 6) had been consistently unsupportive of Hurley initiatives from the time of his appointment as Vicar Apostolic in 1946. They regarded this American programme as inappropriate for their rural Zulu congregations. Deacon Mthethwa, however, disputes the idea that there were places for which Renew was unsuitable: 'There was no way Renew could not be introduced anywhere . . . outside there in the bundus [remote rural areas] . . . Even at the place where the priest comes once after three months, Renew would work'. Renew could easily be adapted for such situations. According to Nadal, eventually all the parishes participated in Renew, even those in the Umvoti deanery. Lay people, who heard glowing reports from neighbouring deaneries, insisted that they were not going to be left out, whatever their priests thought.

Meanwhile, preparations were under way for a national launch of the pastoral plan in every parish on Pentecost Sunday, 14 May 1989. By that time, full agreement had been reached on the vision document. This remarkable booklet, the fruit of years of careful consultation by bishops, priests, religious and lay people across the whole country, described in simple terms what 'Community Serving Humanity' meant. In an introductory letter to their people, the bishops could rightly say that, unlike any previous SACBC document,

> It comes from all of us and is sent to all of us. It comes from you, because many of its original ideas came from you and so did many of the suggestions which have improved and clarified it. It also comes from us bishops who have worked hard on this document and have prayed over it for several years. It is, therefore, truly a document of the whole Church of southern Africa and through it our whole Church is . . . saying, . . . 'This is the vision of our faith, the vision that, with God's help, we want to follow during the coming years'.[8]

Hurley and his Auxiliary Bishop Dominic Khumalo OMI wrote their own special pastoral letter for the launch, indicating their excitement: 'One of us, the Archbishop, has been a priest for nearly 50 years and a bishop for 42. Caution and calm should be associated with his years and experience, but he can honestly say that he is as excited now as he was on the eve of his priestly ordination in July 1939'. Peter Sadie, the national coordinator of pastoral planning, said that Hurley was 'genuinely excited, . . . like a child getting a new present, when the benefits of these programmes began to be realized'.

A few weeks later, Hurley and Khumalo sent out another letter to the archdiocese as an invitation to a great celebration that was to take place at the Westridge Tennis Stadium in Durban on 30 July 1989, to mark Hurley's golden jubilee of priestly ordination and the diocesan launch of the Renew process: 'Doesn't it excite you to experience that for the first time in our history thousands of people in all our parishes are being invited to join together in a great common effort of Christian formation, and are already beginning to respond?'[9]

Attended by about 12,000 people, the Renew launch was a lively and joyful celebration, with marimbas, dancers, Zulu praise songs, an Indian garland for the Archbishop and an *umsinsi* (coral) tree for each participating parish. In a moving ceremony, Hurley renewed his priestly vows before Cardinal Owen McCann, who asked all present to, 'Pray for your beloved archbishop and give thanks for his devoted service over so many years'.

Renew was now well under way in Durban. What was happening in the rest of South Africa? The bishops had decided that there were two ways in which dioceses could implement the pastoral plan: through Small Christian Communities or through Renew. To give other dioceses information about Renew, the theological winter school held in major cities in 1989 was devoted to this topic. The two speakers were Monsignor Kleissler, from Renew headquarters, and Monsignor Nadal, head of the Durban team. Eleven dioceses chose Renew and twelve a home-grown programme on Small Christian Communities. Because there were so many diocesan teams to be trained in Renew, and it would be prohibitively expensive for all to travel to the United States, the training was offered at Oakford over three weeks. Several Anglican dioceses also participated. Hurley was excited about these developments and travelled to Oakford on a few occasions to celebrate Mass and attend training sessions.

As time went by, some problems of the pastoral plan began to surface. A competitive spirit developed between dioceses using the Small Christian Community programme and those involved in Renew—as if each had to prove that their option was better. Resolute efforts were made to share materials and to hold joint training sessions in order to build a more collaborative spirit.

These problems led to a major evaluation of the whole plan through questionnaires and a participatory consultation with bishops, priests, religious and laity working together in diocesan teams. This took place in Durban in August 1992. By this time, there were more than 5,000 Small Christian Communities, or faith-sharing groups, in South Africa—an extraordinary achievement. The consultation led to a document that set out 'the most pressing needs for continued implementation of the Pastoral Plan of the SACBC'. These included attention to the fact that the 'serving humanity' dimension was not well understood or implemented, that an open dialogue was needed with those who found it difficult to identify with the pastoral plan, that a special effort should be made to reach out to priests who had not been involved in formulating the plan or in considering its implications, that the Church should ensure that seminarians were fully prepared for the role they would play once ordained.

Hurley's last meeting as chair of the Pastoral Plan Advisory Committee took place on 9 September 1993, by which time Lobinger had been appointed to succeed him. At the end of the meeting, Lobinger thanked Hurley, 'who had worked so tirelessly over many years to initiate and promote the idea of a pastoral plan. His efforts had finally resulted in the publication of the Vision Document, Community Serving Humanity, and in the introduction of Renew and the Small Christian Community process as a means of implementing this Pastoral Plan through the Conference territories [South Africa, Botswana and Swaziland]'.

HIV/AIDS MINISTRY

For Hurley, ending apartheid was not the only issue to be faced. There was a great new challenge to the Church: HIV/AIDS.[10] He had only in January 1989 become fully aware of the threat it posed to South Africa through a presentation made to the bishops by an English Jesuit, Father Ted Rogers. Rogers had worked for many years in Zimbabwe, formerly Rhodesia. He had become known to Hurley when he (Rogers) was appointed Director of IMBISA.

Almost as soon as Rogers became aware of the HIV/AIDS epidemic in Zimbabwe, he determined to learn all he could about the disease. Then he started to speak in local parishes and set about forming a national organization, 'Youth against AIDS', which brought together young people in youth clubs, now numbering 38, most of them in schools and a few in parishes and orphanages. He trained the leaders and encouraged them to commit themselves to sexual abstinence.

On his appointment as director of IMBISA, Rogers was asked to extend his AIDS ministry to all the countries of southern Africa. When he explained to the South African bishops the looming disaster, his message made a big impact on Hurley. Rogers in turn was impressed that Hurley saw the problem and responded 'more or less instantly'. Though already 73 and near the end of his time as Archbishop of Durban, he immediately invited Rogers to address a meeting of parish representatives in Durban so that the diocese could start working on this huge new crisis without delay.

In July 1989 Rogers addressed a Durban meeting on 'AIDS—the Christian Response'. From the questions, Hurley was able to identify two people who already seemed knowledgeable about the disease and who he thought could be the core of a local awareness effort: Liz Towell, who was working for the national Health Department; and Dr Hermann Schumann, a district surgeon. He invited them to meet him a few days later to discuss the establishment of an AIDS committee. Most of the initial members they recommended were already involved in health work. Once the committee was established, Hurley wanted its members to visit all the deaneries and spread to the parish level the key points from Rogers's presentation.

Towell was so taken up with the committee's work that she soon resigned from her job with the Health Department to work for the archdiocese. Because of Hurley's extensive contacts, especially with Catholic funding agencies, he was able to mobilize resources with surprising speed: within two weeks of Towell's explaining what she would need as a full-time AIDS worker, he had organized a salary, equipment and a vehicle. She began to see that, like Rogers, scientific knowledge was important to Hurley, but he also felt the urgent need to go out and meet the people who were suffering, to comfort and pray with them and their families.

Towell was surprised to find how clearly Hurley understood the problem of women in Africa, 'how powerless [they] were to make decisions about their sexual health' and how difficult it was for them to talk about their problems to their partners and their priests. In these moral and ethical dilemmas, she was impressed to find that Hurley did not stress the official teaching of the Church on AIDS—at that stage it had in any case not yet been fully enunciated—but rather urged people to rely on conscience: 'What is it that you are hearing? What is God telling you to do?' he would ask. He emphasized a message 'of loving and caring for your fellow man . . . That was the biggest thing he wanted: love these people. They were just so shunned, so rejected, so stigmatized that that was really the only thing we were actually asked to do'.

When Hurley invited Towell to address his priests, he opened the meeting by saying that they should feel free to ask any questions because he had asked Towell to be 'as explicit as possible'. Unfortunately, only two of the younger priests asked questions. After these had been answered, Hurley went on to urge the priests to think carefully about the consequence of any course of action for families or couples who were asking how to protect themselves from infection. He strongly urged the priests to start talking about these issues and to encourage their people to be faithful in their relationships.

After his retirement as archbishop in 1992, when he was parish priest of the cathedral, Hurley on several occasions invited Towell to address all the weekend Masses, taking over the time that he would have used for the homily. He encouraged her to be '100 per cent forthright and accurate from the pulpit, about AIDS'. Faced with the AIDS crisis, it seemed that he had overcome some of his embarrassment about sex.

With regard to the use of condoms, Hurley was neither in favour of their random distribution nor of a total ban but, Towell said, agreed that the AIDS committee could make them available in certain situations where, according to their conscience, they thought this advisable. When Bishop Kevin Dowling of Rustenburg was under attack within the SACBC for promoting condom usage in situations in which one partner in a marriage was HIV positive, Hurley publicly supported his view.

As chair of the Diocesan AIDS Committee (later Commission), Hurley gave as much encouragement as possible to Towell and other staff members, as well as to the large number of volunteers who provided home-based care to people with AIDS. 'He was always acutely aware that 99.9 per cent of our volunteers were women who already had a huge job in their homes, under very difficult conditions, but were still giving of themselves to . . . help others, and were also suffering from the disease themselves and could do very little about it'. Even in his old age, when Hurley accompanied these volunteers over rough terrain in the townships or in rural areas, he always insisted on going into the homes of people who were desperately ill, to comfort and pray with them.

The Commission relied on him to thank the volunteers at their annual gatherings and to write personal letters to members of the public who gave even the smallest gifts or donations. The files of the AIDS Care Commission are full of such letters. Hurley would insist on visiting frequent donors to thank them. At the time of his death, in 2004, there were still appointments in his diary to visit people who had been especially generous.

Over the years, Rogers has regularly returned to Durban, always including a meeting with Towell and Hurley so that they could update one another about the struggle against HIV and AIDS.

RESIGNATION

Before the Second Vatican Council, there was no obligatory retirement age for bishops; like the Pope, they could continue in office for life. One of the changes introduced by Pope Paul VI, as a result of discussions at the council, was that bishops should offer their resignation to the Pope at the age of 75. Hurley reached this age on 9 November 1990, and in accordance with Canon Law, which governs the Catholic Church, submitted his resignation to Pope John Paul II.

Subsequently, in a pastoral letter read at all Masses in the Archdiocese of Durban, on 23 June 1991, Hurley informed the priests, religious and laity, that the Pope had accepted his resignation and had asked him to continue in office until his successor was named.[11] In the same letter, Hurley informed the archdiocese that the process of selecting his successor was under way and that he expected it to conclude some time before the end of 1991. This process, he wrote, usually consisted of the Apostolic Delegate making confidential enquiries about possible candidates and forwarding names to the Vatican. The Vatican would then select three and, after a further confidential enquiry, the Pope would choose one and appoint him archbishop.

Hurley asked for prayers to be offered for God's guidance on this process and gave the text of a prayer for this purpose. He ended the letter: 'In the light of what I have mentioned above, I have the joy of serving you for a few more months and of coming very close to completing 45 years as your chief pastor in a territory that has a tradition of long service among its bishops. I am only the fourth in 140 years'.

'WHAT A WAY TO GO!'

In Hurley's years in office as a bishop, one of the most difficult episodes occurred in the last year, while he waited for his successor to be named and installed.[12] It illustrates how he assessed complex situations at this stage of his life and also says something about his personality. A diocesan priest was arrested for being in possession of pornographic videos, a story publicized by local newspapers. The priest's conduct was the subject of scandal in his parish, but parishioners were divided about what should happen to him: some wanted him to be transferred, others felt he should be allowed to stay on. Hurley and his Vicar General, Nadal, were both initially in favour of a transfer.

When Hurley attended a function in the parish, a number of parishioners spoke to him, urging him not to move the priest: 'When we were down, he was there to pick us up. Now he's down, let us pick him up'. Hurley consulted the Parish Pastoral Council, and they agreed. He then called a meeting of the more senior diocesan priests and put to them the dilemma. The priests accepted that their colleague should be allowed to continue serving the same parish.

Two diocesan priests who were not happy with this decision were officials of Durban's Inter-diocesan Tribunal, whose main task was to deal with applications for marriage annulments. Father Rodney Moss presided over the tribunal's work, with authority delegated by the archbishop and the other bishops of what was then known as Natal. Father Massimo Biancalani performed a role equivalent to that of a prosecutor in a civil court.

The tribunal had received about a hundred letters from parishioners, indignant because it seemed that Hurley was protecting the priest. Moss had drawn this to the attention of the archbishop, but Hurley indicated that he had decided to accept the request of the parish council. Moss and Biancalani felt they could not, in conscience, continue their work for the tribunal because, as they saw it, Hurley had not handled the matter justly. They effectively went on strike. Cases piled up, including those from other dioceses in Natal that made use of the Durban tribunal because they did not have the resources to run their own.

After this had gone on for six weeks, Hurley asked Moss and Biancalani to come and see him. They explained their reasons for not wanting to continue on the tribunal, but he brushed aside their arguments. Instead, he ordered them, in terms of their ordination promise of obedience, to take up their work for the tribunal once again. Moss told Hurley that by instructing them to go back to the tribunal, he was violating their freedom of conscience, 'enshrined in Vatican II'.

When Moss saw that Hurley would not change his mind, he agreed to take up his work on the tribunal, provided he could tell whoever he wanted to that he was returning to the tribunal on an instruction from the archbishop. He promised that he would be discreet, and Hurley agreed. Moss commented, 'In very important issues, [Hurley] did not accept opposition. While he was a liberal, in so many ways he was also very traditional'.

According to Moss, Hurley was concerned that the rights of the priest who had misbehaved had been violated. The police had made known the facts of the case more widely than they needed to. Moss criticized Hurley for looking at the individual good of the priest, whereas he and Biancalani felt the archbishop should have transferred the priest for the sake of the parish. Nadal also felt that the priest should have been moved as he and the archbishop had originally agreed. However, at a general meeting of the diocesan priests, called by the archbishop to finalize the decision, it became clear to Nadal that there was something of a personal vendetta against the priest by some of his colleagues. He therefore decided that, as vicar general, he would back Hurley's decision.

In reflecting long after the event, Nadal conceded that Hurley might have been correct in his judgment. The priest would probably have been a broken man if he had been moved. Instead, he was initially suspended for three months. Then, he continued to serve the people effectively as their pastor, and much healing took place in the parish. The priest was highly regarded for encouraging lay involvement in various ministries.

Nevertheless, it was a painful episode for Hurley, especially right at the end of his time in office. According to Nadal, he was 'terribly, terribly depressed at the turmoil that the . . . affair caused among the priests and said: "What a way to go!" ' Nadal urged him not to focus on that one incident, reminding him of all that he achieved at the same time through 'Renew', as a result of which the archdiocese was alive and flourishing.

The priest himself had been impressed by Hurley's compassion. Looking back on these events, about fifteen years later, he said: 'During the time of my enormous problem, . . . he rescued me. He saved me. He was full of compassion and understanding of human frailty.' 'I knew that if I rang him at 2:00 a.m. and asked whether I could come and see him, he would say: "I'll come and see you".' It was a compassion that crossed from the personal to the political throughout Hurley's ministry— but it should be carefully distinguished from the compassion shown to priests rather than to the young people they had abused in the vastly different circumstances of paedophilia, with disastrous effects in many dioceses around the world.

FAREWELL

An estimated 10,000 people were present in Durban's Exhibition Centre on 24 November 1991 to pay tribute to Hurley on his retirement as Archbishop of Durban.[13] The huge congregation gave the archbishop a rousing welcome as he arrived in procession for the 3-hour farewell service with Cardinal Owen McCann of Cape Town, six bishops, seventy priests and deacons and leading representatives of other churches and faiths.

A letter from the Vatican's Congregation for the Evangelization of Peoples paid tribute to Hurley for his dedicated service to the people of South Africa and to the universal Church, for his love of people of all walks of life, and for promoting justice and peace in South Africa. The letter described him as a tireless missionary and evangelizer, who had served loyally under five popes. It cited his humility, warmth, gentleness and sense of humour.

Hurley, who at the time of his appointment in 1946 had been the world's youngest Catholic bishop and, at the time of his resignation, was the longest-serving of its 4,000 bishops, spoke of the influence the Second Vatican Council had had on him and of the unique joy of participating in the pastoral plan 'Community Serving Humanity'. He also expressed gratitude to the many Christians of other denominations through whom, he said, he had encountered Christ during his ministry. He hoped the day was not too far distant when they could share a common baptism, a common biblical faith and communion. He also prayed that the Christian family might grow in appreciation of 'other faiths and ways of life which all in one way or another look to the same loving God'.

The congregation cheered and ululated when, Professor Otty Nxumalo, a praise singer, enumerated Hurley's achievements.

The celebration over and the farewells said, Hurley returned to work for almost a further year, completing more than 45 years of episcopal ministry, before his successor, Bishop Wilfrid Fox Napier OFM, was appointed Archbishop of Durban on 29 May 1992. From that date until 4 October 1992, when Napier was installed as archbishop, Hurley technically ceased to be Archbishop of Durban and became administrator of the archdiocese.

28

Civil War[1]

Hurley's friendship with Chief Mangosuthu Buthelezi, strong in the early 1970s, had all but ended by the time the archbishop reached his last five years in office (1987–92). This was because of profound differences of opinion about political strategies. 'Originally', said Deacon Lawrence Mthethwa, 'the two were really friends because Buthelezi was very strong in saying apartheid is wrong, and Archbishop Hurley was also saying apartheid is wrong, and that was more or less a unifying factor for the two'.[2] Writing about that period, Hurley said: '[Buthelezi] was very popular among the Zulu people and was warmly accepted in Church circles. There was hardly an important church gathering, at least of the Catholic Church, to which he was not invited'.[3]

In 1975, at the prompting of the ANC, Buthelezi re-established Inkatha, which had been founded originally in the 1920s as a national cultural liberation organisation. The re-established Inkatha initially enjoyed the ANC's blessing and encouragement because it hoped that Inkatha would make political breakthroughs for the ANC, particularly in rural Natal. In 1979, however, there was a sharp breakdown in the relationship between the ANC and Inkatha as a result of a meeting in London between leaders of the two organizations. According to Gerry Maré, 'Buthelezi led a high-powered Inkatha delegation to London to prove that he was no "traitor" to the liberation struggle . . . but a recognized leader of another liberation movement'. He did not succeed, and from that time on it was clear that Inkatha would no longer be able to present itself as in some way an internal Zulu wing of the ANC. Inkatha and the ANC became increasingly divided about involvement in homeland government—and later about economic sanctions, to which Buthelezi was strongly opposed.

The ANC embarked on a propaganda onslaught against Buthelezi and Inkatha, describing him as a 'sell-out' and 'a puppet of Pretoria' because of his involvement in homeland politics. Meanwhile, Buthelezi and Inkatha described the ANC as the 'external mission of the ANC', not the 'true' ANC of the 'founding fathers'.

Just how rapidly the relationship between Inkatha and the ANC deteriorated as a result of the London meeting became clear in 1980, when pupils in Durban's KwaMashu township undertook a school boycott as part of a national campaign against overcrowding in schools, lack of equipment and books, and lack of student representation. In other parts of South Africa, the boycott directly confronted the national government, whereas in Natal it challenged the KwaZulu government, which controlled black schools in many parts of the province, including KwaMashu. Inkatha members used violence to compel the pupils to go back to school. It was the first, but far from the last, time that Inkatha resorted to violence to achieve its political objectives despite calling itself a non-violent movement.

In the same year, a German visitor was taken by Diakonia staff to visit the informal settlement at Malukazi, south of Durban, where Diakonia employed a community worker to help the residents solve some of their main problems, especially the lack of running water. After her return to Germany, the visitor wrote about her experience in a letter to the *Frankfurter Allgemeine Zeitung*. She said that, when she had asked the Malukazi community members about Inkatha, there was 'harsh and bitter laughter'. Buthelezi supporters in Germany drew this letter to the chief's attention, and he raised the issue in the KwaZulu Legislative Assembly, using it as an example of what he called Diakonia's negative attitude towards the KwaZulu Government and Inkatha.

When Buthelezi's remarks in the Legislative Assembly were reported in local media, the Diakonia executive, including Hurley, felt that this sort of criticism could hamper Diakonia's work, not only in Malukazi but also in many other communities, especially those controlled by KwaZulu. It was agreed that a Diakonia delegation should meet the chief to clarify the issues. This meeting took place on 3 July 1981, with Diakonia represented by Hurley as one of its patrons, Rev Victor Pillay of the Presbyterian Church as chair, Marlene Volkmer of the Evangelical Lutheran Church of Southern Africa, as Vice-chair, Rev Paul Jali of the Presbyterian Church, an executive member, and myself as director.

We made it clear that Diakonia was not responsible for the letter in the *Frankfurter Allgemeine Zeitung*, our first knowledge of which had been Buthelezi's reference to it in the legislature. Two other documents were of concern to Inkatha: a report published by CIIR and a transcript of evidence I had given to the Buthelezi Commission, which was investigating the possibility of an alternative political dispensation for the province of Natal. The CIIR publication *South Africa in the 1980s* claimed that Inkatha was collaborating with Pretoria. Once again, we informed the meeting that Diakonia was not in any way responsible for the CIIR document. With regard to the evidence given to the Buthelezi Commission, I indicated that the views were simply a reflection of the critical attitude among some young urban black people towards Inkatha and the KwaZulu Government.

It was a difficult meeting despite Hurley's gentle and good-natured challenges to some of the harsher remarks by Inkatha representatives. Chief Buthelezi gave them much more time to make their sweeping allegations than he gave us to reply. One of the most disturbing comments was by Winnington Sabelo, a leading Inkatha member from Umlazi township. He showed his anger at the criticisms of Inkatha that were the focus of the meeting by threatening, while banging his fist on the table, that 'we will come down to Durban and smash up everything there'. This menacing statement was not challenged by Buthelezi or his colleagues. What became clear was that it would be difficult for Diakonia to have a normal relationship with Inkatha in this atmosphere; it was a disillusioning experience for our delegation, especially Hurley, in the light of his friendship with Buthelezi.

Relations between Diakonia and Inkatha worsened over the next few years, not only as a result of this meeting but also because of the launch of the UDF in 1983. As mentioned earlier, its purpose was to oppose the new tricameral parliament and the so-called Koornhof Bills, which established community councils for the African townships. Buthelezi and Inkatha were also opposed to this constitution and new legislation. The real dividing line between them and the UDF, however, was that Buthelezi and Inkatha were controlling the KwaZulu homeland and working 'within the system', a position strongly rejected by the UDF.

The UDF included several church- and faith-based organizations among its hundreds of member organizations. Because Diakonia had been involved in campaigns on local issues together with UDF affiliates based in Natal, and because it shared their opposition to the tricameral parliament and the Koornhof bills, it was invited to join the UDF. In May 1983 Diakonia decided to become an observer member, and in December of that year, after considerable discussion, its council voted overwhelmingly in favour of full membership; Hurley was one of those in favour. This decision would later be reviewed because it increasingly gave the impression that the churches had decided to back one party in a political dispute.[4]

The UDF, informally regarded as the ANC's 'internal wing', was a major threat to Inkatha, which from this point onwards competed directly with the UDF and therefore, in effect, with the ANC. The implications of this situation had not been realized by Diakonia when it became a full member of the UDF.

The ANC and its allies were working on a strategy of making South Africa ungovernable and apartheid unworkable. Carrying out this policy involved attacks on local councillors, tribal chiefs and KwaZulu officials, many of whom were members and supporters of Inkatha. Township residents were often coerced to participate in stay-aways and consumer boycotts. 'This coercion, in many instances, bred a violent backlash from those intimidated into taking part', according to Anthea Jeffery of the SA Institute of Race Relations (SAIRR). Jeffery's claim implies that all the aggression came from, or was started by, the ANC. This was far from being the case: Inkatha was frequently the aggressor, vigorously supported by the police.

Apart from the establishment of the UDF, another major political development of 1983 was the proposal to incorporate two of Natal's oldest townships into the KwaZulu homeland: Lamontville in Durban and Hambanathi, near Verulam, on the North Coast. The proposed move was stoutly resisted by residents' associations in both townships. The residents' associations of Lamontville and Hambanathi were united in the Joint Rent Action Committee (JORAC). This had close links with Diakonia's Housing Programme which supported JORAC's opposition to rent increases. Its meetings were regularly held in Diakonia's meeting room and attended by Diakonia's housing organizer. These links were seen as further evidence of the organization's alleged hostility towards Inkatha and the KwaZulu government, which began to put out the message that JORAC was actually a creation of Diakonia.

Violence broke out at Hambanathi in August 1983, when Inkatha supporters killed three UDF supporters and set thirteen houses alight because the owners were linked to the residents' association. Once more, Diakonia became involved, this time in supporting the victims. August 1983 was also the month in which the UDF was launched in Cape Town, greatly increasing the tension with Inkatha. A further example of the resulting violence was an incident on 29 October 1983 at the University of Zululand, south of Empangeni. The clash arose from student opposition to Buthelezi's proposal to commemorate, on the university campus, the 1884 death of the Zulu king Cetshwayo. According to the TRC Report, a 'large group of Inkatha supporters attacked the student residences, breaking down doors and pulling students out from where they were hiding. Students were dragged out, assaulted and stabbed with traditional weapons'. Five people were killed, four of them students and one an Inkatha Youth Brigade member. Parents and friends of those killed and injured met at the Ecumenical Centre (now known as the Diakonia Centre) in Durban, to plan the funerals and to work out how to respond to these attacks. This was regarded as additional proof that Diakonia was taking sides with Inkatha's opponents. Because Hurley was the founder and a patron of Diakonia, he was inevitably tarred with the same brush.

In 1983 and 1984, Buthelezi made further criticisms of Diakonia in the KwaZulu legislature, citing its membership of the UDF and association with organizations and groupings perceived to be enemies of Inkatha. When the patrons of Diakonia held their annual meeting in November 1984, they agreed that it would be important to meet Buthelezi again. This time, Hurley and Anglican Bishop Michael Nuttall were chosen to represent the organization. Subsequently, the Diakonia Council suggested that Rev B. K. Dludla of the United Congregational Church be added to the delegation, but the meeting never took place.

In the same patrons' meeting, Nuttall raised concern about Diakonia's membership of the UDF, asking how it could play a reconciling role if it was a member of one of the conflicting parties. Other patrons raised similar concerns but thought that withdrawing from the UDF would be equally problematic. Since the UDF was about to re-define itself, the Diakonia Council postponed its decision pending this re-definition. At a special council meeting on 10 April 1985, it was reported that the UDF was becoming more of a political organization than a front. All members would have to apply for re-affiliation. This gave Diakonia the opportunity to re-consider its membership. After much discussion, it decided by a large majority to revert to observer membership as in the first months of the UDF's existence. This did not entirely resolve the problem identified by Nuttall, though he remembers 'how carefully [Hurley] listened to my critique . . . and how he supported the change to observer status. He was keenly open to collegial decisions'.

Hurley was increasingly concerned about the violence, which seemed to be spreading to many parts of the province. Help was needed to understand this phenomenon and its causes. In mid-1985, Hurley approached Professor H. W. van der Merwe, head of the University of Cape Town's Centre for Inter-Group Studies, to undertake a study of the violence.[5] Van der Merwe agreed, saying that he had a good relationship both with the UDF and Inkatha. Hurley asked him to secure their approval for the project. Van der Merwe proposed research on two aspects: interest groups (their goals, policies, ideological leanings, major alliances and divisions) and major issues, such as the sources of conflict.

Between October 1985 and July 1986, van der Merwe made five trips from Cape Town to Durban in connection with the research project requested by Hurley. In the process, he learnt about the different approaches of the two political movements. His aim was to find common ground between them and to suggest ways in which their differences could be overcome.

As a result of this exercise, a meeting between the UDF and Inkatha took place at Hurley's home in Durban on 25 July 1986. Inkatha was represented by its chair, Musa Zondi, Rowley Arenstein and Ntwe Mafole; the UDF by Archie Gumede, one of the UDF presidents, though possibly without an official mandate for his presence, such was the UDF's reluctance to meet Inkatha at that stage.

The meeting began with mutual recriminations but, after an appeal by van der Merwe as mediator, settled down to discuss what could be done about the violence. Unfortunately, he was due to go overseas immediately after the meeting for a year-long sabbatical. No agreement was reached about a mediator to take his place, so no further Inkatha-UDF meetings were held for the next 18 months. Van der Merwe learnt from this experience never to undertake long-term mediation as an individual, but only as part of a team.

Hurley had written to Buthelezi after the 1984 meeting of Diakonia patrons, requesting a meeting. A year later, no reply had been received from the chief, indicating how much their relationship had deteriorated and how little trust Buthelezi had in Diakonia. It was decided at the next patrons' meeting, at the end of 1985, not to proceed with a request for a Diakonia delegation to meet Buthelezi, but that individual patrons could request meetings on behalf of their own churches.

During 1985, according to the TRC Report, Buthelezi was alerted by SADF Military Intelligence about alleged assassination plots against him. This led him to ask his informants to provide him with support 'including offensive paramilitary capacity, in order to take on the ANC/UDF'. As a result, Military Intelligence set up 'Operation Marion' to provide assistance to Inkatha and the KwaZulu government. A key element was training in Caprivi, a narrow strip of land in the far northeast of Namibia. During 1986, some 200 Inkatha supporters were trained there by the Special Forces' arm of the SADF. Planning was done in the utmost secrecy, according to the TRC, and involved the highest levels of the State Security Council and Military Intelligence, on the one hand, and Buthelezi and his personal assistant, M. Z. Khumalo, on the other.

The six-month training included the handling of Soviet-bloc weapons (the use of which might mislead people into thinking that attacks were being carried out by the ANC), heavy-duty weapons such as mortars and rocket launchers, as well as explosives, land mines and hand grenades. The trainees were taught to carry out attacks without leaving a trace, how to avoid arrest, detention and interrogation by police, and how to attack houses with the aim of killing the occupants. These Caprivi trainees continued to be involved in hit-squad activities in KwaZulu and Natal up to the 1994 elections, receiving monthly salaries from the SADF until 1989, when most were enrolled in the KwaZulu police. They then carried out their hit-squad activities under the guise of being official law-enforcement officers and were partly responsible for the dramatic escalation of political conflict in the region.

Despite their refusal to participate in the TRC process, the IFP submitted to the commission a list of over 420 IFP party office-bearers who had been killed, allegedly by members and supporters of the UDF and ANC, between August 1986 and August 1995. Many of these fell outside the TRC's cut-off date of April 1994, and so their deaths were not investigated. The TRC's Durban office, however, conducted an intensive investigation into the 289 listed cases which fell within their mandate. It was unable to corroborate 136 of these because no trace of the individuals could be found despite further information being sought from the IFP. Of the remaining 153 incidents, the commission's finding was that, in 76 incidents, the deceased had indeed been deliberately targeted because they held positions in the IFP.

The commission also found that, especially in the 1980s, large numbers of human rights violations were perpetrated by ANC supporters for which the ANC was 'morally and politically accountable' because it had created a 'climate in which such supporters believed their actions to be legitimate'. These violations included killings, attempted killings, arson and severe ill-treatment committed against urban councillors and rural headmen, members of the IFP and people perceived to be 'collaborators' of the system or enemies of the ANC.

In the latter part of the 1980s, many young people in the rural areas around Pietermaritzburg began rebelling against tribal authorities and openly supporting the UDF. Adults also renounced their Inkatha membership. What attracted them to the UDF was that, as Hurley said, it offered an agenda of liberation, whereas Inkatha offered little more than a stress on the importance of Zulu traditions, especially obedience to the elders. Faced with these defections by young people, Inkatha embarked on a recruitment drive in the Edendale and Vulindlela valleys bordering on Pietermaritzburg. They were assisted by Caprivi trainees, who used intimidation and force. The UDF members violently resisted the recruitment drive, and the conflict escalated dramatically from 1987 onwards, into what became known as the 'Midlands War'.

Faced with this conflict, Rev Dr Khoza Mgojo, national president of the Methodist Church, and president of the Federal Theological Seminary based in the Pietermaritzburg township of Imbali, invited Hurley and Nuttall to meet him and Peter Kerchhoff, organizing secretary of PACSA. They discussed how the churches should respond to the violence that was destabilizing local communities.

These leaders continued to meet regularly, and in 1988 the group was enlarged to include church leaders and ecumenical church workers from the Durban area. Known as the Natal Church Leaders' Group (NCLG) and after 1994 as the KwaZulu-Natal Church Leaders' Group (KZNCLG), it provided a forum where ecumenical action could be agreed on by the churches, including joint pastoral letters, pastoral visits to areas where there had been major outbreaks of violence, and the establishment of the Natal Crisis Fund to assist victims of the violence and help pay for funerals. Where possible, the NCLG mediated between the conflicting parties, difficult though this was because Inkatha leaders claimed that the group favoured the UDF and ANC.

Nuttall said that the NCLG had come into existence out of a 'spontaneous sense of great urgency' on the part of church leaders who were 'seeking to respond pastorally and prophetically to the increasing violence in the province'. Looking back ten years later, Hurley said that the NCLG's existence had greatly helped in strengthening ecumenical relations: 'We established a very warm brotherhood between the church leaders . . . that has survived up to the present time and is still highly regarded by the members who participate'.[6]

Early in 1989, a key year for mediation efforts, Hurley was approached by representatives of COSATU and the UDF with a proposal for a peace conference organized by a 'Committee of Convenors', significant public figures, including himself and Nuttall. COSATU and the UDF requested Hurley's support for the proposal and his assistance in inviting Inkatha to participate.[7] In a letter of 22 March, Hurley outlined the proposal to Buthelezi, listing the suggested convenors. He invited the chief to nominate two or three additional people and to forward their names so that they could be invited to the first meeting at Archbishop's House on 31 March.

Buthelezi's reply, dated 28 March, indicated that he was doubtful about a peace conference, because he feared it would develop into another 'talk shop'. He only wanted to involve himself in peace initiatives if he felt certain they would be effective. He was also angry because he suspected that the proposal had been worked out by COSATU and the UDF and presented to him (Buthelezi) as a fait accompli, with little time to consult the KwaZulu Legislature or to suggest additional convenors. Moreover, he noted that eight convenors had already been appointed (presumably nominated by COSATU and the UDF), whereas he was only invited to suggest two or three names, almost as an afterthought.

Then Buthelezi mentioned that he had been developing his own rather different peace intervention. This was to consist of raising 'a very substantial amount of money' from Christian organizations overseas, to provide for broadcasting and publishing peace appeals in the media, making air drops of peace pamphlets and using loudhailers to present pre-recorded peace messages to communities across the province. The funds would also be needed for monitoring and verifying outbreaks of violence and establishing peacekeeping units in the field. He insisted on 'a complete moratorium on mud-slinging'.

Buthelezi said that if he could be satisfied that the Hurley initiative was 'part of a genuine endeavour to bring about a cessation of hostilities', he would probably suggest amalgamating the two initiatives. Though correspondence was exchanged over the next two months, nothing seems to have come of either initiative. Buthelezi eventually invited a delegation from COSATU and the UDF to meet himself and Inkatha representatives in Ulundi, the capital of KwaZulu. The

UDF and COSATU suggested that Durban would be a more neutral venue. A stalemate resulted.

By the time the Anglican Provincial Synod, the top policy-making structure of the Anglican Church at national level, took place in Durban in July 1989, this remained the position. The synod delegates were extremely concerned that the conflicting parties were not communicating with each other. They resolved that a special delegation should be sent immediately to negotiate with Buthelezi, a fellow Anglican, about peace talks.[8] This consisted of three Zulu bishops, all well known to Buthelezi, one of them a personal friend and one a member of the Zulu royal lineage. Archbishop Desmond Tutu, who was presiding over the synod, suggested that Nuttall, as Bishop of Natal, should also be part of the delegation.

Arrangements were made for the four to have an urgent meeting with Buthelezi. So, while the synod continued its business, the delegation drove to Ulundi to meet the chief. They were successful in persuading him to ask one or two of his colleagues to meet at any agreed venue with UDF and COSATU representatives for an initial, exploratory meeting. Thereafter, the meetings could be at venues, such as Ulundi and the COSATU headquarters in Johannesburg.

Nuttall described Hurley's response to the Anglican initiative:

> Hurley was by now an elder statesman on the church scene though he was still in office as the Archbishop of Durban. During these exacting times he was like a rock in our midst: a rock of stability and long experience, a rock of deep wisdom and grace. Part of his grace was to make room gladly for younger church leaders such as myself to make their own distinctive contribution. A notable example of this occurred in 1989: . . . after failing in an attempt to set up a joint meeting between Inkatha and the UDF, he warmly welcomed and commended an Anglican episcopal initiative, which managed to achieve a breakthrough. Archbishop Hurley had no personal stake in this difficult and delicate enterprise; his sole concern was peace.

In the midst of these mediation efforts, Hurley celebrated the golden jubilee of his ordination to the priesthood and the launch of the Renew process at an outdoor Mass at the Westridge Park Tennis Stadium in Durban on 30 July 1989. Among the tributes paid on this occasion was a gracious letter of congratulations from Buthelezi:

> I am writing to convey my warmest congratulations to you as you rejoice in your fiftieth anniversary of serving your Church. You really have earned black South Africa's respect and, in thinking about your life and commitment to a just society, a host of fond memories welled up from the past.
>
> It is rather sad that we do not meet as often as we used to, but this notwithstanding, I want you to know that my respect for you is totally undiminished. You have earned a respect that nothing can take away from you.
>
> . . . Know that no matter how much we differ on the question of tactics and strategies or about what is good and what is evil in politics, my congratulations to you

are altogether untrammelled. The thoughts I have expressed in this letter are very simple and honestly felt.[9]

Meanwhile, the exploratory meeting agreed to by Buthelezi and the Anglican delegation was facilitated by Nuttall. It was agreed that five-a-side peace talks should be set up as soon as possible. With remarkable speed, they reached consensus about a substantial peace plan. It was to begin with a Conference of Presidents of the ANC, COSATU, Inkatha and the UDF in London. The ANC-in-exile was based there and would not have been allowed into South Africa because it was still banned. The Conference of Presidents which was to have been held in London would be followed by a peace conference and joint public rallies, together with a monitoring and reconstruction programme in KwaZulu-Natal.

Unfortunately, the proposed London conference foundered on the question of numbers. Inkatha insisted on having an equal number of delegates to that of the other three partners combined—ANC, COSATU, UDF—the basis of equality on which the five-a-side talks operated. When this was not accepted, Inkatha wanted to add representatives of its own trade union, the United Workers' Union of South Africa (UWUSA), and of an obscure group known as the Natal PAC-in-exile, each of which would have the same number of representatives as every other group.

This proposal became a major obstacle; but more serious, according to Nuttall, was that Buthelezi had written to Oliver Tambo, president of the ANC, asking to meet him. Tambo had, however, suffered a stroke just a few days after the letter had been written and could not have been expected to reply himself. Was there not someone else who could do so on his behalf? Nuttall felt that the lack of a reply or even of an acknowledgement was a key factor in Inkatha's declaration of a moratorium on the peace process at the end of September 1989. In this situation, violence escalated and began to spread ominously from urban to rural areas. As many as 2,000 lives had been lost in 1988 and 1989; worse was to follow.

The Anglican delegation, anxious to ensure that all would not be lost from their July 1989 breakthrough and that communication be kept open between the conflicting parties, went to see Buthelezi in November. Once again, despite Inkatha's moratorium on peace talks, they were able to persuade him to allow two-a-side talks, with Oscar Dhlomo and Frank Mdlalose as the Inkatha delegates. In time, Alec Erwin and Diliza Mji were appointed to represent COSATU and the ANC respectively, and the group continued to meet into early 1990. Years later, Erwin said that he had, on a number of occasions, asked Hurley to intercede directly with Buthelezi with regard to situations of violence, and that the archbishop had always done so. Unfortunately, there is no record of these interventions, probably made by phone.

Dramatic political developments in the transition to democracy took place early in 1990: the unbanning of the ANC and PAC announced in parliament by President F. W. de Klerk on 2 February 1990, and the release of Nelson Mandela on 11 February. In Natal, these major developments were, however, marred by an escalation of political violence. On 11 March, Mandela was welcomed by a crowd estimated at

100,000, in the grounds of King's Park (now Absa Stadium), Durban. Among the church leaders present to greet him on this occasion was Hurley, who commented:

> He made a dramatic arrival by helicopter and of course received a tumultuous welcome. He spoke for nearly an hour, and what a speech it was—courteous, reconciling, sensitive, creative, forward-looking and without resentment and rancour. It was superb. After 27 years in prison, it was a magnificent plea for peace, understanding and cooperation. I thank God that I was present on such a momentous occasion.[10]

Not everyone in the vast crowd was as impressed. Mandela's call to 'take your guns, your knives and your pangas [like machetes], and throw them into the sea' was too much for some young people, a number of whom showed their disapproval by walking out. Given the violent conflict in the province, they did not feel secure without their weapons.

Two weeks later, on a rain-soaked Sunday, a much smaller crowd, estimated at 8,000 to 10,000, gathered at the same venue to hear Buthelezi. At this rally, David Ntombela, a key Inkatha warlord from the Pietermaritzburg area, who had taken charge of the recruitment campaign that led to the 'Midlands War', made an ominous threat. If buses with Inkatha supporters were again stoned as they passed through the UDF area of Edendale, on their way back to the Inkatha stronghold of Vulindlela, steps would be taken against the culprits.

As buses returned from the King's Park rally, they were indeed stoned again, with tragic consequences out of all proportion to the stoning. In the succeeding days, what came to be known as the 'Seven Days' War' took place in the Edendale area outside Pietermaritzburg.[11] It was a well-prepared response, fed perhaps by humiliation and disappointment about the comparatively poor turnout for the Buthelezi rally. Over the seven days following the Inkatha rally, more than 100 people were killed, some 3,000 houses were destroyed by fire and approximately 20,000 people fled to escape the violence. The vast majority of those killed or injured were from the UDF areas, and most of the properties damaged, burned and looted belonged to their supporters.

The attack started soon after dawn on Wednesday 28 March, with Inkatha leaders going down from Vulindlela in trucks and lorries, escorted by police vehicles and latecomers following on foot. In the late afternoon, groups of armed men could be seen returning with stolen cattle, furniture, TV sets, stoves and clothing. At about 9:00 a.m., when the fighting was at its most intense, Father Tim Smith SJ, parish priest at Elandskop, situated between Edendale and Vulindlela, received calls from the local newspaper, the *Natal Witness*: 'What's going on up there? We hear there is big fighting'. At that stage, all they knew at the church was that no one had gone to work from their area. No buses ran; everything was unusually quiet. Then they began to receive reports of people fleeing by the thousands into Edendale.

Smith phoned Hurley at about 10:00 a.m. to let him know what was happening. Hurley was in a meeting but nevertheless took the call, thanked Smith for letting him know and went back into the meeting. Smith and his colleagues went ahead, finding out what was happening. Suddenly, at about 12:30 p.m., there was Hurley with

Khumalo. In what Smith thought 'a fine pastoral example', they had driven up from Durban—a ninety-minute drive—to show their concern for the clergy and local people. Hurley was keen to go down into the Edendale valley, through the war zone, but was dissuaded because it was too dangerous.

Over the next few days, he was involved with the NCLG in negotiations about a proposed peace rally, in which Mandela had agreed to meet Buthelezi at Taylor's Halt, in the heart of Inkatha-controlled Vulindlela. Given the circumstances, the ANC were totally opposed, and the meeting was called off.

Mgojo described how Hurley accompanied him into some frightening situations.[12] After visiting some of the thousands of refugees accommodated in Edendale churches, they had gone to Taylor's Halt to see David Ntombela, who had led the attack on Edendale. When they arrived at Ntombela's home, they were told that he was not there but were directed to where they could find him, at the huge tent specially erected for the aborted Mandela-Buthelezi rally. 'As we approached the place where we eventually found [Ntombela], he took out his gun from the ammunition belt around his waist. Archbishop Hurley and Bishop Nuttall humbly addressed him'.

Rev Athol Jennings said that he saw, 'again and again at the Church Leaders' Group meetings when people were needed to go and be a presence somewhere, Denis Hurley always seemed to find the time to . . . be a presence on behalf of the NCLG, to say to communities around the province: peace is the way we need to be travelling'.[13]

In the wake of the Seven Days' War, a delegation of the NCLG joined representatives of the SACC in Ulundi on 2 April to meet Buthelezi, leading members of his cabinet and the Inkatha Central Committee. Hurley commented, 'We tried to prevail upon him to implement a peace plan that had been drafted in July 1989 . . . We could not convince him. He kept blaming the other side for the delay, but we . . . have been trying since March last year to persuade him. Now we have to decide what our next move must be'.[14]

Hurley took part in an important meeting with President de Klerk in Cape Town on April 11. The purpose, he said, was to get de Klerk 'to understand the Natal situation'. As it turned out, the delegation—which included Tutu, Nuttall and Boesak, among others—'was well received and the discussion was friendly, but we don't know how well we succeeded'.

Speaking at a press conference after the meeting, Hurley said that one of the demands the church leaders had put to the president was that the police 'must act with impartiality, neutrality and in an effective way' in the violence-torn areas of Natal. He added, 'I think it will take a considerable change of hearts and minds in the security forces before the kind of impartiality we desire is achieved'. He said there had been accusations of police 'taking sides in the conflict and even participating in attacks'.[15]

Over the next few weeks, the NCLG felt under much pressure to exercise their prophetic role and speak out openly about responsibility for the Seven Days' War. They drafted a media statement to be released after their meeting on 4 May 1990. Hurley had been convinced that the time had now come to make a clear statement about the violence, but Rev Frank Chikane, as general secretary of the SACC, happened to be present at the meeting to discuss funding for the Natal Crisis Fund in the light of the huge needs in Edendale. When Chikane heard about the proposed statement, he asked searching questions, based on the efforts he was making at the national level to revive the proposed peace plan drawn up by the five-a-side talks. What exactly would the church leaders' statement achieve? Would they be able to deal with the likely increase in violence? Could they continue to play a mediating role if they spoke out so clearly about the culprits? Was their intention to abandon the peace plan, and if so, what would be their next step in trying to end the violence?

It seemed clear to Chikane that issuing a challenging statement about the origin of the violence might be cathartic for the church leaders in the short term and perhaps give comfort to the victims and even earn praise for the church leaders' prophetic stance. However, it was not part of a carefully thought-out strategy. 'If you are involved in mediation,' Chikane said many years later, '. . . you can't make statements that would negate the objectives of the mediation process'. Nuttall commented that 'it was helpful having someone from outside the actual scene of the conflict bringing wise counsel to local church leaders who were clearly tired and stressed, helping them to retain a longer-term perspective'.[16]

Chikane's questions gave the church leaders much to think about, and they delayed issuing their statement until their next meeting on 23 May, at which a modified version was approved. This 'would not jeopardize Rev Frank Chikane's initiative' by pointing fingers of blame for the violence. The NCLG expressed their full support for what he was doing.

Chikane persisted with his national peace efforts, and on 14 September 1991, more than a year later, a National Peace Accord was signed. Among the signatories were the ANC and the IFP, who committed themselves to change the strategies and tactics used by their supporters. Unfortunately, the Peace Accord and its various peace structures at national, provincial and local levels did little to change the situation, at least in the short term. In the run-up to South Africa's first democratic elections, the violence worsened, with the highest numbers of violent deaths in the last two months before the elections in April 1994. Supporters of the Peace Accord felt that, but for the peace structures, the death toll might have been much higher. Whatever their weaknesses, these structures did at least provide opportunities for meeting and talking. Conflicting parties began to remember their common humanity and to understand each other a little better. Over time, this helped to reduce the violence, though not before more than 15,000 people had been killed.[17]

Hurley was asked to co-chair the Natal Peace Committee with M. C. Pretorius, a leading member of the business community. According to Hurley, Pretorius took control of the structure, running it along business lines that conflicted with the African need to reach consensus by thorough and lengthy discussion. Jennings recalled that, on a number of occasions, Hurley tried to open up discussions in the Peace Committee to avoid hasty decisions that might not enjoy full support, but Pretorius's approach prevailed.

Inkatha threatened to boycott the elections, fearing that it would lose power in Natal. As the date drew closer, analysts were anxious that, if the IFP refused to participate, there was no way the election could take place without bloodshed; and that, if the election did not take place or was delayed for any reason, the townships throughout the country would explode.

To resolve the conflict between the ANC and the IFP, it was eventually agreed that disputed constitutional issues should be referred to a panel of international mediators. When this international effort failed despite the involvement of such high-profile figures as Henry Kissinger from the USA, and Lord Carrington from the UK, there were fears of civil war in Natal. Nevertheless, some still hoped that a further mediation between Buthelezi, Mandela and the National Party government might succeed, especially because of an intense campaign of prayer, including a continuous vigil in the Anglican Cathedral in Pietermaritzburg over several weeks. The highlight of this campaign was the 'Jesus Prayer Rally' on 17 April, days before the election.[18]

While 30,000 people gathered in prayer, Buthelezi was meeting at the stadium with Jacob Zuma (since 2007, president of the ANC), the highest-ranking ANC representative at the rally, and Danie Schutte, Minister of Home Affairs, the top government representative. They were considering a last-ditch set of mediation proposals worked out by Professor Washington Okumu, a Kenyan mediator brought to South Africa by Michael Cassidy of the evangelical organization, African Enterprise. Both Zuma and Schutte were in favour and briefed their parties.

Everything then depended on Okumu's meeting with Mandela in Cape Town and Buthelezi's meeting with the IFP's Central Committee, both scheduled for that evening. Both meetings endorsed the Okumu proposals. The next day, all the key role-players met at the Union Buildings in Pretoria, the administrative seat of government, to discuss the possibility of an emergency session of parliament to ratify the necessary constitutional amendments. On Tuesday, 19 April, with only 9 days before the election, the agreement was signed and the announcement made that the IFP would take part in the elections.

Despite the great logistical challenges that this late entry posed, this news was greeted with immense relief. South Africa had looked into the abyss of a full-scale civil war and at the last minute drawn back. There was much comment about 'divine intervention' that seemed to have saved the day.

Though violence continued for some years after the elections, it never again reached the proportions of the last two months before the poll. Many irregularities in the elections had occurred in Natal, especially in the rural areas. As a result of difficult negotiations, however, an agreement was reached that the IFP would be regarded as the winner. This decision was thought also to have played an important role in preventing increased violence.

After the elections, when a new, democratically elected national government came to power, the police and security forces were brought under tighter control, which reduced the involvement of 'third forces' suspected of having a hand in the violence. The national election results themselves played a role in reducing the violence. Gradually, it seemed that two things became clear to IFP supporters, according to Professor Colin Gardner, former member and Speaker of the Msunduzi City Council in Pietermaritzburg: the ANC had an undeniable majority in the country as a whole; and life under ANC rule was not as intolerable as IFP supporters, like many whites, had feared.[19] Communities had also become weary of violence and the immense destruction it had caused to people and property. Nevertheless, it took years before the violence was brought completely under control.

In his letter of congratulations to Hurley on the fiftieth anniversary of his ordination, referred to earlier, Buthelezi stated that he was under no illusion about 'how much we differ on the question of tactics and strategies or about what is good and what is evil in politics'. By the end of Hurley's time as Archbishop of Durban, he had long rejected the Inkatha strategy and was broadly supportive of the UDF and ANC. He had, however, never accepted the ANC's armed struggle any more than he supported the use of violence by Inkatha. He was as firmly opposed to the civil war that threatened to engulf Natal and KwaZulu at the time of the elections in 1994 as he had been to the apartheid war launched by the National Party government in the 1970s.

29

A Painful Experience

When Hurley ceased to be Archbishop of Durban in 1992, he was asked by his colleagues in the SACBC to continue representing them on ICEL's episcopal board. He had stepped down as chair in 1991 after a sixteen-year stint and reverted to being an ordinary member representing the South African bishops. It was the beginning of his fourth and last decade of involvement with ICEL, one that would prove most difficult for ICEL and, towards its end, one of the most painful experiences of Hurley's life.[1]

There had been difficult years for ICEL earlier: for example, when Cardinal Augustin Mayer had been the Vatican's top liturgical official, prefect of the Congregation for Divine Worship (CDW). In 1988 Mayer had retired at the age of 77. One of his last actions in office was to send a letter to ICEL's eleven-member conferences of bishops, saying that the organization needed to be 'reformed, restructured and redirected'. It was an unsurprising end to his tense relationship with ICEL. John Page, ICEL's executive secretary, recalls that Mayer's letter was simply ignored by most conferences. The US bishops sent back a curt letter, saying, 'We are happy with ICEL as it is'.

Mayer's place was taken by the more friendly and open-minded Cardinal Martinez, who did not pursue Mayer's call for the reform of ICEL but had a more harmonious relationship with the organization, as did his successor, Cardinal Ortas, prefect from 1992 to 1996. Contact between the CDW and ICEL improved during those years to such an extent that, in 1996, Archbishop Agnelo, the CDW secretary, commended ICEL's work and the service it gave to the member bishops' conferences.

As more conservative bishops were appointed during Pope John Paul II's twenty-seven-year pontificate, so some bishops' attitude towards ICEL began to shift. This was more pronounced in the United States, where some argued that ICEL translations were making worshippers less respectful, especially towards the Eucharist. This negative attitude towards ICEL became evident during the votes of the bishops' conferences on each of the eight segments making up the revised missal prepared by ICEL. With only one exception, these segments received substantial—

and in some cases overwhelmingly—positive majorities in the votes of the individual bishops' conferences. This was also true in the United States, though about 25 bishops out of 275 voters mounted an increasingly determined opposition to the ICEL revision of the missal. When the bishops of the eleven conferences came to vote on the segment containing the revised texts of the Order of Mass—the heart of the Roman Missal—again substantial majority votes were achieved in the various conferences. But in this instance the number of 'no' votes from US bishops had increased from 25 to more than 60 of the 225 voters present. At the June 1995 meeting of the US bishops, the dissenting group came close to denying the revision of this segment the two-thirds majority required by church law.

The US Conference did approve the revision with the required two-thirds vote, but by a margin of only seven votes, a fact that was noticed in Rome. It was mentioned by Cardinal Ratzinger (Pope Benedict XVI from 2005) when Archbishop Pilarcyk, Hurley's successor as chair, and Page met him and other officials of the Congregation for the Doctrine of the Faith (CDF) in mid-October 1995. The latter body would have been pleased to know that the most powerful bishops' conference in the English-speaking world was less than enthusiastic about the work of ICEL. This matched the CDF's own disenchantment with the organization, which they thought was pursuing a dangerously liberal agenda.

An example of this was the translation of Psalms. Known as the ICEL Psalter, it had deliberately used non-sexist and inclusive language, avoiding the use of masculine pronouns for both men and women and also for references to God. This text had not been voted on by the conferences but had been published in 1995 simply for study. It proved popular and was widely used by men and women religious for morning and evening prayers. By 1997 the CDW was greatly concerned that the ICEL Psalter had not been submitted to the conferences or to the Vatican for approval, though it had an *imprimatur* (official Catholic permission for it to be printed) from the president of the US Bishops' Conference, Cardinal William Keeler.

Before the Psalter was published with Keeler's *imprimatur*, the review committee of four US bishops, all of whom had degrees in Scripture and were sympathetic to ICEL, insisted that in about forty instances the masculine pronoun should continue to be used for God, because traditionally these verses were regarded as referring to Christ. One of the translators of the Psalter was unhappy with this decision and, without informing Page and another key member of ICEL's staff, in the introductory comments took issue with these US bishops. Page described this as 'a mighty nail in ICEL's coffin' and noted that among those who would have interpreted this as another example of ICEL's 'defiance' was Cardinal Joseph Ratzinger.

Ratzinger put pressure on Keeler's successor as president of the US Bishops' Conference, Bishop Anthony Pilla, to withdraw the *imprimatur* for the Psalter. This was done, and when ICEL asked why, it became clear that the objections were to inclusive language and the use of 'dynamic equivalence': translating according to the sense of the original text rather than literally. The Vatican saw inclusive language as the thin edge of the wedge, an effort to advance feminist theology and to promote the ordination of women, which John Paul II had officially declared taboo for Catholics.

Criticizing a translation because it used dynamic equivalence was regarded as a damning indictment: for the CDF, no further motivation would be needed for its rejection. Dynamic equivalence was no longer acceptable, though it had been officially approved by Pope Paul VI and there was still no new policy document.

The new prefect of the CDW was a Chilean, Cardinal Jorge Arturo Medina Estévez, who took up the post in September 1996. More hardline than any of his predecessors, he was said to have been supportive of the notorious General Augusto Pinochet, who had taken power in Chile by means of a military coup.

It seemed that Medina Estévez, perhaps encouraged in this by Cardinal Ratzinger, felt that vernacular translations were out of control and that he had a special mission to put things right. He focused his sights on ICEL as the structure most in need of his reforming zeal.[2] By this time ICEL was concerned not only about the attitude of the CDW but also about the US bishops, two bodies which seemed to be increasingly of one mind in their attitude to ICEL. ICEL's anxiety was in no way lessened by the appointment of the new Cardinal Archbishop of Chicago, Francis George OMI, as the US bishops' representative on ICEL's episcopal board. It was feared that he was bringing to ICEL something of Medina Estévez's interventionist zeal.

The first ICEL meeting that George attended was on 4 June 1998, arriving just as the meeting was starting.[3] He asked the chair, Bishop Maurice Taylor of Galloway, Scotland, to change the agenda, signalling that he had a really important item that he wanted to have discussed and that the bishops should not waste their time and his. He had just come from Rome, where he had met Medina Estévez, but insisted that he did not speak on behalf of Medina Estévez or the CDW but rather of the US Bishops' Conference. Nevertheless he made it known that Rome was deeply unhappy with ICEL and that there was also 'significant opposition' to the organization among the American bishops. Taylor ruled that the agenda could not be set aside but offered a compromise: George might address his concerns as the last agenda item on the first day.

When George took the floor at the end of that day, his message was dramatic: unless ICEL changed its attitude and some of its staff and experts, it was finished. If the US bishops did not see the changes they and the Vatican were looking for, they would establish their own translation body. The CDW was unhappy that ICEL had exceeded its mandate by composing original texts. Moreover, the document that was the basis for all ICEL's work, the 1969 instruction on translation approved by Paul VI and known as *Comme le prévoit* (as requested), had effectively been rejected by Rome, though George admitted that no new policy was yet in place. But it was becoming well known that Rome wanted an almost literal fidelity to the original Latin. Each word or phrase in the original should be matched by a word or phrase of the translation.

The person most shocked by George's words was Hurley. Forty years of effort by his beloved ICEL seemed on the brink of being wiped out. He faced the difficult task of challenging a cardinal—his brother-Oblate, Francis George—in the meeting rather than privately, because George had delivered his message publicly. When the day's work was over, Hurley went to his room and carefully prepared a handwritten statement in response to what George had said.

No doubt Hurley was experiencing pent-up frustration not only as a result of what George had said, but also because of how ICEL was being treated by the CDW and the US Bishops' Conference, as well as disappointment that there seemed to be a strong move away from the values of Vatican II, especially that of collegiality. Worst of all, it seemed unfair that ICEL was being criticized for its fidelity to the mandate set out in *Comme le prévoit*, which had not been officially withdrawn or replaced; this would happen only later with the promulgation of *Liturgiam Authenticam* ('authentic liturgy').

When the bishops reconvened the next morning, the first hand that went up was Hurley's, requesting Taylor's permission to address the meeting.[4] Reading his prepared statement, and without any of the humour with which he would often lighten meetings, Hurley began by referring to the change that had taken place in the Vatican's translation policy, as reflected by George's presentation. Whereas *Comme le prévoit* of 1969 said that the basic unit of translation could be a word, a phrase, a complete sentence or even a longer passage, what the Vatican now seemed to be demanding, without prior consultation, was that each individual word be regarded as a unit of meaning. Hurley said that he had been present in the Second Vatican Council when collegiality had been discussed in October 1963, and 'I find the attitude reflected in the proposed change in translation practice a distressing departure from the spirit of collegiality [and thus] in favour of authoritative imposition'.

Then came a sentence that Hurley later asked the secretary of the meeting, Jim Schellman, to strike from the official record. Addressing George directly, he said: 'With deep respect and fraternal affection, I must confirm that I found the manner in which you conveyed the change to us a reflection of the attitude of authoritative imposition'. He went on to ask George to give a demonstration of 'fraternal charity and collegiality' by communicating to the CDW what many, if not all, of those present felt about such 'authoritative imposition'.

This was followed by the most painful passage in Hurley's statement: 'We have laboured for something like a dozen years to produce a revision of the Roman Sacramentary [also known as the Roman Missal] in the light of *Comme le prévoit*. In the process hundreds of people have dedicated their expertise and their energy, and ICEL [has] expended a huge sum of money only to discover that all this may now end in frustration and waste'.

In response to the charge that ICEL had exceeded its mandate, he complained that the CDW had never formally communicated this to the organization nor had it given precise examples 'despite our openness at all times'. With regard to George's reference to the CDW's impatience with ICEL's 'misbehaviour' over the years, he recalled that there had been tensions between the organization and two prefects of the Congregation, but 'as soon as they relinquished their posts, the tension evaporated'. Turning to inclusive language, he said that this was an issue that had come to stay; there was no way of ignoring it or removing it from the agenda.

In conclusion, Hurley appealed to George once again:

Your Eminence, you have conveyed to us the attitude of the Sacred Congregation for Divine Worship. It would be a great act of fraternal charity and collegiality to convey to, or to facilitate the communication to the Sacred Congregation, and indeed to the Holy Father, of the attitude respectfully and loyally entertained [by] the oldest and largest mixed commission [that is, representing several bishops' conferences] in the field of liturgical translation with a view to the sort of fraternal dialogue that is the best Christian method of resolving differences.

In an extraordinary echo of Vatican II, Hurley ended his response to George's message with the single Latin word that concluded all interventions in the council: *Dixi*, literally meaning, 'I have spoken' or 'That's the end of my speech' but with the flavour of 'That's where I stand'. Clearly, he attached enormous importance to the Vatican II stand on collegiality, the central issue at stake in this quarrel.

John Wilkins, a former editor of the *Tablet*, writing for the 2 December 2005 issue of the American publication *Commonweal* on the basis of eyewitness accounts of what then happened, described the scene:

In a further intervention, Cardinal George reacted strongly to Hurley. He felt he [George] had been insulted . . . He apologized if anyone had felt attacked by him, but he was telling the members of ICEL things they needed to hear. They must be receptive to criticism of their texts, but they were not listening. That was the road to disaster. It seemed to George that he would have to report to the American bishops that they must choose between ICEL and Rome. Several times he pushed back his chair, causing some of the participants to fear that he would walk out.

The next day Hurley wrote a personal letter to George, apologizing that his words 'hurt you so much'. He explained that what he had said had been said in the spirit of Ephesians 4:15, 'speaking the truth in love' (NRSV). He had been moved to speak

by the vigorous, even vehement manner, in which you spoke about the need to accept the change. The impression you created on me was of impatience, anger and an uncompromising demand that the change be accepted without demur, without any recognition of the right of a body representative of so many bishops in the Catholic Church to dialogue with the Congregation about it. Never before in my experience had anyone spoken in an ICEL meeting in that way, a way that created exceptional tension.

Hurley ended with a postscript in which he generously expressed admiration for the way George had agreed to accompany Taylor for discussions with the CDW.

In an interview a few years later, George said that Hurley had behaved as if ICEL was a 'sacred cow', beyond criticism: Hurley seemed to think it could not or would not change. He (George) had been particularly offended by what he called Hurley's 'sarcasm'—twice referring to him as 'Your Eminence'. He seemed unaware that Hurley had long been accustomed to using such formal titles and did so without irony. He would not have known, for example, that Hurley and McCann had for many years addressed each other, in ordinary conversation, as 'Your Grace'.

What Wilkins described as the Congregation's 'knockout blow' to ICEL, was the publication on 28 March 2001 of *Liturgiam Authenticam*, a new instruction on the translation of Latin texts into the vernacular, published by the CDW. This set of guidelines superseded *Comme le prévoit*, which had guided ICEL's work since 1969. *Liturgiam Authenticam* decreed that translations from Latin should reflect the syntax and style of the Latin. The Congregation's purpose was to avoid a secular tone in translation; they wanted a 'sacral vernacular, characterized by a vocabulary, syntax and grammar that are proper to divine worship'. Their hope was to ensure that translations would not date. Yet ICEL had not in any way been consulted about these new guidelines, despite its expressed openness and availability and decades-long experience of vernacular translation.

One of the most disturbing features of the new instruction was that it also ruled out ecumenical cooperation in liturgical translation. This meant an end to the agreed ecumenical texts for prayers, such as the *Gloria* and the Apostles' Creed. These had been developed by bodies like the International Consultation on English Texts (ICET), representing a number of Christian denominations, with which ICEL had worked closely. These agreed texts were already extensively used in Catholic and other churches. Instead of the agreements on such common translations being affirmed as an example of ecumenical progress, they seemed to be viewed by the CDW as misleading or embarrassing to Catholics. 'Great caution', said *Liturgiam Authenticam*, 'is to be taken to avoid a wording or style that the Catholic faithful would confuse with the manner of speech of non-Catholic ecclesial communities or other religions, so that such a factor will not cause them confusion or discomfort'.

Archbishop Jabulani Nxumalo of Bloemfontein, who has long been involved in translating liturgical texts into Zulu, describes *Liturgiam Authenticam* as 'a travesty of anything to do with culture and language'. Nxumalo holds that language 'is an expression of the soul of the people' and it cannot, therefore, be determined by the conventions of another language, in the way that *Liturgiam Authenticam* would like translations to reflect the Latin original. Each language has its own idiom, its own world view. From his own experience of preaching in English, French and Zulu, Nxumalo realized that you could not just translate a sermon: you would have to 'push the whole thing aside and think it out in the other language from scratch'. So his view was that *Liturgiam Authenticam* 'should just be cancelled; . . . it contradicts my whole experience of working on language, anthropology, translation, and also my knowledge of different languages . . . It just doesn't make sense'.

A few months after the publication of *Liturgiam Authenticam*, in July 2001 a further shock for ICEL was the establishment of a high-level committee of English-speaking cardinals and bishops, known as *Vox Clara* (clear voice), with its own experts. This committee, according to Bishop Arthur Roche, current chair of ICEL, has the responsibility for advising the CDW on texts presented by ICEL.[5] With its establishment, control over English translation of the liturgy has largely passed from a collegial structure established by the bishops, ICEL, to two entirely

Vatican-appointed bodies, *Vox Clara* and the CDW, with a third, the CDF, intervening whenever it thinks necessary. This move by the Vatican seems to have taken place with remarkably little resistance from the English-speaking conferences.

There can have been little surprise among the South African Catholic bishops when, in July 2001, their plenary session received a letter from Hurley asking to stand down as their representative on the ICEL episcopal board, bowing out after an involvement with ICEL that began in 1963.

Hurley's view of *Liturgiam Authenticam* is clear from a careful comparison he made of clauses from the Vatican II constitution on the liturgy, known as *Sacrosanctum Concilium* (1962), with equivalent clauses from the new instruction, indicating the way decisions are to be made about liturgical translations. This comparison, he said, showed how far the Church had moved from the idea of collegiality.[6]

From this time onward, Hurley's correspondence reflects his devastation at what the (CDW) had done to ICEL. He had a particular concern for John Page, ICEL's former executive secretary, who had resigned in the wake of harsh criticism and sustained pressure directed at him by the CDW. Page had served ICEL with distinction from 1972, particularly as executive secretary since 1980.

To his friend Petal O'Hea, Hurley wrote: 'At times I find it difficult to understand the attitude of the Roman Curia. It seems to be more concerned with power than with humble service . . . Why are such people promoted to positions of authority where they seem to be promoting their ego rather than the Church? May the Lord come to our help'.

To Jim Schellman, he wrote: 'It is still hard to deal with the pain caused by all that happened to ICEL last year, . . . the refusal to accept a translation to which so many of us had contributed under John Page's able management over fifteen to twenty years. Mother Church sometimes has ways of making her own martyrs'. Hurley's disappointment about the revision of the Roman Missal must have been all the greater because it was a task that he specially promoted during his 16 years in the chair, and which ICEL had dedicated to him (Hurley). The fruit of that work now gathers dust on a shelf of the ICEL archives as the 'new ICEL' works on a completely new translation that meets the requirements of *Liturgiam Authenticam*, with *Vox Clara* and the CDF to pronounce on its acceptability.

Given the painful thoughts that were preoccupying Hurley, one can imagine his satisfaction on reading a report in the *National Catholic Reporter* of 26 December 2002 about a public meeting at St Anselmo's in Rome addressed by Father Ignacio Calabuig OSM, a Catalan Servite. After finishing his talk, Calabuig, like Hurley a veteran of Vatican II, turned to Cardinal Arinze, Medina Estévez's successor as prefect of the CDW, and said: '"What Rome is doing to good scholars of language—poets and linguists, translators and anthropologists—leading scholars in their fields—telling them that they are unworthy or incapable of translating texts, is wrong." (His voice became louder and more emotional.) "It is wrong, unjust, not right . . . and it must stop!" The whole church broke into sustained applause for a few minutes, and Arinze was frozen, not knowing what to do. One colleague said he (Arinze) turned blue. The entire faculty applauded wildly with everyone else, and no one stopped. It became so uncomfortable that Arinze began applauding too.'[8]

Hurley wrote to a friend: 'The applause that rolled on so long at St Anselmo's continues in Durban, South Africa. Long live Father Ignacio Calabuig . . . [with] *plauso, fragoroso, interminato* [prolonged and deafening applause]'.[9]

30

The Perfect Chancellor

The year 1992 was difficult for South African universities.[1] In the wake of the political changes, following the unbanning of the ANC and PAC, and the release of Nelson Mandela and other political leaders, there were enormous expectations, especially among young black people, confident that tertiary education would now be really accessible to them. This was understandable but unrealistic, because government subsidies were dwindling and fees inevitably rising.

Of 7,500 first-year applicants for Natal University's Durban campus that year, only 2,000 could be enrolled. While 120 first-year medical students were accepted, 1,700 applicants were turned away. Of those admitted to various faculties, 700 were unable to pay their residence or tuition fees, leaving the university with a large debt.

Racial tensions surfaced when a law student, Knowledge Mdlalose, was excluded from the university because he had not achieved the required academic level, failing sixteen of twenty-two first-year law courses over a two-year period. For weeks, there were deep divisions about how his case should be handled. The university was the focus of many negative media reports about militant student protests, damage to property, alleged assaults on campus and sporadic class boycotts.

In the midst of that crisis came another, not unrelated. It had been decided that Nelson Mandela, released from prison just two years earlier, should receive an honorary doctorate from Natal University. The degree would be conferred on him by the then Chancellor, Judge Ray Leon, in his last graduation ceremony. This became a matter of controversy because Leon in 1986 had sentenced to death an ANC member, Andrew Zondo, for bombings at the Amanzimtoti shopping centre, just south of Durban, in which five people had been killed and sixty injured. Students threatened to boycott the graduation unless someone other than Leon conferred the honorary doctorate. The ANC put pressure on Mandela not to attend the ceremony, and it was agreed between him and the university that the doctorate would be conferred later, but no date was specified. Though the issue had been amicably resolved, it was highly embarrassing for the university. The protesting students did not take account of Leon's fine judgment in what became known as the 'Hurley case' (1985): as we have seen in Chapter 25, the first time in South African legal history that a judge had ordered the release of a detainee.

Towards the end of 1992, the process of nominating a new chancellor began.[2] Professor Brenda Gourley, then one of the deputy vice-chancellors, said there was much contention about who should be nominated, all the more perhaps because of the embarrassment of Mandela's withdrawal from the graduation ceremony and the racial tensions stirred up by the Mdlalose case. Colin Gardner, professor of English on the Pietermaritzburg campus, described it as 'a moment of rapid and somewhat chaotic transition in South Africa. The liberation movements had been unbanned, but the first democratic election had not yet been held, and there was uncertainty about the future of the country. Who could the university find to be a symbolic unifying figure?'

Many felt that the time had come for the chancellor to be a distinguished member of the black community. There was, however, no agreement on who would be the ideal candidate. Names were proposed, and various groups lobbied for their candidates. In that period of political change and division, no candidate seemed to enjoy general favour. No doubt the violent conflict between the IFP and the ANC was one of the factors making a selection difficult.

And then Denis Hurley's name was put forward. Gourley said that as soon as his name was proposed, 'everybody agreed and that was the end of it'. She thought it 'absolutely remarkable' that there should be 'unanimity about the choice of an elderly white male'. Gardner regarded it as significant that a secular university had chosen a Catholic archbishop.

What Gourley appreciated was that, from then on, the matter of who would be chancellor was completely uncontentious, despite the difficult climate on campus. Hence she described Hurley as the 'perfect chancellor' for that time. One of the other deputy vice-chancellors (DVCs), Professor Emmanuel Ngara, described him as 'a stabilizing factor, a rallying point'.[3]

There was, however, a point of contention. A certain C. B. Hugo, in a letter to the editor of *NU Focus*, claimed to be puzzled by the appointment because the Catholic Church discriminated against women.[4] 'No promotion is possible for a woman in the church of which Archbishop Hurley is such a prominent member'. Hugo went on to say that '[the] archbishop's silence on the position of women in his own church is deafening'.

This criticism was easy to counter, since Hurley had not been silent. Indeed, on 13 July 1991, the *Natal Mercury* carried a report that he had spoken out in favour of the ordination of women—despite the Vatican's ban on discussion of the issue. When Hurley was installed as chancellor, he was interviewed by the *Sunday Times* and repeated this view 'despite its unpopularity in the Vatican'.[5] Such actions made it extremely unlikely that the Vatican would confer on him a cardinal's hat, and he knew it.

In the same interview, the *Sunday Times* asked Hurley how he responded to his appointment. His reply was that he was 'very surprised, astounded, in fact'. But he had accepted nomination because, over the years, he had felt a warm attachment to the University of Natal: he had known many of its professors, staff and graduates. He admitted that he would have immensely enjoyed being an academic, though he had found his life as a bishop fulfilling. He was attracted to science, especially physics, and had compensated for the lack of academic opportunity in that field by wide reading. He did not mention another link with the university: he had received an honorary doctorate in literature there in 1978.

But the most important reason why he welcomed his appointment was that it gave him a close association with the university at a time of transition in South Africa, when universities and churches were being called upon to play an important role in shaping social attitudes conducive to peace and cooperation between groups and nations.

In nominating Hurley as chancellor, Professor Gourley spoke of the qualities that made him suitable. The university was looking for someone who would symbolise its values. 'Hurley had', she said, 'in his life and work . . . articulated these values in a multitude of ways'. She concluded that 'he is one of a few South Africans in our fraught society whom all sectors of the university would acknowledge as a worthy holder of the office of Chancellor'.

In an article for *Denis Hurley: A Portrait by Friends*, she described him as a 'spiritual vessel, so big-hearted that he could embrace great diversity', a reference not only to his ability to work with people of other races, but also with those of other churches and other faiths and indeed even people of no faith.[6]

The University Council accepted Gourley's nomination at a special meeting on 23 October 1992. Hurley immediately took office and was officially installed in a grand ceremony in the Pietermaritzburg City Hall on 4 March 1993. On that occasion, the University orator, Professor Colin Gardner, presented Hurley to the assembly. He outlined the main achievements of his life and the qualities he had demonstrated in many years of leadership. Gardner concluded with his own understanding of why Hurley had been chosen to be chancellor: 'Because he has exemplified remarkably both the vigorous life of the mind and the ways in which, particularly in a South Africa in a state of crisis, the life of the mind may be infused and be fused with the life of action, the daily life of people and societies. For that, in a nutshell, is one of the central thrusts, perhaps *the* central thrust, of the university's mission statement.'

Gardner gave a light-hearted warning to the new chancellor: 'As he solemnly walks in the academic procession in the company of people many of whom are in red robes, and as the rest of the gathering intently watches his tall figure, he must strenuously resist the long-held habit of bestowing, by the sign of the cross made in the air, a benevolent episcopal blessing'.

Hurley used the opportunity of his installation address to stress his hope that the University of Natal and others would commit 'themselves to a programme of social education designed to help create in black and white South Africans the attitudes necessary to produce a creative and dynamic society'.[8] This would involve 'a huge programme of development projects aimed at initiating the black population into the skills and incentives of self-help and . . . at enlarging the vision of white South

Africans to take in not only the privileged society to which they have belonged, but [also] the whole national community of forty million people'.

Reflecting on Hurley's installation as chancellor and many subsequent university ceremonies over which he presided, Professor Emmanuel Ngara referred to the grace and dignity with which Hurley conducted himself. Another of the DVCs of that time, Professor John Volmink, said that never again would the university have a chancellor who could pronounce and understand the Latin so well; he added, 'His whole presence and his gravitas added a great deal to our ceremonies'.[9]

Both Gourley and Ngara commented that Hurley was generous with his time. During these years, from 1993 to 1998, though he was retired, he had a full-time job as parish priest of Emmanuel Cathedral, so he had much to do besides being chancellor. Yet Gourley said that 'he has been very assiduous about attending graduations'. In addition, he had given a lot of other time to the university. He was willing to be present on other special occasions, and his presence was always welcome because he made appropriate and insightful comments.

The university was much engaged with the larger society. In 1994, for example, eighty-four non-governmental organizations (NGOs) had offices on the campus. Hurley was enormously appreciative and supportive of these links. He also strongly affirmed the integration of community service and violence-prevention programmes into the curriculum and attended a number of related functions to indicate his approval and support.

But the initiative that delighted him most while he was chancellor was the establishment of an Ethics Centre. He associated himself with the centre as often as he could. In his addresses at university functions, he would stress how important it was not just to have intellectual leadership but also leadership of a moral nature, which grasped the main issues of the time and tried to do something about them.

Chancellors do not address graduation ceremonies, but Hurley knew precisely what he would have said if there were such an opportunity.[10] In an interview at the time of his retirement as chancellor, he said:

> I would talk about the need for graduates to dedicate themselves to the task of unity in South Africa. Sharing is a great African virtue, so I would invite them to translate from the African cultural convictions—and apply those principles to a new society and a new economy. It's not easy to do because the new economy chokes you and overwhelms you and you forget where you have come from. The trend today, all over the world, is 'money rules'. And money is the one criterion by which people, jobs and achievements are judged. I react against that. I would encourage them to build up a degree of unselfishness and a social conscience.

Hurley revelled in his years as chancellor, not because of the prominence or prestige the office gave him or the leading role in colourful ceremonies, but because he delighted in academic discussion. Being chancellor gave him unique opportunities to engage with academics of many disciplines. It was a great pleasure for him to meet interesting people, especially the honorary graduands. During his time, they included Judge Richard Goldstone, Deputy President Thabo Mbeki, Cyril Ramaphosa, Ismael and Fatima Meer, Archbishop Trevor Huddleston and, most notably, President Nelson Mandela. Hurley much regretted that the honorary doctorates conferred on Aung San Suu Kyi and Mother Teresa had to be awarded in absentia.

Probably the most interesting ceremony over which Hurley presided as chancellor was the 'reconciliation graduation' in December 1995. In a letter to friends, he described it as a ceremony

> for all the [400] doctors who have graduated from the Durban Medical School over about 25 years [and] had refused to attend graduation rituals because of apartheid. The reconciliation brought them all together in high good mood and happy fellowship. Our Vice-Chancellor Brenda Gourley . . . made an appropriate apology before the function for all the shortcomings of the University in the apartheid years. This address established a marvellous mood in the audience, and from then on things went with a swing.[11]

It could be said that Hurley 'went the extra mile' for the University of Natal. In fact, he went several thousand extra miles. He was a regular visitor to the United States in his capacity as a board member of ICEL. During his time as chancellor, he assisted the university's fund-raising efforts by spending extra time there, introducing the university to his influential contacts. This was especially true in 1999: despite no longer being chancellor, he made an extensive series of visits to Boston, Toronto, New York, Chicago, Notre Dame in Indiana, and Washington, DC. The university had established the Archbishop Denis E. Hurley Educational Fund to support bursaries for disadvantaged students. Hurley, despite being nearly 84, agreed to undertake this demanding speaking tour to promote the new fund.

As we will see in Chapter 31, while in Toronto he developed an unusual form of shingles, which made it impossible for him to use his right hand. He bravely faced the embarrassment of having to give a left-handed greeting to the many people he met at dinners and other functions. His travelling companion, Volmink, was urged by Gourley to persuade Hurley to return to South Africa for the sake of his health. He insisted on completing the itinerary.

After Hurley's first year as chancellor, Gourley had been appointed vice-chancellor and developed a close friendship with him. This was evident to many people, who described the leadership team as 'The Hurley-Gourley Show'. In some of the difficult situations that arose on campus, Gourley appreciated being able to speak to Hurley, who had himself been in the front line over many years. And she greatly enjoyed his fund of jokes for every occasion. Even in the midst of solemn ceremonies, they had a common appreciation of the hilarious: 'So many things happen at graduation that you don't see but either the chancellor has . . . to handle . . . or the vice-chancellor . . . We sit up there next to each other, and students do peculiar things . . . We couldn't laugh out loud. All we could do is . . . acknowledge to each other that we had noticed'.

Some years later, in 2004, Gourley was vice-chancellor of the Open University in England and gave her verdict on Hurley as chancellor. She said quite simply that not only was he the 'perfect chancellor for that time' but in fact 'the best chancellor I have ever known'. She concluded, 'We were extremely fortunate to have him'.[12]

34

A Busy Retirement

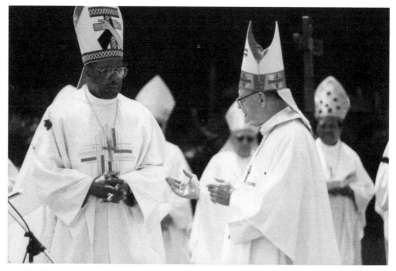

Archbishop Hurley invites Archbishop Napier to be seated on the presidential chair at the latter's installation as Archbishop of Durban—4 October 1992.

A colourful religious ceremony took place at the Westridge Tennis Stadium in Durban on 4 October 1992, the feast of St Francis of Assisi. A Franciscan, Wilfrid Napier, was installed as Archbishop of Durban, in succession to Denis Hurley. Representatives of Napier's three 'families' escorted the new archbishop into the stadium: his family of birth, the Franciscan Order as his religious family, and the family of the Diocese of Kokstad, where he had been bishop for 12 years. A new era was starting: Hurley was handing over the Archdiocese of Durban over after 45 years as its leader. The next day he quietly moved to Emmanuel Cathedral to become parish priest for the first time, a month before his seventy-seventh birthday.[1] Was this a new record for him—the oldest person to become a parish priest for the first time?

Hurley had indicated to Napier that he would be willing to take on this assignment for a few years, to help alleviate the shortage of priests. It was hardly the 'small retirement job' that he had said he would be looking for, though he chose the modest title 'acting parish priest'. He would continue in this post until January 2002, over nine years later, when he would finally retire from active priestly work.

Emmanuel Cathedral is in one of the poorest areas of Durban. At the time of Hurley's arrival there in 1992, the complex consisted of a run-down church, parish centre and priests' house, surrounded by markets, vegetable and fruit stalls, taxi ranks and thousands of the city's poorest commuters. The demographics had changed dramatically from when he had been junior curate over 50 years earlier. Now most parishioners were Zulu-speaking. There was also a large group of coloureds and Indians and a growing number of refugees mainly from Central Africa, but very few whites, though they had been dominant in the 1940s, when he had first been on the staff. It was not entirely a surprise to cathedral parishioners that Hurley had chosen this task for his retirement. He had hinted as much when he attended their annual general meetings.[2]

Clearly, he wanted to continue being active, because at the age of 77, according to cathedral parishioner Huguette Bechet, 'he was a strong man and his mind was clear ... He needed to carry on working, and he had always loved the cathedral'. Charmaine Trycinski, the cathedral secretary, was surprised how much energy he still had and how much time he gave to everything he had to do.[3] Nevertheless, his decision to be parish priest of the cathedral was unusual, because a cathedral is the church of the bishop in office, where he presides over many events, especially during Holy Week and at Christmas as a symbol of diocesan unity. How did Napier feel about having his predecessor as parish priest of 'his church'?

> I would have felt on some occasions that I've got somebody looking over my shoulder and seeing how things are going. But I must pay him his credit ... that only on one or two occasions did he slip into the mould of telling what should be done. But it was just as difficult for him, I think, giving up after all those years [of being] in charge, and then having someone else taking over. But generally I would have said he was exemplary in the way he supported and kept things going.[4]

During his last years in office, Hurley had noticed how the cathedral parish had deteriorated: numbers were down, and the parishioners were apathetic. His aim was to get the parish back on track before a new permanent parish priest was appointed. Bechet felt that in his retirement years Hurley did sort things out and was able to hand over a parish with strong structures when he left in early 2002. Previously it had seemed as if there were two parishes at the cathedral, one Zulu-speaking, the other English-speaking. Hurley worked hard to bring about unity, starting a monthly bilingual Mass, and encouraging the parish pastoral council to develop and implement a mission statement on unity.

Much of his attention was given to encouraging small Christian communities or faith-sharing groups. These met in the members' homes to discuss how they could lead their daily lives in the light of the Scriptures. This was part of the Pastoral Plan and ensured follow-up to the Renew process that he had introduced.

But his concerns were also much wider than the parish's. Members of the neighbouring Grey Street mosque (*Juma Musjid*) noticed that he would come there to pray occasionally in the early morning. Essop Kajee, one of their senior members, said: 'At dawn the silence of the reading of the *Qur'an* is at its best, and His Grace used to come and listen. He would sit there quietly and respectfully while people were saying prayers'. His presence was welcomed as a sign of religious tolerance and concern to improve Christian-Muslim relations, strained in many parts of the world.[5] Paddy Meskin, the national president of the World Conference of Religions for Peace (WCRP), recalls Hurley's presence at inter-faith services at this time: 'He didn't just come and sit at the table and wait to give his prayer and then disappear. He made a point of going to talk to all the different groups. He would go and shake hands with the *imam* or the *moulana*; he would go and talk to the rabbi'.[6]

In his dealings with the poor who came to the presbytery door, Hurley continued his practice as archbishop: giving assistance from his own pocket. His instinct was to trust people, but not all those seeking assistance were trustworthy, as Bechet noted: 'He's a high intellectual: everything comes from his head; but when it comes to the poor, everything comes from his heart . . . He never turned down people, he never rejected [them]'. Among these were the local informal traders, who asked whether they could set up their stalls and sell fruit in Cathedral Mall between the cathedral and what is now the Denis Hurley Centre. Hurley agreed because he saw this as a practical way of helping to create jobs.

A frequent caller at the Cathedral was Denis Strydom, a former trade unionist who was helping workers injured on duty.[7] With Hurley's advice and support, he was able to start a small organization called 'The Association for the Disabled'. If money was needed for transporting disabled people, for repairing their homes or making toilets accessible, or for purchasing wheelchairs, Strydom knew he could obtain support from Hurley, who would always make time to see him. Help was given without fuss or delay.

Not long after Hurley became acting parish priest, the chaplain to people with impaired hearing asked whether it would be possible for them to have a regular Mass at the cathedral. This request had been turned down by the previous parish priest for unknown reasons, but now permission was readily given. Arrangements were also made for a Mass in French for the growing number of refugees from Central Africa. The Missionaries of Charity (Mother Teresa's congregation) initially had nowhere to go when they arrived in Durban while waiting for funding to come through for their work. Hurley made space for the three nuns in the presbytery. Likewise, he provided accommodation for the cathedral housekeeper and the gardener, who had not previously been allowed to live there. Trycinski was struck by how he treated everyone equally, whether it was ambassadors who came to see him or the ordinary workers at the cathedral or homeless beggars. Barry Wood OMI, now Auxiliary Bishop of Durban, notes that in those retirement years at the cathedral, 'he really came off the pedestal and came among the people, and you could relate to him like a brother'.

His compassion, said Bechet, extended not only to the poor but also to the sick, whom he would visit even under difficult circumstances, including a bedridden man who lived on the sixth floor of a block of flats. Because the lift was frequently out of order, Hurley would have to climb the stairs. Sometimes those who took Communion to the sick would return with requests for a visit by Hurley. One of these was from a woman with a lapsed Catholic neighbour who did not want to hear any-thing about God or church. She thought a visit from Hurley might help. Within a few days, Hurley went to see this man and came back with a request that he be taken Communion. The woman who had requested the visit was amazed: 'He went to visit that man, and all the conversation he had with him was about soccer; that's all; he didn't say a word about God to that man, and the next thing that man came and asked me for a Bible, for a rosary, and . . . to go to confession'. This was just one example, Bechet said, of how Hurley converted people not so much by preaching as by the way he related to them.

Among the many visitors Hurley had while at the cathedral was the Oblate Superior General, Father Wilhelm Steckling OMI, who called at the cathedral unannounced to greet Hurley.[8] He found a Mass taking place in a full cathedral, with Hurley preaching in Zulu: 'We couldn't wait until we could say hello to him, but this is the strong impression that remains with me, . . . that even at the age of 80 he was still . . . accepting to be a humble pastor under his successor and really being close to the people, serving the people'.

Hurley chaired the national Justice and Peace Commission of the SACBC, the largest and most active of the commissions, for a number of years after 1987, when he ceased to be president of the Conference, and even after stepping down as Archbishop of Durban in 1992. As chairperson he assisted the commission in pre-senting its reports and proposals to the bishops. He kept up to date with commission activities by attending their meetings, some of which took place over weekends and therefore conflicted with parish duties. Though from 1992 he should no longer have been a member of the Bishops' Conference, his role as chair of the Justice and Peace Commission meant that he attended both plenary sessions and administrative board meetings, of which he had been part since their inception in 1947. Archbishop Buti Tlhagale said that some of the younger members of the conference felt that he stayed on too long and should have made way for others long before he finally did in 2001.

Hurley's attendance at weekend meetings of the Justice and Peace Commission on one occasion led to a confrontation with Bechet, who was in charge of the cathedral's confirmation class. When Hurley announced that he would be late for the confirmation Mass because he had to attend a Justice and Peace meeting, she was angry: what sort of example would the parish priest be giving if he arrived late? Hurley changed his plans and caught an earlier flight so that he was in good time for the Mass.

Undoubtedly the work of the Justice and Peace Commission was a priority for him, along with his parish commitment at Emmanuel Cathedral. The commission was helping the Catholic Church with crucial social issues at a time of transition in South Africa—in the period before 1994, helping to promote the negotiations process, the drafting of the new constitution, and ensuring that the 1994 elections would be free and fair. In the period after 1994, the focus shifted to working for a just economy.

Bishop Kevin Dowling, Hurley's second cousin, who in 2000 succeeded Hurley as chair of the commission, said that he had learnt much from his leadership.[9]

Hurley, he said, insisted that if you were engaging with important social issues that had an international dimension, you needed 'analysis and research of the highest quality'. According to Ashley Green-Thompson, a lay staff member of the commission, 'He set standards that you had to match; . . . he could be quite irritated with shoddy work.'[10]

Dowling was impressed that Hurley could move easily from dialogue with academics invited to advise the commission, to discussions with 'ordinary people from the townships, from squatter settlements, from African villages, and [could] engage in such a human way with them. This showed his ability to link the reality on the ground with the highest ideals of the Church's social teaching'.

Sister Margaret Kelly OP, who led the Justice and Peace staff team for several years, observed that in order to convince Hurley about a particular course of action, you had to be sure that he was thoroughly convinced intellectually.[11] 'This would require that you presented him with the facts, the arguments and the logic. . . . Once that happened, he was more than happy to champion any just cause . . . and defend it to the end, and would never back down because it was an unpopular decision'—except on one occasion. At the request of the Justice and Peace Commission, Hurley, Dowling and Kelly had proposed to the bishops that they should at least discuss the issue of women's ordination, because they had never before refused to discuss a topic. Try as these three might, the bishops were resolute in their refusal to flout the Vatican ban on such discussion. Eventually Hurley turned to Dowling and Kelly and said: "We've won many a battle here. I think this calls for a strategic retreat'.

The highlight of 1994 was the inauguration of Nelson Mandela as South Africa's first democratically elected president. On this occasion Hurley was a special guest: he had been asked by the SACBC to be its representative because of his stand against apartheid since the early 1950s. He regarded it as the second great highlight of his life, after Vatican II. In a letter to his friend Petal O'Hea, he described the occasion:

> The function of the Inauguration was magnificently performed, every person doing his or her part perfectly . . . The mood of the crowd rose to a joyous fever pitch. The final act was the firing of a twenty-one-gun salute and a flyover in tight formation of several SAAF squadrons, the last one consisting of six planes that left trails in the many colours of the South African flag. The crowd was ecstatic. '*Our* air force', shouted the African citizens . . . Lunch followed, very well organized—plenty of food and drink, easy access to supplies and to tables. And by 3:00 p.m. we were climbing onto buses and heading for the airport full of the joy of having participated in perhaps the greatest day in the history of South Africa.[12]

When Brother Jude Pieterse saw Hurley after the inauguration, he noticed 'an excitement I had never really associated with him before . . . He was almost . . . bubbling over, you know. Normally he kept his emotions pretty well under control, but [that day] there was a real joy in his whole approach'.[13]

One of the first policies the ANC put in place was the RDP (Reconstruction and Development Programme).[14] Its aim was to address the immense socio-economic problems brought about by apartheid: violence, lack of housing, unemployment, inadequate education and health care, a lack of democracy and a failing economy. The RDP was to be people-driven, as the policy document stated: 'Development is not about the delivery of goods to a passive citizenry. It is about active involvement and growing empowerment'. Although the RDP had both socialist and neo-liberal elements, it could not be easily categorized as wholly in either camp.

Hurley studied this new policy closely and became increasingly excited about it. It seemed to represent gospel values and to be in keeping with the Church's social teaching. The more he examined the RDP policy document, the more convinced he was that the bishops should put their weight behind it. However, when the document came up for plenary discussion and Hurley was passionately urging its endorsement, one of his colleagues took the wind out of his sails by drawing the conference's attention to a reference that seemed to indicate support for abortion. Somehow this had escaped Hurley's eagle eye, despite the fact that he had read the document five times. He did not, however, feel that the whole policy should be rejected on the basis of this one reference. Hurley rose to his feet and, according to Father Sean O'Leary SMA, a former head of the Justice and Peace Commission, 'in a fiery, angry but very controlled voice' said, 'If you do not accept the RDP, I will resign as the chairperson of the [Justice and Peace] Commission'. Fortunately, a way was found for the bishops to say that, while they had some concerns about the policy document, in general they supported the RDP.[15]

Within eighteen months, however, the government had replaced the RDP with a new policy known as GEAR (Growth, Employment and Redistribution),[16] which Hurley openly criticized:

> It appears that rampant capitalism has been unleashed on an unsuspecting populace ... Along with the dedication to capitalism comes the dedication to high salaries for the top executives. There is no shame about this in South Africa. Liberation campaigners who a few short years ago were keen socialists are now dedicated capitalists pushing for the best salaries they can find. It is sad for South Africa and means that there will be very troubled times ahead as the poor get more and more resentful at not being allowed to share in the prosperity of the country.[17]

Hurley told the Justice and Peace Commission that GEAR was anathema to him: 'We can't allow this to go unchallenged; we've got to talk about it'. He persuaded the commission to call a consultation where it could engage with representatives of government and express the Church's opposition to GEAR. In the consultation Hurley explained to the government representatives how much effort had been invested in getting the bishops to endorse the RDP. 'GEAR is not what we wanted. GEAR is something that seems to favour private-sector-led growth at the expense of human engagement and ownership'. To the commission he said, 'We've got to put our might behind rejecting this'.

Theo Kneifel commented that 'it was fascinating to see how at the very end of his life he became much more insightful into the structures of the economy, of globalization, and I would feel he was at his best in his latest years, [as] good wine ripens with old age. I would say politically, socially, theologically I felt most close to him in [those] very last years.'[18]

Neville Gabriel, a layman who headed the Justice and Peace Commission for several years, worked closely with Hurley on the Jubilee 2000 SA Campaign, the South African expression of a worldwide movement to ensure that poor countries would have their debt to first-world countries cancelled.[19] It was launched in Cape Town on 5 November 1998, with Hurley as one of the main speakers. Gabriel observed that most of the participants were from trade unions and non-governmental organizations (NGOs). Yet what Hurley said seemed to resonate with them, despite the fact that he spoke from a strong faith perspective. Because of his keynote address, many activists in the Jubilee network throughout the country looked to him for leadership. He was elected a patron, along with Anglican Archbishop Njongonkulu Ndungane, Fatima Meer and Dennis Brutus. Gabriel was impressed by how Hurley had applied his theological training and reflection to the structural aspects of the debt issue.

Jubilee 2000 SA was concerned not only with the debts of poor countries but also the so-called 'apartheid debt' accumulated by the previous government in the last few years of its struggle to maintain apartheid. Speaking on the occasion of the Commonwealth Conference in Durban in 1999, Hurley said:

The apartheid debt is quite a sizeable proportion of the total debt that the government is servicing. The most recent annual payment on this debt was R48.2 billion. When we compare this with what was spent on certain social services, we realize how much these social services suffer because of the apartheid debt. The amount spent on health care was R24 billion, on social welfare R18.6 billion and on housing R3.5 billion.[20]

Hurley earnestly requested the government to respond to Jubilee 2000's call for dialogue on the issue.

Another of Hurley's activities while at the cathedral was as a member of the bishops' Church and Work Commission.[21] This was a much smaller body than the Justice and Peace Commission, and there was a feeling among some bishops that it should be phased out and its work merged with Justice and Peace. Its focus on workers and unions was no longer necessary or appropriate: workers were organised, trade unions strong. The staff members of Church and Work, however, pointed out that workers faced new problems because of globalisation, such as mass retrenchments resulting from using casual workers in place of regular employees.

Hurley was asked to join the board of Church and Work to give it more status in the Bishops' Conference. He readily accepted because he agreed that the commission could lose its focus if it merged with Justice and Peace. Hurley strongly supported its opposition to new labour legislation and accompanied a staff member, John Capel, to a meeting with the Minister of Labour, Tito Mboweni (Governor of the Reserve Bank from 1999). The delegation detailed aspects of labour legislation about which the Church was unhappy. One of these was Sunday work, and its representations may have helped prevent Sunday being declared an ordinary day of work. After three years, Hurley reluctantly withdrew from the board because of other commitments. Not long after that, Church and Work lost its independent status.

Hurley's time at the cathedral was busy, with parish duties, university functions, involvement with the national Justice and Peace and Church and Work Commissions and the Jubilee 2000 SA Campaign, and a fair amount of travel as well as frequent invitations to speak on a variety of topics. Whenever he could, he spent his 'day off' working on his memoirs, with the assistance of Professor Joy Brain, the diocesan archivist. To keep himself fit, he continued to use a stationary cycle bought for him in 1980 by Wolfgang and Daisy Losken. He proudly informed them on 7 September 1994 that he had completed his first 10,000 kilometres and asked them to wish him well as he embarked on the second such stretch.[22]

Many awards and honours were given to him during these retirement years. In addition to being appointed Chancellor of the University of Natal (1992), he received the Freedom of the City of Durban (1992) and of Pietermaritzburg (1993). His ninth and tenth honorary doctorates were awarded by the Catholic Theological Union of Chicago (1993) and St Paul's University, Ottawa (1996). He was given the Order of Merit of the Italian Republic (Onorificenza di Grande Ufficiale; 1997) and South Africa's Order of Meritorious Service (Class 1) by President Nelson Mandela (1999); enrolled as a Chaplain in the Order of St John (1997) and named a Paul Harris Fellow of the Rotary Foundation (1998). His golden jubilee of episcopal ordination was celebrated in 1997; the diamond jubilee of his priestly ordination in 1999, and the golden jubilee of his appointment as archbishop in 2001. That year he was one of the community leaders invited to leave their hand prints in special paving in front of the Durban city hall.

The year 2001 also saw Hurley receive an unusual mark of ecumenical respect—a book of tributes compiled by a Presbyterian minister, Rev. Tony Gamley. Entitled *Denis Hurley: A Portrait by Friends*, this included memories by such well-known figures as Desmond Tutu, Wilfrid Napier, Ela Gandhi, Beyers Naudé, Smangaliso Mkhatshwa, Brenda Gourley, Philip Tobias, Fatima Meer and Robert Drinan. Hurley greatly appreciated the gesture and enjoyed travelling with Gamley to launch the book in London, Dublin and Rome.

One honour eluded him: being made a cardinal. He had already been passed over in 1965 when Archbishop Owen McCann of Cape Town was made South Africa's first cardinal. At this time Hans Küng thought that Hurley would have made an excellent member of a 'dream team' to help Paul VI implement the Second Vatican Council, with the portfolio of the pontifical Justice and Peace Commission which would most probably have meant a red hat. 'What a grand, loyal "cabinet"', Küng writes, 'with which the pope could collaborate in an admirable way and efficiently guide the renewal of the church!'[25] It is interesting to speculate what an impact Hurley might have made on the Church's global involvement in justice and peace issues, though Durban and South Africa's loss would have been great.

Hurley was passed over again in 2001, when his successor as Archbishop of Durban, Wilfrid Napier, became the country's second cardinal. Many felt that Hurley was eminently qualified for such an honour, though by this time he had passed the age limit (80) for cardinals to participate in papal elections. Julian

Filochowski, former director of CAFOD in the UK, described him ruefully as 'the best cardinal Africa never had'.[24]

In an effort to understand why Hurley was not made a cardinal, observers mention his public criticism of Paul VI's encyclical on birth control, *Humanae Vitae*, his support for making celibacy voluntary for priests and for the ordination of women. They conclude that Hurley would not have allowed himself to be silenced by being made a cardinal and might have spoken out even more strongly on these and other issues. As a cardinal, his words would have been more in the limelight—so the Pope would have been hesitant about giving him greater prominence. Hurley himself had no doubts about why he would not be made a cardinal. Writing to John Allen, Hebblethwaite's successor as leading English-speaking Vaticanologist, he said, 'You speculate about the possibility of my being named a cardinal. There is no possibility. My comments at the time of *Humanae Vitae* and a short article I wrote for *Theological Studies* have ruled me out permanently'.[25]

Yet Pope John Paul II clearly had a high regard for Hurley. When the Oblate General Chapter of 1986 had an audience with the Pope, out of thousands of present and past members of the Oblate congregation, he put before them the lives of two Oblates whom he said were examples to the whole congregation. The one, an example 'from the past', was Bishop Vital Grandin, an early Oblate missionary bishop among the Inuits in the far north of Canada. The other, an example 'from the present', was Hurley, whom the Pope described as 'the courageous president of South Africa's episcopal conference'.

Sister Margaret Kelly OP said that whenever the bishops went to Rome on their *ad limina* visits, and when Pope John Paul came to South Africa, 'he sang Archbishop Hurley's praises'. 'I suppose the Pope saw [his visit] as an occasion on which to thank Archbishop Hurley because of the way things had worked out in South Africa'.

Dowling gives an interesting account of the bishops' plenary session in January 2001, when Napier's appointment as cardinal was officially announced. An impromptu celebratory dinner had been organized; Hurley, attending his last plenary session, was spontaneously asked to be the main speaker. In a speech that Dowling described as 'vintage Hurley', he began by recalling his presence as a young scholastic in St Peter's Square in 1939, when the election of Pius XII was announced and the new Pope gave his first blessing. Hurley said he had known then that this was 'the closest I would ever get to a papal conclave'—a remark that caused much amusement. He gave no other inkling about how Napier's appointment might have affected him personally but graciously congratulated the new cardinal. 'He was so supportive and welcoming of this [appointment]', said Dowling. 'He was able to let go . . . of his personal feelings and make the person who was the centre of attention feel absolutely affirmed and supported in the way he congratulated him. At the same time [he led] us to see how good this was for the whole Church, that we had a cardinal'.

When Napier arrived back in Durban by air after the announcement, Hurley was at the airport to greet him as he stepped off the plane, to congratulate him once again and loyally to celebrate his appointment as the first cardinal archbishop of Durban.

32

Family

Hurley's immediate family—father and mother, older sister, Eileen, and two younger brothers, Jerry and Chris—was very close, and he had a great loyalty to them. His brothers had large families, fourteen nephews and nieces in all, who with their own children became important to 'Uncle Denis' as his extended family. They had wonderful memories of visits he paid to their homes when they were children:

> After we had rushed to tidy the house when we spotted him walking down the drive-way, Uncle Denis was playful and wonderful. Like a magician he could make his nose crack, break his thumb into two parts and then force it back together. We would bend down and beg him to grab hold of our hands and 'turn us inside out'. He even pretended that having his shoes tied together under the dining room table was a wonderful joke that always took him by surprise.
>
> We teased him when he arrived at our house still wearing his ceremonial purple socks. He always had a great sense of style that possibly started as young as three. His mother told us how he would walk around the house with a tea cosy on his head, practising to be a bishop. And he knew how to enjoy himself with his family. One memorable night, my two elder sisters taught him to jive to a Beatles' record.[1]

Christmases that included Uncle Denis were special:

> We knew that he would bring wonderful presents, beautifully wrapped—both brown and cellophane paper. We did suspect, though, that his secretary took care of the wrapping. One year, the brandy that had been sprinkled on the Christmas pudding wouldn't catch alight. Our parents vividly remember the looks of horror on people's faces as he poured an expensive cognac (which was someone else's precious Christmas present); he spread it over the pudding and set it alight with a great whoosh. Denis always had a great feeling for the ceremonial and the liturgical.[2]

After Christmas dinner there was a traditional backyard cricket match. The family has a photograph from Christmas 1953 showing Denis wearing a large straw hat, flourishing a Don Bradman cricket bat he had won as a schoolboy, while his two brothers sprawled out on the lawn in 'poses of mock desperation'.

> He loved us; of that we were never in doubt. He was interested in everyone and everything we were doing. He always made us feel important, and he kept up to date as all his many great-nephews and nieces were born and grew up . . . They knew him first and foremost not as the archbishop but as Uncle Denis, or just Denis. A few evenings ago we went into his room at Sabon House [the retirement home for priests where Hurley lived at the time of his death]. I think he has kept every photograph of all the kids that we sent across over the years.[3]

When they were still living in South Africa, Chris and Ursula Hurley were part of parish discussion groups and of the Kolbe Association. These involvements gave rise to dinner parties to which they would invite Denis, because he thoroughly enjoyed the lively conversation. Later, when Chris became headmaster of the lay-run independent Thomas More College, there were dinners for guest speakers at the school prizegivings. Denis also enjoyed the stimulating discussions with these speakers. The children, said Ursula, 'used to sit at the table and listen to all the conversation and now and then perk up with what they wanted to say, . . . and he was always very warm'. Ursula felt that these occasions kept him in touch with the realities and intimacies of family life.

It must have been hard for Eileen and Denis when these two large and lively families decided to emigrate to Australia: Jerry, Bobbie and family to Adelaide in 1972; Chris, Ursula and family to Canberra in 1978. One of the main motives was to ensure that their boys would not have to face the dilemma of military service in defence of apartheid. Jerry had been headmaster of Mansfield High School in Durban; in Australia he taught English, history and religious education at Mary McKillop College in Adelaide before he retired. Chris, who had been headmaster of Thomas More College, taught at Marist College in Canberra until his retirement. Denis made several visits to the two families in Australia—opportunities that he and they relished.

Eileen had taught at Port Shepstone and in Pietermaritzburg; at the time she contracted meningitis in 1967, when both Hurley parents died within weeks of each other, she was chief librarian of the Natal Education Department, with an MA degree from Natal University. An active and intelligent woman, who had written several children's books in Afrikaans, she must have found it extremely difficult to be confined to a wheelchair for more than 30 years. Nevertheless, she remained cheerful and kept up correspondence with her whole family. As a result, she probably had the most comprehensive picture of what they were all doing.

In a 1980 letter, Bobbie informed Eileen about a visit Denis had just paid to Adelaide. They tried to get him to rest as much as possible, she said, but the only concession they could manage is that daily Mass would be at 8:00 a.m. rather than the 7:30 a.m. he had suggested.[4] As for the holiday programme over the two weeks, 'he set the pace and had us panting to keep up. We have never looked up so many historical facts, inspected so many monuments, or learnt so much about South Australian beginnings since we arrived'. During a visit in 1985, Denis confessed to Eileen that he had fallen in love with Adelaide because the city was so well planned and has 'an abundance of parks and gardens'.[5]

In the midst of these busy holiday visits, Bobbie found time for some earnest conversations with her brother-in-law.[6] Although Bobbie said with some irony that the Hurley brothers always seemed only to speak to each other about 'nice safe subjects like sport', she was not afraid to raise some real dilemmas about family life. For example, when she had reached the age of 42 and had her eighth child, her blood pressure was 'through the ceiling'. Her Catholic doctor told her that if she had another pregnancy, other doctors would advise her to have an abortion. The only alternative was to go on the pill. So she wrote to Denis and said that over the years she had had seven thermometers, every one of which had been faulty. These were needed for the so-called rhythm method of birth control, the only one officially approved by the Catholic Church because it was not regarded as artificial. She asked whether she should buy another [thermometer]. Denis phoned to thank her for the letter and said: 'What do you think about it?' and she said, 'Oh, I know what I think', and he said: 'Go ahead and do it'.

Ursula Hurley, Chris's wife, also raised challenging issues with Denis, including the case for contraception.[7] These helped him to see, she said, 'what was involved in the intimacies of a marriage relationship', as well as the impact on children and the economic difficulties of families struggling to provide for themselves. Through these debates with Ursula and Bobbie, Denis had his eyes opened.

As the nephews and nieces grew up and became adolescents and young adults, they too began to know and speak their own minds and to make their own way in life. Some of their choices and decisions were difficult for their parents and for their Uncle Denis, as his nephew Jeremy explained:

> But they never judged, not for one moment, and it was a great gift [that] he and they gave us: the gift of unconditional love. It was as though he was a tightrope walker on a rope that was stretched between his fierce loyalty and love for the Church and his fierce loyalty and love for his family. Most of us made the tightrope walk that Denis did very difficult for him at times. I will be ever grateful to him for celebrating our marriage, with our two sons as the ring-bearers, only 13 years ago, and not only doing it in our Australian home in the garden but [also] doing it so beautifully as he welcomed family and friends 'to this wonderful cathedral with its celestial dome and its arboreal columns'.

There were, of course, times of conflict when the young people became 'emancipated from a lot of . . . conservative Catholicism'. On these occasions, said Ursula, Uncle Denis 'always took up an argument, stated the case and was very sensitive to the issues which affect young people . . . So there were a lot of discussions'.

Rarely did Uncle Denis's formal role as archbishop conflict with his role as a member of the family. In Chapter 14 we have seen the difficulties that arose when Jeremy chained himself to a communion rail as a protest. On another occasion, while still at University, Jeremy wrote an article about the Catholic Church's wealth, for a student newspaper.[8] It mentioned how bishops lived in 'palatial mansions' particularly inappropriate in a country with as much poverty as South Africa. This was picked up by a Sunday newspaper that ran a story entitled 'Hurley's Nephew Attacks Church Wealth', featuring a picture of Archbishop's House in Durban.

Jeremy was mortified; 'I was devastated . . . by that incident'. He immediately phoned his uncle and explained that he had not wanted to focus on him as a target; the article had in any case been intended only for a publication with a small student readership. Jeremy remembered Uncle Denis saying: 'Oh, that's OK, it's OK . . . Don't worry'. But Jeremy admitted to me in an interview years later: 'What I was saying was really valid. I knew that as well, so I didn't wish I hadn't done it, because it was true: he lived in a palatial place in Innes Road. It was a lovely old, a beautiful old house—fabulous parlours and chandeliers and stunning gardens, and he shouldn't have been living there, so maybe it *was* aimed at him'. What Jeremy did not say is that most of the house was used for diocesan offices and meetings and soon became too small to accommodate these.

The article caused some tension between Jeremy and his parents. 'It was like attacking the family personally, and you don't do that. You do not do that in the Hurleys. The family loyalty is huge'.

More serious was the conflict that arose in 1978, when Chris lost the position of headmaster of Thomas More College.[9] As Archbishop of Durban, Hurley was patron of the school and also served as a trustee. There were financial problems, and enrolments seemed to be dropping. Some parents, pupils and staff were unhappy about the way Chris ran the school, but there was no allegation of misconduct or neglect. When the trustees proposed that Chris be asked to resign, Denis questioned whether there was sufficient evidence to back the claim that Chris had 'lost the confidence of parents, staff and pupils'. If there was such evidence, this should be put to Chris, and he should be given time to rectify matters. Because it was his brother whose competence was in question, Denis then recused himself from the meeting and abstained from voting. When he heard that the rest of the trustees had voted unanimously to ask Chris to resign, Denis felt there was nothing more he could do.

Chris's family believed that a grave injustice had been done to their husband and father and that the board's decision was unjust. A confidential assessment had been made of Chris's performance, and he had not been told who had said what nor given an opportunity to respond to the criticisms which should have been done according to standard practice in such situations. The family was disappointed that Denis had not come to his brother's defence. At a family meeting, they put the issues to him and showed him certain documents, which they felt proved that Chris had been wrongfully dismissed. Even after this, Denis did not change his stance. The family's hope had been that he would resign from the board as a form of protest while continuing to be patron of the school. He did not, but explained his position at length in a letter to Ursula and Chris, in which he made clear how painful he found the situation and fully understood how much more painful it must have been for them.

One of Chris's sons, also named Denis, was angry about what had happened to his father and years later still felt strongly about it. At the time of his father's dismissal, he was young and impressionable, in the last years of his schooling. As Ursula put it, he was most upset to discover that this 'wonderful and loving uncle could not find it in his heart to say publicly how unjust and incorrect the decision was with regard to his father . . . and there's always been that issue with Uncle Denis'.

After Chris lost his job at Thomas More, he and his family emigrated to Australia, where he was offered a post at Marist College in Canberra. Only Denis and Eileen were left in South Africa, and Chris's daughter Mikaela and her family. Eileen had initially stayed in the Cheshire Home in Queensburgh and later was looked after by the Dominican sisters at Oakford Priory for more than 20 years, by Sisters Dominic Mary and Mary Mannes, fondly referred to by Hurley as 'the heavenly twins'. He made a point of visiting Eileen once a week whenever possible. When travelling, he would try to write to her every week, as did the family in Australia.

A sad family event occurred on 6 January 1996, when Denis's brother Jerry died in Adelaide. Hearing about his brother's serious illness, Denis decided to fly to Australia to be with him but did not get there in time. He arrived on Monday, 8 June, after a lengthy stopover in Singapore for a change of planes, only to hear that Jerry had died on the evening of Saturday, 6 June. Denis officiated at the requiem and the burial.[10]

A few years later, Eileen was moved to Pietermaritzburg, where the Oakford Dominican Sisters had opened the Villa Siena Retirement Centre, with frail care facilities. There she continued to be cared for by 'the heavenly twins'. One of Hurley's regular visits to Eileen had been arranged for 30 May 2003, but at 8:00 a.m. on that day, a telephone message from Villa Siena indicated that Eileen had had a sudden drop in vitality and seemed to be on the point of dying. Denis left immediately for Pietermaritzburg but learned that she had died ten minutes after the phone call. Father George Purves OMI told how Hurley broke down and cried on his shoulder.[11]

Mike Madden, the son of a cousin, who lived near Washington, DC, was struck by the way Denis always tried to make his relatives feel important and to include them in whatever he was doing.[12] He would make sure they were introduced and made to feel welcome. Mike was asked to drive the archbishop when he came to Washington to attend ICEL meetings, to visit his brother Oblates or to receive an honorary doctorate from Georgetown University. 'I was a seventeen-year-old kid . . . and I was treated like royalty, because he was treated like royalty . . . Wherever he went, I had to be part of the occasion'. Denis could have been accommodated in a hotel or with the Oblates, but he made a point of staying with his family, even if he had lots of invitations and 'our dinner was not the nicest he had'.

Like many others, Denis's family noticed that as he grew older, and especially after he was no longer Archbishop of Durban, a warmer and gentler side of his personality became evident.[13] He was more relaxed and approachable and found it easier to show emotion. His niece Mikaela said that he was more able to demonstrate his concern and love for family members. He could speak about how his extended family was important to him and explain that he needed 'the reassurance . . . of human love and contact' that they offered.

Jeremy noticed that Denis was also more outspoken and critical of the Church. In those later years, he had much to say about how love was more important than faith and compliance with laws, to which he thought the Church attaches so much value today. Love made sense of all that he had done in his life, all his emphasis on ecumenism and social justice, his great compassion for people in any difficulty or suffering, his loving relationship with his family. In old age, it became clearer to him than ever that love was the unifying principle. For Jeremy, this was his uncle's great legacy.[14]

33

'The Departure Lounge'

During 2001, Hurley became increasingly aware that it was time to retire as parish priest of Emmanuel Cathedral. His hearing had deteriorated, and he found it difficult to follow meetings; his eyesight was also weakening, and reading liturgical prayers was a problem.[1] He would have liked to continue working at the cathedral but had to be realistic about his ability to provide the ministry needed by a large and demanding parish.[2] Moreover, the writing of his memoirs was moving too slowly, and he needed to devote more time to that task.

Father Alan Moss, the Oblate Provincial, said that Hurley had for some time been speaking about moving to Sabon House, a retirement centre for Oblate priests, commonly referred to by its elderly residents as 'The Departure Lounge'. Long before Hurley moved there in January 2002, Father George Purves, superior of the house, had shown him where he would be accommodated. Some of the priests living at Sabon House were, however, not keen that the archbishop should join their community. They feared that, with an archbishop in residence, they would no longer be free to enjoy the same relaxed community life.

All their worries disappeared in Hurley's first week with them. They were surprised how well he fitted in: according to Father Isidor Freoux OMI, 'He became one of us, . . . like a simple Oblate, . . . like a little novice again'.[3] Freoux was struck that Hurley never complained about anything and always said he enjoyed the food, which Freoux described as 'sometimes very poor'. He did not want to have anything beyond what was provided for other retired Oblate priests. His colleagues noticed that he was usually first in the chapel in the morning and joined in all the times of prayer. They also saw that he was the last to serve himself at table.

At meals he was a good communicator, 'sharing freely with anybody and everybody', according to Moss. He was happy to discuss philosophy, theology, science (including quantum physics), history and some of his personal experiences, not to mention cricket and rugby. Of course, the Second Vatican Council was his favourite topic. Though he was knowledgeable on many subjects, he did not force his knowledge on people. In some ways a private person, he always 'had a friendly

318 GUARDIAN OF THE LIGHT

and reassuring smile for those around him' and got on well with every member of the community. 'When others were tiresome and cantankerous, he had a joke or chatted in a most friendly manner'. When Moss was feeling depressed on one occasion, Hurley came to affirm him and shared stories about himself, going back to being lost in a cave and later years when he had sometimes felt 'let down in higher places'.

He lived a humble life and worked from his simple bedroom, with help from the provincial's secretary, Pat Maycock. The volume of his incoming and outgoing mail showed that he was keeping up an extensive international correspondence. He received many phone calls and visits from people of high and low positions, including beggars. Purves said, 'He was no different from anyone else in his own mind. If there were duties to be done, he would do them. If there was a timetable to be followed, he did that. If the community were asked to participate in something, he would do his duty, . . . presiding at the Office and the Eucharist; . . . [he took] his turn at giving the homily. In fact, he was the most obedient member of the community'.

Much of Hurley's time at Sabon House was taken up with his memoirs, 'a joyful occupation'[4] though frequently interrupted by preparations for the many talks he was asked to give, and by keeping up with his correspondence and meeting those who came to see him. Moss felt that Hurley was ambivalent about the memoirs for two reasons: he was embarrassed to devote so much time to writing about himself, and the task was lonely. It was made more difficult by the paralysis of his right hand, caused by the shingles mentioned in Chapter 30, and also by a burglary in which his dictaphone and five cassettes were stolen.[5] This meant that two chapters had to be redrafted. He had been apprehensive about the 'much more difficult haul of covering the years from 1965 to 1992, . . . a tangled time in South Africa'. Sadly, he died before even starting on that period.

One of his relatives criticized the Church for not making better provision for him in his retirement yet recognized that he would never have asked for that; his personal needs were simple. Charles Yeats, the conscientious objector who is now an Anglican priest, visited Hurley at Sabon House together with his father and was impressed by the simplicity of the retirement centre. 'To think of such a great man accepting in his retirement the very humble community and house in Durban . . . almost brought tears to our eyes, and I remember it being profoundly moving to my father'.[6]

Hurley did have a criticism of life at Sabon House, but it had nothing to do with the accommodation or the food. As an archbishop, he had interacted continually with a great variety of priests, nuns, brothers and laypeople; as indicated in earlier chapters, he had been deeply involved in international events such as the Second Vatican Council, Synod of Bishops and IMBISA, as well as Vatican committees and ICEL; for more than half a century he served on the SACBC and its commissions. These experiences meant that he was used to engaging with the Church in all its diversity. By comparison, Sabon House seemed to be a restrictive environment, with its concerns confined mostly to those of the Oblate congregation.[7]

ORDINATION OF WOMEN

As stated in Chapter 30, Hurley was in favour of women's ordination and believed that the Catholic Church would one day ordain women. At a workshop, he had lunch with Jackie Reeve, the South Africa desk officer from the UK funding agency CAFOD, and Huguette Bechet, from the cathedral. In a light-hearted and joking way, Reeve and Bechet mentioned an ex-nun from South Africa who, with several other women in Germany, had recently been ordained without authorization from Rome.

Hurley told Reeve and Bechet that this was no joking matter and that he felt the women had made 'a mockery of two sacraments—the Eucharist and ordination'.[8] Dina Cormick of Women's Ordination South Africa (WOSA) received a similar response when she mentioned these ordinations to him.[9] 'That's the wrong way to do it, it's absolutely not right. They shouldn't have done that,' he said. Though in favour of women's ordination, he wanted it to be officially approved by the Church. He thought this should and would happen in the future. 'I became so involved in struggles for human rights. I think women have the human right to enter the Catholic priesthood, and I believe one day they will'.[10]

When the Durban branch of WOSA organized protests about the Vatican ban on the ordination of women, Cormick said that Hurley would come over to the protestors in a friendly way or call out from his place in the procession, 'Be patient, sisters. It will happen'.

Another indication of his positive attitude towards women's ordination was that he attended a service in which an Anglican woman friend was ordained a deacon, and another woman ordained a priest, at St Thomas's Anglican Church in Durban on 15 December 2002.[11] Hurley participated in the clergy procession and sat in the sanctuary for the service. At the end, he was invited to address the congregation. In a brief speech he said how much he had enjoyed being present and how at home he had felt, concluding with these words, 'Hasten the day when our two churches can be one,' greeted by loud and prolonged applause.

To one friend he wrote, 'An extraordinary feature of this ordination is that I kissed both the priest and the deacon in the sanctuary after the celebration. Both are women!' To another, 'I found the ceremony very pleasing and very impressive. Please don't tell the Pope'; and to a third, 'When will that [the ordination of women] happen in the Catholic Church? When I get to heaven I shall do my best to promote the idea'.

COMMUNITY OF SANT'EGIDIO

Hurley's relationship with the Rome-based Community of Sant'Egidio became especially important to him in the last few years of his life. Between 2000 and 2004 he attended eight of their conferences and assemblies in various parts of Europe.

The Community of Sant'Egidio derives its name from a church in the Trastevere area of Rome, which they made their headquarters.[12] Founded by a group of young lay people inspired by the Second Vatican Council, the Community believes that it is only possible to understand the gospel by serving the poor. This they do through their work with the homeless, the elderly, gypsies, refugees, AIDS sufferers and many others.

As members of a lay community, they work and lead normal family lives. Within these constraints, they give part of each day to serving and befriending the poor. Central to their community life is prayer, and each evening they gather for worship in the Basilica of Santa Maria in Trastevere, and because of the growth in their numbers, simultaneously in several other Roman churches, and indeed in the many other cities and countries where they are represented.

Over the years, they have come to realize that the poor are the first casualties of war: this has stimulated their interest in promoting peace. As a result, Pope John Paul II asked them to help in organizing the World Day of Prayer for Peace, held in Assisi in 1986. Since then they have organized a similar event each year in a different European city. The Community has also had a growing realization that many wars are based on religious conflict. This led to their commitment to ecumenical and interfaith dialogue. Their work has now spread to sixty countries, a number of which are in Africa, including South Africa, where they are represented in several cities. They are most famous for successfully promoting the Mozambican peace accord.

The Sant'Egidio community first heard of Hurley at the time of his Namibian trial. They were attracted by his friendliness: whenever they phoned his office in Durban, they were put through to him immediately and were warmly greeted by him. Whenever he was in Rome, he would attend their evening prayers, and they would include special intercessions for South Africa. They were struck by his 'evangelical passion and enthusiasm' and enjoyed his company at meals after their evening prayers. When he was charged for statements he had made about the *Koevoet* unit in Namibia, they decided to organize a campaign for the charges to be dropped, collecting signatures from Roman parishes at Sunday Masses and presenting these to the South African Embassy in Rome.

Their mutual friendliness was based on the Second Vatican Council: they felt that Hurley provided a living link with this source of their own inspiration. He was touched by the warmth of their friendship, their concern for marginalized groups and the connection they made between prayer and solidarity. 'Never had he experienced such love', said Father Purves. He was especially moved by the welcome they always gave him. Archbishop Jabulani Nxumalo said that Sant'Egidio made up for something in his own life![12a] Though Hurley was afraid that the Church might stray from its commitment to the council's decisions, he trusted that Sant'Egidio would keep those decisions alive.

Members of Sant'Egidio felt that they had learnt much from him. Leone Gianturco, responsible for the community's work in Africa, described Hurley as 'a constant witness to Vatican II'. He also informed them in a personal way about the suffering of people under apartheid. Through him they met many Catholic bishops from South Africa, as well as other Christian leaders from that country, like Desmond Tutu and Beyers Naudé. As Don Giorgio Ferretti, who was assigned to take care of Hurley on his visits, said, 'He was the first to introduce us to Africa, and today Sant'Egidio is a very African reality; . . . we have to thank him for a universal vision of the Church, but also a universal vision of Africa'.

Early in 2003 Hurley attended a Sant'Egidio event held in Genoa, from which the delegates travelled to Rome for a special audience with Pope John Paul II. After the Pope's address, the bishops present were introduced to him one by one. Hurley was the last in line. When his turn came to speak with the Pope, John Paul said, 'Ah Hurrrley (*sic*), welcome; and how are you?' They exchanged a few friendly words, which included the Pope asking, 'How old are you actually?' The other bishops, all of them younger than Hurley, remarked that he and the Pope seemed to be on very friendly terms. 'You can imagine how pleased I was', Hurley said.[13]

Towards the end of the same year, Hurley attended the Sant'Egidio assembly in Aachen, Germany. The bishop of that city, Heinrich Mussinghoff, wrote about what attracted Hurley to these gatherings. 'I think the Archbishop enjoyed the international community of bishops and priests, and even the ecumenical friendship between Catholic, Orthodox, Protestant and Oriental bishops . . . [Recently] the Community of Sant'Egidio is promoting African bishops so that we European people do not forget Africa and feel responsible for the dignity of black peoples. I think this was a source of . . . special joy to him'.[14]

At the end of the Aachen event, Hurley had arranged to be taken to see his friend, Marly Soltek, in Cologne. Giorgio Ferretti and Roberta di Bella were to drive him there. As it turned out, Giorgio was unable to go, but his place was taken by a young woman called Manuela who, like Roberta, came from Genoa. They were only able to leave Aachen at about 8:30 p.m., and it was late when they reached Cologne and found the Soltek home. Hurley joked that it was fortunate they were not at any point stopped by the Cologne police, who would have been intrigued to find an 87-year-old archbishop travelling the streets of Cologne late at night, accompanied by 'two dazzling Genoese beauties'.[15]

For some time the Sant'Egidio community had been encouraging Hurley to visit Mozambique to see their HIV/AIDS work, and he had promised to do so. Eventually, this became possible towards the end of 2003, when Denis York, the husband of his niece Mikaela, was visiting Maputo in the course of his work as a veterinary scientist. Hurley went along for the two-day trip. He met two young doctors from the community, Graziola and Paola, 'who are up to their ears in the care of the stricken', as well as other members supervising a medical laboratory. 'Thank God', Hurley wrote; 'the bad news we sometimes hear about the Church is amply compensated for by the good news we hear from other quarters'.[16]

Hurley's last trip to a Sant'Egidio event was to a gathering in Rome early in 2004. He told the community about a suggestion he had made during the Second Vatican Council. Noting that the Church has a Congregation for the Doctrine of the Faith, which keeps a watchful eye on the orthodoxy of theologians, he had said that it was more important to have a 'Congregation for Love'. Having seen the work that Sant'Egidio was doing, he no longer thought this was necessary: Sant'Egidio was the Church's 'Congregation for Love'.

Without knowing it, the Community of Sant'Egidio was accompanying him in the last days of his life. Ferretti said he had never seen Hurley so happy. He was deeply impressed and challenged by the addresses given by members of the community, especially on the theme that the basic starting point for the Christian is the gospel and love for the poor. Hurley told Giorgio that, if it were possible, he would like to start his life all over again, because he had understood things he had never before understood. 'In those [last] days in Rome, [as] a bishop of the Second Vatican Council, with great enthusiasm he showed his gratitude for having seen the council fulfilled in the charisma [sic] of the Community of Sant'Egidio. He was happy in those days, and we were [affirmed] by his words, by his friendship and by his joy'.

During this last visit, Hurley stayed at the Oblate General House in the Via Aurelia, as he often did when in Rome. On this occasion he met with the Justice and Peace group of the General House. At a reception afterwards, Father Wilhelm Steckling, the Superior General, sat next to Hurley. As they were having a drink, Hurley said quite casually, 'You know, more and more I realize that love is the only thing that matters. Love makes the difference. Paul said that out of faith, hope and love, love is the most important thing. Sometimes we want to turn it around, . . . saying that faith comes first. We should return to the original message: give love the place of honour. Love is the distinguishing mark of the Christian'.

Coming right at the end of Hurley's life, these words reminded Steckling of St John, who in his old age would be asked by people to tell them about the life of Jesus. John would say: 'Well, Jesus said, love each other as I have loved you', and they would say, 'But we know that already; tell us something more', and John would say, 'No, no, but this is the important thing'.

Steckling said that he was 'in profound wonder and surprise as to how such deep thoughts [could be triggered] in the course of an informal conversation at a social event'. But he realized that for Hurley 'the profane and the sacred . . . had been fused into a wonderful unity long ago, during the many years in which believing in God and listening to the cry of the poor had become for him one thing'.[17]

LAST DAYS IN DURBAN

Hurley arrived back from Rome at midday on Tuesday, 10 February. He was met at Durban airport and taken to Sabon House by Father George Purves, who said, 'From the moment he arrived, . . . he was full of joy and full of enthusiasm'.[18] That evening Hurley and Nadal had dinner with Sister Donna Ciangio OP, who had helped to bring the Renew process to South Africa and was keen to see him before she returned to the United States. He was full of stories about how Sant'Egidio was promoting peace negotiations in several trouble spots. It was also exciting for him to hear how the 'Follow Me' process, a successor to Renew, was progressing in the Durban Archdiocese. The serious part of the evening over, Nadal began to tell stories, imitating local accents: 'We were laughing so hard that we just couldn't . . . catch our breath. It was a very, very happy time'.[19]

The next day Hurley attended a clergy study day and on the Thursday afternoon had guests for tea: Sister Marie-Henry Keane OP, Prioress General of the Newcastle Dominicans, out from London on a visit, together with Sister Catherina OP, from Durban North.[20] Once again, Hurley's conversation was about Sant'Egidio, the

Second Vatican Council, and how priestly training could be brought more in line with the Council's vision.

After these joyful subjects, the conversation moved on to his sadness about what the Vatican had done to ICEL. During this discussion there was 'a kind of pessimism and defeatism' in him, which Keane had never seen before. She thought he might be tired from his journey, so she began to prepare to go. 'What's the hurry?' was his response; he wanted the sisters to stay, which they did for a while longer. In that remaining time, Keane cheered Hurley by telling him that the many people with whom he had shared the vision of Vatican II would not allow it to die.

That evening, Hurley was out again, this time for a social function with diocesan priests. One of the priests said to Nadal, 'Do you have any stories for us?' Nadal was well prepared for this moment, having brought a collection of schoolboy howlers. Hurley laughed so much at these that he said to Nadal, 'For God's sake, stop it, stop it, stop it'.[21]

Friday, 13 February, was the day of the golden jubilee of Our Lady of Fatima School, which had been started by the Newcastle Dominicans. That morning while waiting to be taken to Durban North for the celebration, Hurley was full of humour and interest in everything that was going on. Purves said to him, 'Gee, you're amazing. You're just back from Rome and you're here, there and everywhere.'

In Sister Marie-Henry Keane's introduction to the Jubilee Mass, which Hurley concelebrated with Cardinal Napier later that morning, she thanked him for his role in the establishment of the convent in 1954 and for his support over the years. After Mass, Hurley participated in the tea, meeting and chatting with old friends. Father Derrick Butt, whose church was close to Sabon House, was asked by one of the teachers to take the archbishop home.

During the drive from Durban North to Sabon House in south Durban, a journey of about 15 kilometres, Hurley talked almost constantly.[22] He and Butt spoke about many things, including Hurley's recent visit to Rome, the community of Sant'Egidio and their role in the Mozambican peace process, and his own trip to Mozambique a few weeks earlier. Once again he mentioned how sad he was because of what the Vatican had done to ICEL, but he did not at any stage say that he was feeling sick or in any pain.

As Butt drove along Nicolson Road, a broad double-carriageway with an island in the centre and lined with trees, Hurley asked the names of the trees. When they turned down Penzance Road, close to Sabon House, Hurley said, 'Isn't it wonderful that we have all these beautiful trees and flowers . . . ' Those were his last words, and then he fell silent. Butt said: 'I noticed his right hand move towards me, and when I looked at him, he seemed to be having some sort of attack. I held his hand and asked him if he was all right, but there was no response. I stopped at the side of the road, but he had a glazed, unfocused look. He was also taking short inward breaths every few seconds. I then decided to continue the journey to Sabon House, . . . which was only a few minutes away'.

After being driven into the grounds of Sabon House, the archbishop was still taking short inward breaths. Butt called for help, and a number of the resident clergy and staff gathered around the car. The doctor was called as well as emergency medical care. Father Duncan Mackenzie OMI anointed him, and within five minutes the nurse aide said there was no pulse; Hurley died still sitting upright in the passenger seat at about 11:30 a.m. When three paramedics arrived about 15 minutes later, they certified that he was dead.

It was an extraordinary end to an extraordinary life. Hurley, who had lived life to the full, seemed determined to do so to the end.

The Newcastle Dominican sisters had given much help to his family in his youth; he had attended their schools at Umzumbe and Newcastle. His first Mass had been said at their convent in Rome. Now his last Mass had been said at the fiftieth anniversary of their convent school in Durban North.

One of the few to have received the Freedom of the City of Durban, he had spent his last half hour being driven through its streets, from north to south, admiring the beauty of its trees and flowers.

Faithful to duty, he died, having completed this last assignment, literally with his boots on, surrounded by his brother Oblates.

'THAT MAN IS WITH GOD TODAY'

Dirk Benjamin is a homeless person who has lived rough on Durban's streets for the past 21 years.[23] He had, however, found a friend in Hurley, to whom he frequently turned for help. He would wash the archbishop's car, and Hurley would give him food, clothes and money, as he did for many other Durban 'outies'. He had great compassion for those in any form of difficulty, probably from his own experience of family crisis in the 1920s. When Benjamin heard about Hurley's sudden death on 13 February, he said, 'I reckon that right now he's already with God, no stops, no delays. That man is with God today'.

This was one of hundreds of messages that streamed in from all over the world when it became known that Hurley had died. They came from the great and the ordinary.[24] One from Hawaii put it simply, 'He did his very best as the Archbishop of Durban'. Another, from Khabarovsk in the Russian Federation, spoke of Hurley's 'extreme kindness, his gentle funny wit and above all his enormous heart and deep faith'. From Accra in Ghana, Father Peter Lwaminde of SECAM (which links the bishops' conferences of Africa and Madagascar) said, 'His dedication to episcopal ministry, his simplicity and gospel-filled style of life were just admirable'. From Tokyo came a message written by Archbishop Ambrose de Paoli, a former Apostolic Nuncio in South Africa: 'He was a gift to his country, he was a gift to the Church, perhaps not so much recognized as some would like. But he is with the One whose recognition counts the most'. Jacques Briard of Belgium described him as 'my South African uncle' and Cardinal Cormac Murphy O'Connor wrote from London, 'I had a very real affection for him'.

Many referred to the archbishop's qualities, including Dr Beyers Naudé, who called him 'a wonderful man in every respect, both as a pastor and as an individual'. A fellow Oblate, Father Benny Baillargeon, wrote from the United States, 'Despite his rank in the Church and his many achievements in the world, he always remained a humble priest, an admirable member of our Oblate family, a most loving brother of us all.' Sister Marie-Henry Keane OP described him as 'the Nelson Mandela of the Church'.

Famous people paid tribute to him. Archbishop Desmond Tutu prophesied that 'his name will be etched in gold in the annals of our motherland'. Former President Thabo Mbeki looked to Hurley 'as a continuing inspiration as we deepen our democracy and seek to deliver a better life to all our people'. Ela Gandhi, granddaughter of the Mahatma, said, 'His absolute commitment to the cause of the poor and the downtrodden has been an inspiration to us. He was an epitome of kindness'. Reverend Frank Chikane, Director General in the President's Office said, 'For those of us who were involved in the bitter struggle to remove apartheid, Archbishop Hurley's life, work and witness saved us from a consuming [and] bitter hatred against whites'. For Fatima Meer, Hurley 'lives on in our hearts, in our minds and consciences'. Former Springbok cricketer, Pat Trimborn wrote: 'The great scorer has declared your innings closed, an innings of immense fortitude and brilliance'.

People of other faiths and other churches were loud in their praise. Essop Kajee of Durban's Juma Musjid mosque said, 'Go well, Your Grace. Your Lord awaits you with open arms'. The Chief Rabbi of South Africa, Cyril Harris, said that he was 'always captivated by [the archbishop's] intellectual honesty and passion for justice'. For Anglican Bishop Rubin Phillip, it had been 'a personal privilege to have known such a giant of the Christian faith'. Former Presiding Bishop Louis Sibiya of the Evangelical Lutheran Church in Southern Africa recalled the archbishop's relationships with other churches: 'He loved us, and we loved him'.

Not a few of the messages shared Dirk Benjamin's certainty that Hurley was already receiving his heavenly reward. Anne Marrian wrote from Toronto, Canada, 'Heaven is blessed by the Arch's arrival'. The Daughters of Charity told their Oblate brothers, 'You now have a saint as your mediator in heaven'. Sister Sue Rakozcy IHM urged that prayers be said to Hurley 'for the future of the Church'.

As these and other messages poured in, elaborate preparations began for Hurley's lying-in-state in Emmanuel Cathedral and for his funeral, delayed for two weeks to make it possible for the family to travel from Australia, Ireland and the United States. The intervening days provided an opportunity for a new tomb to be prepared in the cathedral's lady chapel next to the grave of Hurley's predecessor, Henry Delalle OMI, and for requiem masses and memorial services to be held in many churches and Church institutions. Most important of these took place at the South African Council of Churches' headquarters in Johannesburg; St. Mary's Cathedral in Cape Town, where Hurley had been baptized; and Sacred Heart Cathedral, Pretoria.

The City of Durban (known as the eThekwini Municipality from 2000), which had conferred the Freedom of the City on Hurley in 1992, held a civic memorial service in the Durban city hall, at which Mayor Obed Mlaba presented the archbishop's younger brother Chris with a framed copy of the freedom scroll.

Most moving of the various memorials was, however, the lying-in-state in Emmanuel Cathedral, with which Hurley had been closely connected from 1940 and where he would be buried. During these two days, thousands of people of all faiths and races, young and old, streamed past the embalmed body, in a cathedral filled with flowers. Organizations with which Hurley had been closely involved took turns to explain how he had supported and encouraged their work. With their banners and uniforms they provided a colourful panorama of the archbishop's ministry. Notable were the Community of Sant'Egidio which had sent representatives from Rome; the University of KwaZulu-Natal, of which he had been chancellor; the Legal Resources Centre, of which he was an ardent admirer; the National Union of Mineworkers, one of many unions he had supported; the Diakonia Council of Churches, Sinosizo Aids Project, KwaThintwa School for the Deaf, and The Association for the Disabled, all of which he had founded. Many congregations of nuns, brothers and priests also participated, as well as a wide range of Church organizations and Catholic schools.

Hurley had frequently taken part in protest stands organized by the Black Sash against repressive apartheid laws and they had made him an honorary member. It was fitting therefore that about thirty members, wearing their distinctive black sashes, gathered around his body. This time they were not protesting but honouring Hurley with placards such as 'Champion of the Poor', 'Voice for Truth', 'Icon of Justice', all as a tribute to the archbishop's 'unflagging dedication to human rights, social responsibility and justice'.[25]

On the last night of the lying-in-state, it was the turn of the poor to fill the cathedral and to sing, pray and view the body throughout the night in a solemn farewell to their defender and advocate, on whom they had bestowed the highest Zulu honour, *isicoco*—a headdress made of leopard skin—on the diamond jubilee of his priestly ordination. The Zulu congregation of Emmanuel Cathedral and members of many other parishes, some quite distant, were there in force for *umlindelo*, the traditional all-night vigil preparing for the funeral. Bishops and priests joined in, and Chief Buthelezi made a second visit to the lying-in-state.

The next morning, more than 5,000 people made their way to the Absa Stadium for the 3½ hour 'Mass of the Resurrection' in honour of Hurley.[26] To the sound of African drums, the ceremony began with an entrance procession of about 150 deacons, priests and bishops, including the Apostolic Nuncio, Archbishop Blasco de Collaco, and the preacher and principal celebrant, Cardinal Wilfrid Napier. Among the dignitaries were the Deputy President, Jacob Zuma; the first lady, Zanele Mbeki; the Minister of Education, Kader Asmal; the Anglican Archbishop of Cape Town, Njongonkulu Ndungane; and the president of the South African Council of Churches, Rev Russel Botman.

Speaker after speaker paid tribute to Hurley as a person of exceptional intellect, humanity and courage. They referred to him as an outstanding churchman, tireless in his efforts to overcome poverty and injustice, a prophetic leader in the struggle against apartheid. He was described as the bishop of all the people of Durban, of whatever church or faith, even those of no religious belief. Though Hurley was well known nationally and internationally and had received many honours, they said he had remained humble and simple in his lifestyle, full of humour, compassion and kindness. He had indeed been a guardian of the light.

There were many moving moments in the lengthy service, for example when symbols of the archbishop's life—his Oblate cross, priestly stole and bishop's mitre—were placed on the coffin; when children presented cards and flowers to express their sympathy to the Hurley family; when a group of young Indian women danced with incense around the coffin; when hundreds of white balloons were released as a symbol of the archbishop's love of peace; when lively hymns in Zulu and English, some composed by Hurley, were sung to the accompaniment of organ and marimbas; when a young Zulu priest spontaneously sang a solo after communion, giving thanks for the encouragement he had received from Hurley; when officers of the Durban Fire Brigade, in full ceremonial uniform with brightly polished brass helmets, escorted the coffin as it left the stadium for the burial in Emmanuel Cathedral.

The simple burial service in the cathedral was attended by members of the Hurley family, bishops, priests, deacons, nuns and members of the Diocesan Pastoral Council. The beautiful anthem *Salve Regina* was sung in honour of Mary, and the service concluded with Hurley's best-known hymn, 'God our Maker, mighty Father, All creation sings your praise', a fitting conclusion for the funeral of someone whose last words had been a thanksgiving for the beauty of nature. Hundreds came forward to sprinkle rose petals on the coffin before the tomb was closed.

NOTES

ABBREVIATIONS

(These abbreviations are for the notes only. Abbreviations for the text are on pages xi and xii)

Publications

BD – *Business Day*

CA – *Cape Argus*

CP – *City Press*

CT – *Cape Times*

DN – *Daily News*

FT – *Financial Times*

IT – *Irish Times*

NCR – *National Catholic Reporter*

NM – *Natal Mercury* (later, *TM = The Mercury*)

NW – *Natal Witness* (later, *TW = The Witness*)

PN – *Pretoria News*

RDM – *Rand Daily Mail*

SC – *Southern Cross*

SS – *Sunday Star*

SS(S) – *Southern Star (Skibbereen)*

ST – *Sunday Times*

STrib – *Sunday Tribune*

TC – *The Citizen*

TG – *The Guardian*

TM – *The Mercury*

TO – *The Observer*

TS – *The Star*

TT – *The Tablet*

TW – *The Witness*

WA – *Windhoek Advertiser*

WM – *Weekly Mail*

Names

BH – Bobbie Hurley

BS – Bertie Simpkins

CC – Colin Collins

CD – Celia Dodd

CG – Colin Gardner

CH – Chris Hurley

D&MM – Dolly & Mike Madden

D&POS – Dennyo & Pauline O'Sullivan

DEH – Denis Eugene Hurley

DK – Dominic Khumalo

EB – Eric Boulle

EH – Eileen Hurley

FMcM – Frederick McManus

GC – Geoffrey Chapman

GD – Geoffrey Durrant

GdeG – Geoff de Gersigny

GM – Geneviève-Marie

HD – Harold Dainty

J&BH – Jerry and Bobbie Hurley

JH – Jerry Hurley

JP – John Page

PH – Patrick Holland

PK – Paddy Kearney

POH – Petal O'Hea

RBK – Robert Blair Kaiser

UH – Ursula Hurley

W&DL – Wolfgang and Daisy Losken

ARCHIVES AND LIBRARIES

AAD – Archives of the Archdiocese of Durban

ADCC – Archives of the Diakonia Council of Churches

APC – Alan Paton Centre, UKZN, Pietermaritzburg

EGML – E. G. Malherbe Library, UKZN, Durban

KHL – Khanya House Library (SACBC, Pretoria)

OAC – Oblate Archives, Cedara

OGHA – Oblate General House Archives, Rome

LETTERS

Letters are indicated by the initials of the people concerned; thus, for example, DEH/DK indicates a letter from Denis Eugene Hurley to Dominic Khumalo.

INTERVIEWS

Interviews are indicated by the use of colons. Thus 'DEH: 19/10/87' refers to an interview with DEH on 19/10/87.

RESOURCE MATERIALS

Many letters and interviews were used in writing this book. Apart from the Hurley interviews recorded for the Alan Paton Centre at the UKZN, a CD of all the other interview transcripts has been given to the Archives of the Archdiocese of Durban and the Oblate Archives at Cedara. Letters, unless otherwise indicated, are in the author's private archive. See also *www.archbishopdenishurley.org*.

PART ONE: "A BOY OF GREAT PROMISE"

CHAPTER 1. SKIBBEREEN

1. Information about Skibbereen is from Fisher, D. (1965), *Archbishop Denis Hurley*; from *SS(S)*, 22/10/32; and from *Fodor's 2001, Rough Guide* and *Let's Go* guidebooks to Ireland.

2. Hickey, P. (1993), 'Famine, Mortality and Emigration: A Profile of Six Parishes in the Poor Law Union of Skibbereen, 1846–7', in O'Flanagan, P. and Bultimer, C. G. (eds), *Cork: History and Society: Interdisciplinary Essays on the History of an Irish County* (Cork: Geography Publications).

3. Family information in this chapter is based on Kearney, P. (ed.) (2006), *Memories: The Memoirs of Archbishop Denis E. Hurley OMI* (Pietermaritzburg: Cluster Publications); and DEH: 13/09/99 and 14/03/03; D&POS: 26/02/04, 01/03/04 and 06/09/04; CD: 10/03/05; D&M M: 29/06/05; CH: 12/06/03 and 16/09/05. Another important source was the 'Hurley Family Chronicle', an unpublished, undated document about the Hurley and O'Sullivan families, by E. Hurley.

4. The description of Inchindreen is from DEH: 13/03/03 and that of the Hurley families living close to Ballynacarriga Castle from DEH: 14/03/03. The report on DEH's grandfather's funeral is from *SS(S)*, 30/12/16.

5. Information about the Land League is from Hickey, D. J. and Doherty, J. E. (eds) (2003), *A New Dictionary of Irish History from 1800* (Dublin: Gill & Macmillan). The general history of Ireland in the nineteenth century is from Ó hEithir, B. (2003), *The O'Brien Pocket History of Ireland* (updated edn) (Dublin: O'Brien).

CHAPTER 2. LIGHTHOUSES

1. Information about South African lighthouses is from Williams, H. (1991), *Southern Lights: Lighthouses of Southern Africa* (Portnet: Portnet publication); and S. Baillie-Cooper's website on Lighthouses of South Africa. The section on Cape Point is based on Odden, E. and Lee, N. (1983), *Cape Point* (Cape Town: Don Nelson); and Pinchuck, T. and McCrea, B. (2005), *The Rough Guide to Cape Town and the Garden Route* (London: Rough Guides). Information about the old and new lighthouses at Cape Point is from Walker, M. (1998), *Simon's Town: A Post Card History, 1900–1913* (Cape Town: self-published); and Biggs, D. (1998), *This Is Cape Town* (Cape Town: Struik). The size of Robben Island was given in *Getaway*, March 2007, p. 72.

2. Details of Denis Hurley's lighthouse service are from DEH: 13/09/99 and *Memories*, pp. 14 and 16. The Hurleys' life at Cape Point and on Robben Island is described in *Memories*, pp. 16–21; 'Eileen and Denis Recalling Early Days, Starting with Cape Point and Moving on to Robben Island', unpublished 12/06/97 (OAC); 'The Earliest Days of the Archbishop', by EH, unpublished and undated (OAC); EH: 10/12/2000; 'Progress from School to Priesthood', by DEH, unpublished and undated (OAC); and DEH: 13/09/99 and 14/03/03.

3. The description of the Hurley family life on Robben Island is from *Memories*, p. 19. Qualities of DEH's father are described in DEH: 14/03/03 and DEH/EH: 27/04/68 as well as in a conversation with C. Mtshali (02/05/05).

4. The reference to DEH's drawing Union Castle liners at Robben Island is from DEH/Cecilia Madden: 24/06/02. Information on the spiritual atmosphere of the Hurley home is from *Memories*, p. 19.

5. Life at Hood Point, East London, is from *Memories*, pp. 21–2; from 'Eileen and Denis Recalling Early Days: East London' as well as 'Progress from School to Priesthood', by DEH (both in OAC); and DEH: 13/09/99 and 14/03/03.

6. The primary sources for information about life at Clansthal are J. Hurley's unpublished and undated memoirs and 'Eileen and Denis Recalling Early Days: Memories of Clansthal', 28/05/98 (OAC). CH's comment about the toilets at St Elmo's convent and school is from his memoirs (2007), 'The Dad's Story' (unpublished, copy from M. York).

CHAPTER 3. HIGH SCHOOL

1. The main sources for this chapter are *Memories*, pp. 25–32; DEH: 13/09/99 and 18/08/03, as well as DEH & EH's 'A Further Stroll down Memory Lane', 19/11/98 and 03/12/98 (OAC).

2. Details about St Thomas's School are from H. Dainty: 27/03/04 and B. Simpkins: 19/10/04; from *Sursum Corda* school magazine, 1927–29; and from the 1928 School Diary of BS.

3. Information about the cave incident is from 'Three Boys in a Cave', by J. Ryan, compiled for the Prioress General of the Newcastle Dominicans, May 1928.

4. The anecdote about DEH's visit to the shrine of St Thérèse of Lisieux is from an email DEH/R di Bella: 28/02/03 and from Geneviève-Marie, 20/06/06.

5. Official documents about D. Hurley senior's mental illness are in the KwaZulu-Natal Archives in Pietermaritzburg.

6. The report on CH's response to his father's return at the end of December 1930 is from CH: 26/02/04 and 16/09/05.

7. The account of DEH's experience on the Pietermaritzburg station, seeing a white woman chatting to an Indian woman, is from W. Slattery: 05/08/04.

8. Recollections about St Charles's College are from DEH's unpublished and undated article 'St Charles's College: Memories and Reflections'; from Waldman, J. (ed.) (2002), *Together Standing Tall* (Pietermaritzburg: Board of Governors, St Charles's College).

9. Comments by EH on her mother's attitude to DEH's vocation to the priesthood are from EH: 10/12/2000.

CHAPTER 4. IRELAND AND ROME

1. DEH's travel to Ireland is based on *Memories*, p. 34, and DEH: 09/11/99.

2. CH's memory of his mother on the train coming back from Durban is from the launch of DEH's (2005) *Vatican II: Keeping the Dream Alive* (Pietermaritzburg: Cluster Publications), in Canberra, Australia, 16/09/05.

3. DEH's visits to family and friends and his training at Cahermoyle are also covered in *Memories*, pp. 34–8; DEH: 16/09/05 and 26/05/03.

4. E. Boulle's recollections of 'taking the discipline' are from a telephone conversation, 22/05/05.

5. DEH's response to the political views of the Irish novices at Cahermoyle and scholastics at Belmont House, Dublin, are based on DEH: 09/11/99.

6. R. Ryan's comments on DEH as a novice are from the OGHA.

7. DEH's excitement about being sent to Rome is from a family letter of 15/10/33 (OAC).

8. The account of DEH's studies in Rome is based on *Memories*, pp. 38–46; DEH interview with C. Rickard: 08/11/85; DEH: 06/01/97, 09/12/99, 26/05/03 and 23/06/03.

9. DEH's account of how he began to appreciate scholastic philosophy is from DEH/POH, 16/10/97.

10. Comments from the DEH contemporary, J. Gervais, are from JG: 15/06/05.

11. Descriptions of Rome in the 1930s are taken from DEH family letters of 22/10/33, 10/02/34, 20/05/34 and 09/07/39 (OAC).

12. The number of times DEH probably saw Pope Pius XI is based on PH's diary, May 1935–May 1939 (OAC).

13. DEH's comment about Oscar Romero was made to the author.

14. Material on Cardijn and the Young Christian Workers is from DEH: 06/01/97 and from Fierez, M. (1974) *Cardijn* (London: Young Christian Workers).

15. DEH's comments about fascist behaviour towards other people in Italy are from G. and S. Chapman: 23/4/05, as is the reference to DEH's wanting to become a military chaplain.

16. The dates of Hitler's state visit to Rome are from Ridley, J. (1997), *Mussolini* (London: Constable), p. 287. Hitler's wish to meet Pius XI is from J. Allen's column, 'The Word from Rome', *NCR*, 17/05/04.

17. The 'media profile' that described what his fellow scholastics thought of DEH is by C. Neal, *Ottawa Citizen*, 17/02/87.

18. Reports on DEH during his scholasticate years are from the OGHA.

19. DEH's reflections on leaving SA in 1932 and returning in 1940 are from his interview with A. C. Henriques: 28/10/96.

PART TWO: PRIEST, BISHOP, ARCHBISHOP

CHAPTER 5. CATHEDRAL AND SCHOLASTICATE

1. Information about DEH's arrival in Durban in July 1940 is from *Memories*, p. 46; and DEH/POH: 16/07/93.

2. DEH's meeting with his brother Jerry is from DEH: 23/06/03, from J. Hurley's diary and J. Frost's article, 'Chasing Mussolini through Africa', *NW*, 19/07/2000.

3. DEH's appointment to Emmanuel Cathedral is from DEH: 23/06/03. His regret about this appointment, from DEH's interview with C. Rickard: 08/11/05.

4. D. Khumalo's memories of DEH's visit to Inchanga in July 1940 are from DK: 11/11/04.

5. Information about Durban in the war years is from Johnston, P. (1997), *The Durban Chronicle* (Durban: Urban Strategy Department); from Durban Publicity Association (1954), *Durban: Southern Africa's Garden City*; Jackson, A. (2003), *Facts about Durban* (second edn) (Durban: FAD Publishing).

6. For references to Durban's 'legal segregation' in the late nineteenth century, see Swanson, M. W., 'The Rise of Multiracial Durban: Urban History and Race Policy in South Africa, 1830–1930' (unpublished PhD dissertation, Harvard University, 1964), pp. 285–9; Swanson, M.W. (1983), 'The Asiatic Menace: Creating Separation in Durban, 1870–1900', *International Journal of African Historical Studies*, 16, 401–21.

7. Details about Emmanuel Cathedral in the 1940s are from DEH: 06/01/97; POH: February 2004; N. McNally and D. Martin and family: 11/08/05; also from telephone conversations with A. Danker and D. Goad, 09/03/07.

8. The P. Lander (now O'Hea) response to DEH's first sermon in Emmanuel Cathedral is from POH: February 2004; and from conversations with her in May 2006.

9. The sermon on 'The Social Problem of South Africa' and the address on 'Gospel Simplicity and the Colour Bar' are from the AAD.

10. The description of DEH's relationship with the Cathedral altar servers is from N. McNally: 22/06/04; and D. Martin and family: 11/08/05.

11. The account of wedding arrangements is from H. Eccles: 10/08/05.

12. The description of DEH on his motorbike is from J. Warrack/PK, 26/10/05.

13. The story about the convict received into the church on his deathbed is from DEH's unpublished report 'Today you will be with me in Paradise, Luke 23:43' (OAC).

14. DEH's attendance at a meeting concerning the establishment of black trade unions is from DEH: 23/06/2003. Information about the ICU is from Wickins, P. L. (1978), *The Industrial and Commercial Workers' Union of Africa* (Cape Town: Oxford University Press); as well as from Rosenthal, E. (1978), *Encyclopaedia of Southern Africa* (Cape Town: Juta). Information about

the unionization of African workers in early 1943 is from D. Hemson of the Human Sciences Research Council, Durban.

15, Comments on St Joseph's at the time of its foundation are from R. de Sylva: 12/09/03.

16. Accounts of the activities of the Pietermaritzburg Parliamentary Debating Society are from DEH: 04/11/2003 and 02/01/04; as well as L. Weinberg: 03/11/2003. Comments on the friendship between DEH and G. Durrant are in DEH: 22/09/2000; a conversation with DEH: 04/11/2003; as well as GD: 18/06/05. Comments on DEH are from R. Albino: 05/09/06. DEH's speech in the Parliamentary Debating Society that led to a fierce debate with R. Albino is entitled 'That the establishment of Corporative Society and not Communistic is the only reasonable solution of the social problem' (AAD).

17. DEH's appreciation of what he had learnt from the Pietermaritzburg Parliamentary Debating Society is from DEH: 04/11/03 and 02/01/04.

18. The story about the debate involving Voortrekker Hoërskool is from D. Kocks: 21/10/04.

19. DEH's use of speech training exercises provided by P. O'Hea is from POH: February 2004; as well as from conversations with her in May 2006.

20. The establishment of a debating society at St Joseph's is from the Codex Historicus of St Joseph's (OAC).

21. The regular discussions about the South African situation are from DEH: 23/06/03.

22. Information about the Italian POWs who came to live and work at St Joseph's in 1945 is from C. Struve: 22/09/03; J. O'Brien: 13/11/03; as well as former POW F. Perego: 27/12/03.

23. The assessment of DEH as superior of the scholasticate is from the same sources, as well as from R. de Sylva: 12/09/03.

CHAPTER 6. YOUNGEST BISHOP

1. An account of the day DEH heard he was to be bishop is in 'Father Hurley, Come to Durban', in *Memories*, by DEH, pp. 47–54. Further information is from DEH: 13/01/97.

2. Speculation about who would succeed Delalle is from B. Smith: 27/06/05; and J. Patterson: 12/12/05; and article in *NM*, 15/01/60.

3. Information about the French Oblate priests was obtained from I. Freoux: 28/06/04; B. Smith: 27/06/05; J. Patterson: 12/12/05; D. Khumalo: 11/11/2004; J. Nxumalo: January 2005; P. Rowland: 29/09/07; and B. Wood: 21/11/05; as well as from J. Brain on the basis of her discussion with H. St George.

4. The French priests' attitude to DEH was described in DK: 11/11/04; and B. Wood: 21/11/05.

5. The story of DEH's counselling a young woman considering a religious vocation is from M. de Lourdes: 29/07/04.

6. For press accounts of DEH's episcopal ordination, see *DN*, 19/03/47; and *SC*, 26/03/47.

7. The comment by 'a former student from Prestbury' is from the unpublished diary of R. de Sylva (OAC).

8. An account of possible reasons for tension with Sormany was given by A. Danker in January 2006.

9. The story about Cabon building the large church in Ladysmith as a future cathedral is from C. Desmond: 27/09/07; as also the Breton priests not having a common language with the Zulu professionals and therefore having to become fluent Zulu speakers.

10. DEH's early visits to urban and rural parishes of the Natal Vicariate are described in *Memories*, pp. 51–52.

11. DEH's contact with Catholic councillors in 1947 is based on DEH: 6/01/97 and 13/01/97; as also his view on segregation before 1948—also practised by the Catholic Church—and how he saw change coming through an evolutionary process.

12. A report on his address to the Pietermaritzburg Parliamentary Debating Society is from the *DN:* 14/01/48.

13. Comments about M. Lucas's attitude towards political activism are in DEH: 13/01/97; and his urging DEH not to criticize the government is in a letter dated 28/07/49 from Correspondence with Apostolic Delegates (AAD). Crucial to understanding the Catholic Church's approach to social issues in South Africa from 1947 to 1951 is Abraham, G. (1989), *The Catholic Church and Apartheid* (Johannesburg: Ravan).

14. The Zulu-Indian conflict of 1949 is described in DEH: 31/01/97; as well as in Davenport, R., and Saunders, C. (2000), *South Africa: A Modern History* (London: Macmillan), p. 384; and *The Readers' Digest Illustrated History of South Africa* (Cape Town: Readers' Digest Association of South Africa), p. 384; and Johnston, P. (1997), *The Durban Chronicle.*

15. DEH's overseas fund-raising visits are described in '1950: Overseas', *Memories*, pp. 69–78; and his fund-raising methods from D&MM and C. Madden: 02/06/05.

16. The comment about how DEH's overseas travels helped him to become less shy and more relaxed is from M. Bergin: 18/10/04.

17. The description of DEH's return to South Africa as archbishop is from '1950: Overseas', in *Memories*, p. 78.

CHAPTER 7. OUT OF THE SHADOWS

1. DEH's description of the Catholic Church coming 'out of the shadows' is from DEH: 13/01/97.

2. The account of the Marian Congress is also based on DEH: 13/01/97; as well as *Memories*, pp. 79–83; a special 1952 issue of *Caritas* about the Marian Congress; (1952), *Catholic Youth and Family*, 6, (4), (May); NM, 01/05/52; and SC, 07/05/52.

3. The press report on the reception of the pallium is from SC, 15/08/51.

4. J. Hennemann's comments on racial segregation and apartheid are from Abraham, *The Catholic Church and Apartheid*, p. 23.

5. Information about the police shooting eighteen people at a Communist Party protest is from Watson, W. (2007), *Brick by Brick: An Informal Guide to the History of South Africa* (Claremont, SA: New Africa Books).

6. Reflections on the SA Catholic Bishops' silence on apartheid can be found in *Memories*, pp. 84–7.

7. References to the June 1952 statement on race relations are from SACBC (1969), *The Bishops Speak* (Pretoria: SACBC), Vol. 1, *Pastoral Letters, 1952–66*. Other information and comments about this statement are from *Memories*, pp. 88–95; DEH: 13/01/97; minutes of the Administrative Board and plenary sessions of the SACBC, Khanya House Library, Pretoria, as well as Abraham, *The Catholic Church and Apartheid*; and S. O'Leary: 07/09/04.

8. The difference between fundamental and contingent rights is from Ojakaminor, E. (1966), *Catholic Social Doctrine: An Introductory Manual* (Nairobi: Pauline Publications Africa).

9. DEH's response to *Die Kerkbode* is from STrib, 19/10/52.

10. Information about the Defiance Campaign of 1952 is from Davenport and Saunders, *South Africa: A Modern History*, pp. 386–7; the comment on the Suppression of Communism Act is from the same text, p. 384.

CHAPTER 8. DEFYING VERWOERD

1. The most important resource for this chapter was DEH's 'Mission Schools and Bantu Education', in *Memories*, pp. 96–110. Another helpful resource was Abraham, *The Catholic Church and Apartheid*, Chapter 4. Other sources used were B. Flanagan's 'Education: Policy and Practice', in Prior, A. (ed.) (1982), *Catholics in Apartheid Society* (Cape Town: David Phillip); Hunter, P., 'The Reorientation of Educational Policy in South Africa since 1948' (unpublished thesis, University of California, Los Angeles, 1963); P. Christie and C. Collins's 'Bantu Education: Apartheid Ideology and Labour Reproduction', in Kellaway, P. (ed.) (1984), *Apartheid and Education* (Johannesburg: Ravan); and R. G. Clarke's interview with DEH: 02/09/81, from transcript supplied by Clarke.

2. Information about the Eiselen Report is in the Union Government Series of 1951, pp. 43–55, in EGML of the UKZN, Durban.

3. Pius XI's view on Catholic education is from his encyclical letter *Divini Illius Magistri*, as quoted by Abraham, *The Catholic Church and Apartheid*, p. 63.

4. Information about the Bishops' Campaign was obtained from 'Resisting Bantu Education', in *Memories*, pp. 111–8; from SC issues for September and October 1954; and from DEH: 31/01/97. Praise for the Bishops' Campaign by the LP is from *SC*, 28/12/55; and praise by Verwoerd, from *SC*, 15/02/56.

5. Professor Tim Dunne supplied the estimated 2009 value of the funds raised by the Bishops' Campaign (e-mail of 14/11/2008).

6. DEH's overseas travels in 1956 are from 'Overseas Interlude', in *Memories*, pp. 119–22; reports about major addresses at Notre Dame and Philadelphia are from *SC*, 12/09/56 and 07/11/56 respectively. Further information about DEH's US fund-raising visit of 1956 is from DEH/J. McGrath: 24/11/2003.

CHAPTER 9. HOW TO OPPOSE APARTHEID

1. DEH's overseas travels in 1956 were reported in *DN*, 04/04/57; his comments on restrictive apartheid legislation in *NM*, 01/05/57.

2. Information about the Congress of the People is based on Watson's *Brick by Brick* and DEH: 31/01/97.

3. For an excellent treatment of the 'Church Clause', see 'The Church Clause and Condemnation' in Abraham, *The Catholic Church and Apartheid*.

4. For DEH's response to the legislation, see *NM*, 25/02/57. The bishops' proclamation about the 'Church Clause' is in *SC*, 24/07/57.

5. The 1957 statement on apartheid is in *The Bishops Speak*, 1:13–7. DEH's address to the Pretoria Kolbe Association was reported in *NM*, 27/08/59. DEH's view of racial integration as scripturally based is from *SC*, 26/10/60.

6. DEH's views on the SAIRR and his collaboration with Prof Hansi Pollak in opposition to the Cato Manor removals are covered in DEH: 31/01/97; and *DN*, 23/06/59.

7. The views of various political parties on the franchise are from Davenport and Saunders, *South Africa: A Modern History*; and DEH's opposition to a universal franchise from *SC*, 17/06/59.

8. DEH's address to the Durban Parliament in May 1959 was covered in *NM*, 26/05/59.

9. DEH's urging blacks not to adopt an uncompromising stance is from an address to the Durban Parliament, *SC*, 14/10/59.

10. The full text of the SACBC 1960 pastoral letter is in *The Bishops Speak*, 1:18–29.

11. Reports of L. Boyd's speech on PP policy are from *SC*, 27/01/60 and 25/05/60. The LP criticism of the SA Catholic bishops' closeness to the PP is from *SC*, 23/03/60.

12. Descriptions of the Sharpeville shootings are from Davenport and Saunders, *South Africa: A Modern History*, pp. 413–4; as well as from *Readers' Digest Illustrated History of South Africa*, pp. 401–3. Statements about Sharpeville are from DEH: 14/05/97; likewise comments on sabotage. Reports on the Cape Town march and the referendum of 1960 are from Davenport and Saunders, *South Africa: A Modern History*, p. 414.

13. DEH's views on leaving the Commonwealth are from DEH: 14/05/97.

14. Reports on the Natal Convention are from SC, 03/05/61 and 24/05/61; as well as from files of the APC and from Brookes, E. H. (1997), *A South African Pilgrimage* (Johannesburg: Ravan). C. Gardner also shared his memories of this event.

PART THREE: THE GREATEST EXPERIENCE OF MY WHOLE LIFE

CHAPTER 10. GOOD NEWS

1. Information from T. Müller: 31/07/05 and 09/11/05; from P. Nadal: 05/09/03, 24/10/05 and 27/07/06; from O. Hirmer: 08/08/05; and from Sister A. St Amour IHM who explained the new catechetical approach.

2. The definition of mortal sin is from *The New Dictionary of Theology*, Editors Komonchak, JA, Collins, M. and Lane, D.A., p. 961.

3. DEH's address to the Eichstatt Conference, 'The Role of the Bishop in Catechetical Renewal', July 1960, and his paper, 'The Catechetical Renewal', prepared for the Study Weeks of January 1962, are available in the AAD.

4. The DEH letter to T. Müller in which he described his meeting with C. Van Hoeck is in the AAD, 21/07/62.

5. D. Scholten's comments about DEH are from D. Scholten: 14/03/05 and 15/03/05.

6. Comments about DEH's role at Katigondo are from S. and G. Chapman: 23/05/05 and 24/05/05.

7. The DEH correspondence with J. Hofinger is in the AAD (Catechetics, 1965–67).

8. F. Wilson in telephone conversation, 03/03/07.

9. Information about the People of God series is from *SC*, 02/07/69 and from S. and G. Chapman 23 and 24/05/05.

10. How DEH's reading prepared him for the council is from DEH, *Keeping the Dream Alive*, pp. 1–5; also from DEH: 10/02/97 and 01/12/03.

11. Information about Teilhard de Chardin is from Speaight, R. (1968), *Teilhard de Chardin: A Biography* (London: Collins); Grim, J. and Tucker, M. E., 'Teilhard de Chardin: A Short Biography', in Fabel, A., and St John, D. (2003), *Teilhard in the Twenty-First Century: The Emerging Spirit of Earth* (Maryknoll, NY: Orbis), pp. 15–25; Kaufmann, L. (2005), 'Teilhard de Chardin: Introduction', *Grace and Truth*, 22, (2), (August), 3–7; as well as from the following unpublished papers by DEH: 'Pierre Teilhard de Chardin' (undated), in OAC; and others in AAD: 'The Spiritual Vision of Teilhard de Chardin', Father P. Holland Memorial Lecture, 11 November 1968; 'Man and Evil', First Open Winter School, University of Natal, 17 July 1974; 'Teilhard de Chardin: Reconciler of Church and World', Alliance Française, Durban, 20/04/78.

12. Reference to DEH's first seeing the name Teilhard de Chardin is from an email to Prof U. King, 28/03/03. DEH's comment that Teilhard had 'won my heart completely' is from DEH/P. Roach, 03/12/02.

13. Nugent, R. (2002), 'From Silence to Vindication: Teilhard de Chardin and the Holy Office', in *Commonweal*, 25/10/02, 15–7.

14. Hurley's response to reading *Le Milieu Divin* and *The Phenomenon of Man* is described in DEH's 'Teilhard de Chardin: Reconciler of Church and World', p. 13.

15. Teilhard's 'compulsion to seek unity and his opposition to all forms of dualism' is from 'Teilhard de Chardin: Reconciler of Church and World', pp. 3, 16, 36; and his view of creation is from p. 13.

16. The account of Geneviève-Marie's reading 'The Mass on the World' for DEH is from GM: 23/09/04 and 20/06/06.

17. P. Tobias's contact with Teilhard is from P. Tobias: 09/07/04, the transcript of the SATV conversation between Tobias and DEH in 2001; as well as Tobias, P. V. (2005), 'Teilhard de Chardin, Denis Hurley and the South African Connection', *Grace and Truth*, 22, (2), 8–13.

18. P. Tobias: 09/07/04.

19. Information about the Holy Office's formal warning is on p. 34 of DEH's 'Pierre Teilhard de Chardin' (undated). DEH's response to the warning is from DEH/P. Roach, 03/12/02.

20. DEH, 'Pierre Teilhard de Chardin', 36.

21. F. Lobinger: 05/08/05.

22. T. Kneifel: 29/02/04.

CHAPTER 11. SECOND VATICAN COUNCIL

1. The most important source of information about the Second Vatican Council is the five-volume work edited by Alberigo, G. (1995–2006), *History of Vatican II* (Maryknoll, NY: Orbis).

2. Information about Pope John XXIII calling the Second Vatican Council is from *Memories*, p. 151; and DEH: 31/1/97.

3. DEH's initial surprise at the calling of the council is from DEH: 30/01/97.

4. The suggestions DEH made for the council agenda are from DEH, *Keeping the Dream Alive*, pp. 7–9.

5. Speculation on possible reasons for DEH's selection to serve on the Council's CPC are from Denis, P., 'Archbishop Hurley's Contribution to the Second Vatican Council', in Denis, P. (ed.) (1997), *Facing the Crisis: Selected Texts of Archbishop Denis E. Hurley* (Pietermaritzburg: Cluster Publications), p. 233.

6. DEH's understanding of the 'progressive' and 'conservative' camps in the Council and Pope John's intuition about the need for a Council are based on 'The Struggle of Vatican II', *Church*, Spring 2001. pp. 18, 19; as well as DEH: 10/02/97.

7. DEH's excitement about Cardinal Suenens's proposal concerning the agenda of the Council is from DEH, *Keeping the Dream Alive*, p. 15; as is DEH's writing to Cardinal Suenens to express his concerns about the council.

8. DEH's description of the opening of the council is from Hurley, D. E., 'council Reminiscences', in (2003) 'Abbot Butler and the Council', Papers given at a Symposium at Heythrop College, Kensington, London, on 12/10/02, *The Downside Review*, 121, (422), (January), 53–6; also *Memories*, pp. 153–4.

9. Novak, M. (1965) *The Men Who Make the Council: Portraits of Vatican II Leaders* (Notre Dame, Indiana: University of Notre Dame Press).

10. The account of the first working day of Vatican II is from *Memories*, pp. 154–5. The strategy for dealing with the elections to the commissions is from DEH: 01/12/2003.

11. Information about the Commission for Seminaries, Studies and Catholic Education is from Denis, *Facing the Crisis*, pp. 247–54; as well as from Hurley, D. E., 'The Training of Priests', in Hurley, D. E., and Cunnane, J. (eds) (1967), *Vatican II on Priests and Seminaries* (Dublin and Chicago: Scepter Books). Further information is from Hurley, D., 'The Commission on Seminaries, Academic Studies and Catholic Schools', in *Keeping the Dream Alive*, pp. 147–57; Greiler, A., 'Denis Hurley and the Seminaries' Commission', pp. 234–9; and Greiler, A., 'Notes from Conversations [with DEH] on 7, 8 and 17 March 1997' (AAD).

12. DEH's first speech at Vatican II is from Fisher, D. (1965), *Archbishop Denis Hurley (The Men Who Make the Council)* (Notre Dame, Indiana: University of Notre Dame Press), p. 32.

13. Analysis of the two crucial debates with which the first period of the council ended is in *Memories*, p. 156.

14. DEH's critique of the procedure of the CPC and of the council, and of the standard of the documents, is described in 'The Struggle of Vatican II', p. 19. DEH's visits to progressive cardinals to express his concerns about the council are described in DEH: 01/12/2003.

15. The discovery that the council was predominantly 'progressive' is from Fisher, *Archbishop Denis Hurley*, p. 33.

16. The informal programme of lectures during the Council is described in 'The Struggle of Vatican II', p. 19; as well as in RBK: 20/06/05.

17. The 'Bob Kaiser Academy' is described in RBK: 20/06/05. P. Hartubise's account of DEH's role is from P. Hartubise: 14/06/05.

18. P. Akal: 21/05/04 and B. Gaybba: 04/05/04.

19. The account of Hurley's visits to Chenu and Congar is from Sister Geneviève-Marie: 23/09/04 and 20/06/06. She said that the visits took place on 4 December 1987.

20. The section on the founding of ICEL is from McManus, F., 'ICEL: The First Years', in Finn, P. C., and Schellman, J. M. (eds) (1989), *Shaping English Liturgy: Studies in Honor of Archbishop Denis Hurley* (Washington, DC: Pastoral Press); also Shelley, J. (1989), *Paul J. Hallinan: First Archbishop of Atlanta* (Wilmington: Michael Glazier); and DEH: 01/12/03; FMcM: 28/06/05; and JP: 06/09/04.

21. The description of bishops complaining about the council's procedures is from DEH/EB & GdeG: 05/11/62.

22. Information about the second session of Vatican II is from *Memories*, pp. 157–61. The response to DEH's speech about the role of priests is from Fisher, *Archbishop Denis Hurley*, p. 36.

23. Material on the Third Session is based on *Memories*, pp. 162–8; and *Keeping the Dream Alive*, pp. 73–120.

24. Information about the establishment of the Synod of Bishops is from Alberigo, G. (2006), *History of Vatican II*, Vol. 5, *The Council and Transition: The Fourth Period and the End of the Council, Sept. 1965–Dec. 1965*; and from Hebblethwaite, P., 'The Synod of Bishops', in Hastings, A. (ed.) (1991), *Modern Catholicism: Vatican II and After* (New York: Oxford University Press).

25. Other material on the Fourth and Final Session is from *Memories*, pp. 168–75; and DEH, *Keeping the Dream Alive*, pp. 121–46. DEH's response to the Holy Office's warning is in DEH/P Roach, 03/12/02.

CHAPTER 12. ARCHBISHOPS CLASH

1. PH/DEH: 17/11/63 is in the PH file in OAC.

2. The press report 'Demonstration of Unity in Incarnation' is from *SC*, 01/01/64; the report about PH's sermon is from 'Priest to Speak in Presbyterian Church', *SC*, 25/03/64;

3. J. C. Garner's criticism of ecumenical events in South Africa, from 'Ecumenism in South Africa: Goodwill and Dangerous Muddle-Headedness', *SC*, 08/04/64.

4. The second ecumenical service, '2,500 in Durban City Hall for Second Unity Demonstration', is in *SC*, 15/04/64.

5. The DEH Hoernlé Memorial Lecture is in Denis, P., *Facing the Crisis*, pp. 58–76. A report on the lecture is from *SC*, 22/01/64.

6. Information about Whelan is from DEH: 25/08/03; J. Patterson: 12/12/05; B. Hinwood: 07/07/05; C. Collins: 20/10/05; and D. Scholten: 14/03/05–15/03/05.

7. McCann's conversation with DEH about Whelan's attitude towards him (DEH) is from DEH: 28/08/83; and from A. C. Henriques's interview with DEH: 28/10/96, which also has useful information on J. McGeogh.

8. The genesis of Whelan's interview is in B. Hinwood: 07/07/05; and *SC*, 26/02/04; as well as in 'Who Put the Questions?' *SC*, 26/02/64.

9. *SC*, 19/02/64.

10. Whelan's full interview was published in *SC*, 19/02/64; many articles and reports about the interview appeared in *SC*, 26/02/64. The *Catholic Herald* comment is from *Pretoria News*, p. 474; the comment by D. Koka from *The World*, 21/2/64. The SACBC statement reaffirming its position on race relations appeared in *SC*, 04/03/64.

11. Information about DEH's contact with McCann after the Whelan statement is from M. Shackleton: 25/02/05. D. Woods's telegram to DEH is from the OAC.

12. The article criticizing the *SC* ban on comment about the Whelan-Hurley clash is from '"Challenge" Calls for Freedom of Speech in the "Southern Cross"', *SC*, 20/05/64.

13. C. Collins's comments on what happened in the bishops' discussion of the Whelan-Hurley clash, as well as DEH's response, is from CC: 20/10/05.

14. DEH's correspondence with J. McGeogh: 01/04/64 is from AAD; likewise DEH's letters to A. Samorè and Cardinal Agagianian. DEH/CC, 18/11/64, about the SA Embassy in Rome, was given to me by CC.

15. P. Nadal to the author: 10/12/08.

16. DEH/OMcCann is dated 01/02/64, but since it expresses the hope that McCann had a 'happy and profitable Easter', that date must be incorrect. The letter is in the AAD.

17. DEH's view on whether racism would be on the agenda of the council is from 'South African Archbishop holds Ecumenical Council should deal with Racism', NCWC News Service, 10/10/63.

18. Quotations from council documents on race are from Abbott, W. H., and Gallagher, J. (eds) (1967), *The Documents of Vatican II* (London: Geoffrey Chapman), pp. 206 and 668.

19. The Pastoral Letter of July 1966 is from *The Bishops Speak*, 1:43–52.

20. DEH's 'Panegyric for the Funeral of Archbishop William Patrick Whelan OMI: 14 February 1966' is in AAD.

CHAPTER 13. HUMANAE VITAE

1. The principal sources of information on the *Humanae Vitae* controversy were the following *SC* reports: 'Birth Control Ban to Stay', 31/07/68; 'Hans Küng on Conscience', 02/08/68;

'Non-Acceptance "Grave Act of Disobedience"—Australian Bishops', 07/08/68; 'Amazing Reactions to Pope's Decree', 07/08/68; 'I don't think I have ever felt so torn in half', 07/08/68. Other helpful coverage is from Friday, R. M., 'Birth Control', in *The New Dictionary of Theology*, pp. 129–32; and DEH's (1969) unpublished 'Circumstances Alter Cases', address at the Theological Winter School, Durban, in AAD.

2. DEH's comment to Father Albert Danker OMI about losing his mitre was passed on to me by Danker on 22/02/07.

3. A. Nolan: 03/03/04.

4. J. Nxumalo: Jan. 2005.

5. The debate about priestly celibacy is from the *ST*, 'Let priests marry—Hurley', 06/08/68; and 'Abp Hurley supports optional celibacy', *SC*, 09/10/68.

6. DEH's correspondence with Pope Paul VI (1969–70) is from the OAC.

7. DEH's letter to Dr John Marshall was emailed on 30/12/2002.

8. The DEH article that narrowly escaped Vatican censorship appeared in (1974) *Theological Studies*, 35, 154–163. Further information is from W. Burghardt: 04/06/05; as well as from Burghardt, W. (2002), *Long Have I Loved You* (Maryknoll, NY: Orbis); and from DEH/WB, 12/08/02.

CHAPTER 14. IMPLEMENTING VATICAN II

1. The main source of information about catechetical and liturgical renewal as well as structural changes to draw lay people into a consultative process is Abrahams, M., 'Denis Hurley and the Reception of Vatican II', in DEH's *Keeping the Dream Alive*, pp. 240–52; also M. Abrahams: 11/05/05 and 19/10/05.

2. Elizabeth Johnson's involvement in the theological winter school of 1987 is from: 07/06/05. The account of the influence of her book *She Who Is* is from H. Ennis: 28/01/05.

3. M. H. Keane's comments on the DEH Vatican II lectures are from 'Vatican II: Keeping the Dream Alive' in the DEH book of the same title, pp. 261, 264.

4. M. Mdluli's comments are from M. Mdluli: 25/08/04.

5. B. Wood's comment is from B. Wood: 21/11/05.

6. M. Birks: 26/09/04.

7. Information about the establishment of parish councils is from 'Parish Councils' D-Day in Durban', *SC*, 26/02/67.

8. Report about the first diocesan synod is from 'First Catholic Diocesan Synod held in Durban', *SC*, 25/12/68. Comments on the synod are from interviews with J. Nxumalo: Jan. 2005; O. Nxumalo: 24/03/2004; E. Higgins: 09/07/04; and M. Mdluli: 25/08/04.

Limehill – A Case Study of Activism

9. Information about the Limehill removal is from Desmond, C. (1971), *The Discarded People* (Harmondsworth: Penguin); as well as from C. Desmond: 08/12/2003; and P. Rowland: 06/08/05; 'Africans moved from mission farm: Need for aid continues', *SC*, 27/03/68; 'Hurley comment on 'Enemies of SA' statement', *SC*, 12/02/69; and B. Robinson's 'Butting-in at Limehill', *SC*, 15/01/69.

IMBISA

10. The origins of IMBISA are from AAD, IMBISA Box file no. 2. Further information is from T. Rogers: 22/09/06.

11. Information about the conflicts between Portuguese- and English-speaking bishops in IMBISA, and how DEH responded to these, is from I. Linden: 14/09/04; M. Hippler and G. Thie: 28/09/04; and C. Corcoran: 23/05/05.

12. DEH's comment about lengthy meetings with Angolan and Mozambican bishops to secure agreement on IMBISA's joint pastoral letter is from DEH/I Linden: 14/09/04.

13. The incident at the 1996 Harare consultation on the Church's social teaching is from P. Henriot: January 2005; and D. Martin: 27/05/05. P. Henriot's response to D. Martin's comment on the AMECEA statement is from a conversation on 30/01/08.

Synod of Bishops

14. Information about the Synod of Bishops is from W. McConville's entry in *The New Dictionary of Theology*. Information about individual Synods 1967 to 1985 is from Hebblethwaite, P., 'The Synod of Bishops', in Hastings, *Modern Catholicism: Vatican II and After*.

15. DEH/POH, 20/10/71 concerns discussion of clerical celibacy at 1971 synod.

16. DEH/W. Burghardt: 12/08/02 concerns the threat that DEH would not be allowed to attend the Synod of 1974.

17. DEH's comment about the dinner he attended with the Cardinal Secretary of State is from DEH/EH, 17/10/74.

18. DEH's comment about procedural problems at the Synod of 1974 is from DEH/J&BH: 30/09/74. The news about his election to the Synod Council is from DEH/J&BH: 10/11/74.

19. DEH's story about 'fast bowling' in the English B discussion group (Synod of 1977) is from DEH/EH: 08/10/77.

20. DEH's description of the meal that the African bishops had with Pope John Paul II is from DEH/J&BH: 11/10/80.

21. DEH's comment about the synod requiring 'test match temperament' is from DEH/J&BH: 01/12/85.

22. DEH's assessment of the Synod of Bishops is from DEH/T. Fox, 08/05/03.

CHAPTER 15. LEADER OF ICEL

1. Information about ICEL is based on Page, J., 'Promoter of English in the Liturgy', in Gamley, A. M. (ed.) (2001), *Denis Hurley: A Portrait by Friends* (Pietermaritzburg: Cluster Publications). 'What Is ICEL?' Presentation to the National Conference of Catholic Bishops, USA, 17/06/93; as well as Hurley, D. E., 'The International Commission on English in the Liturgy', 1977, AAD; and McManus, F., 'ICEL: The First Years'; and Page, J., 'ICEL, 1966–89: Weaving the Words of Our Common Christian Prayer', in Finn and Schellman, *Shaping English Liturgy*.

2. Comments on Hurley's role as chair of ICEL are from Page, J., 'An Appreciation of Denis Hurley, Archbishop-Emeritus of Durban, South Africa', *NCR*, 20/02/04. Also from A. Boylan: 25/05/05; E. Clancy: 19/09/05; J. Fitzsimmons: 02/07/05 and 29/05/05; M. Fowler: 03/06/05; K. Hughes: 23/06/05; T. Koernke: 03/06/05; T. Krosnicki: 03/06/05; F. McManus: 28/06/05 and 29/06/05; G. Ostdiek: 22/06/05; J. Page: 06/09/04 and 21/06/05; D. Pilarcyk: 03/06/05; J. Schellman: 01/06/05; M. Taylor: 12/09/04; D. Trautman: 28/06/05; R. Weakland: 13/06/05.

3. Page's comments about the episcopal board's communication with member conferences and the US bishops' perception of ICEL as a 'bully' are from email, JP/PK, 24/04/07. Chapman's references to occasions when several of the member conferences went their own way with regard to translation is from email, GC/PK, 15/04/08.

4. The draft letter from Cardinal Basil Hume is in the OAC.

5. Father Chris Walsh's letter is dated 28/07/87 and is in the ICEL correspondence files at AAD.

6. Page's comments on the decree *Sacram Liturgiam* (1964) are from his email, JP/PK: 24/07/07.

7. Chapman's comments on Hurley's role in the survival of the original ICEL is from email, GC/PK, 15/04/08.

CHAPTER 16. CLOSE ENCOUNTERS

1. E. Boulle's memories of DEH are from: 18/09/03 and 23/09/03 as well as from 'A Universal Man: A Personal Memoir of Denis E. Hurley OMI', Parts II and III, *OMI Update: KwaZulu-Natal, South Africa*, April to June 2004.

2. GC/PK, 07/04/08. Chapman writes that Hurley told him that the 'capacity to relate to people had been "knocked out" of him' during his training in Ireland. The prevailing view at the time was that priests in training should keep lay people, especially women, at a distance.

3. The deaths of young people at St Clement's just before Father Canevet's death were confirmed by K. Mlambo: 04/01/05.

4. J. Mathias's memories of DEH are from J. Mathias: 05/01/06; and email, JM/PK, 20/01/08 concerning the KwaThintwa school.

5. P. Nadal: 05/09/03 and 24/10/05.

6. P. Akal's story about DEH contacting the Natal rugby team coach in Australia is from P. Akal: 21/05/04.

Reminiscences are from:

7. M. Mdluli: 25/08/04.

8. L. Mthethwa: 19/01/05.

9. A. Piper: 16/02/04.

10. T. Cooke: 13/01/05.

11. P. Mabaso: 01/02/05,

12. R. Mahlangu: 17/10/04.

PART FOUR: PROPHETIC LEADER

CHAPTER 17. STIRRINGS OF RESISTANCE

Black Consciousness

1. Information about the Black Consciousness Movement is from Roberts, M. (1996), *South Africa 1948–1994: The Rise and Fall of Apartheid* (Harlow: Longman); Phillips, I. (1992), *South Africa: World History Series* (London: Collins); and Biko, S. (1988), *I Write What I Like* (Harmondsworth: Penguin); and Pityana, N. B., Ramphele, M., Mpumlwana, M. M., and Wilson, L. (eds) (1991), *Bounds of Possibility: The Legacy of Steve Biko and Black Consciousness* (Cape Town: David Philip).

2. For protests by black priests, see Mkhatshwa, S., 'That Man Hurley', in Gamley, *Denis Hurley*; also *RDM*, 23/01/70; *SC*, 28/01/70, 11/02/70, 24/02/71 and 28/07/71; and S. Mkhatshwa: 12/11/03.

The 1973 Strikes

3. Sources for the Durban dock-worker strikes of 1969 and 1972 and the Durban strikes of 1973 are Bonnin, D., Hamilton, G., Morrell, R., and Sitas, A., 'The Struggle for Natal and KwaZulu: Workers, Township Dwellers and Inkatha, 1972–1985', in Morrell, R. (ed.) (1996), *Political Economy and Identities in KwaZulu-Natal: Historical and Social Perspectives* (Durban:

Indicator, 1996); Du Toit, D. (1981), *Capital and Labour in South Africa: Class Struggles in the 1970s* (London and Boston: Kegan Paul); Fisher, F., and Maré, P. G. (1977), *The Durban Strikes 1973* (Durban and Johannesburg: Institute for Industrial Education & Ravan).

4. DEH's meeting with worker leaders in 1971 is from R. Lambert: 05/09/05; and emails, RL/PK, October 2006.

The Church and Just Wages

5. Reports on the decision to hand over the mission schools to the KwaZulu Territorial Authority are from *SC*, 14/02/73.

6. The bishops' national decision about the schools is from *SC*, 21/02/73.

Confronting Security Police

7. Coleman, M., (ed) (1988), *A Crime against Humanity: Analysing the Repression of the Apartheid State*. (Cape Town: David Phillip), pp. 58–59.

8. The Hurley-Meer meeting with F. Steenkamp is from Meer, F., 'Man of the Pulpit—Man of the People', in Gamley, *Denis Hurley*; also from F. Meer: 01/11/03; and *SC*, 10/11/71.

Pilgrimage against Migrant Labour

9. The 'Pilgrimage for Family Life' is from *ST*, 17/12/72; *CT*, 17/12/72; *CA*, 7/01/73 and 15/01/73; and A. Jennings: 16/11/05. Press cuttings provided by N. Hudson.

10. DEH's speech on migrant labour at the Durban Parliamentary Debating Society is from *SC*, 14/03/73. The reference to the DRC Synod is from *CA*, 11/01/73.

Defying School Segregation

11. Information about the open schools is from Christie, P. (1990), *Open Schools: Racially Mixed Catholic Schools in South Africa, 1976–1986* (Johannesburg: Ravan); Flanagan, B., 'Educational Policy and Practice', in Prior, *Catholics in Apartheid Society; Boner, K.* (2000), *Dominican Women: A Time to Speak* (Pietermaritzburg: Cluster Publications); as well as DEH: 31/10/97; P. Koornhof: August 2005; M. O'Sullivan: 28/05/05; J. Pieterse: 28/03/04 and 10/03/06; E. Quinlan: January 2005.

12. The comment that G. Hickey feared the talking 'would go on for ever' is from K. Boner: 04/11/06.

13. G. Hickey/O. McCann is in the Open Schools file of the Cabra Dominican Archives, Springfield Convent, Cape.

14. M. Kelly's article on the 'Open Schools' Experience' is from *SC*, 20/05/79.

15. Pope Paul VI's support for the open schools is from *WA*, 22/01/77.

16. Information about the Permanent Black Priests' Solidarity Group is from Mukuka, George (1997) 'The Impact of Black Consciousness on Black Catholic Clergy and their Seminary Training', School of Theology, University of Natal. *http://www.wkzn.ac.za/sorat/theology.bct/vat8.htm*. Comments of the Permanent Black Priests' Solidarity Group are from the Report of the Resource Team on Open Schools, January to October 1977 (AAD).

Soweto, 16 June 1976

17. Information about 16 June 1976 is from Kane-Berman, J. (1978), *Soweto: Black Revolt, White Reaction* (Johannesburg: Ravan).

18. DEH's address on mobilizing for peace is taken from the *New Zealand Tablet*, 1976.

19. The later SACC comment on DEH's speech can be found on *http://www.sacc.org.za/about/celebrate7.html*.

Diakonia

20. Information on the original vision of Diakonia is taken from DEH's address to the Synod, Archdiocese of Durban, 23–24 May 1974.

21. *Seek*, June 1976; and from *SC*, 11/04/76.

CHAPTER 18. 'NO' TO APARTHEID WAR

1. For the 1974 SACC Conference at Hammanskraal, see de Gruchy, J. W. (1979), *The Church Struggle in South Africa* (Cape Town: David Philip).

2. For information about South Africa's border war, see 'South Africa: Skirting Borders of Country's Memory, *BD*, 19/07/07. A right-wing perspective on the war can be found in Steenkamp, W. (1992), *South Africa's Border War, 1966–1989* (Oxford: African Books Collective).

3. For information about the militarization of South Africa in the 1960s and 1970s, see 'Conscripts on the Run', *New African*, March 1979, 72–4. Also Law, L., Lund, C., and Winkler, H., 'Conscientious Objection: The Church against Apartheid Violence', in Villa-Vicencio, C. (ed.) (1987), *Theology and Violence: The South African Debate* (Johannesburg: Skotaville).

4. For the text of the SACC resolution on conscientious objection and DEH's response, see Methodist Church of Southern Africa (undated), *Church and Conscience* (Methodist Church of SA, Christian Citizenship Department), loaned by R. Steele.

5. The SACBC Administrative Board's resolution about the Defence Further Amendment Bill is from their Minutes of 25/07/04.

6. C. Clark's article about DEH's statement is from *ST*, 08/09/74.

7. Further detail of that statement is from *CA*, 09/09/74.

8. DEH's sermon of 08/09/74 is from the 'Broadcast Sermons' file, AAD.

9. D. Worrall's response is from *CA*, 11/09/74.

10. Response to DEH's statement is from *ST*, 15/09/74.

11. Hurley's sympathetic attitude to the 'boys on the border' is from P. Nadal: 26/11/06.

12. The list of objectors between 1979 and 1989 is from Centre for Intergroup Studies (1989), *Conscientious Objection*, Occasional Paper No. 8 (Rondebosch: University of Cape Town).

13. Information about C. Yeats's 1981 trial is from C. Yeats: 24/05/05, from his book (2005) *Prisoner of Conscience* (London: Rider); from Yeats, C., 'He Stayed on to Support Me', in Gamley, *Denis Hurley*; from Swart, C., 'Amazing Witness at Court Martial', in *Campus*, undated; and from 'Why I Admire Yeats', *NM*, 13/05/81. The account of Yeats's interactions with DEH is from Gamley, *Denis Hurley*. The church leaders' statement in support of Yeats is from 'Church Call for Alternate to Military Service', *DN*, 13/05/81.

14. L. Goemans: 07/07/04.

15. 'A Heavy Price for a Noble Ideal', *DN* 27/08/82.

16. DEH's praise for N. Mitchell is from 'A Heavy Price for a Noble Ideal', *DN*, 27/08/82.

17. R. Steele's invitation to DEH to chair the media conference at which nineteen COs declared their conscientious objection to military service is from the CO file, in AAD. N. Mitchell gave me a copy of the letter he received from DEH. DEH's message at the End Conscription Campaign Festival of June 1985 is from OAC.

18. R. Cawcutt's story about military chaplains is from R. Cawcutt: 24/02/05.

CHAPTER 19. LEADING THE BISHOPS

1. Sparks, A. (1990), *The Mind of South Africa: The Story of the Rise and Fall of Apartheid* (Johannesburg: Jonathan Ball); Phillips, *South Africa*; Roberts, *South Africa 1948–94*.

SACBC President

2. The comparison between DEH's first spell as SACBC leader (1952–61) and his second (1981–87) is based on DEH: 28/11/97.

3. Comments on DEH's leadership are based on the following: H. Ennis: 28/01/05; B. Tlhagale: 10/11/03; E. Lafont: 10/09/04; F. Lobinger: 05/08/05; W. Napier: 26/08/05; J. Nxumalo: January 2005; S. O'Leary: 07/09/04; N. Pistorius: 29/12/04; P. Rowland: 06/08/05; W. Slattery: 05/08/04.

No Cause for Celebration

4. The SACBC statement on the Republic festivities is from 'Cause not to celebrate Republic Day—bishops', *SC*, 17/05/81.

5. Hurley's pastoral letter, 'Why my Church is boycotting the Republic Festival', *ST*, 10/05/81; and 'Hurley snubs festival', *NM*, 11/05/81.

6. A. Paton's article is from *DN*, 25/06/81; and the Clive Derby-Lewis statement, from *TC*, 11/05/81.

'Ich Will Ein Mensch Zein'

7. U. Koch: 28/09/04.

8. T. Perez: 26/02/05.

9. H. Zingel: 27/09/04.

CHAPTER 20. NAMIBIA

1. Information about Namibia is from the CIIR (1985), *Profile of Namibia* (London: CIIR); and from Phillips, *South Africa*.

2. The account of the bishops' visit to Namibia in 1981 is based on interviews with H. Steegmann: 27/09/04; M. Aitken: 28/10/03 and 19/03/05; and I. Linden: 14/09/04; as well as Roman Catholic Church, Vicariate of Windhoek (1983), *The Green and the Dry Wood* (Windhoek: Oblates of Mary Immaculate).

3. The findings of the bishops' visit to Namibia are from (1982) *Report on Namibia* (Pastoral Action, No. 27) (Pretoria: SACBC); as well as from Sparks, A., 'Namibians are tortured', *TO*, 16/05/82; 'Bishops' Delegation finds most Namibians back SWAPO', *SC*, 30/05/82; and 'Namibia Report', *TT*, 22/05/82.

4. DEH's visits to the Western Contact Group are described in *The Green and the Dry Wood*.

5. This account is based on 'The Catholic Church and Namibia', *EcuNews*, February 1983; 'Sparks fly as bishops talk on Namibia', *SC*, 13/02/83; 'Hurley defends bishops' report at meeting of 1,000', *RDM* and *TS*, 01/02/83.

6. The banning of the Namibia report was covered in 'Banned report on Namibia reflected "suffering" in war', *TS*, 19/01/83; *SC*, 30/01/83; and *RDM*, 25/05/83.

7. Information on the SACBC press conference that led to the charge against DEH comes from the transcript 'SACBC Press Conference 1983—Hurley Address', *Koevoet* Trial File, BIO—11/T/5/3, OAC.

8. Information about the trial is from 'The Story of My Trial', a one-page memorandum by DEH, Namibia files, AAD; 'Archbishop Hurley Charged', Dossier by CIIR, 15/10/84 AAD; 'SAP may charge Catholic Leader', *RDM*, 05/02/83 and 09/02/83; 'Criminal charges face SA church leader', *Catholic Herald*, 18/02/83; *WA*, 04/07/83.

9. The report on DEH's first court appearance on 19/10/84 is based on 'Telex from SACBC', 19/10/84 in CIIR Dossier, AAD.

10. Hurley's attitude towards the Namibia case is from B. Currin: 06/07/04; and email, GC/PK: 07/04/08.

11. For information about how the legal team was inspired by DEH, see Currin, B., 'Trial of an Archbishop', in Gamley, *Denis Hurley.*

12. Currin's view on the availability of witnesses is based on a telephonic conversation: 11/02/07.

13. B. Currin's view of the prosecution's anxiety is from email BC/PK, 10/01/06. D. Kuny's view of the case is from D. Kuny: 15/02/06.

14. 'Mandela's Letter from Jail', S.C. 09/07–15/07/08.

15. Drinan's conversation with the SA Ambassador to the USA is based on Drinan: 01/06/05. For report on J. Malone's letter protesting DEH prosecution, see *SC*, 09/12/84.

16. Information about Gastrow's involvement came from DEH/POH, 01/03/85.

17. The report on DEH's trial on 18/02/85 is based on 'State man booed in Hurley case', *PN*, 19/02/85; 'Applause for acquitted Hurley', *CT*, 19/02/85; and *SC*, 03/03/85.

18. Lamont, D. (1977), *Speech from the Dock* (London: K Mayhew with CIIR).

19. The media conference after the trial is based on a transcript by C. Rickard, and DEH: 28/11/97.

20. DEH's civil claim is based on Currin and Kuny interviews; 'Hurley sues AG and Ministers', *NM*, 04/12/86; 'R25,000 damages for Hurley', *CT*, 03/03/87; and DEH/A Campbell: 08/06/87.

CHAPTER 21. IN THE SHOES OF THE WORKERS

1. Reports about the Study Day on 30/01/82 are from Appendix E to minutes of SACBC Plenary Session of 26/01/82–03/02/82 KHL; also from 'Bishops told of union struggles', *SC*, 21/02/8.

2. 'Catholic Church to back black unions', *TS*, 05/02/82.

3. Launch of Diakonia's 'Worker Rights Statement' was reported in 'Churches take stand on exploited workers', *DN*, 17/10/83; and 'Hurley hits "exploitation"', *NM*, 18/10/83.

4. Information about the St Joseph the Worker Fund and use of Emmanuel Cathedral for a worker meeting are from R. Lambert: 05/09/05; A. Erwin: 06/07/04; as well as Erwin, A., 'A Walk in the Garden', in Gamley, *Denis Hurley.* Information about the priests' response to the worker meeting in Emmanuel Cathedral is also based on E. Boulle: 23/09/03; and L. Kaufmann: 02/03/85.

5. The account of the BTR-Sarmcol Strike is based on 'Victory! BTR-Sarmcol', in (undated) *Worker Solidarity*, Issue 9. Information about DEH's involvement with the Sarmcol workers was obtained from P. Dladla: 31/10/05 and L. Kaufmann: 02/03/05, as well as from DEH/J & BH, 18/10/86.

6. Information about the land bought for the Sarmcol Workers' Co-operative with funds provided by *Misereor* is from T. Cooke.

CHAPTER 22. POLICE CONDUCT IN THE TOWNSHIPS

1. The account of events in the Vaal Triangle on 03/09/84 and the following months is based on Noonan, P. (2003), *They're Burning the Churches* (Bellevue: Jacana Books); and P. Noonan: 10/10/06.

2. Information about police conduct is based on SACBC (1984), *Report on Police Conduct during Township Protests: August–November 1984* (Pretoria: SACBC); as well as P. Noonan: 10/10/06; and S. Crowe: 11/11/03.

3. Reports on the media launch are from *TG*, 07/12/84; *FT*, 07/12/84; and *IT*, 07/12/84.

4. DEH's comments on 'crisis ministry' in the Vaal Triangle are from *EcuNews*, January/February 1985.

5. Information about discussions with the police concerning the report is from DEH's presidential report to the SACBC, 22/01/86.

CHAPTER 23. NEW POLICY DIRECTIONS

Meeting the ANC

1. DEH's meeting with O. R. Tambo at the Railway Hotel, Paddington, London, is from I. Linden: 14/09/04; and emails, I. Linden, 23/03/07. Additional information was supplied by A. Nolan.

2. DEH's comments on how the crisis had intensified since September 1984 are from DEH/J&BH, 19/04/86. DEH's 1986 comments on change in SACBC's approach are from *TC*, 'RC plans to talk to black movements', 27/01/86. Motivation for talks with ANC are from 'ANC has important role, says Hurley', *NM*, 01/02/86; and 'Whites must become aware', *NM*, 17/02/86. Information about the *Kairos Document* is from its preface, in [A group of theologians] (1985), *The Kairos Document: A Theological Comment on the Political Crisis in South Africa* (Third World Theology) (London: Catholic Institute for International Relations; British Council of Churches).

3. Information about contact with the ANC-in-exile is from 'Hurley to meet the ANC', ST, 13/04/86. A full account of the SACBC delegation's talks with the ANC is from 'Visit to ANC in Lusaka, 14–16 April 1986'; as well as the 'Joint Communiqué of the Meeting of the SACBC and the African National Congress, Lusaka, April 16, 1986.'

4. DEH's personal impressions of the ANC delegation are from DEH: 17/04/98.

5. Napier's recollection of Hurley's questions during ANC discussions are from W. Napier: 26/08/05.

6. 'Prelate sees options for SA: Talk or collapse', *SC*, 22/06/86.

Sanctions

7. The introduction to this section is based on Phillips, *South Africa*; and Davenport and Saunders, *South Africa: A Modern History*.

8. The SACBC view on sanctions is outlined by Orkin, M. (1987), *Sanctions against Apartheid* (Cape Town: David Philip; London: Catholic Institute for International Relations); as well as SACBC report of 24/02/87, 'The South African Situation and the Question of Economic Pressure' (AAD).

9. Information about the Durban clergy meeting on sanctions is from 'Rebel Priests meet in Durban', *CT*, 01/05/86.

10. The special plenary on sanctions is from Pistorius, N., 'Economic pressure—bishops exercised utmost responsibility', *SC*, 25/05/86; and Rai, K., 'Read the bishops' letter carefully, then decide', *SC*, 08/06/86.

11. Information concerning public meetings to explain the bishops' decision on sanctions is based on an advertisement in *CT*, 20/05/86, 'Catholic Bishops Call Meetings'.

12. DEH's view of the sanctions issue is based on Linden, I., 'Refusal to sit on the fence', in Gamley, *Denis Hurley*; I. Linden: 14/09/04; and W. Napier: 26/08/05.

13. Comparison with views of D. Tutu, B. Naudé and A. Paton is based on correspondence with C. Gardner.

14. Information about when Tutu became committed to sanctions is from Allen, J. (2006), *Rabble-Rouser for Peace* (Johannesburg: Random House).

15. Desmond, C. (1986), 'Sanctions and South Africa', *Third World Quarterly*, 8, (1) (January).

CHAPTER 24. MOBILIZING THE CHURCH

Pastoral Planning

1. This section is based on F. Lobinger's one-page outline notes, 'The History of the Pastoral Plan', as well as his paper titled 'A Pilgrim Church Searches for Its Way', presented at St Augustine's Seminary, Roma (Lesotho), in 1992. Other helpful material from F. Lobinger: 05/08/05; O. Hirmer: 08/08/05; and P. Sadie: 01/05/07.

Christians for Justice and Peace

2. Papers on CJP are in Historical Papers Department, William Cullen Library, University of Witwatersrand.

3. For a summary of DEH's address to 1983 SACC National Conference, see 17/1/85—1 in CJP file, AAD.

4. For Church leaders' discussion of DEH's proposal, see their minutes, 7/02/84–8/02/84, AAD.

5. 'Report of a meeting of interested persons', 08/05/84, CJP file, AAD.

6. For outline of aims and objects of CJP and proposed methods of operation, see 'Christians for Justice and Peace', undated printed leaflet with CJP logo and charts, in William Cullen Library, Witwatersrand University.

7. P. Storey's comment about the possibility of the South African Church splitting before end of 1980s is from minutes of Church Leaders' Meeting, 7/02/84–8/02/84.

8. For resolution of BECLC, see CJP file in AAD; and press clip, 'Black Clerics revolt in SACC', SS, 01/12/85.

9. S. Brittion's comments on the decision to disband are from S. Brittion, 02/12/85, CJP file, AAD.

CHAPTER 25. REASON TO BELIEVE

1. Information about context in Durban, August 1985, is from TRC (1998), *Truth and Reconciliation Commission of South Africa Report* (Cape Town: Juta).

2. The most helpful source for this section is Rickard, C., 'Reason to Believe', in Gamley, *Denis Hurley*. Also DEH/J&BH, 11/10/85 and 08/04/86.

3. Details of Appeal Court's decision is based on report in *BD*, 23/05/86.

CHAPTER 26. THE PRICE OF PROPHECY

1. Information about B. Edwards's attack on DEH in Natal Provincial Council taken from 'Hurley accused of waging "holy war"', *NM*, 17/05/84; 'Hurley considers action against NRP MPC', *NW*, 18/05/84; 'Hurley may sue detractors', *SC*, 17/06/84; and B. Edwards: 05/01/04.

2. Reference to DEH in StratCom listing discovered by TRC, from 'TRC unearths who's who of township unrest', *NM*, 05/11/97.

3. Smear of DEH in US publication, *Family Protection Scoreboard*, reported in 'Twisted Picture', *STrib*, 03/05/87.

4. Information about the special plenary session in July 1986 is from 'Minutes of a special meeting of bishops held on 9 and 10 July 1986'.

5. Napier's comments on the bishops' emphasis on unity is from W. Napier: 26/08/05.

6. Account of meeting with P. W. Botha is from S. Crowe (of the SACBC Communications Dept), 'Report on meeting of the SACBC with the State President on 17 November 1986'; as well as a statement by DEH about the same meeting, DEH: 15/07/98.

7. Account of J. Mees's controversial advice to the South African bishops is from 'Hurley crosses swords with Pope's envoy', *STrib*, 25/01/87; from W. Napier: 26/08/05; and from 'Minutes of the official opening of the SACBC Plenary Session, 19/01/88, p. 23, KHL.

PART FIVE: 'IN OLD AGE, THEY WILL STILL BEAR FRUIT'

CHAPTER 27. LAST YEARS IN OFFICE

Protest Marches

1. Information about the situation in South Africa in the late 1980s is from the *Reader's Digest Illustrated History of South Africa*; and from Roberts, *South Africa 1948–1994*.

2. The Standing for the Truth Campaign is from SACC (1993), 'Come Celebrate! 25 years of the SACC', Chapter 12; and from Allen, *Rabble-Rouser for Peace*.

3. For analysis of the protest marches of 1989, see du Pisani, J. A., Broodryk, M., and Coetzer, P. W. (1990), 'Protest marches in South Africa', *Journal of Modern African Studies*, 28, (4), 573–602.

4. For details of 'Red Flag Row', see *DN*, 23/09/89; 'The Communist flag issue', *DN*, 19/10/89; 'Churches debate dilemma of red-flag marches', *DN*, 19/10/89.

'Community Serving Humanity'

5. Information about the Pastoral Plan and DEH's involvement in its preparation was obtained from F. Lobinger: 05/08/05; through telephonic conversations with him during 2007; and through 'A Pilgrim Church Searches for Its Way: The Pastoral Plan of the Southern African Catholic Bishops' Conference'.

6. Minutes of the Pastoral Plan Advisory Committee for the period 1987–93 were loaned by E. Charbonneau, Grail Centre, Johannesburg.

7. Information about Renew was obtained from D. Ciangio and T. Kleissler: 08/06/05; P. Nadal: 05/09/03, 24/10/05 and 27/07/06; L. Mthethwa: 19/01/05; A. Piper: 16/02/04.

8. The quotation from the Vision Document is from SACBC (1989), *Community Serving Humanity: Pastoral Plan of the Catholic Church in Southern Africa* (Pastoral Action, No. 50) (Pretoria: SACBC).

9. Quotations from the Pastoral Letters of DEH and D. Khumalo are from 'A Pastoral Letter from the Archbishop and Bishop Dominic Khumalo for Pentecost Sunday, 14 May 1989', News Bulletin of Catholic Archdiocese of Durban, May 1989; and 'Please join in the journey of Renew': A pastoral letter to the people of the Catholic Archdiocese of Durban, with an invitation to the Mass of 30 July 1989, AAD.

HIV/AIDS Ministry

10. This section is based on interviews with L. Towell: 13/01/04 and 17/02/04; and T. Rogers: 22/09/06.

Resignation

11. DEH's letter 'To the Clergy, Religious and Laity of the Archdiocese of Durban, to be read at Mass on 23 June 1991', published in Archdiocese of Durban (1991), *News Bulletin of Catholic Archdiocese of Durban*, No. 269, (June).

'What a Way to Go!'

12. This section is based on P. Nadal: 24/10/05 and 27/06/06; R. Moss: 19/10/04 and 16/02/05; M. Biancalani: 31/01/07; and the priest concerned: 21/10/03. The parishioners' plea to DEH not to move the priest is from an interview with A. Moss (not related to R. Moss): 18/06/04.

Farewell

13. This section is based on 'Thousands praise Hurley', *DN*, 25/11/91; and '10,000 at Durban prelate's farewell', *SC*, 08/12/91.

CHAPTER 28. CIVIL WAR

1. The main sources for this chapter were the *Truth and Reconciliation Commission of South Africa Report*, Vols 2, 3 and 5; Jeffery, A. J. (1997), *The Natal Story: Sixteen Years of Conflict* (Johannesburg: SA Institute of Race Relations); and Maré, G. (2000), 'Versions of resistance history in South Africa: The ANC strand in Inkatha in the 1970s and 1980s', in *Review of African Political Economy*, 27, (83), 63–79.

2. L. Mthethwa's assessment of Buthelezi and DEH's friendship in the early 1970s is from L. Mthethwa: 19/01/05.

3. DEH's assessment of Buthelezi in the 1970s is from a report, DEH/J. Mees: 09/10/85.

4. Diakonia's decisions regarding membership of the UDF and its delegation to Chief Buthelezi are from Diakonia Council Minutes, 1981–85, ADCC, as well as a press release provided by M. Volkmer which indicated that the latter had appeared in the *Frankfurter Algemeine Zeitung* on 20/11/80.

5. Information about van der Merwe's peacemaking is from his book, van der Merwe, H. W. (2000), *Peacemaking in South Africa: A Life in Conflict Resolution* (Cape Town: Tafelberg).

6. DEH's assessment of the ecumenical value of the NCLG is from DEH: 28/09/98.

7. Information about the DEH peace initiative of 1989 is from the correspondence file 'Natal/KwaZulu Peace Initiative', in the AAD.

8. The Anglican peace initiative of 1989 is from Nuttall, M. (2003), *Number Two to Tutu: A Memoir* (Pietermaritzburg: Cluster Publications). His comment on DEH's response is from 'Living in Heady Times', in Gamley, *Denis Hurley*. Erwin's comment about asking Hurley to intercede with Buthelezi is from A. Erwin: 06/07/04.

9. Buthelezi's letter to DEH on the fiftieth anniversary of his ordination as a priest is from *DN*, 31/07/89.

10. Letter to POH.

11. Information about the Seven Days' War and DEH's visit to Elandskop parish is from Smith, T. (1991), *They Have Killed My Children: One Community in Conflict 1983–1990* (Pietermaritzburg: Pietermaritzburg Agency for Christian Social Awareness); and from T. Smith: 16/02/05.

12. K. Mgojo's comments about DEH are from 'Umehlwemamba—The People's Bishop', in Gamley, *Denis Hurley*.

13. A. Jennings: 16/11/05.

14. DEH's comments about the Ulundi meeting with Buthelezi on 02/04/90 and the de Klerk meeting in Cape Town on 11/04/90 are from DEH/GM, 27/04/90.

15. Comments by DEH at the press conference after the de Klerk meeting are from 'Church leaders urge police impartiality', *SC*, 29/04/90.

16. M. Nuttall's comment on F. Chikane's intervention at the NCLG meetings in May 1989 is from email, MN/PK, 17/09/07. Chikane's comments are from F. Chikane: 13/09/07.

17. The statistic for the number killed in the violence is from email, GC/PK: 07/04/08.

18. Information about the IFP's last-minute participation in the elections of 1994 is from Cassidy, M. (1995), *A Witness for Ever: The Dawning of Democracy in South Africa; Stories behind the Story* (London: Hodder & Stoughton).

19. C. Gardner's views on the role of the 1994 election results in reducing violence are in email, CG/PK, 27/09/07.

CHAPTER 29. A. PAINFUL EXPERIENCE

1. The main sources of information about ICEL between 1991 and 2002 are the ICEL files in the OAC; J. Page: 06/09/04; J. Schellman: 01/06/05; M. Taylor: 12/09/04; as well as J. Wilkins (2005), 'Lost in Translation', *Commonweal*, (December); and an anonymous report 'ICEL and the Congregation: A History', 2000; as well as emailed comments, JP/PK, 24/08/07.

2. Comments about M. Estevez's motivation for reform of vernacular translation are from JP/DEH: 18/02/98. Nxumalo's comments on *Liturgiam Authenticam* are from J. Nxumalo: January 2005.

3. An important source of information about the clash between DEH and F. George at the ICEL meeting on 04/06/98 is 'George tells ICEL Rome wants change', *NCR*, 17/06/98.

4. DEH's response to F. George's presentation at the ICEL meeting of 04/06/98 is in the OAC; and DEH's letter of apology to F. George in the AAD.

5. A. Roche: 22/01/07.

6. DEH's comparison of *Liturgiam Authenticam* with *Sacrosanctum Concilium* can be found in Hurley, D., *Keeping the Dream Alive*, pp. 188–194.

7. DEH's correspondence with various friends about what happened to ICEL between 2001 and 2002 is from the OAC.

8. The account of Father I. Calabuig's address at St Anselmo is from JP/DEH, 15/06/04.

9. DEH's response to the Calabuig address is in DEH/RT, 09/01/03.

CHAPTER 30. THE PERFECT CHANCELLOR

1. Information about the 1992 problems at the University of Natal comes from Ramjathan, K. (1993), 'Straddling the Great Divide', *WM* (March); as well as from press clippings in the UKZN Archives, especially 'Tough year ahead for universities', *NM*, 13/02/93.

2. For the process surrounding Hurley's nomination as chancellor, see B. Gourley: 15/09/04; and C. Gardner/A. Moss, 15/08/04. Gourley's motivation for nominating Hurley is from *SC*, 08/11/92.

3. Comments by E. Ngara from E. Ngara: 27/10/03.

4. Hugo, C. B. (1993), in *Natal University Focus*, 4, (2).

5. DEH's interview with C. Rickard, 'Hurley's lifelong search for truth', appeared in *ST*, 07/03/93.

6. B. Gourley's article 'The Perfect Chancellor' appeared in Gamley, *Denis Hurley*.

7. The text of C. Gardner's 'Laudation' Address, 04/03/93, is from the UKZN Archives.

8. Hurley's installation address is from 'Time to cultivate a commitment to change', *NW*, 05/03/93.

9. Volmink's comments on DEH, especially his visit to the US, are from J. Volmink: 17/10/03.

10. 'Farewell, dear friend', *Natal University Focus*, 9, (3) 1998.

11. DEH's description of the 'reconciliation graduation' is from DEH/W&DL, (undated).

12. B. Gourley: 15/09/04.

CHAPTER 31. A BUSY RETIREMENT

1. DEH's move to Emmanuel Cathedral is described in DEH/GM, 11/01/93.

2. DEH's hints about going to the cathedral after his retirement are from H. Bechet: 26/12/03; as also comments about DEH's need to remain active, information about the Mass for people with impaired hearing, the French Mass for refugees and assistance to the Missionaries of Charity.

3. Trycinski's comments about DEH's energy and how he treated people with equal respect are from C. Trycinski: 17/06/05. Wood's comments on DEH 'coming off the pedestal' once he had retired are from B. Wood: 22/11/05.

4. Napier's comment about DEH in retirement is from W. Napier: 26/08/05.

5. The story about DEH visiting the Grey Street mosque is from G. Ardé's article 'Polishing Durban's Gems', in *TM*, 06/07/05; as well as a letter from E. Kajee, 22/04/04; and a telephonic interview with him: 22/10/06.

6. P. Meskin: 13/04/05.

7. D. Strydom: 23/12/03.

8. W. Steckling: 03/09/04.

9. K. Dowling's comments on DEH's leadership of the Justice and Peace Commission are from K. Dowling: 09/08/04; as also the account of DEH's speech at the celebration for W. Napier.

10. A. Green-Thompson's comment on DEH's high standards is from A. Green-Thompson: 30/08/04; as also his reflection on DEH's excitement about the RDP.

11. M. Kelly's comments on DEH's need to be intellectually convinced before he could speak out about issues are from M. Kelly: 27/05/05 and 28/05/05; as also her comments on Pope John Paul II's high regard for DEH.

12. DEH/POH, 22/05/94.

13. J. Pieterse: 10/03/06.

14. For the RDP, see ANC (1994), *The Reconstruction and Development Programme: A Policy Framework* (Johannesburg: Umanyano Publications).

15. S. O'Leary's report on DEH's response to the SACBC's hesitation in endorsing the RDP is from S. O'Leary: 07/09/04.

16. For discussion of GEAR, see Hirsch, A. (2005), *Season of Hope: Economic Reform under Mandela and Mbeki* (Pietermaritzburg: UKZN Press).

17. DEH's comment about the danger of high salaries, characteristic of the GEAR era, is from DEH/GM, 30/12/96.

18. T. Kneifel: 29/02/04.

19. N. Gabriel: 12/11/03.

20. DEH's concern about the 'Apartheid Debt' is from an address of 13/11/99 on the occasion of the Commonwealth Conference in Durban.

21. DEH's membership of the Church and Work Commission is from M. Hippler and G. Thie: 28/09/04; and J. Capel: 18/02/05.

22. The account of DEH completing the first 10,000 kms on his stationary cycle, is from DEH/W&DL, 20/07/94 and 07/09/94. In earlier years it is said that he used to do Canadian Air Force exercises every day.

23. Hans Küng's 'dream team' is listed on p. 334 of Küng, H. (2003), *My Struggle for Freedom* (translated by John Bowden) (London: Continuum).

25. DEH/J. Allen: 07/03/03.

24. J. Filochowski: 13/09/04.

CHAPTER 32. FAMILY

1. From a tribute by his nephew Jeremy at DEH's funeral on 28/02/04.

2. Jeremy Hurley, 28/02/04.

3. Jeremy Hurley, 28/02/04.

4. DEH's visit to Australia in 1980 is described in BH/EH, 29/04/80.

5. DEH's view of Adelaide is from DEH/EH, 21/04/85.

6. B. Hurley's discussion with DEH about contraceptives is in BH: 13/06/03; and Jeremy Hurley: 08/06/03.

7. UH's conversations with DEH and mention of dinners to which DEH was invited are in UH: 16/09/05.

8. JH: 08/06/03.

9. CH's resignation as headmaster of Thomas More College is from the 1978–79 box file on the College in AAD; as well as from UH: 16/09/05; and a telephonic conversation with former Thomas More staff member, P. McKay, on 14/09/07.

10. Information about J. Hurley's death and funeral is from DEH/POH, 21/01/96; and DEH/W&DL, 15/02/96.

11. DEH/H. Eccles: 18/08/03; as well as from notes prepared by DEH for order of service at Eileen's funeral.

12. M. Madden: 02/06/05.

13. Family impressions of how DEH changed in old age are from Eeva Hurley: 26/02/04; M. York: 26/01/04; and Jeremy Hurley: 08/09/05.

14. DEH's emphasis in his later years on the importance of love is from Jeremy Hurley: 08/09/05.

CHAPTER 33. 'THE DEPARTURE LOUNGE'

1. DEH/L. Towell, 07/05/02.

2. The report of DEH's desire to continue working at Emmanuel Cathedral is from A. Moss: 18/06/04; as also the account of DEH's life at Sabon House. See also G. Purves: 06/08/04.

3. I. Freoux: 28/06/04.

4. DEH's comment about writing his memoirs is from his email, DEH/GM, 18/03/03.

5. Information about the theft at Sabon House is from an email, DEH/UH&CH, 27/08/02. DEH's comment about how difficult the years 1965–92 would be to cover in his memoirs is from DEH/L. Stirton, 30/01/04.

6. C. Yeats: 24/05/05.

7. Comment about life at Sabon House is from DEH/GM, 21/05/03.

The Ordination of Women

8. J. Reeve's conversation with DEH about the ordination of women is from her email, JR/PK, 15/12/05.

9. DEH's response to D. Cormick's comment on women's ordination and various WOSA protests, is from D. Cormick: 17/02/04.

10. DEH's comment about women's ordination as a human rights issue is from DEH/C. Haupt, 25/11/02.

11 DEH's attendance at an ordination of women in the Anglican Church, from DEH/M. Hatchings, 08/01/03; and emails, DEH/D&POS: 31/12/02; and DEH/R. di Bella, 23/12/02.

Sant'Egidio

12. Information about Sant'Egidio is from an article by Offer, C. J., Archdeacon of Norwich, contained in DEH/R. di Bella, 02/05/03. Other information about the community and its relationship

to DEH is from L. Gianturco: 03/10/04; G. Ferretti and R. di Bella: 27/02/04 and 02/03/04; and Father M. Zuppi: 30/09/04.

13. DEH's account of his conversation with Pope John Paul II at an audience with the Sant'Egidio community is from emails, DEH/C. Trycinski, 01/04/03; DEH/G. and S. Chapman, 10/04/03.

14. HM/PK, 24/08/04.

15. DEH/S. Eakins, 02/11/03.

16. The account of DEH's visit to Mozambique is from DEH/D. Donnelly, 20/08/03.

17. W. Steckling's comments about DEH are from his 'Message to Cardinal Napier on the Death of Archbishop Hurley'; and from W. Steckling: 03/09/04.

18. Last days in Durban, G. Purves: 06/08/04.

19. D. Ciangio: 08/06/05.

20. Information about the tea with Sisters M. H. Keane and Catherina, from January 2005 and 22/12/04 respectively.

21. The diocesan priests' social function was described by P. Nadal: 24/10/05.

22. DEH's last trip from Durban North to Sabon House is from D. Butt's 'Archbishop Denis Hurley OMI: Final Moments'; and from D. Butt: 20/02/04.

'That Man Is with God Today'

23. D. Benjamin's story is from Harper, P., 'Man of God and his 'outie' friend', STrib, 29/02/04.

24. The extracts from messages received after DEH's death are adapted from those read at his funeral on 28/02/04.

25. The account of the Black Sash stand at the lying-in-state is from 'Women of Black Sash to stand again with Denis Hurley', TM, 27/02/04. Information about the all-night vigil is from S. Ndlovu: 13/10/07 and 15/10/07.

26. Details of the DEH funeral are from 'Archbishop Hurley laid to rest', Challenge (April/May 2004); and G. Purves (2004), 'Celebrating a life: The funeral service of Archbishop Denis Hurley OMI', unpublished article, DAC.

SELECT BIBLIOGRAPHY

Abbott, W. M. and Gallagher, J. (1967), *The Documents of Vatican II*. London: Geoffrey Chapman.

Abraham, G. (1989), *The Catholic Church and Apartheid: The Response of the Catholic Church in South Africa to the First Decade of National Party Rule, 1948–1957*. Johannesburg: Ravan.

Ackroyd, P. (1998), *The Life of Thomas More*. London: Chatto & Windus.

Alberigo, G. (1995, 1997, 2000, 2003, 2006), *History of Vatican II* (English version edited by J. A. Komonchak) (Vols 1–5). Maryknoll, NY: Orbis.

Allen, J. (2006), *Rabble-Rouser for Peace*. Johannesburg: Random House.

Allen, J. L. (2000), *Cardinal Ratzinger: The Vatican's Enforcer of the Faith*. New York: Continuum.

Archdiocese of Durban (1987), *Archbishop Hurley: Fortieth Anniversary as Bishop of Durban*. Durban: Archdiocese of Durban.

Archdiocese of Durban (1989), *Guardian of the Light: Tributes to Archbishop Denis Hurley OMI on the Golden Jubilee of His Priestly Ordination, 1939–1989*. Durban: Archdiocese of Durban.

Brain, J. B. and Bechet, H (1999), *So Well Thy Words Become Thee*. A Selection of the published writings of Archbishop Denis Hurley OMI, compiled in two unpublished volumes on the occasion of the 60th Anniversary of his Ordination to the Priesthood.

Brain, J. B. (1975), *Catholic Beginnings in Natal and Beyond*. Durban: T. W. Griggs & Co (Pry) Ltd.

Brain, J. B. (1982), *Catholics in Natal II 1886–1925*, Durban: Archdiocese of Durban.

Brockman, J. R. (1989), *Romero: A Life*. Maryknoll, NY: Orbis.

Brookes, E. H. (1997), *A South African Pilgrimage*. Johannesburg: Ravan.

Brown, W. E. (1960), *The Catholic Church in South Africa: From Its Origins to the Present Day*. London: Burns & Oates.

Burns, A. T. and Wales, S. (2006A), *Your Servant for Jesus' Sake: Essays in Honour of Bishop Kevin Dowling CSSR*. Merrivale, South Africa: Redemptorist Pastoral Publications.

Butler, C. (1999), *Basil Hume: By His Friends*. London: Fount.

Cassidy, M. (1995), *A Witness for Ever: The Dawning of Democracy in South Africa; Stories behind the Story*. London: Hodder & Stoughton.

Christie, P. (1990), *Open Schools: Racially Mixed Catholic Schools in South Africa, 1976–1986*. Johannesburg: Ravan.

Clarke, B. (2008), *Anglicans against Apartheid, 1936–1996*. Pietermaritzburg: Cluster.

Clingman, S. (2005), *Bram Fischer: Afrikaner Revolutionary*. Cape Town: David Philip.

Colenso, J. W. (1982), *Bringing Forth Light: Five Tracts on Bishop Colenso's Zulu Mission*. Durban: Killie Campbell Africana Library.

Collins, P. (ed.) (2001), *From Inquisition to Freedom: Seven Prominent Catholics and Their Struggle with the Vatican*. London: Continuum.

Dhupelia-Meshtrie, U. (2004), *Gandhi's Prisoner: The Life of Gandhi's Son, Manilal*. Cape Town: Khwela Books.

————. (2003), *Sita: Memoirs of Sita Gandhi: Growing Up at Phoenix and in the Shadow of the Mahatma*. Durban: Local History Museum.

Davenport, R. and Saunders, C. (2000), *South Africa: A Modern History*. London: Macmillan.

Denis, P. (ed.) (1997), *Facing the Crisis: Selected Texts of Archbishop Denis E. Hurley*. Pietermaritzburg: Cluster Publications.*

Desmond, C. (1971), *The Discarded People*. Harmondsworth: Penguin.

Fierez, M. (1974), *Cardijn*. London: Young Christian Workers.

Finn, P. C. and Schellman, J. M. (eds.) (1990), *Shaping English Liturgy: Studies in Honor of Archbishop Denis Hurley*. Washington, DC: Pastoral Press.

Fisher, D. (1965), *Archbishop Denis Hurley* (in the series 'The Men Who Make the Council'). Notre Dame, Indiana: University of Notre Dame Press.

Gamley, A. M. (ed.) (2001), *Denis Hurley: A Portrait by Friends*. Pietermaritzburg: Cluster Publications.

Gevisser, M. (2007), *Thabo Mbeki: The Dream Deferred*. Johannesburg: Jonathan Ball.

Gutierrez, G. (1993), *Las Casas: In Search of the Poor of Jesus Christ*. Maryknoll, NY: Orbis.

Hastings, A. (ed.) (1991), *Modern Catholicism: Vatican II and After*. New York: Oxford University Press.

Hebblethwaite, P. (1994), *John XXIII: Pope of the Council*. London: Fount.

————. (1993), *Paul VI: The First Modern Pope*. London: Harper Collins.

Hickey, D. J. and Doherty, J. E. (eds.) (2003), *A New Dictionary of Irish History from 1800*. Dublin: Gill & Macmillan.

Hickey, P. (1993), 'Famine, Mortality and Emigration: A Profile of Six Parishes in the Poor Law Union of Skibbereen, 1846–7', in O'Flanagan, P. and Bultimer, C. G. (eds.), *Cork: History and Society: Interdisciplinary Essays on the History of an Irish County*. Cork: Geography Publications.

Howard, A. (2005), *Basil Hume: The Monk Cardinal*. London: Headline.

Hughes, K. (1991), *The Monk's Tale: A Biography*. Collegeville, MN: Liturgical Press.

Hurley, D. E. (2005), *Vatican II: Keeping the Dream Alive*. Pietermaritzburg: Cluster Publications.

Hurley, D. E. and Cunnane, J. (eds.) (1967), *Vatican II on Priests and Seminaries*. Dublin and Chicago: Scepter Books.

Hyslop, J. (2004), *The Notorious Syndicalist: J. T Bain, a Scottish Rebel in Colonial South Africa*. Johannesburg: Jacana.

Johnson, E. A. (1992), *She Who Is: The Mystery of God in Feminist Theological Discourse*. New York: Crossroad.

Kairos Theologians (1985), *The Kairos Documents: A Theological Comment on the Political Crisis in South Africa (Third World Theology)*. London: Catholic Institute for International Relations; British Council of Churches.

---

*Note J. Brain's outstanding Bibliography of Hurley's writings pp. 256–282.

Kane-Berman, J. (1978), *Soweto: Black Revolt, White Reaction*. Johannesburg: Ravan.

Kearney, P. (ed.) (2006), *Memories: The Memoirs of Archbishop Denis E. Hurley OMI*. Pietermaritzburg: Cluster Publications.

Komonchak, J. A., Collins, M. and Lane, D. A. (eds.) (1992), *The New Dictionary of Theology*. Dublin: Gill & Macmillan.

Küng, H. (2003), *My Struggle for Freedom: Memoirs*. Translated by John Bowden. London: Continuum.

———. (2008), *Disputed Truth: Memoirs*. Translated by John Bowden. London: Continuum.

Kwitny, J. (1997), *Man of the Century: The Life and Times of Pope John Paul II*. New York: Henry Holt.

Linden, I. (1980), *The Catholic Church and the Struggle for Zimbabwe*. London: Spottiswoode Ballantyne.

Maré, G. and Hamilton, G. (1987), *An Appetite for Power: Buthelezi's Inkatha and the Politics of 'Loyal Resistance'*. Johannesburg: Ravan.

Noonan, P. (2003), *They're Burning the Churches*. Bellevue: Jacana Books.

Nuttall, M. (2003), *Number Two to Tutu: A Memoir*. Pietermaritzburg: Cluster Publications.

Oblates of Mary Immaculate (1982), *The Green and the Dry Wood*. Windhoek: Oblates of Mary Immaculate.

Ojakaminor, E. (1996), *Catholic Social Doctrine: An Introductory Manual*. Nairobi: Pauline Publications Africa.

Orkin, M. (1987), *Sanctions against Apartheid*. Cape Town: David Philip; London: Catholic Institute for International Relations.

Prior, A. (ed.) (1982), *Catholics in Apartheid Society*. Cape Town: David Phillip.

Rees, W. (ed.) (1958), *Colenso: Letters from Natal*. Pietermaritzburg: Shuter & Shooter.

Romero, O. (1993), *Archbishop Oscar Romero: A Shepherd's Diary*. Cincinnati: St Anthony Messenger Press.

Romero, O. (1988), *The Violence of Love*. San Francisco: Harper & Row.

Ryan, C. (1990), *Beyers Naudé: Pilgrimage of Faith*. Cape Town: David Phillip.

Southern African Catholic Bishops' Conference (1982), *Report on Namibia*. Pretoria: SACBC.

———. (1966, 1980, 1985, 1988, 1990), *The Bishops Speak* (Vols. 1–5). Pretoria: SACBC.

———. (1984), *Report on Police Conduct during Township Protests: August–November 1984*. Pretoria: SACBC.

Smith, T. (1991), *They Have Killed My Children: One Community in Conflict, 1983–1990*. Pietermaritzburg: Pietermaritzburg Agency for Christian Social Awareness.

Sobrino, J. (1989), *Archbishop Romero: Memories and Reflections*. Maryknoll, NY: Orbis.

Sparks, A. (1990), *The Mind of South Africa: The Story of the Rise and Fall of Apartheid*. Johannesburg: Jonathan Ball.

Speaight, R. (1968), *Teilhard de Chardin: A Biography*. London: Collins.

Third World Christians (1989), *The Road to Damascus: Kairos and Conversion*. London: CIIR and Christian Aid, Washington: Center of Concern.

Tolle, E. (2001), *The Power of Now*. London: Hodder & Stoughton.

TRC (1998), *Truth and Reconciliation Commission of South Africa Report*. Cape Town: Juta.

Yeats, C. (2005), *Prisoner of Conscience*. London: Random House.

INDEX

Aachen, Germany, 321
Abbeystrewery cemetery, Skibbereen, 3
abortion, 142, 307, 313
Abraham, Garth, 66, 335, 366
Abrahams, Mervyn, 144, 341
Absa Stadium (Durban), 326
Abyssinia (now Ethiopia), 33
Administrative Board of the Southern
    African Catholic Bishops' Conference, 55,
    64, 65, 76, 77, 82, 83, 99, 182, 201, 217,
    258, 305, 335, 345
Aida Parker Newsletter, 256
African Committee, Marian Congress, 61
African Methodist Episcopal Church, 197
African National Congress (ANC), 48, 57,
    58, 63, 68, 80, 88, 153, 196, 242, 298, 306,
    348, 351, 353
  ANC in exile, 210
  civil war, 275–288
  meeting with the ANC, 238–241
  banning, 89, 181, 241
  RDP policy, 306
  Robben Island, 10
  unbanning, 297
African National Congress Youth League, 57,
    63, 186,
Agagianian, Cardinal, 131, 340
Agnelo, Archbishop, 289
"Agricultural Exhibition Train", 15
Ahern, Barnabas, 144
AIDS Care Commission, Archdiocese of
    Durban, 271
Aitken, I.C. 248
Aitken, Marilyn, 193, 217, 346
Akal, Patrick, 116, 176, 339, 343
Albert Park, Durban, 62
Albino, Ronald, 48, 49, 334
Alfrink, Cardinal, 109
Aliwal Shoal (KwaZulu-Natal), 14
Allard, Bishop Marie Jean François OMI, 61
Allen, John, journalist on National Catholic
    Reporter, 310, 333, 353

Allen, John, biographer of Desmond Tutu,
    348
Amnesty International, 223
ANCYL see African National Congress
    Youth League
Angelicum (St. Thomas's Dominican
    University), 287
Anglican Church, 11, 57, 63, 72, 90, 197,
    203, 204, 205, 206, 244, 268, 282, 283,
    351, 354
Anglican Church schools, 73, 77, 90,197,
    203, 204, 205, 206, 244, 268, 282, 283,
    351, 354
Anglican Diocese of Namibia, 204
Anglican Provincial Synod, 282
Anglo-American empire, 88
Apartheid
  Bantu education, a cornerstone of, 72
  bishops' memorandum and meeting with
      P.W. Botha, 258
  Black priests' call concerning apartheid
      in the Catholic Church, 182–183
  change of heart by Church, 210
  debt, 308, 353
  entrenchment, 63
  evil, 83, 129, 210, 214
  existence in Durban, late 19th century,
      42–43
  gradualist position, 45, 50, 66, 67, 83, 86
  grand Apartheid plan, 70–71
  Namibia see Namibia
  opposition to, 80–91
  protest marches, 263–265
  repeal of certain laws, 208
  sanctions see sanctions
  school segregation, defying, 189–193
  Soweto uprising, 194–196
  strikes see strikes
  structural sin, 214
  war, resistance to, 199–207
  Whelan-Hurley conflict about, 128–133
Apostles' Creed, 294

Archbishop Denis E. Hurley Educational
  Fund, 301
Archbishop of Westminster (1955), 77
Archbishop of Sydney (1955), 77
Archbishop of Toronto (1955), 77
Archbishop's House (Innes Road, Durban),
  173, 175, 229, 281, 314
Archdiocese of Durban
  boycott of Republic Festival, 212
  direct mailing appeal for funds, 178, 257
  Follow Me process, 322
  Golden Jubilee, Hurley's, 268
  HIV/AIDS ministry, 269–271
  Hurley appointed archbishop, 59
  Napier installed as archbishop, 274
  Parish councils, establishment of, 147
  Pastoral council, establishment of, 147
  Hurley's resignation, pastoral letter
    announcing, 271
  Pastoral plan, implementation of, 265, 266
  People's Hymn Book, published by, 146
  pulpit exchange, 125
  Renew *see* Renew
  Synod, 1968, 148
  Synod, 1974, 196
Arenstein, Rowley, 279
Arinze, Cardinal, 295, 296
Aristotle, 114
Asiatic Land Tenure and Indian
  Representation Act of 1946, 43
Asmal, Kader, 326
Association for the Disabled, 304, 326
Association of Member Episcopal
  Conferences in Eastern Africa
  (AMECEA), 155, 342
Association of Men and Women Religious in
  the Archdiocese of Durban, 95
Association of Women Religious (AWR),
  189, 190, 192
Attorney-General of the Northern Transvaal
  (circa 1985), 226
Aubert, Roger, 101, 110

Baillargeon, Father Benny OMI, 324
Ballynacarriga Castle, West Cork, 4, 331
Balmes, Father Hilaire OMI, 37
Banks, Monsignor Marius OFM, 218
Bantu Administration Act, 1956, 81
Bantu Affairs Department, 149, 150
Bantu Authorities Act, 1951, 68

Bantu Education Act, 1953, 67, 71, 72, 74,
  75, 76, 77, 79
Bar Abbas (St Peter's), 119
Bar Jonah (St Peter's), 119
Basilica of Santa Maria, Trastevere, 320
Batzofin, Saul, 203
Baum, Gregory, 116
Bax, Douglas, 200
Bea, Cardinal Augustin, 111
Bechet, Huguette, 303, 304, 305, 319, 352
Beethoven, 146
Belgian Oblate Scholasticate, 29
Belmont House, Dublin, 26, 27, 28, 332
Benedict XVI, Pope, formerly Cardinal
  Ratzinger, 290, 291
Benjamin, Dirk, 324, 325, 355
Bergin, Sister Marie HF, 335
Bernardin, Cardinal Joseph, 145
Bester, Charles, 203
Biancalani, Father Massimo, 272, 350
Biko, Steve, 181, 182, 188, 195, 196, 343
Bill, François, 187
Birks, Moira, 146, 341
birth control,
  approval of rhythm method, 313
  Humanae Vitae, 134–138, 140, 157, 310
  Vatican II, 121, 124, 156
Birth Control Commission, 134, 138
Bishops' Conference of England and Wales,
  167
Bishops' Department of Catholic Schools,
  189, 193
Biyase, Bishop Mansuet, 218, 239
Black bishops, appointment of, 184
Black Consciousness Movement (BCM),
  181, 182–184, 187, 188, 193, 194, 195,
  196, 199, 250, 343, 344
Black education/schooling *see* Mission schools
Black Ecumenical Church Leaders'
  Consultation (BECLC), 249, 250
Black priests 182, 183
Black Priests' Solidarity Group, 193, 344
Black Prince (Ship), 5
Black Sash, 149, 150, 326, 355
black theology, 193
Boesak, Allan, 257, 285
Boipatong, Vaal Triangle, 234
Bokenfohr, Bishop John OMI, 77
Bonelle, Marie-Therese, 173
Boner, Sister Kathleen OP, 189, 190, 344

Bophelong, Vaal Triangle, 234
Bordeaux, 35
Border War, 199, 201, 202, 345
Botha, M.C., 149, 150
Botha, P.W., 209, 240, 257, 349
    accusations against Hurley, 202–203
    attitude towards Hurley 258, 259
    Minister of Defence, 200
    Namibian issue, 219, 220, 223, 224
    Rubicon speech, 241
    Southern African Catholic Bishops'
        Conference meeting with, 258
    State of Emergency, 257
    stroke and resignation, 264
Botman, Rev Russel, 326
Boulle, Father Eric OMI, 27, 170, 171, 173,
    230 329, 332, 339, 343, 347
Boyd, Leo, 56, 87, 203, 337
Boylan, Monsignor Anthony, 164, 342
Boyle, Bishop Hugh, 183
Brain, Joy, 309, 334
Breton priests, 43, 52, 53, 55, 267, 334
Briard, Jacques, 324
Brink, André, 177
British Commonwealth, 35, 89, 90, 241, 308,
    337, 353
Brittion, Sue, 249, 250, 251, 349
Brookes, Edgar, 90, 91, 337
Bruce, David, 203
Brutus, Dennis, 308
BTR-Sarmcol rubber factory, Howick, 231,
    232, 233, 347
Buffalo River Harbour (East London), 13
Bugnini, Father Annibale, 114
Burghardt, Father Walter SJ, 141, 142, 143,
    157, 341, 342
Butelezi, Archbishop Peter OMI, 153, 183,
    202, 218, 258
Buthelezi, Chief Mangosuthu, 351
    delayed involvement in 1994 elections, 287
    Inkatha 209, 275, 276, 277, 285
    KwaZulu-Natal Church Leaders' Group
        281, 285
    meeting with Anglican bishops, 282, 283
    Peace Conference, 1989, 281, 282
    Rally, King's Park, Durban, 1990, 284
    relationship with ANC, 186, 275, 276
    relationship with Diakonia, 276, 277, 278
    relationship with Hurley, 186, 275, 277,
        279, 282, 288, 326
    sanctions, 242
    South African Council of Churches, 285
Buthelezi Commission, 276
Butler, Christopher, Bishop OSB, 144
Butt, Father Derrick OMI, 323, 355

Cabon, Father Henri OMI, 52, 55, 334
Cabra Dominicans, 189, 190, 344
Cahermoyle, County Limerick, Ireland, 25,
    26, 27, 35, 332
Calabuig, Father Ignacio OSM, 295, 296, 352
Caledon Square police station, Cape Town, 89
Camara, Archbishop Helder, 154
Canevet, Father Ernest OMI, 170, 343
canon law, 148, 158, 271
Cape Dutch Reformed Church Synod, 188
Capel, John, 308, 353
Cape Point, Western Cape, 9–12, 331
Cape Point lighthouse, 9, 10, 331
Cape Recife, Cape Colony (Eastern Cape), 5,
    8, 10
Cape St Francis lighthouse, Cape Colony
    (Eastern Cape), 5
Cape Times (newspaper), 129, 191
Cape Town City Hall, 264
Cape Town Diocesan seminary, 154
capitalism, 32, 109, 307
Caprivi trainees, 279–280
Cardijn, Father Joseph, (Canon, Cardinal),
    32, 47, 245, 332
Cardinal Patriarch of Lisbon (1974), 158
Caritas (newsletter), 50, 335
Carnarvon Castle (ship), 24, 25
Carrington, Lord, 287
Carter, Bishop Alexander, 113
Cassari, Monsignor Mario, 259
Cassidy, Michael, 287, 351
Castel Gandolfo, Lazio, Italy. 33, 139
Castletownshend, West Cork, 4
Catechetics
    catechetical renewal course, 96
    children's books, 100
    Hofinger, Father Johannes SJ, see
        Hofinger, Father Johannes SJ
    Müller, Sister Theodula CPS see Müller,
        Sister Theodula
    new catechetics, 95–98, 101, 145, 146
    penny catechism, 95
    People of God series (Religious Education
        Programme), 212

Study Conference on Mission Catechesis, Eichstatt, 97
study weeks, 98–99
syllabus, 97, 98, 100, 101
Cathedral Mall, 304
Cathedral of the Holy Nativity (Pietermaritzburg), 287
Cathedral of the Sacred Heart (Bloemfontein), 133
Catherina, Sister OP, 322, 355
Catholic Action, 50, 58, 97, 108, 146
Catholic African Teachers' Federation, 75
Catholic African Union (CAU), 46, 69, 74,
Catholic Bishops' Campaign, 77, 78, 79, 185, 212, 336
Catholic schools
  Bishops' Department of Catholic Schools, 189
  children of black diplomats admitted, 189–190
  financial crisis, 185
  focus on white education, 189
  integration, 189–193
  Pope Paul VI's support for open schools, 192
  religious instruction, 100
  Springfield Convent (Cape Town), 190, 344
Catholic Fund for Overseas Development (CAFOD), 153, 310, 319
Catholic Herald (newspaper), 129, 340, 346
Catholic Institute for International Relations (CIIR), 153, 217, 227, 243, 276, 346, 347, 348
Catholic Men's Society, 44
Catholic Schools' Association, 97
Catholic Students' Mission Crusade, 78
Catholic Theological Union of Chicago, 309
Catholic University of America, 145
Cato Manor, (KwaZulu-Natal), 58, 85, 86, 88, 336
Cawcutt, Father (later Bishop) Reginald, 207, 345
Celebration Hymnal, 146
celibacy, 36, 124, 136, 137, 138, 140, 141, 156, 157, 310, 341, 342
Central Preparatory Commission (CPC), 91, 101, 108, 109–113, 115, 136 338, 339
Cetshwayo, King, 278
Chalcedon, 106

Challenge, (Catholic periodical), 130
Chapman, Geoffrey, 33, 97, 99, 100, 165, 169, 170, 222, 330, 332, 337, 340, 342, 343, 347, 355
Chapman, Mrs. (dressmaker), 7
Chapman, Sue, 33, 99, 332, 337, 355
chastity, 26, 36, 96
Chenu, Marie-Dominique OP, 107, 111, 117, 339
Cheshire Home, 315
Chicago, 301
Chikane, Rev Frank, 249, 263, 286, 325, 351
Children of Mary, 45
Christ the King Cathedral, Johannesburg, meeting at, 220
Christian Council of South Africa (later SACC), 64
Christian Institute, 149, 151, 188, 200, 244
Christian-Muslim relations, 304
Christian National Education (Nationalist Policy), 68
Christian Social Union (Bavaria), 215
Christians for Justice and Peace, 99, 212, 245, 247–251, 263, 349
Church as the Body of Christ, 27, 35, 101, 108
Church and Work Commission, 308, 309, 353
Church Clause, 81–83
Church in the Modern World, The (Gaudium et Spes), 104, 121, 123, 132, 148, 245
Ciangio, Sister Donna OP, 266, 322, 350, 355
civil disobedience
  admission of black children to schools, 191, 193
  after 1950–1951 legislation introduced, 63
  bishops threaten, 201
  church, 83
  Gandhian non violent methods, 68
  1960, 89
  Pacem in Terris of John XXIII, and, 132
  Standing for the Truth campaign, 264
Clansthal, South Coast (KwaZulu-Natal), 13–16, 17, 21, 331
Clark, Caroline, 201
Clarke, R.G., 336
Clayton, Archbishop Geoffrey, 82
Cobh, Cork, 5

Coetsee, Kobie (Minister of Justice), 224
Coetzee, Lieutenant Colonel Ignatius, 254
Colgan, Father John, 10
Collaco, Archbishop Blasco, 326
collegiality, 120–122, 137, 141, 152, 154, 156, 157, 160, 164–165, 229, 244, 292, 293, 295
Collins, Colin, 97, 130, 131, 329, 336, 340
Collins, Kitty, 6
Colosseum, 29, 33
Comme le prévoit, 291, 292, 294
Committee of Church Representatives on Bantu Resettlement, 149, 150
condoms, 270
Commonweal (publication), 101, 293, 338, 352
Commonwealth Conference, Durban, 1999, 308, 353
communism, 32, 34, 48, 63, 80, 81, 87, 122, 154, 202, 213, 215, 219, 239, 240, 258, 259, 264, 265
Community of Sant'Egidio, 319–322, 323, 326, 354, 355
Community Serving Humanity, 247, 265–269, 273, 350
Conference of the Presidents, 283
Congar, Father Yves OP, 107, 111, 117, 339
Congregation for Divine Worship (CDW). 162, 163–165, 166, 167, 168, 289, 290, 291, 292, 293, 294, 295
Congregation for the Doctrine of the Faith (CDF), 104, 121, 158, 162, 290, 291, 295, 321
Congregation for the Evangelization of Peoples, 273
"Congregation for love", 321
Congregation for Seminaries and Universities, 113
Congregation of Rites, 168
Congress Alliance, 80, 86
Congress for a Democratic South Africa (CODESA), 91
Congress of Democrats, 80
Congress of South African Trade Unions (COSATU), 281, 282, 283
Congress of the People, 80–81, 86
Conscientious objection, 200–207, 318, 345
Conscientious Objector Support Group (COSG), xi, 203, 206
conscription, 199, 203, 206, 207, 345

Constantine, 123
Constantinople, 106, 107
Constitution on the Sacred Liturgy (Sacrosanctum Concilium) (1963), 121, 145, 168
Contact (Liberal Party newsletter), 77
Convocation of Churches in South Africa, 1988, 263
Cooke, Tony, 170, 178, 343, 347
Coopération Internationale pour le Développement et la Solidarité (CIDSE), 225
Coovadia, Ishmael, 239
Corcoran, Cathy, 153, 342
Cormick, Dina, 319, 345, 354
Coughlan, Father Noel OMI. 62, 144
Council of Trent (1545 to 1563), 106,109
Crimean War, 4
Criminal Law Amendment Act, 68
Cromwell, Oliver, 4
Cronin, Peter Paul OMI, 29
Crowe, Sarah, 237, 347, 349
Cullen, Bishop A.H., 125
Cullen, Archbishop Paul 4
cultural boycott, 241
Curran, Charles, 144
Currin, Brian, 222, 223, 226, 227, 347
Cyprian, 211

Daily Dispatch (East London) (newspaper), 130
Daily News (Durban) (newspaper), 213
Dainty, Harold, 18, 330, 332
Damiano, Archbishop Celestine, 83
Danger Point lighthouse, 4, 6
Daniel, Archbishop George, 210, 218, 258
Danker, Father Albert OMI, 43, 101, 135, 174, 333, 334, 341
Daughters of Charity, 325
Davis, Thurston, 116
Dawjee, (Projectionist), 18
Day, Dorothy, 123
de Bruyn, Trevor, 187
Declaration of Commitment on Social Justice and Race Relations within the Church, 246
Defiance Campaign in 1952 (ANC), 68, 264
Defiance Campaign in 1989 (MDM), 264
Defence Further Amendment Bill, 201
de Gersigny, Geoff OMI, 339
de Klerk, F.W., 220, 264, 283, 285, 351

de Klerk, Colonel P.J., 205
Delalle, Bishop Henri OMI , 18, 22, 24, 25, 26, 43, 51, 52, 53, 54, 55, 325, 334
Delease, Leslie, 19, 20
De Lourdes, Sister Marie OP, 54, 334
de Mazenod, Bishop Eugene of Marseilles, 29
de Mazenod Circle, 29
Denis, Philippe OP 108, 113
Denis Hurley Centre, 58, 304
de Paoli, Archbishop Ambrose, 324
Derby-Lewis, Clive, 213, 346
Desmond, Father Cosmas OFM, 149–152, 244, 334
De Sylva, R., 334
detainees, 89, 187, 197, 209, 218, 229, 235, 236, 252–254, 257, 298
de Valera, Éamonn, 12
Development and Peace, Canadian Catholic Organisation for, 213
de Villiers, Andrè, 125
de Villiers, F.J., 73
Devitt, Father Brian OMI, 50
Devonport, England, 5
Dhlomo, Oscar, 283
Di Bella, Roberta, 321, 332, 354, 355
Diocesan AIDS Committee (later Commission), 269, 270
Diocesan Pastoral Council, 147, 148, 327
Diakonia Centre, 278
Diakonia Council of Churches, 175, 279, 326, 330, 345 347
    boycott of Republic Festival 212
    Brittion, Sue 249–250
    Buthelezi, Chief Mangosuthu and, 276, 277, 278, 351
    Christians for Justice and Peace, 249, 250
    constitution, 197
    establishment of, 196–198, 345
    Housing Programme 277–278
    inaugural meeting, 197
    Inkatha, relationship with 277–278
    Mdluli, Joseph, call for judicial inquiry into death, 197
    UDF, relationship with 277–278, 351
    victims of violence, 278
    worker rights statement, 229, 347
    Yeats, Charles, employed by, 204
Dias, Bartholomew, 9
Diekmann, Godfrey, 144

Dladla, Philip, 231, 232, 233, 347
Dlamini, Kuzwayo Jacob, 234
Dludla, B.K., 278
dock worker strike, 1971, 185
Dodd, Celia, 331
Dominican Sisters, 15, 17, 21, 22, 34, 54, 145, 172, 315
Doms, Father Heribert, 123
Donnelly, D., 355
Dowling, Father Kevin CSSR (now bishop), 193, 270, 305, 306, 310, 353
Drakensberg Mountains, 17, 19, 173
Draper, Sarah, 7
Drinan, Father Robert SJ, 224, 309, 347
Dublin, 26, 27, 28, 309
Dun Laoghaire, port of Dublin, 26
Dunlop Rubber Plant (Durban), 46
Durban Central United Church, 197
Durban City Council, 43, 48, 56, 85, 86, 264
Durban City Hall, 55, 62, 91, 125, 126, 264, 309, 325, 340
Durban Exhibition Centre, 273
Durban Fire Brigade, 327
Durban Parliamentary Debating Society, 86, 188, 336, 344
Durban Point Prison, 45–46
Durrant, Geoffrey, 48, 330, 334
Durwell, Father Xavier CSSR, 101
Dutch Reformed Church (DRC), xi, 67, 68, 188, 244

Eakins, S., 355
East Asian Pastoral Institute, Manila, 99
East London West Bank Government School (Eastern Cape), 13
Eastern Church, 106
Eberhard, Anton, 203
Eccles, Hugh, 45, 333, 354
Ecclesiam Suam, 141
economic sanctions, see sanctions
Ecumenical Centre (now Diakonia Centre), Durban, 278
Ecumenical Councils, 139, 340
Ecumenism, 125–126, 139
Edendale, 280, 284, 285, 286
Education Council of Association of Religious (ECAR), 190, 192
Edwards, Brian, 256, 349
Eichstatt, Germany, 97, 99, 107, 112, 337
Eiselen, Werner, 70, 71, 73, 336

Eiselen Commission, 1951 70–71, 73
Elandskop, (KwaZulu-Natal), 284, 351
Elizabeth, Queen, Consort of George VI, 55
Elizabeth, Princess, 55
Emmanuel Cathedral, Durban, 33, 42, 47,
    49, 50, 58, 236, 298, 333, 347. 352, 354
    Archbishop Hurley, installation of, 62
    bilingual mass, introduction, 303
    demographics, 303
    Evening of reflection on the Death of
        Joseph Mduli, 198
    funeral of Archbishop Hurley, 325–327
    interfaith service in, 264
    Junior curate (Hurley), 41, 52
    1940s, 43
    Parish priest, Hurley as, 300, 302, 305,
        317
    radio sermon from, 202
    trade union meeting in, 230
    white parishioners, dominated by, 43,
        303
    withdrawal of charges against Hurley,
        announcement, 224
Emmanuel Church, Unit 14, Sebokong, 236
Enda, Sister OP, 17
End Conscription Campaign (ECC), xi, 206,
    345
English College, Rome, 118
Ennis, Father Hyacinth OFM, 145, 341, 346
Entraide et Fraternité, Belgium, 213
Ephesus, 106
Erwin, Alec, 229, 230, 283, 347, 351
Eshowe diocese, (KwaZulu-Natal), 72, 73
Essery, Etienne, 203
Estévez, Cardinal Jorge Arturo Medina, 291,
    295, 352
Esztergom, Administrator of, 158
Etchagaray, Cardinal Roger, 155
Ethics Centre. University of Natal, 300
Evangelical Lutheran Church, 149, 197, 276,
    325
Evangelii Nuntiandi, 156
Evaton, Vaal Triangle, 234

Fabricius, Hans, 222, 227
Faith sharing groups, 266, 303
False Bay, Western Cape, 9
Familiaris Consortio, 156
Family Protection Scoreboard, (Magazine),
    257, 349

Farr, Charlie, 20
Fascism, 32, 34
Faurè, Ray, 225
Feast of Mary's Immaculate Conception,
    Rome, 1933, 31
Feast of St. Denis, 223
Federal Theological Seminary, Imbali, 280
feminist theology, 145, 290,
Fenian Movement, 4, 6, 28
Ferretti, Don Giorgio, 320, 321, 355
Fianna Fáil Party (Ireland), 12
Filochowski, Julian, 310, 353
Fitzgerald, Archbishop Joseph OMI, 33, 136,
    152, 153, 157, 158, 192, 203
Fitzsimmons, Father John, 162, 164, 166, 342
Flanagan, Father, 13
Flanagan, Sister Brigid HF, 96, 223, 336, 344
Florian, Brother FMS, 23–24
"Follow Me" process, 322
Fons Vitae, educational institute for nuns,
    144
forced removals, 85, 149–151
The Forum, Rome, 29, 30
Fowler, Mary, 162, 342
Fox, Tom, 342
Frances, Sister Jane OP, 193, 201
Franco, General Francisco, 33, 34
Frankfurter Allgemeine Zeitung, 276
Fransen, Piet, 144
Fratres Maristae a Scholis (Marist Brothers),
    see Marist Brothers
Freedom Charter, 80–81
Freedom March, Durban, 264
Freeman, Cardinal, 158, 159
Frelimo (liberation movement,
    Mozambique), 199
Freoux, Father Isidor OMI, 317, 334, 354
Frere Road Presbyterian Church, 125
Friends of the Soviet Union, 48
Frings, Cardinal Joseph, 109, 120, 121, 215
The Furrow (Irish Theological Journal), 101,
    112, 113
Fulda, Germany, 214

Gabriel, Neville, 308, 353
Gandhi, Ela, 309. 325
Gandhi, Mahatma, 68, 230, 325
Gandhi Settlement, 230
Gardner, Colin, 288, 298, 299, 329, 337, 348,
    351, 352

Garner, Bishop, later Archbishop, John, 64, 82, 83, 126, 135, 183, 340
Gastrow, Peter, 224, 347
Gaybba, Brian, 243, 339
Geneviève-Marie, Sister OSA, 103, 117, 332, 338, 339, 351, 352, 353, 354
Genoa, 321
George, Cardinal Francis OMI, 291. 292, 293, 252
George VI, King, 55
Georgetown University, Washington, DC, 266, 315
German Catholic Bishops' Conference, 215
German Synod, 1975, 215
Gervais, Father Jacques OMI, 30, 36, 332
Ghetto Act, 43
Gianturco, Leone, 320, 355
Gillick, Father John SJ, 144
Girls' Collegiate, Pietermaritzburg, 49
Glencree, Wicklow Hills, Ireland, 28
Gleneagles Agreement, 241
Goemans, Loek, 203, 345
Goldstone, Judge Richard, 300
Goodwin, Mrs W.M., 20
Grail, The, 193, 217
Gregorian chant, 54, 124
Gottschalk, Bishop Manfred, 218, 219, 220
Gourley, Brenda, 298, 299, 300, 301, 309, 352
Grandin, Bishop Vital OMI, 310
Graphic, The, magazine, 13
Gray, Mr., 14
Green, Bishop Ernest, 98
Green-Thompson, Ashley, 306, 353
Gregorian University, 31, 32, 35
Grey Street, Durban, 57, 58
Grey Street Mosque (Juma Musjid), Durban, 303, 325, 353
Greyville Racecourse, 62
Grimshaw, Archbishop Francis, 117, 118, 119
Group Areas, 42–43, 82, 149
Group Areas Act of 1950, 43 63, 68, 82, 127, 208
Growth, Employment and Redistribution (GEAR), 59, 307, 353
Guild of Our Lady of Mercy, 45
Gumede, Archie, 279

Hallinan, Archbishop Paul J., 116, 117, 118, 119, 339
Hambanathi, KwaZulu-Natal, 277, 278

Hammanskraal, 182, 183, 194, 199, 201, 246, 345
Hands, Miss (teacher) 11
Hani, Chris. 213
Harare, 154, 155, 156, 168, 342
Häring, Bernard CSSR, 144
Harris, Cyril, Chief Rabbi, 325
Hartubise, Pierre OMI, 116, 117, 339
Hastings, Adrian, 144, 339, 342
Hathorn, Peter, 203
Haushiku, Bishop Bonifatius, 220
Havenga, Nicolaas, 28
Hebblethwaite, Peter, 122, 157, 158, 159. 160, 310, 339
Hennemann, Bishop Francis SAC, 63, 335
Henriot, Father Pete SJ, 155–156, 342
Henriques, A.C. OMI, 333, 340
Henry, Brother FMS (St. Charles College, Pmb.), 24
Hertzog, James Barry Munnik, 28
Heunis, Chris, 258
Hibberdene, Natal (KwaZulu-Natal), 15, 192
Hickey, Mother Geneviève OP, 190, 344
Hiddingh Hall, Cape Town, 127
Higgins, Eddie, 148, 341
Hill, Father Francis OMI, 55, 59, 62
Hilton College, KwaZulu-Natal, 203
Hinwood, Father Bonaventure OFM, 340
Hippler, Michael 154, 342, 353
Hirmer, Bishop Oswald, 98, 100, 247, 337, 349
hit-squad activities, 280
Hitler, Adolf, 33, 36, 56, 333
HIV/AIDS, 269–271, 320, 321, 350
HMS Pearl (ship), 5
HMT Devonshire (ship), 41
Hobart, Tasmania, 117
Hoechst (Company, Germany), 215
Hoernlé Memorial Lecture, 127, 128, 129, 130, 340
Höffner, Cardinal Joseph, 215
Hofinger, Father Johannes SJ, 97–99, 337
Holland, Father Patrick OMI, 17, 18, 34, 47, 50, 51, 54, 125, 126, 330, 332, 337, 340
Holy Office, now Congregation for the Doctrine of the Faith (CDF), 102, 103, 121, 338, 339
Holy Rosary Convent, Port Elizabeth, 191
Hood (battle cruiser), 13
Hood Point lighthouse, 12–13

House of Assembly, SA, 150
Howell, Father Clifford SJ, 101, 146
Huddleston, Father Trevor, 57, 301
Hudson, Norman, 187, 344
Hughes, Ralph, 25, 26
Hughes, Sister Kathleen RSCJ, 164, 342
Hugo, C.B., 298, 352
Hugo, Father Charles OMI, 18, 19
Humaine, Antoine OMI, Canadian, 36
Humanae Vitae, 134–143, 157, 158, 310, 340
Humanisme Integrale, by Jacques Maritain, 101, 121
Hume, Cardinal Basil, 158, 159, 167, 342
Hurley, Bobbie, 173, 312, 313, 329, 330, 342, 347, 348, 349, 354
Hurley, Christopher (Chris) (b.1922), 11, 15, 17, 22, 25, 173, 311, 312, 314, 315, 325, 329, 331, 332, 354
Hurley, Denis (grandfather), 3, 4
Hurley, Denis (father), b.1880, 4, 5, 7, 8, 11, 311
Hurley, Denis (nephew), 314–315
Hurley, Archbishop, Denis Eugene
    AMECEA, participation in Vatican-
        sponsored meeting, 155
    admiration for Teilhard de Chardin, 102–104
    anti-Hurley smears, 256–257
    appointed archbishop, 59
    Archbishop Denis E. Hurley Educational
        Fund established, 301
    attitude towards creation, 103
    Bantu Education Act, concern about, 72
    Bantu Resettlement, chair of committee
        on, 149
    belief in intellectual freedom, 104
    Belmont House, 28–29
    birth, 10
    birth control, 156, 313
    bishop-designate, 53
    Bishops' Church and Work Commission,
        board member of, 308
    black bishops, appointment of, 184
    Black Sash, honorary member of, 326
    Border war, 201–202
    Botha, P.W., meeting with, 1986, 258–259
    Buthelezi, Chief Mangosuthu, friendship
        with, 186, 275, 277
    Catechetical and Liturgical Commission,
        appointed to chair, 97

catechetical article in *The Furrow*, 101, 112, 113
    catechetical renewal, 96–100
    Catechetics and Education Department,
        chair of, 146
    Catholic African Union, address to
        regional council, 69
    Catholic Students' Mission Crusade,
        address, 78
    Catholic Theological Union of Chicago,
        honorary doctorate (1993), 309
    Cato Manor, rezoning of, 85–86
    celibacy, call to be made optional, 136
    Central Preparatory Commission,
        appointment to, 108
    Chancellor of the University of Natal,
        298–301, 309
    charges against Hurley for remarks about
        Koevoet, 220–226, 237
    Charles Yeats's defence witness, 205
    Chenu and Congar, relationship with, 117
    Christians for Justice and Peace *see*
        Christians for Justice and Peace
    civil claim against Minister of Law and
        Order and Justice, 226–227
    clash with Whelan regarding apartheid,
        128–133
    collegiality, 137–138, 141
    Commission on Seminaries, Academic
        Studies and Catholic
        Education, elected to, 112–113
    communism, attitude towards, 265
    Community of Sant'Egidio, relationship
        with, 319–322
    Community Serving Humanity, vision
        document, 269
    Congregation for Doctrine of the Faith,
        summoned to meet with, 158
    conscientious objectors, support for, 201,
        206–207
    death, 323–324
    Desmond, Cosmas, support for, 151–152
    detention of Paddy Kearney, 252–255
    detentions, visit to head of security
        police, Frans Steenkamp, 187
    Development and Peace, guest of, 213
    Diakonia, founder and first chairperson
        of, 196–197, 299
    Diocesan Pastoral Council, establishment
        of, 147, 148

Diocesan Synod, establishment of, 147–148

Disabled, Association for the, 304, 326

disagreement with Whelan over Catholic mission schools, 74

dock workers, 1971, support for, 184–185

East London, 13

Ecumenical acts of witness, Durban City Hall, 125–126

Eichstatt address, 97, 107, 112

Emmanuel Cathedral
  installation as Archbishop, 62
  junior curate, 41–47
  lying in state, 325–326
  parish priest, 302

embarrassment about sexual matters, 174, 177, 270

Entraide et Fraternité, Belgium (1988), guest of, 213

episcopal ordination, 54–55

farewell as archbishop, 273

father and mother's deaths, 148

first Mass, 34, 324

Freedom March, Durban, 1989, 264–265

Freedom of the City of Durban, 309, 324, 325

Freedom of the City of Pietermaritzburg, 309

French (Breton) priests unsupportive of Hurley's initiatives, 52, 53, 55, 267

fund raising tour of Europe and North America, 59

HIV/AIDS ministry, 269–271

Hoernlé Memorial lecture, 127, 128

honorary doctorate, Georgetown University, 266, 315

honours and awards, 309

GEAR, criticism of, 307

golden jubilee celebration of Hurley's ordination, 282, 288, 309

government attitude toward Hurley, 258

Humanae Vitae statement, 135–136

Hurley, Chris, dismissal from Thomas More School, 314–315

hymns composed by, 146, 327

ICEL, 295
  participation and leadership, 119, 161–169

special award, University of Notre Dame's Centre for Pastoral Liturgy, 1989, 164

resignation. 295

IMBISA, participation in 153–155

Jubilee 2000 SA Campaign, patron of, 308

Justice and Peace Commission, chair of, 305–306

Kolbe winter school, address, 69

Koornhof, Piet, meeting with, 192

KwaThintwa School for the Deaf, 172, 326, 343

KwaZulu-Natal Church Leaders' Group, praise for, 280–281

language skills, 117

last days in Durban, 322–324

lay ministries, promotion of, 146–147

Limehill forced removals, opposition to, 149–152

liturgy, stickler for correctness, 146

majority rule, 195

Marian Congress, 61

Mandela, Nelson
  Hurley attends presidential inauguration of Nelson Mandela, 306
  message sent to Hurley via Archbishop Stephen Naidoo, 223

Mass of the Resurrection for Hurley, 326

Mass of the Rubber Bullet, Sebokeng, 236–237

meeting with black priests, protesting about how they were treated by Catholic Church 1970, 182

memoirs, writing, 16, 63, 309, 317

migrant labour debate, Durban Parliament, 188

Misereor, 1983, guest of, 213

mission schools, handing over to KwaZulu authorities, 186

Natal Convention, involvement in, 90

Natal Peace Committee, co-chair, 286

Namibia, leads SACBC delegation to, 217–219

Namibia report, addressed gathering at Cathedral of Christ the King, Johannesburg (1983), 220

Notre Dame University, address, 78

novice, 26–28

Oblate Scholasticate, superior of, 47–51

Open School Movement, leadership of, 192

opposition to armed struggle of ANC, 287

opposition to civil war in KwaZulu-Natal, 287

opposition to the Church Clause, 82–84

Order of Merit of the Italian Republic, 1997, 309

Order of St John, enrolled as Chaplain in 1997, 309

ordination as priest, 34

ordination of women, support for, 298, 319

overseas visit, 1956, 83

papal primacy, 114, 120, 137, 138, 139, 141

parish councils, establishment of, 147

Pastoral Institute, chair of. 144

pastoral planning and, 246–247, 263, 265, 267, 269

Paul Harris Fellow (Rotary Foundation), named 1998, 309

People of God series, 100

People's Hymn Book published, 146

personal attributes, 171–178, 273

Philip Tobias, friendship with, 103–104

Pilgrimage for Family Life, involvement in, 188

police, approach to, 237

Police Conduct during Township Protests, report on, 235

Pope John XXIII, audience with, 1959, 107

Pope John Paul II
    audience with, 310, 321
    high regard for Hurley, 310
    meal with Hurley, 159

Pope Paul VI
    audience with, October, 1968, 137
    correspondence with, 136–141

Pope Pius, XII
    audiences with, 78, 107
    coronation, 34

position regarding Vatican II, 160

preparation for Vatican II, 101

prophetic leadership
    ANC, meeting, 238–241
    apartheid war, opposition to, 199–207
    Christians for Justice and Peace, 247–251

Diakonia, establishment of and involvement with, 196–198

leading the bishops, 208–215

migrant labour, pilgrims against, 187–188

Namibia, 216–217

Paddy Kearney, support for release of, 252–255

pastoral planning, 245–247

police conduct in townships, Hurley's response to 234–237

price of prophecy, 256–259

sanctions, 241–244

school segregation, defying, 189–193

security police, confronting, 186–187

Soweto, 1976, 194–196

strikes, 1973, 184–185

support for workers, 228–233

qualified franchise, support for 86–87

RDP, enthusiasm for, 306–307

racial prejudice
    as a school boy, 25
    as a novice, 28
    how difficult it was to overcome, 58
    reacting against a fascist way of treating people, 33
    overcoming prejudice through meeting other students in Rome, 35

radio sermon, 202

Renew, launch and implementation of, 265–269, 282

Republic celebrations, pastoral letter regarding 212–213

resignation 271

retirement, 302–310

Robben Island, 11–12

Roman Missal, revision of, 162, 289, 290, 292, 295

Rome, studies in, 29–37

Roomse gevaar pamphlet, 68

Sabon House, life at, 317–318

SACBC delegation to Lusaka, 239–241

SACBC chair (later titled president), 97

SACBC president, 210–212

SAIRR, appointed president of, 127

SAIRR (Durban), address, 69

sanctions and, 241–244

Skibbereen, visit to, 26

South Africa's Order of Meritorious Service (Class 1), awarded 1999, 309

Southern Cross, writings in, 15, 58, 135, 144

Soweto crisis, SACC address on need for peace mobilization, 194

St Charles's College, Pietermaritzburg, 22–24

St Paul's University, Ottawa, honorary doctorate, 1996, 309

St Thomas's Boys' School, 17–20

St. Elmo's Convent, 15–17

Study Conference on Mission Catechesis, address, 97

Synods of Bishops
    elected in 1967, 1974, 1977, 1980, 1985 to attend, 156, 157
    Hurley's opinion of, 159, 160

Tambo, Oliver, meeting with, 238–239

Theological Issues, article in, 143

township unrest and, 234–237

trade unions and, 227–233

tributes, 309, 324–326

UDF-Inkatha meeting at Hurley's home, 279

Vatican II, *see also* Vatican 11
    appointment to the CPC, 124
    clerical celibacy, 124
    Commission on Seminaries, Academic Studies and Catholic Education, 112, 113
    disarmament, 124
    implementing decrees of, 144–160
    inaugural meeting of CPC, 91
    oral interventions at Second Session, 120
    prominence at, 114
    religious freedom, 120, 123
    submission of agenda suggestions, 107–108

vernacular Mass, introduction of, 144–145

Verwoerd, Hendrik, meeting with, 75–76

Yeats, Charles, support for, 203–204

Hurley, Eeva, 354

Hurley, Eileen, 5, 8, 10, 13, 15, 16, 17, 18, 21, 22, 24, 41, 48, 148, 311, 312, 315, 331, 332, 342, 354

Hurley, Helena (*née* O'Driscoll) (b.1895), 4

Hurley, Jeremiah (Jerry) (b.1929), 11, 14, 15, 17, 22, 25, 41, 89, 173, 311, 312, 315, 330, 333, 342, 348, 349, 354

Hurley, Jeremy (b.1951), 152, 313, 316, 353, 354

Hurley, Mikaela (York), 315, 321, 331

Hurley, Theresa May (*née* O'Sullivan), 3, 6, 7, 8, 10, 11, 12, 311

Hurley, Randall, 4

Hurley, Ursula, 173, 312, 313, 314, 315, 330, 354

Hurley and Another v The Minister of Law and Order, 252–255, 297–298

Hurley Family Chronicle, 5, 6, 331

Hurth, Father Franz SJ, 35, 123

Huss, Father Bernard CMM, 46

Hymn of the Universe by Teilhard de Chardin, 102

Ich will ein Mensch sein campaign, 213–215

Imbali, 280

Immorality Act, 208

Immorality Amendment Act, 63

Incandu River, KwaZulu-Natal, 17, 19

Inchanga mission, KwaZulu-Natal, 42, 43, 333

Inchindreen, West Cork, 4, 5, 7, 331

Industrial and Commercial Workers' Union of Africa (ICU), 46, 63, 333

Inkamana, KwaZulu-Natal, 72

Inkatha , 209, 231, 252, 275–285, 287, 288, 343, 351

Inkatha Freedom Party (IFP), xi, 280, 286, 287, 288, 298, 351

Inter-diocesan Tribunal, Durban, 272,

International Commission on English in the Liturgy (ICEL),117–119, 161–169, 212, 289–294, 295, 301, 315, 318, 323, 339, 342, 343, 352,
    advisory committee, 161–164, 166, 167
    approbatio, 164
    board, 164
    chair of for 16 years, 161, 162
    collegiality, a characteristic of, 164, 165
    Congregation for Divine Worship and, *see* Congregation for Divine Worship
    consultations with the Congregation for the Doctrine of the Faith, 162
    full breviary, 162
    independence, 165
    link with bishops' conferences, 165
    Order of Christian Funerals, 167–168

recognitio, 162
scholars, 163, 164
translation of the Roman Missal, 162
International Commission of Jurists (ICI), 223
International Consultation on English Texts (ICET), 294
Inman, Bishop Vernon, 149
Institute for Contextual Theology, 249
International Court of Justice in The Hague, 216, 219
Inter-Territorial Meeting of Bishops in Southern Africa (IMBISA), 152–156, 168, 269, 318, 341, 342
Ireton, General Henry, 4
Irish National League, 6
Irish Republican Army (IRA), 5
Italian prisoner of war (POW) camp, Hay Paddock, KwaZulu-Natal, 50

Jali, Rev Paul, 276
Jeffery, Anthea, 277, 351
Jennings, Rev Athol, 187, 188, 285, 286, 344, 351
Jerusalem, 106, 247
Jesus Prayer Rally, 287
Job Reservation Act, 127
John XXIII, Pope, 34, 110, 111, 112, 124, 132, 134, 338
    announcement of general council 106–107
    appoints Hurley to CPC, 108
    Birth Control Commission, 134
    death, 119
    encounter with Hurley, 107
    Hurley's opinion of, 109
    illness, 115
    opening address at Vatican II, 109
    Pacem in Terris, encyclical letter, 132
John Paul II, Pope, 156, 159, 265, 271, 289, 290, 320, 342, 353, 355
    African bishops, meeting with, 155
    audience, Hurley's, 321
    ordination of women and, 290
    politics, Hurley's call to Pope to clarify his position on, 259
    regard for Hurley, 310
    Synod of Bishops, called special session, 145
    Zimbabwe, visit to, 153

Johnson, Elizabeth, ii, 144, 145, 341
joint communiqué of ANC and SACBC, 241, 348
Joint Rent Action Committee (JORAC), 277, 278
Jones, Beryl, 172
Joliffe, Mr. 49
Jubilee 2000, 308–309
Justice and Peace Commission (National), 157, 210, 211, 217, 223, 305, 306, 308
Justice and Peace Commission (Vatican), 155

Kairos Document, 1985, 239. 349
Kaiser, Robert Blair, 116, 330, 339
Kajee, Essop, 303, 325, 353
Kampala, Uganda, 99
Katatura township, Windhoek, 217
Katigondo, Uganda, 99, 337
Kaufmann, Father Larry CSSR, 231, 232, 337, 347
Keane, Sister Marie-Henry OP, 145, 322, 323, 325, 341, 355
Kearney, Paddy, 252–255, 342, 343, 344, 347, 351, 352, 354, 355
Keeler, Cardinal William, 290
Kelly, Father Sheldon OMI, 61, 62
Kelly, Sister Margaret OP, 190, 306, 310, 344. 353
Kenya, 41
Kerautret, Father Joseph OMI, 52, 53, 55
Kerchhoff, Peter, 249, 280
Kerkbode (Dutch Reformed Church publication), 67
Khanya House, SACBC headquarters, 225
Khanyisa, catechetical institute, 144
Khumalo, Dominic, Bishop OMI, 42, 53, 173, 176, 267, 268, 285, 329, 330, 333, 334, 350
Khumalo, M.Z., 279
King William's Town Dominican nuns, 172
King's Park (now Absa Stadium), Durban, 173, 284
Kissinger, Henry, 287
Kistner, Wolfram, 257
Kleissler, Monsignor Tom, 266, 268, 350
Kliptown, 80–81
Kneifel, Theo, 105, 307, 338, 353
Knox, Cardinal, 158
Koch, Ulrich, 214, 215, 346

Kocks, Denise (*née* Ferreira), 49, 334
Koernke, Sister Theresa, 164, 342
Koevoet (police para-military unit), 217, 219, 221–227, 256, 320, 346
Koka, Drake, 129, 340
Kolbe, Monsignor Frederick, 15
Kolbe Association, 65, 69, 84, 312, 336
Koornhof, Piet, 191, 192, 209, 277, 344
Koornhof Bills, 209, 277
Kotze, Victor, 188
Kuiper, Father Vincentius, 35
Krosnicki, T, 342
Küng, Father Hans, 116, 135, 309, 340, 353
Kuny, Denis SC, 222, 223, 225, 227, 347
Kwa-Mashu, KwaZulu-Natal, 85, 276,
KwaThintwa School for the Deaf, 172, 326, 343
KwaZulu Government, 276, 278, 279
KwaZulu-Natal Church Leaders' Group (KZNCLG), 280, 281, 285, 286, 351
KwaZulu Territorial Authority, 186, 344
Kyi, Aung San Suu, 301

Lambert, Rob, 184–185, 229, 230, 344, 347
Lamont, Bishop Donal O.Carm, 152, 225, 347
Lamontville (KwaZulu-Natal), 197, 277
Land League (Ireland), 4, 6, 28
Lateran Councils (I–IV), 106
Latin American Bishops, 99
League of Nations, 216
Leakey, Louis, 104
Lefebvre, Archbishop Marcel, 111, 156
Legal Resources Centre, 252, 253, 326
LeGrange, Louis, 236
Lennoxton, KwaZulu-Natal, 17
Lenten Campaign (*Ich will ein Mensch sein*), 213–215
Leo XIII, Pope, 31, 32, 49, 64, 185
Leon, Judge Ray 254, 255, 297
Leonine College, Rome, 34
Leper Colony, Robben Island, 10, 11
Le Voguer, Father R. OMI, 46
L'Henoret, Father Joseph OMI, 43, 44, 47
Liberal Party (LP), xi, 77, 85, 86, 87, 90, 244, 336, 337
liberation theology, 257
Liénart, Cardinal Achille, 109, 112
Lille, France, 112
Limehill, forced removals, 149–151, 341

Linden, Ian, 153, 217, 238, 239, 243, 342, 346, 348
Little Sisters of Jesus, 175
Liturgiam Authenticam, 292, 294, 295, 352
Liturgical Consilium, 163
Lobinger, Father (later, Bishop) Fritz, 100, 105, 247, 269, 338, 346, 349, 350
Losken, Daisy & Wolfgang, 309, 352, 353, 354
Louwfant, Father John, 182
Loxton's Drift, KwaZulu-Natal, 19
Lucas, Archbishop Martin SVD, 51, 54, 55, 57, 62, 64, 65, 68, 69, 83, 259, 335
Lumen Gentium, 122
Lusaka, 210, 238, 239, 248
Lusitania (ship), 9–10
Lutheran World Federation, 225
Lwaminde, Father Peter, 324

Mabaso, Philip, 170, 178, 343
Mabona, Father Anthony, 182
McCann, Archbishop (later, Cardinal), 64, 109, 128–131, 135, 173, 182, 190, 203, 258, 268, 273, 294, 309, 340, 344
    Bishops' Conference, President, 97
    deputation to Verwoerd, 75
    qualified franchise, support for, 182
    response to Church Clause, 82
    response to Sharpeville, 88
    vote of no confidence, 183
McConville, W, 156, 342
McDonagh, Enda, 144
McGeogh, Archbishop Joseph, 130, 131, 340
McGough, Michael, 29
McGrath, Father John OMI, 336
McKay, Peter, 354
McKenzie, Father Duncan OMI, 324
Mackinnon, Father Angus OMI, 26, 52, 242
McManus, Monsignor Frederick, 119, 330, 339, 342
McNally, Norman, 45, 333
Machibisa mission, Pietermaritzburg, 101
Madden, Cecilia, 331, 335
Madden, Dolly, 331, 335
Madden, Mike, 315, 331, 335, 354
Mafole, Ntwe, 279
Magisterium, 139, 141, 142, 143
Maharaj, Mac, 239
Mahlangu, Father Raphael, 170, 178, 343
Malan, D.F., 76
Malan, Magnus, 258

Malone, Bishop James, 224, 347
Malukazi, 276
Mamelodi, 257
Mandela, Nelson, 153, 223, 229, 287, 301,
    309, 325, 347, 353
  ANCYL, leader, 57
  honorary doctorate from University of
    Natal, 297–298
  Hurley's trial, support at time of, 223
  imprisonment on Robben Island, 10
  inauguration, 306
  Mandela/Buthelezi rally, aborted, 285
  release from prison, 283–284
  treason trial, 81
  Umkhonto we Sizwe, formation of, 89
Mannes, Sisters Mary and Dominic Mary
    OP, 315
Manning, Cardinal, 158
Mansfield High School, Durban, 312
Marcoux, Hervé OMI, 36
Maré, Gerry, 275
Marella, Cardinal Paolo, 122
Margaret, Princess, 55
Maria Ratschitz Mission, KwaZulu-Natal, 149
Marian Congress, 61– 62, 212, 335
Mariannhill, 46, 54, 72, 73, 95, 136
Marist Brothers, 23
Marist College, Canberra, 312, 315
Maritain, Jacques, 101, 120
Mark of Zorro (film), 18
Marmion, Dom Columba OSB, 27
Marrian, Anne, 325
Marshall, Dr John, 138, 341
Marshman, Colin, 19,20, 21
Martin, David, 45, 333, 342
Martin, Bishop, later Archbishop, Diarmuid,
    155, 156, 342
Martinez, Cardinal, 289
Marty, Cardinal, 158
Mary McKillop College, Adelaide, 312
Mathias, Julie (formerly Rainsford),
    170–176, 343
Matthews, Tony, 254
Mass Democratic Movement (MDM), 263,
    264
Mass of the Resurrection for Hurley, 326
Mass of the Rubber Bullet, 236–237
The Mass on the World, by Teilhard de
    Chardin, 103
Mavundla, Father Jerome OMI, 42, 51, 54

May, William E., 96
Maycock, Pat, 318
Mayer, Father, later Cardinal, Augustin OSB,
    113, 289
Mazenod School, Chesterville, 79
Mbeki, Thabo, 238, 239, 300, 325
Mbeki, Zanele, 326
Mboweni, Tito, 308
Mdlalose, Frank, 283
Mdlalose, Knowledge, 297, 298
Mdluli, Joseph, 197–198
Mdluli, Sister Michael OP, 145, 148, 341, 343
Medellín, Colombia, 99, 245, 246, 248
Meer, Fatima, 187, 301, 308, 309, 325, 344
Meer, Ismael, 301
Mees, Archbishop Jan, 259, 349, 351
Meidner, Hans, 90
Mellett, Leon, 221
Mental Hospital, Robben Island, 10
Meran, KwaZulu-Natal, 149
Merrivale, KwaZulu-Natal, 233
Mersch, Emile, 101,
Meskin, Paddy, 304, 353
Metal and Allied Workers' Union (MAWU),
    229, 231, 233
Methodist Church, 57, 90, 149, 188, 197,
    206, 248, 249, 259, 280, 345
Mgojo, Rev Khoza, 248, 280, 285, 351
"Midlands War", 280, 284
migrant labour, 126, 142, 186, 188, 344
military chaplains, 37, 41, 42, 200, 207, 332,
    345
military intelligence, 279
military service, 199, 200, 202, 203, 204
Mirror, The, 13
Misereor, 154, 197, 213–215, 233, 247
mission schools, 85, 128, 185, 212, 214, 336,
    344
  Bantu Education Act, stipulations
    regarding, 72
  conciliatory approach, 73
  Eiselen Report, 73
  evangelizing, nature of, 72
  fundraising, 77–79
  handing over to KwaZulu authorities,
    186
  memorandum and meeting with
    Verwoerd, 75
  National party, concern regarding, 70
  Father St George's proposal, 76

state subsidies, 71–72
statistics, 1973, 72, 79
wages, paying inadequate, 186
Missionaries of Charity, 304, 352
Mitchell, Neil, 203, 206, 345
Mji, Diliza, 283
Mkhatshwa, Father Smangaliso, 182, 183, 223, 235, 239, 309, 343
Mkhize, Raphael, 79
Mlaba, Obed, 325
Mlambo, Khosi, 345
Moetapele, Father David, 182, 183
Mokoka, Father Clement, 182
Moll, Peter, 203, 204
Momphati, Ruth, 239
Montanelli, Carlo, 50
Montebello, 145, 148, 177
mortal sin, teaching young children about, 95–97, 337
Moses, 99
Moss, Father Alan OMI, 317–318, 350, 352, 354
Moss, Father Rodney, 272, 350
Mossel Bay, 25
Mount Minto, site of lighthouse on Robben Island, 11
Mozambican Peace Accord, 320
Mpophomeni (Howick township), 231–232
Msunduzi City Council, 288
Mthethwa, Deacon Lawrence, 170, 177, 267, 275, 343, 350, 351
Mtshali, Father Cletus, 331
Müller, Sister Theodula CPS, 95–100, 337
Munnik, Dr Lapa, 190
Murphy-O'Connor, Cardinal Cormac, 324
Murphy, Roland, 144
Mussinghoff, Bishop Heinrich, 321
Mussolini, 31, 33, 34–36, 333
Mxenge, Victoria, 252

Nadal, Paul, Monsignor, 36, 100, 131, 144, 170, 174–177, 202, 266–268, 272–273, 322, 323, 337, 340, 343, 345, 350, 355
Naidoo, Archbishop Stephen CSSR, 217, 223, 258
Nala, June-Rose, 229
Namibia, 96, 100, 152, 199, 246, 256, 279, 321, 346, 347
atrocities, 217
Bishops' report, 218–220

British mandate to govern, 216
Hurley's trial, 221–227, 237, 320
Inkatha, supporters trained in Caprivi Strip, 279
military effort in, 204–206
Napier, Cardinal Wilfrid Fox, OFM, 211, 212, 244, 303, 323, 326, 346, 348, 349, 353, 355
archbishop, appointed, 274
cardinal, appointed, 309, 310
installation as archbishop, 302
meeting with P.W. Botha, 1986, 258
preacher at "Mass of the Resurrection", 326
SACBC delegation to Lusaka, 239–240
Natal Carbineers, 41
Natal Church Leaders' Group (NCLG), 280, 281, 285, 286, 331 see also KwaZulu-Natal Church Leaders' Group (KZNCLG)
Natal Command, 204
Natal Convention, 90, 91
Natal Council of Churches, 149, 196, 197
Natal Crisis Fund, 281, 286
Natal Education Department, 312
Natal Indian Congress (NIC), 48, 58, 85, 86
Natal Indian Organization (NIO), 85, 86
Natal Mercury (newspaper), 20, 298
Natal PAC in exile, 283
Natal University, 85, 90, 254, 297–301, 309, 352
Natal University College, 46, 48
Natal Vicariate, 41, 43, 50, 54, 55, 59, 61, 65, 334
Natal Witness (newspaper), 284
National Catechetical and Liturgical Commission, 96
National Catechetical Commission, 98, 175
National Catholic Federation of Students (NCFS), xii, 210
National Catholic Reporter (publication), 295, 333, 342, 352,
National Party (NP), 42, 48, 56–58, 63, 64, 68, 70–71, 77, 79, 83–86, 89, 90, 126, 128, 129, 149, 181, 186, 216, 238, 258, 263, 264, 287, 288
National Peace Accord, 286
National service, 199, 204, 206
National Union for the Total Independence of Angola (UNITA), 199
National Union of Mineworkers (NUM), 326

National Union of South African Students (NUSAS), xii, 103, 181
National University of Ireland, 28
Native Abolition of Passes and Co-ordination of Documents Act, 1952, 63
Native Laws Amendment Bill, 1957, 81–82
Native Urban Areas Act, 1923, 58
Naudé, Beyers, 188, 200, 203, 244, 250, 257, 309, 320, 324, 348
Nazism, 33, 34
Ndungane, Archbishop Njongonkulu, 308, 326
Neal, Sister Augusta SND, 189
Necklacing (method of punishment), 209–210
Neo-scholasticism, 109
New Republic Party, 256
Newcastle, KwaZulu-Natal, 17, 18, 20, 22, 23
Newcastle Academy, 17, 22
Newcastle Dominican Sisters (SA), 15, 17, 34, 322, 323, 324, 332
Newton, Mr, (headmaster), 11
Ngara, Professor Emmanuel, 298, 300, 352,
non-governmental organisations (NGOs), 308
Nicaea, 106 (council)
Nicholson, Chris, 252–255
Nicholson Road, Durban, 323
Nkadimeng, John, 240
Nolan, Father Albert OP, 135–136, 238, 341, 348
Noonan, Father Paddy OFM, 234–237, 347
Notre Dame University, Indiana, 78, 111, 301, 336
    Centre for Pastoral Liturgy, 164
Ntombela, David, 284–285
NU Focus (publication), 298
Nuttall, Bishop Michael, 264, 265, 278, 280, 281, 282, 283, 285, 286, 351
Nxumalo, Otty, 148, 274, 341
Nxumalo, Archbishop Jabulani OMI, 148, 211, 212, 274, 294, 320, 334, 341, 344, 346, 352

Oakford Dominican Sisters, 54, 315
Oakford Priory, 58, 268, 315
Oblate General Chapter, 310
Oblate General House, Rome, 312, 332, 333
Oblate International Scholasticate in Via Vittorino de Feltre, Rome, 29–30
Oblate Scholasticate, Prestbury, 52, 54

Oblates of Mary Immaculate, 22, 23, 25, 26
O'Brien family, 26
O'Brien, Father Jack OMI, 51
Ochs, Father John OMI, 61
O'Donovan, Gerry, 17
O'Driscoll, Helena, 4
O'Hea, Petal, née Landers, 44, 49, 157, 295, 306, 330, 332, 333, 334, 347, 351, 353, 354
O'Keefe, Father Vincent SJ, 142, 143
Okumu, Professor Washington, 287
Olduvai Gorge, East Africa, 104
O'Leary, Father Sean SMA, 66, 211, 307, 335, 346, 353
Olivier, Judge Pierre, 231
Olympic Games, 241
Open schools, 191–193, 344
Open University, 301
Oppenheimer, Harry, 88
Operation Marion, 279
Operation Palmiet, 234
Order of Christian Funerals, 167–168
Order of Mass (text), 290
ordination of women, 290, 298, 306, 310, 319, 354
Örsy, Ladislas, 144
Ortas, Cardinal, 289
Ostdiek, Father Gil, 162, 164, 342
O'Sullivan, Dennyo, 331, 354
O'Sullivan, Eugene, 10
O'Sullivan, Jeremiah, 6
O'Sullivan, Kitty (née Collins), 6
O'Sullivan, Mother Marian, 191, 344
O'Sullivan, Pauline, 331, 354
O'Sullivan, Theresa May, 3, 6
O'Sullivan family, 6, 7, 331
Our Lady of Fatima School, 323
Ovamboland, Namibia, 217, 218

Pacelli, Cardinal Eugenio, see Pope Pius, XII
Pacem in Terris (encyclical letter), 132
Paddock, Billy, 203
Page, Dr John, 162, 289, 290, 295, 330, 339, 342, 343, 352
Palatine Hill, Rome, 30
pallium, 62, 335
Pan-Africanist Congress (PAC), 10, 88, 241, 283, 297
    armed struggle, 89
    banning, 89, 181

papal infallibility, 107
papal primacy, 114, 120, 137–139, 141, 156
parish councils, 147, 232,
Parker, Aida 256, 257, 272, 341
pass books, 46, 63, 68, 88, 89, 208
Passion Play (Durban), 62
Passion Play (Oberammergau), 62
Pastoral Institute, 144,
Pastoral Plan Advisory Committee, 265, 269, 350
pastoral planning, 99, 142, 212, 245–247, 248, 263, 265–269, 273, 303, 349, 350
Pastoral Planning Working Paper, 246, 247
potato famine, Ireland (1847–1851), 3, 8, 330
Paterson, Adrian, 203
Patterson, Father John OMI, 334, 340
Paton, Alan, x, 212–213, 344, 346, 348
Paul VI, Pope (formerly Cardinal Montini), 109, 119, 121, 124, 134–141, 156–160, 163, 168, 182, 192, 271, 291, 309, 310, 341, 344
Pegging Act, 43, 56,
Penzance Road, Durban, 323
People of God series (religious education programme), 100, 120, 212, 337
People's Hymn Book, 146
Perego, Franco, 50, 51, 334
Perez, Thora, 214, 346
Permanent Black Priests' Solidarity Group (PBPSG), 193
Peruisset, Father Louis OMI, 36
Phenomenon of Man, by Teilhard de Chardin,102, 103
Phillip, Bishop Rubin, 325
Phoenix National and Literary Society, 4
Piazza Venezia, 33, 111
Pierre Teilhard de Chardin Association of Great Britain and Ireland, 103
Pieter Faurè (steamer), 10
Pietermaritzburg, (KwaZulu-Natal), 22
Pietermaritzburg Agency for Christian Social Awareness (PACSA), 249, 280, 351
Pietermaritzburg City Hall, 90, 299
Pietermaritzburg, Freedom of City of, 309
Pietermaritzburg Mental Hospital, 21
Pietermaritzburg Parliamentary Debating Society, 48, 49 86, 188, 334, 335
Pietersburg, 82, 98
Pieterse, Jude, 192, 193, 306, 344, 353

Pilarcyk, Archbishop Daniel, 163, 290, 342
Pilla, Bishop Anthony, 290
Pillay, Rev Victor, 276
Pinochet, General Augusto, 291
Piper, Andy, 170, 177, 266, 343, 350
Piscine Hill, Rome, 31
Pistorius, Noel, 243
Pius IX, Pope, 4, 137
Pius XI, Pope, 31, 332, 333, 336
    death, 34
    education, teaching on, 72
    encyclical against communism, 32
    encyclical against fascism, 32
    encyclical against Nazism, (*Mit Brennender Sorge*) 32, 33
    laity, 121
    Quadragesimo Anno, 32, 49, 185
Pius XII, Pope (formerly Cardinal Eugenio Pacelli), 77
    election and coronation, 34, 310
    Hurley's audiences with, 78, 81
    message to Marian Congress, 62
    opposition to communism, 81
Police Act, 221, 225
Pollak, Hansi, Professor, 85, 86, 336
Pollsmoor Prison, 223
Pontifical Commission for Justice and Peace, 154, 155, 156
poor, 32, 33, 45, 134, 142, 148, 154, 178, 196, 210, 213, 223, 231, 244, 245, 248, 303, 304, 305, 307, 308, 320, 322, 325, 326
Popular Movement for the Liberation of Angola (MPLA), 199
Population Registration Act, 1950, 63
Port Nolloth, Cape Colony (Western Cape), 5
Presbyterians, 57, 60, 90, 125, 197, 200, 203, 296, 248, 276, 309
Prestbury, Pietermaritzburg, 49
Pretoria Kolbe Association, 84, 336
Pretoria Magistrates' Court, 224
Pretoria Mental Hospital, 21
Pretorius, M C, 286
Prison, Robben Island, 10
Pro-Cathedral, Skibbereen, 7
Progressive Federal Party, 224
Progressive Party (PP), 56, 85, 87, 88, 203, 337
Prohibition of Mixed Marriages Act, 1949, 65, 206

Promotion of Bantu Self Government Act, 1959, 126
prophecy (biblical), 181
prophetic ministry, 100, 181, 195, 198, 205, 210, 215, 244, 256–259
protest marches, 263–265
Protestantism, 12, 20, 63, 67, 68, 72, 109, 321
Psalter, 209
Public Safety Act, 1953, 68
Puebla (Mexico), 245, 246, 248
Purves, George, OMI, 315, 317, 318, 320, 322, 323, 353, 354, 355

Quadragesimo Anno, 1931, 32, 49, 285
Queenstown (now Cobh), 5, 23
Queenstown naval base, 5
Quinlan, Sister Evangelist RSM, 192, 344

Rai, Kevin, 243
Railway Hotel, Paddington Station, 238
Rakoczy, Sister Sue IHM, 325
Rahner, Karl, 116
Ramaphosa, Cyril, 300
Ramokwa, Peter, 240
Rand Daily Mail (newspaper), 126, 182
Ratzinger, Cardinal, *see* Benedict XVI, Pope
Reconstruction and Development Programme (RDP), 306, 307, 353
Reece-Edwards, Hugh, 176
Rees, John, 200
Reeve, Jackie, 319, 354
Reeves, Bishop Ambrose, 72, 73, 81
Reformation, 106, 109, 120, 121
refugees from Central Africa, 303, 304
religious tolerance, 304
Renew Process, 170, 265–269, 273, 282, 303, 322, 350
rent increases, protest about, 209
Renown (Battle cruiser), 13
Republic Festival, 212, 213, 346
Repulse (Battle cruiser), 13
Rerum Novarum (of new matters), 1891, 31–32, 49, 64, 185
Resettlement Aid Fund, 150
The Resurrection, by François Xavier Durwell, 101
Rickard, Carmel, 253, 254, 255, 332, 333, 347, 349, 352
Riegler, Bishop, 73
Riffel, Father Peter OMI, 77

rights (human), 67, 69
Rin Tin Tin (film), 18
Riotous Assemblies Act, 1956, 81
Roach, P, 338, 339
Robben Island, 10–15, 25, 181, 192, 242
Roche, Bishop Arthur, 294, 352
Roets, Frans, 225
Rogers, Father Ted SJ, 153, 269, 270, 271, 341, 350
Roman Curia, 107, 110, 112, 145, 295
Roman Missal, 162, 289, 290, 292, 295
Romero, Archbishop Oscar, 32, 332
Rondebosch Common, 188
Roomse gevaar, 57, 62, 67–68, 70, 73, 222
Rossiter, George, 19–21
Rotary Foundation, 309
Rowland, Bishop Paschal OFM, 149, 334, 341, 346
Rubicon speech, 241
Rugambwa, Cardinal Laurian, 99, 111, 114
Ruppell, Hartmut, 222, 227
Russell, David, 188
Russell, Archbishop Philip, 204
Russia, 48
Ryan, Father Richard OMI, 1, 26–28, 332
Ryan, Sister Josephine OP, 18, 332

Sabelo, Winnington, 276
Sabon House, 312, 317, 318, 322, 323. 354, 355
sabotage, 89
Sacerdotalis Coelibatus (1967), 140, 157
Sacred Heart Cathedral, Pretoria, 325
Sacrosanctum Concilium, 118, 121, 168, 295
Sadie, Peter, 267, 349
St Andrew's Centre, 197
St Anselmo, Rome, 295, 352
St Armour, Sister A IHM, 337
St Augustine's School, Durban, 58
St Charles's College, Pietermaritzburg, 13, 22–24, 51, 52, 332
St Clement's, Clermont (KwaZulu-Natal), 170
St Denis, 223
St Dominic's Priory, Port Elizabeth, 191
St Elmo's Convent, Umzumbe, KwaZulu-Natal, 15–17, 23, 331, 332
St Francis de Sales, Oblates of, 233
St Francis of Assisi, 44, 302
St George, Father Howard OMI, 73, 75, 76, 230, 334

St George's Anglican Cathedral, Cape Town, 264
St Henry's Marist College, 45
St Jacques Dominican community, 117
St John, 322
St Joseph the Worker Fund, 229, 233
St Joseph's Church, Morningside, Durban, 56, 104
St Joseph's Scholasticate, Pietermaritzburg, 49–51, 53, 64, 65, 105, 334
    Caritas (Newsletter), 50
    chair of sociology, Catholic action and actualities, 50
    establishment of,47
    first black student, 51
    social issues included in curriculum, 50
St Joseph's Theological Institute, Cedara, 144
St Louis des Invalides (hospital), 117
St Mary's Cathedral, Cape Town, 10, 325
St Mary's Church, Pietermaritzburg, 22, 52, 152
St Paul, 27, 35, 84
St Paul's Church, Morningside, Durban, 56
St Paul's University, Ottawa, 116, 309
St Peter, 83
St Peter's Basilica, Rome, 30, 31, 34, 35, 111, 112, 116, 118, 119, 124,
St Peter's Catholic Seminary (Hammanskraal), 193, 199
St Peter's Old Boys' Association (SPOBA), 182
St Thérèse of Lisieux, 20, 332
St Thomas Anglican Church, Durban, 319
St Thomas Aquinas, 109, 114
St Thomas Boys' School, 13, 17–20, 23, 332
Salazar, Antonio de Oliveira, 49
Salem, Massachusetts, 6–8, 59
Salve Regina, (hymn), 327
Samorè, Archbishop Antonio, 131, 340
sanctions, 88, 206, 210, 220, 235, 238, 240, 241–244, 275, 348
São Tomé e Príncipe, 152
Sarmcol Workers' Co-operative (SAWCO), 233, 347
Savage, Jooste and Adams, 222
Schellman, Jim, 162–164, 292, 295, 339, 342, 352
Schillebeeckx, Edward, 144
Schiller, Friedrich 146
Scholastic theology, 101,114

Scholten, Father Dominic OP, 98, 182, 337, 340
Schoombie, Willem, 49
Schumann, Herman, 269
Schutte, Augustine, 188
Schutte, Danie, 287
Scorpio (right wing group), 188
Scott, Father Michael, 57
Scottsville, Pietermaritzburg, 23, 48, 49
Sebokong, Vaal Triangle, 234
security forces, 181
security police, 150, 186–187, 197, 198, 217, 229, 252–254, 259, 344
sedia gestatoria, 31
seminary education, 97
Separate Representation of Voters Act, 1951, 68
Separate Amenities Act, 208
"Seven days' war", 284, 285, 351
She Who Is, by Elizabeth Johnson, 145
Sharpeville, 88, 89, 181, 186, 194, 209, 234, 337
Sharpeville Six, 234
shingles, 301, 318
Sibiya, Bishop Louis, 325
Sibiya, Micca, 231
Sibiya, Phineas, 231
silent movies, 18
Simpkins, Bertie, 18, 21, 329, 332
Simonstown, Western Cape, 5, 10
Sinosizo AIDS project, 326
Sistine Chapel, 34
Sisulu, Walter, 57
Sketch, The, 13
Skibbereen, West Cork, Ireland, 3–8, 26
Slater, Raymond, 203
Slattery, Bishop William OFM, 211, 212, 332, 346
Small Christian Community program, 268–269
Smith, Father Tim SJ, 284, 351
Smuts, Jan Christiaan, 28, 41, 55, 56
Soares de Resenda, Bishop Sebastiano, 114
social justice, 27, 46, 64, 84, 145, 175, 189, 196, 245, 246, 259, 265, 316
Society of St Pius X, 156
Society of St Vincent de Paul, 45
Soltek, Marly, 321
Somalia, 41
Somerville, Boyle,Vice Admiral, 4, 5
Sophiatown, 77

Sormany, Father Leo OMI, 42–44, 47, 52, 54, 55, 334
Sounds of Soweto (music group), 214
South Africa in the 1980s, (CIIR Publication), 276
South African Air Force (SAAF), 306
South African Broadcasting Corporation (SABC), 150
South African Catholic Laity Council, 214
South African Communist Party (SACP), 63, 213, 239, 240, 264, 265, 335
South African Council of Churches (SACC), 235, 248, 264, 286, 325, 326, 328, 344, 345, 349, 350
  Buthelezi, Chief Mangosuthu 285
  Catholic Church, 64,
  Chikane, Frank, 263, 286
  conscientious objection, 200, 201, 345
  Convocation of Churches in South Africa, 263
  Hurley, Denis Eugene, speaker at conferences of, 194, 195, 247
  National conference, (1976) 194, 195
  National conference, (1974) 199
  National conference, (1983) 247
  National Peace Accord, 286
  Soweto uprising, 1976, 194
  Standing for the Truth Campaign 263, 264, 350
South African Defence Force (SADF), 42, 200, 202, 204, 217, 256, 279, 280
South African Embassy, Rome, 131, 320, 340
South African Embassy, Washington, 224
South African Indian Council (SAIC), 68, 80
South African Institute of Race Relations (SAIRR), 44, 69, 73, 74, 85, 127, 149, 277, 336
South African Light Service, 5
South African Press Association (SAPA), 129, 221, 225
South African Referendum, 1960, 89
South African Students' Organization (SASO), 182
South African Television (SATV), 104, 338
Southampton, 26
Southern African Catholic Bishops' Conference (SACBC), 96–98, 109, 125, 128, 130, 132, 145, 152, 153, 156–159, 168, 214, 237–242, 258, 265, 267, 268, 270, 289, 295, 305, 306, 318

  ANC-in-exile, and, 239–241
  basis of first statement on race relations, 50
  Church and Industry Department, 228
  Church and Work Department, 229
  Community Serving Humanity, see Community Serving Humanity
  condom use and, 270
  conscientious objection and, 201
  Department of Press, Radio and Cinema, 128
  Hurley as president, 168, 210–212, 217, 228, 238, 245, 247, 256, 259, 263
  Justice and Peace Commission, see Justice and Peace Commission
  Namibia and, see Namibia
  Native Affairs Department, 73
  official policy on race relations, 130
  police conduct in townships, and, 235–237
  sanctions, see sanctions
  support for Hurley, 223
  unity, 258
  worker struggle, backing for, 238
  Zwane's influence on, 184
Southern Cross (newspaper), 15, 58, 62, 65, 77, 87, 126, 129, 130, 135, 144, 183, 184
South West African Bar Council, 226
South West African People's Organisation (SWAPO), 10, 199, 216–220
Soweto, 72, 182, 184, '97, 105, 206, 209, 214, 239, 245
Soweto uprising, 194–196
Sparks, Allister, 208, 209, 345, 346
Speech from the Dock, by Bishop Donal Lamont O.Carm, 225
sports boycotts, 241
Springfield Convent (Cape Town), 190, 344
SS Africa (ship), 78
St John, 322
Standing for the Truth Campaign, 263–265, 350
Star of the Sea Catholic Church, Robben Island, 12
State Security Council (SSC), 257, 279
States of Emergency, 68, 89, 209, 239, 249, 257, 258, 263, 264
Steckling, Father Wilhelm OMI, 305, 322, 353, 355
Steegmann, Father Heinz OMI, 217, 346

Steele, Richard, 203, 204, 345
Steenkamp, Frans, 187
Steyn, Colonel, 237
Storey, Rev. Peter, 249, 259, 349
Strategic Communications (StratCom), 257, 349
Strauss, Frans Joseph, 214
strikes, 1973, 184–185
Stroessner, General Alfredo, 259
Struve, Father Charles OMI, 51, 334
Strydom, Denis, 304, 353
Stubbs, Father Louis, 62
Study Project on Christianity in Apartheid Society (SPROCAS), 195
Stuhlmueller, Carroll, 144
Suenens, Archbishop, later Cardinal, 110, 111, 115, 121, 338
Sunday Times (newspaper), 136, 201, 298
Suppression of Communism Act, 1951, 63, 68
Surgeson, Joseph OMI, 18
Swart, Chris, 204. 205, 345
Swaziland, 152, 217
Swiss Catholic Lenten Fund, 100
Syllabus of Errors, 137
Symposium of Episcopal Conferences of Africa and Madagascar (SECAM), 324
Synod of Bishops, 122, 136, 137, 141, 143, 145, 146, 152, 156–160, 318, 339, 342
Synod of Durban Archdiocese, 147–148, 196

Table Bay, Cape Town, 10, 12
Tambo, Oliver, 89, 238–240, 283, 348
Tara, Ireland, 28
Tardini, Cardinal, 107, 108
Taylor, Archbishop Robert Selby, 188
Taylor, Bishop Maurice, 291, 292, 293, 342, 352
Taylor's Halt, 285
Teilhard de Chardin, Pierre, 102–105, 121, 337, 338
temporal power, 137
Tertiaries (lay group associated with Franciscan Order), 44, 45
Theological Studies (journal), 141, 143, 157, 310, 341
Theresa, Mother, 301, 304
They're Burning the Churches, by Father Paddy Noonan OFM, 234
Thie, Dr Gunter, 154, 342, 353
Thomas More Academy, 36

Thomas More College, Kloof, KwaZulu-Natal, 312, 314, 315, 354
Time magazine, 116
Timol, Ahmed, 187
Tlhagale, Archbishop Buti, 211, 305, 346
Tobias, Professor Phillip, 103, 104, 309, 338
Toms, Ivan, 203
torture, 187, 197, 217, 218, 231, 235
Towell, Liz, 269, 270, 271, 350, 354
townships
    local council system, 209
    police conduct in, 234–237
    unrest, 1984–1985, 210
trade unions, 46–47, 90, 184, 185, 193, 208, 228–230, 232, 283, 304, 308
Trading and Occupation of Land (Transvaal and Natal) Act of 1943, 43
Traglia, Archbishop Luigi, 34
transalpini cardinals, 109, 112
Trautman, D, 342
tricameral parliament, 208, 209, 277
Trimborn, Pat, 325
Truth and Reconciliation Commission (TRC), 252, 256, 257, 278–280
Trycinski, Charmaine, 303, 304, 353, 355
Tshwete, Steve, 239
Tutu, Archbishop Desmond, 100, 225, 244, 248, 257, 282, 285, 309, 320, 325, 348, 351
Tutu, Leah, 225

Ubi Spiritus ibi libertas, 54, 104
Umkhonto we Sizwe (Spear of the Nation), 89
Umlazi, KwaZulu-Natal, 85, 252, 277
Umvoti Deanery, 267
Umzimkhulu, 183
Umzumbe, KwaZulu-Natal, 15, 16, 17, 21, 22, 35, 324
Union Castle liners, 14
Ulundi, KwaZulu-Natal, 281, 282, 285, 351
Union Buildings, 75, 258, 287
Union Defence Force, 42
United Congregational Church of Southern Africa (UCCSA), 57, 90, 149, 197, 206, 248, 278
United Democratic Front (UDF), 209, 247, 252, 263, 277–284, 288
United Nations (UN), 67, 88, 216, 219, 220, 241
United Nations Conference on Population, 141

United Party (UP), 56, 85, 86
United Workers' Union of South Africa (UWUSA), 283
Universal Declaration of Human Rights, 1948, 67
University of Cape Town (UCT), 99, 127, 279
University of Cape Town, Centre for Inter-Group Studies, 279
University of Natal, 85, 90, 254 297–301, 309, 352
University of Notre Dame, Indiana, 78, 111, 301, 336, 339
University of Notre Dame, Indiana. Centre for Pastoral Liturgy, 164
University of KwaZulu-Natal (UKZN), 326
University of Tübingen, Germany, 135
University of Zululand, 278
Urban Areas Act see Native Urban Areas Act
US Bishops, 165, 267, 289–291, 342
US Bishops' Committee on Liturgy, 165
US Bishops' Conference, 224, 290–292
US Congress, 224

Vaal Ministers' Support Group (VMSG), 234, 237
Vaal Triangle unrest, 209, 235, 241, 242, 256, 347, 348
Van der Merwe, H W. 279, 351
van Gijlswijk, Archbishop Bernard, 63
van Hoeck, Bishop Clemens, 82, 98, 337
Van Niekerk, Sybrand, 191
Van Riebeeck, Jan, 11, 68
Van Velsen, Bishop Gerard, 107, 136
Vatican, 33, 35, 84, 107, 109, 117, 118, 121, 155, 157, 158, 164–166, 168, 220, 241, 259, 271, 289–292, 295, 298, 306, 308, 318, 319, 323, 341
   Congregation for the Evangelization of Peoples, 273
Vatican Council, First, 1869–1870, 106
Vatican Council, Second, 91, 95, 99, 102–105, 106–124, 125, 131, 133–140, 144–148, 152, 156, 160–162, 164, 165, 170, 181, 189, 201, 210, 232, 271–273, 292, 293, 306, 309, 317–323, 332, 338, 341, 342
   adult education, 116–117
   Central Preparatory Commission see Central Preparatory Commission

Church as a living community, 124
Church debate, 115
"Church in the Modern World", 121, 123, 138, 142, 245
clerical celibacy, 124, 136
closing, 124
Commission on Seminaries, Academic Studies and Catholic Education, Hurley elected to, 112–113
Declaration on Religious Liberty, 122
Dogmatic Constitution on Divine Revelation, 115
election of council commissions, 112
establishment of the Synod of Bishops, 122
final session, 122–124
first session, 114–115
founding of ICEL, 117–119
Hurley's prominence at, 128
marriage, 123
Message to the World debate, 114
nuclear weapons, 123–124
opening of the Council, 111–112
religious freedom, 120, 122. 123
Revelation and the Church debate, 114
Sacrosanctum Concilium, 118, 121, 168, 295
second session, 119–121
Theological Commission, 114
third session, 121–122
war, 123
Vatican Justice and Peace Commission, 155
Vatican Radio, 241
vernacular liturgy and texts, 108, 117, 118, 119, 124, 145, 146, 165, 166, 168, 291, 294
Verulam, 277
Verwoerd, Hendrik, 63, 70–77, 80, 82, 89, 126, 194, 336
   clarification of Bantu Education Policy 74
   criticism of Catholic Schools, 76
   meeting with Hurley, Whelan and McCann, 75–76
Viallard, Father Gabriel, OMI, 47, 48,
Vicars Apostolic, 18, 59, 61, 64, 267
Victor Emmanuel II Monument, 33
Viger, Gerard, 51
Villa Rosa Chapel, 34
Villa Siena Retirement Centre, 315
Villani, Piero, 50

Villot, Cardinal, 157
Vistarama Missionary Exhibition, 79
Viveiros. Michael, 203
Vlok, Adriaan, 258
Vogt, Father Wilfred OMI, 50
Volkmer, Marlene, 276, 351
Volmink, Professor John, 300, 301, 352
Voortrekker Hoërskool, Pietermaritzburg, 49, 334
Voortrekkerhoogte, Pretoria, 206
Vorster, B.J., 194, 201
voting
    qualified franchise, 69, 85, 86, 87, 88, 182
    right to vote, 67
    universal franchise, 85, 86, 87, 182, 185
Vox Clara, 294, 295
Vulindlela, 280, 284, 285

Wall Street Stock Exchange collapse, 22, 25
Walsh, Father Chris, 167, 343
Ward, Barbara, 157
Warrack, J, 333
Warwick Castle, (ship) 41
Wasbank, KwaZulu-Natal, 149
Washington, DC, 145, 161, 163, 224, 266, 391, 315
Weakland, Archbishop Rembert OSB, 165, 342
Wessels, Rev. M., 248
Western Contact Group, 220, 347
Westridge Tennis Stadium, 268, 282, 302
Whelan, Archbishop William Patrick OMI, 64, 73–77, 84, 128–131, 133, 340
The Whole Christ, by Emile Mersch, 101
Widenham, KwaZulu-Natal South Coast, 103
Wilkins, John, 293, 294, 352
Williams, Father, 41
Williams, Harold, 13, 331
Wilson, Professor Francis, 99, 188, 337

Windhoek Diocese, 220
Witwatersrand University, 204
Wojtyla, Cardinal, 159, see also John Paul II, Pope
Women's Ordination South Africa (WOSA), 319, 354
Wood, Bishop Barry OMI, 53, 145, 304, 334, 341, 353
Woods, Donald, 130, 340, 341, 353
Worrall, Denis, 202, 345
Work of Our Redemption, by Clifford Howell SJ, 101
Worker Rights Statement, Diakonia publication, 198, 229
World, newspaper, 129
World Alliance of Reformed Churches, 83
World Conference of Religions for Peace (WCRP), 304
World Day of Prayer for Peace, Assisi, 1986, 320
World War 1, 10, 12, 14, 41, 216,
World War 11, 35, 41, 42, 47, 89, 95, 199, 216

Yeats, Charles, 203, 206, 318, 345, 354
Yeats, W.B, 191
Youghal, East Cork, 26
Young Christian Students (YCS), 210
Young Christian Workers (YCW), 32, 47, 121, 133, 184, 210, 332, 357
Young, Archbishop Guildford, 117–119
Youth Against AIDS, 269
York, Denis, 321

Zingel, Heribert, 215, 346
Zoghby, Bishop Elias, 114
Zondi, Musa, 279
Zondo, Andrew, 297
Zwane, Bishop Mandlenkosi, 184
Zuma, Jacob, 287, 286, 326
Zuppi, Father Matteo, 355